The Collected Letters of St. Teresa of Avila

VOLUME ONE

The Collected Letters
of
St. Teresa of Avila

VOLUME ONE

1546 –1577

Translated, with an introduction by
Kieran Kavanaugh, O.C.D.

ICS Publications
Institute of Carmelite Studies
Washington, D.C.
2001

ICS Publications
2131 Lincoln Road, NE
Washington, DC 20002-1199
800-832-8489
www.icspublications.org

Library of Congress Cataloging-in-Publication Data

Teresa, of Avila, Saint, 1515-1582
[Correspondence, English]
The collected letters of St. Teresa of Avila / translated by Kieran Kavanaugh.
p. cm.
Includes bibliographical references and index.
ISBN 0-935216-27-8
1. Teresa, of Avila, Saint, 1515-1582--Correspondence. 2. Christian saints--Spain--Avila--Correspondence. I. Kavanaugh, Kieran, 1928- II. Title.

BX4700.T4 A31 2001
282'.092--dc21
[B]

2001039191

Contents

Abbreviations

References to St. Teresa's other writings are from *The Collected Works of St. Teresa of Avila*, trans. Kieran Kavanaugh, O.C.D., and Otilio Rodriguez, O.C.D., 3 vols. (Washington, D.C.: ICS Publications, 1976–85). The following abbreviations will be used in referring to her works:

F	*The Book of Her Foundations* (vol. 3)
IC	*The Interior Castle* (vol. 2)
L	*The Book of Her Life* (vol. 1)
M	*Meditations on the Song of Songs* (vol 2)
SC	*A Satirical Critique* (vol. 3)
ST	*Spiritual Testimonies* (vol. 1)
W	*The Way of Perfection* (vol. 2)

Other abbreviations:

BMC	*Biblioteca Mistica Carmelitana*, ed., Silverio de Santa Teresa, 20 vols (Burgos: El Monte Carmelo, 1915–35)
CN	Carmelite Nuns of the Observance
DCF	Discalced Carmelite Friars
DCN	Discalced Carmelite Nuns
MHCT	*Monumenta Historica Carmeli Teresiani*, Insitutum Historicum Teresianum (Rome: Teresianum, 1973–)

Introduction

Introduction

St. Teresa's correspondence makes up nearly one half of her known writings. Her letters have left us with a treasure-trove of vivid narratives about her times, along with illuminating insights into her personality. Only those letters written by Teresa in the last couple decades of her life have reached us, however, those decades representing the same period in which she wrote her major works. It is not difficult to admit that her career as a spiritual author flowed from her mystical experience of God. But while spiritual needs prompted Teresa's classic works, it was the many other needs of her daily life that drove her to letter-writing. Her letters, as a rule, do not give us the kind of teaching and testimony we have grown accustomed to in her other works. Rather, they show us a different facet of Teresa, a Teresa immersed in the relationships and grim business matters thrust upon her by her vocation as a foundress and reformer.

Certainly she had written honestly and openly the story of her life and work in her two books, *The Life* and *The Foundations*. Despite the openness of these works, however, she wrote in the knowledge they would be read by her confessors and eventual censors. Her letters exhibit an even greater candor, and we benefit from many more details that were not meant for the public, nor even for her confessors or censors. Even at that, many personal details in her *Life* were not meant for broadcast. A keen observer of the reality around her as well as within, Teresa focuses light on many of the struggles in both the Carmelite order and the church of sixteenth-century

Spain. She introduces us to major personalities who have left their mark on history.

In addition, historians benefit from the letters because many of the gaps in the outline of events that is presented in her *Foundations* are filled in through her letters. Through them we also gain better knowledge of the chronology of events in her life and of how she related to the diverse people she dealt with. A number of everyday particulars that compilers and editors of those times considered unimportant are today prized. Her worries, her troubles and triumphs, her expressions of sadness and joy, can all be discerned there. With a compelling spontaneity, the letters disclose a Teresa in a complex variety of circumstances. We walk with her year by year, day by day—even hour by hour sometimes. Without question we have before us a rich collection of documents, unbroken in their sequence, revealing in confidential tones a personal history that touches the furthest reaches of her soul.

Despite the fact that the letter-writing was a necessity, any reader can easily see that, though a lover of solitude and prayer, Teresa possessed a heart magnanimously open to others. Ever willing to communicate with them on many levels different from the decidedly spiritual level mainly found in her other writings, she pours herself out to her family members, her religious sisters and brothers, to friends, theologians, advisors, patrons of the nobility, and business people. She had to travel and buy and sell. The ever-present burden of fund-raising wearied her. Problems sprang up over jurisdiction, stirring her to write to Rome and even to King Philip II. She had to chose prioresses, advise and comfort them, and discuss the nettlesome pros and cons ever present in the selection of new postulants, as well as doubts about dowries and other material needs. People's health was always a disquieting concern for her.

A Daily Torment

The extraordinary gifts of grace bestowed by God on this Spanish Madre fortified her for a demanding ministry of service which entailed heavy responsibilities that drew her contemplative soul into a maelstrom of activities. Because of the limited means for travel and communication in the sixteenth century, the organization of a reform like hers, with its unavoidable business matters, had to be dealt with chiefly through correspondence, a chafing duty that became one of Teresa's greatest trials. She wrote, "With so many duties and troubles . . . I wonder how I'm able to bear them all. The biggest burden is letter-writing" (Ltr. 39.1). This is the often repeated confession of a woman overwhelmed with worries. Difficult as writing a book was for her, she preferred it to the letter-writing, a drudgery that cost her more than all the pitiful roads and sorry weather experienced on her journeys through Spain.

What proved painful for Teresa has proved a treasure for us, a collection claimed by scholars to be unparalleled in Spanish literature even to this day. With their humor and delicacy, the letters on the surface do not betray the inner self-coercion they hide. Held bondage by her correspondence, Teresa worked at it day after day, often far into the night by the light of a poor little oil lamp. The pile of letters to be answered was enough to drive her mad. Yet, even though she could be busy answering them until two in the morning, she was up with the rest of the community at five in summer, and six in winter.

Eventually the burden and the lack of sleep took its toll, and she fell into the alarming exhaustion of 1577, precisely in the most intense period of her correspondence. "But I wrote you yesterday, and the labor of letter-writing this winter has so weakened my head that I have been truly sick" (Ltr. 188.1). The doctor issued orders that she not continue writing after midnight and that she get a secretary. Subsequently following this advice, whenever she felt especially exhausted she turned for help to a secretary. When a letter from Teresa is written in another's hand, we can usually attribute it to poor health at the time. "I beg your forgiveness that this is written in someone else's hand, for the bloodletting has left me weak, and my head can't do anything more" (Ltr. 28).

The use of a secretary became more common after the exhaustion of 1577. "You should know, *mi padre*, that my heavy correspondence and many other duties that I tried to handle all alone have caused a noise and weakness in my head. And I have been given orders that unless it's very necessary I should not be writing letters in my own hand" (Ltr. 187.5). Sometimes Teresa begins the letter herself, gives it to the secretary to continue, and then adds some final words in her own hand. If she needed a special guarantee because of the uncertainty that surrounded the mail, she again turned for help to a secretary to make copies. She would order duplicates, triplicates, and even quadruplicates to be made and sent by different means. In that way she could sustain some hope that at least one would reach its destination.

Even in her tortuous travels she seized every moment she could find to work on her correspondence. With her longing for the day when she could be free for more prayer and solitude, her forced confinement in the Carmel in Toledo would have been like a paradise—except for the heavy load of correspondence. It is hardly a surprise that sometimes she didn't know what day it was, that she nearly sent to Gracián's mother a letter she wrote to the bishop of Cartagena, or that she did actually get some addresses mixed up.

The Quantity of Letters

How many letters did Teresa write? The answer to that question is not an easy one, unless you respond that no one knows. Most of her letters have not survived. Some of them she directed to be destroyed, those that if intercepted could have given her trouble. Fortunately Gracián paid little heed to her warnings and saved a good part of Teresa's correspondence. But Anne of Jesus, submissive to Teresa's orders, burned what must have been a captivating collection. One of the letters to her, however, a severe letter, did escape the fire, although by Anne's mistake. On another occasion, in an act of renunciation, it is told, John of the Cross burned a cherished packet of letters from Teresa. Whether or not this is so, none of her letters to John have been conserved.

But how could many of Teresa's correspondents have known the value that a letter from Teresa of Jesus would one day have? Teresa herself generally destroyed letters written to her. Today we regret the loss of all that must have scintillated in her letters to St. John of Avila, Doña Guiomar de Ulloa, St. Peter of Alcántara, St. Francis Borgia, St. Luis Beltrán, St. Pius V, and many other collaborators, friends, and benefactors.

Undoubtedly, because of the defects of the postal system, numerous letters were clearly lost. Judging by Teresa's own complaints, a quantity of her letters simply vanished along the road. At times they vanished because someone suspected that money was enclosed. Simple carelessness, the way in which autographs have been treated by their owners down through the centuries, further contributed to the loss of letters. In sum, Teresa wrote hundreds of letters more than those that have reached us.

In his fourth edition of Teresa's letters, Tomás Alvarez has located 468 letters. From all that has been said and from Teresa's own words about her correspondence, this number presumably amounts to only a fraction of those she wrote. Among editors, Vicente de la Fuente in the eighteenth century estimated that she wrote about 1200 letters; Silverio in the nineteenth raised the number to 5,000; while Efrén/Steggink put the number at 15,000. It could easily have gone higher, as high as 25,000 according to Rodríguez-Egido.

Formalities and Content

Upon examination, the existing autographs, with their evenly spaced lines, absence of crossed-out words, and margins increasingly large according to the social category of the recipient, suggest a much more tranquil setting than was actually the case. Teresa always had other letters to write, many things to worry about, and many matters to attend to. Time was lacking, or it was getting late; or the messenger was waiting and in as much of a hurry as she was to finish, for the mail carrier or the muleteer who would ultimately deliver the letter was also waiting and also in a hurry. "[I wrote] in such a hurry that I don't know what I said" (Ltr. 175.11). Who would deduce, if she didn't confess it outright in a letter to her brother Lorenzo (Ltr. 177.12) that she didn't take the time to reread her own letters or even, in this case, reread his before answering it? Despite the many demands on her time, and the tedium of the letter-writing itself, she convincingly leaves her recipients with the impression that it is with the greatest pleasure that she writes to them.

Regardless of her simplicity, openness, and surprising intimacy at times, Teresa follows rigidly the rules of letter-writing acceptable in her day. At the letter head we find the Christian symbol for the name of Jesus: JHS, in which a cross is made from one of the vertical stems of the letter H. The greeting is usually a variant of one of two formulas: "May the Holy Spirit be with your honor" (or your lordship, your paternity, your reverence, and so on), or "May Jesus be with your honor." Throughout a letter she will continue to use, almost scrupulously, the opening form of address, such as "your honor" or "your reverence." (In this English version, I have, for the most part, translated the title of address literally only at the beginning or again at the end of the letter and in the body settled simply for "you" to avoid a rhetorical repetition that can be painful to read for the modern reader. And the higher the dignity of the person to be catered to, the more frequent becomes the repetition of the form of address. Teresa made careful use of all the formalities of her times in addressing others. Even her own brother and sister are addressed as "your honor" (*vuestra merced*, which could also be translated "your worship"). Bordering on exasperation at sixteenth-century Spain's penchant for titles of honor, in her *Life* she jokes, "Just for the titles of address on a letter there's need for a university chair" (37.10). Despite her jests, she is hardly ever careless in the use of titles. Religious men and women are addressed as "your reverence," or sometimes, in the case of priests, "your paternity." In instances where she feels greater confidence, she uses "*mi padre*" (my father), or "my daughter." Bishops receive a "your lordship"; the inquisitor general is greeted as "your most illustrious lordship."

There were, as well, the *maestro*, the *licenciado*, the *doctor*, and the rector. The title *maestro* (master) was used in two senses. In the proper sense it referred to a teacher who had received a degree to teach. Secondly, it was sometimes used for a very learned person, as when someone notably erudite was called by the people a *maestro*. The title *licenciado* (licentiate) was given to someone for having earned a licentiate degree, which paved the way for the doctorate degree. In addition to using the title "doctor" for someone who received the doctorate, the people were apt to give the title "doctor" to someone out of respect for his person or learning. And finally "rector" was a title used for Jesuit superiors, or for directors of schools.

The point that Teresa understood so well is that in her social and business contacts, the cultivation of friends depended on a thorough knowledge of the intricacies of courtesy. Knowing the way to present a petition in writing became indispensable to her for her work as a foundress. Not only the high nobility, but nobles of minor rank, clergy and members of the middle-class depended on letter-writing in their business and personal affairs. Those who could not afford a secretary for these matters studied the manuals for letter-writing and composed the letters themselves.

Teresa's usual tactic in making requests or suggestions, providing advice, or warning, was to be exquisitely polite, and her letters are filled with expressions of courteous respect. She apologizes, lightens the blow, suggests options, and then often distances herself to acknowledge the independence of her addressees to act as they see fit. But her politeness never prevents her from also being colloquial in her style. Through her letters we acquire a better sense of the language of daily conversation.

Written in response to special situations, her letters cover a multiplicity of topics. From beginning to end, however, she is returning to the problems of her new Carmelite communities of both friars and nuns. The events surrounding her reform are the basis for a narrative of joys and conflicts. Conflicts arose, understandably, with the Carmelite friars of the observance, but more surprisingly they did so even with her own discalced friars. These many frictions stirred up fears within her that her letters might be stolen, so she often used code names for different individuals lest her candid words be read by others for whom they were not intended.

Another topic that posed sobering concerns for Teresa was bodily health, her own and that of others. Well known is her caution in her *Way of Perfection* against "complaining about light illnesses": "If you can tolerate them, don't complain about them" (ch. 11). Nonetheless, she speaks freely of her own illnesses, indeed deploring them, but worrying much more over the health of others. She becomes noticeably upset when others are sick, especially those who are leaders in her communities. She scolds them when they fail to inform her of their illnesses. In her other writings Teresa's major concern is with spiritual health; in her letters she focuses more on physical health and well-being. As a result, her letters furnish an informative document about the medical practices of her day.

Though Teresa did not neglect to consult medical doctors and respected their advice, she was also an enthusiast for popular medicine. She welcomed all the varieties of medicinal remedies—except, of course, sarsaparilla water. The most frequently used remedy, even among professionals, although to our minds strange, was recourse to purges and bloodletting.

Mainly as a result of her own long, woeful history of illness, Teresa had acquired an uncommon knowledge of medicine. With remarkable insight, she grasped the import in care for the sick of cleanliness, appropriate climate, special nourishment, and comfort—all of these clashing with the austere practices exacted in her time of discalced nuns. She summed the matter up with her own sensible maxim, ". . . it is better to cater to yourself than to be sick" (Ltr. 114.6). This was her principle in dealing with the sick, but she was not so careful in dealing with her own health.

It goes without saying that Teresa's correspondence covered a rich variety of other topics. Her letters give us a hint of what her conversation must have been like: simple yet multifaceted. Each represents one part, a splendid part, of a dialogue with another. There are her usual digressions, parenthetical insertions, afterthoughts, repetitions, and so on.

Since most of the historical background for the letters constituting this volume can be found in the introductions I've already written for volumes one through three of *The Collected Works of St. Teresa of Avila*, there would be no point in repeating all of this information here. The biographical pieces at the end of this volume are intended to provide additional information about many of the persons appearing on the pages of this correspondence, whose lives in themselves were often fascinating.

The Materials

Motivated by respect for the recipients of her letters, Teresa chose paper of the best quality, with its watermark still perceptible. If she inadvertently began on a piece of poor-quality paper, she felt no scruple in leaving the rest blank, telling the reader to pass on to the next page (cf. Ltr. 48.3). The ink, too, had to be the finest. A bad pen would simply not do, and vexedly she would change it for another—and change it again, if necessary, within the same letter. Annoyed, she complained to her brother about the poor quality of pens in Toledo: ". . . they are a nuisance and make my task harder" (Ltr. 185.1). The remarkable state in which her autographs are preserved gives testimony to her generous care for quality, a care prompted by the esteem she bore toward her correspondents.

Addressing and Mailing

Teresa concluded her letters with greetings to others, a prayer, a plea for prayers, or a promise of prayers. After she signed and dated them, more often without precision (thereby creating puzzles to be solved by her editors), but very precisely when she wanted to follow the best protocol, there remained the task of folding them. Before doing so, however, she often thought of other things to say, not surprisingly, and added postscripts in any free space she could find—even the king could receive a postscript. Envelopes had not yet been invented. Generally, as was the custom, Teresa wrote on large sheets of paper 8 ½ " by 12" which were folded. She used a smaller size when only intending to write a note. One section of the paper was left blank so that when the letter was folded the blank section provided the space for writing the address. The address was more or less detailed to match the status of the addressee. She goes to great lengths to be sure she is using the appropriate titles in the address.

Once the address was written out, if the letter was to be sent by the official mail, it was marked with the cost, agreed on with the carrier as part or full payment. This amount was to be paid by the receiver on the letter's arrival. The ends of the folded paper were glued together with paste or wax and then imprinted with Teresa's seal, bearing the anagram JHS. She had another seal, consisting of a skull, which she used only when she didn't have her preferred one with her. When these procedures were completed, Teresa was still liable to think of some other news she wanted to add, which she then wrote on the outside.

The Postal System

When Teresa's task was finished and her letters ready to go, she had no choice but to hand them over to uncertainty, the carriers not always being reliable. They might open the packets if they suspected something valuable within, and then destroy the letters; or they might lose them, or themselves be the victims of robbery before reaching their destination.

As a matter of fact, it was during Teresa's lifetime that the official mail was converted into a service open to the public. You could deposit your mail at one of the postal houses, although you could never be sure it would arrive at its destination. Teresa felt more at ease when her houses were situated in places linked with this network of public service. She deplored the trouble she had to go through to communicate with her out-of-the-way monasteries, like Malagón and Beas.

The muleteers were those she trusted more, especially with valuables, and they could carry heavier packages. But, lamentably, the cost was higher. She valued them also because they went to places not covered by the ordinary postal service.

In delicate business matters needing prompt attention, when she could not chance any delay or uncertainty, she hired special messengers—or her correspondents did. Because of the high cost, she did this only as a last resort.

Relatives, friends, friars, nuns, other members of the clergy also, carried letters for her on their travels. Another means to which she had recourse was the help of a prioress in one of her communities. She would send her a packet of letters to distribute or have distributed.

Teresa prized Toledo as a center for communications. In the commerce carried on with the Americas, the road passing along from Seville to Toledo to Madrid was a primary route, later extended to Medina del Campo and Valladolid.

The amount of time for letters to reach their destination depended on the place and season of year. In August, a round trip between Madrid and Toledo took five days, and from Toledo to Seville, eight days. But letters to America or to Rome required a good store of patience. The first step for a letter to America was to keep informed about when the fleet was to set sail so that a letter could be there in time. This was only the first obstacle to be surmounted. If the letter did finally arrive at the other shore, it then had to travel over land. The safest solution was to send many copies of the letter by different routes.

Before she began receiving support from the Spanish monarchy, Teresa's correspondence with the general of the Carmelites was substantial, regardless of the fact that only a few of these letters have been preserved. To Teresa's disappointment, the letters from the general were especially slow in reaching her. One of them took as many as 150 days to arrive. Another took over a year, 374 days to be precise. And many never made it to their destination.

What may come as a surprise to a present-day reader is that correspondence in sixteenth-century Spain was a luxury. Because of her longings to live a life of poverty, it pained Teresa to have to engage in a task like this. The postal system, which was less reliable, had a fixed rate, but the other methods put Teresa in the undesirable position of paying expensive fees. In certain circumstances the fees were downright exorbitant. The official mail cost about a quarter of a day's salary, limiting its service for the most part to paper and money. Teresa received packages on various occasions that included much more than paper or money: potatoes, lemons, butter, quince, marmalade, melons, coconuts, crucifixes, preserves, balsam, spices, and fresh fish. She found herself obliged to admonish the prioress of Seville: "But the portage costs so much that there is no reason for you to be sending me anything any more; it's a matter of conscience" (Ltr. 222.1).

Another perhaps novel fact for us is that the portage or postage was not paid by the sender but the receiver. The sender would write the amount for the postage on the outside of the letter or packet of letters with the understanding that the recipient was obliged to pay. Sometimes in pressing matters Teresa took pains to urge her correspondent to put down a generous amount for postage, and she had to coax others that they not neglect writing to her, that she would gladly pay the postage. There were times when she felt obliged to apologize for the postage, but then found an excuse for herself in the weighty nature of the contents. Never one for haggling over the postage, she did feel uneasy about the possibility that others might have to pay beyond their means to receive a letter from her.

Autographs, Copies, and Editions

Nothing of the kind of enthusiasm prompted by Teresa's other writings was shown toward her letters, neither by Philip II nor by her numerous friends and followers. It took time before people came to value the letters. Because of the many and difficult travels he was obliged to undertake after her death, Padre Gracián entrusted a packet of letters from Teresa to the care of his sister, who was then prioress of the monastery in Consuegra. This packet was handed on to her brother Tomás Gracián at the beginning of the seventeenth century in the hope that it would serve usefully in the process of Teresa's beatification. Not being used in this process, however, the packet was broken up and regrettably the letters were dispersed far and wide. Two small collections from Gracián's packet are conserved today, one in the Carmel of Seville, the other in the Carmel of Corpus Christi in Alcalá de Henares. Although autographs were lost, fortunately there were people interested enough to make copies of many of them.

If this happened with the correspondence for which special efforts toward preservation had been made, what could be expected for many of the other letters received from Teresa by different people. To our benefit, though, there were persons who did know the value of what they possessed. They took careful measures so that those who succeeded them after their death knew what to do with these precious mementos. An example here are the letters written to María de San José. A dear friend of Teresa's, she was the recipient of many precious letters from her revered foundress. Two years before her death, María de San José went to Lisbon, Portugal, to make a foundation there. She carried with her a cherished keepsake, her letters from Madre Teresa. Later these letters passed into the hands of Doctor Francisco Sobrino, who then became bishop of Valladolid. Two of the bishop's sisters were members of the community of Carmelite nuns in Valladolid, which explains how the Carmel in Valladolid has in its possession an invaluable collection of letters written by Teresa to María de San José.

The oldest codified copy of the letters dates from the middle of the seventeenth century and is found in Manuscript 12.763 in the National Library of Madrid. The copyist made a selection from a group of letters more doctrinal in character. Nonetheless, this copy has merit for its integrity and fidelity to the autographs; a comparison of autographs with this copy shows how trustworthy the codex is. On the exceptional occasions when something is suppressed, an indication of this is carefully provided. In the preparation of critical editions this codex has proved a trusty guide when the autograph is missing.

Another codex (12.764) in the same library, intended for the first edition of Teresa's letters, shows a troublesome tampering with the text. Much of the material covering internal affairs was omitted, supposedly because Teresa would not have wanted such material presented to the public. What the editors thought should be presented to the public were her "divine and heavenly teachings." This was the criterion in 1654, and this codex was the basis for the first edition of Teresa's letters published in 1658 in two volumes by Juan Palafox. It contained sixty-five letters. But they are immersed in and almost drowned by Palafox's innumerable notes written, in the baroque style of the times, for the purpose of bringing into relief the seemingly sparse doctrinal content. The letters seem to end up as not much more than a springboard for Palafox's long-winded efforts to edify.

Nonetheless these volumes pleased the public, so much so that in 1674, 108 more letters were published. Since, however, the diligent Palafox had died, Pedro de la Anunciación prepared the commentary, this time with more critical rigor and with unadorned notes. This richer volume, praiseworthy by our standards, did not please the public the way Palafox's did and met with less success. Not until the eighteenth century were more of Teresa's letters published, again filled with spiritual commentary, bringing the total to about 371 letters. The excellent critical work done in that century on Teresa's correspondence by Manuel de Santa María and Andrés de la Encarnación went unappreciated and ignored in the publications of her letters at that time.

In the nineteenth century Marcel Bouix in France and Vicente de la Fuente in Spain brought out more complete and acceptable editions of Teresa's letters, but still there were many defects.

The twentieth century saw the beginning of a much more critical approach and an assiduous effort to establish the exact chronology. Padre Silverio de Santa Teresa was the major player in the enormous task of securing the correct text of the Teresian writings. A further advance in the critical study of Teresa's letters, qualitatively and quantitatively, was made in the Efrén/Steggink critical edition of the complete works of St. Teresa published by the Biblioteca de Autores Cristianos in three volumes (Madrid 1959).

Teresa's letters put forth the same difficulties that most correspondence does when only one side of the picture may be had. We wonder what is motivating the responses or reactions, we ask what is being alluded to or to whom one is referring. But in Teresa's case the frustration mounts because of the four-centuries distance in time, and this made worse by the lack of care for, or curiosity about, them in the beginning. There are little events and large ones, great dramas and small ones, which we don't know enough about, the toils, the travails, the complexities hidden in the background, preventing us from an understanding that satisfies. And then there are the many people appearing on stage. Reading the letters of Teresa has been compared to reading a Russian novel. In fact it is even more difficult to keep straight all the characters, their many tiny worlds, that make their way onto her pages. I have found no greater help with this problem than in the most recent volume of the letters of St. Teresa edited by Tomás Alvarez (*Santa Teresa Cartas*, fourth edition, Burgos 1997). Taking Silverio's critical edition as a basis, attentive to the considerable progress made in research since then, he has given us a text that lays before us the best information research now gives. We have an answer for at least a good number of questions about persons, places, and events that arise as one reads. I have also chosen to follow his numbering of the letters—the numbering varies from editor to editor—which in his fourth edition follows a chronological order.

It goes without saying that the heading for each letter, which presents the name of the addressee, the places where the letter is sent to and from, and the date are the work of editors. These are not always certain, which means that discrepancies are found when comparing the editions of different editors. I have chosen to follow Tomás Alvarez's judgment in these matters also. If the autograph is still extant, I included information about the place where it may be found. Finally, after a short introduction, intended to indicate only briefly the thrust of the letter, the actual text of Teresa's begins. If the address is still extant, it precedes the letter's initial words of greeting.

Obviously Teresa did not number her paragraphs; numbering was done by Silverio in his critical addition. I have followed this numbering since it serves a practical purpose in presenting references.

The best introduction that I know of to the letters of St. Teresa is the one authored by Luis Rodríguez Martínez and Teófanes Egido appearing in *Introducción A La Lectura De Santa Teresa* (Madrid: Editorial de Espiritualidad, 1978), pp. 427–72. I found the abundant material presented there extremely helpful in the planning and writing of this introduction.

Among the many who have encouraged me to bring this volume to completion, I want to mention the special assistance I received from Mrs. Tina Mendoza who painstakingly compared my translation of each letter with the Spanish text giving me many excellent suggestions toward a better or more exact rendering. I am grateful for her constant readiness to help. I must also mention my debt of gratitude to Dr. Carol Lisi for her careful editorial assistance and valued work in the page design and layout.

Kieran Kavanaugh, O.C.D.
Carmelite Monastery
Washington, D.C.

The Letters

Letters 1–23 (1546 –1569)

1. To Alonso Venegrilla, Gotarrendura

Avila, 12 August 1546 (?)

(Autograph: DCN, Calahorra [Logroño])

Venegrilla took care of the pigeon-house that Teresa's family owned in Gotarrendura (1546-49), about ten miles north of Avila.

❖❖❖❖

Señor Venegrilla:

Santos García[1] brought ten bushels of wheat. Would you do me the favor of paying for the wheat, for I don't have the money. Señor Guzmán[2] will be pleased with this and will reimburse you, for that is what he usually does.

Doña Teresa de Ahumada

Would you kindly send me some little pigeons.

---

1. Santos García was probably a farmhand at Gotarrendura.
2. Martín de Guzmán was Teresa's brother-in-law, the husband of María de Cepeda.

2. To Don Lorenzo de Cepeda,[1] Quito (Ecuador)
Avila, 23 December 1561

(Autograph: DCN, Santa Ana, Madrid)

Teresa is living outside her monastery in the home of Doña Guiomar de Ulloa in Avila. From there she is supervising the renovation of the house bought for her first foundation. She is in dire financial need. Unexpectedly several Indians who were Lorenzo's friends brought letters and money. A mysterious promise made by St. Joseph is fulfilled. Deeply moved, Teresa writes in haste before Lorenzo's messenger leaves.

1. Jesus. Señor. May the Holy Spirit be always with your honor, amen, and repay you for the care with which you have so diligently come to the help of all. I hope in the majesty of God that you will gain much in his eyes. Certainly all those to whom you sent money received it at such an opportune moment that I was greatly consoled. I believe that it was God who stirred you to send me so much. The amount of money brought by Juan Pedro de Espinosa and Varrona[2] (which I think is the name of the other merchant) would have been enough to keep a poor worthless nun like myself who goes about in patches—which I now consider an honor, glory to God—out of need for some years.

2. I have already written you a long letter about a matter that for many reasons I could not escape doing, since God's inspirations are the source. Because these things are hard to speak of in a letter, I mention only the fact that saintly and learned persons think I am obliged not to be cowardly but do all I can for this project—a monastery of nuns. There will be no more than fifteen nuns[3] in it, who will practice very strict enclosure, never going out or allowing themselves to be seen without veils covering their faces. Their life will be one of prayer and mortification as I have written more at length in a letter to

you. I will write another for Antonio Morán to bring when he leaves.

3. That lady, Doña Guiomar,[4] who is also writing to you, is a help to me. She is the wife of Francisco Dávila, of Salobralejo, if you recall. Her husband died nine years ago. He had an annual income of 1,000,000 maravedis. She, for her part, has an entailed estate in addition to what she has from her husband. Although she was left a widow at the age of twenty-five, she has not married again but has devoted herself very much to the Lord. She is deeply spiritual. For more than four years we have been devoted friends, closer than if we were sisters. She still helps me very much, for she contributes a good portion of her income. At present she is without funds, so it is up to me to buy and prepare the house. With God's favor I have received two dowries beforehand and have bought the house, although secretly. But I did not have the means to pay for the work that still needed to be done. So by trusting in God alone (for God wants it to be done and will provide), I entered into an agreement with the workers. It seemed a foolish thing to do. But then His Majesty comes along and moves you to provide for it. And what amazes me is that the forty pesos you added was just what I needed. I believe that St. Joseph—after whom the house will be named—wanted us to have the money,[5] and I know that he will repay you. In sum, although the house is small and poor, the property has a field and some beautiful views. And that's sufficient.

4. They have gone to Rome for the papal bulls, for although the house belongs to my own religious order, we are rendering our obedience to the bishop.[6] I hope the foundation will give the Lord much glory, if he allows it to come about. I believe without a doubt that it will, for the souls that are planning to enter will give an excellent example of humility, as well as penance and prayer. They are choice souls. Will you all pray to God for this project, for by the time Antonio Morán departs, everything will be completed, with God's favor.[7]

5. Antonio Morán came here and was a great consolation to me. He seemed to be a loyal and highly gifted man. I was especially consoled to learn about all of you, for one of the great favors the Lord has granted me is that he has given you understanding of what the world is, and so you have chosen to live quiet lives. Now I know, too, that you have taken the path of heaven. This is what I wanted most to know, for up until now I was always in dread. Glory to the One who does all. May it please him that you always advance in his service. Since there is no measure to his remunerations, we should never stop trying to serve the Lord. Each day we will advance at least a little further, and with fervor. It seems, and so it is, that we are always at war, and until we are victorious, we must not grow careless.

6. All those with whom you have sent money have been reliable men. But Antonio Morán has surpassed them all. He has sold the gold at a higher price without charge, as you will see, and has brought the money here from Madrid despite his poor health—although today he is better, for it was caused by an accident. I notice that he thinks highly of you. He also brought the money from Varrona and did so with great care. Rodríguez came here too, and has done everything well. I will write to you through him, for perhaps he will be the first to leave. Antonio Morán showed me the letter you had written him. Believe me, I think that all this care is not only the fruit of his virtue, but also the result of God's inspiration.

7. Yesterday my sister María[8] sent me the enclosed letter. When they bring her the other money, she will write again. The help came just in time for her. She is a very good Christian and undergoes many trials. If Juan de Ovalle[9] initiates a lawsuit, it would destroy her children. Certainly he doesn't have as much a claim as he thinks he does, even though the sale of everything went badly and proved a disaster. But Martín de Guzmán also had good intentions—God rest his soul—and the judge ruled in his favor, even though not well enough. I cannot bear that anyone should now claim what my father—may he

enjoy eternal glory—sold. And the rest, as I say, would only kill María, my sister. God deliver me from the self-interest that brings so much harm to one's relatives. It has reached the point here that it's a wonder if there's a father who cares about his son or a brother who cares about his brother. Thus I'm not surprised by Juan de Ovalle; rather, he has done well by setting this litigation aside for now out of love for me. He is by nature good, but in this case it would be unwise to trust in that. When you send him the 1,000 pesos, you should ask him for a written promise to be given to me; and the day that he reintroduces the lawsuit, 500 ducats will go to Doña María.[10]

8. The houses at Gotarrendura are still not sold, but Martín de Guzmán received 300,000 maravedis from them, and it was only right that this amount went to Juan de Ovalle. Along with the 1,000 pesos you sent, he is taken care of and will be able to live here. For this is what he has done, he has come here and now needs to remain. He would be unable to live here other than badly and for only short periods of time without help from over there.[11]

9. His marriage is a good one. But I must tell you that Doña Juana is so honorable and trustworthy that she makes you want to praise God, and she has the soul of an angel. I've turned out to be the worst sister; the way I am, you ought not even acknowledge me as your sister. I don't know why you're all so fond of me. I say this in all truthfulness. Juana has undergone many trials and born them well. If you can send the money without placing yourself in need, do so quickly, even if little by little.

10. The money you sent was allocated as you will see from the letters. Toribia[12] is dead as is also her husband. It was a great help for her children, who are poor. The Masses have been said according to your intentions—some of them before the money arrived—and by the best persons I could find, all of them excellent. I was edified by the intentions for which you had them said.

11. I am staying in the house of Señora Doña Guiomar during these business affairs.[13] It makes me happy to be with persons who speak to me about you; indeed, it is my pleasure. One of this lady's daughters, who is a nun in our monastery, had to come out and stay with her mother, and our provincial ordered me to be her companion.[14] Here, more than at my sister's house, I am at liberty to do the many things I need to do. All the conversation here is about God, and we live in great recollection. I will remain here until given other orders, even though it would be better for me to stay here so as to handle the above business matters.

12. Now to speak of my dear sister, Señora Doña Juana,[15] for although I mention her last, she is not so in my heart. That is certain, for I pray to God for her as intensely as I do for you. I kiss both your hands a thousand times for all the kindnesses you have shown me. I don't know how to repay you other than by praying fervently for our little boy.[16] And this is being done, for the saintly friar Peter of Alcántara has promised to do so (he is the discalced friar about whom I wrote you), and the Theatines[17] and other persons whom God will hear are doing so.[18] May it please His Majesty to make the child better than his parents, for good as you are, I want more for God. Continue writing to me about your joy and resignation to God's will, for that makes me very happy.

13. I mentioned that when Antonio Morán leaves I will send along for you a copy of the patent letters of nobility,[19] which they say couldn't be better. I'll take great care in doing this. And if this time it gets lost on the way, I'll keep sending others until one arrives. For some foolish reasons it was not sent (it was the responsibility of a third party who did not want to—I'll say no more). I'll also send you some relics, for the reliquary isn't worth much. I kiss my brother's hands a thousand times for what he has sent me. If it had come at a time when I wore gold jewelry, I would have been very envious of the medal, for it is extremely beautiful. May God keep you and your wife for

many years. And may he give you a happy new year, for tomorrow is New Year's Eve for 1562.[20]

14. Since I spent a long time with Antonio Morán, I began this letter late; otherwise I would say more, but he wants to leave tomorrow. I will write again through Jerónimo de Cepeda,[21] and since I'll be doing so soon, it doesn't matter that I don't say more here. Always read my letters yourself. I went to great lengths to use good ink. This letter was written so quickly; and, as I say, it is so late that I cannot take time to read it over. My health is better than usual. May God give you health in body and soul, as I desire, amen.

15. I'm not writing to Hernando de Ahumada or Pedro de Ahumada[22] for lack of time; I will do so soon. Your honor should know that some very good persons who are aware of our secret—our new undertaking—have considered it a miracle that you sent so much money at such a time. I hope that when there is need for more, God will put it into your heart to help me, even though you may not want to.

Your devoted servant,

Doña Teresa de Ahumada

---

1. Teresa's younger brother Lorenzo de Cepeda departed for America in 1540 and took up residence in Quito, where he became a wealthy man.
2. There were four merchants who brought money from Lorenzo: Pedro de Espinosa (perhaps related to Lorenzo's wife), Varrona, Antonio Morán (praised in nos. 2, 4, & 7 of this letter), and Alonso Rodríguez (no. 6). In thinking that Lorenzo was stirred by God, Teresa is alluding to what she tells in L. 33.12.
3. Cf. WP. 2.9, and note 5.
4. Guiomar de Ulloa was the widow of Francisco Dávila, a large property owner, who left her a small fortune, which she used mostly for charitable works.
5. Cf. L. 33.12.
6. Teresa placed her first foundation under obedience to the bishop of Avila on account of the difficulties the Carmelite provincial had about accepting it. See L. 33.4.14,16; F. epil.

7. The project suffered a delay so that the foundation did not take place until 24 August 1562.
8. Teresa's older sister María, the widow of Martín de Guzmán y Barrientos, had shown Teresa hospitality on their farm in Castellanos de la Cañada when Teresa had become sick as a young nun. See L. 3.3; 4.6; 5.3.
9. Juan de Ovalle, Teresa's brother-in-law, was the husband of Juana de Ahumada.
10. All this litigation in the family stemmed from the fact that Alonso de Cepeda had not divided his goods equally between the children of his first and second marriages.
11. Teresa's sister and brother-in-law had come from Alba de Tormes to Avila to help Teresa with her new foundation. See L. 33.11; 36.5.
12. Toribia worked for Don Alonso as a housemaid.
13. Teresa became acquainted with Guiomar de Ulloa through her daughter, Antonia de Guzmán, who was a nun with Teresa at the monastery of the Incarnation in Avila. Antonia, sometimes accompanied by Teresa, used to leave the monastery for long visits with her mother. A close friendship then began between Teresa and Doña Guiomar.
14. That is, a traveling companion to Antonia de Guzmán.
15. Juana Fuentes y Espinosa was Lorenzo's wife. Born in Perú (1539), she married Lorenzo in 1556. She died in childbirth in 1567, leaving seven children behind.
16. The little boy, probably Lorenzo's oldest son, died in 1563.
17. In Spain, the Jesuits were at first called Theatines.
18. The autograph ends here.
19. These patent letters were given by the chancery of Valladolid in favor of Teresa's father and uncles after suit was brought against them for not paying taxes. They claimed exemption because of their noble status (1519-22).
20. It was 24 December. In Avila the new year began on Christmas Day, until 1564 when the date for beginning the new year was changed to 1 January.
21. Teresa's younger brother(1522-75) who was returning from Spain to America.
22. Hernando (1510) and Pedro (1521) are Teresa's brothers. Both went to America; only Pedro returned, in 1575.

3. To the Lords of the Town Council, Avila

Avila, 5 December 1563

(Autograph: DCN, Medina del Campo)

This letter speaks of the consolation the sisters find in their hermitages, places of solitude in their garden where they can praise God and pray for the city. A lawsuit was initiated against the nuns because one of the hermitages was constructed at a site harmful to the city's water supply.

Most Honorable Lords:

1. Since we received information that the little hermitages constructed on our property would cause no damage to the city's water ways, and the need was very great, we never thought your honors would be disturbed. What we did only serves for God's praise and provides us with a place apart for prayer, for it is in these hermitages that we beg God in a special way to preserve this city in his service.

2. Aware that your honors are displeased—which distresses us all—we beg you to come and see. We are prepared to comply with all the documents, promises, and pledges your lawyers might require so as to be sure that no damage will be done at any time; and we have always resolved to act in this way.

3. If despite this your honors are not satisfied and want the hermitages removed, may you first consider the benefit and not the harm that may come from them. What we want most to avoid is that you be displeased. We would be distressed if we had to go without the consolation we find in them, for it is spiritual.

4. May our Lord keep and preserve you, most honorable gentlemen, in his service, amen.

Your unworthy servants who respectfully kiss your hands,

The poor sisters of San José

4. To Juan de San Cristóbal, Avila

Avila, 9 April 1564

(Autograph: DCF, Avila)

A letter of agreement for the sale of some dovecotes. Since the request in Letter 3 was rejected, Teresa decided to make this purchase and convert the dovecotes into other hermitages that would not be a threat to the city's water supply.

⁂

1. This day, Quasimodo Sunday,[1] 1564, Juan de San Cristóbal and Teresa of Jesus entered into agreement on the sale of a group of dovecotes for 100 ducats free of tithes or duties.

2. The amount will be paid in this manner: 10,000 maravedis now and 10,000 by Pentecost Sunday; the remainder will be paid by St. John's feast of this year.

In confirmation of the above, I place my signature.

Teresa of Jesus

---

1. The Octave Sunday of Easter. Since the request in Ltr. 4 had been rejected, Teresa decided to make this purchase.

5. To Padre García de Toledo, Avila (?)

Avila, 1565

(Autograph: El Escorial)

This letter accompanied the second draft of Teresa's Life *and appears in that work as the epilogue. García de Toledo, one of her directors, had urged Teresa to expand on the first draft and now was in a hurry to read what she had written in her second draft. Teresa advises him to hurry in the service of the Lord.*

1. May the Holy Spirit be always with your honor, amen.

It wouldn't be wrong for me to exaggerate this service[1] I have rendered you in order that you feel obliged to take great care to pray to our Lord for me. For I certainly must have the right to ask this of you from what I have undergone in writing about myself and calling to mind so many of my miseries; although I can truthfully say it was more difficult for me to write about the favors His Majesty granted me than about my offenses against him.

2. I did what you commanded me and enlarged upon the material.[2] I did this on the condition that you do what you promised by tearing up what appears to you to be bad. I hadn't finished reading it after the writing was done when you sent for it. It could be that some of the things are poorly explained and others put down twice, for I had so little time I couldn't read over what I wrote. I ask you to correct it and have it transcribed if it is to be brought to Padre Maestro Avila, for it could happen that someone might recognize my handwriting.[3] I urgently desire that he be asked for his opinion about it, since this was my intention in beginning to write. If it seems to him I am walking on a good path, I shall be very consoled; then nothing else would remain for me than to do what lies within my power. Nevertheless, do what you think best, and remember you are obliged to one who has so entrusted her soul to you.

3. I shall recommend your soul to our Lord for the rest of my life. So do me the favor of hurrying to serve His Majesty; for you will see, from what is written here, how well one is occupied when one gives oneself entirely—as you have begun to do—to him who so immeasurably gives himself to us.

4. May he be blessed forever! I hope in his mercy that you and I will see each other there where we shall behold more

clearly the great things he has done for us, and praise him forever and ever, amen.

This book was finished in June 1562.[4]

---

1. The service was either her having written for him or having sent him the *Book of Her Life*.
2. Padre García encouraged Teresa to give free reign to her pen (see L. 30.22;37.1).
3. Teresa is referring to St. John of Avila. In the end, with the help of Doña Luisa de la Cerda, she sent him the autograph itself rather than a copy.
4. This date, according to Domingo Báñez, refers to the completion of the first redaction. The second redaction was finished toward the end of 1565.

6. To Don Gaspar Daza, Avila

Toledo, 24 March 1568

Gaspar Daza was a priest in Avila of whom Teresa speaks in her Life *(23.6-9). Now he is an admirer and defender of the little monastery of St. Joseph's. Writing from the palace of Doña Luisa de la Cerda in Toledo, Teresa had just come from Alcalá where she had assisted María de Jesús in a foundation for Carmelite nuns there (see L. 35.1-2). Teresa is directing her eyes now toward her next project, the foundation in Malagón. The autograph, now lost, was torn and parts were missing.*

1. The relics of the young shepherd saints[1] that were brought to Alcalá moves us to praise our Lord. May he be blessed for everything. Indeed, sir, it is so easy for His Majesty to make saints that I don't know why you are so amazed up there that he should grant some favors to those who live in solitude. May it please the Lord that we know how to serve him, for he knows so well how to repay.

2. I was most happy that you were pleased . . . which will not be enjoyed save by one who truly understands how sweet the Lord is.[2] May it please God to preserve you for me many years as a help to those sisters.[3]

3. Do not allow them to speak with one another about the kind of prayer they experience, nor should they get involved in such matters, or speak about Concepción,[4] for each one will want to add some foolishness of her own. They should let her be, for when she cannot do all the work, they can find another and the two can share the work, for God will provide food . . . .

4. Your mother and sister must remember little of me. I will write to the abbess,[5] if I can. May God give her health. I already wrote to Madrid for the coarse wool. I don't know whether I am forgetting something. At least, I won't forget to pray for you. Please do the same for me and ask the Lord that this new house[6] for his service may be founded. Next Tuesday, I think, we will be going for certain. Today is the vigil of Our Lady of the Incarnation. My regards to Padre Lárez, Brother Cristóbal, and to Maridíaz.[7]

Your unworthy servant and daughter,

Teresa of Jesus, Carmelite

---

1. She is alluding to the solemn transfer of the relics of Justus and Pastor from Huesca to Alcalá, 7 March.
2. Cf. Psalm 34:8.
3. The nuns at St. Joseph's in Avila.
4. She was probably the *demandadera* (one who serves an enclosed monastery of nuns by answering the door and running errands).
5. The abbess of the Cistercian nuns in Avila.
6. The foundation in Malagón.
7. Cf. L. 27.17 and note 13.

7. To Doña Luisa de la Cerda, Antequera

Malagón, 18 May 1568

After the death of her husband, Luisa de la Cerda received permission from the Carmelite provincial to have Teresa to stay with her. She later offered to provide funds for a foundation of Teresa's in Malagón. Teresa has been in Malagón since the beginning of April. She is worried about her manuscript and urges Doña Luisa to send it without delay to St. John of Avila.

1. Jesus be with your ladyship. I would have liked to have had more time for this letter, and thinking that I would have it today, I waited until now; for tomorrow, 19 May, I'm leaving. But I have had so much to do that no time is left. I will write through Pablo Hernández.[1] Although I have received no word about him since he left here, I'll inform him of all that you asked me to tell him. I've praised our Lord that your trip went so well.[2] We prayed very much for it here. May His Majesty be pleased that the rest of the trip turn out as well.

2. I am feeling fine and each day I feel better in this town, and so do all the others. None of the sisters is dissatisfied, and every day they please me more. I tell you that of the four who have come, three experience deep prayer, and have many other gifts.[3] They are such that you can be sure that even though I'm going away, nothing that has to do with perfection will be lost, especially considering the persons who will be here with them . . .[4] May God keep him here for many years, for with him I have no worry about anything.[5] The parish priest[6] kisses your hands, for he is the type—I don't know how to say it—who doesn't send greetings. As you directed me, I gave your greetings to him. We owe him a great deal.

3. I cannot understand why you have not yet sent Maestro Avila what I entrusted to you![7] Do not delay any longer, for love of the Lord, but send it right away through a messenger—they

tell me it's only a day's journey. To wait for Salazar[8] would be foolish; if he is rector, he wouldn't be able to leave to visit you, and even less go to see Padre Avila. I beg you, if you have not sent it, to do so at once. Indeed, this has distressed me, for it seems that the devil is interfering. And the Reverend Licentiate[9] has been a great temptation, for I had told him to bring it when he went. I believe that the devil will get mad if this saint sees it. I don't know the reason . . .[10] I beg you to send it at once and do what I asked of you in Toledo. Realize that it's more important than you think . . .[11]

---

1. One of Teresa's Jesuit confessors.
2. Doña Luisa had journeyed to the south of Spain in search of a spa for her son, who was suffering from kidney stones.
3. The four nuns had come from Teresa's monastery of St. Joseph's in Avila.
4. Here something is missing from the text.
5. She is probably alluding to the community's confessor, Tomás Carleval.
6. Juan Bautista, the parish priest in Malagón.
7. Teresa is speaking of *The Book of Her Life*. She wanted Maestro Avila (St. John of Avila, who was living in Montilla) to read it and give his opinion of it.
8. Gaspar de Salazar, a Jesuit who knew Teresa when he was rector in Avila and who was now rector in Marchena.
9. The Reverend Licentiate Velasco who was in the service of Doña Luisa.
10. Here there is another omission in the manuscript.
11. The rest of the letter is missing.

8. To Doña Luisa de la Cerda, Antequera

Toledo, 27 May 1568

Teresa is writing late at night from the Toledan palace of Doña Luisa de la Cerda. She had recieved a letter sent from Andalusia by Doña Luisa, but nothing was said in it about her book (the Life*). She presents a positive report on life at the palace and gives information about Malagón and the plans for* *a school of Christian doctrine. Having arrived very sick and been confined to bed, Teresa improved after being bled twice. Although still in a weakened condition, she plans to leave the next day for Avila by way of Escalona.*

1. May Jesus be with your ladyship. Today, the feast of the Ascension, the licentiate[1] gave me your letter. When I learned that he had come, I was very anxious, until I read it, for I wondered about its contents. Glory to our Lord that you are doing well, as is also Don Juan, and my lords.[2]

2. As for the rest, don't worry in the least about it. But even though I say this, I myself was disturbed and told him that he had done the wrong thing. He is very confused, in my opinion; indeed, one cannot understand him. On the one hand he desires to serve and says that he loves you very much, which is true, and on the other hand he doesn't know how to behave consistently. He also suffers from a little melancholy, just as Alonso de Cabria.[3] But what contradiction in the things of this world! He could be serving you and doesn't want to; and I, who would enjoy doing so, cannot. Things like these, and other worse things, we as mortals have to endure. We never manage to understand the world, but we don't want to leave it.

3. I'm not surprised that you are distressed. I've already understood that you would have to suffer much, seeing that you have not the kind of temperament that gets along with everyone. But since this is for the service of the Lord, try to bear it and talk it over with this Lord, for he will not leave you alone. That the licentiate has left you will not seem bad to anyone here, but they will feel sorry for you. Try to cast aside your worries. See how much we care about your health. Mine has been very bad these past days. Were it not for all the comfort you have provided for me in this house, it would have been worse. I needed this, for with the sun along the road, the pain I was suffering when you were in Malagón increased to such a

point that when I arrived in Toledo they had to bleed me twice. I wasn't able to move in bed because of the pain moving up from my shoulders to the back of my head. The next day I had to undergo a purge. And so I was delayed here eight days as of tomorrow, for I came Friday.[4] I'm leaving in a very weakened condition—for they drew much blood—but feeling better. I felt very lonely when I found myself here without you, my friend. May the Lord be served by everything. Everyone has treated me very well, including Reolín.[5] Indeed, I was delighted over how you took such care of me up here, even though you are down there. I pray fervently to the Lord for you. I am well now, although weak.

4. The priest from Malagón accompanied me;[6] it is remarkable how indebted I am to him. Alonso de Cabria does so well under his administrator[7] that he didn't feel like coming with me. He said that the administrator would miss him very much. Since I had such good company and he was tired from the previous trip, I did not press him. You should know that the administrator does a superb job. They say he's beyond all expectations. Alonso de Cabria never finishes praising him, and so, too, the others. Lord Don Hernando[8] is also very happy with him.

5. Carleval has left, and I don't think he'll return . . .[9] They say that the Lord has wanted Alonso de Cabria to work for the monastery and that the hospital would pay the expenses. And that is true because Carleval's brother[10] came. I tell you that I am most happy to leave him there. Other than my Padre Pablo,[11] I don't know who I could have left that would match him. We are lucky to have him. He is a man of prayer, with deep experiences of it. He is very happy, but it's necessary to make some further provisions for him. Because I've written to you in Malagón about all this, I'll say no more. Here they tell me great things about this padre I'm speaking of.

6. The sisters are elated. We agreed to bring in a woman who is very much a *teatina*.[12] The house will provide her

meals—since we must give alms we might as well do it this way—and she will teach needlework gratis to young girls with the intent of teaching them Christian doctrine and how to serve the Lord, something highly beneficial. Padre Carleval also sent for a young man, and Huerna, as they call him, to assist them. And he and the parish priest will teach the doctrine. I hope in the Lord that this will be of great benefit. Truly, I have come away highly pleased, and may you be so also. Be assured that my absence will take nothing away from the religious observance of the house, for with the spirit of the sisters and with such a confessor,[13] and the priest, who will not neglect them, I hope in God they will advance each day, and I don't doubt that.

7. As for the other chaplain, no one wants to tell him not to say Mass.[14] You might write to him about it, although Padre Pablo is looking for someone to tell him, but I would not want you to forget to do so yourself. The administrator says that he will arrange things so well for him that he will be much better off than previously; but since it is he who must console him, he does not want to be the one to tell him. I beg you not to forget this. They have already given a third of the money to the licentiate; Miranda gave it to him. Send your instructions in writing about who should reimburse Miranda for these payments. May the devil not concoct a scheme that would make us lose a man like this. And he certainly will try, for Miranda will do him as much harm as he possibly can. May you understand the importance of this, and not allow it.

8. I was so busy today that I didn't have time to write; now it's late into the night, and I feel very weak. I brought the lady's saddle that you kept in the fortress—I hope you won't mind—and I bought another good one here. I already know that you will be happy that it is a help to me on these journeys since it was there without being used. At least, I'll be traveling with something that is yours. I hope in the Lord that I shall be re-

turning on it; and if not, I will send it to you as soon as you return.

9. I've already written to you in Malagón that I think the devil is trying to prevent Maestro Avila from seeing what I entrusted to you.[15] I wouldn't want him to die before seeing it; that would be too much to bear. Since you are so near him, I beg you that through one of your messengers you send it to him sealed. Write to him and highly recommend it to him, for he wants to read it and will do so as soon as he can. Fray Domingo[16] now wrote to me here that when I arrive in Avila I should send it to him by a private messenger. I'm distressed—I don't know what to do, for, as I told you, I would be greatly harmed, if they found out.[17] For love of our Lord, please attend to this quickly; realize that if you do, you will be rendering our Lord a service. And as a favor to me, be brave in those strange lands. Recall how our Lady and our Father St. Joseph went about in Egypt.

10. I'm going to go by way of Escalona, for the marchioness is there and she has sent for me.[18] I told her that you had bestowed so many kindnesses on me that I didn't need anything further from her, but that I would stop to see her on the way. It will be for only half a day, if possible, no more. I'm doing this because Fray García,[19] who promised her, urged me to do so, and I won't be going out of my way. Señor Don Hernando and Señora Doña Ana[20] graciously came to see me, and Don Pedro Niño[21] and Señora Doña Margarita[22] as well; and other friends and various people came, some of whom tired me out. Those from your house are very recollected and solitary. Would you write to the señora directress;[23] you now see what you owe her. I did not see her, although she sent me gifts, for I was confined to bed most of the time. I must go to see the señora prioress[24] tomorrow before leaving, for she is insisting that I come to see her.

11. I was not going to speak about the death of my lady the Duchess of Medinaceli[25] in case you had not heard about it. Afterward, I thought that by the time this reaches you, you will

know about it. I would not want you to grieve over it, for the Lord has granted a favor to all those who truly loved her—and granted one to her—in that he brought her so quickly to himself; with the sickness she had, they would have seen her die a thousand deaths. Such was her ladyship's life that she will live forever, and the hope of seeing her again, you and I together, helps me to live deprived of her presence. I kiss the hands of all my lords; Antonia[26] kisses yours. Give my best regards to Señor Don Juan; I pray for him very much. May His Majesty keep watch over you for me and and guide you always. I'm very tired, and so I'll say no more.

Your unworthy subject and servant,

Teresa of Jesus, Carmelite

12. They've already given authorization to our "eternal *padre*."[27] That's the way it is: on the one hand I'm annoyed, and on the other I see that the Lord wants it so and that you suffer trials alone. The padre will surely write to you when he finds a messenger. I will leave this letter with Doña Francisca[28] giving her urgent instructions. If I find someone going that way, I will write from Avila. I forgot to mention that our padre told me of a nun who is very devoted to reading and gifted in ways pleasing to him. She has no more than 200 ducats, but the nuns are so much alone and the needs of a monastery in its beginning so great that I said they should take her. I prefer having her to taking in foolish nuns, and if I could find another like her, I wouldn't take any more. May your ladyship remain with God; I'd rather not bring this to an end, nor do I know how I'm going to bear being so far from someone to whom I'm so indebted and love so much.

---

1. It seems Velasco resigned from the service of Doña Luisa.
2. Juan Pardo de Tavera, Doña Luisa's son, and the others in their circle
3. Alonso de Cabria Pecellín, a priest in the service of Doña Luisa, who enjoyed a benefice in Paracuellos.
4. She arrived from Malagón on the 19th and will leave for Escalona on the 28th.

5. Gabriel de Reolí, a Toledan and friend of St. Teresa's.
6. The licentiate Juan Bautista.
7. Doña Luisa's administrator, Juan de Huidobro de Miranda.
8. Doña Luisa's brother, Hernando de la Cerda.
9. Doctor Bernardino Carleval, a disciple of St. John of Avila's and professor at the university of Baeza. The manuscript is illegible here for about three lines.
10. The Carmelite Tomás de Carleval.
11. The Jesuit Pablo Hernández.
12. An expression referring to a woman given to acts of piety and under the guidance of Jesuits, who at first were called Theatines.
13. Probably Tomás Carleval, confessor at the Carmel in Malagón.
14. Teresa now wanted the Mass to be said each day by the Carmelite, Padre Carleval. She was trying to find another better benefice for the former chaplain.
15. Teresa had consigned the *Book of her Life* to Doña Luisa, who was to care for its safe delivery to St. John of Avila.
16. Fray Domingo Báñez who had already rendered his official judgment of the book and didn't see any need to submit it for an opinion to St. John of Avila.
17. The group of theologians and directors in Avila who had already approved the book.
18. Doña Juana Lucas de Toledo, the Marchioness of Villena and the Duchess of Escalona, a near relative of Padre García de Toledo's.
19. Padre García de Toledo, one of the Avila group who approved the *Life*.
20. Ana de Thienlloye, wife of Doña Luisa's brother, Hernando de la Cerda.
21. Pedro Niño de Conchillos y Rivera, an in-law relative of Doña Luisa's.
22. Margarita de Centellas y Borja, St. Francis Borgia's sister.
23. Ana de Silva, directress of a school for young ladies from the nobility.
24. The prioress of the Jeronimites of San Pablo.
25. Juana Manuela de Portugal, who died 1 May 1568.
26 Antonia del Espíritu Santo, one of the original nuns from San José in Avila, who accompanied Teresa on her journeys.
27. A humorous yet respectful name for the Jesuit Pablo Hernández.
28. Probably the daughter of the founder of Teresa's monastery in Toledo, Alonso Ramírez.

9. To Doña Luisa de la Cerda, Antequera

Avila, 9 June 1568

Teresa, in an exhausted condition, had arrived in Avila eight days prior to the date of this letter. She had traveled from Malagón to Toledo and through Escalona to Avila. She writes about her arrival, but also mentions again the matter of her manuscript, the Life.

1. Jesus be with your ladyship. I arrived here in Avila very tired on the Wednesday before Pentecost, for, as I wrote to you,[1] I was in such a dreadful state of health that I wasn't ready for traveling. And so we journeyed at a slow pace. The priest[2] accompanying us was a great comfort to me; he's so gracious about everything. A relative of mine is passing through; as a child, he suffered from stone and was cured by the waters of the spring down there[3] and has never suffered a relapse. This good news made me so happy, because I hope in our Lord the same thing will happen to Señor Don Juan. May His Majesty heal him, which is what we here are begging him to do. I kiss his honor's hands and those of all my lords.

2. I've found out that Doña Teresa, the daughter of the Marchioness of Velada has become a nun[4] and is very happy. I visited the Marchioness of Vellena last Sunday. She was most gracious, but since my Señora Doña Luisa is all I need, the courtesy mattered little to me. May the Lord bring you here to me safely and in good health. In regard to what I entrusted with you,[5] I beg you once more, for reasons about which I've already written you, not to neglect it, for it is a very important matter for me. Since I left a long letter in Malagón for you and another in Toledo, this one is for no other purpose than to let you know that I arrived safely, and so I've nothing further to say.

Today is Wednesday.

Your ladyship's unworthy subject and servant,

Teresa of Jesus, Carmelite

---

1. In Ltr. 8.
2. The priest from Malagón, the licentiate Juan Bautista.
3. Fuentepiedra, a spring near Antequera from which Doña Luisa's son, Don Juan Pardo de Tavera, was seeking a cure from kidney stones.
4. Doña Teresa de Toledo, the daughter of the Marchioness of Velada, Doña Lucas de Toledo, joined the Cistercian nuns of Santa Ana in Avila.
5. Her *Life*, which she wanted delivered to St. John of Avila.

10. To Doña Luisa de la Cerda, Antequera

Avila, 23 June 1568

Teresa is preparing for her journey to Valladolid to make her fourth foundation. She is still concerned about her book, which has now been delivered to St. John of Avila. She is happy with her Carmels in Avila and Malagón.

1. May Jesus be with your ladyship. The messenger is in such a hurry that I don't know how I'm going to manage sending you even these few lines, although my love for you is helping me find the time. Oh, my lady, how often I think of you and of your trials, and so I take care in praying to our Lord for you. May it please His Majesty to give health quickly to those lords so that I will not feel so far away from you, for if I knew you were in Toledo, I think I'd be content. I am well, glory be to God. I will go from here to Valladolid after the feast of St. Peter.

2. Remember, since I entrusted my soul[1] to you, that you send it to me by messenger as quickly as you can, but not without a letter from that holy man,[2] so that we may know his opinion, as we agreed in our conversation together. I'm afraid that when the *presentado* Fray Domingo[3] comes, for they say

he is coming this summer, I'll be caught red-handed.[4] For love of our Lord, after that saint has seen it, send it to me, for there will be time for us to see it together when I return to Toledo. Don't worry about having Salazar[5] see it, unless an exceptional opportunity arises, for it's more important that you send it back to me.

3. From your monastery[6] they write me that everything is going very well and that they are making progress, and I believe it. Everyone here thinks that those sisters are so very fortunate in having such a confessor—for they know him.[7] They marvel and so do I at the manner in which the Lord brought him there. I think the Lord did so for the benefit of souls in that place, for they say he does much good. And this he has done wherever he has been. Surely, he is a man of God. Everyone here esteems the house in Malagón highly, and the friars[8] are very happy. May the Lord bring me back there with you.

4. I find that the sisters here have made exceptional progress. All of them kiss your hands, and I, those of both Señor Don Juan[9] and my ladies, for I have no time to write more. Tomorrow is the feast of St. John; we will pray fervently to him for our foundress and patroness, and for our patron.[10]

Your ladyship's unworthy servant,

Teresa of Jesus

Unless you want them to pass through the superior, address your letters, and what I entrusted to you, here.

---

1. *The Book of Her Life*, which she wanted St. John of Avila to read.
2. St. John of Avila.
3. The Dominican theologian Domingo Báñez.
4. She is being facetious here. Thinking his approval was sufficient, Báñez did not want her *Life* to be read by others.
5. The Jesuit Gaspar de Salazar, former rector in Avila.
6. Teresa's Carmelite foundation in Malagón, which Doña Luisa had endowed.

7. Tomás de Carleval.
8. The Carmelites of the observance in Toledo.
9. Juan Pardo, Doña Luisa's son.
10. Doña Luisa, by reason of the endowment, is considered the foundress and patroness of the Carmel in Malagón and Don Juan, its patron.

11. To Don Cristóbal Rodríguez de Moya, Segura de la Sierra

Avila, 28 June 1568

Don Cristóbal, a wealthy widower, was trying to decide whether to found a Teresian Carmel or a Jesuit school. His two daughters and he wanted spiritual direction from the Jesuits. A Franciscan friend of Teresa's interceded in favor of the Carmel. At this point Teresa wrote the following letter, but in the end Don Cristóbal decided in favor of the Jesuits. The authentic text of the letter is incomplete. The first nine numbers of the text have undergone some decided tampering. Because some of the thought is still Teresa's, they are presented here in a note. Numbers 10-13 are authentic.[1]

10. When I heard about this matter, I was closer to you, for in May I left that place for where I am now. Our Lord, who so ordained things, must have known this to be better. By leaving everything in his hands—your desires and mine, since all must be directed to his glory—the Lord will ordain that what is for the best will come about.

11. I am sending through this messenger a request to the licentiate Juan Bautista, who is the priest in Malagón, that he pay you a visit. During the time I was there, he was most gracious and helped in everything, both spiritual and temporal, for the Lord gave him talents in all these matters. He will in-

quire about your aims and inform you about our way of life (for, as our confessor, he came to know all about it). In this way we won't be left in the dark on a matter so important. I don't think he'll refuse this act of charity.

12. You can speak with him about your concerns as with one who is completely familiar with my goals. Whatever he says in my place and agrees to, you can believe as though it were I speaking. May the Lord direct everything and make your honor his great servant, something I will beg of His Majesty from now on. The news that Father Guardian[2] gave me about the works our Lord does through you obliges me to do this.

13. You are also especially obliged to pray for Father Guardian. He traveled a number of leagues for this matter only, and this he did on foot and discalced, which makes it more praiseworthy, as does the fact that he has devoted himself to my project as if it were his own. Indeed it is for the glory of our Lord and the honor of the glorious Virgin Mary.

Written in Avila in the monastery of St. Joseph, 28 June 1568.

Your honor's unworthy servant,

Teresa of Jesus

---

1. [Paragraphs 1 - 9]

1. *Our Lord has brought together in these houses persons who amaze me and leave me completely confounded, for those chosen must be persons of prayer, suited for our way of life. If they are not, we do not take them. God gives them ordinarily a joy and happiness so great that they seem to be in a paradise on earth.*

2. *This is a fact, as your honor can learn from many people, especially if any members of the Society of Jesus who have been here pass through. For they know me and have seen this. They are my fathers to whom, after our Lord, my soul owes every good it possesses, if it does possess any.*

3. *And one of the things that attracts me to those ladies and to serving you in every way I can, is that they have conversed with these fathers. Not every spiritual person satisfies me as being suited for our monas-*

teries, but those who have had these Fathers as confessors do. Almost all those who are in our houses are their daughters—I don't remember any that I have accepted who were not. They are the ones who suit us. For since these Fathers nurtured my soul, the Lord has granted me the favor of having their spirit planted in these monasteries. And so, if you are familiar with their rules, you will see that in many things in our constitutions we are like them. For I received a brief from the pope to draw up constitutions, and when Our Most Reverend General came here, he approved them and gave orders that they be observed in all the monasteries founded by me. And he ordered that the fathers of the Society be preachers for the nuns and that no major superior could hinder them from doing so; and that if they wanted, they could be the nuns' confessors. But the fact is that they have a rule forbidding this, and so, except on rare occasions, we cannot confess to them. Nonetheless they frequently speak to us and give us counsel and do us much good.

4. *I had the same desire that those ladies have, to submit the house to the direction of these fathers, and I tried to do it. I know for certain they will not accept a monastery, even were it the wish of the princess, for they would have to care for too many in the kingdom; so, it's something impossible.*

5. *I praise God that like no other order we have a freedom to speak with them, a freedom that we are sure will never be taken from us.*

6. *Now with the favor of our Lord, monasteries of the primitive rule like ours, dedicated to prayer and mortification, to which we must be given, are being founded. Our Most Reverend Father has given permission for this, and there are persons and friars filled with zeal as well as a great many houses. But if I learn that a house of ours would appeal to that town, I will perhaps try to found one there, for I have the authority and patent letters for doing so. The monasteries that I found are subject only to the general or any of his delegates.*

7. *It is very important that with our Lord's help these monasteries always make progress in perfection. And be assured that, with respect to lax monasteries where there is no prayer, I have sought in every possible way that we persevere in what we have begun.*

8. *I ask you as well as those ladies, for the love of our Lord, not to forget me in your prayers. As for this matter at hand, take special care to go through with it, if it is for the service of God; if not, then set it aside. We here shall do likewise.*

9. *If it seems to you too rigorous that we abstain from meat, the foundation could be made like the one made on Palm Sunday in Malagón. It could be easily done since there are bulls enabling us to do so. We*

approved their having an income in Malagón and eating meat, since there was no possibility of doing otherwise in that place. With regard to income, the Council allows freedom.

2. Antonio de Segura who was then guardian of the Franciscans in Toledo. He was a friend of Teresa's and a member of the Alcantarine Franciscans.

12. To Don Alvaro de Mendoza, Avila

Medina, 6 July 1568

(Autograph: BN, Madrid)

Teresa has stopped off in Medina on her way to making a foundation in Valladolid. This has been made possible through a gift of property from Bernardino de Mendoza, recently deceased. In these circumstances she received a locution from the Lord telling her to hurry, that the soul of Don Bernardino would be suffering in purgatory until the foundation was made (cf. F. 10.1-3). The autograph is in bad condition, the first page of the letter is missing.

1. All these sisters kiss your lordship's hands many times.

For a year now we have been hoping that you would come to visit my Señora Doña María. Señor Don Bernardino assured us of this, and we were very happy about it.[1] Our Lord did not will it. May it please His Majesty that I will see you in that place where there will be no separation. The psalms were recited this year on the same day, and this we will always do gladly.[2] May our Lord always guide you and for his greater service preserve you for many years.

2. Señor Fray García[3] is doing very well, glory to God. He is always gracious to us, and each day he is more dedicated to your service. He has undertaken an office given him by his provincial, that of novice master—a lowly task for someone of his authority. But it was not given him for any other reason than that his spirit and virtue benefit the order and imbue those

souls with that spirit. He accepted the office with so much humility that he was most edifying. He has much work to do. Today is 6 July.

Your lordship's unworthy servant,

Teresa of Jesus

Would you do me the favor of sending this padre[4] quickly. It could be that a letter from you would be helpful.

---

1. Don Bernardino and Doña María were the brother and sister of Don Alvaro de Mendoza, the bishop of Avila.
2. Possibly the office of the dead for Don Bernardino who had died in Baeza at the beginning of 1568.
3. García de Toledo, the Dominican friend of St. Teresa's, was the destinee of her *Life* (cf. L. epil).
4. She is probably referring to Julián de Avila who through recourse to Don Alvaro was seeking to hasten the steps toward a foundation in Valladolid.

13. To Don Francisco de Salcedo, Avila

Valladolid, September 1568

Francisco de Salcedo was the "saintly gentleman" (L. 23.6) who collaborated with Gaspar Daza in the spiritual direction of Teresa at the beginning of her mystical life. Teresa is now sending John of the Cross to Avila with letters of recommendation from her to her friends to prepare for the foundation in Duruelo.

To The Most Honorable Señor Francisco de Salcedo.

My lord,

1. Jesus be with you. Glory to God that after six or eight letters dealing with business matters that couldn't be avoided, I have a little time to rest from them by writing these lines to let you know I receive much consolation from your letters. Do not

think that writing to me is time lost, for now and then I need this, provided that you don't keep telling me that you are old, which leaves me in total dismay. As though there were some security in being young! May God let you remain here until I die; afterward, so as not to be there without you, I will beg the Lord to bring you there quickly.

2. Would you speak to this padre,[1] I beg you, and help him in this matter, for although he is small, I know that he is great in the eyes of God. Certainly we will miss him very much here, for he is wise, and just right for our way of life. I believe our Lord has called him for this task. There's not a friar who does not speak well of him, for he had been living a life of great penance, even though he is young. It seems the Lord is watching over him carefully, for although in trying to get everything settled we met with a number of troubles—and I myself must have caused trouble at times by becoming annoyed with him—we never saw an imperfection in him. He's courageous, but since he is alone, he needs all that our Lord gives him for taking this work so much to heart. He will tell you how we are getting along here.

3. The generous sum of six ducats seemed to be no small thing, but I would give much more to see you. Surely you are worth a higher price than I; who is going to value a poor lowly nun? In addition, you are to be prized more in that you can give *aloja*,[2] wafer cookies, radishes, and lettuce, that you have an orchard and take the place of your servant—I know about it—to bring us apples. The *aloja* here, they say, is very good, but since I don't have Francisco de Salcedo here, we don't know what it tastes like nor do we have the means of knowing. I'm telling Antonia[3] to write you, for I'm not able to go on at length. Remain with God. I kiss the hands of Señora Doña Mencía[4] and Señora Ospedal.[5]

4. May it please the Lord that the improved health of that married gentleman continue. You shouldn't be so incredulous, for prayer can do all things, and the kinship he has with you

will do a lot. Here, we will help with our widow's mite. May the Lord bring it about as he can. Indeed, I think the illness of his wife is more incurable. The Lord can cure it all. I beg you, tell Maridíaz, and the Flemish woman, and Doña María de Avila[6]—for I would very much want to write her, and surely I don't forget her— when you see them, to recommend me and this monastery to God. May His Majesty keep your honor many years for me, amen. For, in passing, it might be said that this year could go by without my seeing you again, the Princess of Eboli[7] being in such a hurry.

Your lordship's true and unworthy servant,

Teresa of Jesus, Carmelite

5. I beg again as an alms of you that you speak to this padre and counsel him on what you think about his mode of life. The spirit the Lord has given him has greatly encouraged me, and his virtue, among so many troubles, makes me think we have a good beginning. His prayer is deep and he has good intelligence. May the Lord lead him on.

---

1. Fray John of the Cross, who is preparing for the discalced life in Duruelo.
2. *Aloja* was a popular drink made from water, honey, and spices.
3. Antonia del Espíritu Santo (Henao), one of the first four nuns at St. Joseph's in Avila.
4. Mencía del Aguila, Francisco de Salcedo's wife and a relative of Teresa's.
5. One of Salcedo's maids, the oldest. She was much respected and given the title "Lady."
6. Maridiaz was Teresa's friend and known in Avila for her penance and recollected life. The Flemish woman was Ana Wasteels, who became a Carmelite at St. Joseph's (Ana de San Pedro). María Dávila, the latter's daughter, also became a Carmelite at St. Joseph's (Ana de los Angeles).
7. Ana de Mendoza (the Princess of Eboli) was in a hurry for Teresa to make a foundation in Pastrana. Teresa did not pass through Avila until February or the beginning of March.

14. To Doña Luisa de la Cerda, Toledo

Valladolid, 2 November 1568

(Autograph: DCN, Bordeaux)

The first site selected for the foundation in Valladolid proved to be an unhealthy one. Teresa and the nuns became ill. As a result, they moved to the house given them by María de Mendoza. Teresa was living in this house when she received St. John of Avila's approbation of her book and the news that Doña Luisa had returned to Toledo.

To the Very Illustrious Doña Luisa de la Cerda, my lady.

1. May Jesus be with you, my lady and friend. However much this Doña Luisa may travel, she is still my lady. I have told Antonia[1] to write to you about all that is happening, in regard both to my poor health and all the rest. My head is in such a condition that only God knows how I can write this. But knowing that you and my lords have arrived in good health so consoles me that my writing these lines is not taking much effort. May the Lord be blessed for everything; I prayed a great deal for all of you. I'm also much consoled that you are happy with your monastery.[2] And I find that you are right, for I know that our Lord is genuinely served there. May it please him that the nuns serve you as they ought. And may our Lord keep you and allow me to see you again, since I did not die.[3]

2. With regard to the book,[4] you have worked everything out so well that it couldn't have been done better. So I'm forgetting all the anger this caused me. Master Avila[5] wrote to me at length, and he is satisfied with everything. He says only that some things should be explained further and that some terms should be changed. This will be easy to do. You have done a good work; the Lord will repay you for this and for the other favors and good deeds you have done for me. I greatly rejoiced in receiving such good news, for this is an important matter.

One recognizes who it was who counseled that the book be sent.

3. I would very much like to write to Padre Pablo Hernández,[6] but I'm really not able to do so. I think I'll be rendering him a greater service if I do not make myself sick. I beg you to tell him about what's going on here that he might pray to the Lord for me and for all these business matters, for I do the same for him. I also beg you to send Sister Antonia's letter to the prioress of Malagón[7] along with this one, if you do not object. Otherwise, have someone write her that she should not become involved in the matter that I wrote about in a letter sent to her through Miguel,[8] for the general[9] has written to me again, and it seems that things will be going better. Note that it's very important you give her this message.

4. I kiss the hands of Señor Don Juan[10] and my ladies many times. I welcome them back and also you; your return, I repeat, has made me happy. Give my best regards to Señor Don Hernando and Señora Doña Ana, and also to Alonso de Cabria and Alvaro del Lugo.[11] You already know that with me you must lose something of your noble status and gain in humility. May it please the Lord that I might see you again, for I surely want to. My health and everything else I do fare better in your region than up here.

5. With regard to moving, it's important to be very careful about choosing a healthy site, as you can see from what's happening to us here because of the unhealthy location, even though the house is very pleasant.[12]

6. I was happy that you gave an alms to that young girl.[13] When it comes to your desire, you ought not bother about whether there is room or not, for everything belongs to you. Señora Doña María de Mendoza[14] kisses your ladyship's hands many times. Before I had read to her what you wanted me to tell her, she begged me to convey this to you. She is not at home now. I will pass on what you wanted me to tell her, for she truly deserves it. Tell me whatever you think appropriate

concerning the licentiate, our Padre Velasco,[15] and remain with God. May he grant you all that I desire for you, amen.

Today is the day following the feast of All Saints.

Your ladyship's unworthy servant,

Teresa of Jesus, Carmelite

---

1. Antonia del Espíritu Santo, who returned with Teresa from Malagón.
2. The monastery of Malagón
3. She had been sick of a very high fever as had all the nuns who had gone on the foundation of the new monastery in Valladolid.
4. *The Book of Her Life*, which she had entrusted to Doña Luisa to send to St. John of Avila for his opinion.
5. St. John of Avila had previously written to Teresa (2 April 1568) that since she had already given her book to others to examine there was no need for his opinion. Nonetheless, because of her persistent desire for his approval, he read the book and gave his judgment in a letter of 12 September 1568 (See BMC 2: 207-10).
6. A Jesuit who helped her in Toledo and Malagón.
7. Ana de los Angeles (Gómez).
8. Miguel Lescano, a messenger.
9. General of the order, Giovanni Battista Rossi (Rubeo).
10. Juan Pardo de Tavera, Doña Luisa's son.
11. Hernando de la Cerda and his wife Ana de Thienlloye; Alonso de Cabria Pecellín, a priest in Doña Luisa's household in Paracuellos; Alvaro de Lugo, a priest administrator in the hospital of Tavera de Toledo.
12. Doña Luisa was planning to build a new monastery for the nuns at a new site in Malagón. The new building was not finished until the end of 1579. In Valladolid, the nuns became sick because the monastery was too damp from being close to the river.
13. María de las Vírgenes (de la Torre).
14. The bishop of Avila's sister, who offered her house to the nuns in Valladolid thus enabling them to move from the unhealthy site (cf. *F.* 10.6).
15. The priest who had recently left Doña Luisa's service.

15. To Padres Luis de Guzmán and Pablo Hernández, Toledo

Valladolid, 2 November 1568

Through this formal statement addressed to two Jesuits, Teresa grants the powers to work toward a foundation in Toledo.

1 I, Teresa of Jesus, prioress of St. Joseph's in Avila, have received from the Most Reverend General, Master Fray Juan Bautista Rubeo, sufficient patent letters for founding and accepting monasteries of the primitive rule of the holy Order of Our Lady of Mount Carmel. I have been informed that in the city of Toledo, moved by the grace of our Lord and aided by the Blessed Virgin, patroness of our order, some persons want to give this order an alms consisting of a house together with a church and four chaplains and everything else necessary for the divine service in the church. I am of the opinion that our Lord will be served and praised by this, and I therefore accept the offer as a work of charity and alms and sign my name below.

2. And if it should be necessary to negotiate certain matters regarding this agreement, as usually happens, I declare that if Father Superior[1] and Padre Pablo Hernández are willing to do me this charity of working toward an understanding in these matters, I will accept the obligation to fulfill all that they arrange. And if they themselves should not want to enter into these negotiations, I will accept whomever they appoint; we must not fail in reaching an agreement since my going to that city would please the Lord.

3. And because these things are my desire, I declare that I will carry them out and attest to this with my signature.

Valladolid, 7 December 1568.

Teresa of Jesus, prioress
St. Joseph's in Avila
Carmelite

1. Luis de Guzmán, S.J. It was he who arranged for the dowries of the two daughters of Diego de San Pedro on their entrance into the Carmel of Toledo.

16. To Doña Luisa de la Cerda, Toledo

Valladolid, 13 December 1568

(Autograph fragment: DCF, Seville)

From Valladolid Teresa sets in motion her plans for a foundation in Toledo. She regrets being separated from Doña Luisa and asks for help to obtain a license from the administrator of the diocese for a foundation there. Being ill, she writes only with difficulty.

To the very illustrious Doña Luisa de la Cerda, my lady.

1. May Jesus be with your ladyship. I have neither time nor energy to write much, for, by myself, I am now writing to only a few persons. I wrote to you a short while ago. I am in a wretched state. When I am with you and in your city my health is better; although the people here do not abhor me, glory to God. But since my desire is to be there, so the body would want to be there also.

2. What do you think about how the Lord arranges things so that I can be at rest? May his name be blessed, for he has wished to work things out through persons who are such servants of God that I think His Majesty will be greatly served through this. For the love of His Majesty you might try to obtain the license. I don't think the administrator[1] should be told that it's for me, but that it is for a house of discalced nuns. And he

should be told of the great good they do wherever they are. At least this is true for our nuns in Malagón, glory to God. And you will see that soon you will have this servant of God there with you, for it seems that the Lord does not want us to be separated. May it please His Majesty that we may be together in glory, with all my lords, of whom I ask for prayers. Write and tell me how your health is, for you have been very negligent in doing me this favor. The sisters here kiss your ladyship's hands.

3. You can't imagine how many indulgences[2] and benefits we have obtained through the foundresses of this order. These favors are without number. May the Lord be with you.

Today is the feast of St. Lucy.

Your ladyship's unworthy servant,

Teresa of Jesus, Carmelite

---

1. Don Tello Gómez Girón, who was administering the diocese while Archbishop Carranza was in Rome. The license was granted 8 May 1569.
2. The indulgences and privileges granted by Rome to the founding benefactors of monasteries of the order.

17. To Diego Ortiz, Toledo
Valladolid, 9 January 1569

Diego Ortiz was co-executor for an estate from which Teresa hoped a Carmel could be founded in Toledo. She promises to come to Toledo as soon as possible (see F. 15.1-5).

1. Jesus. May the Holy Spirit always be in your soul, and may he give your honor his holy love and fear, amen. Padre Doctor Pablo Hernández[1] has written me about the favor and alms you are granting me by wanting to found a house for this holy order. Indeed, I believe that our Lord and his glorious Mother,

my Patroness and Lady, has moved your heart to so holy a work, which I hope His Majesty will make good use of. And I hope you will as a result receive many spiritual blessings. May it please the Lord to accomplish this, as all the sisters and I beg him; and from now on the entire order will be praying for you. This has been a great consolation for me, and so I desire to meet you that I might offer myself in your presence as your servant; may you consider me so from now on.

2. Our Lord has been pleased to free me from the fever. I am hurrying as much as possible so that when I leave here things will be to my satisfaction, and I believe that with the grace of our Lord the work will soon be finished. I promise you that I won't lose time, or pay attention to my illness should the fever return, but will leave at once. It is only right that, since you are doing everything, I should do my part, which is nothing, and endure some trial. We ought not strive for anything else, those of us who seek to follow the one who, without deserving any trials, always lived in the midst of them.

3. I do not think I will gain only one benefit from this work, for according to Padre Pablo Hernandez I stand to gain much from knowing you. Up to this point I have been sustained by the prayers of others, so I beg you for the love of our Lord, not to forget me in yours.

4. I think that unless His Majesty ordains otherwise I will be in that city, at the latest, two weeks after the beginning of Lent.[2] Even though I will leave here soon, I will be stopping for a few days at the monasteries that the Lord has been pleased to found during these past years. My stay will be as short as possible, since that is your desire; although in matters that are so well taken care of, I will have nothing else to do but behold and praise our Lord. May His Majesty always guide you and give you life and health and the increase of grace that I beg of him, amen.

Today is 9 January.

Your honor's unworthy servant,

Teresa of Jesus, Carmelite

---

1. The Jesuit who was helping Teresa with the foundation in Toledo (see F. 15.1).
2. Lent began that year on 23 February, and she arrived in Toledo on 24 March.

18. To Alonso Ramírez, Toledo

Valladolid, 19 February 1569

Alonso Ramírez was the brother of Martín Ramírez, the founding benefactor for the foundation in Toledo. Designated as his brother's executor, Alonso wrote to Teresa urging her to come to Toledo. Having recuperated from the fever caused by the unhealthy location along the Rio de Olmos, Teresa was staying at the house of María de Mendoza and preparing to set out on her next journey.

1. Jesus. May the Holy Spirit be with your honor and repay you for the consolation your letter brought me. It came just when I was most concerned about finding someone through whom I could send a letter and give you news of myself, for it is only right that I not neglect you. I will be delaying a little more than I said in my letter,[1] but I assure you I will not be wasting a moment. Fifteen days have not gone by since we moved from our other house.[2] The move was made in a very solemn procession and with much devotion. May the Lord be blessed for everything.

2. Since Wednesday I have been staying with Señora Doña María de Mendoza; because she has been ill, she hasn't been able to see me, and I needed to talk to her about some mat-

ters. I thought of staying for only a day, but the weather got so cold, with snow and ice, that it seemed traveling would have been unbearable; so I have been here until today, Saturday. I will definitely leave for Medina on Monday, with the Lord's help. And despite my hurry I will be staying there and at St. Joseph's in Avila more than fifteen days because of some business matters I must attend to. So I think I will be detained longer than I had said. You will forgive me, for from what I have mentioned here, you will see that I cannot help the delay. It will not be a long one. I beg you not to proceed with buying a house until I arrive; I want it to be suitable for our purposes since both you and he who is in glory[3] are giving us the alms.

3. With regard to the licenses, the one from the king will be gotten easily, with heaven's help, even though some trouble might arise. My experience is that the devil bears up badly with these houses, and so is always persecuting us. But the Lord can do all things, and the devil is routed.

4. Here we have met with very great opposition, and from the most renowned persons in this locality; at present everything has been ironed out. You shouldn't think you must give our Lord only what you now have in mind, but much more. His Majesty shows his gratitude for good works by asking for more, and it's nothing to give money, for doing so causes us little pain. When they throw stones at you and your son-in-law[4] and all of us who take part in this effort, as was almost done in Avila when St. Joseph's was founded, then the work will prosper. And I will be sure that the monastery will suffer no loss, nor will those of us who undergo trials, but that much good will come about. May the Lord guide everything as he sees is fitting. You should not be sad. It made me sad not to have *mi padre* here.[5] If necessary, we will try to have him come. Indeed, the devil is already beginning. May God be blessed, for if we do not fail him, he will not fail us.

5. I truly long to see you, for I think this will bring me much consolation, and then I will respond to the kindnesses you show

me in your letter. Please God I will find you and your son-in-law in good health. I earnestly beg both of you for prayers. You see, with my wretched health, I need them for these journeys, although the fevers have not returned. I will take care—and I am doing so—of what you asked of me, and these sisters likewise. All of them beg for your prayers. May the Lord always lead you by the hand, amen.

Today is 19 February. Written in Valladolid.

Your honor's unworthy servant,

Teresa of Jesus, Carmelite

6. Would you, in charity, have the enclosed letter given to Doña Luisa[6] as well as my best wishes. I don't have time to write to Señor Diego de Avila,[7] and even the letter to Señora Doña Luisa is not written in my hand. Would you tell her about my health, please, and that I hope to see her soon. Don't be disturbed about the licenses, for I hope in the Lord that everything will turn out very well.

---

1. She is referring to a letter written to Diego Ortiz (Ltr. 18), Don Alonso's son-in-law.
2. This occurred 3 February (see F. 10.7).
3. Martín Ramírez, Don Alonso's brother, who left a bequest for a foundation of Teresa's in Toledo (see F. 15.1).
4. Diego Ortiz.
5. The Jesuit Pablo Hernández.
6. Luisa de la Cerda. The autograph of only this last part of the letter is conserved, in San Pablo de los Montes (Toledo).
7. Perhaps a relative of the archdeacon of Avila, Francisco de Avila.

19. To María de Mendoza, Valladolid

Toledo, End of March 1569

María de Mendoza, the bishop of Avila's sister, helped Teresa with the foundation in Valladolid and continued to help her afterward. In Toledo, Teresa is staying with Luisa de la Cerda and working toward a foundation in that city. She had received some bad news about a trial Doña María was undergoing and is writing for more specific information.

⁂

To the most illustrious Doña María de Mendoza, my lady.

1. Jesus. May the Holy Spirit be with your ladyship. Indeed, I have been very sad on this trip. I'm sorry to be so far away from that place.[1] On top of all this, the lord bishop has written me that you are suffering a great trial, but he has not mentioned what it is.[2] With such anxiety aboout you, I would have tried not to leave, had it not been the eve of my departure. I found help by entrusting the whole matter to our Lord. The thought came into my mind—I don't know how—that it has to do with some conflict the administrator[3] caused my Lady Abbess.[4] This consoled me somewhat, for although a soul may be tried, God could be allowing this so as to enrich it. May His Majesty take care of the entire matter as I beseech him to.

2. I was most happy to learn that your health is much better. Oh, if you had the interior dominion that you have in exterior things, how little would all that we call trials here below matter to you. What I fear is the harm they do to your health. I beg you to write me—there should be many messengers coming to this city—and tell me in particular what the trouble was, for I am worried about it. I arrived here safely on the vigil of our Lady.[5] Señora Doña Luisa was overjoyed.[6] We spent a lot of time talking about you, which is a pleasure for me, for since she loves you so much she doesn't tire of this.

3. I tell you that the renown you have here is remarkable; may it please the Lord that your deeds will match it. They do nothing else but call you a saint and continually speak your praises to me. May the Lord be praised for your giving them such an example. In what way do you think it is given? In suffering so many trials. In this way the Lord, by means of the fire of love that he sets in your soul, begins to kindle it in others. So, be brave. Look at what the Lord suffered this time of year.

Life is short, a mere moment of trial remains for us. O my Jesus, and how I offer to him the pain of my being separated from you and unable to know about your health as I would like!

4. My founding patrons[7] here are very gracious. We are already seeking to get the license.[8] I would like to proceed quickly, and if they give it to us promptly, I think everything will go well. I would like to speak of many things to my lady Beatriz and to my ladies, the countesses.[9] I often think of my angel Doña Leonor;[10] may the Lord make her his servant. I beg you to give my greetings to Father Prior of San Pablo and to Father superior.[11] The provincial of the Dominicans is preaching here.[12] He has a large following, and rightly so; I have not yet spoken with him. May our Lord guide and preserve you for many years, amen.

Your ladyship's unworthy servant and subject,

Teresa of Jesus, Carmelite.

---

1. The place was Valladolid, which she left on 22 February (cf. Ltr. 18.2).
2. The bishop of Avila, Don Alvaro de Mendoza, Doña María's brother.
3. Doña María's administrator, Juan Bernaldo.
4. Abbess of Las Huelgas Reales of Valladolid, Doña María's cousin Ana Quixada de Mendoza.
5. On 24 March, the vigil of the Annunciation.
6. Luisa de la Cerda
7. Alonso Alvarez Ramírez and Diego Ortiz.
8. The licence was not granted until 8 May (see F. 15.5).
9. Doña Maria's sister Beatriz de Mendoza. The countesses were Leonor de Castro and Beatriz de Castro (mother of the former).
10. The child Leonor de Castro, Countess Leonor's granddaughter.
11. Prior of the Dominicans of San Pablo (Valladolid), Alonso de Hontiveros; superior of the Jesuits, Juan Suárez.
12. Juan de Salinas.

20. To Doña Juana de Ahumada, Alba de Tormes

Toledo, 23 July 1569

(Autograph fragment: DCN, Rochefort, France)

The last lines of a letter that Teresa most likely wrote on returning from the foundation in Pastrana after stopping off in Madrid, where she probably met the princess of Portugal.

I kiss these ladies' hands. Fortunately there is the opportunity to do this. I'm saying nothing to Señor Juan de Ovalle because this letter is meant also for him.

I believe it's 23 July. Yesterday was the feast of the Magdalene. I have spoken with the princess of Portugal many times and have been delighted, for she is a servant of God . . . .[1]

1. Before arriving in Toledo, Teresa spent 10 days in Madrid, having been given hospitality at the *Descalzas Reales* (see F. 17.5). There she was able to speak with Doña Juana de Portugal, the sister of King Philip II.

21. To Simón Ruiz, Medina del Campo

Toledo, 18 October 1569

(Autograph: DCN, Medina del Campo)

A business man, with an important role in the public life of Medina, Simón Ruiz supported Teresa's foundation in that city. His niece, Isabel de los Angeles, had entered the Carmel there and desired to turn over all her possessions to it, a desire which was being opposed by her relatives.

1. Jesus. May the Holy Spirit be always with your honor, amen. Mother Prioress[1] has already written me of how everything was done, and others also have written. May our Lord be praised forever. I have been greatly consoled—above all with the good news Mother Prioress tells me about Sister Isabel de los Angeles.[2] May it please our Lord to watch over her and Sister San Francisco[3] as well, with whom the community is also very happy.

2. It is no wonder that this caused a stir and aroused devotion. Because of our sins, the world is such that among those with the means to be well-off, as they think, only a few embrace the cross of our Lord; and it would be a much heavier burden for them to have to remain in the world. Here, too, from what I see, the news we received from up there will benefit us. I share in your happiness and that of Señora Doña María.[4] Please remember me in your prayers.

3. It's clear she was in good company from the way she has understood the truth. As for the rest, certainly in anything that is of service to our Lord, the devil will try to use his power under the guise of many attractive colors. He has done a great deal here. In some way the nuns are right. They think that since they have to live on alms in these houses they would find themselves in trouble were others to see that the well-off take an interest in us. It may be possible to get along for a while, but soon the truth will be known. In sum, these are serious matters and an agreement cannot be reached so quickly.[5] Glory be to the Lord since all has turned out so well. May it please His Majesty to give you all a long life to enjoy, and that you build a house for so great a King, for I hope in His Majesty that he will repay each of you with another house that will have no end.

4. I have received good news about Padre Fray Juan de Montalvo,[6] although I have not seen a letter from him since I've arrived here. I thought he was up there. You are doing us a great favor by leaving the matter of the chaplain in such good hands. If the one of whom you speak has the required qualities, it matters little that he is young. May our Lord direct this as he has directed everything else.

5. As for the nuns, you are right; that is what is appropriate. For now, they must take no more than two. I am writing to Mother Prioress about this because our number should not exceed thirteen, and when these two enter, that number will have been reached. May His Majesty choose them and always

protect you, amen. Would you please send these letters without delay to Mother Prioress.

Today is 18 October, the very day in which I received your letter.

Your honor's unworthy servant,

Teresa of Jesus, Carmelite

---

1. The prioress of Medina, Inés de Jesús.
2. The niece of Simón Ruiz, after being left an orphan, was educated by him and his wife and later became a Carmelite nun.
3. María de San Francisco had been reared by Isabel de los Angeles and entered Carmel with her.
4. María de Montalvo, Simón Ruiz's first wife.
5. Isabel de los Angeles wanted to give all her possessions to the monastery without conditions. Her relatives on the other hand objected and wanted to be patrons of the monastery. Teresa disapproved of the latter and eventually moved Isabel to Salamanca.
6. An Augustinian friar, probably María Montalvo's brother.

22. To Doña Juana de Ahumada, Alba de Tormes

Toledo, 19 October 1569

(Autograph: DCN, Toro, Zamora)

Teresa is sending her sister Juana letters from their brother Lorenzo, who plans to return to Spain from America. She anticipates and shares in the joy that Juana will have from reading them.

1. Jesus. May the Holy Spirit be with your honor. I am sending money to Avila so that they may send this messenger to you, for these enclosed letters[1] will bring you much happiness. I was overjoyed by them, and I hope in the Lord that my brother's arrival will bring you some relief—a great deal—from your trials. So many holy intentions cannot help but bring about much good, and I would rather see him and his family live

peacefully in their own home than that they have the endowment of these other offices, for I see flaws in each of them. May the Lord be blessed who has so directed matters. I repeat that I am especially happy for Señor Juan de Ovalle[2] and you. In sum, my letters must have been good for something, but yours have been of little help.[3]

2. I wrote to Gonzalito through the inquisitor Soto.[4] I still don't know whether the letter was delivered to him; I have received no news of him. Do you see now what God is working in Lorenzo de Cepeda? He seems to be looking more to his children's salvation than to amassing a fortune. O Jesus, how much I owe you—everywhere that I look—and how little I serve you! No happiness for me is greater than to see my brothers, whom I love so much, receive the light to desire what is best. Didn't I tell you to leave it all in the Lord's hands, that he would take care of it? So I advise you again to place your affairs in his hands, for in everything His Majesty will do what most suits us.

3. I'm writing no more for now because I've written a great deal today, and it is late. Indeed, I am happy in thinking about the joy you will have. May the Lord give us joys where they will last, for all those of this life are suspect. I am well and am in a hurry to buy the house;[5] things are moving along. Regards to Beatriz.[6]

Today is the nineteenth of October.

Yours,

Teresa of Jesus

---

1. The letters were from their brother Lorenzo de Cepeda in America in which he tells of his plans to return to Spain. In them he probably promised to help Juana financially.
2. Juana de Ahumada's husband.
3. In previous letters to Lorenzo, Teresa had begged financial help for Juana.
4. Teresa's nephew Gonzalito who was then 12 years old. Francisco de Soto y Salazar had blessed the Ovalle-Ahumada marriage.

5. A house for their foundation in Toledo, to which they moved, from their temporary house, in May 1570 (see F. 15.7-9).
6. She was Teresa's niece, younger than her brother Gonzalo.

23. To Doña Juana de Ahumada, Alba

Avila, Middle of December 1569

Juan de Ovalle has arrived in Toledo on his way back from Seville. He has collected a good sum of money sent by Lorenzo to be deposited in Spain. He has also collected a hundred pesos each for Juana and Teresa. As a result Teresa speaks to her sister about money matters and her own thinking regarding the demands of poverty. As a foundress she had permission to dispose of money.

1. Jesus be with your honor. I would be foolish to deprive you of the joy of reading a letter from me by not spending some time to write you when so good a messenger[1] is available. Blessed be the Lord who has arranged things so well. May it please His Majesty to do the same in everything else.

2. Don't you see how, even though you didn't want it, circumstances made it necessary for my brother[2] to come here? And it may be that he will have to come again to get the money,[3] although there may be someone through whom he can send it. He will bring you news about your son.[4] Everything that could bring one joy is going well now; may the same be true regarding the soul's progress. Go to confession in preparation for Christmas and pray for me.

3. Don't you see that however much I try, His Majesty doesn't want me to be poor?[5] I tell you, indeed, that in a certain sense this gives me great displeasure, but it removes the scruples I undergo when I have to spend something. I am thinking now of some little things I got for you, of what I paid and what was left and the greater amount I spent on the needs of the order, and, so as not to go around with these scruples, to keep ac-

count of what I have to spend otherwise. For if I do have money, I cannot keep anything when I see the great need at the Incarnation.[6] And no matter how much I try, I cannot get fifty ducats for what I claim is necessary, not for getting what I want but for what pertains to the greater service of God. That is the truth. May His Majesty guide us and make you holy and give you a happy Christmas.

4. I don't like these plans of which my brother[7] speaks. It would involve going outside your own house and spending more than he would make. And you would be alone, and we would all be anxious. Let us wait now to see what the Lord does. Try to please the Lord, for he will take care of your affairs. And don't forget that all things come to an end. Don't fear that your children will be left in want if you seek to please His Majesty. My regards to Beatriz.[8] May he watch over you all. Amen.

5. One thing I ask you out of charity is that you do not love me for the sake of what you can gain in the world but because I pray for you. When it comes to anything else, there's nothing I can do—regardless of what Señor Godínez[9] says—and it distresses me. I follow the one who governs my soul, and not whatever happens to enter the head of this one or another. I say this so that you may respond when something is said to you. You should understand that if we consider how the world is now and the state the Lord has placed me in, the less you think I do for you the better it is for me; and this is fitting for the service of the Lord. Certainly, even if I should do nothing, it would be enough for someone to imagine the least little thing so as to say about me what I hear said about others. So you have to be careful in regard to the little thing you mentioned to me.

6. Believe me that I truly love you and that sometimes I put together some trifle for a moment in which it will bring you pleasure. But explain when someone mentions it to you that I must spend what I have at my disposal for the order, for it belongs to the order. And how do others have a say in this

matter? Realize that someone as exposed to the world as I am has to be careful even in the way she practices virtue. You'd be unable to believe the trouble I have. But, then, I do things so as to serve God. His Majesty will watch over you and your affairs for me.

7. May God keep you; I've gone on at length and the bell for Matins has rung. I assure you that when I see a postulant bringing with her something of value, I think of you and Beatriz, but I would never take anything, not even by paying for it with my money.

Yours,

Teresa of Jesus

---

1. Juana's husband, Juan de Ovalle, who was returning from Seville to Alba.
2. Juan de Ovalle.
3. The money sent by Lorenzo.
4. Gonzalo de Ovalle.
5. She is alluding to the money brought for her by her brother-in-law from her brother Lorenzo in Seville (cf. Ltr. 24.11).
6. The monastery of the Incarnation in Avila.
7. Juan de Ovalle had some investment plans in mind.
8. Juana's daughter.
9. Gonzalo Godínez, Juan de Ovalle's brother.

Letters 24–38 (1570–1571)

24. To Don Lorenzo de Cepeda, Quito (Ecuador)

Toledo, 17 January 1570

(Autograph fragment: DCN, San Clemente (Cuenca)

Teresa is happy over the news that her brother has decided to return to Spain. Writing from Toledo, she gives him advice about places to live and the education of his children. She adds news about her foundations and also about many of their friends and relatives. Included is an account of how she is using the money sent her by Don Lorenzo.

1. Jesus. May the Holy Spirit always be with your honor, amen. I have written you letters by four different avenues, and in three of them I enclosed a letter for Señor Jerónimo de Cepeda.[1] Because at least one of them will surely arrive, I'll not respond now to everything you have told me, nor will I say more about the good resolve[2] our Lord has placed in your soul, about which I have praised His Majesty. It seems to me to be a sound decision. Indeed, the motives you mentioned made me think more or less of others there might be, and I hope in the Lord that this will all be for his greater service. In all of our monasteries we are praying especially and unceasingly that since your intention is to serve our Lord, His Majesty will bring

you safely to us and guide you toward what will be most beneficial for your soul and for your children.[3]

2. I have written earlier that already six convents have been founded, and two houses also of discalced friars of our order. I consider the latter to be a great favor from the Lord, for they are making splendid progress in the way of perfection. As for the communities of nuns, they all resemble St. Joseph's in Avila, for they all seem to be one. And it heartens me to see how our Lord is so truly praised and with such purity of soul.

3. At present I am in Toledo. It will be a year on the vigil of our Lady's feast in March[4] that I have been here, although from here I made a trip to Ruy Gómez's villa; he is the prince of Eboli. A monastery for friars and one for nuns was founded there, and they are doing very well.[5] I returned here to finish the work of getting everything in order for this house, which will be a very important monastery. My health has been much better this winter. The climate here is wonderful. If there were no other disadvantages—you would not find it a good place for the education of your children—you could settle here; at least I sometimes find myself wishing this because of the good climate. But there are places in the region surrounding Avila where you could reside during the winter months. This is what some do. As for my brother Jerónimo de Cepeda, I think, instead, that when God brings him back, he will enjoy better health if he settles here. His Majesty's will is done in all things, for I don't think I have had such good health in forty years, and I am keeping the observance with everyone else, which includes not eating meat except in cases of great necessity.

4. A year ago I had the quartan fevers, but they have left me feeling better. I was engaged in making the foundation in Valladolid, and Señora Doña María de Mendoza, the widow of secretary Cobos, smothered me there with amenities.[6] So when the Lord sees that it is necessary for our good, he gives health; when it is not, sickness. May he be blessed for everything. I was distressed that the illness you had was in your

eyes, which is a painful thing. Glory to God that there has been so much improvement.

5. Juan de Ovalle has already written you about his trip to Seville.[7] A friend of mine gave him such good instructions that on the very day he arrived he withdrew the silver. He brought it here where they will give him the money at the end of this month of January. The account of the duties that had to be paid was carried out in my presence; I will enclose it here. I did no small thing in managing these affairs. I have become so adept at bargaining and managing business affairs for these houses of God and of the order that I am abreast of everything. Since I consider your business affairs to be those of our Lord, I rejoice in knowing how to handle them.

6. Before I forget, after I wrote to you, Cueto's son died, who was still very young.[8] There is no trusting in this life; so I am consoled every time I think of how well you understand this.

7. When finishing here I would like to return to Avila, for I am still prioress there and don't want to anger the bishop,[9] for I owe him a great deal as does the whole order. I don't know what the Lord will do with me; I may have to go to Salamanca where they are giving me a house. Although I am tired, the good these houses bring about in the towns where they are located makes me, in conscience, want to do all that I can. May the Lord so help with his grace that I will be given encouragement.

8. In my previous letters I forgot to tell you about the good facilities Avila has for the education of children. The Jesuits have a school where they teach grammar and hear the confessions of the students once a week and make their students so virtuous that it is something to praise God for. The students also learn philosophy and afterward for their theology go to Santo Tomás.[10] There is no reason to go elsewhere for studies and training in virtue, and the whole city is so Christian that it is an edification to outsiders: much prayer, many confessions, and a life of great perfection among the laity.

9. The good Francisco de Salcedo is there. You did me a great favor in sending such a nice gift to Cepeda.[11] That saint never stops expressing his gratitude to you, and I don't think I'm exaggerating by calling him a saint. The elderly Pedro del Peso[12] died about a year ago—he was well advanced in years. Ana de Cepeda[13] greatly appreciated the alms you sent her. With it she will indeed be rich, for other people help her since she is so good. She will not be lacking a place to stay, but she has such strange traits that she is not suited for community. God leads her by that path. I have never dared to take her into one of these houses, and not because of any lack of virtue in her, but because I see that she lives the life that best suits her. Nor will she stay with Señora Doña María[14] or anyone else, and this is good considering her goals. She seems to live like a hermit, and with that goodness and dedication to much penance that she has always shown.

10. The son of Señora Doña María, my sister, and of Martín de Guzmán has made his profession and is advancing in holiness.[15] And the daughter Doña Beatriz has died, as I have already written to you. Doña Magdalena, who was the youngest, lives in a monastery as a secular. I would love to see God call her to be a nun. She is very pretty. I haven't seen her for many years. Now they are speaking about a marriage for her with a certain widower who has a primogeniture. I don't know how things will turn out.

11. I have already written to your honor about how your assistance to my sister[16] arrived just in time. For I have been frightened by the trials of poverty that the Lord has given her, and she has born it so well that he now wants to give her relief. I have no needs but a surplus of everything, and so what you sent me in alms I will share with my sister, and the rest will go for good works according to your intentions. Because of some scruples that I had, your help came just at the right time, for these foundations make demands on me. However careful I am about using everything for them, I could give less away,

such as in courtesy offerings to the learned men whom I must consult about my soul. In sum, the matter concerns trifles, but I was very relieved not to have to appeal to others. They would not fail to help me, but it pleases me to be free in dealing with these gentlemen so as to be able to tell them my opinion. And the world is so selfish that I, in a way, have a horror of possessing anything. So, I will not keep for myself anything of what you sent, but I will keep my freedom by giving some of it to the order. I have all the permissions I need from the general and provincial[17] for receiving nuns, transferring them, and helping one house with the resources of another.

12. They are so blind in trusting me that I don't know how this trust could have come about, and there are people who will go so far as to lend me one or two thousand ducats. So, just at a time when I have come to abhor money and business affairs, the Lord desires that I deal with nothing else, which is no small cross. May it please His Majesty that I serve him in this manner, for all things will pass away.

13. Indeed, I think it will be a relief for me to have you here; since very few things of the earth provide me with it, perhaps our Lord wants me to have this consolation and that we both work together for his honor and glory and bring some profit to souls. For what greatly grieves me is to see so many souls lost, and I am very anxious about those Indians. May the Lord give them light. There is so much misery here and over there that, since I travel in many regions and speak to many persons, I don't know what to say except that we are worse than animals; we do not understand the great dignity of our soul and we undervalue it with things as cheap as those of earth. May the Lord give us light.

14. You can speak with Padre García de Toledo, whom I miss very much in my business affairs; he is the nephew of the viceroy.[18] If you should need anything from the viceroy, know that he is a strong Christian, and it was a great stroke of fortune that he wanted to go over there. I put letters for him in the

previous packages I sent. I also enclosed in each some relics for you for your journey. I strongly hope they will get there.

15. I hadn't thought of going on at such length. I want you to know of the favor God bestowed on Señora Doña Juana[19] in granting her such a death. Here we have recommended her to the Lord and offered prayers for her soul in all of our monasteries. I hope in the Lord that she has no need of more. You should try very hard to put aside this grieving. Remember, it is those who do not recall there is an everlasting life that feel such pain when someone departs from the miseries of this life.

16. Best regards to my brother Jerónimo de Cepeda; this letter is for him too. You made me very happy in telling me that you have given orders so that he can return here within a few years, and I hope, if possible, that he will not leave his children there but that we will all be together here, to help one other so as to be together forever.

Today is 17 January 1570.

Your unworthy servant,

Teresa of Jesus, Carmelite

17. Concerning the Masses, many have been said and the rest will be said. I took in a nun who had nothing for a dowry, not even a bed, and I offered this to God that you and your children will arrive in good health. Give my regards to them. I am making a similar offering for Señor Jerónimo de Cepeda. I receive many nuns in this way, if they are spiritual, and then the Lord sends others who provide the means for them all.

18. In Medina someone entered with a dowry of 8,000 ducats,[20] and another entered here with 9,000 without my asking for anything. And these cases are so numerous that one can only praise God. If someone has the spirit of prayer, she seeks nothing else, so to speak, than one of these houses; and the number of nuns in them does not exceed thirteen. Since ac-

cording to our constitutions we do not beg for alms, but we eat what is brought to the turn for us, which is more than sufficient, our number must be small. I think you will be made very happy when you see these houses. With regard to all that is given, no one demands an accounting, nor does anyone see it but me, and that means more work for me.

19. Give my best regards to Señor Pedro de Ahumada. Because he can receive news about me from your honor and I have so little time, I am not writing to him. I am very concerned about Agustín de Ahumada since I do not know how he is faring in his relationship with our Lord. I pray a great deal for him. And I send regards to Señor Hernando de Cepeda.[21] A daughter of his sister's recently married rather well.

---

1. Teresa's brother who is also in America.
2. A resolve to return to Spain.
3. Lorenzo's children are now without a mother.
4. She arrived in Toledo 24 March 1569.
5. The town was Pastrana (see F. 17).
6. Teresa had been sick during the months of January and February 1569. Francisco de los Cobos had been a secretary of Charles V.
7. Juan de Ovalle, Teresa's brother-in-law, went to Seville to draw out 2,020 silver pesos sent by Lorenzo from Quito (22 November 1569). Teresa of Jesus and Juana de Ahumada were each to be given 100 silver pesos. The rest was to be invested from which 120 ducats were to be paid annually to Doña Juana.
8. Diego Alvarez de Cueto, a resident of Avila. Nothing is known of the son here mentioned.
9. Don Alvaro de Mendoza.
10. The Jesuits conducted the school of San Gil from 1554 in Avila and the Dominicans that of Santo Tomás from 1482.
11. One of Lorenzo's cousins.
12. A brother of Teresa's father's first wife.
13. Probably Teresa's cousin.
14. She is perhaps alluding to María de Cepeda, a nun at the Incarnation in Avila.
15. Teresa's older sister, Doña María, was now deceased. Her son was Fray Juan de Jesús, who made his religious profession in the

Franciscan reform of St. Peter of Alcantara. Beatriz and Magdalena de Guzmán were his sisters.

16. Doña Juana de Ahumada.
17. The general was Padre Giovanni Battista Rossi (Rubeo); the provincial of Castile was Padre Alfonso González.
18. Teresa's friend Padre García de Toledo had departed for Peru the previous year as religious adviser to the viceroy Francisco de Toledo.
19. Doña Juana de Fuentes y Espinosa, Lorenzo's wife who had died 14 November 1567.
20. She is alluding to Isabel de los Angeles, niece of Simón Ruiz.
21. Pedro and Agustín Ahumada were brothers of Teresa's in America. Hernando de Cepeda was a cousin.

25. To Padre Antonio de Segura, Cadalso de los Vidrios
Toledo, February-March(?) 1570

(Autograph: The Canonesses of St. Augustine, Paris)

This friend of Teresa's was a member of St. Peter of Alcantara's Franciscan reform. In 1568 while Father Guardian of the Franciscan house in Toledo, he advised Teresa in regard to a plan she had for a foundation in Segura de la Sierra. After gently complaining of his failure to visit their house, Teresa commends to him her nephew, young and recently professed in the same reform, fearing that this nephew might be overworked.

To my very reverend padre in Christ, Fray Antonio de Segura, guardian of the house of Cadalso. To be delivered at the aforementioned house.

1. Jesus. May the Holy Spirit be with you *mi padre*. I don't know how to put in words what little attention we should pay to the things of this world and how little I understand it. I say this because I never thought you would so forget Teresa of Jesus, and since you are so close this couldn't be due to a poor memory. It's hard to believe that you were here and ne-

glected to visit this house,[1] which is yours, and give it your blessing.

2. Now Padre Julián[2] has written me that you are the guardian there in Cadalso. However weak your memory, you could inquire about me now and then. May it please the Lord that you not so forget me in your prayers, for if you remember me in your prayers I will endure the rest; miserable though I am, I do not forget you in mine.

3. He also wrote me that my nephew[3] is coming here, although just in passing. If he has not gone yet, I beg you to have him write to me at length about how he is doing interiorly and exteriorly, for in the measure that he practices obedience along the way, he will be either very proficient or distracted. May God strengthen him, for they are not dealing with him as I thought they would, his being a relative of mine. If it's necessary for me to get his superiors to look kindly toward him, please let me know. For with friends like Señora Doña María de Mendoza[4] and others similar to her, it will be easy to get them to consider allowing him to have a little respite.

4. If you should be passing by, be sure that you do not fail to visit this house, which is yours. May the Lord guide us on the path to heaven. I am well, and we are doing well, glory to God. Since I don't know whether or not Fray Juan de Jesús is there, I am not writing to him. May God give him interior strength, which he will surely need, and may the Lord also be with you.

Your reverence's unworthy servant and daughter,

Teresa of Jesus, Carmelite

5. Our Padre Fray Bartolomé de Santa Ana[5] will be spending all of this Lent with Doña Luisa[6] in Paracuellos.

---

1. The Carmel in Toledo founded in 1569.
2. Julián de Avila, chaplain at St. Joseph's (Avila).

3. Fray Juan de Jesús (Guzmán) of the Alcantarine reform of Franciscans, son of Teresa's sister María de Cepeda and Martín de Guzmán y Barrientos.
4. Benefactress of Teresa's Carmel in Valladolid (cf. F. 10.6).
5. Also a member of the Alcantarine Franciscan reform.
6. Teresa's friend, Luisa de la Cerda.

26. To Diego de San Pedro de Palma, Toledo

Toledo, 15 July 1570

Don Diego's two daughters received the habit of discalced Carmelite nuns in Toledo without permission from their father. Teresa writes immediately to him and their mother and obtains a highly favorable response.

1. Jesus. May the Holy Spirit be always with your honor. For some days your daughters—and our sisters—have been wanting to receive the holy habit of our Lady. Knowing that you have not been opposed to this, I decided to give it to them today, after observing the spirit and fervor with which they were asking me for it. I think this will be for the glory of God.[1]

2. I beg you, out of charity, to accept this and to consider the favor His Majesty has shown you in giving you daughters he has chosen to be his brides. They are very consoled. Their only concern is for the sorrow this might have caused the both of you. For love of our Lord, may they not sense anything that could cause unrest to their souls so well prepared for this state. You will have them here—something perhaps better than if they were elsewhere—for your consolation, and you can consider all the nuns of this house to be your servants and *capellanas*.[2]

May our Lord be always with your soul, and may he guide you, amen.

Your honor's unworthy servant,

Teresa of Jesus, Carmelite

1. The two new sisters were Juana del Espíritu Santo and Isabel Bautista.
2. The Spanish term for this type of "servant" is *capellana*, similar to the old English term "beadsman" or "beadswoman" (one who prays for the soul of another). Still today in many Carmels the nuns choose to be "capellanas" for specific individuals.

27. To Diego de San Pedro de Palma, Toledo

Toledo, 11 August 1570

This official statement was required because of the quick acceptance of Don Diego's two daughters into the Carmel in Toledo.

Since Padre Don Luis, superior of the Society of Jesus,[1] came to an agreement with Señor Diego de San Pedro de Palma on what should be given in alms to this house because the latter's daughters have entered here as nuns,[2] I, Teresa of Jesus, a Carmelite nun, and the nuns of this house hereby grant with my signature attached the necessary permission required by the lawyer for the daughters of Señor Diego de San Pedro to renounce their share of their inheritance.

Signed in St. Joseph's in Toledo on the eleventh day in the month of August, 1570.

Teresa of Jesus, Carmelite nun

1. The superior of the Jesuits in Toledo was Luis de Guzmán
2. The two daughters were Juana del Espíritu Santo and Inés Bautista (cf. Ltr. 26).

28. To Diego Ortiz, Toledo

Toledo, Middle of August 1570

Diego Ortiz did not want to speak to Teresa about the meaning of some stipulations made in the contract for the foundation in Toledo. On the eve of her departure for Avila, she writes to him to clarify her understanding of what was stipulated. She has been ill and uses a secretary for this letter with the exception of the last paragraph.

To the very magnificent Señor Diego Ortiz, my lord.

1. Jesus. May our Lord bestow his divine grace on your honor. I had very much wanted to meet with you during these days, and so I sent word beseeching you in this regard. Since you are not going to grant me this favor and the time has arrived for my departure (which I believe will be tomorrow), I want to tell you about what we began discussing the other day in regard to the sung Masses on Sundays and feast days. I have been thinking about the matter these days, for I had not given it much thought before you spoke to me; nor did I think it necessary to speak about it, for my intention seemed clear in the written agreement. But they tell me I must clarify some things.

2. What I intended was that the chaplains be obliged to sing a Mass on feast days, for then our constitutions prescribed this, but not that the nuns be obliged to sing, for in their rule this is optional. Even if the constitutions do prescribe singing, they do not on this matter bind under any sin. How could I make this an obligation for the nuns! I wouldn't do it for anything, nor did you or anyone ask me for such a thing. I spoke in this way for the sake of our convenience.[1] If in writing this down I made an error, it wouldn't be right to demand of them what should be voluntary. And since they are willing to serve you and ordinarily sing the Masses, I beg you that when some need arises for them you consider it a good thing to allow them their

freedom. I beg your forgiveness that this is written in someone else's hand,[2] for the bloodletting has left me weak, and my head can't do anything more. May our Lord keep you.

3. Señor Martín Ramírez[3] pleased me very much. May the Lord be pleased to make him his servant and keep you for the good of all. You will be doing me a great favor if you clarify the matter concerning the Masses. And since the Mass is sung almost every day without the nuns' being obliged, it would be right for you to remove this scruple of ours and make the nuns and me happy in a matter that has so little importance, for we all want to serve you.[4]

Your unworthy servant,

Teresa of Jesus

---

1. Teresa wanted the sung Masses, stipulated in a contract made with Diego Ortiz, to be the responsibility of the chaplains; that is, the priest celebrating Mass would sing the usual parts without any sung response from the nuns. According to her own constitutions (no. 2), but not the rule, the nuns were to sing at Mass on Sundays and feast days.
2. A secretary was writing this letter for Teresa.
3. He was the son of Diego Ortiz and Francisca Ramírez. Teresa told the nuns that whenever "Martinico" came to the monastery they should call her. She enjoyed speaking with him because he was a very virtuous young man (BMC 5: 419).
4. Diego Ortiz did not yield to Teresa's wishes, as might have been expected. He was a difficult man to deal with (cf. F. 15.4).

29. To Doña Catalina Hurtado, Toledo

Avila, 31 October 1570

Doña Catalina Hurtado was the mother of two young women who had entered the Carmel in Toledo the previous July. Having befriended Teresa, she began sending her gifts.

Teresa is ill and cannot express her gratitude in her own handwriting.

1. Jesus. The grace of the Holy Spirit be with your honor and watch over you for me, amen, and repay you for the care you take in giving me gifts. The butter was exquisite, like everything your hands have made for me. Whenever you have some more that is good, I will accept it with pleasure if you remember me, for it is very beneficial to me. The quince were also exquisite; it seems you have no other care than to give me gifts. On my part it is a gift to see a letter from you and know that you are well. As for me, I am not so well right now. I have a pain in my jaw and my face is a little swollen, and that is why this letter is not in my handwriting. But I don't think this will matter at all to you.

2. Pray for me, and don't think it provides me little joy to have a daughter[1] like the one I have had up until now and will have always. I will not forget to pray for you, and the sisters will do the same. All those in this house kiss your hands, especially the subprioress[2] who owes you so much. Pray for her, for her health is not good. May the Lord keep you for me and give you his Holy Spirit.

October, the end of the month.

I beg for the prayers of those ladies, your sisters. May God give health to the one who is ill, for I am beseeching him to do this, and I ask the same for you, my daughter.

Your honor's unworthy servant,

Teresa of Jesus

1. Juana del Espíritu Santo, one of Doña Catalina's two daughters, who was a discalced Carmelite nun in Toledo.
2. María de San Jerónimo, subprioress of St. Joseph's in Avila.

30. To Doña Isabel de Jimena in Segovia

Salamanca, End of 1570

(Autograph: DCF, Teresianum, Rome)

Teresa replies to an aspirant who sought to enter one of her monasteries. A Jesuit wrote a letter recommending her. Teresa writes warmly to Doña Isabel who was giving up her wealth in order to serve God.

To the very magnificent Señora Doña Isabel de Jimena, my lady.

1. Jesus. May the Holy Spirit be with your honor always and give you the grace to understand how much you owe the Lord. Despite dangers so dangerous as youth, wealth, and freedom, the Holy Spirit gives you light to want to leave them aside. And the things that usually frighten souls, such as penance, enclosure, and poverty, enabled you to understand their value and also the delusion and loss that would have been yours had you followed after the former dangers. May the Lord be blessed and praised forever.

2. This is the reason you have so easily persuaded me that you are very good and capable of being one of our Lady's daughters by entering her holy order. May it please God that you will advance so far in your holy desires and works that I won't have to complain of Padre Juan de León.[1] He sent me information that left me so satisfied that I didn't need to know anything more. I am so consoled with the thought that you will become a great saint that I would be very satisfied in just having you without anything more.

3. May the Lord repay you for the alms you have resolved to give wherever you enter, for the amount is large.[2] Doing this must be very consoling to you since you are doing what the Lord counsels— to give yourself to him—and what you have to the poor for love of him.[3] Considering what you have re-

ceived, I don't think you could have fulfilled your obligation with a smaller amount. Since you are doing all you can, your offering is no small matter nor will what you receive in return be small.

4. Since you have seen our constitutions and rule, I have nothing to say but that if you carry on with this decision you may enter at whatever time you settle on, and you may choose from among our houses the one you prefer. In all of this I want to please my Padre Juan de León, leaving the choice to you. Truly, I would have liked you to take the habit in the house where I am living, for I certainly desire to make your acquaintance. May our Lord direct everything for his greater service and glory, amen.

Your honor's unworthy servant,

Teresa of Jesus, Carmelite

---

1. A Jesuit residing at the time in Segovia where Isabel lived who had highly recommended her to Teresa.
2. For a dowry she brought 3,000 ducats as well as other things for the church. This was the Isabel (de Jesús) who, as a novice in Salamanca, sent Teresa into ecstasy with her singing so beautifully a song about how hard life is without God (cf. ST. 12; M. 7.2; IC. VI.11.8).
3. Cf. Mt. 19:21.

31. To Alonso Alvarez Ramírez, Toledo

Alba de Tormes, 5 February 1571

Teresa desires to keep informed about the foundation in Toledo through the founder's brother. In the midst of many trials, she has recently established the monasteries in Salamanca and Toledo.

To the very magnificent Señor Alonso Alvarez Ramirez, my lord.

1. Jesus be with your honor. If I had as much time at my disposal as you, I wouldn't be negligent about writing, as you are. But I do not neglect to recommend you to the Lord. Since I have learned about your health from other sources, I can bear with your silence. May our Lord grant you health, as is in his power and as I desire, so that you and Señor Diego Ortiz[1] and Señora Francisca Ramírez may rejoice in that most precious work, which as I am told, is now the church with its chaplains. May God be praised forever.

2. I rejoiced over the pleasant manner in which our most Reverend General[2] brought the matter to a conclusion. He is a wise and holy man. May God preserve him. His Majesty knows how willingly I would have remained in our monastery in Toledo. Ever since I left it, I tell you that I have not had a day without heavy trials. Two monasteries have been founded, glory to God, and this house is the smaller one.[3] May it please His Majesty that it be of some service to him.

3. I don't know why the body of Señor Martín Ramírez—may he be in glory as I desire and beg the Lord—has not been transferred.[4] I beg you to let me know why, and if any progress has been made in the project you once mentioned to me. O Lord! How often have I remembered you in the business affairs that have arisen here and how many times I have asked for blessings on you. For it was enough to say something once to you all, even in jest, for something to get done. May our Lord keep you for many years and allow me to enjoy your presence, for I certainly love you in the Lord.

4. It would be good if Señor Diego Ortiz were to write to me now and then. When you do not want to write, tell him to write for you. I kiss your hands many times and those of Señora Francisca Ramírez; and my regards to our little angels.[5] May our Lord guard them, especially our patron,[6] and may he keep you in his hands and give you all of the good I beseech him to bestow on you, amen.

Today is 5 February.

5. I forgot to mention that Juan de Ovalle and my sister kiss your hands. Juan de Ovalle never finishes speaking of what he owes you; and what must I owe!

Your honor's unworthy servant,

Teresa of Jesus, Carmelite

6. About the favor you have done me in lavishing so much attention on Isabel de San Pablo,[7] I am saying nothing. I owe you so much in return that I am leaving it to the Lord to thank and repay you. You have done a great charity. May the Lord be blessed for everything. Tell Señor Diego Ortiz that I beg him not to fail to place my lord St. Joseph at the door of the church.

---

1. Diego Ortiz was Alonso Ramírez's son-in-law and a collaborator with his wife in the foundation in Toledo.
2. The Reverend General Giovanni Battista Rossi approved the agreement that was drawn up between Teresa and Alonso. The agreement runs for nine large pages of close print in BMC 5: 413-21; for Rossi's approval see MHCT 1: 104-07.
3. The two monasteries were those founded in Salamanca (1 November 1570) and Alba de Tormes (25 January 1571).
4. The remains of Martín Ramírez (founding benefactor of the Carmel in Toledo) lay in the church of Santa Justa. It had been stipulated that they be transferred to the Carmel.
5. The children of Francisca Ramírez and Diego Ortiz.
6. She is referring to the oldest child, Martín. She calls him "patron" because he was named "Martín" after his grandfather who was the founding benefactor of the Carmel in Toledo. This child died in the odor of sanctity; the process for his beatification was begun in Toledo.
7. This daughter of Teresa's cousin Francisco de Cepeda went on the foundation in Toledo.

32. To Diego Ortiz, Toledo

Salamanca, 29 March 1571

While looking for a house to buy in Salamanca, Teresa received a letter from Toledo with good news about construction of the monastery church in Toledo.

To the magnificent Señor Diego Ortiz, my lord.

1. Jesus. May the Holy Spirit be ever in your soul and repay you for the charity and favor you have shown me with your letter. You would not be losing time if you wrote me many, for this could help to spur us on in the service of the Lord. His Majesty knows that I would rather be down there, and so I'm in a great hurry to purchase a house here.[1] It's a weighty burden, although there are many for sale and at a low price. So I hope in the Lord this matter will be settled soon. My haste is equal to the joy that will be mine in seeing Señor Alonso Ramírez.[2] I kiss his honor's hands and those of Señora Doña Francisca Ramírez.[3]

2. Surely your honors must find great joy in your church, for I share in your happiness through the good news I receive. May our Lord allow you to enjoy many years with as much dedication to his service as I beg of him. Allow His Majesty to work and do not be in such a hurry to see everything done, for he has already granted us a great favor in what has been accomplished in just two years.

3. I don't understand what has been written to me about the controversy with the curate and chaplains—at Santa Justa I suppose.[4] I beg you to let me know what this is all about.

4. I am not writing to his honor Señor Alonso Ramírez; there's no reason for tiring him, since I'm writing to you. Because I am not able to serve your honors in the way I ought, I beg the Lord to repay and to preserve you for many years and to make those angels[5] very holy—especially my patron—for we are in

great need of this; and may he always keep you in his care, amen.

Today is 29 March.

Your honor's unworthy servant,

Teresa of Jesus, Carmelite

---

1. There was a delay before she found one. She did not, in fact, return to Toledo until 1575 when she was on her way to Beas.
2. He was one of the founding benefactors of the Carmel in Toledo (see F. 15.1-5).
3. Diego Ortiz's wife.
4. Martín Ramírez was interred provisionally in the church of Santa Justa.
5. Diego Ortiz's children.

33. To Diego Ortiz, Toledo

Avila, 27 May 1571

Diego Ortiz was insisting on his right to have certain Masses sung in the church of the Carmelite nuns in Toledo at which the nuns would participate. His letters, filled with justifications for his requests, are severe in tone. Teresa's answer is tactful but firm.

1. Jesus. The grace of the Holy Spirit be with your honors, amen. You show me so much kindness and charity through your letters that even were your last letter more severe, I would have felt well repaid and obliged once more to serve you. You say that you sent me a letter through Padre Mariano[1] that I might know the reasons for your request. Because you have given me such good ones and you know so well how to put forth the value of what you want, I'm afraid my reasons are of little weight. And so I'm not thinking of defending myself, but as with those who have a hopeless case I will shout and cry out and remind you that you are always more obliged to favor or-

phan daughters and minors over chaplains. For, in the end, everything is yours—how much so—even the monastery and those living in it, but not those who, as you say, are in a hurry to finish quickly, and sometimes with little devotion.

2. You have done me a great favor in agreeing to that matter concerning Vespers, for it's a subject about which I can do nothing. As for the rest, I am writing to Mother Prioress[2] to do as you ask, and I am sending her your letter. Perhaps by leaving everything in her hands and those of Señor Alonso Alvarez,[3] we will gain more. The two of them can work out an agreement among themselves. I kiss your honor's hands many times. I was very sorry to learn of the pain in your side from which you suffered. Here we offered it to the Lord, and so I pray for all of you and for those angels.[4] May God make them his own and preserve them.

3. There is one thing that would seriously inconvenience the nuns and be burdensome to them: a Mass to be said before the High Mass when a saint's feast is being celebrated, especially if there is a sermon. I don't know how that can be arranged. It should matter little to all of you that on such a day the feast be celebrated at the High Mass; and a little before it, the low Mass by the chaplain could be celebrated. The need for this will not arise often. Try to put up with this opposition to your desire and do me this favor, even though the day may be a festive one; of course, I'm not referring to ceremonies requested by one of you. Know that this matter is not important, and you will be doing the nuns a good deed and me a great favor.

4. After the letter to our Father General[5] went out, I realized that there was no reason for it; anything Father Visitator[6] does is as valid as something done by the pope, for no general or general chapter can undo it. The visitator is very learned and well informed, and your honor will enjoy dealing with him. I think that without doubt he will make a visitation of the monastery there this summer, and he will be able to set up firmly

what you ask for. I will speak to him about this when he passes through here. Well, I will not depart in the slightest from what you see as serving best for greater stability nor from anything by which I might serve you. I am sorry I am not in a place where I could show you my good will from close at hand. I earnestly recommend myself to the prayers of Señora Doña Francisca Ramírez.[7] I no longer have a fever, glory to God.

5. You can indeed write to me all that you want, for I know the spirit in which you write. My only pain would be to cause you pain. For surely I would not want to cause you any or that anyone in that house do so. As for the rest, nothing that you have ever said has caused me any harm, nor will it. May our Lord bestow on you all the spiritual blessings that I ask His Majesty for, and may he always guide you.

Today is the Sunday after the Ascension.

Your honor's unworthy servant,

Teresa of Jesus

---

1. The discalced Carmelite, Ambrosio Mariano de San Benito.
2. The prioress of the Carmel in Toledo, Ana de los Angeles.
3. Alonso Alvarez Rodríguez, another one of the founders in Toledo.
4. Diego Ortiz's children.
5. Giovanni Battista Rossi who had already approved the contract for the foundation (see BMC 5: 422).
6. The Dominican Pedro Fernández.
7. Diego Ortiz's wife.

34. To Doña María de Mendoza, Valladolid

Avila, Middle of June 1571

Teresa sent Doña María two letters, but only this second one has been preserved. She has words of praise for the new apostolic visitator, the Dominican Pedro Fernández, who was quite strict with her. She misses the consoling presence of Doña María.

❧❧❧❧

1. Jesus be with your ladyship. When they gave me your letter, I had already written the enclosed. I kiss your hands many times for your care in showing me kindness; this is nothing new. I had very poor health after I arrived here, but now I am all right. And since I have His Excellency[1] present, all goes well, although the peace he brings me would be still greater if you were present; I would have the solace of speaking to you about many things. For a number of reasons[2] I don't think this will be possible as soon as I thought.

2. You will be discussing all of this with Father Visitator,[3] as was written to me, which makes me very happy. He is your devoted servant and I was consoled to observe how fondly he speaks of you, and so I believe that in everything he will do what you request. I beg you to show him every kindness and to convey that regard you usually have for such persons. He is the highest superior we now have, and his soul must merit much before the Lord.

3. As for accepting those nuns,[4] I indeed see the kindness you are showing me. But since Padre Suárez,[5] of the Society, writes to me and is the one they should speak to and learn from in matters concerning our order and the required dispositions, there is no reason for delay. They should seek permission from Father Provincial[6], and you should request him to receive them; otherwise, ask it of Father Visitator who will grant it immediately. I make out better with him than I do with our Father Provincial; however much I write to him, he doesn't want to answer me.

4. I am sorry about the illness of my lady abbess.[7] May God be blessed because in one way or another you are never without a reason for being distressed. All of us here are praying for her, and for you as well. There is no need to ask this of me

when I have such a good bell to awaken me, which is love. May it please our Lord that the illness not be serious and that you will soon be well. All the sisters here kiss your hands many times.

5. They have written me that you are deeply spiritual. This was nothing new to me. But I would be happy if I were closer and could delight—were I not what I am—in speaking of spiritual things with you. This Father Visitator brings me life, for I don't think he is deceived by me as are all others; God wishes to enlighten him about how miserable I am, and so he catches me in imperfections at every step. I am very consoled by this and seek to make them known to him. It is a great relief to be transparent before one who stands in the place of God. In this way I will benefit from the time I am with him.

6. You must already know that they want Fray Domingo[8] to go to Trujillo, for they've elected him prior there. Those in Salamanca[9] have petitioned their Father Provincial[10] to leave him where he is. It is not known what the provincial will decide. The climate there would be hard on his health. When you see Father Provincial of the Dominicans, scold him for not coming to see me when he was in Salamanca, for he stayed there a good number of days. It's true that I do not have much love for him! This letter is going to end up tiring you out. I'm adding one other, no more. But since I am consoled by speaking with you, I wasn't being careful.

Your ladyship's unworthy servant and subject,

Teresa de Jesús, Carmelite

---

1. The bishop of Avila, Don Alvaro de Mendoza, Doña Maria's brother.
2. She is probably alluding to the attitude of the provincial, Angel de Salazar, who imposed Doña Teresa de Quesada on the nuns in Medina as prioress. This was done after they had elected, on Teresa's recommendation, Inés de Jesús as prioress. Teresa was ordered by the provincial to return to Avila at once.
3. The visitator of the Carmelites in Castile was the Dominican Pedro Fernández, who at first was very cautious in dealing with Teresa,

testing her spirit to see if it was authentic. In the end he said that she was a good woman, and Báñez noted that coming from his mouth that comment was hyperbole (BMC 18:9).

4. Some aspirants were waiting to be accepted in the Valladolid Carmel.
5. The Jesuit Juan Suárez who was superior of the Jesuit house in Valladolid.
6. Angel de Salazar.
7. The abbess of the Huelgas Reales of Valladolid, Doña Ana Quixada de Mendoza.
8. The Dominican Domingo Báñez.
9. The Dominicans in Salamanca.
10. Provincial of the Dominicans, Alonso de Hontiveros.

35. To Padre García de San Pedro, Toledo
Medina del Campo, August (?) 1571

(Torn Autograph: DCN, Loeches)

García de San Pedro, a priest in Toledo, had a niece who had recently made profession in the Carmel; he was also spiritual director of one of the nuns. Teresa explains one of her policies for portresses.

1. . . . I should extend my best wishes . . . nonetheless both made me happy. Some day would you go to see for me the nun who recently received the veil[1] and speak at length with her and ask her to pray for me, as well as for all these business matters connected with the order. May the Lord make her very holy, and Señora Doña Catalina[2] as well; give her my regards.

2. It is a special mortification for me to see the reputation we have for our poverty while we live in comfort, for as the nuns will affirm we have plenty of food and good accommodations. Some little things . . .such that we do not make a big issue of it . . . we have more than we need . . ., and we send it to our discalced brothers . . . Fray Gregorio[3] who is . . . .

3. I believe that Beatriz[4] will be an honor to you since you do so much for her progress. I was most consoled by what your honor said and that she has not disappointed Mother Prioress.[5] You tell me that at the turn[6] she is a person of few words. Would you tell the prioress—for I forgot—to let her remain in that office; reserve is an important virtue for the portresses in our houses. Here I have forbidden Alberta,[7] who is the portress, to speak except in response to what she hears; and if they ask or speak about other things she is to say that she does not have permission for this. In such a way people are more edified than by a lot of talk.

4. Since I am writing a long letter to Mother Prioress (fortunately I can do so since there are no other letters to write) and she can tell you whatever I've not mentioned here, I'll say no more than to ask you not to fail to write to me from time to time, for your letters bring me much consolation. May God be pleased to give you what I desire for you.

Your honor's unworthy servant and daughter,

Teresa of Jesus, Carmelite

---

1. Juana del Espíritu Santo, the daughter of Diego de San Pedro and Catalina Hurtado, made her profession 15 July.
2. Catalina Hurtado.
3. The identity of this Fray Gregorio is unknown.
4. Beatriz de San Miguel (Andrada) who had been under the spiritual direction of García de San Pedro. She made her profession on 14 August 1571.
5. Ana de los Angeles was prioress in Toledo at the time.
6. The "turn" is a revolving barrel by which objects or messages are received from or exchanged with those living outside the monastery.
7. Alberta Bautista was turn sister at the Carmel in Medina.

36. To Doña Catalina Balmaseda, Medina del Campo

Medina del Campo 5 October 1571

This note of acceptance was written the day before Teresa left to assume her new position as prioress at the Incarnation in Avila.

Jesus

My daughter and my lady,

1. To receive God's help is better than early rising.[1] You are hereby being admitted to this house with the approval of all the sisters. I would have liked to give you the habit before departing, but that is not possible since I will be leaving early tomorrow morning. We will meet sometime in the future.

Your honor's servant

Teresa of Jesus

1. A popular saying in Spanish was *A quien madruga, Dios le ayuda* (God helps the early riser). Teresa changed it around to *Más vale al que Dios ayuda que el que mucho madruga* (To receive God's help is better than early rising).

37. To Doña Guiomar Pardo Tavera, Paracuellos

Avila, 22 October 1571

(Autograph: Biblioteca Nacional de Lisboa)

Teresa responds at once to the sad news about the grave illness of Doña Guiomar's brother, Luisa de la Cerda's son. He in fact died the same day.

1. Jesus. The Holy Spirit be with your honor. The Lord did not want me to enjoy receiving your letter, because the reason

for your sending it took away my happiness. May God be blessed for everything.

2. It is evident that the Lord is loved in that house since he is giving it trials in so many ways. When trials are born with such patience as they are there, he is enabled to give more favors. A great favor it is just to begin to understand what little attention should be paid to a life that continually manifests itself as perishable, and to understand how much the life that never ends should be loved and sought. May it please our Lord to give health to Señora Doña Luisa and Señor Don Juan;[1] we are beseeching the Lord for this here.

3. When there is an improvement, I beg you to take away the sorrow that you have now given me. Ask Doña Isabel and Doña Catalina[2] to pray for me. I beseech you to have courage so that you can in turn give it to Señora Doña Luisa.[3] Surely, to stay longer in that place[4] would be to tempt God.

4. May His Majesty guide you and give you all the good I both desire and ask of him for you, amen; and the same goes for Señora Doña Catalina.

Today is 22 October. I received your letter today.

Your honor's unworthy servant,

Teresa of Jesus

---

1. Luisa de la Cerda and her son, Juan Pardo de Tavera.
2. Luisa de la Cerda's two sisters: Isabel Manuel de la Cerda and Catalina de la Cerda.
3. Luisa de la Cerda.
4. Paracuellos was not a healthy place in which to live (cf. Ltr. 38.3).

38. To Doña Luisa de la Cerda, Paracuellos

Avila, 7 November 1571

Doña Luisa de la Cerda's son (who was thought to be suffering from kidney stones) had died sixteen days previous to this letter, and Teresa writes to console her friend. She has been prioress at the Incarnation in Avila for about a month, sent there under obedience. Her responsibilities for the 130 nuns are many and troublesome, but an inner calm remains with her.

To the very illustrious Señora Doña Luisa de la Cerda.

My lady in Paracuellos,

1. Jesus. May the grace of the Holy Spirit be with your ladyship. Since I have been in this house of the Incarnation—a little over three weeks now—I have written you three times.[1] I don't think any of my letters has reached you. I share so much in your trials that when this suffering is added to the many I have here, I'm no longer worrying about asking our Lord for any more. May he be blessed for everything, for it truly seems that you are among those who will enjoy his kingdom since he gives you to drink from the chalice through so many illnesses, both your own and of those you love.

2. I once read in a book that the reward for trials is the love of God. For so precious a return, who will not love them? So I beg you to do so and to note how all things pass away quickly; journey by detaching yourself from everything that does not last forever.

3. I had already learned that you were ill, and so today I have tried in every way to learn about your health. May the Lord be blessed that you have improved. Come away from that region, for the love of God, for it is clearly bad for the health of all.[2] My health is good—may he be blessed—compared to what it usually is. But with all the work I have, I wouldn't be able to hold up without better health than I usually have. My responsibilities are so many and so pressing, inside and outside the house, that I have little time even to write this.

4. May our Lord repay you for your kindness and the consolation your letter brought me, for I tell you that I need some of this. Oh, my lady, as one who has known the calm of our houses and now finds herself in the midst of this pandemonium, I don't know how one can go on living, for everywhere there is suffering. Nonetheless, glory to God, there is peace, which is no small thing. Gradually I am taking away the nuns' diversions and freedom, for even though these nuns are so good—certainly there is much virtue in this house—changing a habit is death, as they say. They bear it well and show me much respect. But where there are 130 nuns, you will understand the care that is necessary to keep things in order. I am somewhat concerned about our own monasteries; but since I was obliged to come here under obedience,[3] I hope that our Lord will not allow me to fail in my duty, but that he will care for them. It doesn't seem that my soul is disturbed in the midst of this whole Babylon, which I take to be a favor from the Lord. Human nature grows tired, but it is all little next to my offenses against the Lord.

5. I was sorry to learn of the death of the good Doña Juana.[4] May God take her to himself, and indeed he will, for she was most worthy. I really don't know why we should feel sorry about those who depart for a safe haven, whom God draws out of this world with its dangers and instability. We are loving ourselves rather than those who go to enjoy a greater good. I commend myself to the prayers of my ladies.

6. I tell you that I keep you ever present and that it was not necessary for you to awaken me with your letter; I would rather be half asleep than see myself so imperfect as to fail to be afflicted over your sufferings. May our Lord give you eternal happiness and rest because for some time now you have given up happiness and rest in this life, though you do not yet appreciate the value of suffering. The day will come when you will understand what you have gained and that for nothing in the world should you ever want to lose it.

7. I'm very much consoled in knowing that my Padre Duarte[5] is there. Now that I am not able to serve you, it brings me joy to know that you have so much good support to help you undergo your trials. The messenger is waiting, so I cannot go on any longer, save to kiss the hands of my ladies many times.

8. May our Lord lead you by his hand and take those fevers away quickly. May you be given the strength to please His Majesty in everything, as I beg of him, amen.

Written at the Incarnation in Avila, 7 November.

Your ladyship's unworthy servant and subject,

Teresa of Jesus

---

1. Teresa had taken over her office of prioress at the Incarnation in Avila on 6 October. Insisting on their right to vote for a prioress, the nuns in Medina, despite the provincial, received permission from the visitator Fernández, a higher authority, to vote for Teresa. After Teresa was elected prioress of Medina, the provincial, in apparent retaliation, managed to convince the visitator to appoint Teresa as prioress of the Incarnation in Avila. The nuns at the Incarnation vehemently resisted having Teresa imposed on them as prioress, without an election. They tried to bar the provincial from entering their monastery. Not until they were asked by the provincial did they agree to accept Teresa.
2. The place was Paracuellos del Jarama, between Madrid and Alcalá.
3. She had been appointed prioress by the apostolic visitator, Pedro Fernández.
4 Juana de Toledo Pacheco was the daughter of the second count of Oropesa.
5. Padre Duarte, from Alcalá de Henares, was a Jesuit confessor to Doña Luisa.

Letters 39–57 (1572–1573)

39. To Doña Juana de Ahumada, Galinduste

Avila, 4 February 1572

Teresa writes from the monastery of the Incarnation, which was in financial straits. She has had bad health since she arrived there. Juan de Ovalle, contrary to her hopes, had not passed through Avila on his way to Madrid; also, he was in conflict with the nuns of Alba over a roadway.

1. Jesus be with your honor. It seems as though you are in another world, living far off in that place.[1] God deliver me from it and from this place as well, for almost from the time of my arrival I've had poor health. So as not to be telling you about this, I've preferred not to write. Before Christmas I suffered from fevers and a sore throat, and was bled and purged twice. Since before Epiphany I've been down with the quartan fevers, but I've not experienced any nausea; and on days when I've been free of them, I've been able to go to choir with the others and sometimes to the refectory. I don't think the fevers will last. Since I see the improvement the Lord has brought about in this house,[2] I try not to stay in bed except when I have the fever, which lasts all night. The chills begin about two, but they are not excessive. Everything else is going well, with so many duties and troubles that I wonder how I'm able to bear

them all. The biggest burden is letter-writing. I have written four times to the Indies, for the fleet is leaving.

2. I'm amazed by your indifference in seeing me with so many trials. I've been waiting each day for Señor Juan de Ovalle, who, I'm told, will be passing through here on his way to Madrid, for it is important to send my brother what he has requested.[3] Now it's too late, nor do I know what to say. Everything should be easy for you; certainly it will not look well.

3. I've been told that Señor Juan de Ovalle and Señor Gonzalo de Ovalle are those who oppose giving a narrow passageway to the monastery.[4] I can't believe it. I wouldn't want us to become involved in haggling. This doesn't look right for women, even though there may be a reason, and those lords would be greatly discredited, especially since the matter pertains to me. Furthermore, I don't think the nuns were aware of the reason; at least one should not turn their simplicity into a fault. Would you inform me about what is going on, for, as I say, this is the news that reached me, and it could be incorrect. Do not be sorry about my illness, for I don't think it will amount to anything; at least it is not interfering much with my duties, even though it does cost me somewhat.

4. I miss you here very much, and I find myself alone. I need some *reales*, for I don't take any food from the monastery provisions except bread;[5] try to send me some. I kiss the hands of those lords and of Beatriz. I would be very happy to have her here. I already know that Gonzalo is well. May God watch over him. Agustín de Ahumada is with the viceroy; Fray García has written me about it. My brother has arranged marriages for two of his nieces—and very good ones at that. They will be secure on his departure. The clock will soon strike twelve and I'm very tired so—no more.[6]

Yesterday was the feast of St. Blase; the day before, of our Lady.

Your honor's devoted servant,

Teresa de Jesus

---

1. Galinduste was a little town near Alba de Tormes where Doña Juana used to spend the winter with her family.
2. The monastery of the Incarnation in Avila.
3. A probable reference to Lorenzo de Cepeda, who could have had some official business at the Court.
4. Apparently the Ovalle brothers were in opposition to the nuns' receiving from the municipality a narrow passageway on the border between the monastery and the Ovalle houses. The passageway served for drainage, and they feared that if given to the monastery it would be enclosed, which would put their houses in danger of flooding.
5. The Incarnation was suffering from such lack of material resources that there was not enough food to provide all the nuns with their daily ration. At the Incarnation a good percentage of the nuns came from families of a high social class, and the nuns were not obliged to give up certain possessions. There was a distinction between goods held in common and individual goods. In speaking of the poverty of the monastery, one is referring to what was held in common.
6. Beatriz and Gonzalo were Doña Juana's children; Agustín de Ahumada was Teresa's brother. The viceroy of Peru was Don Francisco Alvarez de Toledo, a cousin of Fray García de Toledo's. It was Teresa's other brother, Lorenzo de Cepeda, who, with his wife's financial support, arranged marriages for nieces Leonor and Juana. These latter were daughters of Teresa's brothers, Agustín and Jerónimo; they all lived in the Indies.

40. To Doña Juana de Ahumada, Galinduste

Avila, February-March 1572

(Autograph: Dominican Nuns Havana Cuba)

Teresa encourages her sister to bear her trials and assures her of prayers. Her sister's husband Juan de Ovalle has just passed through Avila on his return from Madrid. The

Incarnation, where Teresa is the prioress, would be happy to have some turkeys.

1. Jesus...the Lord. The muleteer is coming...thus there is no time to say more. You should reflect that in one way or another those who are going to be saved will have trials, and God does not give us a choice in the matter; and perhaps he gives you who are weak the smallest. I couldn't know better what you are going through, even if you were to try to explain or write it in a letter; and so I pray to God for you with great care. It seems I love you more now than ever, although my love for you is always great.

2. You will be receiving another letter from me.[1] I don't think you have become worse, even though it seems so to you. I beg you for the love of God and me to go to confession frequently. May he be with you, amen. Señor Juan de Ovalle will tell you the rest; he left in a hurry.

Send the turkeys since you have so many.

Your unworthy servant,

Teresa of Jesus

1. This doesn't seem to be the previous letter, since Juan de Ovalle had just visited Teresa and is on his way back from Madrid, where he had taken care of some business matters for Lorenzo de Cepeda.

41. To Doña María de Mendoza, Valladolid

Avila, 7 March 1572

(Autograph: DCN, Valladolid)

The nuns in Valladolid must have written that they were being pressured by Doña María and some Jesuits to receive two aspirants who showed no signs of a vocation. With cautious tact Teresa strongly presents her position on the matter. Her health has been bad since she arrived at the

Incarnation, but she is happy that matters there are improving despite her illnesses.

⊰⊰⊱⊱

To the most illustrious Señora Doña María de Mendoza. My lady.

1. Jesus. May the grace of the Holy Spirit be always with your ladyship, amen. I have often thought of you during this weather we're having and have feared lest its harshness do damage to your health. And I believe it did. May God be blessed, for we will one day see eternity without changes in the weather. May it please His Majesty that we live this life in a way that will enable us to enjoy so great a blessing. My region has proved such a trial for me that it doesn't seem I was born here. From the beginning of my stay,[1] I don't believe I've had as much as a month and a half of good health. The Lord saw that without my health I wouldn't be able to get anything straightened out, so His Majesty does it all. I do nothing but pamper myself—especially three weeks ago when on top of the quartan fevers I suffered from a pain in my side and from quinsy. Just one of these afflictions would have been enough to kill me if God had so willed, but it doesn't seem there is anything capable of rendering me this blessing. After having been bled three times, I am feeling better. The quartan fevers have gone away, but there's a fever I have that never goes away, and so I am going to be purged tomorrow. I'm vexed at seeing myself in so miserable a condition, for I do not leave my little corner, nor can I, unless for Mass. What causes me the most suffering is a painful jaw, which I have had for about a month and a half.

2. I am giving you an account of all these illnesses so that you will not fault me for having failed to write you, and you will see that these are the favors the Lord gives me in answer to what I am always asking him for. Indeed, from the time I arrived it seemed to me impossible to endure so much tribulation with such poor health and so weak a constitution; for even

without the responsibility of this house there are always many business matters that arise with respect to our monasteries and many other things to exhaust me. Thus you see that all things can be done in God who gives us the power, as St. Paul says.[2] He gives me many illnesses all together, and nonetheless I so carry out all my duties that I sometimes have to laugh to myself; and he leaves me without a confessor and so alone that there is no one with whom I might talk things over for the sake of some relief, and I have to be on my guard about everything. But in matters concerning my bodily comfort there has been no lack of compassion or someone to care for me. The people here have given me much in alms; thus it is only the bread I eat that comes from the house, and even this I'd rather not take. We are about to deplete the alms given us by Doña Magdalena,[3] for until now they provided a meal (with the help of alms from you and others) for the poorest nuns.

3. Since I now see the nuns to be so tranquil and good, it would grieve me to have to see them suffer, for they are indeed just like what I said. Our Lord is to be praised for the change he has wrought in them. The ones who were most forbidding are now the ones who are more satisfied and accepting of me. During this Lent there are no women visitors, nor men, even though they be parents, which is something very new for this house. Nonetheless, they accept it all with much peace. Truly, there are great servants of God living here, and almost all the nuns are improving. My "prioress"[4] is working these marvels. That you might understand that this is so, our Lord has ordained that I be in such a condition that it doesn't seem I've come here for any other reason than to abhor penance and think only about my own comfort.

4. Now, that I might suffer in every way, Mother Prioress[5] of your monastery writes me that you want her to admit an aspirant and that you are displeased because they told you I did not want to accept her. She wants me to send her the authorization to accept this one and another that Padre Ripalda[6] is

presenting. I think there has been a mistake. I would be distressed if it were true that you were displeased with me, for you may give me orders and scold me. I cannot believe that you would be displeased with me and not tell me, unless you pretended to be so in order to avoid some trouble. I would be very much consoled if this were true, for I know how to get along with those fathers of the Society. They wouldn't accept anyone unsuited for their order just to do me a favor. If you should want to give decisive orders, there would be no need for further discussion, for clearly you can give orders for this house, and the others too, and you must be obeyed by me. I would then request permission from Father Visitator or from Father General[7] because it is against our constitutions to accept anyone with such a defect, and I would not be able to grant a permission contrary to the constitutions without the consent of one of them. These two aspirants would have to learn how to read Latin well, for we are ordered not to accept anyone who does not know it.

5. To satisfy my conscience I cannot neglect to mention to you what, after recommending the matter to the Lord, I would do in this case. I am setting aside, as I say, your desires, for I must be ready to submit to them in everything so as not to oppose them, and I'll say no more about this. I only beg you to consider the matter carefully and desire what is best for your house,[8] for when you see that she does not fit in there, you will regret it. In a house where there are many nuns, one can overlook whatever defect there may be; but where there are so few, it makes sense to be selective. I've always noticed that you have this same outlook. Furthermore, I have found everywhere so many aspiring to be nuns, and I have not dared to send any of them to your monastery, for I wanted one who would be as excellent a nun as I would want there, and I did not find her. So, in my opinion, neither of these two should be accepted, for I do not see in them either holiness or fortitude or much discretion or many talents—gifts that would be beneficial to the house. Well, if the house would be the loser, why

do you want to accept them? To help them, there are many monasteries where, since the numbers are large, as I say, the defects could be more easily tolerated. There in your monastery, anyone who is accepted should be capable of being prioress or holding any other office that is given to her.

6. For love of our Lord may you consider the matter well and see that it is always better to look after the common good than some particular good, and since the nuns have to be enclosed and live their lives together, and bear with one another's faults, along with the other austerities in the order, the worst trial for them would be someone imposed on them whose vocation is not certain. You should favor them in this matter just as you favor us in all other matters. If you give the orders, you can entrust this matter to me, for, as I say, I know how to deal with the Fathers of the Society. If you should still persist in your wishes, what you enjoin will be respected, as I have said, and if the matter does not turn out well, the responsibility will lie with you. I don't think the one mentioned by Father Ripalda would do badly were we dealing with some other order, but the nuns are just starting out there and so must be careful not to bring discredit on the house. May our Lord ordain what is for his greater glory and enlighten you so that you do what is most fitting; and may he preserve you many years for us, as I beseech him, for I do not neglect praying for you, however ill I might be.

7. I kiss the hands of her excellency, my lady the duchess,[9] many times, and of my lady Beatriz,[10] and of my ladies, the countess and Doña Leonor.[11] Write to me—I mean may you give me orders—and what pleases you will be done, for I believe that by leaving everything to your conscience my own conscience will feel assured, but not without effort. In none of our houses will any nun be found with so noticeable a defect,[12] nor would I accept her for anything. I think it would be a continuous mortification for the other nuns, for since they are always together and love one another so much, this would

cause them incessant grief. They already have the good Magdalene there;[13] and that is enough, please God.

Today is 7 March.

Your ladyship's unworthy servant and subject,

Teresa of Jesus, Carmelite

Mother Subprioress[14] kisses your ladyship's hands many times. I get along well with her.

---

1. She took up her office of prioress at the Incarnation in October, 1571.
2. Philippians 4:13.
3. Doña Magdalena de Ulloa, who had been the governess of Don Juan of Austria, on account of her charity was called "God's almsgiver."
4. Our Lady. When Teresa took over her new duties, she placed a statue of Our Lady of Clemency in the prioress's chair in the choir to signify to the nuns that she was entrusting the rule of the monastery to the Blessed Virgin Mary.
5. María Bautista.
6. The Jesuit Jerónimo Ripalda.
7. Pedro Fernández was the visitator and Giovanni Battista Rossi, the general.
8. María de Mendoza was the founding patron of the Carmel of Valladolid.
9. The Duchess of Osuna, Leonor Ana de Guzmán y Aragón.
10. Doña María's sister, Beatriz Sarmiento de Mendoza.
11. The Countess of Lemus, Beatriz de Castro, mother of Leonor de Castro y Portugal, wife of Doña María's brother, Diego Sarmiento de Mendoza.
12. It seems that this candidate had only one eye and another facial deformity. Neither of the two candidates showed signs of a vocation to the Teresian Carmel. Their families may have been seeking to escape a burden by having them placed in a monastery.
13. María Magdalena Gutiérrez, a niece of the Dominican court preacher Juan Gutiérrez; she made profession 15 August 1571
14. Isabel de la Cruz (Arias), subprioress at the Incarnation.

42. To Doña María de Mendoza, Valladolid

Avila, 8 march 1572

(Autograph: Capuchin nuns, Bilbao)

Teresa learns after her letter of the previous day that one of the aspirants has more positive recommendations than was thought. She writes to both the Father Visitator and Doña María to accept her into the Carmel of Valladolid. She also prays that the Lord might give Doña María greater inner freedom.

To the most illustrious Señora Doña María de Mendoza, my lady, Valladolid.

1. Jesus. May the Holy Spirit be always with your ladyship, amen. Since I wrote to you yesterday, this letter is only to let you know that today they brought me letters from the Duchess of Osuna and from Doctor Ayala[1] urging that one of those young ladies be received;[2] and a Father from the Society[3] who went there to inquire about this has written me a good report on one of them. The other one would be frightened by the austerity. That is why it is good that the one who speaks to aspirants describe the austerity with candor. Nothing more was said about that other one. I have written that the one could be accepted right away. And I mentioned that I had written you about what must be done to give her the habit at once, and that they should inform you as soon as she arrives in Valladolid.

2. I am writing to our Father Visitator,[4] telling him of your desire to receive her and begging his paternity to send you his permission along with this letter. I think he will do so, and if he doesn't, you should immediately write again to him in such a way that no mistake can be made about your request. From what I understand, Father Visitator will not fail to make you happy whenever he can. May our Lord give us the happiness that will last forever and may he always guide you.

3. Today the bishop[5] sent word that he is better and that he will visit us. Do not be troubled. When will I see you with more freedom? May our Lord bring this about. It is true that we need to help each other. May it please God that when I see you I will find you more in control of yourself, for you have a spirit suited to being so. I think it would be beneficial for you to have me close to you, as it is for me to have our Father Visitator present. As my superior, he tells me the truth,[6] and I—daring as I am and habituated to having you put up with me—would do the same with you. I recommend myself to the prayers of my lady, the duchess. The sisters here are fervent in their prayers for you.

Your ladyship's unworthy servant and subject,

Teresa of Jesus, Carmelite

4. You never mention how you get along with Padre Fray Juan Gutiérrez;[7] some day I will speak to you about it. Please give him my regards. I don't know whether his niece made her profession.[8] It is Father Visitator who gives permission for those who are to make it. Would you inform Mother Prioress[9] about this fact, for I forgot to do so.

---

1. The duchess was Leonor Ana de Guzmán; Ayala could have been a priest in the family service.
2. See Ltr. 41.4-6.
3. Juan Alvarez.
4. Pedro Fernández.
5. Alvaro de Mendoza, the bishop of Avila and Doña María's brother.
6. Cf. Ltr 34.2.
7. Juan Gutiérrez was a Dominican residing in Valladolid.
8. His niece was the "good Magdalene" of Ltr. 41.7.
9. María Bautista, prioress of the Valladolid Carmel.

43. To Doña Juana de Ahumada, Alba de Tormes

Avila, 27 August 1572(?)

Juan de Ovalle is still convalescing and should not try to travel. Teresa is extremely busy, but her health has improved.

To my lady and sister Doña Juana de Ahumada.

1. May Jesus be with your honor. I am well, although so busy that I would rather not have to write you now. Blessed be God that Señor Juan de Ovalle is well. By no means should you allow him to come here, for that would be a risk for him. It would have been better had you sent the letters to the Indies by the same way you sent the packages, for the letters you send never reach their destination over there. My greetings to Señora Doña Magdalena, who I was happy to hear is better, and to the children.[1]

2. Fray Diego[2] is here, although I haven't seen much of him. If he can, he will go to visit you. Mother Prioress and my companion are well.[3] As for myself, I am feeling so much better that I would be surprised if it lasted. May the Lord do his will, and may he be with you.

Today is the vigil of St. Augustine. It would be a great mistake for Señor Juan de Ovalle to try to do any traveling.

In the Incarnation....[4]

Yours truly,

Teresa of Jesus

1. Doña Magdalena de Toledo, of the family of the Count of Oropesa, was a Benedictine nun in Alba de Tormes. Doña Juana had two children, Gonzalo and Beatriz.
2. Fray Diego de Cepeda was a relative of Teresa's who belonged to the Alcantarine Franciscans.

3. The prioress was María de San Jerónimo at the Carmel of St. Joseph in Avila. The companion was Isabel de la Cruz, subprioress at the Incarnation.
4. This passage was illegible in the autograph, which is now lost.

44. To Padre Antonio Lárez, Avila

Avila, 1572

A fragment from a note of condolence written to the Jesuit rector of San Gil in Avila after the sudden death of a brother Jesuit.

Your lordship ought not grieve the sudden death of Padre Hernandálvarez del Aguila, for there is someone who has seen him in heaven among the holy confessors there.

45. To Doña Juana de Ahumada, Alba de Tormes

Avila, 27 September 1572

(Autograph: DCN, Palencia)

The situation at the Incarnation continued to improve, and Teresa's health is fairly good. The nuns are benefiting a great deal from Fray John of the Cross's spiritual direction. But the financial problems are still a cause for worry. Teresa and her sister Juana are awaiting the arrival of Lorenzo from America, which they think might be any day now.

1. Jesus be with your honor. Blessed be God that Señor Juan de Ovalle is well, for the weakness will pass. The tertian fever has been everywhere. Around here,[1] that's all one finds, although it has left me alone. Everything is daily getting better, glory to God. I have been well this summer. I don't know what the winter will bring, for it is already starting to cause me some

disturbance; but when there's no fever, one can put up with it all.

2. Regarding the purchase of the house, I would like to know what was done.[2] From Oropesa they wrote me of the news that the fleet had arrived in Sanlúcar, although this is not certain. I know nothing more. As soon as I know anything about my brother, I will inform you. I have the Perálvarez house ready for him.[3]

3. I am displeased by those fasts of the prioress.[4] Tell her so, and that this is why I do not want to write to her or have anything to do with her. God deliver me from anyone who wants to do her own will rather than obey. If I can be of help to Señora Doña Ana, out of consideration for Señor Don Cristóbal, I'll do so gladly.[5] We have discussed her staying in the house where Doña Sancha used to live, but it is in such a state that no one could live in it. Here in the Incarnation, no one may enter except as far as the portress's office,[6] nor can the service women go out. Her sisters, I believe, though they would like to help her, could do little for her. Because for five years they have eaten nothing but the bread supplied by the monastery, they are drained of energy—and Doña Inés is almost always sick.[7] They deeply regret their lack of energy. As for myself, you already know they are so bound by precepts that there is little I can do.[8]

4. Give my best regards to the subprioress. I don't have time to write any more. Isabel Juarez is the one who came from Malagón, and most unwillingly, according to what they say. But having once expressed the desire, she was sent by the prioress; and I think that at some other time the prioress herself will come. I have many cares—may God provide for them. My regards to Señor Juan de Ovalle and to my dear children. You don't tell me what Beatriz's illness was. May God be with them.[9]

Today is 27 September.

Yours,

Teresa of Jesus

The discalced friar who is confessor here is doing great good; he is Fray John of the Cross.[10]

---

1. The monastery of the Incarnation in Avila. Teresa has been prioress there for a year.
2. It seems she is alluding to the house in Alba that was the cause of a litigation between the Ovalles and the Carmelite nuns in that city (cf. Ltr. 39.3).
3. The brother referred to is Lorenzo de Cepeda, who in fact did not return from the Americas with this fleet. The Perálvarez house belonged to Pedro Alvarez Cimbrón, who was soon to become a good friend of Lorenzo's.
4. The prioress was Juana del Espíritu Santo, superior of the Carmel in Alba de Tormes. She had transferred to the discalced Carmelites from the Incarnation and accompanied Teresa on the foundation in Toledo. She was prioress in Alba when Teresa died there.
5. Cristóbal Chacón was an old friend of Teresa's father. His three daughters were Ana, Sancha, and Inés. The latter two were nuns at the Incarnation.
6. The portress had a room, or sometimes a chair, next to the turn where she communicated unseen with people who came to the monastery.
7. Although there were rich monasteries, the Incarnation was a poor one. The daily ration of food for each nun in 1565 was 5 1/4 ounces of bread and about 4 ounces of meat. This does not mean that all the nuns lived on this ration alone.
8. She is alluding to the severe orders given her by the visitator Pedro Fernández regarding the reform of the Incarnation.
9. The subprioress of Alba was María del Sacramento, who joined Teresa from the Incarnation. Isabel Juárez had gone from the Incarnation to Malagón and was sent back by the prioress to the Incarnation. The children were Juana's children, Gonzalo and Beatriz.
10. Teresa had arranged for St. John of the Cross to come to the Incarnation as confessor to the large community.

46. To Doña Mariana Juárez de Lara(?), Avila

Avila, End of December 1572[1]

Doña Mariana had to wait six years before she received the consent of her parents to enter St. Joseph's in Avila. She made profession 9 January 1576.

1. Jesus. The grace of the Holy Spirit be with your honor. It has not been necessary for me to see you first to value as a very great favor the opportunity you offer me of kissing your hand. For after having learned how well you comprehend all that is good, I myself would have sought to procure the joy of meeting you, if possible. Thus, I beg you to believe that you will be doing me a great favor by coming here to meet me. And if you should come at a time in which we can be together for a longer period, my joy will increase. I had so little time on the feast of St. Thomas[2] that I was happy when you put the visit off for another day.

2. With regard to what you say, it would seem rather to increase one's joy than impede it. There was no time to deal with matters of the soul and all the other things that would have added greatly to the joy. And how much you ought to do in the service of our Lord since you are in possession of such good doctrine. It truly seems that you deserve this. May it please our Lord that you lose nothing by coming to speak with this wretched servant. So be careful about what you are doing, for once you have extended your favor to her, you are obliged not to take it back. In all matters much is to be gained by being attentive in the beginning; then the end will be a good one. In this case, I think the end will have to be a good one. In sum, set the day and hour in which you would like to come, and

you will be doing me a great favor by your visit. May our Lord always be your light and guide.

Your honor's unworthy servant,

Teresa of Jesus

1. Silverio gave December 1574 as the date of this letter and was unable to identify the addressee. Efrén-Steggink identify her as Mariana de Lara and set this earlier date.
2. 21 December.

47. To Martín Dávila Maldonado Bocalán, Salamanca

Avila, 1 February 1573

The monastery of the Incarnation, where Teresa was prioress, had many financial woes and many sick nuns as well. Teresa sends this note of gratitude and a receipt for a donation of fowl from a friend of hers that was sent by Don Martín. The latter's daughter Leonor de Jesús entered the Carmel in Salamanca in September of that same year.

To the very magnificent Señor Maldonado Bocalán, my lord.

1. Jesus. The grace of the Holy Spirit be always with your honor, and may he repay you for your charity and care in sending us the donation given by Señor Don Francisco.[1] May it please our Lord to preserve you for many years and further the improvement that you are beginning to experience.

2. For not knowing where to address my letter, I did not ask you to send me the poultry. The indigence of this house[2] is so great and there are so many sick nuns that we really needed it. I, too, have been very sick, although I am better now. The donation that we have again received was most consoling to me. May God be blessed for everything. The one who brought the poultry performed his task very well.

3. So I affirm that I received today, on the eve of Our Lady of the Purification in the year 1573, sixty-two birds, and in confirmation of this, I sign my name. May the Lord always lead your honor by the hand, and may His Majesty give you as many blessings as possible, amen.

Your honor's servant,

Teresa of Jesus, prioress

I have already written to Señor Don Francisco about the care you have for us and the good condition in which the poultry arrived.

1. Don Francisco de Fonseca, Lord of Coca and Alaejos.
2. The monastery of the Incarnation, where Teresa is prioress.

48. To Gaspar de Salazar, Cuenca

Avila, 13 February 1573

Padre Salazar was Teresa's confessor and friend at the time she founded her first monastery, St. Joseph's in Avila. Here she writes to him about the improved spirit at the Incarnation where she was appointed prioress by the visitator. She asks Salazar for a favor in response to an urgent request from Avila's mayor.

To the Very Magnificent and Reverend Señor Gaspar de Salazar, rector of the house of the Society of Jesus in Cuenca. My lord and my Father.

1. Jesus. The grace of the Holy Spirit be with your honor always, amen. I am delighted that the occasion has arisen in which I can send you news of myself, since you are so neglectful in sending me news about yourself. May it please our Lord that you enjoy the health I beg of him for you.

2. Many days and even months had gone by without my having received a letter from you filled with good counsel and advice. Your letter came just at the right time, for I was greatly encouraged, although your prayers must have brought me even greater benefit. I want you to know that in this house[1] the Lord has bestowed so many favors that I can assure you I no longer have any more reason to be distressed over resistance to obedience and recollection here than at St. Joseph's.[2] It seems the Lord is giving these souls so many graces altogether that I am stupefied. So was Father Visitator[3] who found nothing to correct in the visitation he made a month ago. Would you give thanks to the Lord for that. In the monastery of Our Lady of Mt. Carmel,[4] he appointed discalced friars as prior, subprior, porter, and sacristan. And one of them, who is very saintly, has been the confessor here for some time.[5] He has done much good; and all of them are to my liking.

3. This decision has been an exceptionally good one. If this house[6] were entrusted completely to them—as I hope in the Lord it will be—there would be no need for me to stay here any longer. Pray for this, that a proper remedy will be found for everything. Up to the present I have had many trials and duties, and in the winter poor health, for this house aggravates my illnesses. I consider it all worthwhile when I see the favors that His Majesty has granted me. I had a strong desire that you might know about these things, and if I could see you it would be a great consolation to me. (Pass on to the next page, for I got a bad piece of paper.) May the Lord do his will in all things.

4. The lord mayor here, whom I very much want to please, came to urge me—and afterward continued pressing me—to ask you that a monastery there (I think he said they were discalced, but anyway you have much influence there) might accept a daughter of Juan de Buedo and Leonor de Hermosa for the religious life. They say that the young lady and her parents meet all the requirements. Would you find out if this is so and, out of love for God, help her. You would be rendering a

service to God, and a great favor to me, for I cannot accept her in any of our monasteries; the necessary disposition is lacking.

5. Everyone is doing very well in Malagón. Brianda de San José is now prioress; the former prioress has returned to her house here. I'm writing no more for I am certain you will do all you can for me. I am at present enjoying better health than usual. Don't forget to keep me in your prayers, and I, though wretched, will do the same for you.

My confessor is Padre Lárez.[7]

Today is 13 February 1573.

Your honor's unworthy servant and daughter,

Teresa of Jesus

---

1. The monastery of the Incarnation
2. The new discalced monastery that St. Teresa founded in Avila.
3. Pedro Fernández, who had appointed Teresa prioress at the Incarnation. In a letter to the Duchess of Alba, he praises the work being done by Madre Teresa: "In the monastery of the Incarnation there are 130 nuns who are living in the same peace and holiness as the 10 or 12 discalced Carmelites of the other monastery, so much so that I am both amazed and consoled. This is all due to the presence of the Madre...." See MHCT 1:137-139.
4. The monastery of the friars of the observance in Avila.
5. St. John of the Cross.
6. The monastery of the Carmelite friars in Avila. It was not Fernández's intention to turn the monastery into a house for discalced but that its members observe their own rule in greater holiness. Cf. MHCT 1:139.
7. Padre Lárez was rector of the Jesuit College of San Gil in Avila.

49. To Doña Juana de Ahumada, Alba

Avila, 9 March 1573

Teresa writes hurriedly since the carrier is waiting. There are a number of allusions with no sure meaning.

1. Jesus be with your honor. I have no longer been sending letters with this messenger, yet I am delighted that he is here so that he can bring this letter from my brother which was given to me while I was at Vespers. Glory to God that he is well, and we can be sure now of his coming as you will see. Please God, Señor Juan de Ovalle is well. Since this messenger's coming was so certain, a few lines could have been sent to let me know how he is. I am fine, and everything is going well, glory to God.

2. It's only right that immediate steps be taken to obtain those documents and take possession. I don't know where that city is of which he speaks, whether it is far away. My brother[1] will certainly know. Since as the saying goes, "Wait no longer than a Creed[2] and a messenger leaves for Madrid," try to act as quickly as possible to track down this lord, who must be involved with litigations, so that the documents will be ready. May the Lord intervene in everything and make you very holy.

3. It seems to me the letter is from a brother-in-law of our uncle Ruy Sánchez's son.[3] I will try to write through this messenger, for he must be reliable; and you, too, write to me.

Today is 9 March.

Regards to my dear children.[4]

Your reverence's servant,[5]

Teresa of Jesus

---

1. Her brother-in-law, Juan de Ovalle.
2. The amount of time necessary to recite the Apostles Creed.
3. Ruy Sánchez was an uncle on her father's side.

4. Juana's children.
5. Here Teresa (or the copyist) must have been distracted, since she would hardly refer to her sister as your reverence.

50. To Padre Juan Ordónez, Medina(?)

Avila, 26 March 1573

(Autograph fragment: DCN, Rochefort, France)

...I am writing now. Give my best regards to Señor Asencio Galiano and to Doña Elena.[1]

May the Lord be with your honor always.

Today is Thursday of Easter Week.

Your honor's unworthy servant and subject,

Teresa of Jesus

1. Elena de Quiroga.

51. To Madre Inés de Jesús, Medina del Campo

Avila, Beginning of May 1573

The prioress in Medina consulted Teresa with respect to a nun whom they believed was possessed. Teresa responded by sending St. John of the Cross who had gained a reputation in Avila as an exorcist. His most noted exorcism took place in May 1574. Teresa did not return to Avila from Segovia until the end of September, and so this note was probably written in October or November.

My daughter: I am very sorry about Sister Isabel's[1] sickness. I am sending you the saintly Fray John of the Cross, for God has given him the grace to cast out devils from persons having them. Just recently here in Avila he has driven out three legions of devils from a person, demanding that they identify themselves, and they obeyed at once. What they fear in him is so much grace accompanied by so much humility.

---

1. Sister Isabel de San Jerónimo (Alvarez) died 23 November 1582 of a brain illness from which she suffered for a number of years. According to Alonso de la Madre de Dios, John's early biographer (1600), St. John of the Cross, "on seeing her, concluded that her affliction was not a work of the devil but the beginning of an illness that would cause insanity. Afterward, when it grew worse they understood its nature." The last two sentence are missing from some copies of this letter.

52. To the King Don Philip II, Madrid

Avila, 11 June 1573

(Autograph: Capuchin Friars, Jerez)

Teresa writes from the Incarnation where she has been prioress for almost two years. She wants a favor from the king, but we do not know the details of what it was. The letter presents to the king her intermediary, Juan de Padilla, an influential but somewhat over-zealous reformer.

To His Sacred, Catholic, Imperial Royal Majesty, the Lord King.

1. Jesus. The grace of the Holy Spirit be always with your majesty, amen. I truly believe that your majesty is aware of the everyday care I take to recommend you to our Lord in my poor prayers. Since I am so miserable a person, this may be of small service, but by stirring the sisters of these discalced monasteries of our order to do so, I may be of some help to you; for I know that they serve our Lord. And in this house where I now reside, the same is done,[1] together with praying for our lady the queen and for the prince[2]—may God give him long life. And the day in which his highness was pronounced heir,

special prayers were offered. This we will do always. Thus, the more this order increases, the more your majesty will gain.

2. As a result, I dare to beg your majesty for your favor in certain matters about which the licentiate Juan de Padilla,[3] in whom I'm confiding, will speak to you. Would you give credence to him. Seeing his true zeal, I felt confident in entrusting this affair to him. If it were made public, great harm would be done to what we are aiming after, which is all for the glory and honor of our Lord. May His Divine Majesty preserve you for many years, as many as are needed by Christendom. It is a great relief that in its trials and persecutions, our Lord God has as great a defender and help for his church as is your majesty.

From this house of the Incarnation in Avila, 11 June 1573.

Your majesty's unworthy servant and subject,

Teresa of Jesus, Carmelite

1. She alludes to the Carmels she has been founding and also to the Incarnation from where she writes this letter.
2. The queen is Anne of Austria; the prince, Don Fernando, born 5 December 1571 and pronounced heir in May of 1573. He died at the age of seven, 18 October 1578.
3. Juan Calvo de Padilla, a zealous reformer.

53. To Padre Juan Ordóñez, Medina del Campo

Avila, 27 July 1573

(Autograph: DCN, Toro [Zamora])

Doña Elena de Quiroga and her daughter Jerónima, who both wished to enter the Medina Carmel, had plans to use funds from Jerónima's estate to found a school for young women and place it under the care of the discalced Carmelite nuns in Medina. Negotiators in the matter were the Jesuit Juan Ordónez and, on the part of the visitator, Domingo Báñez, and Teresa herself. Surprisingly Teresa does not oppose the project outright, but she has many misgivings and wants the opinions also of both the Jesuit provincial and Baltasar Alvarez. She writes from the Incarnation; her health in that house has been bad.

✣✣✣✣

To the Very Magnificent and Reverend Señor Padre Ordóñez of the Society of Jesus, my lord.

1. Jesus. The grace of the Holy Spirit be with your honor. I would like to have a good deal of time and health to mention some things that, in my opinion, are important. But I am in such a state that, after the departure of the young lad, I got even worse than before, incomparably so. Just writing this will cost me much effort. And I get so tediously long that, however much I may want to keep this short, I will go on at length. This house of the Incarnation is noticeably bad for my health. Please God some merit will come from my being here.

2. Since this matter of ours seems to be nearing the decisive step, I have become much more concerned, especially after seeing our Father Visitator's[1] letter today, in which he refers the matter to Padre Maestro Fray Domingo[2] and me. He writes to transfer his powers in this regard to us. I am always apprehensive in matters in which I have to decide; it seems at once that I am going to make a mistake over the whole thing. It is true that beforehand I had recommended everything to the Lord, and they have done so here.

3. It seems to me, *mi padre*, that we have to look carefully at all the drawbacks, for if the thing doesn't work out, you and I will be held responsible before God and the world—have no doubt about it. Therefore don't bother about whether the matter is concluded in more or less than fifteen days. What you say in your letter about the prioress made me happy, that she should not become involved in the matter except in the two areas you specified. For, believe me, it is very necessary to proceed in such a way that to achieve one good we do not remove another, as you say.

4. As for there being so many, as you often said, this has displeased me. I know there is as much difference between teaching young women together and teaching young men as there is between black and white. And if we want to do something good, there are so many disadvantages in a large number that I am not able to recount them now. I only say that the number should be fixed, and if it passes forty, that will mean too many, and things will become chaotic, with some of them disturbing others so that no good will come from it. In Toledo,[3] I found out, there are thirty-five, and that is the limit. I tell you that in no way is it necessary or suitable to have so many young women and so much noise. And if on this account some do not want to give alms, proceed slowly, for there is no rush, and seek to form a holy community, for God will help you; we must not fail in substantial matters for the sake of alms.

5. In choosing those suitable for entering, it will also be necessary to have two other votes besides that of the prioress. One should be very careful on this point. If the prior of San Andrés[4] accepts this task, it would not be a bad thing; he could have an administrator or be administrator himself along with another. They would take care of the record of expenditures, for the prioress should not get involved in this—neither see it nor hear about it—as I said before. It will be necessary to consider the qualities required of those who will be entering and the number of years they expect to remain. You and Padre Maestro[5] could look into that; and everything you submit to him should first be presented for consultation to Father Provincial of the Society of Jesus and to Padre Baltasar Alvarez.[6]

6. Many other things will be necessary, but we've already dealt there with some, especially not going out. Those that seem to me extremely important are the first two, for I have experience of what it is for many women to be together—God deliver us!

7. With respect to what you say—I think the prioress[7] has written me concerning it—about not getting free of the rent

payment for now, you should understand that Lady Doña Jerónima[8] cannot enter, nor do I have the authority to allow her to enter, without her first getting rid of the mortgage. Or Señora Doña Elena[9] should assume it as a part of her estate, in such a way that the monastery doesn't waste a thing on paying rent and remains free. I know that Father Provincial[10] gave permission only on this condition, and not to respect it would be deceptive, in my opinion. In sum, I cannot do it. I can well see how all of this is a heavy burden for Señora Doña Elena. But there's a way out: she can delay work on the church, or Señora Doña Jerónima need not enter so quickly. The latter is preferable, for she would be older.

8. The thought comes to mind that we ought not build too much on a foundation that may crumble, for we don't know if this lady will persevere. Your reverence should consider everything carefully. It makes more sense to spend a few years on the work so that it will last rather than to do something that becomes a laughingstock. And that would matter little if virtue were not discredited.

9. It is also necessary to consider, if we now accept this means, to whom we should be bound for it doesn't seem there is anything certain for the present, and Father Visitator will ask what need there is of drawing up a contract. I would have been free of considering all these things if Father Visitator had done so. Now I have to make myself into the expert I'm not.

10. I beg you to give my regards to Señor Asensio Galiano,[11] and give him this to read. He's always doing me favors in everything, for I am most happy that my letters are now safe. This wretched health of mine makes me slip into many faults. Ana de San Pedro[12] prizes her daughters too highly to send them there; it doesn't even enter her mind. The day after tomorrow I will leave, provided some other sickness does not strike me down, and it would have to be a serious one to keep

me back. All the letters have been delivered to San Gil;[13] no response has yet come. Tomorrow, Tuesday, I'll try to get one.

Your honor's unworthy servant and daughter,

Teresa of Jesus

Ask my Father Rector to remember me in his prayers.

---

1. The visitator was the Dominican Pedro Fernández.
2. The Dominican Domingo Báñez.
3. She is alluding to a school for young women founded by Cardinal Siliceo.
4. The Dominican monastery in Medina del Campo.
5. Domingo Báñez.
6. The provincial of the Jesuits was Juan Suárez. Baltasar Alvarez had been Teresa's confessor during the time of doubt about her mystical life (cf. L. 28.14).
7. The prioress was Inés de Jesús.
8. Señora Jerónima de Villarroel y Quiroga actually received the habit 31 January 1575. At the time Teresa wrote this letter, Jerónima was only 12 years old. She received the habit at age 14 with the name Jerónima de la Encarnación.
9. Elena de Quiroga, Jerónima's mother. She also later entered the Carmel of Medina, 4 October 1581.
10. The provincial of the Carmelites of the Observance, Angel de Salazar.
11. A contractor in Medina who had been a guarantor for Teresa when she bought a house there for her foundation.
12. Ana de San Pedro (Wasteels), the Flemish widow and nun at St. Joseph's in Avila. She had two daughters living in Avila.
13. The Jesuit school in Avila.

54. To Pedro de la Banda, Tozos (Salamanca)

Salamanca, 2 August 1573

(Autograph: DCF, Alba de Tormes)

Pedro de la Banda had offered his house to the Carmelite nuns for the foundation in Salamanca (F. 19.7,10). Since it belonged to an entailed estate, a license from the king was required. Teresa had arrived two days before writing this letter. She has the license from the king, but the owner is absent.

1. Jesus. May the grace of the Holy Spirit be always with your honor, amen. I have come here to proceed at once toward getting these sisters settled. I don't have much time and because of this and also because the desirable season for constructing walls is nearly over, I was sorry not to find you here. The license from the king has arrived, and it's necessary to have it verified at once.

2. I beg you please to come quickly; since the matter is so important, I hope in God that you will not become irritated with me. May the Lord guide everything for his greater service and may he always lead you by the hand.

3. The house seems good to me, although more than 500 ducats will be necessary before entering it. Nonetheless, I am pleased and I hope in our Lord that you will be pleased in seeing it put to such good use. May the Lord grant you many years. Remember, the work has to begin during the good season and so it's a pity to see these days wasted.

4. For the love of God do us the favor of coming at once. And if you delay, I beg you to agree to our beginning to make the partition walls, for more than two hundred are needed; this will do no harm to the house. If afterward the agreement is not finalized (which is why I hope in God you will come quickly), the loss will be ours.

5. When you arrive, everything can be worked out. May His Majesty give you a long life so that you may ever gain more merit for eternal life.[1]

Today is 2 August.

Your honor's unworthy servant, who kisses your hands,

Unworthy,

Teresa of Jesus

1. Pedro de la Banda was not very cooperative; he didn't return until a month later. When he did come and saw what the nuns had done, Teresa writes, he "was so furious that I didn't know what to do with him" (F. 19.10).

55. To Don Francisco de Salcedo, Avila

Salamanca, 3 August 1573(?)

(Autograph: DCF, S. Teresa al Museo, Naples)

It seems this note was written to Francisco de Salcedo, who had visited Teresa in Salamanca and was now returning to Avila. She was entrusting to him several letters for Medina and a message for the provincial.

1. Jesus. May the Holy Spirit be with your honor and repay you for the charity you have done me today. I thought I would have been able to speak with you, not so as to complain, for I had no motive for that, but for my consolation. See that you do not forget me in your prayers. That will now leave me all the more obliged to you by reason of the poverty of my own prayers.

2. I beg your honor to be very careful with these letters and to give them to Padre Lárez,[1] for several of them deal with a most important matter. May the Lord go with you.

3. Tell our Father Provincial[2] that the ones I am enclosing for Medina should be delivered only by a person who is very trustworthy, for they deal with the business matter[3] I spoke about to you the other day, and there could come upon us many anxieties and obstacles to the service of God. They should be

delivered to Padre Ordóñez[4] as soon as possible. If this cannot be done, would you send them back to me.

Your unworthy servant,

Teresa of Jesus

1. Antonio Lárez, a Jesuit in Avila.
2. The provincial of the Carmelites was Angel de Salazar.
3. This probably refers to the foundation of a school for young women in Medina, a matter with which Teresa was dealing at the time.
4. Juan Ordóñez, a Jesuit in Medina, was involved with the foundation of a school for young women in Medina (cf. Ltr. 49).

56. To Pedro de la Banda, Salamanca

Salamanca, 8 October 1573

The nuns moved into the house owned by Pedro de la Banda on 28 September. Eight days later Teresa signed the purchase and sales agreement. But the demands of the former owner continued, and Teresa responds with this note. Three years later the purchase of the house was still not finalized (see F. 19.11).

To the Illustrious Señor Pedro de la Banda, my lord.

1. Everything your honor said is being carried out according to your wishes. From what everyone says, I am not obligated to all of this until the license arrives. But our having entered the house obliges me to comply with your orders, and please God you will be satisfied with everything.

2. May our Lord give you calm[1] that you may serve him better, and may he always lead you by his hand.

Today is 8 October.

Your honor's unworthy servant,

Teresa of Jesus

1. This prayerful wish may have been prompted by Pedro de la Banda's angry reaction on his return to Salamanca at finding the nuns in his house (see F. 19.10).

57. To Doña Juana de Ahumada, Alba de Tormes

Salamanca, 14 November 1573

In this letter to her sister, Teresa speaks about her health, the business affairs concerning the new house in Salamanca, and the entrance of a new member into the community.

1. Jesus. May the grace of the Holy Spirit be with your honor. I have praised our Lord that Señor Juan Ovalle[1] despite this humid weather is better. May it please His Majesty that he continue to improve. My quartan fevers are continuing, and what is worse, the pain of the preceding winters is returning. Last night I slept but little. I believe they will bleed me again. God must have so ordained that it wouldn't appear that everything was the result of being at the Incarnation. The truth of the matter is that this sickness came upon me there, and I have never been without some aftereffects. Perhaps I would fare better there where you are living, and even here the pain up until now has not been as severe as in Avila—in no way. And if it should come to that, I would be able to bear it better because I don't have as much work.

2. The business affairs with Pedro de la Banda are on good course. Nonetheless, I fear there will be some delay because it is necessary to take the matter to Madrid.[2] Once the authorization is given, I will attend to the workmen, for they have not finished. It seems God wants me to remain here, for there is no one in the house who understands construction or business matters.

3. Yesterday we gave the habit to a young woman of high quality.[3] And I believe she will have something she can con-

tribute to us, and even a great deal. She's made to order—the daughter of Martín de Avila Maldonado, and her mother is Doña Guiomar de Ledesma. This has been a source of happiness for us. She is delighted and we are with her.

4. This letter is also for Señor Juan Ovalle; give him my regards, and give them also to my daughters. Doña Antonia sends you greetings—she is well now, without the quartan fevers—and the prioress also sends them. Greetings to the sisters there, especially the youngest one, for I don't think I'll be able to write, nor do I have anything in particular to say except to ask that they pray for me.[4] May His Majesty make you a saint.

Your servant,

Teresa of Jesus

5. May the Lord repay you for what you do for me, for you are right about what you think is suitable. I have been very happy in learning about the improvement of Señor Juan Ovalle and that you are in good health, and those angels as well.

---

1. Juana's husband.
2. Because the property involved an entailed estate, the purchase and sales agreement now had to go to Madrid for the royal approval. The approval was ultimately denied.
3. This young woman took the name Leonor de Jesús. She made her profession 13 November 1574 and died some months afterward, 14 June 1575.
4. Mentioned here are Antonia del Aguila, a nun from the Incarnation who had accompanied Teresa to Salamanca; the prioress in Salamanca, Ana de la Encarnación; the sisters (her daughters) in the Carmel in Alba, the youngest in the community being probably Inés de la Cruz; and those angels, Juana's two children, Gonzalo and Beatriz de Ovalle.

Letters 58–78 (1574)

58. To Padre Domingo Báñez, Valladolid

Salamanca, Beginning of January 1574

Although Teresa is sick with the quartan fevers, her manner is sprightly. The letter deals with four separate dramas going on at this time in Teresa's life: the question of a school for girls in Medina; the capricious princess of Eboli; the bizarre story of Casilda de Padilla; and the purchase of a house in Salamanca. She jests with Báñez over his letter-writing habits.

To my Padre and Señor, Maestro Fray Domingo Báñez.

1. Jesus. May the grace of the Holy Spirit be with your honor and in my soul. When I was sick I wrote you a long letter telling you about the ups and downs of my health, and sent it by way of Medina—I don't know why they didn't deliver it. Now I would also like to write at length, but I have many letters to write and I am feeling cold, for it is the day of the quartan fever.[1] I've been without it, or half without it, for two days. But since the pain I used to have along with it hasn't returned, it all amounts to nothing.

2. I praise our Lord for the news I hear about your sermons, and I am very envious. And now, since you are the superior of that house,[2] I feel a longing to be there. But when have you ceased being my superior? If I were there, though, it seems to

me I would experience a new joy. But since I don't deserve anything but the cross, I praise him who gives it to me always.

3. I was delighted with those letters of Father Visitator to you, *mi padre*.[3] Not only is that friend of yours a saint, but he knows how to show it, and if his words do not contradict his deeds, he proceeds very wisely. And although what he says is true, he will not fail to admit her,[4] because between lords and lords the difference is great.

4. The Princess of Eboli as a nun was something to cry over.[5] That angel there,[6] as a nun, can be of benefit to other souls, and the greater the outcry, all the more! I find no drawbacks. The worst that can happen is that she leave, but the Lord in the meantime will have drawn out, as I say, other benefits and perhaps have stirred some soul who otherwise without this means might have been condemned. Great are God's judgments, and there is no reason for us to deny admission to one who loves him so authentically when she is in the danger that all these illustrious people are in. Nor should we refuse to bear the trial of some disturbance in exchange for so great a good. To make her wait, it seems to me, would be like going along with the world and copying its ways, and it would be a torment to her. It is clear that even if she did change her mind[7] during the thirty days, she would not say so. But if such a delay would placate her parents, justify her cause, and provide for the waiting period your honor desires—it would be no more, I repeat, than a delay—may God be with her. For it is impossible for whoever gives up much not to receive much from God since he gives so much to us who have given up nothing.

5. I am greatly consoled that you are there to lend support to the prioress[8] and that she may do what is right in all matters. May he be blessed who has thus arranged everything. I hope in His Majesty that all things will go well. This business with Pedro de la Banda[9] is never-ending. I believe I'll have to go first to Alba so as not to lose time, for there is a danger in this matter that the conflict is between him and his wife.[10]

6. I greatly pity the nuns in Pastrana. Even though the princess has returned home, they are like captives, for the prior of Atocha[11] went there and did not dare visit them. Now she is also mad at the friars.[12] I don't know why they should have to put up with such slavery. I am doing well with Padre Medina.[13] I think that if I were to speak with him often, everything would soon be smoothed over. He is so busy that I hardly see him....

Doña María Cosneza[14] told me that I shouldn't prize him as highly as I do you....

7. Doña Beatriz[15] is well. Last Friday she repeatedly offered to do something for me; but now I don't need anything, thanks be to God. She told me about the goodness you have shown her. The love of God permits many things; if it is in the least bit lacking, everything would be finished. Your difficulty, it seems, is to write at length; mine is to be brief. Nonetheless, you do me a great favor because I do not grow sad when I see a bundle of letters and yours is not among them. May God keep you. It doesn't seem this letter should....[16] May it please God that my excess will not be tempered by your silence.

Your honor's servant and daughter,

Teresa de Jesus

---

1. In the quartan fevers, the fever returned every fourth day.
2. A professor at the college of St. Gregory (Valladolid), he was appointed its regent.
3. The letters referred to were those in which the visitator, Pedro Fernández, deferred the matter of the school for young women in Medina to the decision of Báñez and Teresa. Fernández and Báñez had been companions together in the novitiate.
4. In her *Foundations* (ch. 11), Teresa tells the story of Casilda de Padilla, how she escaped from her family and entered the Carmelite cloister in Valladolid before she had reached the age of 12. The family in their great opposition finally got a court order to take her out of the monastery. They had recourse to Báñez and tried to get him to overcome Teresa's resistance. Eventually, Casilda escaped again and entered the monastery. She was professed a week after her fifteenth birthday, 13 January 1577.

5. When the Prince of Eboli died, the princess announced that she was going to become a nun and entered the monastery of the discalced Carmelites in Pastrana, bringing her maids with her and totally disrupting the contemplative life of the nuns. Growing to dislike the prioress and the rest of the nuns, she eventually left, but continued to cause them trouble.
6. Casilda de Padilla
7. This refers to the actual situation in which the family wanting to keep her outside of the monastery for thirty days, sought the help of Báñez.
8. Maria Bautista (Ocampo), Teresa's cousin, who was a great admirer of Báñez's.
9. The business refers to the purchase from Pedro de la Banda of a house for the nuns in Salamanca (cf. F. 19.7–12).
10. The house actually belonged to Pedro de la Banda's wife. She wanted it sold so she could use the money to help her two daughters (cf. F. 19.10).
11. The Dominican prior of Atocha in Madrid, Hernando del Castillo, a friend of the deceased prince, went to Pastrana to try to appease the princess, but in vain.
12. The discalced Carmelite friars in Pastrana, a foundation that had also been patronized by the prince and princess.
13. Bartolomé de Medina, a Dominican professor at Salamanca, had strongly opposed Teresa, but as he got to know her he softened his attitude.
14. One of Báñez's directees and admirers.
15. Beatriz Sarmiento de Mendoza, the sister of Don Alvaro de Mendoza, bishop of Avila.
16. A part is missing because of deterioration in the text of the autograph.

59. To Madre Ana de la Encarnación, Salamanca

Alba de Tormes, Middle of January 1574

Ana de la Encarnación (Tapia), Teresa's cousin, was a nun from the Incarnation. Teresa at this time was prioress in Salamanca and was again sick. She sends kind regards and messages of concern, adding that she is sending a trout to

Padre Medina. She mentions the enjoyment she has in her views of the river.

❖❖❖❖

For Mother Prioress in Salamanca.

1. Jesus be with your reverence. Let me know how you are and how all the nuns are as well, and give them my regards. Tell them I would like to be enjoying their company along with that of the nuns here. I believe I will have less difficulty here than I thought. And from my hermitage,[1] and also from where I sleep, there's a view of the river—I can enjoy it while in bed, a most refreshing experience for me. I have felt better today than usual. Doña Quiteria[2] has her customary fever; she says she misses all of you. They have brought a doctor here for Señora Doña Jerónima,[3] for she is still sick. Pray for her there, as we are doing so here; I am worried about her. May God guide you.

2. The duchess[4] sent me this trout today. It looked so good that I got this messenger to deliver it to my Padre Maestro Fray Bartolomé de Medina.[5] If it arrives at dinner time, send it to him at once through Miguel,[6] and this letter as well. And if it arrives later, send it to him anyway to see if he's willing to write a few lines.

3. Don't neglect to write me about how you are, and don't neglect to eat meat these days. Tell the doctor about your infirmity and give him my best regards. Anyway, may God be always with you, amen.

4. Give my regards to my Padre Osma[7] and tell him I greatly miss him here. Let me know how Juana de Jesús[8] is, for she had a very pale face the day I left.

Today is Wednesday after the twelfth, and I am yours,

Teresa of Jesus

5. How is the countess?[9] And the magistrate's wife?[10] Send someone to find out and let me know about it. I will write about how your sister[11] is, for I did not want to send Navarro[12] until I knew; through him I will also send you something. He will bring these sixteen *reales*, if I remember tomorrow, for today I also forgot. If Lescano should ask for something, give it to him, for I will repay you. I told him that if he needs something you would give it to him. I'm quite sure he will not ask.

---

1. In the Carmels founded by Teresa there were little chapels or cells in the garden or on the top floor of the house; there the nuns could enjoy a more intense solitude. From this hermitage she had a view of the river Tormes.
2. Quiteria Dávila (1526–1607) was a nun from the Incarnation whom Teresa brought with her to Salamanca.
3. Jerónima de Villarroel y Quiroga, Cardinal Quiroga's niece, entered the Carmel of Medina the following year.
4. The Duchess of Alba, María Enríquez.
5. The Dominican professor of theology at the University of Salamanca who had at first opposed Teresa.
6. The messenger's full name may have been Miguel Lescano, the one Teresa refers to in no. 5 as Lescano.
7. The identity of this priest in Salamanca is unknown.
8. Juana de Jesús (Guerra) received the habit in Avila in 1570 and then was transferred to Salamanca, where she made her profession.
9. The Countess of Monterrey, María Pimentel (cf. F. 19.10).
10. Doña Mariana who helped Teresa in the foundation of Salamanca (cf. F. 19.10).
11. Inés de Jesús, a cousin of Teresa's originally from the Incarnation and at the time prioress of Medina.
12. One of Teresa's messengers.

60. To Don Alvaro de Mendora, Valladolid

Alba de Tormes, January–February 1574

(Autograph: DCN, Santa Ana, Madrid)

This letter reflects two Family dramas: the Padilla family's opposition to young Doña Casilda's becoming a discalced Carmelite nun (a matter in which Don Alvaro and his sister don't dare interfere); and the marriage of Don Fadrique with Doña Magdalena de Guzmán, which Don Alvaro opposes. Teresa learns of the first through the prioress in Valladolid and of the second from the Duchess of Alba.

1. Jesus. The grace of the Holy Spirit be always with your lordship. Blessed be God that you are in good health. May it please His Majesty that you continue to improve, as I beg him.

2. It would be a consolation for me if I had the time to write you at length, but I have so little that I didn't want to begin. María Bautista[1] will give you news of me, since I cannot do so here in this letter. When she writes, she gives me the news that I desire and informs me about you, glory to God, and with this I can get along without seeing any letter from you. I have written some letters. With one of them, I already know that, for a certain reason, they did not give it to you; with the others I don't know what happened. I have received only one from you since I have been here. (I mean I received it in Salamanca).[2]

3. I have already told the duchess[3] what you directed me to tell her. She gave me an account of the matter and said that she had never thought you knew about the recent events. She certainly deserves that one not lose her friendship.[4] Nor can I write to Señora Doña María.[5] I kiss her ladyship's hands many times, but it seems to me that our Lady defends her daughters better than her ladyship does her subjects, judging from what they tell me about her silence in these matters. May the Lord help that little angel,[6] for what he is doing for her is now something truly new in the world. I think this is the reason he has ordained that she find herself alone and with these struggles: that his favor toward her be better known. This makes me praise His Majesty greatly.

4. Now, since you have many saints there,[7] you are beginning to recognize those who are not, and so you are forgetting me. Nonetheless, I believe that in heaven you will see that you

owe the sinner[8] more than you do them. I would be more willing to send best wishes to Señora Doña María and my lady the countess[9] if it were for something else than this wedding; although I am consoled that it is taking place so quickly.

5. May it please our Lord that it be for his service, and may your lordship and Señora Doña María rejoice in it for many years. I kiss the hands of Señora Doña Beatriz and my lady the duchess many times.[10] May our Lord always guide you.

Your lordship's unworthy servant and subject,

Teresa of Jesus

6. I beg you to inform me whether Father Visitator has given the permission for me to spend some days at St. Joseph's; the prioress will write to me.[11]

---

1. The prioress in Valladolid.
2. Teresa adds this sentence in the margin of the letter.
3. María Enríquez, the Duchess of Alba.
4. The matter in question was the planned marriage of the duke's heir, Don Fadrique with Doña Magdalena de Guzmán, a lady from the royal court. The marriage never took place and the attempt to proceed without the royal permission brought about the imprisonment of Don Fadrique and Don Fernando, the duke.
5. María de Mendoza, Don Alvaro's sister. Despite her friendship and close contact as benefactress with the nuns in Valladolid, she avoided any confrontation with the wealthy members of Doña Casilda's family.
6. Casilda de Padilla (cf. F. 11).
7. The Carmelite nuns in Valladolid are the saints.
8. The sinner is Teresa.
9. The countess (of Lemus) is Leonor de Castro y Portugal to whom Teresa sends her good wishes on the occasion of her marriage with Diego de Sarmiento de Mendoza, the count of Rivadavia and brother of Don Alvaro and Doña María.
10. Doña Beatriz is Don Alvaro's sister. The duchess is Leonor Ana de Guzmán of Osorno.
11. Teresa will be passing through Avila on her way to the foundation in Segovia. She needs permission from Pedro Fernández, the visitator, to stay with the nuns of her first foundation in Avila. She is still offi-

cially prioress of the Incarnation. María Bautista is the prioress in Valladolid.

61. To Padre Domingo Báñez, Valladolid

Salamanca, 28 February(?) 1574

Though still prioress of the Incarnation in Avila, Teresa is in Salamanca entangled in the efforts to purchase a house for the nuns there. She has happily received a novice recommended by Báñez and notes that lack of a dowry has never kept her from receiving those, such as this novice, in whom she sees a vocation. Both the new novice and the Dominican Fray Melchor Cano receive high praises. She is preparing for a new foundation in Segovia.

To my Most Reverend Señor and Padre Maestro Domingo Báñez, my lord.

1. Jesus. May the grace of the Holy Spirit be with your honor and with my soul. There is no reason to be amazed at anything that is done for love of God, for my love for Fray Domingo is such that whatever seems good to him seems so to me and what he wants, I want as well. I don't know where such enchantment will end.

2. Your Parda[1] has made us happy. She is so outside herself with joy since her entrance that it makes us praise God. I don't think I will have the heart to take her as a lay sister, knowing how you have helped her. So, I have decided that they teach her how to read and on the basis of her progress we will make our decision.

3. My spirit has well understood hers even though I have not spoken to her. And there is a nun who cannot resist the deep prayer that this new sister stirs in her. Believe me, *mi padre*, it is a pleasure for me every time I accept someone who brings in nothing and is received for love of God alone;

otherwise those who don't have anything would have to renounce their vocation for lack of means. I see that God does me a special favor allowing me to be a means to their salvation. If I could accept all in this way, I would be overjoyed. But I don't recall ever having refused anyone pleasing to me because she didn't have a dowry.

4. It made me particularly happy to see how God grants you such great favors as to use you in works like this of sending us a postulant. You have become the father of those of little means, and the charity the Lord gives you for this work makes me so happy that I will do anything I can to help you in deeds of this kind. But the flood of tears of the one who accompanied her![2] I thought it would never end. I don't know why you sent her here to me.

5. Father Visitator[3] has given the permission, and it is the beginning of more to come with the help of God. And perhaps I will be able to accept the whimpering one,[4] if it should please you. But I have too many for Segovia.

6. Parda found a good father when she found you. She says that she still doesn't believe she is living in our house. Her happiness is something to praise God for. I praised him also on seeing your little nephew who came with Doña Beatriz,[5] and I rejoiced in meeting him. Why didn't you tell me beforehand?

7. It also pleases me that our new sister lived with my saintly friend.[6] My friend's sister writes to me making generous offers of help. I tell you I have been deeply touched. It seems I love my friend much more than I did when she was alive.

8. You will have already heard that you received a vote for prior at San Esteban; the present prior received all the rest.[7] I was edified to see such unanimity. Yesterday I was with a padre named Fray Melchor Cano,[8] who is from your order. I tell you that if there were many spirits in your order like his, they could found some contemplative monasteries.

9. I wrote to Avila that those wanting to make such a foundation should not lose heart if they don't find the means here, for I have a great desire that there be a beginning. Why don't you tell me what you have done? May God make you as holy as I desire. I want to speak to you some day about those fears you have; they only make you waste time, and for want of humility you don't believe me. Fray Melchor does better, for after I spoke with him in Avila, he says, it benefited him and he doesn't believe an hour passes that he doesn't think of me. Oh, what a spirit, and what a soul God has in him! I was highly consoled by him. It seems I have nothing more to do than tell you about the spirit of others. Remain with God and beg him to give me a spirit that will never stray in any matter concerning his will.

It is Sunday night.

Your honor's daughter and servant,

Teresa of Jesus

---

1. María Pardo y Cifuentes who took the name María de Jesús.
2. María de los Santos was the one accompanying her.
3. The Dominican Pedro Fernández who as visitator could give Teresa permission to make a foundation in Segovia.
4. María de los Santos.
5. Beatriz Sarmiento de Mendoza, the sister of Don Alvaro de Mendoza. Báñez's nephew would have accompanied Doña Beatriz as a page.
6. This friend of Teresa's was the saintly Maridíaz in Avila who died in 1572. María de los Santos, "the whimpering one," was her niece.
7. The prior was Juan de las Cuevas, who most probably cast his vote for Báñez.
8. Baltasar de Prego Cano took the name Melchor after his uncle, Melchor Cano, a theologian at the Council of Trent and author of the once famous treatise *De locis theologicis*. This nephew Fray Melchor died in the odor of sanctity in 1607.

62. To Some Aspirants, Avila

Segovia, Middle of March 1574

(Autograph: DCN, Talevera de la Reina Toledo)

Two young women in Avila wanted to enter St. Joseph's even though their parents would not give them permission. Teresa counsels them to wait and pray for their parents' change of heart.

1. Jesus. The grace of the Holy Spirit be in your souls, and may he grant that your good desires be lasting ones. It seems to me, my ladies, that Doña Mariana, the daughter of Francisco Juárez, has had more courage, since for six years she has had to bear the displeasure of her mother and father and has been relegated to a small town.[1] How much she would give to have the freedom you have in being able to confess at San Gil.[2]

2. It is not as easy as you think to receive the habit in this way. Even though you are determined in your desire, I do not think you are so holy that you will not afterward grow tired of suffering the loss of your father's favor. Thus, it is preferable that you pray to our Lord for your father and leave the matter to His Majesty, who can change hearts and provide other means. And when we are most detached, he will so arrange things that everyone will be pleased. Right now, what must be fitting is to wait. His judgments are different from ours.

3. Be content with knowing that a place is being reserved for you, and abandon yourselves into God's hands so that his will may be done in you. This is what perfection consists of, and the rest could be a temptation.

4. May His Divine Majesty bring about what he sees as best. Certainly, if it were a matter of my will alone, I would at once

comply with your desires. But, as I said, there are many things that have to be considered.

Your honors' servant,

Teresa of Jesus

1. Mariana Juárez de Lara did finally enter St. Joseph's in Avila in 1574.
2. San Gil was the Jesuit school in Avila.

63. To Madre María Bautista, Valladolid

Segovia, 14 May 1574

(Autograph: DCF, Monte Carlo [Monaco])

Letters from María Bautista and Padre Báñez had arrived. The former was undergoing many trials from Casilda de Padilla's family in Valladolid. The affair was having its repercussions on the Castilian nobility. The discalced Carmelite friars had arrived in Andalusia contrary to their Father General's wishes. Teresa had been suffering many ills, but now she had somewhat recovered and was in good humor.

1. Jesus be with you, my daughter. Your messenger is such a great traveler that although I thought he would arrive from Madrid tomorrow—for I sent him there not knowing with whom I could entrust these business matters—he returned today, Thursday. Together with your letter, I have to respond to some letters from Avila, so I won't be able to send them off until tomorrow at noon. Neither my eyes nor my head are up to doing any better; and please God the messenger will be able to leave tomorrow. I would have preferred to write to you at a leisurely pace and to Señora Doña María.[1] Now I am almost well, for the syrup about which I am writing to our padre[2] relieved me of that torment of melancholy and I think it also took away the fever completely.[3]

2. The letter you sent written in your own hand made me laugh a little, for the melancholy had gone away. Don't tell Padre Fray Domingo, for I'm writing him a humorous letter; perhaps he will show it to you. I was certainly delighted with his letter and with yours, and even more so with yours in learning how that saint[4] is now at rest and of her beautiful death. I am amazed that anyone could be grieving rather than envying her for such a great blessing. I am sorry about the great trial you have had, my daughter, and still must endure with so many business affairs and such important ones, for I know what it is.[5] But I don't think you would feel any better if you had the quiet you speak of, but worse. Of this I am very certain, for I know your temperament and I accept the fact that you will have to suffer trials because in one way or another you must become a saint; and this desire you have for solitude is better than having the solitude.

3. Oh, if you could see the agitation going on—although in secret—in favor of the discalced friars. It is something to praise the Lord for. And it was all stirred up by those who went to Andalusia—Gracián and Mariano.[6] My delight is greatly tempered by the grief this will give our Father General,[7] since I care for him so much. On the other hand, I see that without such favor we would be lost. Pray for this whole affair. Padre Fray Domingo will tell you what is happening and you will also find this out from some papers I am sending you. Whatever you write to me, you must send with a trustworthy person, very trustworthy; this is something most important, even if you have to delay sending it for a few days. It is to our disadvantage that Father Visitator[8] is so far away. There are business matters that I believe I will have to send him by messenger, whatever the cost, for the substitute superior would not be able to handle matters like these. May Father Visitator be our superior for many years.

4. With regard to Padre Medina,[9] have no fears; even if it were something worse I wouldn't be disturbed—rather it made

me laugh. I would be more sensitive to even a half word from Padre Domingo. This other one doesn't owe me anything, so I am not bothered that he cares little for me. He has never dealt with these monasteries so he doesn't know our situation. He cannot be equated with Fray Domingo who loves them as if they were his own and who has truly sustained them. You have had a real tumult to contend with, but there isn't a prioress who would not do the same for her house.

5. My best regards to Doña María de Samaniego[10] and tell her that this world makes us realize that we can trust only in God. I believe all that you write about her and her sister. But it's good that more was not done, for we have to be grateful, and it would have shown a terrible lack of gratitude even to the bishop.[11] As time goes on, the Lord will arrange matters in another way and we will be able to do something for the consolation of those ladies; I saw clearly that it would not please Señora Doña María.[12] I thought of writing to her; I don't think it will be possible. Doña María Cibrián[13] is dead; commend her soul to God. Send my fond regards to the prioress at the monastery of the Mother of God,[14] for much charity has been shown us here through her recommendation. And since I am not up to writing on account of my eyes, ask her to pardon my not writing. Take care of your health, for I wouldn't want you to have to pay for all the trouble and the bad nights you've had.

6. Oh, how I long to travel up there some day, for we are not far away, but I don't see how this will be possible. Regards to my Casilda.[15] If you think it appropriate, let her read the enclosed letter from her aunt, for I sent her aunt the one Casilda wrote to me. For some time I have been close to her and I would trust her in any matter. I think I've forgotten something. God be with you and may he who binds us in such intimate friendship preserve you for me. I don't know how I bear that close friendship you have with my padre.[16] See how you have fooled me; I think you are a great servant of God. May he make you a saint.

Today is 14 May.

7. Tell my good María de la Cruz[17] that I long to see her, and also Estefanía.[18] Pablo Hernández[19] was amazed by her, and he is right.

Yours,

Teresa of Jesus

8. I have just learned of the counsels that Isabel de San Pablo[20] is giving you—she made me laugh with her monasteries. She lifted my spirits in the midst of this sickness of mine; her temperament and good humor brought me joy and enlivened and helped me to pray. I assure you she will show great ability in everything else, and if she has the health she could easily be entrusted with the charge of a monastery.

---

1. María de Mendoza.
2. Padre Domingo Báñez.
3. In Segovia she had suffered for three months from many bodily and spiritual ills: nausea, fevers, melancholy (depression), darkness of soul, and dryness (see F. 21.4).
4. Beatriz de la Encarnación. See Teresa's account of her life and death in F. 12.
5. A reference to the many problems the prioress had to undergo relative to Casilda de Padilla's vocation and the family's opposition (see F. 10.8–16; 11).
6. Jerónimo Gracián and Ambrosio Mariano de San Benito.
7. The general of the Carmelite order, Giovanni Battista Rossi, who had just written a serious warning to Gracián (see the letter of 26 April 1574 in MHCT 1:170).
8. Pedro Fernández.
9. The Dominican Bartolomé de Medina, a professor of theology at Salamanca. Before he got to know Teresa well, he had an unfavorable opinion of her.
10. The identity of this person is unknown. The autograph ends at this point.
11. Don Alvaro de Mendoza, the bishop of Avila.
12. María de Mendoza.
13. She was probably a nun at the Incarnation.

14. The prioress of this Dominican monastery in Valladolid was Doña María de León.
15 Casilda de Padilla.
16 Padre Domingo Báñez.
17. María de la Cruz, one of the four first discalced Carmelite nuns at St. Joseph's in Avila.
18 Estefanía de los Apóstoles, a saintly lay sister (see F. 11.1).
19. A Jesuit confessor and friend of Teresa's.
20. She was the daughter of Teresa's cousin Francisco de Cepeda and among the first to be professed at St. Joseph's in Avila.

64. To Antonio Gaytán, Alba de Tormes

Segovia, 30(?) May 1574

(Autograph: DCN, Toledo)

Antonio Gaytán met Teresa in Alba de Tormes. Undergoing a conversion of life, he became her collaborator. Teresa here reports on the situation of the foundation in Segovia, of which he was a part. She also responds to his questions about prayer and in this respect calls him "my son."

1. Jesus. May the Holy Spirit be with your honor, my son. I'm not fortunate enough to have the time to write you at length, but I assure you I have the desire to do so. Your letters bring me happiness in knowing about the favors the Lord grants you, which each day become greater. He is repaying you now for all the work you have done here.

2. You should not tire yourself with a great deal of thinking, nor should you be concerned about meditation. If you haven't forgotten, I have often told you what you should do and how this is a greater favor from the Lord. And to be always praising him and desiring that everyone do so is the greatest effect of the soul's being occupied with His Majesty. May it please the Lord that you, and I as well, may know how to repay something of what we owe him and may he give us much to suffer, even if it comes from fleas, goblins, and traveling.

3. Antoño Sánchez[1] was ready to give us the house without further word, but I don't know what you and Padre Julián de Avila[2] had done with your eyes that you wanted to buy it in the condition that it was in. It's a good thing he had not wanted to sell it. Now we are negotiating to buy one near San Francisco, on the Calle Real in the best part of the suburb, near the market place. It is very nice. Let us pray for this.[3]

4. All the nuns send their best regards. I am better; I was going to say "well," because when I am without the usual ailments, this means good health for me. May the Lord give you health and preserve you for us.

Your honor's servant,

Teresa of Jesus

---

1. The owner of the houses rented by Antonio Gaytán and Julián de Avila for the foundation in Segovia. The houses did not meet with Teresa's approval.
2. The chaplain at St. Joseph's in Avila, who frequently accompanied Teresa on her foundations.
3. The negotiations were successful, and the nuns moved to the new house, where they are still located (see F. 21.8–11).

65. To Don Francisco de Salcedo(?), Avila

Segovia, 4 June 1574

(Autograph: Vda. de Claudio Porrero. C. Antonio Maura, 12, Madrid)

The addressee of this letter is uncertain. Teresa asks him to pay Padre Julián de Avila for the expenses of the journey to Segovia for the new foundation there.

1. Jesus. May the grace of the Holy Spirit be always with your honor. It's a wonderful thing when one finds oneself in need to have a good treasurer like you. At present I am in great need and so I beg you to give Señor Julián de Avila[1] whatever you can spare from your accounts; it will go to pay the cost of

the travel, which was borrowed. As a receipt you can use this letter with my signature. And will you pray for me as I do for you, despite my wretchedness; the same to Señor Maestro and my good sister, Señora Catalina Daza.[2]

2. It makes me feel very lonely to be so far from those I love so much. If I hadn't resolved to live with the cross, I would be suffering a great trial. May our Lord give you the peace I desire for you along with much holiness.

The date is the fourth of June in the year fifteen hundred and seventy-four. From this house of St. Joseph in Segovia.

Your honor's unworthy servant,

Teresa of Jesus, Carmelite

---

1. Julián de Avila, chaplain at St. Joseph's in Avila, had accompanied Teresa on the foundation made in Segovia along with Antoñio Gaytán and St. John of the Cross.
2. She is referring to Gaspar Daza and his sister (cf. L 23.7–9).

66. To Madre Ana de la Encarnación(?), Salamanca

Segovia, 30 may 1574

(Autograph Fragment: Cathedral of Las Palmas [Canary Islands])

This fragment is from a letter that may have been addressed to Ana de la Encarnación, the prioress in Salamanca.

1. ...recommend to God his business affairs and those of Don Fadrique.[1] Concerning my brothers,[2] I don't know anything. You show me great charity in being concerned, for they have to come by sea. Isabel de Jesús[3] will tell you about anything not mentioned here, so I'll add no more.

Today is Trinity Sunday, and I am yours,

Teresa of Jesus, Carmelite

1. Don Fadrique Alvarez de Toledo was the Duke of Alba's son.
2. She is probably referring to her brothers in America who were planning to return to Spain.
3. Isabel de Jesús (Jimena) made her profession in Salamanca and in 1574 went as subprioress on the foundation made in Segovia.

67. To Don Teutonio de Braganza, Salamanca
Segovia, Middle of June 1574

(Autograph fragment: Parroquia Santa María, Viana [Navarra])

Teresa responds to Don Teutonio who had sent gifts to her and the sick nuns and proposed a foundation of discalced Carmelite friars in Salamanca. He also notified Teresa of the death of the king of France. Teresa has recovered from a critical illness that lasted two months. She is following the situation in France with much interest and also shows enthusiasm for the foundation of her friars in Salamanca.

1. Jesus. The grace of the Holy Spirit be with your lordship. I am happy that you arrived safely and in good health. But after such a long journey your letter seemed to me short indeed.[1] And then you mention nothing about the purpose of the trip, about how those things which were the reason for your going there turned out. That you are unhappy with yourself is nothing new; nor should you be surprised at suffering some tepidity, considering the hardships of traveling and the impossibility of regulating your time. When your calm returns, your soul will experience it also.

2. My health is now better than it was. If I knew how to complain as well as you do, you would consider your sufferings a trifle. The extremely serious illness lasted two months.[2] And it was of a kind that had repercussions on my interior life so that I felt as though I had no being. Interiorly, I am now better; exteriorly, I have the usual ailments.

3. I am well provided for by you. May our Lord repay you, for what you sent was of benefit not only to me but to other sick sisters as well. Some nuns from Pastrana were quite ill, for the house there was very humid.[3] They are better and are choice souls with whom you would be delighted to speak, especially the prioress.[4]

4. I had already learned of the death of the King of France.[5] It greatly grieves me to see so many troubles and how the devil goes about winning over souls. May God provide a remedy and may our prayers be efficacious. We take great care to beg this of His Majesty, and I beg him to repay you for the concern you show in favoring and caring for our order.

5. Father Provincial (I mean Visitator) has gone so far away that not even by correspondence have I been able to deal with what you ask about making a foundation there of discalced friars.[6] A foundation there would be most beneficial, although the devil for that reason may want to hinder it. The favor you are doing for us is most useful, and it comes at the right moment. The visitators have been reconfirmed in office[7] (and not for a limited time and with more powers than before) and they can authorize the founding of monasteries. I hope then that it will be the Lord's will. For love of God, may you not give up the idea.

6. Soon, I believe, Father Visitator will be close at hand. I will write to him; they tell me he will pass through there.[8] You would do me a favor by speaking with and telling him your opinion about everything. You can speak with him in all openness, for he is very good and deserves that we so speak to him. And through your intervention he may decide to do so. Until you see what he does, I beg you not to give up.[9]

7. Mother Prioress[10] recommends herself to your prayers. All the nuns continue to be solicitous in praying for you, and they will also do so in Medina and wherever they may want to please me. I am sorry about the poor health of our Father Rec-

tor.[11] May the Lord grant him health and to you, all the holiness I beg for you, amen.

8. Tell Father Rector that we are praying especially for his return to health and that I am getting along well with Padre Santander,[12] although not with the Franciscan friars. We bought a house just right for us, but it is near theirs and they have entered a lawsuit against us.[13] I don't know how it will all end up.

Your lordship's unworthy servant and subject,

Teresa of Jesus

---

1. We do not know what journey Teresa is speaking of. She had only recently met Don Teutonio, probably in Salamanca.
2. These were the sufferings Teresa spoke of in F 21.4.
3. The community in Pastrana escaped to Segovia in order to free themselves from the troublesome Princess of Eboli. They arrived in Segovia 7 April 1574.
4. Isabel de Santo Domingo.
5. Charles IX died 30 May 1574.
6. The visitator was the Dominican Pedro Fernández. Teresa was interested in a foundation of discalced Carmelite friars in Salamanca.
7. They were reconfirmed by the nuncio, Ormaneto, 8 May 1574.
8. Salamanca.
9. A foundation for discalced Carmelite friars was not actually made in Salamanca until 1581.
10. Isabel de Santo Domingo.
11. The Jesuit Baltasar Alvarez, one of Teresa's first directors (cf. L 28.14).
12. Luis Santander was the Jesuit rector in Segovia.
13. A settlement was reached relatively quickly (cf. F. 21.8–10).

68. To Madre María Bautista, Valladolid

Segovia, End of June 1574

(Autograph Fragment: DCN, Seville)

In this confidential letter Teresa shares with María Bautista intimate thoughts that would be understood only by the recipient. She comments on other matters concerning her

Carmels and sends some medicine for the prioress of the Dominican nuns.

1. Jesus. May the Holy Spirit be with your reverence, my daughter. If the prioress of Medina[1] had not informed me that you are well, I would have been feeling sorry for you, thinking that you must be ill since you haven't written for so long. May God be blessed, for I greatly desire your good health. Let those who are ill bear it cheerfully so that, God willing, it will be beneficial to their souls.

2. You perhaps know that the Lord took to himself Isabel de los Angeles,[2] the one about whom there was all that trouble in Medina, and by such a death that if any nun were to undergo a similar one she would be considered a saint. Certainly she went to be with God, and here I remain, someone who has become useless. Three weeks ago I had a terrible cold along with many other ailments. Now I am better, although not entirely well, and very happy about the news I am writing to Padre Fray Domingo.[3] May they give thanks to the Lord, for we have done this here. May he be praised for everything.

3. Would you send this letter to the prioress of the convent of the Mother of God,[4] for I am enclosing here some medicine that I think helped me. I am distressed about her illness, since I have suffered so much from it in these recent years; that pain is without mercy. But what an idea you had to send me the scorzonera![5] I hardly ate any, for I had been left with a loathing for anything sweet. Nonetheless, I have greatly prized your care in sending things to the sisters and to Isabel,[6] who already through her courtesy and love seems fully mature.

4. How foolish you are in the excuses you make regarding the hands and all the rest! Until we meet once again, I don't dare tell you about the intention I have in everything. You should know that every day I feel greater freedom, and if I were sure that that person commits no offense against God, I would have

no other fears. I have seen many great falls and many dangers in this matter, and I greatly love that soul—it seems God has given me this concern. And the simpler she is, the more fear I have for her. So, I am happy that she is pleased to be in a safe place, although in this life there is no such thing; nor is it good that we feel safe, for we are at war and surrounded by many enemies.

5. Look, my daughter, when I am without such a serious illness as I have had here, I become very frightened if I feel the least stirring of attraction toward something. This is for you alone, because those who do not understand me will have to be guided according to their own spirit. And indeed, if there is anyone with whom I can allow this stirring, it is with the one to whom I am writing, but however small this may be, a free soul feels it very strongly, and perhaps God wants it to feel this to safeguard the part that is necessary for his service. Oh, my daughter! We are in a world that you will never completely understand, even when you are as old as I. I don't know why I am writing these things without having a trustworthy person to send this letter with; I'll give a good tip.

6. Everything you do for Doña Guiomar[7] is well done, for she is holier than you realize, and has her fill of trials. It's good the other one left in such peace. May it please God that things go better with the other one we received, despite my fear. Those who give up their own home to come to us don't find it easy to adapt to ours, although for now it seems she will do all right. Isabel[8] will write to you about it.

7. I had written as far as this and not found a messenger. Now they tell me there is one and that I should send my letters at once....[9]

1. Inés de Jesús.
2. Isabel de los Angeles, whom Teresa admired, was the niece of Simón Ruiz, a well known banker in Medina del Campo.
3. Domingo Báñez.
4. María de León, prioress of the Dominican convent in Valladolid.
5. A medicinal herb.

6. Isabel Bautista Ortigosa, a lay sister in Valladolid.
7. Doña Guiomar de Ulloa was a collaborator with Teresa in the foundation of St. Joseph's in Avila.
8. Probably Isabel de San Pablo who at this time was helping Teresa with her correspondence.
9. The rest of the text is missing.

69. To Don Teutonio de Braganza, Salamanca

Segovia, 3 July 1574

(Autograph: DCN, San José Santiago [Chile])

Don Teutonio has been ill and is undergoing a cure. Teresa pleads with him not to use pompous titles in addressing her. She assures him of her prayers and urges him not to worry. In answer to his questions, she gives him some advice about prayer. Once more she brings up the matter of the foundation for her friars in Salamanca.

To the Very Illustrious Señor Don Teutonio De Braganza, my lord.

1. Jesus. The grace of the Holy Spirit be with your lordship. I tell you definitely that if you address your letter to me again with those titles, I won't reply.[1] I don't know why you want to displease me, although I was not so aware of this displeasure until today. Find out from Father Rector[2] how he addresses letters to me, and don't add anything more, because the titles you use are against the spirit of our order. I am glad that he is well, for I was concerned about him. I beg you to give him my best regards.

2. This seems a difficult time of the year for you to be seeking a cure. May it please the Lord that the cure be successful, as I am begging him. May His Majesty bring back your servants in good condition. I am already beseeching him for this. But I would rather you weren't so troubled—what will this distress

do to your health? Oh, if we understood well these truths, few things would trouble us on this earth.

3. I sent the letter at once and wrote to Father Rector[3] telling him how important it was to me that he act quickly. I owe him a great deal. He arranged everything for a house we have already bought,[4] glory to God—tell Father Rector[5]—which is a very good one, close to the one where we are living now, which is in a good location. It belongs to a gentleman named Diego de Porras. Padre Acosta[6] will describe it for you; give him my regards and tell him that his novices grow happier each day, and we with them. They ask for your prayers and for those of the nuns. But what bad manners I have to be asking you to deliver these messages. Truly, it's your humility that bears with all this.

4. With regard to the desire you experience to cut short your prayer, pay no attention to it. Instead praise the Lord for the desire you have for prayer and believe that this is what your will wants—and love to be with God. Melancholy dislikes being treated with severity. It is best to use less severe means and at times relax outdoors where you can walk and see the sky; your prayer will suffer no loss because of this; it's necessary that we bear our weakness and not try to constrain our nature. Everything amounts to seeking God, since it is for him that we search out every kind of means, and the soul must be led gently. In this regard and in everything else, my Father Rector[7] will better discern what is appropriate for you.

5. They are awaiting Father Visitator,[8] for he is on his way. May God reward you for your care in wanting to favor us.[9] I will write to you when I find out where he is. What is important is that you speak with him, for he will pass through there. I am better now; may it please the Lord that you will be so also and that the cure will be of great benefit to you.

Today is 3 July.

Your lordship's unworthy servant and subject,

Teresa of Jesus, Carmelite

---

1. Although Teresa was careful to use the pompous titles of the times in addressing others, she did not want anybody using them with her.
2. Baltasar Alvarez, then rector of the Jesuits in Salamanca.
3. Luis de Santander, rector of the Jesuits in Segovia.
4. The house for the foundation in Segovia, accepted by Padre Santander in the name of the Carmelite nuns (see F. 21.8).
5. Baltasar Alvarez, rector in Salamanca.
6. Diego de Acosta, who was a Jesuit professor of theology in Salamanca and later provincial.
7. Baltasar Alvarez.
8. Pedro Fernández. The matter concerning a foundation for discalced Carmelite friars in Salamanca had to be discussed with him.
9. By his interest in helping toward the foundation in Salamanca.

70. To Madre María Bautista, Valladolid

Segovia, 16 July 1574

(Autograph Fragment: DCN, Soria)

In the morning Teresa received letters from María Bautista and Báñez; she now hurries to send off her reply in the afternoon of the same day. María Bautista longs to see her but Teresa cannot go to Valladolid. She thinks a limit should be placed on the number of lay sisters in a community. In Segovia she is having trouble with the canons of the cathedral chapter. She has been suffering from stomach problems and feels old and tired; at the same time she is most concerned about María Bautista's health as well as Báñez's.

For my daughter, Madre María Bautista, prioress of the Conception monastery.

1. Jesus be with you, my daughter. Your annoyance made me smile. I assure you it is no pleasure for me to have to give

up seeing you. In fact, seeing you would be such a pleasure for me that it seems to me a lack of perfection to try to go there without any compelling reason. Moreover, if Padre Maestro[1] is there, what need is there for me? So, if I am given orders to go there, I will go; if not, I'll have nothing to say. I really think I can be of service wherever I go, even when it seems there is no need. But since you are so prudent, perhaps I'd have nothing more to do than rest. I'm no longer good for much else.

2. With regard to the lay sister, there is nothing to say; the deed is done. But I tell you it is a hard thing to have to see so many lay sisters for every three nuns, as they say. It makes no sense. I believe we will have to get Father Visitator to set a limit as we have for the choir nuns.[2] I don't know what excuse you have for not telling me how sick you are; this grieves me. It's very foolish for you to be worried about perfection when you should be pampering yourself, for your health is important to us. I don't know what *mi padre* is doing; take note that I will be very annoyed if you do not obey María de la Cruz[3] in this case.

3. I am very discreet in similar things. The truth of the matter is that I have never been very perfect, and now I think I have a greater motive, since I am old and tired; it would frighten you to see me. These days my stomach has been weak, so the nuts you sent arrived at a good time. Although there were still some left from others that had been sent to me, these are very good. You eat the ones that remain for love of me, and give my best regards to the Countess of Osorno.[4] It seems to me that I received only one letter from her, and I wrote one; but I will write again as soon as I can. Today they brought me three packets of letters and yesterday a good number of them. Since my confessor is at the grille and says I should send this messenger boy off quickly, I won't be able to write at length.

4. Oh, how the letter from *mi padre* saddens me! You should find out at once whether the power the visitator has is in writ-

ing. How these canons[5] weary me; and now they want authorization from the prelate so as to oblige us to pay rent on the land. If *mi padre* is able to give it, it must be in writing and notarized. He should consider how far his powers extend; and if he can give it, let him send it to me at once, for goodness' sake, if he doesn't want the canons to be annoyed with me. We would now be in the house if it were not for a miserable 3,000 maravedis, and perhaps there would be time left over for me to be sent to your monastery. I would like that, even if it were just to see what this nun of yours is like. Tell María de la Cruz that her letter made me happy and that the gift I now ask of her is that she surround your reverence with care.

5. Don't fail to communicate with the rector,[6] for I assure you he may be a greater friend of yours than anyone else may be; indeed, these fathers are helpful. The rector[7] here made the purchase, and he went to the chapter about it, and took care of everything very well. May God likewise take care of you, my daughter, and do not be angry with me, for I have told you why I am not coming to Valladolid. It would be a lie for me to say I don't want to. If I were to come, all the dealings with the nobility and all the commotion would greatly tire me; but I would put up with it all in order to see you.

6. Last night I wrote you a few lines, and now I've written a lot considering the hurry I am in to finish. All the nuns send their regards. May God make you holy. The replies that you make in the letter from *mi padre* are very amusing; I don't know whom to believe. Don't tire yourself trying to get him to write to me; if you tell me how his health is, I will be very satisfied with that.

7. Tell me where he is from because if it is Medina,[8] he will be doing wrong not to pass by this way. This messenger boy came today, July 16, at ten o'clock. I am sending him back at

four. Why don't you tell me about the business affairs of Señora Doña María.[9] Give her my best. May God keep you.

Your servant and still....[10]

Teresa of Jesus

1. Domingo Báñez, whom she calls *mi padre* throughout the rest of the letter.
2. In the constitutions for the discalced Carmelite nuns of 1581 the number of lay sisters was not to exceed three. The Dominican Pedro Fernández was the visitator.
3. She was one of the four first discalced Carmelite nuns and accompanied Teresa on the foundation in Valladolid.
4. The saintly María de Velasco y Aragón with whom Teresa had a close friendship.
5. The canons of the cathedral claimed the right to exact rent from the property on which the houses bought from Diego Porres stood. The matter was not settled until February 1579.
6. The rector of the Jesuits in Valladolid was Juan Suárez.
7. The rector of the Jesuits in Segovia was Luis Santander.
8. Báñez grew up in Medina del Campo but was actually born in Valladolid.
9. María de Mendoza.
10. The autograph ends here without being completed.

71. To Madre María Bautista, Valladolid

Segovia, 11 September 1574

The visitator ordered Teresa to return to Avila to prepare for a foundation in Beas de Segura, ruining the chances of a trip to see María Bautista in Valladolid. Teresa is hoping that the nuns in Segovia will be in their house before she has to leave. Her health is better. She is in immediate need of money.

1. Jesus. May the Holy Spirit be with your reverence, my daughter. From the letter of Padre Maestro Fray Domingo,[1] you will see what is happening and how the Lord has arranged matters in such a way that I will be unable to see you. I assure

you I deeply regret this, for it is one of the things that would now give me consolation and pleasure. But this disappointment will pass away also, as do all the things of this life; when I think of this, I can bear well anything that displeases me.

2. My best regards to my dear Casilda[2] (for I also regret not being able to see her) and to María de la Cruz.[3] On some other occasion the Lord will so arrange things that more time will be available than there would have been at present. Take care of your health (now you see how important that is and how it saddens me that you are ill); and try to be very holy, for I tell you, holiness will be necessary if you are going to bear the trial you have there. I no longer have the quartan fevers. When the Lord wants me to do something, he then gives me better health.

3. I will be going at the end of this month;[4] and I am still afraid that the nuns here won't be established in their house when I leave. We have agreed to give the chapter[5] six hundred ducats at once; from one of the sisters we have a very good title to an income worth six hundred and thirty. Well, we haven't been able to find anything about this title; no one will accept it or take it as collateral. Pray for this; it would make me very happy not to have to leave the nuns before they are settled in their house. If Señora Doña María[6] had given the money, they would have readily accepted the title, for it is very good and safe. Let me know if this might be possible, or if there is anyone who might accept it or who would give us a loan on good collateral worth more than a thousand. And pray for me, since I have to make such a long trip and in winter.[7]

4. The end of this month, at the latest, I will go to the Incarnation. If you want to send something, write to me, and don't be sad about not seeing me. Perhaps it would make you sadder to see me, I'm so old and worn-out. Give my regards to all. Isabel de San Pablo[8] would very much like to see you. These canons have mortified us all. May God forgive them.

5. Do you know anyone there who could lend me some *reales*? I don't want them as a donation but only until I am

paid what my brother[9] gave me, for they say it has now been collected. To go to the Incarnation without a cent would be a mistake.[10] And here there is nothing available since they have renovations to complete on the house. Whether little or much, try to get something for me.

6. Now they have spoken to me of two nuns[11] with very good dowries who would like to enter here. They would bring more than two thousand ducats each; this could go to pay for the house, which cost four thousand, and to pay the six hundred to the canons, and still more. I am telling you this that you might praise the Lord, for he has granted me a favor; and the two women being received are so good. I have not heard anything about Doña María's business affairs; write to me about them, and send her greetings from me, and let us see if she sends something.

7. Glory to God that my Padre Fray Domingo is well. If by chance Padre Maestro Medina[12] passes through, give him this letter from me for he thinks I am angry with him, according to what Father Provincial says,[13] because of a letter he wrote me. It was a letter deserving thanks rather than anger. He must be wondering also if I know what he said to the other person, although I said nothing to him about it. Our Father Visitator told me she was already a nun and had no more than a thousand ducats for a dowry. Write to me about how she is doing and what Father Visitator says. Well since she is from his order, he will be patient.

8. I wrote to you a short while ago. I don't know whether you received it. It is not right for you to go so long without writing to me, for you know how delighted I am with your letters. May God be with you. It's strange how difficult I am finding it not to be able to see you—I had still been hopeful.[14]

Today is 11 September.

Yours,

Teresa of Jesus

1. Domingo Báñez.
2. Casilda de Padilla.
3. María de la Cruz had come from St. Joseph's in Avila to the foundation in Valladolid.
4. She in fact left Segovia on 30 September.
5. The cathedral chapter of canons.
6. María de Mendoza.
7. She is referring to the projected foundation in Beas de Segura. She left for Beas in February 1575.
8. At the time, Isabel de San Pablo was helping Teresa with her correspondence.
9. Probably Lorenzo de Cepeda who had sent Teresa money from America.
10. The monastery of the Incarnation in Avila was in dire need of funds. Teresa's term as prioress at the Incarnation was to expire on 6 October.
11. The names of these two were Beatriz del Espíritu Santo and Francisca de la Encarnación.
12. A Dominican professor at Salamanca, Bartolomé de Medina.
13. Pedro Fernández was a Dominican provincial as well as the apostolic visitator of the Carmelites in Castile.
14. She in fact did get to see María Bautista before the trip to Beas. At the end of December, the matter concerning Casilda de Padilla required Teresa's presence in Valladolid.

72. To Don Teutonio de Braganza, Salamanca
Segovia, 15 September 1574

(Autograph: DCF, Santa Ana, Genoa, Italy)

Matters in Segovia are settled and Teresa is thinking of her coming travels. Her term as prioress at the Incarnation will end 6 October, so she is unable to go to Salamanca as Don Teutonio requested. The nuncio has given permission for a foundation of discalced friars in Salamanca.

1. Jesus. May the grace of the Holy Spirit be with your lordship. I was greatly consoled to learn about the state of your health. May it please our Lord that you continue to improve. I

have prayed much to His Majesty for you; would you now do the same for me. I need your prayers because of the long distances I will have to be traveling.[1]

2. I am writing to Father Rector about the command Father Visitator has given me;[2] you may ask him about it. He told me to write to you about how he had given me orders to stay at St. Joseph's. He also told me that Father Prior of Atocha had written him that the nuncio said that because it seemed to him a good thing he was giving permission for the monastery.[3] He didn't tell me to write about this to you; he must have thought that you knew of it from the nuncio. I have learned that he desires to please you in everything, which made me happy. And I would be glad if that cleric were to stay in your house, if that's agreeable to you.[4]

3. Padre Gómez has been here several times, which seems to me a good thing. He told me he wanted to know if that person[5] who left here was in agreement with you, for he knew that he was in Salamanca. I urged him to pray for you since your health was bad, and he took on the obligation. We are also praying for the matter you entrusted to our prayers, that our Lord will bring about what will be for his greater service. May His Majesty show his power, and may he guide you. I didn't really have the time to write to you today, so I won't enlarge on this.

Today is 15 September.

Your lordship's unworthy servant and subject,

Teresa of Jesus, Carmelite

---

1. She was concerned about the long trip to Beas.
2. Baltasar Alvarez was the Jesuit rector in Salamanca. Teresa wants Don Teutonio to know about Pedro Fernández's orders for her to return to Avila because he was urging her to come to Salamanca to help the nuns settle a lawsuit with Pedro de la Banda.
3. The Dominican prior of Atocha in Madrid was Hernando del Castillo. The nuncio was Nicolás Ormaneto. The monastery refers to a projected foundation of discalced Carmelite friars in Salamanca.

4. The identity of this cleric is unknown.
5. The identities of this person and Padre Gómez are also unknown.

73. To María Bautista, Valladolid

Segovia, End of September 1574

The problems in Segovia have been resolved and Teresa is ready to move on, but she will not be able to go to Valladolid. María Bautista is deeply disappointed and Teresa tries to console her. She also gives a list of those who will be going with her to Beas. Ana de Jesús (Anne of Jesus) will be the prioress there.

1. Jesus. May the Holy Spirit be with your reverence, my daughter. Knowing of your own disappointment seems to console me for having to leave without seeing you. Well, the Lord can arrange things in ways that we don't now foresee, and then we'll have more time together. Certainly, while I have been here, there has been no possibility of doing anything else. A short visit becomes very tiring. One does nothing but visit and one even gives up sleep so as to continue talking—and idle words are never lacking—for great is the desire to be with you. But many things I would like to speak to you about cannot be discussed by letter; one of them is the desire not to humiliate Maestro Medina.[1] Believe me, I have my reasons for this and have seen some good results; don't fail, then, to send him the letter, and don't be bothered, even if he seems less friendly; he isn't obliged to us, nor does anything he might say about me matter in the least. Why doesn't he say it directly to me?[2]

2. I want you to know I told Father Provincial[3] that they had worked things out well in taking Samanó[4] from us. Do you know what I realize now? God wants you to be poor but with honor, for he gave you Casilda, who is poor but worth more than all the money in the world.[5] It seems that Father Visitator has become aware of this and wanted to explain things to me, at

least he made many excuses for Orellana;[6] so I believe it was Casilda who wanted this. I become angry when I have to speak of this blessed soul.

3. I wrote you a letter after the one that you answered and sent it with a Theatine[7]—or I don't know with whom—or better, it was with the one who usually brings messages to the prioress of the Mother of God.[8] In it I told you that we have found the money and that everything is concluded, glory to God.[9] I am in a hurry for us to move before I leave. I don't know if things will be ready. There is little to do, and the house is next to this one. Do not worry. God reward you for your advice. I believe I understood what you crossed out. You should know that Beas is not in Andalusia, but five leagues this side, for I know that I cannot make foundations in Andalusia.[10]

4. The book[11] arrived here, I think, two or three days after the bishop left for Madrid.[12] I have to send it to him there, but I don't know where he is staying. So, I am sending it to you to give to him just as it is when he leaves, but give him this letter addressed to his lordship right away. In it I include a message for Señora Doña María.[13]

5. I am bringing Ana de Jesús[14] as prioress, who is from Plasencia and whom we received at St. Joseph's; she has been living in Salamanca and is there now. I don't at present see anyone else who would be good for your region. The truth is they are saying wonderful things about the holiness and humility of one of the two ladies who are sponsoring the foundation;[15] they are both good. No one should be brought there who is going to be an imperfect example, for from what they say that house will mark the beginning of much good. I mention this for the nun who is with you.

6. Another foundation, please God, will be made soon. But someone who doesn't get along with you would have a bad effect on a new foundation. Nonetheless I would have very much wanted to bring her along. Four of those who came from Pastrana[16] will be going, and still that is not many, because

with the two who are now going to enter we would have twenty-two here. The one with 1500 ducats is entering Saturday, and all are amazed by her fervor; I don't know where it will end up. Those nuns who are here, I assure you, are all extremely good. With six going from here, along with the prioress,[17] who is not a native of this town, and the subprioress,[18] a sufficient number of nuns will still be left. There are, in fact, four lay sisters, who are extremely good. Still, one will be forced to transfer more of the nuns, for I understand there are some very good women who would like to enter. You see now how one could hardly fail to make a foundation in Beas! And still another monastery is needed.

7. You think, my daughter, that you were showing me great consideration in advising me not to go. My departure will take place this coming winter, for God has so willed. Considering the harm it caused me, I don't know how I suffered the cold of this region. Don't think I suffered little from it here. It may be that....[19]

---

1. Bartolomé de Medina.
2. Apparently, Padre Medina made some critical remarks about Teresa, which María Bautista did not explicitly mention.
3. Pedro Fernández, provincial of the Dominicans and visitator of the Carmelites.
4. Nothing is known of her except that in the end she entered the Dominican order. She had probably been from a family of considerable wealth and wanted to follow in Casilda's footsteps.
5. Casilda de Padilla, who was poor because her wealthy family opposed her vocation (see F. 10–11).
6. Juan de Orellana, a Dominican who was later noted for his denunciation of Teresa's writings to the Inquisition.
7. A Jesuit.
8. María de León, prioress of the Dominican nuns in Valladolid.
9. The money with which to buy the houses belonging to Diego de Porras. She signed the purchase agreement on 28 September.
10. Although Beas was not in the civil province of Andalusia, it was included in the ecclesiastical province. Teresa had not wanted to make a foundation in Andalusia (see F. 24. 2–5).
11. The autograph of *The Book of Her Life.*

12. The bishop of Avila, Don Alvaro de Mendoza.
13. María de Mendoza.
14. Ana de Jesús (Anne of Jesus), for whom St. John of the Cross wrote his *Spiritual Canticle.*
15. The two ladies were siblings: Catalina and María Sandoval y Godínez (see F. 22.4–20).
16. The Carmelite nuns, who had escaped from Pastrana and the Princess of Eboli's clutches, settled in Segovia.
17. Isabel de Santo Domingo, who had come from Pastrana.
18. Isabel de Jesús (Jimena), who had come from Salamanca.
19. The autograph is cut off here, and the remainder of the letter is missing.

74. To Mateo de las Peñuelas, Avila

Segovia, September 1574

(Autograph: DCN, Incarnation, Avila)

Mateo de las Peñuelas as procurator for the Incarnation, managed its properties and was most sensitive to its situation of poverty. As a collaborator with Teresa, he had been assisting her for three years to find remedies for the monastery's worrisome financial situation. Teresa expresses concern over the illness and troubles of Francisco de Salcedo.

1. Jesus. The grace of the Holy Spirit be with your honor. I assure you that your letter delighted me; it seems you wrote it for no other purpose. May God reward you for the goodness you have shown me through it and by all that you say. As for the rest, these days I have not even been thinking of myself, much less of food. When I have a free moment, I tell you, I grow more concerned than when I was there.[1] I don't know how you can say that I inspired courage, for it was you who gave courage to all of us, and so I beg you to continue doing so.

2. It made me very sorry to learn that they are beginning to use the bread.[2] The proceeds from its sale would have pro-

vided me with my only collateral. I fear lest we lose on the one hand what we gain on the other. I have already given orders that they buy bread; that should be possible through what accrues from the sale.[3] I am looking around here to see if I can scrape something together for my return. In sum, I hope in the Lord that we will not want. So, would you continue helping us in your usual way? I will serve you by praying to the Lord for you; please do the same for me. I am well and have so many letters to write that I can't say more.

Yours,

Teresa of Jesus

3. Out of charity would you visit Francisco de Salcedo[4] for me, and tell him I have been distressed over his illness but was delighted to learn from this messenger that he is not bothered at all by the litigation. After I wrote to him, they told me that he was taking it very hard, and this grieved me. He must not have received my letter. Be very careful about letters sent to the little villages; such care is necessary.

---

1. At the monastery of the Incarnation in Avila, where she is still prioress.
2. This would be the bread made from grain just harvested from the properties belonging to the Incarnation through the dowries of the nuns. But these properties did not provide enough income to feed all of the nuns.
3. As prioress of the Incarnation, Teresa was responsible for the financial situation of the monastery, and had the authority to give orders from a distance.
4. Francisco de Salcedo is the "saintly gentleman" of Teresa's *Life*. After his wife died, he was ordained a priest (1570). He is now embroiled in a litigation that will bring his estate to ruin.

75. To Don Antonio Gaytán

Segovia, Final Months(?) 1574

Antonio Gaytán had written for counsel about prayer and his desire for solitude.

To the Magnificent Señor Antonio Gaytán, my lord.

1. Jesus be with your honor and repay you for the book you sent, which is just right for me. I would need more time to answer your question—I mean about what touches on prayer—although the substance of the answer is that this is a very common way of proceeding by those who have reached contemplation. I have often told you this, but you forget it. You have to realize that just as there are different seasons on this earth, so there are in the interior life, and it cannot be otherwise. So don't be troubled— you are not at fault.

2. As for the rest, I cannot be a judge, since I am an interested party; and also my natural inclination has always been toward the state of solitude, although I have not merited to have it, and since this is the state proper to our order, I could be giving counsel appropriate for myself but not for what is fitting for you. Speak about this clearly with Father Rector,[1] and he will see what is best; and try observing to which one your spirit has the greater leaning. May God keep you, for I am writing so many letters that I don't know how I have been able to say this much, and the messenger is waiting.

3. As to my departure, there is nothing new; I don't know how it could be possible this year. God can do all. Pray much to His Majesty for me, as I do for you, and keep me always informed about yourself.

Your honor's unworthy servant,

Teresa of Jesus

1. The rector of the Jesuits in Salamanca, Baltasar Alvarez.

76. To Padre Domingo Báñez, Valladolid

Avila, 3 December 1574

For two months Teresa had been back an Avila after having made the foundation in Segovia. Báñez is preparing the community in Valladolid for their coming elections. Teresa's health is better despite the cold weather of Avila. The text that has come down to us is incomplete.

1. ...I tell you, *mi padre*, I think my joys are no longer of this kingdom, for what I want I do not have, and what I have I do not want. What is missing is that the happiness I used to experience in dealing with my confessors is no longer present; one would have to be more than a confessor. Anything less than what the soul desires does not fulfill it. Certainly, it has been a relief for me to write this. May God grant that your honor always find your relief in loving him.

2. Tell your "poca cosa,"[1] who is concerned about whether the sisters will vote for her or not, that she is thereby meddling and lacking in humility. For what you and those of us who look after the welfare of that house believe is best will be done rather than what one nun thinks, for we have more interest in a good choice. It is necessary that the nuns be made to understand these things. When you see Señora Doña María, give her my regards for I have not written for some time. It is a good thing that I am better in the midst of this cold weather.

I think it is 3 December, and I am your honor's daughter and servant.

Teresa of Jesus

1. María Bautista, the prioress in Valladolid, was this nun who called herself *poca cosa* (of little worth). Báñez also began referring to her in this way. She was afraid the nuns would reelect her as prioress. As things turned out she was reelected.

77. To Doña Ana Enríquez, Toro

Valladolid, 23 December 1574

Ana Enríquez was the daughter of the marquises of Alcañices and a good friend of Teresa's. The difficulties with the family of Casilda de Padilla occasioned the visit by Teresa to Valladolid. Her health is good, she is happy with the community and, especially, with the sermons of Domingo Báñez. She is preparing for the long trip to Beas.

1. Jesus. The grace of the Holy Spirit be with your honor always. It would have been a great consolation for me to find you here, and I would have considered the journey well spent had it given me the opportunity to enjoy your company for a longer time than in Salamanca. I do not deserve this favor from our Lord. May he be blessed forever. This prioress[1] has enjoyed your company fully. After all, she is better than I and most dedicated to serving you.

2. I was most happy that you had my Padre Baltasar Alvarez[2] there for several days to provide you with some relief from so many trials. May the Lord be blessed that you are enjoying better health than usual. Mine is now much better than it has been in recent years, and that is saying a lot for this time of year. I have found souls of such quality in this house that I had to praise the Lord. And although Estefanía[3] certainly is a saint in my opinion, the talent of Casilda[4] and the favors the Lord has granted her after she took the habit have pleased me greatly. May His Majesty lead her forward. For we should have high regard for souls that he takes to himself in so short a time.

3. Estefanía's simplicity in everything except what pertains to God amazes me, for I perceive through her words the wisdom she has in regard to the Truth.[5]

4. Father Provincial[6] has visited this house, and the election has taken place. They have reelected the prioress,[7] and from

St. Joseph's in Avila we are going to bring the subprioress elected by them, whose name is Antonia del Espíritu Santo. Señora Doña Guiomar[8] knows her; she is a very good soul.

5. The foundation in Zamora has been set aside for now, and I am going to make the long trip for which I had left before.[9] I have already thought of giving myself the joy of passing through your region so as to pay my respects to you. I haven't received a letter from my Padre Baltasar Alvarez in a long time. Nor have I written to him; certainly not so as to mortify myself, for I never make any progress in this or, it seems, in anything else. But I haven't written because of the torment of having to write so many letters, and when I think of writing one just for my own satisfaction, there is never time. Blessed be God, for we will have security in our eternal enjoyment of him. Here below, certainly, with this flux of separation and change of every kind, we cannot rely much on anything. With this hope for the end, I go through life; they say we do so with many trials, but it doesn't seem so to me.

6. Mother Prioress here is telling me about my "custodian."[10] His affability is as pleasing to me as it is to her. May our Lord make him very holy. I beg you to give him my regards. I often pray to the Lord for him and for Señor Don Juan Antonio[11] as well. Don't forget me in your prayers, for love of the Lord, for I am always in need. We can now be at ease about Doña Guiomar, as you say and she herself confirms. I would love to know something about the successful event so as to make a better judgment and share in your joy. May our Lord in this Christmas season grant your soul all the great joys that I beg of him for you.

7. On this feast of St. Thomas,[12] Padre Fray Domingo preached a sermon here in which he spoke of trials in such terms that I found myself wanting to have many and that the Lord would give them to me in the future. His sermons are for me a sheer joy. They have elected him prior. It is not known whether he will be confirmed.[13] He is so busy that only briefly

have I been able to benefit from his presence. But if I were able to see you for as much time, I would be happy. May the Lord bring this about, and may he give you as much health and rest as is necessary to gain that which has no end.

Tomorrow is Christmas Eve.

Your honor's unworthy servant and subject,

Teresa of Jesus

---

1. The prioress of Valladolid, María Bautista.
2. A Jesuit and former confessor to Teresa.
3. Estefanía de los Apóstoles, a lay sister.
4. Casilda de la Concepción (Padilla, cf. F. 11).
5. As an example, one day the king, Philip II, visited the monastery and entered the cloister and asked Sister Estefanía what she would like. She answered that she would like a little hermitage next to the kitchen where she could go and be recollected in prayer when free in the kitchen. When they agreed, she suggested: "Your reverence has so many business matters to attend to that I'm afraid you'll forget; let me tie a knot in your scarf so that you will remember." The hermitage still exists and is dedicated to Our Lady of Mount Carmel.
6. Pedro Fernández, the Dominican provincial and visitator of the Carmelites.
7. María Bautista.
8. Guiomar de Ulloa, a spiritual friend of Teresa's (cf. L. 24.4; 30.3), who had property in Toro.
9. She had been planning to make a foundation in Beas. She journeyed to that foundation by way of Medina, Avila, and Toledo the first part of January.
10. It seems Doña Ana had a son who highly esteemed Teresa, even appointing himself her protector.
11. This person has not been identified.
12. 21 December.
13. She is referring to the Dominican, Domingo Báñez; actually his election was not confirmed and he remained in Valladolid.

78. To Doña Inés Nieto, Madrid

Valladolid, 28 December 1574

Doña Inés Nieto was the wife of Don Juan de Albornoz, secretary to the Duke of Alba. She had just sent some good news to Teresa, perhaps of the return of her husband and the duke from Flanders. Teresa speaks of the monastery's need for a dowry from aspirants and thanks Inés for a statue.

1. Jesus. The grace of the Holy Spirit be with your honor. Although I have not written until now, you can be sure that I do not forget you in my poor prayers before our Lord, and learning of your happiness made me happy. May it please our Lord that you will enjoy many years in his service, for I hope in His Majesty that nothing will impede you from this service, even though there may be obstacles. All those things considered good in this miserable life are obstacles. That you spent these past years for God will be of great benefit to you in judging each thing according to its true worth and counting it as something that will soon pass away.

2. Some time ago Señora Isabel de Córdoba[1] spoke to the prioress of this house,[2] who considers her to be very dedicated to God's service. And so I arranged to speak to her. She told me she is a rather close relative of Señor Albornoz's,[3] which is the reason why I would like her to enter here. However since this house is in the process of being adapted and Doña María Mendoza[4] is the foundress, we will need the help of some alms in order to receive her. Since she told me that Señor Albornoz had promised to help her become a nun, I told her that I thought he would be even more willing to do so if she were to enter this house. Indeed, even were I to want a different arrangement, I wouldn't be able to do anything, because of Doña María and also the nuns. Since the number of nuns is small and there are many aspirants, and they are in need, it would be harmful for the nuns not to take in those who can help them. She told

me that she has property but that it is of a kind, she is informed, that cannot be sold. When some means are found, even if less than what could be received from others, I will do what I can, for I certainly want to serve you and Señor Albornoz as I ought, for whose prayers I beg. In my prayers, although miserable, I will do what you have asked.

3. May our Lord reward you for the statue. You indeed owe it to me. I beg you to keep it well protected until I ask you for it. That will be when I am more settled in one monastery than I am now; there I will be able to enjoy it. May you do me the favor not to forget me in your prayers. May our Lord grant you all the spiritual blessings that I beg of him, amen.

Today is the feast of the Holy Innocents.

Your honor's unworthy servant,

Teresa of Jesus, Carmelite

---

1. A widow for 20 years, she was being recommended to the Carmel by Juan Albornoz. In the end, she entered the Carmel of Santa Ana in Madrid.
2. María Bautista (Ocampo), a relative of Teresa's, was prioress.
3. Juan de Albornoz, the husband of Doña Inés.
4. The bishop of Avila's sister, who helped Teresa with the foundation in Valladolid (see F. 10.6).

Letters 79–100 (1575)

79. To Don Teutonio de Braganza, Salamanca

Valladolid, 2 January 1575

(Autograph: DCF, Concesa [Milan, Italy])

Teresa answers a letter from Don Teutonio, who has just returned from a business trip that was not entirely successful. He is interested in the Teresian foundations and has a number of possible sites in mind. He had defended Teresa's travels outside the cloister, for which she was being criticized. He had warned her to be careful in dealing with a certain person. And finally, he had sought advice about some difficulties in his spiritual life. Teresa is in Valladolid seeking to resolve the issue concerning Casilda de Padilla. She is about to undertake a trip through Medina, Avila, and Toledo on her way to Beas, but will be unable to go to Salamanca until her return, which she mistakenly thinks will be in April.

1. Jesus. The grace of the Holy Spirit be with your lordship always and give you many more good years, as many as I desire, and with the holiness I beg for you. I have been waiting a long time to see your handwriting and find out whether you are in Salamanca, for I didn't know where to write to you. And now I don't know if I'll have the time to write at length, as I

desire, since I have a very reliable messenger for this letter. I praise our Lord that you are better. My health has been good, which is a lot for this time of year.

2. May His Majesty repay you for the care with which you undertook all that I had asked of you.[1] Well, it seems to me that our Lady, the Blessed Virgin, has chosen you to be the protector of her order. It is consoling for me to know that she will repay you in more ways than I could think of mentioning in my prayers, although I continue to pray for you.

3. The monastery in Zamora has been set aside for now:[2] first, because this is not a suitable time of year (it's the time for going to a much warmer region); second, because it doesn't seem that the one who was to give us the house responded to all that we expected of him, and he is absent. However, we have not given up. Furthermore, I have also been considering how troublesome it is for a house founded in poverty to have a founder who is not much inclined to helping, especially if he has the right to build the monastery.[3] It seems to me that it would be better to begin in a different way, by buying a house, but this would require more time. The Lord will provide when it pleases him to do so. You have done me a great favor in obtaining the authorization for me at the right time. When a messenger is available you can send it to me, but it is not necessary to hire one immediately.

4. With regard to Torrijos,[4] don't go to any bother about it. In no way does the place appeal to me. I would accept it to comply with your wishes. But for persons of this kind to be received just because we need the dowry would be something unacceptable in these houses, because then we would not be able to send them away at once if they were not suited to our order.

5. I am sorry that the reason for your having undertaken the trip was not realized. Nevertheless, I hope in the Lord that your words will bear much fruit, even though their effect is not seen immediately. May it please the Lord that the business in Rome

will go well. I have prayed hard for this, if it be for his service; what I hope is that if it is, he will bring it about, because so many prayers are being offered for that intention.

6. With respect to the countess's monastery,[5] I don't know what to say, for I have been hearing about it for a long time. I tell you I would rather found four monasteries of our nuns than try to convert these blessed souls, however holy, to our manner of living, for within fifteen days from the start our manner of life can be set up so that those who enter do not have to do anything more than what they see is done by the other nuns. I spoke with two of them in Toledo and know that they are doing well in the way of life they have chosen. On the other hand, I certainly don't know how I could receive them under my charge, for I believe they conduct themselves with more rigor and penance than mortification and prayer; I mean in general. Nonetheless, if the Lord so desires, I will find out more, since that is what you seem to want.

7. It was most fortunate that you had the marquis so much on your side, for that is important. May it please the Lord that you receive good news. Regarding the business here, now that you are in the midst of it, I hope in him that all will go well. I will not have to worry any more about letters that displease Padre Olea since it is to you that one ought to write.[6] I have been sorry about it, for much is owed to him and in my opinion my letters got into the hands of others. The prioress of Segovia[7] must not have been on guard, thinking that the matter was not important. It made me happy to know how I can write to you when it is necessary and that when the occasion arises you will speak in favor of my travels.[8] Certainly traveling is one of the things that wearies me in life and one of life's greater trials, and above all when I am judged by others to be doing something bad. I have often thought how much better off I would be remaining at rest and not having the general's command.[9] At other times, when I see how the Lord is served

in these houses, everything seems small to me. May His Majesty direct me in doing his will.

8. I tell you there are souls in this house[10] that almost continually, or very frequently, stir me to the praises of God. Although Estefanía[11] is great and, in my opinion, a saint, Sister Casilda de la Concepción[12] amazes me. Certainly I don't find anything in her, exteriorly or interiorly, that would keep her from becoming (with God's assistance) a great saint. What he is doing in her is clearly seen. She is very talented (beyond all possibility for her age) and deeply prayerful, for since she took the habit the Lord has favored her. Her happiness and humility are remarkable; it's a strange thing. Both of them say they will pray for your lordship in a special way.

9. I have not wanted her to write to you: first, because we are being very careful not to let her think we are showing her any special attention (although, indeed, in her simplicity she has little need for this; in many ways she's like another Fray Junípero);[13] second, because I wouldn't want you to pay attention to what we poor women tell you, for you have a good padre who awakens and teaches you and a good God who loves you.

10. With regard to Madrid,[14] I don't know the reason, but even though I see that it would be appropriate to have one of these houses there, a strange resistance wells up in me; it must be a temptation. I still haven't seen a letter from Prior Covarrubias.[15] It would be difficult to make a foundation without permission from the ordinary, because the patent letter I have requires this, and also the Council.[16] But I believe we would have the permission, if this were the only thing in need of our attention. May the Lord advance the project.

11. I will be leaving here after the feast of Epiphany. I am going to Avila along the road passing through Medina, where I don't think I'll stay for more than a day or two; the same goes for Avila, in that I am going on at once to Toledo. I want to finish up this business of Beas.[17] Wherever I am, I will write to

you as often as I find someone who will deliver a letter to you. In your charity, please pray for me.

12. May His Majesty repay you for the care you show the sisters there,[18] for you are showing great charity; they are not without their trials. I would be so happy to be there. But, since you are not located along the way to the next foundation, it would be very difficult for me to go there. Unless I were to receive a command, I wouldn't go; nor must I do anything without approval of the authorities. I think that since the nuns are offering him more,[19] he will be satisfied, for the place is very good and there is room for expansion (the site you mention seems to me to be out of the way), and the church is nice. In sum, the location is what matters most. As for the rest, it wouldn't bother me much if anything of what has been constructed were lost. Your lordship, along with Father Rector,[20] should consider the whole matter as a transaction to be made for our Lady, and we will act accordingly. Lest some change be introduced, I would like to see the plan delayed, in one way or another, until I return from Beas. If possible, I will return in April.

13. Your imperfections[21] do not shock me, for I see myself with so many. Here, I have had more time to be alone than I have had in a long while; it has been a great consolation for me. May our Lord give the consolation to your soul that I ask of him, amen. With regard to the one you told me to make a fuss over, I had already come to this awareness, and of all the rest, but both my obligation to be grateful and your great zeal enable me to endure more than with my temperament I could otherwise bear. Nonetheless, I am on my guard![22] The prioress relies greatly on your prayers.[23] Now that she knows you, she is sorry about how little she understood of the great grace God gave her through your visit.

Today is 2 January.

Your lordship's unworthy servant,

Teresa of Jesus

---

1. The business Teresa requested Don Teutonio to undertake for her is unknown.
2. Teresa set aside this plan after her recent meeting with the visitator, Fernández. She never did get to make a foundation in Zamora.
3. A house founded in poverty did not have a benefice attached to it. The patron or "founder" of a house established with a benefice would agree to endow the monastery with assets that would provide a fixed income. Teresa found that the patron would often be reluctant to endow the monastery with sufficient income.
4. This was another possibility for a foundation, but it never materialized. It seems a foundation was promised on condition that a certain person be accepted as a postulant into the community.
5. The monastery referred to here is unknown, but to become one of Teresa's it would have had to be adapted to the Teresian way of life.
6. The Jesuit Francisco de Olea was opposed to Teresa in certain matters, but the passage is puzzling to historians. Also puzzling are the previous words about the marquis.
7. Isabel de Santo Domingo.
8. Don Teutonio had recommended a reliable messenger to Teresa. He had also spoken in her favor in Madrid to those who were criticizing her for her travels outside the cloister.
9. In a patent letter of 6 April 1571, Father Giovanni Rossi, the general of the Carmelite order, commissioned Teresa to found as many monasteries as she could (cf. MHCT 1:111). She took this commission seriously and mentions it a number of times in her *Foundations* (21.2; 22.2; 27.19).
10. In Valladolid.
11. Estefanía de los Apóstoles (cf. F. 11.1).
12. Casilda de Padilla.
13. Fray Junípero was that companion of St. Francis of Assisi known for his simplicity.
14. The possibility of founding a Teresian Carmel in Madrid.
15. Diego de Covarrubias y Leiva was bishop of Segovia and president of the Council of Castile. Teresa mistakenly wrote *prior* instead of *president*.
16. The patent letter from Giovanni Rossi of 6 April 1571 (MHCT 1:111). The Council referred to is Trent, session XXV.
17. The new foundation she was planning to make in Beas. She traveled there as planned, but instead of returning to Salamanca, she went on to Seville, under obedience, and made a foundation there.

18. Don Teutonio was helping Teresa's nuns in Salamanca in their difficulties over the lawsuit with Pedro de la Banda.
19. The nuns were offering to pay Pedro de la Banda a higher price for his house.
20. The Jesuit Baltasar Alvarez.
21. Don Teutonio turned to Teresa for spiritual direction.
22. What she is referring to is unknown.
23. The prioress of Valladolid was María Bautista.

80. To Don Alvaro de Mendoza, Avila

Beas, 11 May 1575

Teresa is preparing for the trip to Seville which she will undertake in obedience to Padre Gracián. She would have preferred to make her next foundation in Madrid. Her confidential remarks to Don Alvaro reveal only slightly the struggle she was going through at the time from homesickness for Avila and Valladolid and fear of the sizzling Seville summer. The autograph, now lost, was already damaged in the 17th century.

1. Jesus. The grace of the Holy Spirit be with your lordship. Every day I comprehend better what a favor it is from our Lord to understand the good that lies in suffering. This enables me to bear calmly the lack of satisfaction present in the things of this life, for they are of such short duration.

2. You should know that I was hurrying so that I could have a good summer in Avila or Valladolid. Then, Padre Gracián came here, who is the provincial of Andalusia through a commission given him by the nuncio after the counter-brief.[1]...He *has such good qualities*[2] that I would be delighted if he could kiss your hands so that I could find out whether I am fooling myself. He desires very much to do so since I told him about the favor you always show toward the order. It has been a

great consolation for me to see so good a man among the order's members.

3. Well, we are leaving for Seville on Monday of next week.[3] The distance is fifty leagues. I truly believe that he would not have placed me under any obligation, but his desire for this was so great that if I hadn't complied, I would have been left with a disturbing scruple that I wasn't being obedient, something I always desire to be. As for me, I have felt weighed down and am not pleased with having to pass the summer in Seville with this scorching heat.[4] Please the Lord, it will be for his service, for the rest is of little importance. I beg you to bless me and not forget to pray to our Lord for me.

4. They say they will have messengers there, for there are none in this isolated place; I will write you from there. May it please our Lord to keep you well, as I always beseech him. Padre Julián de Avila[5] does the same. He is a real help to me. He kisses your hands many times. We keep you very much present and *the house of St. Joseph*[6] and the quiet I had there. May the Lord be served by everything, and may he watch over you much more than over me. Today is the vigil of the feast of the Ascension.

Your lordship's unworthy servant and subject,

Teresa of Jesus

My health has been good here, much more than usual, glory to God.

---

1. She is referring to a brief of Gregory XIII (13 August 1574) obtained by Rossi, the general of the Carmelites, in which the faculties of the Dominican visitators were revoked. The nuncio in Spain, Nicolás Ormaneto, in turn appointed visitators once again (22 September 1574) to the Carmelites in Andalusia. The two he named were Francisco Vargas, O.P. and Jerónimo Gracián.
2. The words in italics were added by early editors who pointed out that a fourth part of the page of the original was missing.
3. She left 18 May 1575.

4. Of the heat suffered on this journey, Teresa writes: "Even though we did not travel during siesta time, I tell you, Sisters, that since the sun was beating on the wagons, getting into them was like stepping into purgatory" (F. 24.6).
5. Julián de Avila was the chaplain at St. Joseph's in Avila who accompanied Teresa on many of her foundations including this one in Seville.
6. The words in italics are not Teresa's, but were added by early editors where there was a break in the text.

81. To Madre Isabel de Santo Domingo,[1] Segovia

Beas, 12 May 1575

Isabel de Santo Domingo, prioress in Pastrana while Gracián was studying at the University of Alcalá, had been instrumental in his vocation. The Carmel in Pastrana later moved to Segovia to escape from the unpredictable princess of Eboli. Teresa writes enthusiastically to Isabel about her first meetings with Gracián. The next foundation will be in Seville by order of Gracián, who is now Teresa's superior. Though her health has been good, she dreads the thought of the excruciating heat of Seville during the summer. Six nuns will be going with her for this foundation.

1. Jesus. The grace of the Holy Spirit be with your reverence, my daughter. May God be blessed that your letters arrived here, for I had no small desire for them. In this I see that I love you more than I do other very close relatives of mine. But your letters always seem short to me. I was greatly consoled that you are in good health. May the Lord give you the health I ask of him for you. I am very sorry that you have that disturbance added on to those you have by reason of your office.[2] That illness seems to have become so common that it requires a special remedy. May it please the Lord to provide a suitable one.

2. Oh, Madre, how I have desired that you be with me during these days. You should know that in my opinion they have

been the best days of my life, without exaggeration. Our Padre Gracián has been here for over twenty days. I tell you that though I have spoken with him a great deal, I have not yet come to fully grasp the worth of this man. He is without fault in my eyes, and for us better than what we would have asked God for. What you must do now, and all the nuns, is to beseech His Majesty to give him to us for our superior. In this way I could rest from the government of these houses. For I have never seen perfection combined with so much gentleness. May God lead him by the hand and protect him, for in no way would I have wanted to miss seeing him and speaking with him at such length.

3. He has been waiting for Mariano,[3] whose delay made us very glad. Julián de Avila[4] is all enthused about him and so is everyone else. He's a wonderful preacher. I truly believe he has made progress since you saw him,[5] for the great trials he has undergone have benefited him very much. The Lord has so turned things around that I am leaving this coming Monday, with the Lord's help, for Seville. I am writing to Padre Fray Diego[6] in more detail about it.

4. The fact is that this house is in Andalusia,[7] and since Padre Maestro Gracián is provincial of Andalusia,[8] I have discovered that I am his subject without having realized it, and as such I can be given orders by him. A situation came about that when we were ready to go to Caravaca[9] to make a foundation and had been given the license by the Council of Orders, the license turned out to be invalid, and it was decided to go at once to Seville. I would be greatly consoled if I could bring you with me, but I see that for you to leave now would mean the ruin of the house where you are, and there are other drawbacks.

5. I think that before Padre Maestro returns here you will see him, for the nuncio[10] has sent for him, and by the time this letter reaches you he will be in Madrid. While here, I am, and have been, in much better health than usual. How much bet-

ter would it be to pass the summer with your reverence rather than in the sizzling heat of Seville. Pray for us and tell the sisters to do the same and give them my regards.

6. There will be more messengers in Seville and we will write more often; and so I'll say no more, other than that you give my regards to Father Rector and the licentiate[11] and tell them what has been happening and ask them to pray for me. My regards to all the sisters. May God make you a saint.

Today is the feast of the Ascension.

7. San Jerónimo[12] sends her regards. She is going to Seville with five other very talented nuns, and the one who is going to be prioress[13] is very capable.

Your Reverence's servant,

Teresa of Jesus

8. I don't know why there is such a hurry for Juana Bautista to make profession. Let it go for a while longer, for she is very young. But if you think otherwise and are content with her, then go ahead with it. But it doesn't seem to me a bad thing that you give her a longer probation, for she seems sickly to me.[14]

---

1. Though many think this letter was addressed to Inés de Jesús, the prioress of Medina del Campo, Tomás Alvarez thinks it was destined for Isabel de Santo Domingo, who had been influential in Gracián's vocation.
2. She held the office of prioress.
3. Ambrosio Mariano de San Benito, one of the first friars of the reform, who accompanied Gracián to Andalusia.
4. The chaplain of St. Joseph's in Avila who accompanied Teresa on her foundations.
5. Madre Isabel had not seen Gracián since the summer of 1573 when he left the novitiate in Pastrana to go to Andalusia.
6. Probably the Dominican Diego de Yanguas.

7. In making this foundation in Beas, Teresa thought she was making it within the jurisdiction of Castile, but found out through Gracián that Beas was in the ecclesiastical jurisdiction of Andalusia.
8. Gracián was vicar provincial of the discalced Carmelite friars and nuns and apostolic visitator of the Carmelites of the observance in Andalusia.
9. The plan was to make the next foundation in Caravaca.
10. Nicolás Ormaneto.
11. Luis de Santander was the rector of the Jesuits in Segovia. The licentiate was Cristóbal de Herrera, who was a help for the foundation in Segovia.
12. Isabel de San Jerónimo.
13. María de San José Salazar became the prioress of Seville.
14. Juana Bautista made her profession in the Carmel of Segovia 24 June 1575.

82. To Padre Luis de Granada, Lisbon

Beas, May 1575(?)

Teresa had never had the opportunity of meeting Fray Luis de Granada, a Dominican author of spiritual books that she prized. Now, a mutual friend, Teutonio de Braganza, gives her the chance to write him a letter of appreciation.

1. Jesus. May the grace of the Holy Spirit be always with your paternity, amen. Many persons love you in the Lord for having written such holy and beneficial doctrine, thanking His Majesty for giving it to you for the good of souls—and I am one of them.[1] And for my part I know that no amount of effort would have prevented me from seeing the one whose words console me so much, if my state in life and my being a woman had allowed it. Unable thus to see you, I had to search out persons like you for assurance against the fears in which my soul lived for some years. And since I have not merited to meet you, I am consoled that Señor Don Teutonio[2] has ordered me to write this letter, something I wouldn't have dared to do on

my own. But, trusting in obedience, I hope in our Lord that it will benefit me because you will at times remember to pray for me. I am in great need of prayers since I go about exposed to the eyes of the world and with little to show, nothing to verify in the least what they imagine about me.

2. If you understand these things, it will be enough that you grant me this favor and alms; for knowing so well what the world is, you can comprehend the great trial it is for someone who has lived a wretched life. This being so, I have often dared to ask our Lord to grant you a long life. May it please His Majesty to grant me this favor, and may you continue growing in holiness and in his love, amen.

Your paternity's unworthy servant and subject,

Teresa of Jesus, Carmelite.

3. Señor Don Teutonio, I believe, is one of those who are deceived in my regard.[3] He tells me he likes you very much. In recompense for this, you are obliged to visit his lordship; don't think it would be fruitless.

---

1. It is not known which of the books written by Fray Luis de Granada that Teresa read. In her *Constitutions* (no. 8), she recommends them in general; also refers to them in general in her *Foundations* 28.42.
2. Teutonio de Braganza
3. Deceived because of his high esteem for her.

83. To Padre Juan Bautista Rubeo,[1] Piacenza

Seville, 18 June 1575

(Autograph: DCN, Livorno-Antignano [Italy])

Teresa, who always had high esteem for the holiness of her Father General (Rubeo), now finds herself in a difficult situation in her relationship with him because of the discalced friars. They had founded three monasteries of friars in Andalusia without permission of the general and without notifying him, although they did have authorization from the visitator. The general chapter of Carmelites in Ciacenza, Italy (May–June 1575), suppressed these monasteries under pain of excommunication. Teresa writes to explain the state of affairs in Andalusia to Rubeo and to intercede for Gracián and Mariano, who were mainly responsible for what had been done She states her opinion about the decisions taken by the chapter at Piacenza and pleads with the general to look at things in a different light.

1. Jesus. The grace of the Holy Spirit be always with your lordship. Last week I wrote to you at length in the same vein in two letters, each sent in a different way, because I want the letter to reach you.[2] Yesterday, 17 June, I received from you two letters, which I had eagerly desired, one sent in October, the other in January. Although they were not dated as recently as I would have desired, I was much consoled by them and the knowledge that you are in good health. May our Lord continue to give it to you as all your daughters in these your houses beseech him. Each day in choir we pray for you especially, and in addition all the nuns are concerned about you. Since they know of my love for you and they have no other father, they have great love for you. And this is not surprising, since we have no other good on earth. And since all the nuns are happy, they never cease being grateful to you for having encouraged us in the beginning.[3]

2. I wrote you about the foundation in Beas and how another was being requested in Caravaca, and that the license for the latter contained so many unsuitable requirements that I did not want to proceed with it. Now they have given another license similar to that of Beas, in which the nuns are subject to you, and this will be so, God willing, for all the houses.[4] I also wrote you about the reasons for which I came here to Seville to make a foundation. May our Lord be pleased to bring about

my purpose in coming here, which is to rid the discalced friars of the things that provoke you. May God grant me this favor. You should know that before coming to Beas I made many inquiries to make sure it was not Andalusia. In no way would I have otherwise considered coming here, for I do not fare well with these people. And it is true that Beas is not Andalusia, but it is in the province of Andalusia. This I learned only a month after the foundation was made.[5] Since I was here with the nuns, it seemed to me that I should not abandon the monastery. It was one of the reasons for my coming here. But my main desire is the one I wrote about to you, to understand the complicated situation of these fathers, for although they justify their cause (and indeed I don't gather from them anything else than the desire to be your true sons and not displease you), I cannot help but blame them. Now it seems they are beginning to understand that it would have been better for them to have proceeded otherwise so as not to have been troublesome to you. Mariano and I especially argued a great deal, for he is very impetuous.[6] Gracián is like an angel, and were he alone he would have done otherwise. His coming here was by order of Fray Baltasar,[7] who was at the time prior of Pastrana. I tell you that if you knew Gracián you would rejoice to have him as your son, and I know truly that he is, and Mariano is too.

3. This Mariano is a virtuous and penitential man and is known by all for his inventive talents, and you can be sure that he has been moved solely by zeal for God and the good of the order; but as I say, he has gone to extremes and been imprudent. I don't think there is any ambition in him, but he says many things he doesn't mean, and the devil, as you say, stirs up trouble. I have suffered very much from him at times, but since I see that he is virtuous, I pass over it. If you could hear the excuses he makes for himself, you would be satisfied. Today he told me that he wouldn't be at peace until he could prostrate at your feet. I already wrote to you how both of them have asked me to write to you and present their excuses, for they don't dare do so themselves. So I will say nothing here

but what seems to me necessary, since I have already written you about it.

4. First you should understand for love of our Lord that I would not give a thing for all the discalced friars together if they dared even so much as to brush against your robes. This is a fact, because to cause you the least displeasure would be like striking me in the pupil of the eye. They have not seen and will not see these letters, although I have told Mariano that I know you will show them mercy if they are obedient. Gracián is not here, for the nuncio[8] sent for him, as I wrote to you, and believe me if I saw they were disobedient, I would not either see them or listen to them; but I couldn't be any more devoted to you than they show themselves to be.

5. I will now give you my opinion and if it amounts to foolishness, please forgive me. With regard to the excommunication,[9] this is what Gracián has now written to Mariano from Madrid: Father Provincial, Fray Angel, told him that he could not stay in the monastery because he had been excommunicated. So he stayed in his father's house. When the nuncio found out, he sent for Padre Fray Angel and scolded him very much saying that it was an affront to say that those who were in Andalusia through his orders were excommunicated and that anyone saying this should be punished. Gracián then went to the monastery, where he is now residing, and he is preaching in the city.

6. *Mi padre*, and lord, this is not a time for excommunications. Gracián has a brother close to the king who serves as his secretary and of whom the king is very fond. And the king from what I have learned might side with the reform. The calced[10] friars say they don't know why you treat such virtuous men in this way, and that they would like to communicate with the contemplative friars[11] and witness their virtue, and that you by this excommunication prevent them from so doing. They say one thing to you, and here they say something else. They go to the archbishop[12] and say they do not dare pun-

ish them because they will immediately have recourse to you. They are a strange lot. I see the one group and the other, and our Lord knows that I speak the truth, for I believe that the most obedient are the discalced friars, and they will continue to be so. Over there you don't see what is going on here. I see it and feel responsible for it all, for I truly know of your holiness and how fond you are of virtue. The things of the order are going so badly here, on account of our sins; and now that I have seen what is going on here, the friars in Castile seem to me to be very good. Even since I have been here something very distressing happened–in broad daylight the police found two friars in a house of ill-fame and publicly brought them to jail. This was handled badly. I am not surprised by human weaknesses, but I would expect that more consideration be given to avoiding scandal. This happened after I wrote to you. Nonetheless, people are saying that it is good they were arrested.

7. Some friars have come to see me. They seem to be good, the prior especially, who is an excellent man. He came that I might show him the patent letters authorizing me to make the foundation. He wanted to have a copy. I asked him not to start a litigation, for he saw that I had the authority to make the foundation. For the last patent letter you sent me in Latin, after the visitators came, gives permission and says that I can make foundations everywhere.[13] And this is the way learned men understand it, for you do not designate any house or kingdom, nor are any limits indicated; rather foundations are to be made everywhere. And it even issues a command, which made me push myself to do more than I was able, for I am old and worn out; but this all seems to me to be nothing, including the fatigue I underwent at the Incarnation. I never have good health, nor do I have any desire for it; but yes, I do have a great desire to depart from this exile, even though God gives me greater favors every day. May he be blessed for everything.

8. With regard to the calced friars who were received by the discalced friars, I have already spoken to Mariano about it. He says that Piñuela[14] took the habit deceitfully, for he went to Pastrana and said that the visitator here, Vargas, had given it to him, but it was found out that he had taken it on his own. For some days they have been trying to send him away, and they will certainly do so. The other friar is no longer with them. The monasteries[15] of the discalced friars were founded by orders of the visitator, Vargas, who has the apostolic authority to do so. He holds that for this region the main tool for reform is to have houses of discalced friars. And so the nuncio sending Fray Antonio de Jesús as visitator gave him the license to be a reformer so that he could found monasteries. But he went about it in a better way, for he made no foundation without asking you.[16] And if Teresa of Jesus had been here, perhaps this would have been carried out more carefully, for if they even considered founding a house without your permission they would have been fiercely opposed by me. And in this matter Fray Pedro Fernández, the visitator in Castile, proceeded well, and I owe him much because he was always careful not to displease you. The visitator here has given so many licenses and faculties to these fathers, asking them to make use of them, that if you saw the powers they were given you wouldn't think they were so much at fault. Thus they say that they never wanted to accept Fray Gaspar[17] or have his friendship—who begged them for it—or others; and the house they took over from the order, they later abandoned.[18] And so they say many things in their defense, from which I see that they have not proceeded with any malice. And when I see the great trials they have undergone and the penance they do–for I really believe they are servants of God–it pains me to learn that you disapprove of them.

9. The monasteries were founded by the visitator, and he ordered the friars with grave precepts not to abandon them. And the nuncio gave patent letters of reformer to Gracián and gave him care of the houses of the friars as well, and you say

they ought to observe what the visitator commands; and as you know, the pope says the same in the brief that suppresses the faculties of the visitators. I don't know how everything can now be undone. Besides, they tell me there are constitutions in print prescribing that in every province there should be houses of reformed friars.[19] Whether the whole order is reformed or not is not a concern here. These reformed friars are considered to be saints, whatever may be the case. Truly they are good and live with great recollection and practice prayer. Among them are some distinguished persons, and more than twenty have taken courses–or I don't know what they call them–some in canon law and others in theology, and they are very talented. And in this house together with those of Granada and La Peñuela they say there are more than seventy friars, or so it seems to me I heard. I don't know what would become of all of them or how it would appear now to everybody, considering the opinion they have of them. Perhaps we would all have to pay. They are highly regarded by the king, and this archbishop[20] says that they are the only real friars. Now to make them leave the reform (since you don't want any reformed friars)–believe me that even though you had every reason in the world, it wouldn't seem that you did. Well, if you were to remove them from your protection, they wouldn't want this, nor would you be right in doing so, nor would it please our Lord.

I commend you to His Majesty; as a true father, forget the past and remember that you are a servant of the Blessed Virgin and that she would be displeased if you were to forsake those who by the sweat of their brow desire to bring increase to her order. Matters are now such that much careful thought....[21]

1. Giovanni Battista Rossi, the prior general of the Carmelite order, wrote his name in Latin as Johannes Battista Rubeus. Thus Teresa used a Latinized form for his last name: Rubeo

2. The two letters were lost. Probably this letter also was lost. The autograph in Livorno-Antignano seems to be a copy that Teresa made for herself.
3. When he visited Avila in 1567 he was pleased with the life Teresa had established there at St. Joseph's. "He gave me extensive patent letters, so that more monasteries could be founded, along with censures to prevent any provincial from restraining me" (F. 2.3).
4. The foundation in Caravaca was made 1 January 1576, but Teresa did not go personally on this foundation.
5. Beas lay within the civil jurisdiction of Castile, but at the same time it belonged under the ecclesiastical jurisdiction of Andalusia.
6. Ambrosio Mariano de San Benito was a discalced Carmelite who came down to Andalusia from Pastrana.
7. Baltasar Nieto de Jesús was a troublesome Andalusian Carmelite who after being punished by the general managed to join the discalced friars and become prior of the discalced monastery in Pastrana.
8. Nicolás Ormaneto.
9. The Carmelite chapter of Piacenza, May 1575, gave orders that the monasteries founded without permission in Andalusia were to be abandoned and that those friars made superiors be removed from office.
10. Teresa refers to the Carmelites of the Observance as "calced" friars to distinguish them from the "contemplative" friars who came to be know popularly as discalced friars because they did not wear shoes but went about barefoot or in sandals as a sign of reform and return to the primitive rule. "Calced Carmelites" has never been the official title of the Carmelites of the Ancient Observance, but "Discalced Carmelites," after Teresa's death, became an official title for the discalced friars of the Teresian Carmel. In her letters Teresa often uses the popular terms "calced" and "discalced" to distinguish the Carmelite friars of her time.
11. Rubeo in his patent letter wanted them to be called the "contemplative" rather than "discalced" friars (cf. MHCT 1:65).
12. Cristóbal de Rojas y Sandoval. At this time he was still opposed to Teresa's foundation in Seville (cf. F. 24.16–18).
13. In this letter (6 April 1571) he gives her faculties to make as many foundations in all regions as she could and orders her under holy obedience to devote herself to the work (cf. MHCT 1:110–12). The visitators (Pedro Fernández and Francisco de Vargas) were appointed 20 August 1569.
14. Fray Gabriel de la Peñuela had been punished by Rubeo in 1566.

15. The monasteries of discalced Carmelite friars founded in Andalusia were in Seville, Granada, and La Peñuela.
16. Padre Antonio de Jesús had sought permission from the general for the foundation in Almodóvar del Campo and received a positive reply 21 June 1574 (cf. MHCT 1:186–88).
17. Fray Gaspar Nieto (brother of Fray Baltasar Nieto), former provincial of the Carmelites in Andalusia, who was also troublesome and punished by Rubeo.
18. Teresa is alluding to the monastery San Juan del Puerto (Huelva) of the Carmelites of Andalusia that was given over to the charge of the discalced friars by Vargas in October 1572. But the project failed and Gracián returned the monastery to the Andalusian Carmelites, 18 October 1573.
19. She is referring to the Constitutions of Venice, 1524.
20. The archbishop of Seville.
21. The rest of the text is missing.

84. To Doña Inés Nieto, Madrid

Seville, 19 June 1575

Teresa asks to have sent to her a statue (or painting) of our Lady, offered to her by Doña Inés, for the foundation in Seville.

1. Jesus. The grace of the Holy Spirit be always with your honor.

I have not forgotten the image of our Lady that you have offered me as a gift, which must be very beautiful since Señor Albornós is pleased with it.[1] So I beg you to give it to whomever Padre Maestro Gracián sends for it, for his reverence will take care of sending it to me.

2. I will take care of asking our Lady to keep you close to her, and Señor Albornós as well. Since I am so far away, I don't know whether you did anything more regarding the matter you wrote to me about in Valladolid. My health is good, glory to God, and I'm faring well in this region where obedience has

brought me. I desire very much that you will have good health and always advance along the path that you have begun in the service of our Lord.

3. May it please His Majesty that you make good progress and may he always rescue your honor from the tumult of Madrid, although nothing disturbs the one who truly loves God.

Today is 19 June. From this house of the glorious St. Joseph in Seville.

Your honor's unworthy servant,

Teresa of Jesus, Carmelite

---

1. Señor Albornós is Juan Albornoz, the husband of Doña Inés. In a previous letter to Doña Inés (Ltr. 78), Teresa asks her to keep a statue for her until she gets settled in one monastery. Although Silverio places that letter in the year 1574, Efrén-Steggink give the year 1568 because the content suggests that the foundation of Valladolid was in its initial stages. Doña Inés could have given Teresa more than one statue. It is not always clear whether Teresa is referring to a statue or a painting.

85. To Antonio Gaytán, Alba de Tormes
Seville, 10 July 1575

Antonio Gaytán had accompanied Teresa on her trip to Beas and then Seville. He had also gone to Caravaca to prepare for the foundation there. After a long absence he has returned home. Teresa informs him about the projects in which he had been involved. She is still looking for a house for her community.

1. Jesus. The grace of the Holy Spirit be with your honor, my good founder.[1] The muleteer did not arrive until yesterday. Please God the licentiate[2] is sending the parcel with care, for he promised me earnestly that he would do so. I will send word again, for I have been very concerned. In the package I

am sending two doubloons for the prioress[3] and telling her to pay the rest. Now we are rich; and indeed we were never in want except when we needed something for your return.[4]

2. The archbishop came here and did all that I requested of him. He is giving us wheat and money and showing much kindness.[5] He wants to give us the house of Belén and the church; I don't know what we will do.[6] Things are moving along nicely; don't be troubled. Tell this to my nuns and my sister, for I do not want to write until I have some good news to send about my brothers.[7] You must not fail to write to us, for you know how much your letters console me.

3. I am well, as are all the sisters and the prioress.[8] It is really hot, but the heat is easier to bear than the sun over the inn at Albino.[9] We have an awning in the courtyard, and that helps a lot. I have already written you that a license like the one for Beas was given for the foundation in Caravaca.[10] Since you have given your word, may you now give us the means by which we can act.

4. I assure you that if the founders do not go to bring the nuns from Segovia, nothing will be done. Until we see how matters turn out in Madrid, we cannot do anything.[11] Our good friend Don Teutonio[12] does very well, and it seems that the negotiations will be successful. Pray to God for him and for me. Give my regards to Mother Prioress, to Tomasina, and to San Francisco.[13]

5. Write to me and tell me how our little rascal[14] is, and the condition of your house, whether it remained standing, and how your housekeeper is.[15] Give my regards to anyone you think you should, and remain with God; I already desire to see you, even were it to cost me another round of trials. May His Majesty make you as holy as I beg him to, amen.

Today is 10 July.

Your honor's unworthy daughter,

Teresa of Jesus

---

1. She calls him founder because of his collaboration in the three previous foundations (Segovia, Beas, and Seville) and his trip to Caravaca.
2. Probably the licentiate Cueva y Castilla, friend of the Cepeda's.
3. The prioress of Alba, Juana del Espíritu Santo.
4. According to Julián de Avila, when he and Gaytán were ready to return home Teresa gave them enough money for their travel, but she would have wanted to give them much more to repay them for their services (BMC 18: 201).
5. Initially, when the nuns arrived in Seville they discovered that the archbishop was opposed to the foundation.
6. This place did not prove suitable.
7. Teresa's sister Juana de Ahumada lived in Alba. They were waiting the return of their brothers Lorenzo and Pedro from the Americas.
8. The prioress of Seville was María de San José.
9. When they arrived thirsty in the excessive heat at the inn of Albino, between Ecija and Seville, they found that the innkeepers were out of water and that the only food available was some salty sardines. But in addition to that was their fright and horror over the swearing, fighting, flashing of swords, and firing of muskets going on among the patrons at the inn (cf. BMC 18: 201; *Libro de Recreaciones*, 9).
10. It allowed the foundation to be under the jurisdiction of the order, as Teresa had insisted.
11. Gracián had been called to Madrid by the nuncio Nicolás Ormaneto; Teresa was waiting to learn the results of the meeting.
12. Don Teutonio de Braganza.
13. Carmelite nuns in Alba, Tomasina Bautista and María de San Francisco.
14. Gaytán's little daughter Mariana.
15. While away on the foundation, Gaytán was worried about things back home, so Teresa asks in jest if his house is still standing. He was a widower and so had a housekeeper.

86. To King Don Philip II, Madrid

Seville, 19 July 1575

(Autograph: DCN, Yepes [Toledo])

While Teresa was taken up with the foundation in Seville, the Carmelites held a chapter at Piacenza in Italy (22 May 1575), the results of which were unfavorable toward Teresa and her work. She foresees many difficulties in the making and proposes to the king that he erect a separate province for the discalced friars and nuns. She also asks that Gracián be made its superior.

1. Jesus. The grace of the Holy Spirit be always with your majesty. While much afflicted and praying to our Lord about the affairs of this holy order of our Lady and considering the great need there is that these initiatives God has taken in its regard not crumble, it occurred to me that the best safeguard for us would be that you realize what giving a solid foundation to this edifice entails;[1] even the calced friars would benefit from the increase in numbers.

2. I have lived among them for forty years,[2] and, considering everything, I know clearly that if a separate province is not made for the discalced friars—and soon—great harm will be done, and I think it will be impossible for them to move ahead. Since this lies in your hands and I see that the Blessed Virgin, our Lady, has chosen you to support and protect her order, I have dared to write and beg you that for the love of our Lord and his glorious Mother you give orders that this separate province be formed.[3] It is so important for the devil to hinder this project that he will raise many objections, without any of them being valid, for only blessings of every kind can come from doing this.

3. It would be most beneficial to us in our situation if you would appoint a discalced *padre*, named Gracián, whom I have

recently come to know, to be in charge of us in our beginnings. Although he is young, I was moved to praise our Lord greatly for what he has given to that soul and for the great works he has done through him for the salvation of many souls. And so I believe that the Lord has chosen this friar to bring many blessings to our order.[4] May our Lord so direct things that you will want to render him this service and issue the necessary commands.

4. I kiss your hands many times for the favor you granted me in regard to the license for founding a monastery in Caravaca.[5] For the love of God I beg you to pardon me, for I recognize that I am being very bold. But in reflecting that the Lord listens to the poor and that you stand in his place, I don't think you will become annoyed.

5. May God give you peace and a long life, as I beg him continually and as is needed by Christendom.

Today is 19 July.

Your majesty's unworthy servant and subject,

Teresa of Jesus, Carmelite

---

1. The edifice is her reform.
2. On 2 November 1535, Teresa entered the Incarnation, a Carmelite monastery of nuns in Avila.
3. Teresa simply thought the king had all the powers necessary to issue such orders. King Philip II and Rossi had divergent views about matters of reform.
4. Jerónimo Gracián de la Madre de Dios was 30 years old at the time and had been a priest for five years, but he had been a professed Carmelite for only two years.
5. In her *Foundations* (27.6), Teresa tells of her writing to the king asking that a license be given so that the foundation would be subject to the Carmelite order rather than the council of the Order of Knights, as the first license prescribed. This letter has been lost.

87. To Doña Juana de Ahumada, Alba de Tormes

Seville, 12 August 1575

This letter has a note of excitement because two of Teresa's brothers have returned from America. They will be in Seville within a few days. But the joy is tempered by news of some deaths that occurred on the journey. She advises Juan de Ovalle against coming to Seville at once, and shares news about Gracián's recent appointment.

1. Jesus. The grace of the Holy Spirit be with you, my friend, and permit you to enjoy the presence of your brothers who, glory to the Lord, are now in Sanlúcar. Today they wrote here to Canon Cueva y Castilla[1] asking him to inform Señor Juan de Ovalle in Alba and me in Avila, where they thought I was, of their arrival. I think they will be overjoyed to find out that I am here. But the joys of this life all come with trials so that we do not become absorbed in them. You should know that the good Jerónimo de Cepeda died like a saint in Nombre de Dios.[2] And Pedro de Ahumada is coming, whose wife has died, according to what they have told me.[3] There is no reason to grieve, for I knew about her life. She had practiced prayer for a long time, and her death was of the kind that left everyone amazed, according to what I was told. Lorenzo, also, lost another boy; he's bringing three children and Teresita.[4] They are well, glory to God. I am writing them today and sending them some little things.

2. I am told they will be here within two or three days. When I think of the joy they will experience in finding me so close, it makes me joyful too. I marvel at the ways of God, that now he brings to me here those who seemed so far away. Today I have written to our Padre Gracián in Madrid, for this letter is going by that same route, which is very secure; you will have the news as soon as possible. Do not weep for him who is in

heaven, but give thanks to the Lord that he has brought these others to us.

3. I don't think Señor Juan de Ovalle should start out on his journey until I speak to my brother, because the weather is difficult to bear down here and I must find out if my brother has business that will detain him here. If he will be detained a long while, perhaps you could come along too, and all of you could return together. I will write again soon and in the meantime will tell my brother how I have forestalled Juan de Ovalle from coming, and the weather will then become milder. Give my regards to Señor Juan de Ovalle and let this letter be for him too.

4. You ought also to know that they have given Padre Gracián authority over all the discalced friars and nuns down here and up there as well;[5] no better thing could have happened for us. He is the ideal person as Señor Antonio Gaytán must have told you, whom you must also greet for me, and let this letter be for him too. Regards also to Mother Prioress[6] and all the other nuns. Go and see the lady marchioness for me and tell her I am well and give Señora Doña Mayor the good news about Pedro de Ahumada's return, for it seems to me he was her devoted servant.[7] And give everyone my best. And send this news to Mother Prioress in Salamanca[8] and tell her that the Lord has taken to himself another sister.

5. May His Majesty preserve you for me, my lady. I already told you that I will write at length, for there are reasons for you to be joyful and at peace.

Today is 12 August.

In this letter that I enclose now for you to send, I put the date as the 10th, but I think it's the 12th, the feast of St. Clare. If Padre Gracián should happen to pass through, show him every kindness and courtesy, as if you were showing them to me in a wonderful way.

Your honor's servant

Teresa of Jesus

1. A friend of both Lorenzo and Teresa, who lived in Seville.
2. Now known as Panama, from which they set sail at the beginning of May. Jerónimo de Cepeda, a younger brother of Teresa's, was born in 1522.
3. Pedro de Ahumada, another younger brother (1521–1589), had lost his wife, Ana Pérez, the previous year (1574).
4. She probably means three including Teresita. From Teresa's correspondence we know of two sons: Francisco and Lorenzo. The boy Esteban (1563–1575) died on the journey.
5. She is alluding to the extensive powers given to Gracián by the nuncio, Nicolás Ormaneto. In the next line the adjective before person is missing; editors think it would be "excellent" or "ideal."
6. Juana del Espíritu Santo.
7. The Marchioness of Velada was Juana de Toledo. Doña Mayor de Ovalle was a Benedictine nun in Alba, the sister of Juan de Ovalle.
8. Ana de la Encarnación (Tapia), a relative of Teresa's.

88. To Madre María Bautista, Valladolid
Seville, 28 August 1575

(Autograph: 2 DCN, Lima, Peru)

María Bautista must have written to Teresa about Carmelite postulants and other business matters concerning the nuns in Castile and Andalusia and about Báñez and Gracián. Teresa's answer reveals the close bond between the two nuns and the candid exchanges that took place.

For Mother Prioress María Bautista.

1. Jesus be with your reverence, my daughter. It is a strange thing how almost all letters tire me except yours (excluding

letters from confessors), and answering them even more so. But to receive and answer yours is refreshing. I was greatly relieved to know that your health is better. May God be blessed for everything.

2. You will have learned that my brothers arrived with the present fleet.[1] Lorenzo de Cepeda is the one I'm fond of. And I tell you that even if he were not my brother, he would be worthy of being much loved because he is such a servant of God and so virtuous—a very good soul. He is regaining his strength because he arrived in a very weakened state. It was God's providence that I happened to be here. I never cease rejoicing about this. For many things....[2] Well, I suffer it better. Teresita is eight or nine years old, very charming and beautiful.[3]

3. He wants to remain here through this winter so as not to be separated from me. I have arranged for my sister and her husband to come to join him down here and that he stay in their house when he goes to Madrid where he will necessarily have to go.[4] He has the means on which to live, but he's very tired of everything. His happiness would be to live in solitude. God is granting him many favors. Have the nuns pray that he will find a place to settle that is best....I want to respond to your letter, for I tell you many have arrived that need an answer, especially from Medina.

4. That is the house that is always tormenting me, and now they are asking Asensio[5] to be responsible for the major chapel so that Doña Elena[6] can take responsibility for the church. But the nuns owe him so much and they so need to get out of that choir that I don't know what to say or who will have a place for them.

5. Although you are proud of your novice,[7] I want you to know that if there is agreement about the other nun of whom you speak so highly, you couldn't fail to accept her, for what has been done is already very much. Don't be so particular. It

is enough that she is helpful to the house. Making her wait could do her harm.

6. Believe me that where there is a question of benefit to many souls, certain considerations are of little value; it's enough to send her to a place where she is not known. And she shouldn't think she can find what she is looking for everywhere. In some houses there would be no nuns if so much attention were paid to details. At the beginning of a foundation and for other business matters, adaptations of some sort have to be made, as was the case with St. Joseph's in Avila and all the houses, and as also has to be done there, or you will be left without any nuns....I tell you that if I had understood the situation in the beginning I would not have accepted her, but there was nothing else to do. Since you hadn't written me anything about it, there was no point in your disturbing the others, who knew that I had accepted her. For it was clear that I should have known whether the set number had been reached or not.[8] Don't worry that we will not have a place for her.

7. That you think you know everything is disheartening, and you say that you are humble; and all you care about is your own little house, and you do not consider what is essential for all of them. This would create a state of unrest in which everything could come tumbling down in ruins. She was not the one I wanted to send there; I wanted to send one of Padre Olea's[9] own relatives, and she no longer wants to go. That would be a nice state of affairs, that something be started and then left hanging because you are inflexible! No prioress has ever taken such a stance with me, nor anyone who is not prioress. I tell you that by acting in such a way you will lose my friendship.

8. You should know that I find it displeasing that you think there is no one capable of seeing things as you do; and, as I say, this comes from your being concerned about nothing but your own house, and not about what is important for many others. It is not enough for you to be free, but you must dem-

onstrate this to others. Perhaps that nun will be holier than all. I don't know how from such a spirit you draw out so much vanity. If you were to see what is happening here as regards holding offices and selling them, and the importance given to this, you would be astonished. It is good to consider things carefully, but not with so much drive, for no one will make me believe that this arises from humility. The fault is all mine for not having found out about her from the *padre* himself. Since he had sent me another who was extremely good, I thought this one would be also. Nonetheless it was good to do everything that has been done because we owe him much.

9. In what concerns...Padre Gracián...friendship that I have, for you would be amazed at what is happening. I couldn't have done more, nor am I repentant.[10] If you find faults in him, it will be because you have not spoken much with him and do not know him well. I tell you he is a saint and not at all impetuous, but very cautious. I already have experience of that, and one can trust in him more than in books. You say that since I have him I don't remember my Fray Domingo.[11] They are so different from each other that I am amazed; in the former friendship the only bond is of the soul. Speaking with him is like speaking with an angel, which he is and has always been; and although the other is also, I don't know what the temptation may be—something is very different. Blessed be God that he is better. Give him my regards.

10. Oh, what kind of life that person must be making you live who you say is worse than I, although I understand that all my fears come from the fear that you will lose your holy freedom. If I had assurance in this regard, I know that nothing, save for ingratitude, would matter to me, as is the case with the one who is there now. You should know that when I was there last I came away more assured than ever that you have nothing against me, and this did me much good, and continues to do so daily...since this other friendship, as I say, rather gives freedom. It's something remarkably different and the submission

does not come from the will but from understanding that one is doing the will of God, as I have said.

11. Why don't you tell me whether the person who approved the large book also considered the small one good.[12] Would you mark for me any passages that should be removed, for I'm very glad they haven't burned them, and I would be very happy if the large one were preserved for when...knowing what I know...to benefit many souls. As for myself, what else would matter? I want the glory of my Lord and that there be many to praise him, and I certainly would want them to know my misery.

12. One of the things that make me happy to be here and willing to remain longer is that nobody has any idea of that farce about my sanctity which I was subjected to up there. This allows me to live and move about without the fear that that tower of wind is about to fall on top of me...for a long time has passed without seeing her.

13. If something worse were to come about, I would also regret that. Give him my best regards.[13] I tell you I have to force myself not to write to him. Have no fear that anyone will take away this friendship for it has cost too much.

14. Regarding Catalina de Jesús,[14] Padre Gracián will have already been there, to whom I have written that he might observe her carefully. I am most consoled that it is he who will take account....

As for the rest, I say that it is the feast of St. Augustine. I am repeating the date so that you don't have to go looking for it.

15. A candidate wants to enter who is rich and good. If she enters, we will at once look for a house. You should know that

many of these sisters embroider. One who has entered does exquisite work with her hands.

Your reverence's,

Teresa of Jesus

16. Guard those notebooks[15] carefully. In some there is good material for preparing for profession and on how to deal with temptations, if there are any. Let my Casilda read them and afterward...have the enclosed letter brought to Doña Guiomar,[16] for I spend my time writing to her and the letters get lost, and then she complains, with reason. I should like to write to the subprioress, Dorotea de la Cruz, but so many letters have arrived that I am tired. In one way or another I'll see that she leaves, although I cannot be persuaded...and the submission does not come from the will but from understanding that one is doing the will of God, as I have said.[17]

---

1. The two brothers are Lorenzo de Cepeda and Pedro de Ahumada. They arrived in Sanlúcar on 12 August.
2. The autograph was torn and so parts of this letter are missing.
3. She was born on 27 October 1566 and is Lorenzo's daughter.
4. Her sister and brother-in-law were Juana de Ahumada and Juan de Ovalle; they lived in Alba de Tormes.
5. Asensio Galiano was a contractor in Medina del Campo and a friend of Teresa's.
6. Doña Elena de Quiroga, who became a discalced Carmelite nun in Medina in 1581, owned a house next to the nuns which they desired for their church.
7. Casilda de Padilla, the daughter of the chief governor of Castile, escaped from home and entered the Carmelite monastery before she was 12 years old (see F. 11).
8. Only a fixed number of nuns was allowed in each Carmel.
9. Francisco de Olea, a Jesuit friend, had presented other postulants for Carmel that were not always suitable.
10. Padre Jerónimo Gracián was in Castile at the time and had been appointed commissary of the discalced friars and nuns by the nuncio, Nicolás Ormaneto. For an understanding of what Teresa is referring to here, see her ST. 35; 36; 38; 39.

11. Fray Domingo Báñez. In ST. 36.3, she speaks of Báñez when she feels resistance to the inspiration to make a vow of obedience to Gracián: "The remembrance of one [confessor] especially made me put up strong resistance, since it seemed to me I was offending him."
12. The large book is her *Life*, which had been denounced to the Inquisition and judged favorably by Báñez, one of its censors. The small book could be the *Way of Perfection* or her *Meditations on the Song of Songs*, which had also been reviewed by Báñez and approved 10 June 1575.
13. Domingo Báñez.
14. Catalina de Jesús had made her profession in Valladolid in 1572. She was at the time undergoing severe spiritual trials.
15. They were probably lost.
16. Doña Guiomar de Ulloa, an old friend from Avila.
17. She repeats the exact words that appear at the end of no. 10.

89. To Padre Jerónimo Gracián, Avila

Seville, 27 September 1575

After his brief encounter with Teresa in Beas, Gracián was called to Madrid by the nuncio and in turn, starting in Castile, began to carry out the task given him. Teresa meanwhile made her foundation in Seville. She writes to Gracián to inform him about the attitude of the Carmelites in Andalusia to his new authority over them and about the entrance of Teresita in the Seville Carmel.

1. Jesus. The grace of the Holy Spirit be with your paternity, *padre mio*. Since you will probably be on your way back here and this letter will not reach you in Madrid,[1] I will not go on at length. Yesterday Father Provincial of "those of the cloth" was here with a master, and then the prior came, and after that another master.[2] The previous day Fray Gaspar Nieto[3] was here. I found that all of them are determined to obey your paternity and help you in suppressing any sinful abuses, as long as there are no extreme solutions taken in regard to other matters. I

assured them from what I know of you that you will carry out your office with gentleness, and I explained to them my opinion.

2. I was not unhappy with the reply they made about the *Motu*.[4] I hope in the Lord that everything will work out very well. Padre Elías[5] feels more encouraged and at peace. I tell you that by beginning without noise and proceeding gently you will be able to accomplish much, but one shouldn't try to accomplish everything in a day. Indeed, it seems to me they are reasonable people. May they be so also up there in Castile! You should know that Macario is so terrible, from what they tell me, that I was deeply afflicted over what concerns his soul.[6] They wrote me saying that now he has to go to Toledo. I have asked myself if he doesn't want to return to his lair[7] because the visitation has already been made there and thus he wouldn't have to meet my Eliseo,[8] and that wouldn't displease me until he becomes more reasonable. Surely, seeing good souls so deceived makes me fear.

3. We called in Doctor Enríquez, who is one of the most learned men in the Society of Jesus, about Teresica.[9] He says that among other things sent to him by the Council was a declaration made by a commission of cardinals on this subject. It went like this: one cannot give the habit to anyone under twelve years of age, but a child can be reared in the monastery itself. Fray Baltasar, the Dominican, also said this. She is already here with her habit, for she looks like the house's little elf.[10] And her father is outside himself with joy, and all the nuns are delighted with her. She has the disposition of an angel, and she is adept at entertaining in recreation, telling her stories about the Indians and her voyage by sea better than I could do. I am happy that she will not be a burden to anyone. Now I want you to see her. God has granted her a great favor and she will know how to please you. I don't think God wants this soul to be reared among the things of this world. I now see the charity you have shown me. For, besides being great in itself, it has been shown

in such a way as to remove from me every scruple. And that makes it much greater.[11]

4. It seems now that I have gained a little in charity, for although your absence is so painful for me, I would be pleased, in exchange, if you could help the Incarnation and stay another month to attend to the needs of that house.[12] Eight days would be sufficient, if you leave Fray John there. I know that as things are now, if they see a man who has a good head they soon yield, even though they do a lot of shouting in the beginning. I feel great pity for them, and if the nuncio wanted to do a great work, he could do so in this way. May God provide a remedy, for he can.

5. There is no help for Laurentia[13] from confessors as there was formerly, and since she found relief only in this, now she is without any. With what delicacy our Lord mortifies one, for the confessor that he gives to her has so many obligations that she fears she will enjoy his presence only rarely.

6. It is as hot here now as it is up there in June and even hotter. You have done well to delay. I have written to the good Padilla concerning the Incarnation. Would you please inform my Padre Olea and give him my regards.[14] I have written three letters to him. Would you find out whether he has received them. Oh, Jesus, how little it would take to save so many souls! I am amazed at how I now desire this, for one of the things I hated most was to see you charged with that heavy task. Now it is easier for me to accept this. May God provide and protect you.

Today is 27 September.

Your paternity's unworthy subject and servant,

Teresa of Jesus

---

1. Gracián, with his new powers from the nuncio, had been making official visitations of the Carmels in Castile and now had to return to Seville to make visitations in Andalusia.

2. "The fathers of the cloth" was another name, besides "calced," that Teresa used in referring to the Carmelites of the observance. Their habits were made of better material than those of the discalced friars. The provincial's name was Agustín Suárez; the prior's, Vicente de la Trinidad. The provincial had recently returned from the general chapter at Piacenza.
3. Gaspar Nieto was a former provincial, and a brother of Baltasar, to whom Teresa will refer in no. 2.
4. The *Motu* (3 August 1575) was the brief from the nuncio appointing Gracián commissary of all the Carmelites in Andalusia and of just the discalced Carmelite friars and nuns in Castile.
5. The subprior of the Carmelite monastery in Seville.
6. Macario is the code name for Baltasar Nieto, a troublesome friar who joined the discalced Carmelites in Pastrana. The general chapter of Piacenza had expelled him from the order. For an account of the disturbances caused by the Nieto brothers in the Andalusian province see Smet, 2.10–16.
7. The discalced monastery grounds in Pastrana had caves which served as cells in the early days.
8. Because of his large and balding head, Gracián was called Eliseo by Teresa. This code name of hers evoked the thought of the prophet Elisha (Eliseo).
9. "Teresica" and "Teresita" are diminutive forms for Teresa.
10. Enrique Enriquez, S.J. and Baltasar de Vargas, O.P. were two canonists consulted about allowing Lorenzo's daughter to live in the monastery with the nuns. In regard to their reply, cf. *The Acts of the Council of Trent, Reformatio regularium, ch. 17.* Though Teresita did not receive the habit officially and thereby enter the novitiate, she did wear a nun's habit.
11. Gracián had asked Teresa to consult with canonists before accepting Teresita into the Seville Carmel.
12. Gracián had faculties to visit only the discalced Carmelites in Castile. Teresa desired that the nuncio grant him faculties to make a visitation of the Carmelite nuns at the Incarnation in Avila where Teresa had lived for many years and where St. John of the Cross was then confessor.
13. Laurentia is Teresa's code name for herself, used for the first time in this letter. Through a special inspiration from God, she had taken Padre Gracián as her spiritual director. She may have taken the name Laurentia after her brother Lorenzo to whom she felt very close.

14. Juan Calvo de Padilla was a priest who had become involved in the task of ecclesiastical reform. Francisco de Olea was the Jesuit who assisted the nuns at the Carmel in Valladolid.

90. To Padre Baltasar Alvarez, Salamanca

Seville, 9 October 1575

(Autograph: Cathedral in Genoa)

Teresa has been in Seville four months but the nuns still do not have their own house. On the other hand, neither do the nuns in Salamanca, who have been there for five years. Teresa continues to have the interests of that Carmel at heart and enlists the help of Julián de Avila, Gaspar Daza, and probably Baltasar Alvarez, S.J.

1. Jesus. The grace of the Holy Spirit be with your honor, *padre and señor mio*. Padre Julián de Avila and also Señor Maestro wrote me about the house of Juan de Avila de la Vega which is for sale.[1] It is just right for us, both the price (which Padre Julián de Avila says will be little more than 1,000 ducats) and the location, which for our purpose is excellent. That it is close to you is sufficient.

2. I really think that it will be so old that there will be immediate need for repairs. That matters little if there is ample space and a well. I beg you to begin at once to confer about buying it, but without looking too eager because then they will raise the price.

3. My brother[2] is going to Madrid and you can notify him there to send you the authorization. May the Lord direct matters, for it would be a great thing to have our own house. Because I have many letters to write I cannot go on at length. May God preserve you for me for many years and give me the opportunity to see you.

4. I think there is so much to do down here that I will have to stay a long while. I am well, and my brother kisses your hands many times.

Today is 9 October.

Your honor's unworthy servant and true friend,

Teresa of Jesus

---

1. Julián de Avila was the chaplain at St. Joseph's in Avila; the Maestro was Maestro Gaspar Daza, a priest in Avila and friend of Teresa's. Juan de Avila de la Vega was a gentleman from Salamanca.
2. Lorenzo de Cepeda, recently back from America, went to Madrid on business in October and then returned to Seville staying there until June 1576.

91. To Padre Jerónimo Gracián

Seville, October 1575(?)

These two fragments probably belong to different letters, whose date is uncertain. Perhaps they are a response to an inquiry by Gracián during his first visitation of the Carmels in Castile from August through October 1575. For similar responses, see Ltr. 92.

…As regards the house, it is better, in my opinion, to take as prioress someone from the community than to bring in a nun from outside.…

…If the matter concerns the soul's health, priority should be given to that. But in matters concerning bodily health, there are many disadvantages that follow from such a principle. In a letter written a short time ago I mentioned many that came to mind.…

92. To Padre Jerónimo Gracián, Toledo

Seville, October 1575(?)

Teresa had received letters from John of the Cross, praising Gracián, and from Gracián asking her advice concerning his first visitation to the Carmels in Castile. The first part of the letter is missing.

1. ...If she wants, you would be doing much good for the house by leaving her there; if she doesn't, let her come down here and she can go with the nuns as far as Malagón.[1] But truthfully, I hope no one ever does me this favor. There is no house more in need of talented persons than Toledo. The prioress there will soon end her term of office, but I don't think there is another who would be better for that house.[2] Although she is very ill, she is careful, and even though she is friendly with "the cats," she has many virtues.[3] If you think it a good thing, she could resign, giving as a reason the hot weather of that region that is killing her, which is evident, and another election could be held. But I don't know who could go there as prioress, for almost all of them love her so much that they wouldn't adapt easily to another, in my opinion, although there will never be lacking someone who is contentious—that's for sure.

2. You should be careful, *padre mio*, in this matter, and believe that I understand women's nature better than you. In no way is it fitting that you let a prioress or subject think it is possible to transfer someone from her house except in the case of making a new foundation. And truly, even for this reason I see that this expectation does so much harm. I have often desired that the time for making foundations were to end so that all the nuns could settle down. And believe me when I tell you this truth—and if I die, don't forget it—that for people who are enclosed, the devil doesn't want anything else except to foster the opinion that something like a transfer is possible. There is

much to say about this, for I have the permission from our Father General,[4] which I asked for, since sometimes the weather will be bad for a nun and she can then be transferred to another region. Nonetheless I have afterward seen so many disadvantages in this that unless a transfer is for the good of the order I don't think it should be allowed. It is better that some die than that all be harmed.

3. There isn't any monastery that has the full number of nuns; rather some are far short of the full number, and in Segovia I believe they are three or four short, for I paid close attention to this. In Malagón I gave the prioress I don't know how many permissions to receive different nuns, warning her to be very careful, for we took some nuns away from there and left only a few. You should revoke these permissions, for it is better that they have recourse to you.[5] And believe me, *mi padre*, now that I don't feel obliged, for I know the care with which you consider things, it will be a great consolation for me to be relieved of that obligation. As things stand now we can proceed with more order, but the one who had to make foundations with nothing but air at her disposal needed help from all sides and had to be obliging.

And you should believe that they gain a great deal from being attached to the Society of Jesus—even though some mistakes might be made in this respect—as time will tell and I will show you. At least these Fathers have been my main help and I would never fail to recognize this. I wouldn't want you to impede the nuns in Valladolid from sending something from the garden, for they have a surplus and the others are poor. And believe me, *mi padre*, being gracious even in trifling matters cannot be avoided with some persons. This is the only thing that seemed to me a little rigorous in the visitations, even though—since they were made by you—there must have been a reason.

4. Seneca is delighted and says that he has found more in his superior than he could have desired; he is giving great

thanks to God.[6] I wouldn't want to do anything else. May His Majesty keep you for many years.

5. I tell you I am angry about those falls you have; it would be good if they tied you to the saddle so that you couldn't fall.[7] I don't know what kind of donkey that is, nor why you have to go ten leagues in a day, which on a pack saddle is killing. I am worried about whether you have thought of putting on more clothes, for it is now getting colder. Please God the fall didn't do you any harm. Since you are fond of helping souls, consider the harm that many would suffer by your loss of health and, for love of God, take care of yourself.

6. Elías now has less fear.[8] The rector and Rodrigo Alvarez are very hopeful that everything will work out well.[9] As for me, all the fear I previously had has left me, for I cannot feel it even were this my desire. My health has been wretched recently. They have purged me and I am well, better than I have been in four or five months; I got to the point where I couldn't go on.

Your paternity's unworthy servant,

Teresa of Jesus

---

1. She is speaking about the transfer of a nun to another monastery, perhaps from Toledo to Malagón. That nun could travel with those who were on their way from Segovia to make a new foundation in Caravaca. They would be passing through Toledo and Malagón.
2. The prioress was Ana de la Encarnación. She had previously been a member of the community at the Incarnation in Avila and was one of the original nuns of the first foundation, St. Joseph's in Avila.
3. "The cats" was a code name, probably for the Carmelites of the observance.
4. Giovanni Battista Rossi (Rubeo).
5. The prioress in Malagón, Brianda de San José, had received these permissions because Teresa had taken a number of nuns from Malagón for the foundations in Beas, Seville, and Caravaca.
6. Seneca is Teresa's code name for St. John of the Cross. Seneca, Lucius Annaeus (4 B.C.–65 A.D.), born in Córdoba, was a Roman Stoic philosopher whose writings both in verse and prose reached a high ethical and religious standard. In the 16th century countless editions,

translations, and commentaries sprung up. Luis de Granada, O.P. used him in his sermons and spiritual writings. Stoic teaching seems to lie in the background of some of John's observations (cf. *Ascent of Mount Carmel,* Bk. 3, ch. 6). Teresa often used the diminutive "mi Senequita."

7. Gracián was not good at riding animals; on the other hand he admired the way Teresa rode.
8. Elías is Padre Juan Evangelista, prior of the Carmelites of the observance in Seville.
9. The rector of the Seville Jesuits was Francisco Arias. Rodrigo Alvarez, also a Jesuit, was the one for whom Teresa wrote two accounts of conscience (see ST. 58;59).

93. To Doña María de Cepeda, Avila

Seville, 24 October 1575

María de Cepeda was a second cousin of Teresa's. She and her two sisters had been nuns at the Incarnation in Avila. They all transferred to the Teresian reform, but María soon had to return to the Incarnation because of poor health. Teresa is writing to tell her about the family members who had come to Seville from America and from Alba de Tormes.

1. Jesus. The grace of the Holy Spirit be with your honor. Today my sister, her husband, and children arrived to see my brother Lorenzo. He had just departed for Madrid, although he left his children here and will return this winter. Afterward he will go directly to Avila. He arrived very weakened and sick; he is better now. We spoke much about your honor. Agustín remained over there.[1]

2. Sister Beatriz de Jesús has become so fond of the prioress in Malagón that she has begged me not to transfer her, but the prioress has had bad health. May God be pleased to give her good health, for all the nuns are happy with her and with her disposition. I am not so happy with Señor Luis de Cepeda, for it would be good if at times he sent me word of himself. I received a letter from Isabel de San Pablo today.[2] May God

make them his servants, and may he preserve you for many years. I have had better health here than up there. My best regards to all the ladies there.

Today is 24 October.

Your honor's unworthy servant,

Teresa of Jesus

---

1. Juana de Ahumada and Juan de Ovalle had come to Seville to be with Lorenzo de Cepeda and his children. Another of Teresa's brothers, Agustín, had stayed in America.
2. Beatriz de Jesús and Isabel de San Pablo were sisters of Maria de Cepeda; Luis de Cepeda was their brother. The prioress of Malagón was Brianda de San José.

94. To Doña Inés Nieto, Alba de Tormes

Seville, 31 October 1575

Teresa's sister Juana de Ahumada and her husband had arrived in Seville to be with their brother Lorenzo who had recently returned from America. They had probably brought a statue with them, a gift from Doña Inés. In the letter Teresa asks that Doña Inés's husband, who was the duke's secretary, intercede in favor of her sister's son Gonzalo, who was aspiring to become one of the duke's pages rather than remain a page in the service of the duchess.

1. Jesus. The grace of the Holy Spirit be with your honor. I wrote the enclosed letter some days ago. This one is to beg Señor Albornós[1] to do me the favor of helping my nephew Gonzalo[2] in every way he can. I would like to know that he has something to gain by my being the servant of your honors, and so I beg you to help me in this regard.

2. I am writing to my lady, the duchess, to ask her grace to have him removed from the list of her pages, for I think he is a

grown man. And I know that Señor Albornós can do a great deal. Since the pages live together, I have a real fear they will make him leave for some far off place, saying that he is too old to be a page. If I knew that he would be serving the Lord, it wouldn't matter to me, but the situation in Italy[3] is dangerous. May His Majesty protect him as he can and grant you a safe delivery.

3. I was happy to learn more details from my sister[4] about you and about that angel[5] you have. May God preserve him for us and grant your honors what I beg of him for you. The more I look at the statue the more beautiful it seems, and the crown is lovely. I am thinking of bringing it with me when I return.[6]

Today is the last day of October.

Your honor's unworthy servant,

Teresa of Jesus

1. Don Juan de Albornoz was Doña Inés's husband and the Duke of Alba's secretary.
2. Gonzalo, 19 years old, was the son of Teresa's sister Juana de Ahumada and her husband Juan de Ovalle.
3. She was afraid he would be enlisted in the duke's regiment and be sent to Italy.
4. Juana de Ahumada had brought news of Doña Inés to Seville.
5. Doña Inés's grandson.
6. She had spoken of this statue in the two preceding letters to Doña Inés. As things turned out, she left the statue with the nuns in Seville.

95. To Madre Ana de San Alberto, Seville

Seville, 24 November 1575

(Autograph: Archivo del Ayuntamiento, Caravaca [Murcia])

Caravaca was the first foundation made by Teresa in which she delegated her powers to another Carmelite nun. In this memo she carefully instructs Ana de San Alberto how to proceed.

Jesus. Memo of what must be done in Caravaca.

1. When your reverence arrives, set up the enclosure in your house and let no one enter. While waiting for the grilles to be put up, speak with outsiders in the place where the grilles will be erected, or at the turn, and try to have the grille put up at once.

2. It is necessary before Mass is said—I mean before taking possession of the house—to put up a bell and have a lawyer look at the contract in which these ladies[1] agree to provide an income for the monastery. And show him the certified patent that you have from our most reverend Father[2] in virtue of which, in addition to the power of attorney given you by me,[3] you may accept the monastery without any onus or financial obligation or anything else, for that is how it is given in the contract.

3. When the contract is agreed on—and Padre Ambrosio[4] will watch that everything is done correctly—and you and those ladies have signed it, the Blessed Sacrament may be reserved.

4. Note that the license given by the king[5] must also be noted in the contract, for I don't believe it is necessary to have a license from the bishop. The bell must be rung at Mass in order to take possession of the house. It isn't necessary to bless the church, since it isn't properly speaking a church. Once possession of the house has been taken, those ladies will be able to receive the habit whenever they so desire.

Teresa of Jesus

1. Four ladies sponsored and helped prepare for the foundation in Caravaca (cf. F. 27.1).

2. There was a letter of authorization for the foundation from the general of the order and one from Gracián appointing Ana de San Alberto prioress.
3. For the notarized delegation of power to Ana de San Alberto, see BMC 6.266–67.
4. Ambrosio de San Pedro accompanied the nuns on their journey to Caravaca under orders from Gracián.
5. Teresa had not wanted the foundation to be subject to the Order of Knights of Santiago and so requested and received permission from the king that this requirement be dispensed with (cf. F. 27.2–6).

96. To Padre Jerónimo Gracián, Seville

Seville, End of November 1575

(Autograph: Archivo Histórico Nacional, Madrid)

Gracián has returned to Seville, appointed by the nuncio, Ormaneto, as apostolic visitator of the Carmelites, but his authority is being strongly resisted by the Carmelites of the observance. One of them is a retired bishop and friend of Teresa's. She has just spoken to him and is now feeling scruples for having said too much and having failed in charity.

To our Father Visitator.

1. Jesus. May the grace of the Holy Spirit be with your honor, *padre mio*. Oh, if you could see how unsettled and scrupulous I am today! I tell you I am indeed wretched, and what is worse I never mend my ways. Today I told the bishop what Fray Angel had done in Alba.[1] It didn't seem to him to amount to anything, for he asked me what harm could come from his governing these monasteries and in what way he could do us harm. I also told him something about Medina, for since they are not keeping things secret, I didn't believe it mattered. And I added that it would be good for him to know about certain things because, in my opinion, he doesn't know the nature of them. Nevertheless, I feel so scrupulous that if someone doesn't

come tomorrow to hear my confession I will not receive Communion. What a nice addition to the other worries I now have concerning you.

2. I told him the rest. He had thought that Padilla[2] had written me about it. I let him think so. He says that all the lords of the world could not make them obey unless jurisdiction were had over them, and that includes the archbishop of Granada, to whom they are very close. He says that if they tell him something, they do so only to know whether he agrees with them, and that they don't pay any attention to what he tells them; and also that he is under no obligation to try to get them to obey and he doesn't offend anyone by not wanting to get involved, and that there is no reason for them to pay any attention to him. He says that the substance of the matter doesn't lie in such things, but that there are other means that could be appropriately used.[3]

3. At one point I think he said that if there are censures they will obey. He didn't say this clearly, nor should any attention be paid to it, for perhaps this is just my impression. We are praying earnestly for this intention. All things considered, it would be better for them to obey so as to remove the scandal being given in the city, where they must have many supporters. May God give them light.

4. You should hold off, even if they do not obey, from delivering letters of excommunication, so that they may have time to reflect. This is how I see it. You will know better because you are there; but I wouldn't want it to seem that "you have cornered the king."[4]

5. He says that the friar they sent to Madrid went to Rome and did not speak to the nuncio.[5] They must know already that they do not have a good cause.

6. Tell me how you are, for I now see that you are not without worries. Your worries are an affliction to me, and the help

you get from me is my wretchedness, as you see. May God make me improve and may he watch over you.

7. Nevertheless, the bishop told me, since I told him about it—I mean about Fray Angel[6] because he didn't think the other things were very important—that Fray Angel was free to do so and that I should inform the nuncio who is a higher authority. The more I think about your writing to the general[7] and showing him all the respect you can, the better such an approach seems to be. I don't think it would appear wrong to anyone. It is already enough that things are being done against his will; one can at least write some kind words and pay some attention to him. Consider, *mi padre*, that we promised obedience to him and that nothing would be lost by doing what I say.

Your paternity's unworthy daughter,

Teresa de Jesus

8. My brother[8] brought the enclosed letter. Tell me how your brother[9] is, you never tell me anything about him; and send someone here tomorrow to hear my confession. Not for many years have I had as much distress as I've had since this reform began, for here and there I am always saying more than I would like, without saying what I desire to say.

---

1. The bishop is Diego de León, a Carmelite who had been prior of Seville and a theologian at the Council of Trent. He was at this time retired. In 1574, he obtained permission from the general of the Carmelites to found a discalced Carmelite monastery for friars. Fray Angel de Salazar was the Carmelite provincial of the Castile province. He seems to have made visitations of the discalced Carmelite nuns in Alba and Medina. He must have imposed some ordinances that Teresa disagreed with.
2. Juan Calvo de Padilla
3. She is referring to the resistance that the Carmelites were putting up against Gracián's commission as visitator.
4. An expression taken from the game of chess. She didn't want Gracián to force them into submission.

5. Pedro de Cota, prior of Córdoba, and Luis de Navarrete, prior of Utrera, went to Rome to petition the pope to revoke the authority given Gracián by the nuncio, Ormaneto.
6. Angel de Salazar, provincial of Castile.
7. Padre Giovanni Battista Rossi (Rubeo).
8. Lorenzo de Cepeda.
9. Antonio Gracián, who was seriously sick at the time and died in April 1576.

97. To Diego Ortiz, Toledo

Seville, 26 December 1575

Diego Ortiz has a business matter pending in Madrid. He has asked Teresa for help through Gracián, whose father and brother work as secretaries to the king.

1. Jesus. The grace of the Holy Spirit be with your honor, amen. May God be blessed that you are in good health and the whole household as well. I greatly desire that Señor Alonso Alvarez's[1] health will be restored, for indeed I love him tenderly in the Lord. I am praying for him and telling the sisters to do so as well, and we are also praying for you.

2. I kiss his honor's hands, and he may count this letter as also for him and know that wherever I am he has in me a true servant. And I beg you to tell the same to Señora Doña Francisca Ramírez.[2] Since I receive word of all of you from Mother Prioress,[3] I have neglected to write. And, indeed, I often have so much to do that I am not able to write. Here my health has been good, glory to God. As for the rest, I am happier when up there among Castilians; with these people down here, I don't feel comfortable.

3. I spoke to our Father Provincial[4] about the matter you entrusted to me. He says that it would be necessary for him to be there and that since his brother[5] has been very sick in bed for many days it isn't possible for him to do anything. I have

discussed it here with others, but it seems doubtful that anything could be achieved. So, if there is a tribunal up there and you would stand to lose by any delay, do not hesitate to have recourse to it. In my own business affairs I have little luck in Madrid, even though we do all we can. May the Lord be pleased to do what he sees is necessary, for I see how important this is for us. What a hardship that with all the other trials your honors have in this affair, another one should come along.

May His Majesty watch over you and guide you by the hand, amen; and the same to Señor Alonso Alvarez.

Today is the 26th.

Your honor's unworthy servant,

Teresa of Jesus, Carmelite

---

1. Diego Ortiz's father-in-law.
2. Diego Ortiz's wife.
3. Ana de los Angeles, prioress of Toledo.
4. Jerónimo Gracián.
5. Tomás Gracián, the king's secretary.

98. To Madre María Bautista, Valladolid

Seville, 30 December 1575

(Autograph Fragment: Colegiata de Pastrana)

Two letters from María Bautista have arrived filled with advice for Teresa, which makes her laugh. Teresa gives news about her family. The work of the reform is going badly in Andalusia. Teresa herself is given orders to choose a monastery for herself and stay there. Though the climate of the region is good for her, she desires to go back to Castile.

1. Jesus be with you, my daughter, and may he give you as many good years as I ask of him. I tell you that you make me

laugh when you say that on another day you will say what you think about some things. As usual you have advice to give! On the last day of the Christmas feasts,[1] they gave me the letter that came by way of Medina, and before that the other containing one from *mi padre*.[2] I have found no one through whom I could send a reply. I was overjoyed to receive the news about Señora Doña María,[3] for since the bishop[4] wrote that she was sick with fever, I have been very worried, and so we all have been praying much for her. Tell her this and give her my best regards. May God be blessed who has made her well. My regards also to her daughter and all the others.

2. The letter was written more out of devotion than a desire to fulfill an obligation.[5] I would like to be so disposed toward him that whatever I say will be courteous. It is a strange thing that the affection I have for this other *padre* of ours[6] causes me no embarrassment as though he were no person. Actually, he doesn't know that I am now writing to you. He is doing well. Oh, what trials we undergo with these reforms! There's no obedience; he has excommunicated them; there is another uproar. I tell you I have had much more suffering than happiness since he has been here; things were going much better before.

3. Were I allowed I would already be there with you, for they have notified me of the mandate of our most Reverend *Padre*.[7] That is, I must choose a house and remain there permanently and make no more foundations, for I can no longer go out, because of the Council.[8] Clearly this is due to annoyance over my having come down here. I have reached the conclusion that the mandate came at the request of the friars of the cloth.[9] They think it will do me much harm. And it so pleases me that I doubt whether it will be granted. I would like to choose your house for some reasons that cannot be mentioned in a letter, except for one, which is that you and *mi padre*[10] are there. Father Visitator has not allowed me to leave here because for now he has more authority over me than our

most Reverend Father General. I don't know where it will all end up.

4. It would be very good for me now not to be involved in all the turmoil of these reforms. But the Lord does not wish to free me from these kinds of trials; they are most displeasing to me. Our *padre*[11] tells me I may leave when summer comes. As for what pertains to this house—I mean his foundation—there is no longer any need of my presence. As for my health, clearly this region is better for my health and even in a way for my quiet since here they do not have that inflated opinion of me that they do up there. But there are other reasons why I believe it will be better for me to settle down up there; being closer to our other houses is one of them. May our Lord guide matters, for I don't think I have a personal opinion; wherever they send me I will be happy.

5. My brother[12] has returned—and very sick; the fever, however, is now gone. He didn't meet with success in any of his business affairs, but since his possessions here are now safe, he has more than enough to live on. In the summer he will return to Castile, for this was not the right season. He is delighted with his sister[13] and with Juan de Ovalle—they seek to please him and show him every courtesy—and they are delighted with him. He stopped by here for only a moment and so I didn't say anything about that other matter, but I believe it will be necessary to do no more than mention it and he will do it. As for the children's needs,[14] one page will be more than enough.

6. My brother says that, if the page comes here, his mother can feel assured that he will be treated as though she were with him, and if he is capable and virtuous he can study with them at San Gil,[15] and he'll be better off than elsewhere. And as soon as I said that you desire this, Juan de Ovalle said he would take care of the matter, which made me laugh, for whatever he imagines I want, he is pleased to do. And thus I have succeeded in promoting so close a bond of friendship between

my brother-in-law, his wife, and my brother that I hope in God they will gain much. My brother will not lose thereby, for he is at peace.

7. Juan de Ovalle has been extremely kind to him; the children never stop praising him. I say this because that boy,[16] if he comes—I mean here—in the event that they will not be in Avila by April, there will be no one to teach him anything else but virtue. If I were able to arrange everything, I would be delighted to remove any worry from *mi padre*,[17] for considering his character, I am amazed at how much he takes this to heart; God must have inspired him since the parents of the boy had no other solution. I would be very sorry if he went to Toledo. I don't know why he would rather stay there than in Madrid. I fear it won't come about. May God ordain whatever will be for his service, which is what is important. I am sorry for you,[18] and my desire to stay in your house has greatly diminished. I indeed believe, as I have said, they will send me to the place where there is most need.

8. With regard to his sister, there is no use speaking about it until our *padre* goes there, and indeed I am afraid that in trying to free them from one expense we will get them involved in a greater one. Since she was reared there for her whole life, I don't know how she would get along here, and from what I have been half given to understand, she doesn't get along well with her sisters. What I mean is that she must be somewhat bent on having her own way. May it not be a sanctity made of melancholy! Well, our *padre* will look into everything and until then, nothing should be said.[19]

9. By now you will have received my letter in which I told you that I sent a nun from here as prioress for Caravaca.[20] The nun from your house accepted it with much joy, and so the prioress of Malagón,[21] where she has remained, writes me that she is happy. I tell you she must be a good soul. She wrote me wanting to know about you, and she speaks much about what she owes you and speaks of you with much love. The house

was founded before Christmas, as far as I know; I haven't heard anything.[22]

10. I believe it will be good if you say nothing about the page to *mi padre* until I speak to my brother. Write and tell me how old he is and if he knows how to read, because it's necessary that he go with them to school. My best regards to María de la Cruz[23] and to all, and to Dorotea.[24] And why don't you say anything about how the chaplain is?[25] Look after him, for he is a good man. And how is the arrangement of the room working out and do you find it satisfactory both in winter and summer? As usual, despite what you say about the subprioress, you are not more submissive.[26] O Jesus, how we do not know ourselves! May His Majesty give us light and watch over you for me.

11. With regard to matters concerning the Incarnation, you can write to Isabel de la Cruz,[27] for I can help much more from down here than from up there, and this I am doing. And I hope in God that he will give life to the pope, the king, the nuncio, and our *padre* for one or two years,[28] and everything will be settled. If any of them should die we would be lost, since our most reverend Father General is of the present mind; yet God would resolve the matter in another way. Now I am thinking of writing to him and offer to serve him more so than before, for I am very fond of him and owe him much. It grieves me greatly to see what he is doing because of bad information. Everyone here sends you their best regards.

12. The situation here is not suited to composing songs. Do you think things are going so well? Pray much for our *padre*, for a serious person told the archbishop[29] today that perhaps they will kill him. They are in a state that arouses pity, and even more when one sees the offenses committed against God in this region on the part of nuns and friars. May His Majesty provide a remedy and free me from every offense, for up there I don't know....[30] But if God is to make some use of me, my life matters little; I would like to have many lives.

Tomorrow is New Year's Eve.

Yours,

Teresa of Jesus

13. The weather is such here that I would have to go in search were I to want cold weather at night. May the Lord be praised for this. At least for my health, it is a good region, and nonetheless I do not desire to be here. My brother's becoming a friar[31] has gone nowhere nor will it.

---

1. 27 December.
2. Domingo Báñez.
3. María de Mendoza.
4. The bishop of Avila, Don Alvaro de Mendoza.
5. She is probably alluding to a letter of hers to Báñez.
6. Jerónimo Gracián had returned to Seville and resumed, with much opposition, the visitation of the Carmelites of the observance.
7. The general of the order, Giovanni Battista Rossi (Rubeo). She is alluding to the decision of the recent general chapter in Piacenza (May 1575) to suppress the foundations made by the discalced Carmelites in Andalusia without permission from the general and the orders she received in Seville toward the end of 1575 to retire to one of her monasteries in Castile.
8. The Council of Trent established rules for the enclosure of nuns as a tool of reform.
9. The Carmelites of the observance.
10. Domingo Báñez.
11. Jerónimo Gracián.
12. Lorenzo de Cepeda who had gone to Madrid on business.
13. Juana de Ahumada.
14. Lorenzo's sons, Francisco and Lorenzo. She is alluding to the page that Padre Domingo Báñez had proposed for them.
15. The Jesuit school of San Gil in Avila.
16. The page.
17. Domingo Báñez.
18. María Bautista was a great friend of Padre Báñez's.
19. This person's identity is unknown.

20. Ana de San Alberto.
21. Brianda de San José.
22. The founding nuns of Caravaca arrived there 18 December 1575.
23. One of the first four nuns at Teresa's first foundation in Avila.
24. Dorotea de la Cruz.
25. Pedro Xalame.
26. Antonia del Espíritu Santo was also one of the four first nuns in Avila. Teresa had desired that María Bautista obey the subprioress in matters that pertained to her health.
27. From the Incarnation in Avila, she had been the first prioress of Valladolid. But when Teresa was appointed prioress at the Incarnation (1571), she called her back to be subprioress there.
28. St. Pius V, Philip II, Nicolás Ormaneto, and Jerónimo Gracián.
29. The archbishop of Seville, Don Cristóbal de Rojas y Sandoval.
30. The text is torn here.
31. Don Lorenzo had been thinking of joining the discalced Carmelite friars.

99. To Padre Jerónimo Gracián, Seville(?)

Seville, December 1575(?)

In this fragment it seems Gracián is trying to prevent a postulant from entering because of an insufficient dowry.

Your paternity should not think, as I have written at other times, that wealth and all other qualifications are found together in one individual. I repeat that if I had not made adaptations—by considering the small number of postulants entering—you would not now have any nuns at all either for the one need or for the other.

100. To Tomás Gracián, Madrid

Seville, December 1575

Tomás Gracián, Padre Jerónimo Gracián's brother and a secretary to Philip II, testified at the process for Teresa's canonization that he received the following words from her while Padre Gracián was suffering some persecutions as apostolic visitator (BMC 20.288).

⁂

Our *padre*[1] is very happy with the persecutions he is now undergoing, but they are child's play in comparison with the many that are still to come for him. Yet, in the end our Lord will deliver him from them....

1. Jerónimo Gracián.

Letters 101–171 (1576)

101. To Doña Ana Enríquez (?), Valladolid

Seville, January 1576(?)

(Autograph Fragment: DCN, Arco Mirelli, Chiaia [Naples])

This letter consists of two worn fragments that perhaps do not belong together. The destinee and the date are uncertain.

1. Jesus. The grace of the Holy Spirit be always with your honor. I already see that I do not merit the favor you do me if one looks at the many days it has taken me to respond. But I know that the desire I have of seeing you very holy....The prioress doesn't write anything now about my Señora Doña Mariana,[1] and so I think she must have left.

2. I hope in the Lord that wherever she may be she will greatly serve His Majesty. I desire to do the same, and so we will see each other where there will be no fear of absences. I want to know where.[2]...

Your honor's unworthy servant and subject,

Teresa of Jesus

1. A postulant who has not been identified.
2. What follows comes from another fragment.

102. To Padre Juan Bautista Rubeo, Cremona

Seville, January–February(?) 1576

(Autograph fragments: Parish of Esquivias [Toledo]; DCN Santa Ana, Madrid; DCF, Santa Teresa al Museo, Naples)

Gracián has returned to Seville with new powers from the nuncio. The Andalusian and Castilian friars who were present at the chapter of Piacenza have returned to Spain. Teresa learns in a twisted version the decision made in her regard. In Avila Fray John of the Cross is arrested for the first time. Teresa has written a number of letters to the general, but doesn't know whether he has received them. She tries to clear the air and get the general and Gracián to enter into direct dialogue. She manifests her sad conviction that the general no longer pays any attention to what she has to say. She makes an autograph copy of this letter for herself.

1. Jesus. The grace of the Holy Spirit be always with your lordship, amen. After I arrived here in Seville, I wrote to you three or four times,[1] and I did not write any more because the fathers who returned from the chapter told me that you would not be in Rome, that you had gone to visit the Mantuans.[2] May God be blessed that the chapter is over. In those letters I also gave you an account of the monasteries that were founded this year,[3] which are three: Beas, Caravaca, and this one here. You have in them subjects who are great servants of God. Two of the houses were founded with an income; the one in this city was founded in poverty.[4] We still do not have our own house; but I hope in the Lord that we will. Because I am certain that one of these letters must have reached you, I am not going to give a detailed account of everything in this one.

2. I also mentioned how different speaking with these discalced fathers—I mean Padre Maestro Gracián and Mariano—is from what one would imagine through what I heard in Castile. Certainly they are your true sons, and I would dare say that, substantially, none of those who insist they are your true sons would surpass them. Since they have asked me to be an intermediary so that you may look favorably toward

them again, for they did not dare write to you,[5] I begged you in those letters as earnestly as I could, and so I beg you now, for the love of our Lord, that you do me this favor and believe my words. There is no reason for me to say anything but the complete truth, aside from the fact that I would consider it an offense against God not to speak the truth. And even if it were not an offense against God, I would consider it a great evil and betrayal with respect to a father I so love.

3. When we stand before the judgment throne, you will see what you owe your true daughter Teresa of Jesus. This alone consoles me in these matters; for I well know there must be some who say the contrary. And so, in every way that I can I will try to make all understand, I mean all those who are not prejudiced, that I am your true daughter and will continue to be this as long as I live.

4. I have already written to you about the commission Padre Gracián received from the nuncio and how he was called to Madrid.[6] You must know by now how he was again given the task of visitator to the discalced friars and nuns and to the province of Andalusia. I know very definitely that with regard to the latter, he tried to refuse in every way he could—although this is not being mentioned, it is true—and that his brother, the secretary,[7] was also opposed because nothing would come of it but a great trial.

5. But if these fathers would have listened to me after it had become a fact, everything would have been done quietly and as though among brothers. And I did all I could to foster this attitude.[8] For, apart from the fact of it being the correct attitude, these fathers have helped us in every way since we have been here. And, as I wrote to you, I find gifted and learned persons here of the kind that I would love to have in our province of Castile.

6. I am always fond of making a virtue out of necessity, as they say, and so I would have wished that when they decided to resist they would have considered whether or not they would

be able to win out. On the other hand, I am not surprised that they are tired of so many visitations and innovations that, for our sins, have been taking place for a good number of years.[9] May it please the Lord that we know how to profit from this, since His Majesty is waking us up. Yet, since the visitator is from the same order, there is less humiliation. And I hope in God that if you show favor to this *padre* in such a way that he understands that he is in your good graces, everything will proceed very well. He is writing to you and has a great desire for what I said and not to displease you, for he considers himself your obedient son.

7. What I again want to ask you, for love of our Lord and his glorious Mother (whom you so love, and this *padre* does also since he entered the order through his devotion to her) is that you answer him and do so with gentleness and leave aside the things of the past, even though he may have been somewhat at fault, and receive him as your son and subject, for he truly is. And poor Mariano is also, although sometimes it is not evident. I am not surprised that what he wrote to you differed from what he intended, since he doesn't know how to express himself. He confesses in fact that he never intended either in word or in deed to offend you.[10] Since the devil gains so much when things are interpreted according to his own wishes, he must have pushed these fathers to conduct their affairs badly without their meaning to do so.

8. But note, it is characteristic of sons to make mistakes and of fathers to forgive and overlook faults. For the love of our Lord, I beg you to do me this favor. See how this would be appropriate for many reasons that perhaps you would not understand over there as I do here. And even though we women are not good for giving counsel, we sometimes hit the mark. I don't know what harm could come of it and, as I say, there can be many advantages. And I don't see that any harm could come from your being receptive to those who would very willingly cast themselves at your feet, if you were present, for God

never fails to forgive. And no harm can come from your making it known that you are pleased that the reform be carried out by one of your subjects and sons, and, as though in exchange for this, you are happy to forgive him.

9. Would that there were many to whom this task could be entrusted! But apparently there are none with the talents of this *padre* (for I am certain that if you were to see him you would agree). Why don't you show that you are pleased to have him as your subject and let everyone understand that this reform, if carried out correctly, is being done with your approval and with your advice and counsel? And were others to understand that you are pleased with this work of reform, everything would proceed more smoothly. There are many more things I would like to say in this regard, but I think it will be more to the point for me to beg our Lord to give you understanding of what is appropriate for you to do; because for some time now you have paid no attention to my words. I am fully certain that if I am mistaken in my words, my will does not intend to be.

10. Padre Fray Antonio de Jesús is here, for he couldn't get out of coming.[11] Nonetheless, he also has begun to defend himself as have the other fathers. He is writing to you. Perhaps he will be more fortunate than I in getting you to believe us, as would be fitting, with regard to all I am saying. May our Lord provide, as he can, in keeping with our need.

11. I learned of the general chapter act in which I am ordered to remain in one house and not go out. Father Provincial, Fray Angel, had sent it here to Padre Ulloa with orders that he notify me.[12] He thought that it would cause me much grief, which was the intention of these fathers in procuring it, so it was kept from me. It must have been little less than a month ago that I was able to get them to give it to me, for I had heard of it from elsewhere.

12. I assure you that from what I understand of myself, it would have been a great gift and happiness for me if you had

sent it to me with a letter to let me know that you were feeling sorry about the great trials I was undergoing in making these foundations—for I am not much for suffering—and that as a reward you were ordering me to rest. For even taking into consideration the way it did come, it consoled me greatly to know I could live in peace.

13. Since I have such great love for you, I could not help, sensitive as I am, feeling hurt that the order should come as though to someone very disobedient and in such a way that Padre Fray Angel could publish it in Madrid before I knew anything about it, as though they were using force with me. And so he wrote me that I could have recourse to the papal chamber, as though that would bring me great relief. Indeed, even if the work of making foundations, a task you had given me, had not cost me such great trials, it wouldn't enter my mind not to obey, nor would God allow me to find any happiness in going against your will. For I can truthfully say—and our Lord knows this—that if I experienced some relief in the trials and anxieties and afflictions and slander that I have suffered, it was in the thought that I was doing your will and making you happy. And now, too, it will bring me relief to do what you command.

14. I wanted to carry out the orders at once. It was close to Christmas and since the journey is so long, they wouldn't allow me, knowing that you would not want to put my health at risk. So, I am still here, but with the intention of remaining in this house only until after the winter passes. I have little in common with the people of Andalusia. And what I beseech you is that you don't forget to write to me wherever I may be. Since I will no longer have business to attend to—which will certainly bring me great happiness—I am afraid you will forget me, although I will not give you the chance to do so. Even though it may tire you, I will not fail to write to you for the sake of my own peace of mind.

15. In these parts they have never understood, nor do they understand, the Council or *Motu proprio*[13] as having taken away

from prelates the authority to allow nuns to go outside to do things for the good of the order, for many reason for doing so may occur. I do not say this in regard to myself, but so that you will not have any scruple about the past, for I am not good for anything (and not only am I ready to stay in one house, for this will give me some relief and rest, but even stay in a prison cell if that would make you happy—and gladly for the rest of my life). For even though I had the patent letters, I never went anywhere to make a foundation—for otherwise, clearly, I could not have gone—without a written order or license from the prelate. And so Padre Fray Angel gave it to me for Beas and Caravaca, and Padre Gracián for here, for he had the same commission from the nuncio then that he has now, but he wasn't using it. Yet, Padre Fray Angel said that I was an apostate and excommunicated.[14] May God pardon him for you are a witness to how I strove that you would always be on good terms with him and to make him happy—I mean in matters that would not be displeasing to God—but he has never managed to act kindly toward me.

16. It would be much more to his advantage if he were as ill-disposed to Valdemoro.[15] Being prior in Avila, the latter removed the discalced friars from the Incarnation causing great scandal to the people, and he has so greatly disturbed the nuns—the spirit of the house had been something to praise God for—that it is heart-breaking to see. I have received word that to excuse him they are blaming themselves. Now the discalced friars have returned and, according to what has been written to me, the nuncio has given orders that none of the friars of the observance be confessor to the nuns there.

17. The grief of those nuns has deeply afflicted me, for they are given no more than bread and, on the other hand, so much disturbance that it rouses me to great pity. May God provide a remedy for everything, and may he preserve you for many years to come. Today they told me that the general of the Dominicans is coming here. If only God would give me the grace of

providing an occasion for you to come, although, on the other hand, I would regret the fatigue it would cost you. And so my rest will have to wait for that eternity that has no end, where you will see what you owe me. Please God through his mercy that I will be worthy of it.

18. I commend myself to the prayers of the reverend fathers who are your companions. These subjects and daughters of yours ask for your blessing, and I ask the same for myself.[16]

---

1. Only one of these letters has been preserved, that of 18 June 1575.
2. The Mantuan Congregation was a Carmelite reform that at the time had 42 houses scattered through northern and central Italy.
3. The past year.
4. The houses founded in poverty had no established income, but depended on alms and what could be earned through spinning and other handiwork. This, though not always possible, was Teresa's ideal (cf. L. 35).
5. See Ltr. 83.3.
6. See Ltr. 83.5,9.
7. Antonio Gracián, one of the king's secretaries.
8. She is alluding to the opposition of the Carmelites in Seville to Gracián as visitator.
9. Official canonical visitations of the Carmelites in Andalusia had been made by the general, Giovanni Rossi, by the Dominican Francisco de Vargas, and now by Jerónimo Gracián.
10. It seems that despite Teresa's insistence neither Gracián wrote to the general nor the general to Gracián. But Ambrosio Mariano de San Benito, the one least apt to write a tactful letter, did write and succeeded in offending him.
11. Padre Antonio de Jesús (Heredia) had been sent from Almodóvar del Campo to be prior of the discalced Carmelite friars at Los Remedios in Seville.
12. Angel de Salazar was the provincial of Castile, and Miguel de Ulloa was the prior of the Carmelites of the observance in Seville.
13. Neither the decrees of the Council of Trent nor those of the pope.
14. The nuncio, Nicolás Ormaneto, had given these faculties to Gracián 22 September 1574. Fray Angel de Salazar, the provincial.
15. Fray Alonso de Valdemoro was prior of the Carmelites of the observance in Avila. The discalced friars at the Incarnation were St. John

of the Cross and Francisco de los Apóstoles (or Germán de Santo Matía). They had been seized by Valdemoro and held captive in Medina del Campo until the nuncio intervened and ordered that they be released and return as confessors to the Incarnation.

16. Since the letter is an autograph copy of the text sent to the general, it has no signature.

103. To Don Rodrigo de Moya, Caravaca

Seville, 19 February 1576

Rodrigo de Moya was the father of one of the lady foundresses of Caravaca who allowed the nuns to live in a part of his house while they looked for a permanent one. False rumors had reached Teresa about misunderstandings between him and the prioress. Teresa encourages him regarding some complications that had arisen.

1. Jesus. The grace of the Holy Spirit be with your honor. I was greatly relieved to learn from your letter that matters are quite different from what had been believed here. May God be blessed for everything, for Mother Prioress[1] surprised me and I would have been displeased if she had done anything against your will. I more or less understand what moved the one who told us into thinking she was telling the truth. For me it was really difficult to believe and that is why I wrote to ask you what you had observed. Mother Prioress always tells me of how indebted she is to you, of the comfort you are to her, and the help you give her in everything.

2. As for the price of the house, I am not unhappy nor should you be. In exchange for a house being in a good locality, I never mind giving a third more than what it is worth—and I've even ended up giving a half more. It is so important to have a monastery well located that it would be a mistake to look at the price. Considering the water and the view, I would elsewhere

have very gladly paid much more than what the house cost. Glory to God that you were so successful.

3. With regard to the vicar general,[2] you should feel no regrets, for, as you say, that is not a priority. The monastery was founded with a license from the council of the Order of Knights and a mandate from the king. If the king[3] had not given a mandate—he does me a great favor in this respect because of the good reputation these monasteries have—we may have experienced what happened to the foundress[4] of Beas. For twelve years she sought authorization to make a foundation for another religious order, not knowing about this one, and without succeeding. Nor after a monastery is founded, can it be closed down for light reasons; there is nothing to fear in this regard. Now, I believe, they will send you all the documents, except the one I mention in the letter to Señor Miguel Caja,[5] but I will send that one to you soon. And if I do not send it, the reason will be that the bishop,[6] as he says in a letter that arrived today, will be going there. He will go with the readiness to accept the foundation at once, for he is a good gentleman and has relatives and friends who will help me in every way, and so there is no reason to hesitate.

4. The mistake was in not letting me know immediately, for since I had so often written that I would not make the foundation without the license of the ordinary, I certainly thought that it had been given, for I would not have left without attending to this matter. Since I have mentioned here that they have an income of seven hundred ducats (as Mother Prioress has written me and also written to the bishop), the figure must be true. If a nun is received with a small dowry, it may be used to bring the income to the correct amount, if that is lacking. You should not feel sorry, for our Lord wants us to suffer something; in fact this foundation at first made me suspicious because it came about so peacefully. All the foundations, which our Lord will make great use of, afflict the devil and so there is always something for us to suffer. I rejoiced over the improved health

of our sister and señora.[7] Please God it will last for many years, and may he watch over you and Señora Doña Constanza.[8] I kiss the hands of both your honors many times.

Today is Septuagesima Sunday.

Your unworthy servant,

Teresa of Jesus

---

1. The prioress of Caravaca, Ana de San Alberto.
2. On account of the death of the bishop of Caravaca, the episcopal see was vacant at the time of the foundation.
3. Cf. F. 27.6. The date of the royal dispatch is 9 June 1575.
4. Catalina Sandoval y Godínez (de Jesús).
5. A magistrate in Caravaca and brother of one of the lady foundresses, who in Carmel took the name Francisca de San José.
6. The bishop of Cartagena, Gómez Zapata, who had been appointed 10 February 1575.
7. Don Rodrigo's daughter in becoming a Carmelite took the name Francisca de la Cruz.
8. Although her identity is not certain, she may have been one of Don Rodrigo's daughters.

104. To Madre María Bautista, Valladolid

Seville, 19 February 1576

(Autograph fragment: DCN of Loeches in Madrid)

She is worn out from letter writing and doesn't yet know where she will be sent to live. The nuncio wants her to make more foundations even though she has been forbidden to do so by the general. Báñez's illness distresses her. The nuns in Valladolid are urged to be detached from her coming to live among them.

1. Jesus be with you, my daughter. I wanted to be in a more restful state when writing to you. For all that I have just read

and written amazes me in that I was able to do it, and so I've decided to be brief. Please God I can be.

2. With regard to my going to Valladolid, were they in their right minds when they thought I could make the choice rather than go where I was sent?[1] Our *padre*[2] spoke of Valladolid for reasons that no longer exist, and I don't believe he ever had the intention that I go there permanently; but yes, it was my desire. The nuncio[3] has already written to me to say that I should continue making foundations as before. Our *padre* must have so explained matters that the two came to agree. From the time the nuncio was informed, he has been of this mind. I am determined not to make any foundations unless given orders....now is the time when our *padre* will begin the visitation of the friars, for he still has not begun.[4]

3. My brothers[5] are causing a stir so that I might return with them, especially Lorenzo. He says he will wait here until my orders come, for he thinks our *padre* is softening in his resistance. I only remain silent and ask the Lord to inspire his heart with that which will best fit God's plan and by which I will please the Lord the most, for this is what will make me happy. And do the same up there, I beg you. Tell this to my daughters, and may God reward them for their joy; but let them believe me and never look for happiness in things that are passing, for they will be disappointed, and tell my Casilda[6] the same since I am not able to write to her.

4. In a letter by way of Medina that the prioress[7] will have sent you, I mentioned that I received your letters with the money for portage. Now don't send any more portage until I tell you. With regard to Agustina,[8] do what you have done up until now...it is very small and when one subtracts the dowry that was given and the cost of food, it is nothing. And so her mother has written me again to assure me that the reason does not lie in this but in the desire of her daughter. I also respect this desire, and perhaps it is the true motive. If it is of God, he will enlighten us.

5. I don't know how I've left to the last speaking about my distress over the illness of *mi padre*.[9] I'm afraid he did one of those penances customary during Advent, such as sleeping on the floor, for he doesn't usually suffer this illness. Make him keep his feet well covered. Indeed, this pain is not hard to put up with![10] Once it takes hold, it's a wretched thing and lasts for so many days. Make sure he is dressing warmly enough. Blessed be God that he is doing better. There is nothing that so stirs me to pity as this kind of severe pain, even when in my enemies....Give him my regards and very best wishes.

6. The page[11] is very young if he is no more than eleven years old. If he were twelve, it would be better. I would like him to know how to write before coming here, for he will have to accompany the boys[12] to school at San Gil in Avila and begin his studies. My brother[13] said that since this was an initiative of Padre Fray Domingo's he would accept the page even if there is no need, for I told him how indebted I am to *mi padre*....

7. I would very much like to accept the lay sister[14] for that monastery, but I don't see how. For the good Asensio[15] has asked us to accept one of his servants, and I have to take a lay sister away from Medina so that this servant may live there. The aspirant is as holy as Estefanía[16] and still hasn't received the habit; on the other hand, ask Alberta.[17] If you would accept this saint there, you would be making me happy. I would bet that if Señora Doña María[18] knew her, she would ask me for her. You could accept her in place of Doña Mariana,[19] and I could ask our *padre* to find a place for the latter.

8. It's strange that you have not told me what he himself said, perhaps because he doesn't know where he will be sent. I was waiting to see how....Do all you can to learn about her qualities. If she is good, even though we may not know where to place her, we should accept her. Here we are lacking one, and I would love to have one come from Castile. But it is so far away that I don't see how this could be done. You should know that our *padre* has many sisters, and they are very poor; and

since the Blessed Virgin took him away from his parents whom he was supporting, it's necessary that we help them.

1. In the previous letter to María Bautista, Teresa mentioned her preference for the Carmel of Valladolid as the place where she would remain in compliance with the chapter of Piacenza.
2. Jerónimo Gracián.
3. Nicolás Ormaneto.
4. Gracián had notified the Carmelites of Seville of his powers as visitator on 21 November, but he met with strong resistance and so delayed before beginning.
5. Lorenzo de Cepeda and Pedro de Ahumada.
6. Casilda de Padilla, still a novice in Valladolid.
7. The prioress of Medina was Inés de Jesús.
8. She is probably referring to Agustina del Espíritu Santo, who made her profession in Medina in 1578.
9. Domingo Báñez.
10. An ironical statement made by Teresa in view of Báñez's calm endurance of the illness.
11. He was spoken of in the previous letter to María Bautista.
12. Don Lorenzo's children.
13. Lorenzo.
14. Francisca de Jesús, a cousin of Blessed Anne of St. Bartholomew. She made her profession in Medina in 1578.
15. Asensio Galiano, a contractor and friend in Medina.
16. Estefanía de los Apóstoles in Valladolid. Cf. F. 11.1.
17. Alberta Bautista, at one time a prioress in Medina.
18. Doña María de Mendoza.
19. A postulant who has not been identified.

105. To María Bautista, Valladolid

Seville, 29 April 1576

Teresa has just learned that the nuns in Seville will be able to move into their new house. The letter is meant for the nuns in Medina and Salamanca as well because she wants them to know of a let-up in the troubles the Seville nuns had been undergoing on account of calumnies presented against them to the Inquisition. On the other hand her brother Lorenzo has had to seek sanctuary because of unjust tax demands. She then responds to some of María Bautista's counsels.

❖❖❖❖

1. Jesus. The grace of the Holy Spirit be with you, my daughter. The mail carrier is leaving tomorrow, but because I didn't have any good news to tell you I wasn't going to write. Tonight, a little before we closed the door, they sent word to me that the man living in the house has now agreed to allow us to come the day after tomorrow, the feast of Saints Philip and James,[1] which makes me think that the Lord is beginning to soften our trials.

2. Send this to Mother Prioress in Medina[2] whenever you can for she will be feeling distressed over a letter I wrote to her, even though I did anything but exaggerate our trials. You should know that with the exception of the foundation of St. Joseph's[3] everything has been a trifle in comparison with what I have suffered here. When you learn the details, you will see what I mean when I say that only through God's mercy will things turn out well for us. In fact we can say they already have. The injustices that are the common practice in this area, the deception and the duplicity are a strange thing. I tell you, there is every reason for the reputation this region has. May the Lord be blessed who draws good from everything. On seeing so many instances of this, I have been experiencing a strange joy. If my brother[4] had not been here, we wouldn't have been able to do anything at all.

3. He has suffered very much and most willingly spent his money and supported us in everything, which makes us praise God. How right these sisters are to love him, for they received no help from others, but only more trouble. Now he is in hiding on our account, and it was lucky that he wasn't put in the prison here which is like a hell; and everything is done without justice, for they want us to pay what we do not owe and

take him as surety.[5] The only way to end this is to have recourse to Madrid, for there is no other way out, but he has been pleased to suffer something for God.

4. He is in the Carmelite monastery with our *padre*,[6] on whom trials are falling like hail. Well, I have a hard time trying to hide our own from him, for these are what have tormented him most, and rightly so.

5. That you may know what I am referring to, remember the things I wrote concerning the lies which that nun who left told about us.[7] Well, that was nothing in comparison with what she then accused us of at a most inopportune time and without any reason— you will find out some day. Those to whom she told so much came here without warning—and more than once—and without cause. The source of all this became clear to us through the person who was called in. As for myself, I tell you that God granted me such a favor that I was immersed in delight. My joy surpassed my awareness of the great harm that could come to all our houses. It is a wonderful thing to have a secure conscience and to be free.

6. Her companion[8] entered another monastery. And yesterday it was confirmed to me that this companion went out of her mind, and for no other reason than that she left here. See how great are the judgments of God, who stands up for the truth; and now it is clear that the accusations were all nonsense. And nonsense also was what she said of us, that we tied the hands and feet of the nuns and flogged them—would to God all the accusations had been of that sort. On top of this very serious lie, she said a thousand other things, which made me see clearly that the Lord wanted to try us with affliction so as to bring all to a happy conclusion, as he did. Consequently, don't be sad. Rather I hope we will be able to leave soon, once the nuns have moved to their new house. The Franciscans have shown no more signs of life, and if they do after the nuns have taken possession of the house, it won't matter.[9]

7. The nuns here are great souls, and this prioress has a courage that has amazed me—much more courage than I have.[10] It seems to me that my presence here has been a help to them, for the blows fall on me. She is very intelligent. I tell you that in my opinion she is perfect for Andalusia. And how necessary it was to choose well the nuns who were brought here.

I am well, although at first my health had not been good. This syrup is reinvigorating me. Our *padre* is ailing, but without a fever. He doesn't know that I am writing to you. Pray for him, and that God will bring us through all these affairs happily. Yes, I believe he will. Oh, what a year I've gone through here!

8. Let's come now to your counsels. With regard to the first, the title *"Don"* is given in the Indies to all those who have vassals. But when my nephews arrived here, I asked their father not to call them by that title, and I gave my reasons. He complied and they were calm and unassuming about it. When Juan de Ovalle and my sister came, my reasons were insufficient. (I don't know whether or not they were trying to defend the title of their own son.) Since my brother was not here, for he was absent a long while, and I was not with them when he arrived back, they had so many reasons in favor that all mine proved of little use. True, in Avila nothing else matters but this title, which is a shame. And certainly, the matter touches me deeply because of what it will do to their reputation; as for mine I don't think I ever think about it, nor should it matter to you, for next to the other things they say about me, this is nothing. Out of love for you I will speak to their father again, but I don't think there is any way of changing the mind of their uncle and aunt who have become accustomed to it. I am very embarrassed every time I hear the title used.

9. As for Teresa's letter to Padilla,[11] I don't believe she wrote to anyone except to the prioress of Medina and to you so as to bring joy to the two of you. I believe that one time she did

write to him two or three words. You are convinced that I am blinded by her and my brother, and nothing can make you get this out of your head. Certainly I should be, were I different from what I am. But consider that despite all I owe him, I am happy that he was forced into hiding because he is prevented from coming here often. And it is true that he is something of a bother, although when I tell him to go because our *padre* or someone else is coming, he is as obliging as an angel. Not that I fail to love him dearly, for I do love him, but I would like to be alone. All of this is so, whatever others may think—which matters little.[12]

10. Padilla must have been joking in saying that he was visitator. I know him well. Nonetheless, he's been a great help and we owe him much. No one is without faults—what do you want! I am highly pleased that Doña María[13] is happy with that permission. Give her my best regards, for since it is very late I am not writing to her, and tell her I am sorry that the duchess[14] is not with her. I see that the Lord wants her to have him alone as her company and consolation.

11. I know nothing more about Avila than what you write me. May God be with you. My regards to Casilda[15] and all the sisters and especially to my Padre Fray Domingo.[16] I wished very much that he would have delayed his trip to Avila until I got there; but since the Lord wills that everything be a cross, so be it. Do not neglect to write me. Don't send away that nun you say is so good. Or, maybe she would want to come here, for I would like to bring some nuns down here, if I could. Take note—in my opinion, there is no reason to be troubled, for I believe that everything will go well.

12. Don't forget to send this to Mother Prioress in Medina and have her send it to the prioress in Salamanca,[17] and let it be for all three of you. May God make you saints. I confess that the people in this area are not for me and that I desire to be in the land of promise, if God wills. Although if I knew I would serve him better here, I would gladly remain; although the sinful

abominations that go on here are a painful affliction. You would be frightened by them. May the Lord provide a remedy.

Today is White Sunday. Yours,

Teresa of Jesus

13. Regards to my María de la Cruz and the subprioress.[18] Read this to my María de la Cruz. Have all your nuns pray for us.

1. May 1, the day on which they moved to the new house.
2. Inés de Jesús (Tapia).
3. The first foundation, which was made in Avila.
4. Lorenzo de Cepeda, who provided the community with financial help.
5. Demands were being made on the nuns as buyers of the house to pay the excise, which they were not obliged to pay. Efforts were then made to imprison Lorenzo who had given surety.
6. Jerónimo Gracián.
7. One of the nuns who had enjoyed a reputation for holiness outside the monastery became dissatisfied after entering and had to leave. She tried to compensate for what the people viewed as a defect by calumniating the nuns and accusing them to the Inquisition.
8. Another novice whom this disgruntled nun induced to leave with her.
9. At first the Franciscan friars, who had a house close by, opposed the nuns' move (see F. 25.5–7).
10. María de San José.
11. Teresa is her niece and Juan Calvo de Padilla a priest interested in the reform of religious orders.
12. Cf. ST. 41.
13. María de Mendoza, the bishop of Avila's sister.
14. Probably the duchess of Osuna, Ana de Guzmán y Aragón.
15. Casilda de Padilla.
16. Domingo Báñez.
17. Ana de la Encarnación.
18. María de la Cruz and Antonia del Espíritu Santo (subprioress) had been among the first members of the community of St. Joseph's in Avila.

106. To Ambrosio Mariano, Madrid

Seville, 9 May 1576

(Autograph: DCN, Seville)

Ambrosio Mariano has departed Seville for Madrid, leaving Teresa enmeshed in problems concerning both the acquisition of a house for the nuns and the conflict that had arisen between the Carmelites of Andalusia and the discalced Carmelite friars. The latter conflict arose when Gracián and Mariano arrived in Seville. The first has been wonderfully resolved; the second has been exacerbated by the arrival of Tostado in Andalusia. Mariano was a difficult man to deal with and caused Teresa much suffering.

1. Jesus. The grace of the Holy Spirit be with your reverence. Oh, God help me, how apt is your temperament to lead me into temptation. I tell you my virtue has to be great in order to write you this letter. And what is worse, I fear that something of your temperament will stick to *mi padre*, Licentiate Padilla[1]—may God forgive you both—since he does not write to me or even send regards, although I am so indebted to Licentiate Padilla that however neglectful he is I cannot neglect him. So I ask you to consider this letter as meant also for him.

2. When I consider the embroilment you left me with and how unaware you are of everything,[2] I don't know what to think except *accursed be the man*, et cetera.[3] But since evil is to be repaid with good, I wanted to write this so that you will know that on the feast of St. James[4] we will take possession of the house. And the friars have been as silent as the dead.[5] Our *padre*[6] spoke to Navarro,[7] and he is the one who I think made them keep quiet.

3. The house is such that the sisters never cease thanking God. May he be blessed for everything. All say that what we paid was nothing and are certain that today it would cost 20,000

ducats to build. They say the site is one of the good ones in Seville. The good prior of *las Cuevas*[8] came here twice—he is delighted with the house—and Fray Bartolomé de Aguilar[9] came once before leaving, for I already wrote you that he was going to the chapter. It has been a great blessing that we happened to stumble upon this house, although because of the excise we got into some serious conflict.[10] Well, I think we are going to have to pay everything. My brother had to give us a loan and he is watching over the renovation work, which relieves me of a great burden. The notary was the one who made the mistake in regard to the excise. Our *padre* is delighted with the house and so is everyone else. Padre Soto[11] has serious statements to make—he was just here—and says that since you don't write to me, he will not write to you. The church will be set up in the entrance way; it will look very nice. Everything is turning out perfectly. All of this is in regard to the house.

4. With regard to Tostado,[12] a friar has now come who left him in Barcelona in March. This friar carries a patent letter (for he was a conventual here), which Tostado signs as vicar general for all Spain. Cota[13] came yesterday He is hidden in Don Jerónimo's house, hoping that Fray Agustín Juárez[14] will come today, according to what they say. The first two things are true, for I saw the patent letter and know that the other person is here. The information about the provincial is certain, and they say he is coming to take up his office and bringing with him a *Motu* from the pope[15] which, according to what they say, leaves nothing more to be desired as far as the proposal of the calced friars goes. The prior,[16] also, told me today that one among them in whom he has confidence assured him this was so.

5. His most illustrious lordship our archbishop,[17] his assistant, and his public attorney are of the opinion that our *padre* should hide from them so that he cannot be notified of anything until the orders of the most illustrious nuncio[18] are known, and this for many reasons they consider valid. So he is going to Castile without continuing the visitation and by a different route.

This is not the time to be making visitations,[19] for they are very agitated. May God forgive the one who cuts short so much good, although I certainly believe this is part of God's design for the sake of greater good. May it please His Majesty that they merit to make amends. As for the discalced friars, I have no doubt that they will make much progress in perfection, certain that the Lord disposes all for their greater good. Our *padre* appointed Evangelista,[20] who is the prior of the Carmelite community, vicar provincial. He is now waiting for this blow. I am telling him, however, that since he is not the head, they will not notify him of anything. He has courage, and his assistant is well disposed to help him if something should happen.

6. Tomorrow the prior and the subprior of Los Remedios[21] are going to Umbrete, for the archbishop who is there sent for them. If those two[22] do not carry documents that would annul what the visitator[23] has done—and I don't think they do—much will already be done. May the Lord direct all for his service, and may he free you from the siren's song,[24] and also *mi padre*, Licentiate Padilla, whose hands my brother kisses many times and those of your reverence. I would love, infinitely, to have you here, for I believe you would be delighted to see how well things have turned out.

7. We came three days before the lieutenant[25] left. We became great friends with him and his wife. They all gave us plenty to eat and showed us much kindness. The lieutenant says there is no better house in Seville nor a better site. I don't think one will suffer from the heat in it. The patio looks like it was made of *alcorza*.[26] Now everyone enters through it—because Mass is being said in a room until the church is constructed—and they see the whole house. Off the inner patio there are nice rooms; we are better-off there than in the other house. The garden is delightful, the views magnificent. It cost us a lot of trouble, but I consider it all worthwhile because I would never have imagined it would be this good. Mother Prioress[27] and all the sisters commend themselves to your prayers

and those of my Padre Padilla; as I do to those of Father Provincial, Fray Angel.[28] It amazes me how quickly the latter arrived in Madrid. May it please God that the chapter[29] will result in his service, and it will if it is carried out as you say. May God watch over you despite all your faults and make you very holy. I had not thought the house was such a good one.

Today is 9 May.

8. Would you keep me informed about what is happening, for our *padre* is not here and I have no way of finding out about anything. I wouldn't want you to leave there without learning how all this ends. I tell you that I miss you, for you understand our affairs, and we are now proceeding with care and caution. My regards to Padre Fray Vicente[30] and congratulations to him for his profession.

Your reverence's unworthy servant,

Teresa of Jesus, Carmelite

9. Oh, the lies that circulate down here! It's enough to make you faint. Now they just told me that the visitator[31] for the friars of the cloth is in Carmona—that's how they refer to him—and that in many monasteries they have given him their obedience. Nonetheless, I fear these things from Rome, for I remember the past, even though I do not think they will be to our harm but to our advantage. Those calced friars must have something up their sleeve. They wouldn't be so foolish as to come here, for they still don't know that our *padre* has departed;[32] they think he is here. We are receiving many compliments and the neighbors are jubilant. I would like to see our discalced affairs brought to a conclusion, for after all the Lord won't put up with those other friars much longer; so many misfortunes will have to have an ending.

---

1. Juan Calvo de Padilla, the priest friend of Teresa's who was intensely involved in reform.

2. Mariano left Seville at the time in which the nuns were in a tangle of difficulties regarding the foundation in Seville.
3. Ironical allusion to Jer. 17.5.
4. St. James the Less, 1 May.
5. Probably the Franciscan friars who at first tried to prevent the move (cf. F. 27.5–6).
6. Jerónimo Gracián.
7. This person's identity is unknown.
8. The prior of the Carthusian monastery of Las Cuevas, Hernando de Pantoja.
9. A Dominican.
10. A tax incurred in the purchase of the house through an error made by the notary.
11. An elderly priest benefactor of the nuns in Seville.
12. Jerónimo Tostado was in fact made vicar general of the Carmelites in Spain to help put into force the ordinances of the Chapter of Piacenza. In Barcelona at the time of this letter, he was later, 24 May 1576, appointed provincial of the Carmelites of Catalonia.
13. Pedro de Cota, prior of the Carmelites in Córdoba, had gone to Rome to seek a revocation of the visitation being made by Gracián and claimed to have documents to that effect. According to Gracián, they had no validity (see MHCT 1: 363).
14. Juárez or Suárez was the provincial of the Carmelites of Andalusia. When Gracián began his visitation, Suárez left for Madrid and avoided any meeting with the visitator.
15. She is alluding to what is called the counterbrief of Gregory XIII, 13 August 1574, declaring an end to the visitations being conducted by Dominican visitators and their delegates and subjecting all the Carmelite houses to the authority of the general (see MHCT 1: 192–95).
16. The prior of the Carmelites of the observance in Seville, Juan Evangelista, who was appointed by Gracián. He was also named vicar provincial during the Gracián's absence.
17. The archbishop of Seville, Cristóbal de Rojas
18. Nicolás Ormaneto.
19. Gracián had begun a canonical visitation on 21 November 1575. With the arrival of Cota and rumors about revocation of his authority from Rome, Gracián left for Madrid to consult with the nuncio.
20. Juan Evangelista.

21. Los Remedios was the name of the monastery in which the discalced Carmelites in Seville were living. The prior was Antonio de Jesús (Heredia), first friar of the reform.
22. Cota and Suárez.
23. Gracián.
24. The flattery of Madrid.
25. Reyes de León (lieutenant of the count of Barajas); his wife was Doña Inés.
26. A white paste made of sugar and starch, used in making candy and other sweets.
27. The prioress of Seville, María de San José.
28. Angel de Salazar.
29. The provincial chapter of the Carmelites of Castile, convoked on 12 May at San Pablo de la Moraleja in Valladolid.
30. Vicente de Cristo, who made his profession at Mancera.
31. Jerónimo Tostado.
32. Gracián would have departed one or two days before this letter was written.

107. To Ana de Jesús, Beas

Malagon, Middle of June 1576

These words come from a letter to Ana de Jesús who cited them in her testimony for the process of Teresa's canonization (BMC 18, p. 469). The event took place 6 June 1576 in Seville (cf. F. 25.11–12).

Imagine what I felt, in the presence of all the religious orders and confraternities of Seville, at seeing so great a prelate on his knees in front of this poor wretched woman and refusing to rise before she gave him her blessing.

108. To Padre Jerónimo Gracián, Seville

Malagón, 15 June 1576

(Autograph fragments: CN, Maravillas, Madrid; DCN, Iriepal

[Guadalajara])

She has been in Malagón for four days after a long but relaxed journey from Seville. Problems with the reconstruction of the house and problems in the community have brought her to Malagón. But her chief concern is Gracián and the difficulties she fears he will meet with in Andalusia. She gives suggestions on how to deal with certain situations.

1. The grace of the Holy Spirit be with your paternity, *mi padre*. I am delighted that today a muleteer is available; it puts me at ease to know that I can write to you through so trustworthy a person. I tell you that the thought of your being back in Seville already and that they made you hasten your return fills me with anxiety. I see that the best way I could lessen my anxiety would be to be present there. When I consider that only now and then I will have news about you, I don't know how I will bear it. May God provide a remedy and grant me the great favor of seeing you free of those people.[1]

2. I don't know why they want to inflict penalties on you and all the others when the excommunications of Padre Mariano and Father Prior were enough.[2] I have no other relief than to see that you have Doctor Arganda.[3] Give him my best regards. I would love to see him again. Don't forget to tell him that I beg him not to be so confident that those people will give up seeking their freedom; they will seek it even at the cost of lives, for they say they will have to do this if you return. Even if they don't go that far, it is always good to take precautions against what could come about, since you are dealing with fiery people.[4]

3. You should know, *mi padre*, that you made me very happy on the day I saw you, but I would never regret your not having been present for the foolishness that went on there; for they couldn't have done otherwise had you been there, and all to the detriment of the authority of your office and person.

4. I long to know if you are well after having returned from so long a journey. For love of our Lord, try to write to me as soon as you can and find some way for sending the letters. This will be another trial, that Avila is so disorganized as to make it difficult to receive news about you, save from time to time. The letters must go by way of Madrid or Segovia, or sometimes by Toledo. Look at the roundabout ways we have to resort to and in the circumstances we now find ourselves, for even a few hours without knowing about you seemed to be a long time. Since you know this, it would be a great cruelty for you to neglect writing; and even if you cannot write at length, at least let me know about your health. May our Lord give you the good health needed for the sake of the order.

5. Let me know how things are going and if you were happy to see that the house of St. Joseph's is so perfect and has become so well known because of the festivity with which it was inaugurated.[5] I at once saw that since it would be a restful place to live in, the Lord would not leave me there. May he be blessed forever. Here the setup of the house is bad, and because I've just come from the other one, it has seemed worse.

6. Mother Prioress[6] is better, although not completely well. Her illness grieves me, and it would so even more if there were no hope of her getting better, for it is a dangerous illness. We would lose the best member the order has. From what she says, she has made amends for the faults that she used to have, and she will do nothing without reflection. I love her a great deal and am obligated to love her more at seeing how much she loves you and the concern she has for your health. Don't forget to pray much for her. This house, so to speak, would be lost without her.

7. I sent a messenger at once to Doña Luisa.[7] I am waiting for her and have determined that if she does not do things well, I will arrange to have the nuns transfer to her house in Paracuellos until one is constructed here. Paracuellos is three leagues from Madrid and two from Alcalá and, as it seems to

me, a very healthy place to live, for I very much wanted her to build the monastery there, but she never wanted to. I would much rather that the nuns not have to leave since they have already settled in this place and it is a place of transit. But if nothing else can be done, please God she will acquiesce and that you will approve. I will not await further authorization from you, for I believe we have it and there is no other remedy.[8] To close the monastery as was done in Pastrana would be out of the question. Well, if she doesn't answer favorably now, I will go to Toledo to get some other persons to speak to her. I will not leave there until in one way or another this is all settled. Don't let yourself become troubled about it all.

8. I arrived in good condition. We did the right thing in deciding to come the way we did rather than in covered wagons, for I could choose the time for traveling, and my brother[9] provided me with every comfort. He kisses your hands very much. He arrived in good health and remains so. He's a wonderful man! Would that he would leave me in Toledo and go away until matters in Andalusia are settled! He would also have news from you more often, but there is no way of convincing him. Teresa[10] came with us entertaining us along the way, and never being a burden.

9. Oh, *mi padre*, what a terrible thing happened to me! While we were sitting on a haystack considering ourselves lucky to have found it, next to an inn that we were unable to enter, a large salamander or lizard got in between my tunic and bare arm, and it was the mercy of God that it didn't get in somewhere else, for I think I would have died, judging from what I felt. But my brother got hold of it at once and when he threw it away, it hit Antonio Ruiz right in the mouth. The latter was most helpful along the way, and Diego also. For that, please give him the habit right away,[11] for he is a little angel. I think he brought us a new nun whom I much prefer to Catalina[12] whom I must bring from here. It seems she is doing better, but her anxiety to leave will ruin her health completely. You can rest

assured that she was sick when she performed the good work.[13] She says she did it to bring more honor to the order.

10. Mother Prioress sends you her best regards. She says she doesn't write you so as not to tire you. She's up and about and since she is so fond of taking care of everything and so meticulous, her return to health will be slower. When you go to our house, pay special attention to San Gabriel[14] for me, for she was much afflicted when I left; she is an angel in her simplicity and has a very good spirit—I owe her much.

11. You ought to give orders that the nuns should in no way offer anyone something to eat in the parlor, for this becomes a great disturbance for them. And except for you (for you are not to be included in such considerations, when there is a need), they should do so only reluctantly. I consider it worse when they do so, and this I have stated, and there are many disadvantages in their so doing. And the fact that they wouldn't have food for themselves if they did is reason enough, for the alms are few and the nuns won't say anything but go themselves without eating; and this is the least of the disadvantages. When I was there, I saw to it that they would not be in want and that they would not use up what belonged to the monastery. Things tend to go on as in the beginning, and from such a beginning would come much harm. So, you should realize that this is very important and that it will give the nuns great consolation to know that you want them to observe the ordinances given and confirmed by Pedro Hernández.[15] They are all young, and believe me, *mi padre*, that it is safer for them not to have dealings with the friars. I do not fear anything else in these monasteries more than that. For although now everything is holy, I know where it will all end up if this isn't ruled out from the start. And that is why I insist so much upon it. Pardon me, *mi padre*, and remain with God. May His Majesty watch over you for me and give me patience to endure the long time I must wait before receiving a letter from you.

12. I arrived on the second day after Pentecost; today is the following Friday. I came by way of Almodóvar. Fray Ambrosio[16] had a big celebration for me. I am crushed over the departure of Padre Fray Baltasar[17] for Toledo. I don't know why Padre Mariano[18] exposes him to temptation, for even at a distance the occasions are not lacking. Please God...

13. I got this far when the response of Doña Luisa[19] arrived. She says she will send a very good worker this week. I am disappointed. I forgot to tell you that in Seville Padre Fray Alonso,[20] the subprior, troubled by the harm that it does him to stay in that house, has asked you to send him elsewhere. He is a good man; the right thing to do is give him relief. He would get on well in Almodóvar, I believe, for they have enough to eat; and since the prior is not there, it would be good to have a vicar. Fray Gregorio[21] could take his place, and everything, I think, would proceed well. The more I speak to this *padre*, the more impressed I am. You will see for yourself.

14. What I ask you is that you take care of yourself. I wouldn't want you to be so negligent about yourself that everything ends in ruins. I know that Mother Prioress[22] will take care of your needs. I will provide from up here, nor will I lack the means. I tell you this so that when you need something you will ask the prioress, for she will send you money shortly and whatever you need. I don't know how many *reales* I left with San Gabriel; it was what I had left, which wasn't much. Take note, I wouldn't want to say anything to the other friars, which shouldn't surprise you, for it is evident that you need money, and I am worried about your being down there during the summer. This diligence to provide for you from up here does not mean that down there the prioress and subprioress and all the nuns don't care. But perhaps they will be receiving few alms, and when you see this, you will be very reluctant to accept anything.

15. Please God you are well, and may he watch over you for us. The time of your absence will pass, although badly.

Your paternity's unworthy servant and subject,

Teresa de Jesús

---

1. The Carmelite friars of the observance in Andalusia for whom Gracián had been appointed visitator.
2. Mariano de San Benito, who was in Madrid, and Antonio de Jesús (Heredia), who was prior of Los Remedios, a house for discalced Carmelite friars in Seville.
3. Francisco de Arganda, an officer for the Inquisition in Seville.
4. Since December Teresa had the worry that Gracián might be killed.
5. Cf. F. 25.11.
6. The prioress of Malagón, Brianda de San José.
7. Doña Luisa de la Cerda, the founding benefactor of Malagón.
8. Gracián had given Teresa permission, in a letter dated 6 May 1576, to go to Malagón to finalize matters concerning the construction of a monastery there. His plan was that after finishing this she go to finish out her term in Avila and then to Salamanca where she had been assigned as a conventual by the Dominican visitator, Pedro Fernández (cf. MHCT 1:314–15).
9. Lorenzo de Cepeda.
10. Lorenzo de Cepeda's daughter.
11. Diego de Jesús (Rodríguez), who received the habit in Seville.
12. The new nun was Ana de Jesús (Contreras) who made her first profession in Malagón. Catalina de la Resurección belonged to the community in Malagón.
13. This is said with irony.
14. Leonor de San Gabriel in Seville who had served as Teresa's nurse there.
15. Pedro Fernández, the Dominican visitator.
16. Ambrosio de San Pedro was vicar of the discalced Carmelite friars in Almodóvar del Campo.
17. Baltasar Nieto, who probably did so in an act of disobedience toward Gracián.
18. Ambrosio Mariano de San Benito.
19. Luisa de la Cerda.
20. Alonso de la Madre de Dios, subprior of Los Remedios in Seville.

21. Fray Gregorio Nacianceno who had accompanied her on her journey to Seville and on her return to Malagón.
22. The prioress of Seville, María de San José.

109. To María de San José, Seville

Malagón, 15 June 1576

(Autograph: DCN, Valladolid)

She has been in Malagón four days, after a pleasant journey from Seville provided by her brother Lorenzo. In Malagón the prioress is seriously ill and the house is in a dilapidated condition. Doña Luisa is putting off providing for the needed repairs. The nuns in Seville have financial problems and are involved in a lawsuit. Gracián is about to resume his visitation.

For Mother Prioress María de San José, Seville.

1. Jesus. The grace of the Holy Spirit be with your reverence, my daughter. Oh, how I would like to write a long letter, but since I have other letters to write, I don't have time. I told Padre Fray Gregorio[1] to write a long letter about the whole trip. The fact is that there are not many things to report because we journeyed very well; it wasn't hot, and we arrived in good health, glory to God, the second day after Pentecost.[2] I found Mother Prioress's condition improved,[3] although she is not completely well. Take great care to pray for her. I've spent some enjoyable moments with her. I have kept very much in mind the change that you must still make. Please God, you will not be lacking anything.

2. For charity's sake, I beg you to write me through every means you can so that I may always know how you all are. Don't fail to write by way of Toledo, for I will inform the prioress[4] to send the letters in due time, and perhaps I may have to stay in Toledo for a few days, for I fear that this business with

Doña Luisa[5] will demand much effort before being concluded. Pray for this. My regards to Mother Subprioress[6] and the other sisters. Take good care of San Gabriel[7] for me, for she was beside herself the day I left. Many regards to Garciálvarez[8] and tell us about the lawsuit[9] and everything else, and give us even more news about our *padre* if he has arrived.[10] I am writing him with much insistence that he not allow anyone to eat in the monastery parlor—see that you don't start something—except for himself since he is in such need, and if this can be done without it becoming known. And even if it becomes known, there is a difference between a superior and a subject, and his health is so important to us that whatever we can do amounts to little. Mother Prioress will send some money with Padre Fray Gregorio for this and for any other need that may arise, for she is fond of him and so does this gladly. And it would be good for him to know about this, for I tell you that since you receive little in alms it could happen that you would be depriving yourselves of food so as to give it to others. I desire very much that the sisters not be troubled about anything; that they serve our Lord generously. May it please His Majesty that this be so, as I beg of him.

3. Tell Sister San Francisco[11] to be a good historian of all that happens concerning the friars.[12] Since I've just come from the house down there, this house now strikes me as even worse. These sisters here suffer many hardships. Teresa[13] was a little sad on the journey, especially the first day. She said it was caused by having to leave the sisters behind.[14] On arriving here, she felt as though she had been living with these sisters all her life. She was so happy she could hardly eat supper the day we arrived. I was delighted because I believe her affection for them is deeply rooted. I will write again through Padre Fray Gregorio. I have nothing more to say now other than ask the Lord to watch over you and make you holy so that all the nuns will be so likewise, amen.

Today is the Friday after Pentecost.

4. Give this enclosed letter to our *padre* personally, and if he is not there, do not send it to him unless through a very trustworthy person, which is important.

Yours,

Teresa of Jesus

Teresa is not writing to you because she is busy. She says she is prioress and sends you her best regards.

---

1. Gregorio Nacianceno who accompanied her to Seville and on the return trip to Malagón.
2. They left Seville on 4 June and arrived in Malagón on 11 June.
3. The prioress of Malagón was Brianda de San José.
4. The prioress of Toledo.
5. Doña Luisa de la Cerda, the founding patron of Malagón, who on this day informed Teresa that she was sending a good workman.
6. The subprioress in Seville was María del Espíritu Santo.
7. Leonor de San Gabriel had been Teresa's nurse in Seville.
8. Garciálvarez was a secular priest who helped with the Seville foundation, but he later caused many difficulties for that Carmel.
9. The lawsuit was occasioned by the demand that the nuns pay the excise on purchasing the house in Seville.
10. Jerónimo Gracián was returning from Castile to resume his visitation of the Andalusian Carmelites of the Observance.
11. Isabel de San Fancisco was chronicler for the community.
12. The Carmelites of the Observance in Seville.
13. Teresa de Ahumada, daughter of Lorenzo de Cepeda.
14. She had lived with the sisters in Seville for several months.

110. To María de San José, Seville

Malagón, 18 June 1576

She knows how much the nuns in Seville miss her and wants to help them in their financial difficulties. She is preparing for her trip to Toledo to meet with Doña Luisa who has been lukewarm about the needed repairs for the house in Malagón.

For Mother María de San José, Carmelite and prioresss of St. Joseph's in Seville.

1. May Jesus be with your reverence, my daughter. I tell you that if you experience some sadness over my absence, mine is greater. May the Lord make use of the many trials and the pain it cost me to leave daughters who are so dear to me. I hope that you are all well; I am in good health, glory be to God.

2. You will have already received the letters that the muleteer brought. This one will be short. I thought I would be here for some days yet, but since Sunday is the feast of St. John the Baptist, I have advanced the day of my departure, and so I have little time. Since Padre Fray Gregorio[1] will be my messenger, I am not bothered by this.

3. I am worried that you will be pressed this year into paying the annuity,[2] for by next year the Lord will have provided someone to pay it for you. Santángel[3] has a sister whom Mother Prioress[4] here praises highly and would prefer her to the one who entered. She says a dowry of 300 ducats will be given for the one who has entered (who will have completed a year in August), and that the other sister will give the same amount, with which you would be able to pay the annuity for this year. It is a small amount. But if what they say about her is true, she deserves to be accepted for nothing, so much the more because she is from this region. Speak about this to our *padre*,[5] and if there is no other solution, you could accept her. The trouble is that she is only fourteen years old; for this reason I say she shouldn't be accepted unless nothing else can be done. Think about it.

4. It seems to me for many reasons that it would be good if our *padre* gave orders that Beatriz[6] make her profession at

once. One reason is that it would put an end to her temptations. Give my regards to her and to her mother[7] and to all whom you see and to everyone and to Mother Subprioress[8] and all the sisters, especially my nurse.[9] May God watch over you for me, my daughter, and make you very holy, amen.

5. My brother[10] wrote to all of you the other day and commends himself much to your prayers. He is more measured than Teresa,[11] who cannot manage to love any others as much as she loves all of you. Because Mother Prioress (with whom I am definitely delighted) will be writing and Fray Gregorio will tell you the news, I'll say no more. I believe I'll be in Toledo for some days. Write to me there.

Yesterday was the feast of the Most Holy Trinity.

6. Try to get a letter from our *padre* for me or send a lot of news about him, for I haven't received any word about him. May God make you all saints.

Yours,

Teresa of Jesus

7. With regard to the nun,[12] I have found out more; for the time being she shouldn't be considered.

---

1. Gregorio Nacianceno.
2. An obligation arising from the purchase of the house.
3. Elvira de San Angelo who made her profession in Malagón. Her sister, whose name is unknown, lost interest, it seems, in the thought of becoming a Carmelite.
4. Brianda de San José, prioress of Malagón.
5. Jerónimo Gracián.
6. Beatriz de la Madre de Dios (Chaves), who made her profession 29 September 1576.
7. The mother, Juana de la Cruz, entered the Carmel of Seville also, making profession 10 October 1577.
8. The subprioress in Seville was María del Espíritu Santo.
9. Leonor de San Gabriel.

10. Lorenzo de Cepeda.
11. Lorenzo's daughter.
12. The aspirant who was fourteen years old.

111. To Jerónimo Gracián, Seville

Malagón, 18–22 June 1576

(Autograph: DCN, Innsbruck [Austria])

An Andalusian friar passing through on his way to Madrid has brought alarming news. It confirms Teresa in her idea that Gracián ought to give up the visitation. She is writing shortly before her departure for Toledo. The autograph of the text is torn and incomplete.

1. ...that your paternity is in that place. Today the prior of Carmona[1] passed by with another *presentado*. (Padre Fray Gregorio[2] will tell you about some of the things we had to undergo.) He told me that only Cota[3] had retired to the Carmelite monastery and that the prosecutor of the royal council had taken over his case and that the council was dealing with it. This seems to me a bland way to be dealing with the preposterous things they did, although this *padre* well knows that they were in the wrong. He says he has stated this repeatedly and that he is going to the nuncio to tell him to punish those who were guilty and not make everyone pay. And he is going to petition that you not be the visitator because none of them will obey you and that the nuncio choose someone else.

2. I was thinking whether it might be good if you on your own made this request of both the nuncio and the king, pointing out how those friars have this stubborn notion and feel so much hostility toward you that your visitation could hardly bear fruit...and would be to the satisfaction of everyone. And if they do not grant this request, it would be for me at least a comfort to know that you did what you could to free yourself of the

obligation. The thought that they will have to obey you again and then once more start agitating against you is for me worse than death. Think about it, *mi padre*; when there is nothing else you can do, then proceed under obedience and the Lord will take over.

3. They say that they can take care of their province, that Tostado[4] will take charge. May the Lord bring this about, for it would be good to find some means to deal with so hopeless a people, now that you have put things in order. Oh, Jesus, how hard it is to be far away from all the things happening there. I assure you that for me it is a real cross.

4. I am going to Toledo and I am thinking of staying there until Doña Luisa provides what is necessary for this house. Now she is saying that she will send a workman here, but shows no enthusiasm about it.

I am well....

---

1. Francisco de Cárdenas, a Carmelite of the observance.
2. Gregorio Nacianceno, who had accompanied Teresa on the journey from Seville to Malagón and was now going to return to Seville.
3. Pedro de Cota who had been appointed prior in Córdoba in 1573 and was now being commissioned to organize in Madrid the resistance to Gracián.
4. Jerónimo Tostado, who had been appointed visitator of the Spanish Carmelites by the general in Rome.

112. To María de San José, Seville

Toledo, 2 July 1576

(Autograph: DCN, Valladolid)

Having received a packet of letters from friars, nuns, and other friends in Seville, Teresa begins with a reply to María de San José, who is lonely for her. This she does before having read the other letters. She refers to some of the problems of the three Carmelite communities in Seville (nuns and friars).

For Mother Prioress in Seville, María de San José

1. May Jesus be with your reverence. I assure you that I feel the same loneliness for you that you feel for me. After I wrote the enclosed letter, I received yours. It brought me so much joy that I was deeply touched. And your requests for pardon have pleased me. On the condition that you love me as much as I love you, I pardon you for what you have done or will do. My only complaint now is about how little you wanted to be with me. But I see well that you are not at fault, and this I told Mother Prioress in Malagón.[1] It was only that the Lord, who willed that I have so many trials in Seville, ordained that I be deprived of your company, which gave me relief. Certainly, as an exchange, so that you and the sisters were able to have some peace, I consider them worthwhile, and I would even bear many more for this purpose. And believe me, I love you much; and that since I see in you this same affection, the rest is a trifle to which you should pay no attention. But while I was down there, since I underwent the trials along with your aloofness—while I treated you like a cherished daughter—it was a great suffering not to find in you the same simplicity and love. But certainly with this letter of yours everything is forgotten, and my affection for you is such that I have to temper its excess by recalling the past.

2. I rejoiced infinitely in learning how well everything was done. The terms of the contract must be settled before going ahead, even though they may not offer much security for the future, for it's a hard thing to have a lawsuit on one's hands, especially in the beginning. Let's try to repay quickly the money advanced by my brother[2]—I mean the amount for the excise when the house was purchased. I am as concerned about the house in Seville as when I was there, and even more so, or at

least as much. Oh, how happy your letters made him! He never stops speaking about your discretion. The letters arrived in good condition, but whenever you try to improve your handwriting it gets worse. Since he and Teresa[3] are writing, I am not going to say anything about them. I have written to Father Prior of Las Cuevas,[4] and today I must write to Malagón on business and to our *padre*,[5] and so I don't expect to be able to write in answer to the sisters, especially since there has been no letup of visitors.

3. Because of his charity, I readily believe what you tell me about the good Garciálvarez. Give him my best regards. The letter from Father Prior[6] made me happy. My friends do me a great favor by the way they are treating all of you. Try to get on well with them and when the opportunity arises do something, with moderation, for Mariano[7] and Fray Antonio, for I wouldn't want you to lose their favor. May God forgive them, for the commotion that was caused concerning the other friars could have been avoided and matters resolved in another way. Our *padre* is very distressed. He is well, and the nuncio[8] thought it a good thing that he had not returned down there.

4. You cannot say that I do not write you frequently. May you do the same, for I greatly enjoy your letters. I didn't know anything about what was going on there, for our *padre's* letters are very brief; he surely must be unable to do otherwise. May God be with you and make you very holy. Gabriela[9] writes me that she is not well—for I read her letter after I had written a good part of this one. She says she is suffering from pains in the stomach. Please God it is nothing serious. I don't remember whom I entrusted your care to. Let the subprioress[10] take on this task, and see that you obey her and take care of your health for love of me. It would be infinitely painful to me were you to lose your health. May it please the Lord to grant you good health, as I beg him. My regards to Beatriz's mother and to Delgado.[11] The prioress tells me to send her regards to you.

All the sisters are happy about how well things are going for you. May this always be so.

I believe I've already mentioned that today is the feast of the Visitation.

5. The priest[12] came while I was attending Mass, and after giving his greetings, he went away. I spoke with him, and if he had stayed I would have shown him some courtesy, but he was in the company of others and so had to continue on his journey.

Yours,

Teresa of Jesus

6. Gabriela also writes and says that you keep the house very neat. I would love to see it now. I have not been able to look at whom the letters were from until now. I was glad to receive the one from our good *padre*, Garciálvarez. I will gladly write to him, and those daughters of mine will pardon me if I neglect them so as to fulfill my obligation toward their good benefactor.

---

1. Brianda de San José.
2. Lorenzo de Cepeda, who advanced the money for the purchase of the house.
3. Lorenzo's daughter.
4. Hernando de Pantoja, prior of the Carthusian monastery of Las Cuevas.
5. Jerónimo Gracián.
6. Antonio de Jesús (Heredia), who was prior of the discalced Carmelite monastery called Los Remedios.
7. Ambrosio Mariano de San Benito.
8. Nicolás Ormaneto.
9. Leonor de San Gabriel, who acted as Teresa's nurse in Seville.
10. The subprioress in Seville, María del Espíritu Santo.
11. The mother of Beatriz de la Madre de Dios was Juana Gómez. Inés Delgado was a benefactress of the nuns in Seville.
12. She is perhaps referring to St. John of Avila's disciple, Juan Díaz.

113. To Don Lorenzo de Cepeda, Toledo

Toledo, 9 July 1576

(Autograph: DCN of Santa Ana, Madrid)

This note was not in the form of a letter but was a reminder handed to Lorenzo by Teresa when he left for Avila on 9 July. He brought along his three children. Teresita was to begin her Carmelite life at St. Joseph's, and the two sons their studies. Teresa shows concerns about the two sons.

1. I wouldn't want your honor to forget this, and so I am putting it down here. I have a great fear that if you do not start now to take much care about the education of these boys, they will soon be mixing with some of the haughty crowd in Avila. It's necessary that you make them go at once to the Society, for I am writing about it to the rector as you will see. And if it seems appropriate to the good Francisco de Salcedo and to Maestro Daza, they should wear the student's biretta.[1] Rodrigo's daughter had six children of which only one was a boy. Fortunately for the latter they always insisted on his studies, and even now he is at Salamanca. And this is true also of Don Diego de Aguila's son.[2] Anyway, you will find out there what may be the suitable thing to do. Please God, my brothers will not allow their sons to become vain.

2. You will not be able to see much of Francisco de Salcedo or of the *Maestro* unless you go to their houses, for they live far from Perálvarez, and it is good to have these talks while alone.[3] For now, don't forget that you are not to have a designated confessor or any more than the smallest number of house servants. It's better to have to increase the number in the future than to have to reduce it. I am now going to write to Valladolid to have them send the page.[4] Even if the boys have to go for a while without him, it doesn't matter; for there are two of them and they can go together; I'm now writing for the page to come.

3. You are inclined and accustomed to receiving much honor. You need to mortify yourself in this respect and not listen to everybody, but follow the opinion of these two in all matters, and also of Padre Muñoz of the Society, if you think.[5] But the opinions of the two former are enough for more serious matters and you can adhere to their views. Be careful—sometimes we may start things that can be harmful in ways not immediately obvious. You can gain more favor from God, and even the world, by saving your money so as to give alms, and your sons will also benefit from this. For the present, I wouldn't want you to buy a mule, but an old saddle pony should be sufficient for your travels and domestic chores. There's no reason why those boys can't go around on foot. Make them study.

---

1. The school maintained by the Society of Jesus in Avila was San Gil and its rector Gonzalo Dávila. Lorenzo's boys were Francisco (16 years old) and Lorenzo (14 years old). Francisco de Salcedo and Gaspar Daza were friends and former directors of Teresa's.
2. Diego del Aguila was a friend of the Jesuits at San Gil.
3. The *Maestro* is Gaspar Daza, and Perálvarez is Pedro Alvarez Cimbrón, a cousin of Teresa's.
4. She will write to Padre Báñez who had arranged for a boy to act as page for Lorenzo's two sons.
5. The two are Daza and Salcedo; Luis Muñoz was a Jesuit at San Gil.

114. To María de San José, Seville

Toledo, 11 July 1576

Teresa has received a number of letters from the nuns in Seville. In this response to María de San José, she expresses her chief concerns: the poor health of María, the financial problems of the new community in Seville, the disturbing news about Gracián's official visitations in Andalusia, and the general's accident. She cannot move to Salamanca because of the needs of the Carmel in Malagón.

1. Jesus be with your reverence. You cannot say that I do not write to you often. This letter may perhaps reach you before the one I wrote three or four days ago, I believe. You should know that for now I am remaining here. My brother left the day before yesterday, and I made him take Teresa[1] with him because I don't know whether or not they may want me to take a roundabout route, and I don't want to be burdened with the care of a child. I am well and am feeling rested after all the commotion, for despite my great love for my brother, it bothered me to see him away from his home. I don't know how long I will be staying here, for I am still looking for the best way to bring the work at Malagón to a completion.

2. I was distressed about your illness, and for you to undergo a purge at this time doesn't seem good to me. Keep me informed about your health. May our Lord grant you health as I desire and also grant it to my daughters. I urgently commend myself to the prayers of you all. Your letters delighted me. I have already answered some. I wrote today to my Gabriela and to San Francisco;[2] they know so well how to praise one. Please God they are not lying, and the next time the one shouldn't be telling the same thing that the other is. All three told me about the octave of the Blessed Sacrament, I mean the feast. Anyway, I was not displeased, for it was a pleasure to know that the octave was observed so well. May God reward our Padre Garciálvarez.[3] Kiss his hands for me. I wrote to him the other day.

3. My brother and I were delighted that you got the matter about the excise settled.[4] It is extraordinary how fond he is of you, and I have been affected by it. I was also delighted with the books he sent you and for all the kind care my saintly prior[5] takes of you. May God reward him.

4. I would like you to recount with much detail what those poor friars are doing—I mean whether there is any way of their being pacified—and tell me about the Franciscans.[6] Pray for our *padre*,[7] for he is weighed down with trials. Please God he was right in being so severe with those fathers.[8] Give my regards to Padre Fray Antonio de Jesús and to Padre Mariano[9] and tell them I am striving to reach the perfection they have attained in not writing to me. Tell Padre Mariano that Padre Fray Baltasar and I are close friends.[10]

5. Yesterday, Juan Díaz[11] came here from Madrid. There is no thought of having a monastery here, because Juan Díaz is returning to Madrid. The king has given orders to our *padre* to have recourse to the president of the royal council[12] and to Quiroga[13] for the affairs of our order. Please God everything will go well. I repeat that there is a need for much prayer. Also pray for Father General who was thrown from a mule and suffered several fractures in his leg; this distressed me because he is old.[14] Best regards to all my friends, both men and women. Have them do what is indicated on the enclosed paper.

6. Oh, how pleased I am with the tunics I made from the sheets! They say here that it is like wearing linen. May God make you all saints, and give you health. Look after yourself, for it is better to cater to yourself than to be sick.

Today is 11 June.

Your reverence's servant,

Teresa of Jesus

---

1. Lorenzo de Cepeda and his daughter, Teresita, left for Avila.
2. Leonor de San Gabriel and Isabel de San Francisco.
3. The priest friend and benefactor of the nuns in Seville.
4. The nuns lost the case and had to pay 300 ducats, which was beyond what they could afford. They managed to obtain more time before payment.
5. Hernando de Pantoja, the prior of the Carthusians.

6. The Carmelites of the observance and the Franciscans were subject to their respective visitators.
7. Jerónimo Gracián.
8. She is alluding to the severity with which he resumed his official visitation of the Carmelites of the observance.
9. Antonio de Jesús (Heredia) was the prior of the discalced Carmelite friars in Seville and Ambrosio Mariano de San Benito was a member of this community.
10. Baltasar Jesús (Nieto) was an untrustworthy friar who had transferred from the Franciscans to the Carmelites of the observance and then to the discalced Carmelites. Teresa is using irony here.
11. He was a disciple of St. John of Avila.
12. Diego de Covarrubias y Leiva.
13. Gaspar de Quiroga, the inquisitor and future archbishop of Toledo.
14. The general, Giovanni Battista Rossi (Rubeo), was 69 at the time.

115. To Don Lorenzo de Cepeda, Avila
Toledo, 24 July 1576

(Autograph: Azebedo Continho family, Oporto [Portugal])

In the peaceful surroundings of Toledo she takes up once more some of her writing tasks. She will continue her work on the Foundations, *write* On Making the Visitation, *and later* The Interior Castle. *She asks Lorenzo to send back from Avila some of the things she had already written. She had received a letter from Alba in which Juan de Ovalle manifested some jealous tendencies in regard to Lorenzo.*

1. Jesus. The grace of the Holy Spirit be always with your honor. Oh, what a long fifteen days these have been![1] Blessed be God that you are well; I was greatly consoled. From what you tell me about your servants and the house, I don't think there is anything excessive. I had a good laugh over the master of ceremonies,[2] and I assure you I found it very amusing. You can really trust her since she is a good and wise person.

Give her my fond regards when you see her, for I owe her much, and also to Francisco de Salcedo.

2. I am very sorry about your ailment. The cold will soon begin to bother you. I am better than I have been in years, in my opinion. I have a very lovely little cell, well set apart and with a window looking out into the garden, and not many visitors to take up my time. If I didn't have to write these letters and if there were not so many, I would be so well-off that the condition wouldn't last, for that is what usually happens when things go well for me. If you were here I would lack nothing, but if God favors me by granting you health, the separation can be easily endured. May God reward you for your concern about my health, for my sorrow was relieved when I saw that you are also suffering because of my staying here. I hope in God that I will not have to stay so long and that I can get to Avila by the time the cold weather starts there.[3] Despite the harm the cold can do me, I would not avoid it or delay here one day, for when God so wills he can give us good health anywhere. Oh, how much more for my own happiness do I desire that you be in good health! May God grant it to you, as he can.

3. Juan de Ovalle has written me a long letter in which he insists on how fond he is of you and what he would do to serve you. His only fault was to believe that you favored Cimbrón who he thought had complete control over you; and that was the reason my sister didn't come. Those were feelings of jealousy, I certainly think, for he has a jealous temperament and I suffered much from him because of my friendship with Doña Guiomar.[4] All his complaining is about Cimbrón. In certain matters, he's very childish. He behaved much better in Seville where he showed you much love, and so you should bear up with him for love of God.

4. I wrote to him telling him what I thought and that I saw how much you loved him and that he ought rather to rejoice that Cimbrón was looking after your concerns; and I strongly

urged him to try to please you and send you the money if you ask for it, and I added that each one is better off in his own house, that God perhaps had so ordained, and I blamed him and excused Perálvarez.[5] The trouble is that I think he has to come here and that all my efforts to prevent him from coming will have served for naught. Certainly I feel very sorry for my sister, and so we have to suffer much. With regard to you, I swear his desire to please you and serve you is great. God has not given him more. But he has endowed others with the good dispositions needed to put up with him, and this is what you will have to do.

5. The *agnusdei* is in the little chest, I think; if not, it is in the trunk with the rings.[6] I am telling the subprioress[7] to send the chest to you so that you might take out the papers on the *Foundations* and send them back to the subprioress in a sealed wrapping. They have to send us I don't know what for my companion and also my mantle, which we had sent them in a hurry. I don't know what other papers are in there, but I wouldn't want anyone to see them, and so I would like you to take them out (for it doesn't matter to me if you see them), and the same holds true for the *Foundations*.

6. The key for the little chest broke. Force the chest open and keep it in another larger chest until a key is made for it. In the little chest is a key for a mail pouch that I am sending you, for also in it are some papers, I think, on matters concerning prayer. Feel free to read them and take out the paper on which some details about the foundation of Alba are written. Send it to me with the other papers because Father Visitator has asked me to finish writing the *Foundations*, and I need these papers to know what I have already written and about Alba.[8] It's hard for me to have to take up this task, for the time that I have left after tending to letter-writing, I would like to spend in solitude and rest. It doesn't seem God wants this. May the Lord be pleased to make use of this work.

7. You ought to know that the prioress of Valladolid has written me that Doña María de Mendoza had a copy made of the book the bishop once had, and that he has the copy in his possession.[9] I was delighted for your sake, because when I come we can arrange to have you see it. Don't tell anyone. If he should happen to go there, you could feel free to ask him for it.

8. I will write what you say to Seville, for I don't know if the letter was received. Why bother about four *reales*? Either they were not enclosed in the letter, or the carrier knowing that something was enclosed did not deliver it to them. The prioress[10] here is in much better health than usual; she and all the sisters kiss your hands. We have prayed much for your health. I am sending you some quinces so that your housekeeper may make them into preserves and you can eat them after your meal, and also a box of marmalade, and another for the subprioress at St. Joseph's who, they tell me, is very weak. Tell her to eat it, and I beg you not to give any of yours to anyone but eat it for love of me. And when you finish it, let me know, for it is inexpensive here and I'm not using money from the monastery. Padre Gracián gave me orders under obedience to continue doing as I usually do,[11] for what I had was not for me but for the order. On the one hand I have regretted this; on the other, since there are so many expenses to meet here, even if it involve no more than postage, I rejoiced. It pains me that postage costs so much, and there are many other things to pay for....

1. Lorenzo had left for Avila fifteen days ago.
2. She is probably referring to Lorenzo's housekeeper, Jerónima de Aranda.
3. She was hoping to go there without delay, for she was the prioress of that monastery. In fact, she was not able to return until July of the following year.
4. Juan de Ovalle was Teresa's brother-in-law from Alba de Tormes. Cimbrón was Pedro Alvarez Cimbrón, a cousin of Teresa's and now Lorenzo's confidant. Teresa's sister Juana was kept in Alba by her

husband when perhaps her brother Lorenzo was expecting to see her in Avila. Guiomar de Ulloa was Teresa's friend who collaborated with her and Juan de Ovalle in the foundation of St. Joseph's in Avila.

5. Another name for Cimbrón.
6. An *agnusdei* is a disk made from the wax of Easter candles stamped with the figure of a lamb. *Agnusdeis* are blessed by the pope in the first year of his pontificate and every seven years after. The rings were emerald brought by Teresita from the Americas. The items were lost but later found. Thinking that she would soon be returning to Avila, Teresa had sent ahead with a muleteer her mantle, the first chapters of her *Foundations*, and other private papers.
7. María de San Jerónimo (Dávila).
8. The visitator was Padre Gracián who ordered her to continue writing her *Foundations* which she had interrupted after chapter 19.
9. The prioress of Valladolid was María Bautista. María de Mendoza was the bishop's sister. The book formerly in the bishop's possession was Teresa's autograph of the *Life*, which had been confiscated by the Inquisition the previous year. A copy was made surreptitiously at Doña María's request.
10. Ana de los Angeles.
11. She is referring to the special faculties she had been given in matters pertaining to her vow of poverty.

116. To Padre Jerónimo Gracián, Toledo

Toledo, August 1576

(Autograph fragment: Marqués de Villa-Alegre, Granada)

An exchange of opinions between Gracián, the visitator, and Teresa, the foundress. Gracián wrote down his points from the visitation in the left column of the paper leaving the right column blank for Teresa to answer. Only some of the points treated have been preserved and the columns do not correspond exactly with question and answer.[1]

1. *Question: Whether an aspirant whom Laurencia has offered to admit free may be accepted without a dowry when she can pay one. To Eliseo*[2] *it*

1. ...Seculars in matters of self-interest pay little attention to reason. So it is with this mother prioress[3] who, accustomed to

doesn't seem so, because prelates are not the owners of the monastery's property but administrators. If you consult learned men you will find that this is so. Oh, how they will grumble!

Answer: If we assume that this is for the greater service of God, let them grumble. They already know in Segovia about the poverty of that house and that those who do not have a dowry are received, as is the case with the nun to whom they have just given the habit. And there is no reason to make exceptions for a nun who can afford one.

And the honor of Laurencia who has given her word?

Answer: Let Laurencia point out that she has a superior who will decide and that she can no longer do anything about that matter. And in what touches on the greater service of God, let Laurencia know that, although she finds herself in the middle, this doesn't matter to me, for I would rather that a small thread of honor go to my Jesus and a little bit to my Virgin Mary, my Lady and Mother of my soul, than a hundred thousand Laurencias.

Well what must we do? Are we to start disputes? Those blessed licentiates, Herrera and the other friends there, will start the abundance possessed in Pastrana, has little poverty of spirit left. This is a cause of suffering to me and it will be wherever I find

such a lack. For, glory to God, these houses were founded by trusting solely in Him. So I fear that by beginning to place our trust in human means, we will lose some of the divine means. I do not say this in regard to the present matter, but I know that he would not have placed his daughter[4] there if the spirit of poverty were lacking. We owe him, then, so little that it must be the will of God.

On Making the Visitation came as though taught by God.[5] May He be blessed for everything.

2. Your paternity has no need to give me an order, for I consider the order already given and will carry it out. And, to tell the truth, I will be happy not to have to bother with such tiring matters. The only thing is that I fear that in some houses there is more greed than I would like. And please God they will not deceive you more than they do me. I think I am hurt more by this than anything else. And insofar as I know, I was determined that, even were you not the superior, I would not receive anyone without telling you about it, if you were close by, or even, I believe,

them at the suitable time and authorize it, and God who knows that the property belongs to the poor will settle the matter.

2. A doubt in general: Whether it would be fitting to give Laurencia orders so that from here on she not give her word about receiving any nun without informing Eliseo. And I am referring to all the convents lest we find ourselves obliged to keep the word given by her. And Eliseo promises her in the presence of his Lord never to give permission for anyone unless it be in accord with her will and pleasure.

I say this because in the house in Segovia, we just gave the habit to someone who is nice but has brought nothing else. The house is very poor and there are many nuns whose dowries are of little worth. And even in the other monasteries, although there is much holiness, there are few belongings. And if then Laurencia believes every confessor, and if by the fact that she confesses once or twice to the Fathers of the Society she thinks she is thereby made holy, much harm could come later on. A worthwhile hope is better than a worthless possession.

far away. It's impossible to succeed in every instance. Time will tell. And if we go looking for dowries, we will be even worse.

3. Enclosed is the information from the prioress. When I am well informed, it serves for the good of the houses and their affairs. I don't know how they can say this. May God take care of it and give us light so that from now on we may succeed. But how many excuses I'm making. What is worse, I am really put to the test with the one I mentioned....[6]

1. The text below in Italics is not Gracian's, but added by editors to complete the sense of the torn original.
2. Gracián himself.
3. The prioress of Segovia, Isabel de Santo Domingo, who was previously the prioress in Pastrana.
4. The daughter of one of those "seculars" of whom she spoke.
5. Although probably referring to her own work, she could have had in mind the criteria followed by Gracián in his official visitations (cf. MHCT I:304-310).
6. Either the prioress or someone mentioned in Gracian's text.

117. To Padre Jerónimo Gracián, Almodóvar

Toledo, 5 September 1576

Teresa is undergoing mystical suffering over a sense of God's absence. No priest was available with whom she could consult. Through a special favor from God, the situation was remedied (cf. ST. 60). She confides this to Gracián because of her experience in April 1575 (cf. ST. 36). The text is incomplete and was copied from the autograph by Gracián's sister, María de San José (Gracián).

1. ...Now I want to tell your paternity something, because the messenger is a person I can trust. You already know how Angela took for her confessor the prior of La Sisla,[1] for she believes that in many matters one cannot be without someone to consult. She wouldn't feel sure she was doing right nor would she be at peace. The said person began to see her often, but afterward he almost never came. The prioress and I could not discover the reason for this. Once while the unhappy Angela was speaking to Joseph,[2] he told her that he was the one who held him back, that Doctor Velázquez was better for her since he was learned in canon law and highly educated and that in this way she would find some relief, that he would move him to listen to her and understand (for he hesitated since he is very busy). And since Joseph is so serious a person

as you well know, and he counseled her in similar ways before, she didn't know what to do, having already begun with someone else to whom she owed so much. On the other hand she feared displeasing Joseph.

2. She remained thus undecided for several days, and it was a trial for her not to be able to get your opinion, fearing she might lose her peace by consulting with so many. Padre Salazar[3] then came and she decided to do whatever he might say however much the change would cost her, and she almost complained to Joseph for not having informed her earlier. She told Padre Salazar about everything that was happening. He had been the one who had previously counseled her about the prior of La Sisla. She can discuss everything with Padre Salazar, as you are aware, because he already knows about it all. He told her to do what Joseph said. And this was done, and what Joseph said is being realized. First, that the prior came here and that when the prioress[4] asked him why he was acting in this way, he answered that he did not know, that there was nothing he desired more than to come and that he saw clearly that afterward he would regret not coming. He was not master of himself in this regard nor could he do anything else and he was astonished at his powerlessness.

3. Second, that hardly was it mentioned one day to the other person[5] when he said that no matter how busy he was, he would come every week, and was as happy as if he had been offered the archbishopric of Toledo (although I don't think he would be so happy over the latter since he is so good). Fray Hernando de Medina[6] will tell you about him; don't forget to ask him. That you may see how he is accepting the task, I am sending you this note,[7] for I had contacted him over some doubts I had, which I will not mention since it would take too long; they did not concern prayer.

4. So it is, *mi padre*, that Angela is very happy to have him as her confessor, so much the more since after having met Paul,[8] her soul was unable to find comfort or happiness with

anyone. Now, although not as much as with Paul, she feels settled and satisfied, and her soul is disposed to obey him. It is the greatest relief for her. For accustomed all her life to obeying, and being without Paul, nothing she did satisfied her, nor did she think she was doing right; and even if she wanted to she was not able to submit to another. Believe me, he who was at work in the first instance was so also in the second. For she is as amazed by this new condition as was the prior at feeling himself prevented from doing what he wanted.

5. I tell you that you can rejoice if you desire to give some comfort to Angela. It's enough that she is not as happy as with Paul, for her soul has no other comfort. He[9] was not ignorant of the friendship Joseph had with her, for he had heard a great deal, nor was he surprised. Since he is so learned, he backs everything up with sacred scripture. This affords the poor soul the greatest comfort, for in all ways God has banished from her everything she loves. May he be blessed forever.

6. What we must be careful about now is to prevent the prior[10] from finding out. We can let him think that because of his delays about coming I also at times confess with the other person and that you have informed me that I should do what I am told as though it were being told to me by you for the good of my soul. For I assure you that the desires and impulses this woman has to do something for God are so great that now that she cannot do great works, she needs to find out how she can please God more in what she can do.

Your paternity's unworthy servant and daughter,

Teresa of Jesus

---

1. Angela is a code name for Teresa herself. The prior of La Sisla was Diego de Yepes, a Jeronomite and future biographer of Teresa's.
2. Joseph is a code name for Jesus Christ.
3. The Jesuit, Gaspar de Salazar.
4. Ana de los Angeles.
5. Alonso Velázquez.

6. A friar of the observance who had transferred to the discalced friars and was acting as Gracián's secretary.
7. The note has not been preserved.
8. A code name for Gracián.
9. Alonso Velázquez.
10. Diego de Yepes.

118. To Padre Jerónimo Gracián, Almodóvar
Toledo, 5 September 1576

(Autograph: Discalced Mercedarian Nuns, Toro)

Having the same date as the previous letter to Gracián, this one has a clearly different thrust. Gracián had convoked a chapter for the discalced Carmelite friars and planned to use his powers to form a separate province for them. Teresa sees the difficulties in such a plan and makes some suggestions. She is becoming more concerned that their correspondence be sent through safe channels.

1. Jesus. The grace of the Holy Spirit be with your paternity. Today I sent you some letters through the chief courier. You must not forget to tell me whether you receive them. I believe they will surely arrive in Seville, for he is a brother of one of our nuns.[1]

2. I told you that Tostado[2] left for Portugal the day you arrived here. Infante[3] and another preacher from Andalusia were waiting for him and sent a messenger to Madrid who brought them back this news. Blessed be the Lord who has so ordained.

3. You should know that the members of the Council say that if they are to give the license on the basis of the usual procedure, they cannot do so, for we need to have more convincing reasons. If they see a letter from the nuncio[4] saying that he grants it, they will give it without further discussion. This information was given by a magistrate friend to Don Pedro

González.[5] Write to me through those returning from the chapter about what we can do and whether it would be good to seek counsel from someone in Madrid, like the duke[6] or others.

4. I have begun to suspect they have impeded him with letters from Rome from giving these permissions, for he gave them to Padre Fray Antonio[7] easily, it seems to me. I have also been thinking that if they give this false information to the pope, and there is no one there to counter it, they will get as many briefs as they want against us, and that it is most important that we have some of our friars there. When it is seen how our own live, the prejudice of the others will become obvious. I don't think we ought to do anything until that moment comes. Then our friars can bring back the authorization to found a few houses.[8] Believe me, it's very important to be prepared for what may come about.

5. I am writing this in a hurry and so cannot say any more than that everyone recommends themselves to your prayers; and I to the prayers of all the fathers there, especially Father Prior of Los Remedios,[9] although I'm angry with him. I want to know if Padre Mariano[10] came. May God watch over you and lead you by his hand, amen.

6. I am overjoyed to see what nice weather it is for traveling. I am waiting for Antonio.[11] Don't forget to write to tell me the name of the man to whom I must send the letters going to Madrid, that servant of your father's.[12] Be careful not to forget, and tell me how to address the envelope and if he is someone who should be reimbursed for the postage.

Today is 5 September.

7. We are well and it seems I'm feeling somewhat relieved to see that it is easier to write to you from here.

Your paternity's unworthy daughter and subject,

Teresa de Jesús

8. Be careful, *mi padre*, not to lose the paper I gave you, for you said you would place it in the lining but you did not do so. I would like you to keep a copy of it in your little coffer, for many complications would arise if it were lost.

---

1. Antonio Figueredo was the chief courier of Toledo, not a brother but a cousin of a Carmelite nun in Segovia.
2. Jerónimo Tostado was appointed visitator for the Spanish Carmelites.
3. Padre Juan de las Infantas was named prior of San Juan del Puerto by Gracián.
4. Nicolás Ormaneto.
5. Pedro González de Mendoza was a canon and treasurer of the cathedral. After his escape from prison, St. John of the Cross was cared for by him.
6. The discalced friars would be returning from the chapter in Almodóvar. It had been convoked by Gracián on 26 August. The Duke of Alba was Fernando de Toledo.
7. Antonio de Jesús (Heredia), who received a license to found a monastery in Almodóvar. It was given by the general on 21 June 1574.
8. The friars at the chapter followed Teresa's wish and sent Juan de Jesús and Pedro de los Angeles to Rome.
9. Antonio de Jesús (Heredia).
10. Fray Ambrosio Mariano de San Benito had not attended the chapter.
11. Antonio Ruiz from Malagón.
12. Roque de Huerta was a family friend of Gracián's.

119. To Padre Jerónimo Gracián, Almodóvar

Toledo, 6 September 1576

(Autograph fragment: Scotch College, Valladolid)

Gracián had written to her from Almodóvar proposing a removal of the prioress of Malagón from office because of bad health. In responding, Teresa fills him in on recent news.

1. Jesus be with your paternity. The carrier of this letter has just arrived, but he is allowing me little time, and so I can say

no more than what's needed. I praise the Lord you arrived in good health. I have sent you letters by two different routes, informing you that Peralta[1] left for Portugal on the same Thursday that you arrived here. Santelmo[2] wrote me today—and I am enclosing his letter—that we have nothing to fear, that Methuselah[3] is determined to grant our desire of separating out the eagles,[4] for he sees clearly that this is the fitting thing to do.

2. I received a letter today from Seville about the excitement and enthusiasm aroused down there by the news concerning Peralta and how the whole town is being told that the butterflies[5] will have to submit to him. Indeed, what the Lord has done is fitting. May he be blessed forever. Infante[6] came to speak to me; he wanted a letter for Paul.[7] I told him that Paul wouldn't do anything for me, that he should speak to him himself. He doesn't think he is at fault. I believe that if he had any hope for the return of Peralta,[8] he wouldn't be so submissive.

3. In regard to what you say about the prioress of Malagón,[9] I have already written to you about that. In a matter so serious you ought not leave the decision to me, so much more so because in knowing your desire I would not in conscience be able to oppose it. So I beg you to do what you think best, and consider who you think would make a good prioress there. She would have to have more capabilities than is required for subprioress. I can't think of anyone other than the prioress of Salamanca.[10] I don't know the one you mention and she is still new. The other one mentioned would function very poorly in the role of prioress. This distresses me. Recommend this intention to God and give orders about what to do. The actual circumstances make it difficult to transfer nuns. May the Lord direct things, for necessity has no law.[11]

Today is Thursday, 6 September.

I have no time to write to my Padre Fray Antonio[12] or say anything more.

Your paternity's servant and daughter,

Teresa of Jesus.

---

1. A code name for Jerónimo Tostado.
2. Code name for Francisco de Olea, a Jesuit from Madrid.
3. Code name for Nicolás Ormaneto, the nuncio.
4. Code name for the discalced Carmelite friars.
5. Code name for the discalced Carmelite nuns. Rumors were spreading in Seville that Tostado was to replace Gracián as visitator and that the discalced Carmelite nuns would then come under his jurisdiction.
6. Code name for Juan de las Infantas, an Andalusian Carmelite.
7. Code name for Gracián. Infante wanted Teresa to write him a letter of recommendation to present to Gracián. She declined.
8. A possible return from Portugal.
9. Brianda de San José. She was seriously ill.
10. Ana de la Encarnación.
11. This axiom appears in the Carmelite *Rule of St. Albert*, 13.
12. Antonio de Jesús (Heredia).

120. To Madre María de San José, Seville

Toledo, 7 September 1576

(Autograph: DCN, Valladolid)

This letter deals with safe mail delivery, postage, some financial matters, the selection of new postulants, Gracián's visitation, and other concerns of the Seville Carmel.

1. Jesus be with your reverence. I assure you that since I so enjoy your letters I look forward to receiving them. I don't know why it is that I have so special a love for your house and those who live there, unless it's because I suffered so many trials

there. I am well now, glory to God. The fevers ended up in a bad cold.

2. I saw clearly the trial you would have to undergo because of the words and deeds of those fathers.[1] Even here there has been no lack of trial. But since God has delivered us from Tostado,[2] I hope in His Majesty that we will be shown favor in everything else. I don't believe there is the slightest exaggeration in accusing him of hostility toward the discalced friars and me, for he gave clear signs of this. There is always need for much prayer that God will deliver our *padre*[3] from these men and give them light and restore order in these matters. As long as our most reverend general[4] is so displeased, I tell you there will be no lack of means for us to gain merit.

3. Because you will learn about everything from our *padre*, I'm not saying anything about this, except that I beg you out of charity to write to me, when our *padre* is unable, about what is going on, and give him my letters and send me a summary of his. You see what anxieties one goes through when present there. Imagine what I must go through being so far away. The chief mail carrier here is a cousin of one of our nuns in Segovia. He has come to see me and promises to do wonders for you. His name is Figueredo.[5] He is, as I say, the chief mail carrier here. We have come to an agreement, and he says that if down there you take care to give the letters to the chief carrier, I will receive them in about eight days. What a great thing that would be! He says that by placing the packet for me in a folder addressed to Figueredo, the chief carrier in Toledo, no letter will be lost even if there are many. It's more work for you, but I know that you would take on even more for me, as I would for you.

4. You should know that at times I have such a desire to see you that it would seem I have nothing else to think about; this is true. You can find out down there whether you must use the title *magnífico*[6] or something else. He has an important position. For this reason I am happier to stay here now, for Avila is

an inconvenient place as far as these services go and for other things as well. I'm only sorry because of my brother[7] who finds the separation difficult. You're wrong for not writing to him now and then. In the enclosed letter of his, you will see how bad his health is, although I praise God that he has no fever.

5. I never remember to keep the letters they write me about Teresa.[8] All of the nuns tell of how they are in awe at the perfection they see in her and her inclination to assume the lowest offices. She tells them they shouldn't think that because she is the niece of the foundress they should esteem her more, but less. They are very fond of her; they say any number of things about her. I tell you this so that you give praise to God, for you were the nuns who directed her toward the desire for this good. I am delighted that you pray to His Majesty for her. I love her dearly and also her father, but I assure you I am at rest to be far away. I can't understand why, unless it is that the joys of this life are wearisome for me. I must be afraid of becoming attached to anything in it, and so it is better to remove the occasion; although so as not to be ungrateful for what my brother has done, I would like to be there now because he wants me present for the settling of certain matters.

6. Do not fail to let him know about the excise on the sale of the house,[9] and me too; the information should conform to what is on the enclosed paper. I see clearly that you are not going to have enough money, and so I began dealing with the Nicolao[10] matter so that they will give you at the appropriate time the 400 ducats. I had refused that postulant because they told me she had I don't know what kind of scar. Nicolao wrote me another letter, which I am enclosing. Our *padre* told me she isn't suited for us. Nonetheless, I have not been insistent, because in our present need one could consider if it may not be fitting to give her a try. Perhaps she will turn out to be good. Speak of the matter with our *padre* if you think you need to and find out about her faults, for I spoke to him only a little about this. I see that your income is poor. I was surprised to

learn that Beatriz's mother[11] brought no more than 1500 ducats, although she is such that even if she brought no dowry you would gain a great deal. I am happy that you are making stockings and earning a profit. God helps those who help themselves.

7. In answer to what you say about paying the rent by selling the other things, it would clearly be a very great blessing to be free of that burden. If adding the dowry of Bernalda,[12] I mean of Pablos, the sum should reach 3,000 ducats, you should accept it. Speak about it first with some competent persons. When they added that condition, Padre Mariano[13] told me it didn't matter, that even though it was added they would have to take the money because anything else would be unjust. Inquire about everything; before paying the rent, see that you have money in the house. Let Padre Garciálvarez[14] speak with the different ones, and they should speak about it to our *padre*, for when he is there you needn't consult me about anything, but consult him. Please God Leonor's[15] dowry will not be reduced. Tell me how she is doing—for I am not at all satisfied with her intelligence—and if she shows good will.

8. As for Vanegas,[16] it would be a difficult thing to accept someone now who has nothing for a dowry. This could only be tolerated by doing it for the love of God alone, for no one has been accepted there under the title of an alms, and God will help us. Perhaps he will draw others to help us because of our doing this for him. This should be done only if the family pleads insistently with our *padre* and he gives you orders. You shouldn't say a word. And be careful, my friend, that you are not in a hurry to accept nuns, for your life depends on their being suited for us. This one of Nicolao's seems to be pretty and nothing else.

9. The niece or cousin of Garciálvarez,[17] in my opinion, is certainly all that I told you she is. Caballar[18] told me. I don't believe it is Doña Clemencia,[19] but the other one. You can tell Garciálvarez frankly that they've told you she has suffered from

great melancholy. He told me clearly she is insane, so I said no more. This was my impression, and I don't believe I am mistaken. The other girls have a father, and you will have a hard time getting something. Even were this not so, there would be no reason now to burden the house unless to free oneself at once from debt. Let's wait a little, for with the uproar caused by those friars down there, I am not surprised that no one is entering.

10. Keep track of all that you spend on postage so that you can subtract it from the forty ducats they have sent from St. Joseph's in Avila; and be careful not to do anything else, for that would not show zeal but foolishness. I have a reason for saying this. How can you presume to send money already! This struck me as funny, since I am so worried about what you are going to live on. Nevertheless, it arrived at an opportune time for paying the postage. May God reward you, and for the orange blossom water, which is very good, and for Juana de la Cruz's veil.[20] However, you should not presume to do things like this again, for when I want something I will certainly let you know, and, I think, with greater openness and desire than I would with those in whom I have the greatest trust. For I believe that you and the nuns would willingly do whatever I ask. The one with the beautiful voice never came back. I am carefully watching for someone who would be suitable for your community.

11. Oh, how I hope they will give you the water![21] I have wanted this so much that I can't believe it. I have some hope that Padre Mariano,[22] or our *padre*, will be able to work something out with Fray Buenaventura,[23] since he is the Franciscans' guardian. May the Lord bring it about, for it would be a great relief. You can assuredly believe that it would mean more to me to be down there, now that our *padre* is on his way, than up here, even if I were to undergo some difficult moments because of the bishop.[24] I am amazed by the joy I feel in the thought of returning to you. God does everything for the best.

May he be blessed for everything and keep you for me many years.

12. So as not to sadden you I didn't want to speak to you about my own sorrow over the condition of our prioress in Malagón,[25] although God has drawn profit from worse situations. Apart from how much I love her, her loss is a terrible thing for us at this time. I would have brought her here, but our doctor tells me that though she was given a year to live, she wouldn't live more than a month here. May the Lord find a remedy. Pray hard for her. Her condition is really hopeless. They say it's consumption. Be careful not to drink sarsaparilla water, even though it may be good against hysteria. The prioress[26] and the sisters send their regards.

13. I have been very sorry about the illness of my holy prior,[27] and we are praying for him. Let me know about him and of what has been done about Delgado,[28] and if Beatriz and her sister were left something by their mother that should go to the house, and give my regards to all those you think it fitting, and remain with God. I have gone on at length and am happy to know that you are all well, especially you. I fear for our prioresses when I see the state we have come to. May God preserve you, my daughter.

14. At times I receive letters from Beas and Caravaca. They have no lack of trials in Caravaca, but I hope in God a remedy will be found.

Today is 7 September.

Your Reverence's,

Teresa of Jesus

15. Let us now write more often. See that you don't neglect this or fail to be solicitous at times for our *padre*. He fully agrees with us about not serving meals to the friars. We have insisted on this so much that I wouldn't want him to go to extremes,

and you can determine what his need is and consider how much his health matters to us.

16. How come you never say anything about Fray Gregorio?[29] Give him my best wishes and tell me how the friars are doing—if you don't write me about everything, no one will—and how you are getting on with Fray Antonio de Jesús.[30]

17. I will not answer Nicolao until I hear from you. You should pay half a *real* when you have no more than three or four letters; if you have more, then pay more.

18. Since I know what it's like to be in need and how hard it is to find money there, I did not dare reject entirely Nicolao's recommendation.[31] When you ask our *padre* for his opinion on a matter, you need to inform him about everything without hurrying him; otherwise, because he's so busy, the importance of the matter will escape him.

---

1. The Carmelites of the observance in Seville.
2. Jerónimo Tostado, the visitator appointed by the Carmelite order, whose commission was opposed by the royal council. He had then gone from Madrid to Portugal.
3. Jerónimo Gracián, who at the time was in Almodóvar near Toledo.
4. Giovanni Battista Rossi.
5. Antonio Figueredo.
6. The envelope containing the letters was to be addressed to Figueredo, and the concern is about his proper title.
7. Lorenzo de Cepeda.
8. Her niece is a Carmelite postulant at St. Joseph's in Avila.
9. The excise on the sale of the house was covered with Lorenzo's money.
10. Nicolás Doria was at the time a priest in Seville who became a discalced Carmelite shortly afterward. He was recommending a postulant for the Seville Carmel.
11. Beatriz de la Madre de Dios (Chaves) was a nun in the Seville Carmel whose mother, Juana Gómez, entered the same Carmel the month this letter was written.
12. Bernarda de San José, the daughter of Pablo Matías.

13. Ambrosio Mariano de San Benito.
14. The community's friend and confessor.
15. Leonor de San Angelo, who made profession 18 August 1577.
16. Mariana de los Santos, the daughter of Diego Vázquez and Ana Vanegas.
17. Jerónima de la Madre de Dios was his cousin. She made her profession on 3 February 1578.
18. He has not been identified.
19. This was a mistake. The person is Doña Constancia del Rio, a relative of Garciálvarez's.
20. Juana de la Cruz (Gómez), the mother of Beatriz de la Madre de Dios.
21. She is alluding to a request made to the Franciscans to tap water from their property. The request was not granted.
22. Ambrosio Mariano de San Benito, a member of the discalced Carmelites in Seville, was an expert in water conveyance.
23. Diego de Buenaventura, visitator of the Andalusian Franciscans.
24. She is probably alluding to the Andalusian Carmelite Fray Diego de León.
25. Brianda de San José.
26. The prioress in Toledo was Ana de los Angeles.
27. The prior of the Carthusians (Las Cuevas), Fray Hernando de Pantoja.
28. Inés Delgado, a benefactress of the discalced nuns.
29. Gregorio Nacianceno, a discalced Carmelite friar residing in Seville.
30. Antonio de Jesús (Heredia), prior of the discalced friars in Seville.
31. An allusion to the postulant recommended by Nicolás Doria.

121. To Padre Gracián, Almodóvar

Toledo, 9 September 1576

Gracián is preparing for his trip to Seville, where he will resume his official visitation of the Carmelites there. This letter reflects Teresa's optimism about it.

To our Padre Fray Jerónimo Gracián, apostolic commissary

of the Carmelite Order.

1. Jesus. May the Holy Spirit guide and enlighten your honor, and may your Blessed Virgin accompany you.

I tell you, I believe you should make use of the least culpable among those friars to execute your orders. If that provincial[1] had not carried on so foolishly, he would not have been a bad executioner. I am much more encouraged now than I was that other time.

2. You should know that my good friend Salazar[2] is here. Hardly had I written that I needed to see him than he circled back many leagues so as to come here. He is indeed a friend. I was delighted with his visit. He says that the chief angel[3] is very happy to have a niece[4] among the butterflies and that he esteems them highly, and Salazar told him about the eagles[5] and never stops praising them.

3. The prioress[6] and sisters here send you many greetings. They are praying urgently for your paternity. My Isabel[7] is doing very nicely. The enclosed letter is from Señora Doña Juana.[8] She will be my consolation, although it's a terrible embarrassment for me that this house cannot be set up to provide for her adequately. How come you didn't inform that man Roque[9] about my letters? Now I see that that is the name I wanted to know. Pardon the length of this; it was a way of relaxing. And God be with you.

Yesterday was our Lady's feast. Antonio[10] arrived today.

Your unworthy daughter,

Teresa of Jesus,

4. Rodrigo Alvarez[11] has written to me and said much about you. Don't neglect to keep in touch with them[12] as usual, for charity's sake.

1. Agustín Suárez, provincial of the Carmelites of the observance in Andalusia. He suggested that Gracián make use of the Carmelites themselves to carry out the visitation.
2. Gaspar de Salazar, a Jesuit whom she knew in Avila.
3. The grand inquisitor, Gaspar de Quiroga.
4. Jerónima de la Encarnación had entered the Carmel in Medina del Campo.
5. The butterflies are the discalced Carmelite nuns, and the eagles are the discalced friars.
6. Ana de los Angeles, the prioress of Toledo.
7. Gracián's sister Isabel who entered the Carmel of Toledo when only eight years old.
8. Gracián's mother, Juana Dantisco; she is planning to come to Toledo.
9. The notary Roque de Huerta (cf. Ltr. 118.6).
10. Antonio Ruiz, from Malagón.
11. A Jesuit director of Teresa's in Seville.
12. The Jesuits.

122. To Madre María de San José, Seville

Toledo, 9 September 1576

(Autograph: DCN, Valladolid)

Replying to letters received from Madre María, Teresa answers questions and comments on various matters concerning the Seville Carmel, showing particularly her concern over their poor financial situation. She also sends news about Malagón and Teresita.

1. Jesus. The grace of the Holy Spirit be with your reverence, my daughter. I can truthfully say that your letters are such a consolation. When I read the one and thought there were no more, I myself was surprised by the happiness I felt when I discovered another one; it was as though I hadn't received the first. You should then realize that your letters are a kind of recreation for me. Always send me a separate note listing the

particular items you want me to respond to so that I don't forget anything.

2. With regard to the nuns, our *padre*[1] left word, I think, that Beatriz's mother[2] could enter, and I was delighted. So you are doing well to accept her, and you can give her the habit with my best wishes, for I am especially happy about this. And tell her that I would be happy to be there with her. I already wrote you to accept Beatriz[3] for profession—I will tell our *padre*. And give her my regards and tell her not to forget me on that day.

3. Regarding Garciálvarez's cousins, I don't know if you recall that I was told that one had been melancholic to the extreme,[4] for she lost her mind. I don't believe it is Doña Constanza.[5] Speak about the matter plainly. As for the niece,[6] I know nothing. If suited for us, anyone from his family is preferable to others. Make a thorough inquiry and write for permission from our *padre* when you are fully informed. He will be in Almodóvar for now, as you will have learned, since the discalced friars are holding a chapter, an excellent thing for them to do. Why is it you didn't say anything about Padre Fray Gregorio's[7] illness? I indeed felt sorry in hearing about it.

4. Getting back to the nuns, the aspirant with the beautiful voice of whom I wrote to you never returned.[8] There is another one whom Nicolao[9] highly recommends—and Padre Mariano[10] says that Nicolao will do so much for the house. This aspirant will bring a little over 400 ducats in addition to her trousseau. But she will give them right away. This is what I am trying to bring about, that you receive the interest and be free of worry. And there will even be enough to pay the excise on the sale's agreement. I am so sorry that the affair hadn't been concluded before that other one died; perhaps it's for the best.

5. Be always careful to prefer some agreement;[11] and don't forget this, for our *padre* wrote me that a very learned man in Madrid told him we are not in the right and that even if we were, litigations are always troublesome. Don't forget this.

6. They have told me that this nun is very good. I have urged Juan Díaz[12] to meet with her; if whatever the facial mark they say she has is unsightly she should not be accepted. I was attracted by the dowry money that, it is said, will be given as soon as we want it, for the money from Beatriz's mother and Pablo[13] ought not to be touched; it should be reserved for making the principal payment. If you use it up for other expenses, you will be left with a heavy burden, which is a terrible thing. I would like if possible to send you help from here. I am going to inquire thoroughly about that young lady. They praise her highly, and indeed she is from up here. I will try to meet her.

7. As for what you say about the sermons, it is all right for now. In the present circumstances do what they tell you. In the future you must follow our *Acts*,[14] however annoyed others become.

8. I repeat that I would not want you to sell this sister's goods, but we should look for other means. Otherwise, we will be left with that burdensome debt. It would be onerous to try to pay everything at once with Pablo's money. You would be left in a weakened situation.

9. Oh, how the letter from my daughters[15] pleased us. I tell you it was excellent. Give them my regards and tell them I am obliged to write to Garciálvarez. I am delighted that he is in the present mood. Nonetheless, you should all be careful, for he is so perfect that what we might think is edifying will scandalize him. That region down there is not noted for its simplicity.[16]

10. I am extremely delighted that the bishop is well[17] and have given thanks to God. Tell him this when you see him, and if you don't see him very often, don't worry about it. Now the letters are well done, for each one tells me about something different.[18] I was delighted with them.

11. Teresa[19] is doing very well. The perfection she showed on the journey is something to praise God for; it was astonishing. She didn't want to sleep even one night outside the mon-

astery. I assure you that just as you worked hard with her, she is now an honor to you. I can never finish thanking you for the good training you gave her, nor can her father.[20] He is well. I tore up a letter that she had written me, which made us laugh. In your charity, please always pray for her; I ask this especially of her teacher.[21] They write me that she is still homesick for Seville and praises you all highly. I think that some letters for the assistant[22] will be included with these letters; if not, I'll send them later.

12. Today I wrote to Madrid to ask the Count of Olivares[23] to write. It would be a very fortunate thing if he did. May God bring it about. I'll do what I can. Please God I'll be able to do something. I am greatly consoled to know that the house is cool; in exchange for this, I will be glad to put up with the heat here. Don't send me anything, for goodness' sake, for it costs more than it's worth. Some of the quinces arrived in good condition, but not many. The little fish were good. The tuna was left in Malagón and will do much good. Because they will write to you, I will not mention anything about their trials and the prioress's poor health; although the spitting up of blood has stopped,[24] glory to God. May he watch over you, my daughters, and make you holy, amen.

13. I don't think one dares answer your letter. Nonetheless, I assure you that since you are wearing tunics of worsted wool, you can wear underskirts made of the same material without any imperfection. I much prefer this to fine wool.

Today is 9 September.

Your reverence's

Teresa of Jesus

---

1. Jerónimo Gracián who in those days was presiding over the chapter at Almodóvar.
2. Juana Gómez de Chaves, who would enter the Seville Carmel on 29 September of that same year.

3. Beatriz de la Madre de Dios, daughter of the mother just mentioned. She made her profession on the same day that her mother took the habit.
4. Cf. Ltr. 120.9.
5. Constanza del Rio.
6. Cf. Ltr. 120, note 16.
7. Gregorio Nacianceno, a discalced Carmelite in Seville.
8. Cf. Ltr. 120.10.
9. Nicolás Doria; cf. Ltr. 120.6.
10. Ambrosio Mariano de San Benito, a discalced Carmelite friar in Seville who was also Italian and a friend of Doria's.
11. The agreement would regard the excise they owed from the purchase of the property in Seville.
12. A disciple of St. John of Avila's.
13. Pablo Matías, father of Bernarda de San José.
14. It could refer to either the decisions of the apostolic visitators or the constitutions of the discalced nuns.
15. The Carmelite nuns in Seville.
16. Misunderstandings developed later between Garciálvarez and the nuns.
17. Diego de León, a Carmelite of the observance.
18. Cf. Ltr. 114.2 in which she points out in jest that in writing to her the nuns repeat the same news, instead of each one telling her something different.
19. Her niece, Teresita, who had traveled from Seville to Toledo with her that summer.
20. Teresa's brother Lorenzo.
21. The nun in Seville who had been her teacher and guide, probably María de San José herself.
22. Don Francisco de Zapata, the count of Olivares.
23. Don Enrique de Guzmán.
24. The prioress, Brianda de San José, had a serious illness of the lungs.

123. To Don Francisco de Salcedo, Avila

Toledo, 13 September 1576

(Autograph: DCN, Logroño)

Salcedo has got himself entangled in a litigation that could result in the loss of his property. Teresa sympathizes with him and thanks him for being a benefactor of the nuns of St. Joseph's in Avila.

1. Jesus. The grace of the Holy Spirit be ever with your honor. It seems to me our Lord is treating you as he does the strong, for since you want to be poor he is taking away your income. May he be blessed for everything, for he enriches those he loves by exercising them in suffering.

2. At the time I found out, I felt distressed. I was told of this by our Father Visitator[1] who learned of it from the illustrious president[2] of the Royal Council. Afterward I began to think it is for the best, for it is not possible that our Lord would neglect to care for you now that you are without a livelihood. May our Lord so direct events that you might serve him more. This is what all of us must desire who love you in the Lord, for it is what most suits you. I earnestly beseech God for this; the sisters here do likewise, and those up there will not fail to do the same. It is impossible for God to fail to do what most befits you. So, be very confident and joyful.

3. I have been happy since your servant told me that for a year you have been very well, without having any of your usual ailments. It wasn't Mother Prioress[3] who told me. May God be praised and repay you for the help you are always giving the sisters, which seems inspired by God since you never tire of doing so. The Lord will satisfy this debt we owe you, for he is a very good paymaster.

4. I do not thank you more often for this since I know about you and you about me in another way. But be certain this

doesn't mean any lack of gratitude; if I could serve you even to the point of it costing me my life and peace, I think I would do it....May God grant you peace, as he can here below, so that you will enjoy the eternal rest.

5. The bishop of Troya[4] is not here, and so the chalice is not consecrated. They say he will come soon. I will arrange to send it to him when he comes. Have it repaired there in the meantime. I beg you not to forget to pray for me in your holy Masses. May His Majesty keep you many years, giving you the holiness I beg of him, amen.

Today is 13 September.

Your honor's unworthy servant,

Teresa of Jesus, Carmelite

1. Jerónimo Gracián.
2. Diego de Covarrubias.
3. The prioress of St. Joseph's in Avila.
4. Rodrigo Vázquez from Avila.

124. To Padre Jerónimo Gracián, Seville
Toledo, 20 September 1576

(Autograph fragment: DCF, S. Teresa al Museo, Naples)

She speaks enthusiastically of Gracián's mother, mentioning as well some of her children. Happy with the results of the chapter in Almodóvar, she fears that Gracián will not act quickly enough in sending the two friars to Rome, for the nuncio seems to be approaching his end. She advises Gracián also concerning his visitation in Andalusia and gives him news about the Carmel in Malagón.

1. Jesus. The grace of the Holy Spirit be with your paternity. Do not think, *mi padre*, that you can make things perfect with

one stroke. What fruit can you bring about in the two or three days you stay in those small houses that Padre Fray Antonio[1] could not? Hardly will you have left when they will return to their former ways, and you by doing this are exposing yourself to a thousand dangers.

2. Señora Doña Juana[2] is convinced that you do what I ask of you. Please God that in the present matter this will be so. She spent three days here, although I was not able to enjoy her presence in the measure that I would have liked, for she had many other visitors, especially the canon.[3] They became great friends. I assure you, the qualities God has given her are among the best. I have come across few instances in my lifetime of talent and character like hers, or I don't think any at all. She has a simplicity and openness that put me in seventh heaven. In these she greatly surpasses her son.[4] It would be the greatest consolation to me if I lived in a place where I could converse with her frequently. We got along so well that one might have said we had known each other all our lives.

3. She says she was delighted with her stay here. God willed that she find lodging with a widow who lives alone with her maids. It was very much to her liking and close by, which she considered very fortunate. Her meals were prepared and brought to her from here; and it was providential that you gave me orders to keep money so as not to have to be dependent on what the monastery could provide, which would have been a painful thing for me. It was a small matter, but I was able to do things the way I like.

4. It amused me when you told me to open the grille and lift my veil for her. It seems you do not know me; I would have wanted to open the depths of my heart to her. Señora Doña Juana, her daughter, stayed with her until the last day. She seemed charming to me, and I am sorry to see her among those young girls at the school,[5] because the truth of the matter is that, from what she says, she finds it more difficult there than she would here. I would willingly give her the habit along

with that little angel of mine, her sister,[6] who is as pretty and plump as can be. Señora Doña Juana couldn't get over her surprise on seeing her. Periquito, her brother,[7] for all his intelligence, couldn't recognize her when he came. She is my whole recreation here. I spoke much about her to Señora Doña Juana. On the last day it seems she was somewhat touched, according to what Ana de Zurita[8] told me. She told her that she had spent the night thinking about this and was close to making a decision, but that she wanted to reflect on it more. May God bring it about. Pray for this, for since she resembles you very much, I would love to have her with me.

5. Since Señora Doña Juana observed the happiness and behavior of all the nuns, she has decided to make the effort to send Señora Doña María[9] to Valladolid soon, and I think she has repented for having dissuaded Señora Doña Adriana[10] from going there. She was very satisfied, from what I could tell, and I don't think she is deceitful.

6. Yesterday she wrote me a highly complimentary letter, saying that while she was here she did not experience her pain and sadness. Her letter got torn up along with some others. I can't count the letters that have arrived these past two days. They'll make me lose my mind. I felt bad that the letter was destroyed, for I wanted to send it to you. The day she left she said that the tertian fever had left Señor Lucas Gracián[11] and that he is now well. Oh, what a nice person Tomás Gracián[12] is. I like him very much. He also came here. Today I wrote to him telling him that you were doing well.

7. I was thinking today about which of us two loved you more. I find that Señora Doña Juana has a husband and other children to love, and poor Laurencia has nothing else on earth but this *padre*.[13] May God be pleased to watch over him for her, amen, for I am consoling her as much as I can. She tells me that Joseph[14] has assured her again, and in this way she keeps going, although with trials and without any relief from them.

8. Let's come now to the chapter.[15] The members have returned extremely happy, and I am very happy about all the good that was accomplished, glory to God! As usual, this time, too, you have not been spared great praise. It all comes from his hand; and also, perhaps, the prayers do much good, as you say. I was extremely pleased about the appointment of a *zelator*[16] for the various houses. That is a very good step and will prove beneficial. I insisted with him[17] that he stress manual labor, for it is infinitely important. I said I would write to you about it because the chapter did not deal with this. I told him that it was in the constitutions and the rule[18] and that he could do nothing better than to see to their observance. I was also happy—so much so that I couldn't believe it—that they expelled the ones they did from the order. To be able to do this is very important.

9. I was also very happy over the steps taken to strive in every way possible to become a separate province by approaching our Father General,[19] for it is an unbearable battle to have to go about with the displeasure of one's major superior. If this costs money, God will provide it; let it be given to the two companions. And for love of God, your paternity should make every effort that they not delay in going. Don't take this as a secondary matter, for it is the most important. And if that prior of La Peñuela knows Father General well, it would be a good idea for him to accompany Padre Mariano.[20] And if they cannot obtain any concessions, let them speak with the pope. But the first course of action is the best, and now is the propitious time. And in view of Methuselah's[21] health, I don't know why we are waiting, which is like having nothing to stand on and then one day discovering that we are lost.

10. You should know that a priest friend of mine—who discusses matters of his soul with me—told me today that he is very certain that Gilberto[22] will die soon, and he even mentioned that it could be this year. He said that he had experienced such presentiments about others and that these were

never wrong. This is something possible, although one shouldn't pay attention to such experiences. But since it is not impossible, it would be good for you to keep in mind, for the sake of our concerns, that this could happen. So deal with the visitation matters as with things of short duration. All that Fray Pedro Fernández[23] wanted to have carried out at the Incarnation, he did through the hand of Fray Angel—and he observed from afar.[24] Not for this reason did he cease to be the visitator or fail to do his duty. I always remember how that provincial[25] treated you when you were staying in their house, and so I wouldn't want you to show any ingratitude, if you can avoid it. They complain that you are being directed by Padre Evangelista.[26] Also in this regard, you should be careful, for we are not so perfect as to be unable to feel dislike for some and affection for others.

11. The prioress of Malagón[27] is somewhat better, glory to God, although that means little, according to what the doctors say. I was amazed that you wanted to leave the decision to me about going to Malagón when it is out of the question for many reasons. One of them is that there would be no sense to it, for I do not have enough health to care for the sick, nor that much charity. As for the house, I mean the work on it, I am accomplishing much more here. Since Antonio Ruiz[28] is there, the nuns have nothing to worry about. And even if my presence were greatly needed, this would not be a good time to go as you can see.

12. Another good thing is that you are not giving me orders to go, nor do you think that it would be good for me if I did, and that you are telling me I can do what seems to me best. That would show great perfection on my part, to think that my opinion would be better than yours! When they told me that the prioress had lost her senses and speech—insisting on the seriousness of the situation—I sent word that the direction of the house should be taken up by Juana Bautista,[29] who in my opinion was the best choice. It's so much trouble for me to have to

transfer nuns such a distance that I avoid doing so as long as I can. I wrote to the prioress so that she would know my opinion, if she were in any condition to read it, but said that if she thought otherwise she could choose whomever she wanted, for that would be in accord with the order's rule.

13. She did not want Juana Bautista and chose Beatriz de Jesús,[30] who she said is much better. Perhaps she may be, but I don't think so. Nor did she want Isabel de Jesús[31] to be novice mistress. They have so many novices that I am worried. Isabel has experience and has not formed bad novices; she may not be astute, but she is a good nun. The licentiate[32] didn't think Isabel should be chosen either, but Beatriz now has ended up with everything and she is exhausted. If she can't manage, there are others to choose from, and for this house that would be better, in my opinion, than bringing in a nun from elsewhere while God still preserves the life of the prioress. I have clearly seen that you did everything so as to please her. But if I should be tempted to go, it would be difficult. Hardly do I think of going somewhere, it seems to me, than everybody knows about it. As for me, I can tell you that in a way I would be happy to spend some days there.

14. Doña Luisa[33] was here yesterday, and I think I got her to agree to give 4,000 ducats this year, for she only had to give 2,000. The construction manager says that if she gives this amount, he will build the place for the nuns by a year from this Christmas; that is, they will be able to live there by then. So it seems that God guides you well, for my stay here will be most beneficial, and will even bring me happiness. I experience much happiness when I don't have to see relatives as prioress in Avila.

15. My temperament is strange, for when I saw that in leaving me here you weren't concerned that I had no desire to stay, I felt the greatest happiness. And I felt free about expressing my desires and opinions when I saw that you pay no attention to what I think.[34]

16. I told Isabel's[35] novice mistress to write to you. In case you don't remember her name, the enclosed letter is for you. Oh, how pretty she is becoming. How plumb she's getting and charming. May God make her a saint and watch over your paternity much more than me. Pardon me for making this so long and be patient since you are down there and I am up here. I am well. Today is the vigil of the feast of St. Matthew. Regarding that matter about Rome,[36] I beg you to hurry; don't wait until summer, for the weather is good now, and believe me that this is what is fitting for us.

Your paternity's unworthy servant and subject,

Teresa of Jesus

17. Don't kill yourself over those nuns,[37] for according to what Methuselah[38] says, your office will be of short duration. And the night owls[39] think this also, for they say he told Peralta[40] to hurry so as to be back here within two months, and they say that certainly he will take full charge. Oh, if only this matter[41] were concluded! How welcome that would be, and may His Majesty deliver us from all this confusion.

---

1. Antonio de Jesús (Heredia). He had already worked with Padre Fernández, the visitator in Castile. He could help Gracián by making visitations of the smaller monasteries.
2. Juana Dantisco, Gracián's mother.
3. Alonso Velázquez.
4. Gracián himself.
5. Juana Gracián attended a school for young girls from the nobility founded by Silíceo in Toledo.
6. Isabel Gracián, who was a member of the Carmel in Toledo.
7. Pedro Gracián, Doña Juana's son.
8. The person who showed hospitality to the Graciáns when they stayed in Toledo.
9. This sister of Padre Gracián's entered the Carmel in Valladolid.
10. Another sister of Gracián's; she entered the Conceptionist Franciscan sisters in Madrid.
11. One of the oldest sons in the Gracián family.

12. Another of Gracián's brothers; he was married to Lorenza de Zurita of the family who was showing Doña Juana hospitality.
13. Laurencia is a code name for Teresa herself, and the *padre* is Gracián.
14. The code name for Jesus Christ.
15. The chapter celebrated by the discalced Carmelite friars during the first days of September in Almodóvar del Campo.
16. One appointed to watch over and promote the monastic observance.
17. Juan de Jesús (Roca), whom the chapter appointed as the overseer of the religious observance in the monasteries of the discalced friars.
18. She is referring to words in the rule repeated in the constitutions: "You must give yourselves to work of some kind so that the devil may always find you busy."
19. Giovanni Battista Rossi. Teresa was worried that the discalced friars might try to erect a province without seeking the general's approval.
20. Pedro de los Angeles (prior of la Peñuela) and Ambrosio Mariano de San Benito were the two friars appointed to go to Rome.
21. Nicolás Ormaneto, the nuncio.
22. Probably the nuncio also, who died the following year (18 June 1577).
23. Pedro Fernández, the Dominican visitator of the Carmelites in Castile.
24. Angel de Salazar was the provincial of the Carmelites in Castile.
25. The provincial of the Carmelites in Andalusia, Agustín Suárez.
26. Juan Evangelista, the former subprior of the Carmelite monastery in Seville.
27. Brianda de San José.
28. A merchant from Malagón who was a friend of Teresa's.
29. Juana Bautista Baena made her profession in Malagón in 1569.
30. A daughter of Teresa's cousin, Francisco de Cepeda; she had been at the Incarnation. In a later letter Teresa had to admit that Beatriz was doing extremely well in carrying out the office.
31. Isabel de Jesús (Gutiérrez) had also come from the Incarnation in Avila.
32. Gaspar de Villanueva, who was the chaplain at Malagón.
33. Luisa de la Cerda, the patron founder of Malagón.
34. Teresa was thinking of returning to Avila and had already sent her trunk to the Carmel there.
35. Isabel Gracián.

36. She is referring to the trip of the two discalced friars to Rome to negotiate the establishment of a separate province for the discalced Carmelites.
37. A probable reference to the Carmelite nuns of the observance in Paterna and Seville.
38. The nuncio, Nicolás Ormaneto.
39. Probably the Carmelites of the observance (Paterna).
40. Jerónimo Tostado.
41. The effort by the discalced friars to form a separate province.

125. To Madre María de San José, Seville

Toledo, 20 September 1576

Once the chapter in Almodóvar was finished, Gracián and some of the other chapter fathers visited Teresa in Toledo. Gracián has returned to Seville and Teresa is concerned for his well-being.

For Mother Prioress of St. Joseph's, Seville

1. Jesus. The grace of the Holy Spirit be with your reverence, my daughter. I wrote at length to our *padre*[1] and so I have nothing more to say except that I desire news about you and that the prioress of Malagón[2] is a bit better.

2. My brother[3] wants to know if you received his letters, one of which contained four *reales* to be given to the pharmacist who lives near your house. They are for some ointment my brother received from him when, I think, he had the sore leg. If they didn't arrive, pay for this yourself and don't neglect to write to him, for I think he expects this even though I send him your greetings. My best regards to all the nuns; the prioress[4] sends her regards to you. She will write through the muleteer. I didn't permit her to do so now hoping to pay less postage. More letters have arrived than I expected, and so the cost for postage will be high.

3. I would like to have news about *mi padre*, about the prior of Las Cuevas,[5] and about what has been done in regard to the water.[6] May God in his power provide and watch over all the sisters for me; give them my regards. For goodness' sake remember to tell our *padre* to be careful, and to show him every attention; and add what you spend to the forty ducats[7] and don't be foolish. Do what I'm telling you, and also pay the postage, for I will verify it here. I am asking all the nuns to pray hard for you, although I see there is no need to do so.

Today is the vigil of St. Matthew, and I am yours,

Teresa of Jesus

1. Jerónimo Gracián whom she presumes is in Seville.
2. Brianda de San José, who had been hemorrhaging from the lungs a few days before.
3. Lorenzo de Cepeda, a great benefactor of the Carmel in Seville.
4. Ana de los Angeles, prioress of Toledo.
5. Hernando de Pantoja, the prior of the Carthusians of Las Cuevas who was then old and ailing.
6. The nuns of Seville had requested the Franciscan friars to allow them to tap water from their property.
7. The Carmel of Seville owed the Carmel of St. Joseph's in Avila forty ducats.

126. To Madre María de San José, Seville

Toledo, 22 September 1576

She has not heard from Gracián and does not know if he has arrived in Seville yet. She refers hastily to matters concerning vocations, finances, and kinds of cloth used by the nuns.

For Mother Prioress of St. Joseph's Carmel of Seville, Discalced Carmelite Nuns, San José Street, Behind San

Francisco.

1. Jesus be with your reverence. I wrote you two days ago by way of the chief courier,[1] and so I have nothing to say here except that my brother[2] is now well (for I forgot to mention this) and that the nuns don't want such expensive fine wool. The material they use for the underskirts here is like what you used for Teresa,[3] although coarser, the coarser the better. For goodness' sake, take care to send me news of our *padre*[4] by the means I pointed out in the letter his paternity brought you. I'm longing to know whether he arrived safely and how his trip went. If I was so concerned when he was close, imagine what I feel now!

2. My great desire is that you be careful not to fill the house with nuns unless someone comes along who is suited for the life and able to help pay for the house. I also desire that you reach an agreement about the excise.[5] I assure you that your troubles are of concern to me. Please God, I may see you without any and with the health I desire for you. My regards to all the sisters, and to my nurse,[6] whom I don't forget, especially at night.

3. I am not going to write again to our *padre* now, for as I say I wrote him at length the day before yesterday, and I think he will be so busy that it will be good not to bother him with unnecessary matters. I pray hard for him. Don't fail to do so there. And give my very best regards to Padre Fray Gregorio.[7] You haven't mentioned whether his health is all right now.

Yesterday was the feast of St. Matthew.

Your reverence's,

Teresa of Jesus

We are well.

---

1. Antonio Figueredo in Toledo.
2. Lorenzo de Cepeda.

3. The kind of cloth used to make clothes for Teresa's niece when she stayed in the Seville Carmel.
4. Jerónimo Gracián.
5. The excise they owed for the purchase of the property in Seville.
6. Leonor de San Gabriel.
7. Gregorio Nacianceno who lived in the monastery for the discalced friars, Los Remedios, in Seville.

127. To Madre María de San José, Seville

Toledo, 26 September 1576

She is writing in a hurry to tell that Mariano has arrived and to request detailed news about Gracián and the visitation in Andalusia. She cautions against accepting a postulant without assurance of a dowry.

1. Jesus be with your reverence. The carrier for this letter is in such a hurry that I can't say any more than that I am well and that Padre Mariano[1] arrived late yesterday. I enjoyed your letter. Glory to God that you are all well.

2. Don't accept the daughter of the Portuguese—or whatever he is—if he doesn't first deposit with a third person what he must give you.[2] I have learned that you won't be able to get a cent of it, and this is no time for us to accept a postulant for nothing; be careful not to do otherwise.

3. Give the enclosed letters to our Father Provincial personally.[3] And tell him not to be disturbed. Up here Padre Mariano and I are looking into what is going on down there to see if we can find a solution and we will do everything we possibly can. Tell him as well that after these letters were written I was going to entrust them to the good Antonio Ruiz,[4] who was going to Madrid, when Padre Mariano arrived. I was delighted to see him and to know that the Lord is now so arranging our affairs that those fathers are going to leave before being thrown out.[5]

4. Write to me, for goodness' sake, at once and in detail about what is going on. Don't leave this to our *padre*, for he won't have time. Many greetings to Señor Garciálvarez[6] and tell him that I long to see him. Look at my desires, so seemingly impossible to realize. May God reward him for all the favors he does us and watch over him; and also our good prior,[7] for whom we have prayed hard. I'm happy that he's somewhat better. Tell me also about your health, and tell our *padre* how much I would have wanted Padre Mariano to wait for him.[8]

5. Regards to my daughters,[9] and remain with God, my friend. The nuns in Caravaca have been sick; I am told they have written to you. They are doing well now and already buying a house. Since I have not answered their letter, I'm not sending it on to you. I was delighted with the news from Beas and the accounts of Padre Fray Gregorio;[10] I will write to him.

Mother Prioress in Malagón[11] is very sick.

I think today is 26 September.

Your reverence's,

Teresa of Jesus

---

1. Ambrosio Mariano de San Benito was on his way from Seville to Madrid to work toward implementing the decisions of the recent chapter of the discalced friars in Almodóvar.
2. The daughter was Blanca de Jesús María who did enter the Seville Carmel. She brought with her a dowry of 600 ducats. Sevillan banks were failing that year, which gave rise to Teresa's fears.
3. Jerónimo Gracián.
4. A neighbor in Malagón and friend of Teresa's.
5. These were Carmelite friars in Seville, already fugitives in a way from other religious orders, who chose to leave the Carmelite order rather than undergo expulsion by the visitator Gracián.
6. Confessor and friend of the discalced Carmelite nuns in Seville.
7. The Carthusian Hernando de Pantoja of Las Cuevas, who had been recently sick.

8. It seems Mariano received a commission from the chapter to negotiate in Madrid the establishment of a province for discalced Carmelites.
9. The Carmelite nuns in Seville.
10. Gregorio Nacianceno, a discalced Carmelite in Seville.
11. Brianda de San José who had a relapse in her illness.

128. To Padre Jerónimo Gracián, Seville

Toledo, 5 October 1576

(Autograph: DCF, Treviso, Italy)

In a cell apart, Teresa is enjoying some solitude and has time now for things other than writing letters, such as reading the story of Moses and working on The Book of Her Foundations. She still worries about Gracián's visitation in Andalusia and uses some unknown code names.

1. The grace of the Holy Spirit be with your paternity, *mi padre*. If the letter you sent by way of Madrid had not arrived, I would have been in a fine state, for today is the day after the feast of St. Francis and Fray Antonio[1] has not come; nor did I know whether you had arrived in good health until I saw your letter.

2. May God be blessed that you are well and that Paul[2] is too and interiorly at rest. Surely so complete an improvement seems supernatural. All of that must be necessary for this nature of ours, for such things serve well to humiliate and give us self-knowledge. I prayed earnestly here that the Lord would give him a period of calm, for it seems to me he has enough other trials. Tell him this for me.

3. Right now I am without any trials. I don't know where this will end up. They have given me a cell set apart like a hermitage and very cheerful, and my health is good, and I am away from relatives, although they reach me through their letters. Only my worries about what is going on down there

trouble me.[3] I tell you that as far as what pleases me goes you had a good idea in choosing to let me stay here. And even regarding the worries I mentioned, I feel more confident than usual.

4. Last night I was reading the story of Moses[4] and about the troubles he brought on the king and his whole kingdom with those plagues and how they never touched him. In fact, I was amazed and happy to see that no one has the power to cause harm if the Lord does not wish it. I enjoyed the account of the crossing of the Red Sea, thinking of how much less it is that we are asking for. It pleased me to see that saint in the midst of those conflicts by order of God. I was feeling joy at seeing my Eliseo[5] in the same situation and I offered him again to God. I remembered the favors Joseph[6] has granted me and what he has said about him: Still much more has to be endured for the honor and glory of God. I was consumed with the desire to find myself amid a thousand perils in order to serve him. With these and similar thoughts my life is passing. I've also written the foolish things you will find enclosed.

5. Now I am going to begin writing the story of the *Foundations* which Joseph told me will be for the benefit of many souls.[7] If God helps, I believe this will be so. But even apart from this locution, I had already decided to write the account since you had ordered me to do it. I was delighted that you gave such a long report at the chapter.[8] I don't know how those who have written contrary to what you reported are not ashamed. It is fortunate that those who perhaps would have had to leave against their will are leaving of their own accord.[9] It seems to me our Lord is straightening out our affairs. May it please His Majesty that what we are doing will bring him glory and be of benefit to those souls. You will be doing well if you give orders from your own monastery[10] about what should be done. Then they won't have to be observing whether you go to choir or not; I tell you everything will go better. Here, our

prayers are not lacking; they are better weapons than the ones used by those fathers.

6. I wrote to you at length through the chief courier,[11] and while waiting to know if you have received those letters, I have been writing by way of Madrid. About the matter concerning David, I think he will hoodwink Padre Esperanza,[12] as he usually does, for they are together and his brother has left. Although the presence of Fray Buenaventura[13] can accomplish much, I fear that it will do no more than create obstacles, for the two know about the matter. This is fortunate because, God forgive me, I wish David would return to his first calling. I have learned nothing more since I've been here.

Your paternity's daughter and servant,

Teresa of Jesus

1. Antonio de Jesús (Heredia), prior of the discalced Carmelite monastery in Seville, who attended the chapter in Almodóvar.
2. Code name for Gracián.
3. Gracián's official visitation of the Carmelites in Andalusia.
4. Cf. *Exodus*, 7–11.
5. Another code name for Gracián.
6. Code name for Jesus.
7. She resumes the written account of her foundations at Gracián's request. She had got as far as chapter 19. She wrote chapters 20–27 within the next month, finishing on 14 November 1576.
8. Gracián had given a report of all he had done as apostolic visitator to the conventual chapter of the Carmelite friars of the observance in Seville.
9. She is referring to those friars of the observance who left the order before being expelled.
10. The discalced friars had their own monastery (Los Remedios) in Seville.
11. Antonio Figueredo in Toledo.
12. The identities of David and Esperanza are unknown.
13. Diego de Buenaventura, visitator of the Franciscans.

129. To Madre María de San José, Seville

Toledo, 5 October 1576

(Autograph: DCN, Valladolid)

Because she is worried about the visitation being conducted by Gracián in Andalusia, she reproaches Madre María for not writing. She then comments on a number of other topics: the excise, her brother's purchase of property, the loss of some articles, relations with the Jesuits, negotiations with the Franciscans over water, and other Carmels in the South.

For Mother Prioress of St. Joseph's in Seville.

1. Jesus be with your reverence. I don't know how it is you let the muleteer leave without sending a letter, especially since our *padre*[1] is down there and we would like to get news about him every day. I greatly envy all of you that you have him with you there. For goodness' sake, don't do this any more; and don't fail to write to me about everything that is happening. Our *padre's* letters are short, and when he doesn't have time to write, you should be sure to do so. I've already written to you about the means you can use to send me frequent letters.[2]

2. I was delighted to learn, through the letter that Padre Mariano[3] brought—Fray Antonio[4] has not come—that you and all the nuns are well and that an agreement has been reached concerning the excise.[5]

3. My brother[6] is now well. He is always happy to receive news about you. I've already told you not to fail to write to him now and again. He bought some property—which he was already considering when he was down there—near Avila,[7] I think a league and a half away, or not quite that. It has pasture lands, grain fields, and woods. It cost him 14,000 ducats, but the papers have not yet been drawn up. He says that what has happened down there has taught him a lesson not to close the purchase unless everything is very safe and clear, for he doesn't

want any problems. Pray for him and his sons (who already have opportunities for marriage) that they will serve God.

4. You should know that as soon as I arrived here, thinking that we would leave immediately, the trunk and all the packages were sent ahead with a muleteer. And I don't know if it was in unpacking or how, but Teresa's large *agnusdei*[8] and the two emerald rings are missing, nor do I remember where I put them or if they were given to me. Really, I felt sad to see how everything happened so as to contradict the joy she had in the thought that I would be there with her; she needs me in many ways. Try to remember if these objects were in the house when we left, and ask Gabriela[9] if she remembers where I might have put them, and pray that they may be found.

5. I was very surprised by what you told me about the fathers in the Society.[10] As that other person told you, they are almost as rigorous as we are. It would be good if Padre Garciálvarez[11] were to speak to them. My regards to him and to all my daughters and to Father Prior of Las Cuevas.[12] We are praying hard for his return to health. May it please God to give it to him, for his illness distresses me and I am not going to write to him until I know that he is better. Keep me informed of his condition as often as you have a messenger.

6. It would be good, despite all this, if you were to arrange at times to have someone from the Society hear the nuns' confessions. This would help toward removing the fear they have in our regard. Padre Acosta[13] would be very good, if you could get him. May God forgive them, for if she is so rich, her entry would bring an end to their problems; yet, since His Majesty didn't bring her to us, he will provide. Perhaps there was a greater need for her in the community she entered.

7. I thought that since Fray Buenaventura[14] was there the negotiations about the water would improve, but it doesn't seem there is any easing off. May God permit us to pay for the house; then, having money, you will be able to obtain everything. Let things go for now, since you have good wells. We

would pay highly here for one of them, for this matter of getting water is a real problem.

8. Tell me how the visitation of Fray Buenaventura is going, and what is being done about the monastery they abolished near Córdoba, for I know nothing. I am feeling well and am at your service, as they say. Tell me also whether our *padre* comes to your monastery to eat sometimes and how you cater to him, for he cannot be catered to in his own monastery, nor would it appear right. Send me news about everything, and remain with God, for now we will be able to write often, as is fitting.

9 I was amused by the account of the old woman[15] you have there and how she used the stairs. Tell me if the boy is still there and if you have anyone to do your errands. Mother Prioress in Malagón[16] wrote to me that she is doing better; but that illness is such that a little improvement is not enough to make me happy. Keep her always in your prayers. May His Majesty watch over you, my daughter, and make you a saint, and all your daughters as well. Amen.

10. In the enclosed letter from Sister Alberta[17] you will see how things are going in Caravaca. I was delighted with the letter from Beas (for I hadn't received any news from them in some time) and that that nun who is very rich entered there. Everything is working out well, glory to God. Always pray hard for our *padre*, and for me too, for I am in need.

Yesterday was the feast of St. Francis.

11. Enclosed is the postage, for it's expensive, and be careful to let me know if you do not have the money to take good care of our *padre* when the occasion arises; and don't be proud, for that's foolish. I can send it to you. And take care of your health, if for no other reason than not to kill me, for I tell you

the sickness of the prioress in Malagón is costing me dearly. May God provide by restoring her health, amen.

Your reverence's,

Teresa of Jesus, Carmelite

12. When letters are entrusted to the muleteer, you can enclose the postage. When they are not, you know what usually happens if you enclose it; the letters are at risk of never arriving. I tell you this so that you will never do it.[18]

---

1. Jerónimo Gracián.
2. Through the chief courier of Toledo, Antonio Figueredo.
3. Ambrosio Mariano de San Benito, who arrived in Toledo on 25 September.
4. Antonio de Jesús (Heredia), the prior in Seville who had attended the chapter in Almodóvar.
5. The litigation over the excise had been going on since the purchase of the house.
6. Lorenzo de Cepeda.
7. La Serna.
8. See Ltr. 115.5, n.6.
9. Leonor de San Gabriel, who was Teresa's nurse in Seville.
10. A well-to-do aspirant was discouraged by the Jesuits from entering the Carmelites because she did not have a strong constitution.
11. A priest friend of both the Carmelites and the Jesuits in Seville.
12. The Carthusian prior, Hernando de Pantoja.
13. Diego de Acosta, a Jesuit in Seville.
14. Diego de Buenaventura, the visitator of the Franciscans.
15. She was the sister of Juana de la Cruz (Gómez de Chaves) serving the monastery as doorkeeper.
16. Brianda de San José, whose illness had its ups and downs.
17. Ana de San Alberto, the prioress of Caravaca.
18. This postscript continues on the outside of the envelope, but is now illegible.

130. To Padre Juan de Jesús Roca, La Roda

Toledo, Beginning of October 1576

(Autograph: DCN, Consuegra [Toledo])

Juan de Jesús Roca had been appointed zelator by the chapter in Almodóvar with the mission of promoting the spiritual life of the friars in the discalced monasteries. Teresa had been expecting him to stop off in Toledo, but he merely passed by, sending word to Teresa about his worries concerning the departure of discalced Carmelite friars for Rome.

1. Jesus. The grace of the Holy Spirit be with your reverence, *mi padre*. Your house is so far out of the way that even though I want to, I have no one through whom I can answer you, and so I have waited until the departure of these fathers.

2. Concerning Padre Fray Antonio,[1] perhaps God did us a favor because, as I understand, he suffered from serious melancholy, which, considering our diet, would have become much worse. May God be with him, for what he suffers certainly seems to come more from lack of health than from lack of a good spirit. You can't avoid its becoming known, for they will have to provide for a preacher in Almodóvar.[2] Please God he will return to his order. Neither by his having come nor by his leaving does our own order lose anything.[3]

3. I thought you would pass by on your return, but only a slight detour was enough to prevent you from coming.[4] Your desire to please me must not be very great, for even when you were here before, I got to speak with you only a little. You should know that in a similar measure I have very little influence in doing anything about what you wrote concerning the departure for Rome.[5] For some time now I have been asking that someone go to Rome and haven't even succeeded in getting anyone to write a letter to the one who ought to receive a let-

ter.[6] But it is enough that we do what we can, come what may. And the matter doesn't depend on our Father Visitator,[7] for he has already done what he could; but so many people are making different recommendations that mine count for little. I deeply regret not being able to do more. I thought this trip had been decided on; that is what I was told. May God provide, and for goodness' sake don't neglect to hurry things along; you can do more than I can.

4. Although I sent the letters to Seville and Almodóvar at once, I think Father Prior[8] had already arrived in Madrid and is still there. I also sent the one to Caravaca, which was a lucky thing, for a carrier was about to leave for that region, and there aren't many who go there. I am very sorry about Fray Gabriel's illness.[9] Tell him this and give him my regards, for we are praying for him here. He is a father for whom I have a great affection, although he has little for me.

5. Our *padre* has written me that he arrived in good health and that some of the fathers of the cloth[10] have left and that the conventual chapter was satisfied with him. There is nothing else except that those fathers are being docile and sending intercessors to him. If God watches over him for us, I think he will do much good. Don't neglect to take care to pray for him, and for me too. I entrust myself to the prayers of all the fathers there; the prioress[11] asks for yours. May our Lord make you as holy as I beg of him, amen.

Your reverence's unworthy servant,

Teresa of Jesus

---

1. Antonio de la Madre de Dios, who had transferred from the Jeronimites. He was having problems adapting to his new vocation, because of his health, Teresa thinks.
2. An office that was held by Padre Antonio in Almodóvar.
3. After returning to the Jeronimites, Padre Antonio later rejoined the discalced Carmelites and eventually went on the first mission to the Congo. He was drowned in the shipwreck that ensued.

4. In returning from Almodóvar to La Roda, it would have been easy for him to pass through Toledo, which he did on his way to the chapter.
5. A reference to the projected trip of discalced Carmelite friars to Rome.
6. Their Father General in Rome, Giovanni Battista Rossi.
7. Jerónimo Gracián.
8. The prior of Almodóvar, Ambrosio de San Pedro.
9. Gabriel de la Asunción, prior of La Roda.
10. The fathers of the cloth were the Carmelites of the observance in Andalusia, then undergoing an official visitation by Gracián.
11. The prioress of Toledo, Ana de los Angeles.

131. To Padre Ambrosio Mariano de San Benito, Madrid

Toledo, Beginning of October, 1576

(Torn autograph: DCN, Arco Mirelli, Chiaia, Naples)

Padre Mariano had moved to Madrid but neglected to keep Teresa informed about matters of much concern to her. She sends him some news about the friars.

For Padre Fray Mariano de San Benito, Carmelite, Madrid.

1. Jesus. The grace of the Holy Spirit be with your honor. I tell you I don't know how we can be at peace, since you give me so much occasion for war. You know how distressed I was over the illness of Señor Licentiate Padilla[1] and how the other business matters have been a cause of worry to me. It seems only right that you would have let me know about everything. For the love of our Lord, don't be so lacking in compassion. And tell me also how things in Andalusia are going and of Padre Fray Buenaventura,[2] about whom I am worried.

2. You should know that our Padre Antonio.[3]...for if Padre Fray Baltasar[4] is not to stay there, it definitely will be necessary to send another, as everyone says. Many regards to *mi padre*, Señor Licentiate Padilla. Please God he is continuing to improve. Let me know how he is, whatever the case may be,

and about everything else; and remember you don't have to concern yourself with what regards Malagón anymore. Doña Luisa[5] is very happy and she gives us all the permissions we need....and Antonio Ruiz[6] with his frogs made me laugh.

...of October, and I am your reverence's servant,

Teresa of Jesus

---

1. Juan Calvo de Padilla, an ardent reformer and friend of Teresa's.
2. The visitator for the Franciscans in Andalusia.
3. Antonio de la Madre de Dios, who had transferred from the Jeronimites to the Teresian reform, was suffering from melancholy and new vocational difficulties. He had been the appointed preacher at Almodóvar del Campo but had left there.
4. Baltasar de Jesús (Nieto), the prior of Pastrana.
5. Luisa de la Cerda. Teresa may be referring to a transfer of the community to a healthier location or to the serious illness of the prioress.
6. He was a merchant and friend of Teresa's from Malagón.

132. To Madre María de San José, Seville

Toledo, 13 October 1576

Teresa is worried about the prioress's health. She also shows concern for the safety of the mail. She then comments on a number of points in a letter written to her, showing her interest in all that is taking place in the community of Seville.

For Mother Prioress of St. Joseph's in Seville, my daughter.

1. Jesus. The grace of the Holy Spirit be with your reverence, my daughter. I have been feeling very distressed over your illness. I don't know what to do to keep from feeling it so deeply when a prioress in one of our houses becomes sick. The prioress in Malagón[1] is getting better, glory to God. Take care of yourself, and whatever you do, avoid the sarsaparilla water. And for the love of God, don't let the fever go without taking some remedy for it, something other than purgatives. I

have found some comfort in remembering that sometimes they thought you had the fever but I could see that you did not. May God preserve you for me and give you the good health I ask of him, amen.

2. The packages arrived in good condition and that will always be so with Figueredo's[2] services. The cost of the postage will be safe; you can write on the outside the amount that is enclosed—and don't forget to enclose it. You must tell me how my letters reach you, for I doubt if the ones I sent with Figueredo have arrived there yet. Here they are not in any danger, for he has been alerted to the situation and is a very good man. And although you have responded to some of my letters, I don't remember with whom I sent them. May God watch over you, for you are doing things very well. But it isn't necessary for you to enclose my letters with your responses; I think that would prove tiresome.

3. Oh, how I envy your hearing those sermons,[3] and how I long to be with all of you. Here they say that I love the nuns in the Seville house more than all the others. Certainly, I don't know why, but I do love them dearly. So, I am not surprised by your affection for me, for I have always felt the same way toward you, but it pleases me to hear this. There is no longer any reason to speak of what happened in the past, for I certainly don't believe you were responsible for it. I like your courage, and so I believe God will help you. May he be pleased to grant you health as I beseech him.

4. I was delighted to hear of the clothing and the profession;[4] give them my congratulations, and tell San Francisco[5] her letters are a joy to me, as are those of the other nuns, and ask their pardon for my not answering. The amount of correspondence I had down there was nothing; since I've come up here, it has gotten to be terrible.

5. In regard to Garciálvarez's relatives[6] do what you think best, for he will speak the truth, and anyone from his family could not be bad. If I have time I will write to ask him not to

stop hearing the nuns' confessions, for that is something I regret; if I don't write, tell him for me. I am very sorry about the illness of our good Father Prior.[7] We are praying for him. I am afraid the courier is ready to leave, so I am not writing him. You will lose a lot if you lose him, but God, who lives forever, will be with you.

6. Regarding the prayer of those sisters,[8] I am writing to our padre;[9] he will speak to you about it. When San Jerónimo[10] experiences something, write to me. By no means speak to Rodrigo about it; with Acosta, you can.[11] Give him my best regards, for I get along very well with him, and we owe him much.

7. I was delighted about the settlement over the excise. My brother[12] has purchased an exempt estate at La Serna, near Avila. It is a very nice piece of property, with pasture lands, grain fields, and woods. It cost 14,000 ducats. Since he didn't have that amount then—far from it—this would be the time for you to reimburse a third of what you owe him, and not fail to do so on account of your need of money for food. I hope in God that you will be able to manage without it.[13] If little by little you can collect what the people in the house owe you, that will be great.

8. You don't mention the deputy's daughter;[14] my regards to her and all her sisters, and anyone else you see, and to Delgado[15] and Blas,[16] and remain with God. Send my regards to Fray Gregorio[17] and tell him to keep me always informed about his health. And may God give you back your health, for I liked your work. Nonetheless, you shouldn't try to spin when you have a fever; otherwise it will never leave you, considering how much you move your arm when you spin and how much you spin. Regards to Margarita.[18]

9. If you must have a lay sister, keep in mind that a relative of our *padre's*[19] is agitating to enter; let me know if you can take her. The prioress in Valladolid[20] has seen her. She says she would be a good lay sister. She probably does not know

how to read. Our *padre* doesn't want to become involved in the matter. His little sister[21] is someone special and of a gentler disposition than Teresa; she has unusual ability. I am delighted with her.

Today is 13 October.

Your reverence's servant,

Teresa of Jesus

---

1. Brianda de San José.
2. Antonio Figueredo.
3. Gracián's sermons.
4. On 29 September, 1576, Juana del Espíritu Santo was clothed in the Carmelite habit and her daughter Beatriz de la Madre de Dios made profession.
5. Isabel de San Francisco served as a kind of chronicler or news reporter for the monastery.
6. They were giving signs of a desire to enter the Carmel (cf. Ltr. 122.3).
7. Hernando de Pantoja, prior of the Carthusians.
8. The two nuns whose prayer was a concern of Teresa's were Isabel de San Jerónimo (Ureña) and the recently professed Beatriz de la Madre de Dios. The first had a fragile constitution, the second was somewhat unbalanced.
9. Gracián (cf. Ltr. 136. 9–10).
10. Isabel de San Jerónimo.
11. The two were Jesuits: Rodrigo Alvarez and Diego de Acosta. The first was a consultor to the Inquisition and so Teresa did not want to cause the two nuns anxiety by suggesting they speak with him.
12. Lorenzo de Cepeda.
13. Lorenzo had given the nuns in Seville a loan to help them out of their financial crisis.
14. The deputy was Francisco de Arganda.
15. Inés Delgado, a benefactress of the community.
16. A youth who did errands for the nuns.
17. Gregorio Nacianceno, a discalced Carmelite in Seville.
18. Margarita de la Concepción, a lay sister.
19. Gracián.
20. María Bautista.

21. The child Isabel Gracián who took the habit when only eight and made profession in Toledo at age sixteen.

133. To Padre Ambrosio Mariano, Madrid

Toledo, Middle of October, 1576

(Autograph: DCN Zumaya [Guipúzcoa])

Teresa is anxiously following events both in Andalusia, where Gracián has resumed his visitation, and in Madrid, where Mariano is residing. She hopes for a separate province for her discalced friars and a house in Madrid for them.

For *mi padre*, Doctor Fray Mariano de San Benito, Carmelite, Madrid.

1. Jesus. May the Holy Spirit be with your reverence and reward you for the good news you have given me about the health of our good *padre*, Señor Licentiate Padilla.[1] Please God it will continue for many years. So now you are calling me reverend and señora! God forgive you, for this makes it seem that you and I have turned into calced Carmelites. I was amused by the friendship of the reverend *padre*[2] who came to ask you for a favor. He tried it with me in Avila—and God grant him better health!—although there are twelve hours in a day.[3] Perhaps he has changed.

2. You should know that I've been told—and it is so—that Tostado[4] has sent a messenger here with letters for the provincial, who wants to send a friar there. It seems to me there is a lot of coming and going. I am sorry about the departure of Fray Buenaventura,[5] not to mention the good he was accomplishing. If the foolish things being done against him succeed, everyone will deduce that God is favoring him. And you do not tell me what is being done about that suppressed monastery. O Jesus, how many things you allow!

3. I wish we already had that little house;[6] the rest can be done afterward, God willing. I wouldn't even want to see the walls of the house of those who have so little love for us.[7] I have already said that a letter from the Señor Nuncio[8] would set everything straight. *Mi padre*, let us hurry to do all that we can. And if you are able, take up the matter of a separate province, for we don't know what lies in store for us. And nothing would be lost by so doing, but much would be gained. For goodness' sake, if you receive any news about our *padre*,[9] write to me about it, for I am worried. My greetings to Señor Licentiate Padilla and to Padre Fray Baltasar.[10] The prioress[11] sends hers to them as well, and to you. I was happy to see that that revered *padre* is there. May God be with you always.

Your reverence's unworthy servant,

Teresa of Jesus

---

1. Juan Calvo de Padilla.
2. Perhaps Alonso de Valdemoro, prior of the Carmelites in Avila. It was he who took St. John of the Cross prisoner the first time, in 1576. He was making clumsy efforts to obtain Teresa's friendship.
3. Cf. Jn 11:9. The Spanish expression means that there is plenty of time to improve.
4. Jerónimo Tostado, Vicar General.
5. The visitator of the Franciscans in Andalusia.
6. She is alluding to the plan of the discalced friars to acquire a small house in Madrid from which they could carry on their business matters.
7. Mariano was living with the Carmelites of the observance in Madrid.
8. Nicolás Ormaneto. He did not grant permission for the little house.
9. Jerónimo Gracián, who at this time was continuing his official visitation of the Carmelites in Andalusia.
10. Baltasar de Jesús (Nieto).
11. The prioress in Toledo, Ana de los Angeles.

134. To Padre Jerónimo Gracián, Seville

Toledo, 21 October 1576

She is concerned about what is taking place in Andalusia. Why doesn't Gracián show the documents granting him the authority he is exercising there? She gives her opinion about the proposed foundation of discalced friars in Salamanca, summarizing a letter she had written to Mariano the same day.

1. Jesus. The grace of the Holy Spirit be with your paternity. Yesterday I wrote to you of how those fathers[1] had so calmed down that I praised God for it. You should know that the mandate and the *Motu*[2] had still not been read to them. I feared very much what has now come about, and today one of them came and told me they have reacted strangely. Since they think they are right, they will surely cause a stir. They say what I have often told Padre Mariano[3] (and I am pretty sure I even wrote this to you) that to give commands as a superior without showing where the authority comes from is something that is never done.

2. In regard to what you said in your letter about Padre Mariano, about why you did not send the brief,[4] certainly if there were reason for doubt, it would have been better to think of this beforehand. If only they would free you from that task and leave you free for us discalced friars and nuns.

3. Padre Padilla[5] will tell you how Melchizedek[6] says that according to the council[7] I cannot make foundations and that our Most Reverend Father[8] has expressly declared this. I would like it very much if you could look over this declaration, if possible. As for what he says about my bringing nuns around with me, I do so always with permission from superiors. I have here the very permission Melchizedeck himself gave me to bring nuns to Beas and Caravaca. How is it that he didn't take this into consideration at that time since the declaration had already existed then? If only they'd leave me in peace.

4. May God give you, *mi padre*, the rest I desire for you. Perhaps these fathers will now disgorge all the venom and be better afterward, although in my opinion they were very disposed to obey. This clash has not bothered me. Rather, I enjoy all this opposition, for it is a sign that God will be well served.

5. The enclosed letter for you has to do with the project in Salamanca,[9] for I think they have written to you about it. I wrote to them that the work was not suited to discalced friars. If a place is provided for them there, all right; but not that they be vicars (for I don't think anything else is wanted). Two months is a very short time for such a work. The bishop[10] is not asking this of them. Neither does he show any desire that they be sent to that place, nor are they meant for such works. I would like it if the discalced friars were to be looked upon there as beings from another world and not as friars coming and going in the service of women. We have won over the bishop to our cause without this. But we could perhaps lose him if we accepted such a work. I don't know if good Don Teutonio[11] will do anything, for his chances are limited and he is not a good negotiator. If I were there to stir things up, I truly believe we'd succeed. And perhaps this could be so, if you thought it fitting. I wrote to them about all of this.[12]

6. The prioress[13] and other nuns ask for your prayers and those of the fathers there with you; I ask for those of Fray Gregorio.[14] My Isabel is well and very enjoyable, and Señora Doña Juana[15] and her family are also well. Give my regards now and then, for charity's sake, to the lord prosecutor and to the archbishop, and also to Señora Delgada and to your other women friends, especially Bernarda.[16] Let this request be a standing one. Remain with God, for it is very late.

Today is the feast of St. Hilarion,[17] my father.

Your paternity's servant and subject,

Teresa of Jesus

1. Two Carmelites of the observance passing through Toledo on their way to Madrid.
2. A probable reference to a brief by the nuncio Ormaneto (3 August 1575) appointing Gracián apostolic visitator of the Carmelites of the observance in Andalusia.
3. Ambrosio Mariano de San Benito.
4. She is referring probably to the *Motu* mentioned in no. 1.
5. Juan Calvo de Padilla.
6. Code name for Angel de Salazar, provincial of the Carmelites of Castile.
7. The Council of Trent.
8. Giovanni Battista Rossi, the general of the Carmelites.
9. The foundation of a college for discalced Carmelite friars. It was being planned on the condition that they take under their direction a house for repentant women. Teresa was opposed to this idea.
10. Francisco de Soto y Salazar.
11. Don Teutonio de Braganza.
12. This letter summarizes what she wrote on the same day to Mariano de San Benito.
13. Ana de los Angeles, prioress of Toledo.
14. Gregorio Nacianceno, a discalced Carmelite in Los Remedios.
15. Isabel Dantisco is Gracián's sister and Juana Dantisco, his mother.
16. The lord prosecutor for the Inquisition in Seville was Francisco Arganda; Don Cristóbal de Rojas was the archbishop of Seville; Lady Delgada is Inés Delgado, a benefactress of the Carmelite nuns in Seville; Bernarda de San José (Matías y Ramírez) was a discalced Carmelite nun in Seville.
17. Hilarion was an early hermit whose feast the Carmelites celebrated on 21 October (cf. Teresa's poem to him, no. 22, in vol 3, pp. 398–99).

135. To Padre Ambrosio Mariano, Madrid

Toledo, 21 October 1576

(Autograph: DCN, Seville)

Mariano has sent Teresa some weighty recommendations for the acceptance of both a novice and an aspirant into Carmel. In her response, Teresa also discusses his projects for foundations of discalced friars in Madrid, Salamanca, and Ciudad Real. She doesn't show much confidence in either

Mariano or Don Teutonio as negotiators. The letter is a good example of her dealings with the impetuous Mariano.

1. Jesus. The grace of the Holy Spirit be with your reverence. It's quite clear that you have not understood all that I owe to Padre Olea[1] and how much I care for him, for you have written me about matters that he has discussed, or is discussing, with me. I believe you now know that I am not an ungrateful person. So, I tell you that if in this matter I should have to give up my rest and health, it would already be done. But where a matter of conscience is involved, friendship doesn't suffice, for I owe more to God than to anyone. Would to God the matter involved no more than a lack of dowry, for you already know—and if you don't you should inquire for yourself—that there are many nuns in these monasteries who have brought no dowry, while the dowry of this person is a good one. They are giving 500 ducats, which is enough for her to become a nun in any monastery.

2. Since Padre Olea doesn't know the nuns in these houses, I am not surprised by his disbelief. I know what servants of God they are and the innocence of their souls. I could never believe they would refuse the habit to anyone without many reasons. I know how scrupulous they usually are about these things, and for them to make a decision like that, they would have had to have good reasons.[2] And since we are few nuns, the disturbance caused by those who are not suited for religious life is so great that even someone with an unscrupulous conscience would have a problem about accepting them; how much more would someone who seeks not to displease the Lord in anything.

3. Would you tell me how I could get them by force to take a nun if they do not vote in her favor—and they are not doing so—and if no prelate is even capable of doing this? And don't think this matters to Padre Olea. He has written to me that he

has no greater interest in her than in anyone else he may pass on the street. It's because of my sins that you have been inspired by charity toward something in which I cannot be of help, and I feel badly about it. Even if I were to help, it wouldn't benefit her to stay where she is not wanted.

4. I have done even more in this case than was reasonable. And I asked them to keep her for another year of trial, contrary to their will, so that if I pass by there when I go to Salamanca I can become better informed about the whole matter. I'm doing this as a favor to Padre Olea that he may feel more satisfied. I see clearly that the nuns are not lying, for you know how even in matters of little importance such a thing would be far from their minds. It is nothing new for nuns to leave our communities; it is common. And nothing is lost if they say they didn't have the health for so austere a life, nor have I seen anyone less esteemed on this account.

5. Having learned my lesson by this, I will have to be more careful about what I do from here on. So, the person proposed by Señor Nicolao will not be accepted, even if you are more satisfied with her.[3] I have other information, and I don't want to make enemies in order to do a favor for my lords and friends. It is strange that you would wonder why there is a discussion about this. Were we to behave otherwise, no nun would ever be accepted. I wanted to do him a favor, but I had received new information different from what I had first received, and I know Señor Nicolao desires what is good for these houses over anyone's particular good. So he was at peace with this.

6. For love of God don't speak any more about this. She has a good dowry and can enter some other community—not one in which the numbers are so small that the nuns have to be extremely careful about whom they choose. And if up until now we were not so cautious in some cases—although these are rare—things turned out so badly that from now on we will be. And do not put us at odds with Señor Nicolao, which would happen if we had to send her away again.

7. I was amused by your saying that just by seeing her you will be able to recognize the kind of person she is. We women are not so easy to get to know. After many years of hearing confessions, confessors themselves are amazed at how little they have understood. And it is because women cannot express their faults clearly, and the confessors judge by what they are told. *Padre*, when you desire that one of these houses do you the favor of accepting somebody, send us those who are gifted for this life, and you will see that we will not make an issue over the dowry. When such talent is lacking, I can by no means be obliging.

8. You should know that I thought it would be easy to have a house in Madrid where the friars could stay. And even though the house were not a monastery, it wouldn't be unusual for them to have permission for Mass; it is given to *caballeros* for Mass in their homes. So, I informed our *padre*[4] about this. He told me that it wouldn't be opportune since this could do harm to our cause, and I think he was right. And knowing his will in this matter, you shouldn't have decided to bring so many friars together and set up a church as though you had permission, which has made me laugh. I never even bought a house until I had permission from the ordinary of the place. You know well what it cost me in Seville for not having gotten this permission.

9. I told you often that until you have a letter from the nuncio[5] granting permission, nothing should be done. When Don Jerónimo[6] told me that you asked the friars of the observance, I was dumbfounded. So as not to resemble all of you by trusting them so much, at least for the moment, I have no intention of speaking to Valdemoro.[7] I have a suspicion that any friendship he shows us is not intended for our good but only to catch us in something that he can report to his friends. And I wish you were as suspicious and would not trust him or make use of such friends for this affair. Leave the matter to the One to whom it belongs, that is to God, for His Majesty will take care

of it in his time. Don't be in such a hurry, for that will ruin everything.

10. You should know that Don Diego Mejía[8] is a very good gentleman and that he will do what he says. Since he has decided to speak about the matter, he must have come to know that his cousin will act in our favor. You should realize as well that if his cousin does not do it for him he will not do it for his aunt either. There's no reason to write to her or to anyone else. They are first cousins, and a relative and friend of Don Diego Mejía is to be highly esteemed. And it is also a good sign that the archdeacon[9] has said he will present a report about us, for if he hadn't thought of doing it in our favor, he wouldn't have taken on this task. The matter is moving along well. You should not be stirring things up; you may make matters worse. Let's see what Don Diego and the archdeacon do. I will try to find out if there is anyone here who may be able to intervene. And if the dean[10] can do anything, Doña Luisa[11] will be able to get him to do so.

11. All of this has pleased me greatly and made me believe that God will make good use of this foundation; nothing came about through what we ourselves did. It's very nice that you have the house, for sooner or later we will have the permission. If the nuncio had given it to us, everything would now be over. May it please our Lord to give him the health that he sees is necessary in our regard. I tell you that by no means does Tostado[12] lack confidence, nor am I sure that the One who began all this will give up working through him.

12. Regarding Salamanca, Padre Fray Juan de Jesús[13] is in such a state, because of his quartan fevers, that I don't know what he could do; nor do you say what services he might be able to render. As for the college there, let us begin with what matters most, which is that the nuncio grant his permission. Once he has given it, the main thing is done. If mistakes are made in the beginning everything will be wiped out. What the bishop[14] is requesting, in my opinion—since he knows that

Señor Juan Diaz[15] is in Madrid and what he is doing there—is to have someone in Salamanca who can do the same. And I don't know if our rule allows for your taking on the task of chaplains.[16] It doesn't seem suitable to me, nor do I know what one could accomplish in two months, were the task to be accepted, other than annoy the bishop. Nor do I know how the fathers would manage that kind of governing (for they will perhaps want to set high standards of perfection for that community, and such standards will not be suitable for those people[17]). Nor do I know if the bishop would be pleased to have the friars.

13. I tell you there is more to do than you think and where we plan on gaining we will perhaps lose. Nor do I think our order will be seen as responsible if friars who are to be seen as contemplative hermits take on these chaplaincies—for the friars are not wanted for any other reason—and move about here and there with these kinds of women. I don't know how this will look, even though these women will be rescued from an evil way of life.

14. I raise these objections so that all of you there may consider them and then do what seems good to you, for I submit to that. You will arrive at a better decision. Read this passage to Señor Licentiate Padilla[18] and to Señor Juan Díaz, for I don't know anything more to say than this. Permission from the bishop will always be sure in coming. Otherwise, I don't have confidence in Señor Don Teutonio[19] as a great negotiator—in his good will, yes; in his abilities, no.

15. I have been looking forward to being there so as to move this project along, for I am good at bargaining (if you don't think so, my friend Valdemoro will tell you). I wouldn't want the project to fail from your not explaining it well, for I have greatly desired that you have a house in Salamanca and one in Madrid. That you set aside thoughts of a foundation in Ciudad Real[20] for a more opportune moment made me happy. I see no way in which it could have turned out well. All things con-

sidered, Malagón would be a much better place. Doña Luisa is eager to have you come and will provide well for your needs as time goes on, and there are many large towns in the surrounding area. I know you will not lack food.

16. And to have a justifiable pretext for abandoning the house in Madrid you could transfer it to Malagón. Let them think for now that you are not abandoning it definitively but only until the work on the house is completed. For you would appear irresponsible were you to start something one day and give it up the next.

17. I gave Don Jerónimo the letter for Don Diego Mejía. He will send it with another for the count of Olivares.[21] I will write him again when I see that it's necessary. Don't let the matter be forgotten. And I repeat that if he said clearly he would take it up and has discussed it with the archdeacon and considers it as good as done, he is a man of his word.

18. Now he has written me in favor of an aspirant. Would to God the two we let go[22] had possessed her gifts; we wouldn't have had to refuse them. Father Visitator's mother has inquired about her. In mentioning this, it occurs to me that it would be good, under the pretext of saying something to Don Diego about this nun, to speak to him about the other matter and entrust it to him again. That is what I will do. Send the letter on to him. And remain with God, for I've really been lengthy, as though I had nothing else to attend to.

19. I'm not writing to Father Prior,[23] because I have many other letters to write now, and he can consider this one as being for himself. Best regards to my Padre Padilla. I am giving much praise to our Lord because he is well. May His Majesty be with you always. I will strive to procure the document even if this means talking to Valdemoro—and that would be doing a lot, for I don't believe he would do anything for us.

Today is the feast of the Virgins.[24]

Your reverence's unworthy servant,

Teresa of Jesus

20. Today they gave me other letters from you before Diego[25] arrived. Send this letter to our *padre* with the first messenger; it's for some permissions. I am not writing anything to him about those business matters. So don't fail to write to him yourself about them.

21. That you may see whether or not my nuns surpass yours, I am sending you a section of a letter from the prioress in Beas.[26] See the nice house she has found for the friars in La Peñuela;[27] it has indeed given me great satisfaction. Surely, you would not have found one so quickly. They have accepted a nun whose dowry is worth 7,000 ducats. Two others are ready to enter with just as much. And they have already accepted a woman of illustrious background. She is the niece of the count of Tendilla.[28] The silver objects she has sent, the candelabra, cruets, and many other things, a reliquary, a crystal cross would all take too long to enumerate.

22. And now a lawsuit[29] has been initiated against the nuns there, as you will find out in these letters. See what you can do. It would be important to speak to Don Antonio about this. Mention how high the grates are and that having the window open is more important to us than trying not to bother them. Well, see what you can do.

---

1. The Jesuit Francisco de Olea is recommending an unsuitable aspirant. He will end up becoming angry with Teresa over this question.
2. Padre Olea had harsh words for the prioress in Valladolid for not having procured a favorable vote for the novice.
3. This aspirant was proposed by Nicolás Doria while he was still a secular priest in Seville.
4. Jerónimo Gracián.
5. Nicolás Ormaneto.

6. Jerónimo Manrique, a canon in Toledo, who was highly regarded by Philip II.
7. Alonso Valdemoro, prior of the Carmelites of the observance in Avila.
8. Diego Mejía de Ovando, count of Uceda, a relative of Don Alvaro de Mendoza's.
9. The archdeacon of Toledo, Francisco de Avila.
10. The dean of the cathedral in Toledo, Diego de Castilla.
11. Doña Luisa de la Cerda, Teresa's friend in Toledo.
12. Jerónimo Tostado.
13. Juan de Jesús María Roca, prior of Mancera. The Salamancan project consisted of a house for discalced Carmelite friars in front of a women's refuge. Teresa preferred that they have a house of studies in Salamanca.
14. The bishop of Salamanca, Francisco Soto y Salazar.
15. A disciple of St. John of Avila.
16. Chaplains for the house of refuge.
17. Repentant women living in the house of refuge and rehabilitation.
18. Juan Calvo de Padilla.
19. Don Teutonio de Braganza, who was also interested in the foundation in Salamanca.
20. Another foundation project of the discalced friars not yet realized.
21. Don Enrique de Guzmán.
22. The two women unsuited for the life referred to in nos. 1–6.
23. She is referring either to the prior of the Carmelites of the observance in Madrid, Francisco Ximénez or to Baltasar de Jesús Nieto, prior of the discalced friars in Pastrana.
24. St. Ursula and the virgin martyrs of Cologne.
25. Teresa's mail carrier.
26. Ana de Jesús (Lobera).
27. The discalced Carmelite friars of La Peñuela transferred to El Calvario, not far from Beas, in November of 1576.
28. Don Iñigo López de Mendoza.
29. The nuns in Beas opened a window in the wall connecting their house to the parish church so they could listen to the sermons preached there and attend other church functions. But the priest was contesting their right to do such a thing.

136. To Padre Jerónimo Gracián, Seville

Toledo, 23 October 1576

(Autograph fragment: DCN, Livorno-Antignano)

Teresa begins with a report on the letters that have been received and those that have not. In one of the letters Gracián speaks of his prayer, and Teresa makes some comments about it. She also advises him on how to deal with the unusual experiences of two of the nuns in Seville.

To Padre Maestro Fray Jerónimo de la Madre de Dios, prior of Los Remedios.

1. Jesus. The grace of the Holy Spirit be with your paternity, *mi padre*. Today I received three letters from you by way of the chief courier and yesterday those that Fray Alonso brought.[1] The Lord has repaid me well for the time it took them to arrive. May he be forever blessed that you are well. At first I was alarmed, for they gave me the packets from the prioress[2] and I didn't see any letter from you in either of them. You can imagine what I felt. I was quickly put at ease. Always tell me which ones of mine you receive because you often do not respond to anything I ask you, and then on one letter you forgot to put the date.

2. In another, you ask me how I got along with Señora Doña Juana,[3] but I had written to you about that through the mail carrier from here. I think your answer will come through the letter you say you sent me by way of Madrid, and so I am not very bothered by this. I am well, and my Isabel[4] is our sole entertainment. It's extraordinary how gentle and cheerful she is. Yesterday, Señora Doña Juana wrote me. They are all well.

3. I have praised the Lord much over the way our business affairs are proceeding, but I was astonished by the things Fray Alonso[5] told me they say about you. God help me! How necessary your trip was. Even if you did nothing else there, I think

you were obliged in conscience to do so for the good of the order. I don't know how they were able to publish such great calumnies. May God give them light. If you had someone you could trust, it would be very good for you to grant them the favor of appointing another prior.[6] But since you don't have anyone, I'm amazed at the one who gave you that advice. It would be like doing nothing. How wonderful it would be to have someone there who would not contradict everything. And if there does happen to be someone, it would be a real trial if the present prior refused to step down. Well, they're not known for having a desire to be held in little esteem.

4. It's no surprise. I'm more surprised that with so many things to do Paul has time to attend to the affairs of Joseph with so much calm.[7] I praise the Lord greatly. Tell him that he should now be content with his prayer and not bother with the work of the intellect when God is favoring him in another way, for I am very happy over what he writes me. The fact is that in these interior things of the spirit what is more acceptable and certain is what leaves the best effects. I do not mean immediately with respect to many desires. Even though these are good, they do not at times amount to all that our self-love paints them to be. What I mean by the best effects are those confirmed by works and that the desires for the honor of God become apparent in an authentic solicitude for it and that the intellect and memory be occupied in how best to please him and show him the love one has for him.

5. Oh, this is real prayer, and not some delights for the sake of nothing more than our own satisfaction. And when these kinds of delight are present, they are accompanied by laxity and fears and feelings that we are not being esteemed sufficiently. I would not want any other prayer than that which makes the virtues grow in me. If it should be accompanied by great temptations, dryness, and trials leaving me with greater humility, I would consider it good prayer. That prayer is the best prayer that pleases God the most. It shouldn't be thought

that he who suffers isn't praying, for he is offering this to God. And often he is praying much more than the one who is breaking his head in solitude, thinking that if he has squeezed out some tears he is thereby praying.

6. Pardon me for such a long message, but your love for Paul[8] will enable you to bear it. And if you think what I say is good, tell him about it, and if not, don't. But I speak of what I would like for myself. I tell you works and a good conscience are a great thing.

7. I was amused by what happened to Padre Joanes.[9] It could be that the devil had desired to do him some harm and that God had drawn some good from this. But the greatest caution is necessary, for I am certain that the devil will search out every device he can to harm Eliseo.[10] And so it is good to see one of Patillas's[11] tricks there. Thus I don't think it would be harmful to pay little attention to these things. If the purpose is to make Joanes do penance, God is already giving, and has given, him enough. He's not the only one to whom this happened, for his three councilors have also soon had to pay for it.

8. What Joseph then said for certain was that Clemente[12] did nothing wrong, that if he had a fault it was due to his illness, and that in that region where they sent him he was at peace and that Joseph had previously told him about the trial they had planned to inflict on him. Laurentia[13] learned nothing about it from Joseph, but knew only what the people were saying elsewhere. I don't think Joseph would reveal his secrets in that way, for he is very prudent. For my part I think they are calumniating him and the more I hear it said that he is speaking from other sources—which she couldn't verify—the more it seems to me to be Patillas's project. I am amused to see where he now casts his net. Why did he have to free him from his *beatas* so that his soul would make better progress? It would be good to ask for this freedom from the angel, although I would be happy if Patillas were cast out of this house by the means that are usually used. Be careful, for he will show who

he is. I will place the matter before God. Angela[14] in another letter will tell what she has thought about this matter. It was very wise to deal with this business under the seal of confession.

9. It will be necessary to make San Jerónimo[15] eat meat for a few days and give up prayer, and tell her not to speak to anyone but you, or that she write to me, for her imagination is weak and what she meditates on she thinks she sees or hears. Sometimes, though, what she says will be true and has been, for she is a very good soul.

10. And I think that the same goes for Beatriz.[16] I don't believe that what they write me about the date of her profession is a whim but very good. She, too, should fast only sparingly. Give these orders to the prioress[17] telling her that from time to time she have them give up prayer and occupy themselves with other tasks so that things don't get worse; and believe me, this is necessary.

11. It made me sad that the letters were lost. And you do not tell me whether those that fell into the hands of Peralta[18] were important. You should know that I am now sending a mail carrier. I have greatly envied the nuns for the joy they have had in hearing your sermons. It surely seems they deserve this; and I, the trials. Nonetheless, may God give me many more for love of him. I was troubled that you have to go to Granada. I would like to know how long you will be there, how I should write to you or where. For the love of God, keep me informed.

12. No signed blank sheets of paper[19] have arrived. Would you send me a couple. I don't think I'll need them, for I see the work you have to do; and I would like to take on some of it so as to give you a little more quiet. May God give you the rest I want you to have and the holiness that he can give you, amen.

Today is 23 October.

Your paternity's unworthy servant,

Teresa of Jesus

---

1. The chief courier was Antonio de Figueredo and the other mail carrier was Alonso de la Madre de Dios, a discalced Carmelite from the monastery of Los Remedios in Seville.
2. María de San José, prioress of Seville.
3. Juana Dantisco, Gracián's mother.
4. Isabel Dantisco, Gracián's sister.
5. Alonso de la Madre de Dios.
6. The prior, Juan Evangelista, appointed by Gracián was disliked by his community.
7. She begins to use her code names: Paul, Eliseo, and Joanes are names for Gracián; Joseph refers to Christ.
8. The love Gracián has for himself.
9. Gracián.
10. Gracián.
11. Patillas is a code name for the devil.
12. This seems to be Elías de San Martín, a former class mate of Gracián's, who was later to become the general of the discalced Carmelites.
13. Teresa herself.
14. Another code name Teresa gives herself.
15. Isabel de San Jerónimo, a discalced Carmelite nun in Seville.
16. Beatriz de la Madre de Dios, also a discalced Carmelite nun in Seville.
17. María de San José.
18. Code name for Jerónimo Tostado.
19. These were blank patent letters signed by Gracián, which shows his complete confidence in Teresa.

137. Madre María de San José, Seville

Toledo, October 1576

(Autograph fragment: DCN, Valladolid)

Teresa is writing this letter around 1 a.m. She is repeating what her brother Lorenzo has written to the prioress that day concerning some financial matters. She envies the prioress and worries about Gracián.

1. Jesus. May the Holy Spirit be with your reverence, my daughter. I already answered your letters, which arrived in good condition through the mail carrier, and they were a delight for me. But I am writing again because I'm sorry about your illness. For goodness' sake write me at once about your health and about what you know concerning our *padre*.[1] I have envied your general confession. You certainly didn't have as much to confess as I, for I wouldn't have been able to make it so easily. Blessed be God who loves us all.

2. My brother[2] writes in a letter I received today that he has written you and sent someone to collect a third of the amount you owe him.[3] He is well and the purchase of the property has been finalized. The nuns at St. Joseph's are not faring badly.[4] Teresa[5] writes to me from there. The *agnusdei* and the rings that I was at first worried about have reappeared, glory be to God.[6] I am well, but soon the clock will strike 1 a.m. and so I will not be long. I would like some news about my good prior of Las Cuevas.[7]

3. Last week they sent some fresh tuna from Malagón and it was very good and we enjoyed it. I have not broken the fast since the feast of the Holy Cross;[8] see how well I am! Our prioress in Malagón,[9] who has written me that she is better, did so, saint that she is, to console me. Her improvement has not amounted to anything. Today I received a letter from her, and she is very sick with severe nausea, which makes matters all the worse because of her weak condition. We are praying fervently for her, but my sins are great. I know there's no need to ask you to pray for her, but I'm doing this with all the communities.

4. Doña Guiomar[10] was married today. She is delighted to know that you are doing well, and so is Doña Luisa,[11] who has never shown me such love, and her concern for my comfort is

by no means slight. Pray for them, and give my fondest regards to all the sisters.

5. I am worried about those monasteries[12] our *padre* has charge of. I am now offering him the help of the discalced nuns and would willingly offer myself.[13] I tell him that the whole thing is a great pity; and he immediately tells me how you are pampering him. May God preserve you for me. Warn him not to eat with those friars,[14] for goodness' sake. I don't know why he goes down there, unless to provide us all with trials. I have already told you to take what you spend on him from the sum of money sent by St. Joseph's.[15] You see, it would be foolish to do otherwise. And I know what I am saying. The money will be repaid without your realizing how. Don't do anything else. Let the good subprioress[16] keep track of everything; she could do so even of the water.[17] Regards to her and to my Gabriela.[18] May God be with all of you.

6. With what the sister brings, and as much as you can add to it, pay at once on the house so that you will not have such high interest payments, which are a heavy burden, for even if they don't want . . .

---

1. Gracián, who is involved again in the official visitations of the Carmelites in Andalusia.
2. Lorenzo de Cepeda, from Avila.
3. Lorenzo had advanced the money to purchase the house for the foundation of the Carmel in Seville (cf. Ltr. 132.7).
4. They were benefitting from the financial help provided by Lorenzo.
5. Teresa's niece who was a Carmelite aspirant living at St. Joseph's in Avila.
6. They couldn't be found after Teresa's return from Seville (cf. Ltr. 129.4).
7. Hernando de Pantoja, prior of the Carthusians.
8. The long fast of the Carmelite rule begins on 14 September, the feast of the Triumph of the Cross.
9. Brianda de San José, who was chronically ill.
10. Guiomar Pardo de Tavera, Doña Luisa de la Cerda's daughter.
11. Luisa de la Cerda.

12. The monasteries of the Carmelite nuns of the observance in Andalusia, especially those in Seville and Paterna.
13. She is offering to help in the reform of those monasteries as she did at the Incarnation.
14. With the Carmelite friars of the observance in Seville.
15. The nuns of St. Joseph's in Avila had sent money to help the Carmel in Seville (cf. Ltr. 120.10).
16. María del Espíritu Santo
17. In jest she alludes to the subprioress's extreme detail in keeping the accounts.
18. Leonor de San Gabriel.

138. To Padre Jerónimo Gracián, Seville

Toledo, 31 October 1576

She is continuing to work on her book, which is easier for her than the oppressive task of letter-writing. The nuns in Seville are holding their ground against Padre Olea's insistence that they accept a candidate recommended by him. On All Souls Day she will celebrate her 40th anniversary of receiving the Carmelite habit.

For Padre Maestro Fray Jerónimo Gracián, apostolic commissary for Carmel.

1. Jesus. The grace of the Holy Spirit be with your paternity. *The Foundations*[1] is nearing completion. I think you will be delighted to see it. It makes for pleasant reading. See how well I obey! Sometimes I even wonder if I have this virtue, for if one gives me an order in jest, I want to take it seriously. And I carry out the orders more eagerly than I do this letter-writing, for all the bustle involved is killing me. I don't know how I found time for what I have written, and I have not failed to find some for Joseph[2] either, who is the one who gives me strength for everything.

2. I am also fasting, for the cold in this area is not bad, and so it doesn't do me the harm that it does elsewhere. For goodness' sake, give my Padre Fray Antonio[3] best regards from me; although it would be better, if possible, not to let him know that I am writing so much to you and so little to him. Perhaps I will write him a few words.

3. Had San Telmo[4] taken the matter of his nun as Nicolao did, I wouldn't have had to bear so much. I tell you I don't know what to think, for we are not becoming saints in this life. If you could only see the qualities of the first nun, which make her acceptable, and how San Telmo treats the prioress. May it please God, *mi padre*, that we will have need for no one else but God himself. At least, San Telmo would not get any cooperation from me, even if the whole world were to collapse, since I see how this goes against my conscience. And, nonetheless, he says that he is no more interested in her than he would be in some stranger passing by on the street. What a life! And what would he do if he were interested in her. I would be afraid to take in someone that he proposes.

4. Mariano[5] is frightened by it, and because I think he will write to you, I have mentioned it so you will not worry; we've done more than we should have. Well, he will come to know the truth, and if he doesn't, it matters little. What matters to me for my tranquility is that God keep you very holy.

5. Today is the vigil of All Saints. All Souls Day is the anniversary of my receiving the habit.[6] Ask God to make me a genuine Carmelite nun, for better late than never.

My regards to the prosecutor and to Acosta and the rector.[7]

Your unworthy servant and loyal subject. Blessed be God, for I will always be so, come what may.

Teresa of Jesus

6. The enclosed sheet of paper has a carol in honor of the saints that the nuns are sending you as an expression of their desire to have you here. They say that for some days God has been doing everything they ask of him here. From what I've seen, they are right.

---

1. On Gracián's orders she had resumed writing the *Book of Her Foundations* in the beginning of October. She will conclude this portion of her book on 14 November.
2. Code name for Jesus.
3. Antonio de Jesús (Heredia) who was then prior of Los Remedios where Gracián was residing.
4. Code name for the Jesuit Francisco de Olea, who was insisting that the Carmelite nuns accept a postulant recommended by him. Nicolao (Nicolás) Doria had also proposed a postulant who was not accepted by the nuns.
5. Mariano de San Benito, who was then in Madrid.
6. It was her 40th anniversary.
7. The prosecutor of the Inquisition in Seville was Francisco de Arganda. Diego de Acosta and Francisco Arias were two Jesuits.

139. To Madre María de San José, Seville

Toledo, 31 October 1576

She worries about what is happening to her letters, and urges the prioress to watch for those written to Gracián. Some objects lost on the trip from Seville have been found. Brianda de San José's health is still bad.

1. Jesus be with your reverence, my daughter. For love of God, try to find out when our *padre*[1] receives a letter from me, even though I almost never fail to write to you when writing to him. A letter of his delivered today, written on 22 October, says he hasn't received one from me for a long time—and I don't do any thing but write. I wrote at length especially when I could use the muleteer's services. I wouldn't want someone to get

hold of them. If they were lost, that wouldn't matter so much. Perhaps they are held up in the house of the chief courier down there, for they definitely leave from here. You should inquire there at times to see if they have any letters.

2. Before I forget, the large *agnusdei* and the rings have shown up.[2] The nuns are all doing well in Avila as you will see by these enclosed letters. My brother[3] tells me he was delighted with your letters, and he laughed a great deal and showed them to the nuns at St. Joseph's. He is going to write to you, for he is very fond of all of you. And I tell you that I am too.

3. You tell me that Nicolao[4] is helping you all very much and that he will be confessor to the nuns. That is very good. Be kind to him, and write and tell me whether you are well, and not in roundabout ways but truthfully.

4. As for the health of the prioress in Malagón,[5] I don't know what to say to you but that she is very bad. There has been talk now of bringing her here, but the doctor here says that doing so would only hasten her end. The illness is of the kind for which God alone is the true doctor. The locality does nothing either positively or negatively in such an illness. I am advising them again not to drink sarsaparilla water.

5. I wrote to Garciálvarez[6] and a great deal to our *padre* about him. Tell me in detail how everything is going for you and why you do not make our *padre* eat meat on some days. Be with God, for I wrote to you so recently that I have nothing more to say, except ask that you give my regards to all the nuns.

Today is the vigil of All Saints.

Your reverence's servant,

Teresa of Jesus

---

1. Jerónimo Gracián
2. Cf. Ltr. 137.2.
3. Lorenzo de Cepeda.

4. Nicolás Doria, a priest who will eventually join the discalced Carmelites.
5. Brianda de San José.
6. Confessor to the nuns in Seville.

140. To Madre Maria Bautista, Valladolid

Toledo, End of October(?) 1576

This text is from a declaration made by María Bautista in the process for Teresa's beatification. The soul referred to is María Bautista's father, Diego de Cepeda.

I tell you, my daughter, that before you knew about it, I believe his soul was freed from purgatory. Every day just after I had received communion, he would come to me, and when the news arrived—despite the distance—I understood who it was.

141. To Padre Jerónimo Gracián, Seville

Toledo, November 1576(?)

In this fragment of uncertain date Teresa in all confidence begs Gracián not to be so open with everyone and above all not to read her letters to him in public.

1. Time will bring you to lose a little of your simplicity, which I certainly understand to be that of a saint. But since the devil does not want everyone to be a saint, those who are wretched and malicious like myself would want to remove the occasions of sin. I can express and have much love for you for many reasons, but this cannot be so for all the nuns, nor will all superiors be like *mi padre* with whom one can speak so familiarly. God has entrusted this treasure[1] to you, but you mustn't think that all the others will care for it the way you do. I tell you truly I fear much more the fact that men can rob you than that de-

mons can. And what the nuns see me say and do (because I know whom I'm addressing and my age allows it), they think they can do also, and they will be right. But this does not mean that you should stop loving them, rather that you should love them still more.

2. And the truth of it is that, despite my wretchedness, from the time I began to have daughters like these I have gone about with so much circumspection and vigilance, keeping a watch on how the devil might tempt them through me that, glory to God, I don't think there are any particularly serious things they have been able to note (for His Majesty has helped me). I confess that I have striven to hide my imperfections from them—although there are so many they must have seen a good number—as well as my love and concern for Paul.[2] I often point out to them how necessary he is for the order and that I am under an obligation—as if I could act otherwise if I didn't have this reason.

3. But how tiresome I am! May it not prove a burden to *mi padre* to have to hear these things, for you and I are weighed down with a very heavy load and we have to render an account to God and to the world. And since you understand the love with which I say this, you can pardon me and do me the favor I've asked of you: not to read in public the letters I write to you. Remember that people interpret things differently and that superiors should never be so open about some matters. It may come to pass that I am writing about a third party or about myself and that it would not be well for such matters to be known. There is a great difference for me between speaking of certain things with you and speaking of them with others, even my own sister. Just as I would not want anyone to hear me when I speak with God, or hinder me from being alone with him, so it is with Paul....

1. Teresa's new Carmels.
2. Gracián.

142. To Don Lorenzo de Cepeda, Avila

Toledo, Beginning of November 1576

From Toledo Teresa keeps information flowing between Seville and Avila. The nuns in Seville still owe money to Lorenzo, which Teresa does not forget, nor does she allow them to forget it. Francisco de Salcedo's loss is the occasion for her reflections on the spiritual gain that can come through material loss.

1. ...Now she tells me she has the money she owes you.[1]...She doesn't dare send it to you until you have chosen someone to whom she can entrust it and who will show her a letter from you. Be on the watch, then, for the day when the muleteer leaves there. If he is trustworthy, it would be best for him to bring the money, or better, deliver it. Antonio Ruiz[2] must go...from Malagón. He would be delighted because this is not the suitable time for proceeding with work on the house, and so he has nothing to do in Malagón. It's better that he hurry things along down there. You would be doing him a favor by providing him with a way out of his difficulties, and you would be losing nothing. In beginning this letter, I was thinking more of helping these poor people, who are so good, out of their difficulties, than of your gain. But I would also like to see you become very rich, since you spend it so well. And even this morning the thought came to me that you should not have your boys[3] marry soon, so that you can do more for your own soul. If you begin to get entangled in other expenses, you won't have enough for everything. And, after all, this is the recompense you deserve for all the trouble you went through to earn it: to spend as much as you can in the service of the One...who will give you his kingdom, which death cannot take away. His Majesty....

2. ...interior spiritual trials you are much better prepared...in both natural disposition and spirit.[4]...It's necessary always to

show him much kindness, for he soon thinks he is being a bother. I don't know if I could assert that he is the person in my life to whom I am most indebted in every respect, for I began to be greatly enlightened by him, and so I am very fond of him. I am distressed he doesn't bear the trial sent him by the Lord over this lawsuit with greater courage, for I can't believe that it comes from some other source.

3. Pray that God will enlighten him so that he will not be upset. This is what happens when one is not detached from everything. That which could be for us the greatest gain (the loss of property, which lasts for so short a time and is so undeserving of esteem when compared to what is eternal) disturbs and deprives us of this very gain. We have to realize that anyone to whom God has not granted such a favor will receive no consolation from our speaking like this. Rather he will be consoled if he sees we are sorry about his affliction.

4. Today, while thinking of how God distributes his blessings as he wills, I was amazed that a man like this who has served God so sincerely for so many years should become afflicted about losing goods that he considered as belonging more to the poor than to himself. While I was thinking that this would matter little to me, I recalled how disturbed I became when, while we were in Seville, we learned that you were in danger of losing all that you had brought back with you. And so it is that we never know ourselves. Thus the best thing to do is to forsake all for the All. And then our human nature will not make us slaves of such base things. Those who cannot give up everything should reflect often on how we become the slaves of these things. You should do this too, and remember how your human nature drew you....

1. María de San José to whom Lorenzo had lent money.
2. Antonio Ruiz from Malagón was a trader in livestock and a good friend of Teresa's.
3. His boys were Francisco, 17, and Lorenzo, 14.

4. A second fragment of the letter. It deals with Francisco de Salcedo, now a priest, who was finding it difficult to bear the financial ruin he suffered in a lawsuit.

143. To Madre María Bautista, Valladolid

Toledo, 2 November 1576

María Bautista is ill and inwardly troubled. Teresa shows her concern and tries to take the prioress's mind off her troubles with a good deal of news. Teresa herself is feeling well.

1. Jesus. The grace of the Holy Spirit be with you. If you would believe what I tell you once in a while, we could avoid a lot of trouble. Did I not insist the other day in a letter that you not have yourself bled anymore! I don't know what nonsense has got into you, even though the doctor does give his consent. Your illness has been very distressing to me since the affliction is in your head. Now, about Catalina,[1] you must pray for her, and not because she wants to go there, where I know she is very much loved. I tell you, this woman is a great person. Please God she will not have to pay dearly for all this affection she has for you. This is what passed through my mind, and I'm telling you so that you will repent.

2. I've received all your letters. They arrive in good condition this way. There is no need for you to send money to cover the portage, for I can take care of it with what my brother[2] gives me. I owe him so much in every way. Our Father Visitator[3] is well, for a letter from him arrived two days ago. He is solicitous about writing me, and up to the present he is getting along well with those people.[4] But he carries out his office with much discretion and gentleness. Many days have now gone by since that matter with the Franciscans, and they haven't killed their visitator.[5]

3. The news regarding Bishop Quiroga[6] is true, and we are delighted because our *padre* has an excellent rapport with him. Now the bishop and the nuncio[7] are very sick. Pray for them, for we would miss them very much, and the bishop would be a loss to the entire kingdom. Pray also for Don Juan of Austria, for he went to Flanders disguised as the valet of a Fleming.[8]

4. Oh, how pleased you made me by telling me of the health of Padre Fray Pedro Fernández.[9] I had been disturbed, for I had known about his illness but not about his recovery. I tell you, he does not resemble your friend[10] by ingratitude, for with all he has to do, he takes care to write to me. And in everything, he thinks he's indebted to me, although in this regard your friend is much more indebted to me. Know that the care this friend takes of you will last until he finds someone else who pleases him. Be sure of this, no matter how much you take for granted.

5. If God hadn't held me back, I would have done what you wanted to do some time ago. God doesn't allow me to do this, from which I see that he of whom you speak is God's servant. So it is necessary to love him, for he deserves it, and along with him, all the other servants of God there are on earth. If we think we're worth more than they, we're being really foolish. But this does not mean we should resemble him, but rather that we must always be grateful for the good that is done for us. So, forget about all these niceties and don't fail to write to him, but strive little by little to have an inner freedom, of which, glory to God, I now possess a good deal; but you are not as free as you say. Blessed may he be who is always a true friend when we desire his friendship.

6. The letter will be delivered to Luis de Cepeda.[11] I have already written you that his father also died and of how much we prayed here for his father during the illness. Send me the account you say you have prepared for my brother (for I gave him the one Señora Doña María de Mendoza[12] gave me), and send me the other accounts also with all your recollections.

And, when you are up to it, prepare a report on Estefanía[13] like the one you sent to Avila, for that was very well done. The handwriting should be good, so that I don't have to get someone here to make a copy. And don't entrust it to Juliana,[14] for, because of exaggeration, the silly and nonsensical things she said in the report about Beatriz de la Encarnación[15] were unbearable. But when you are well, write down what you know, for the provincial has ordered this to be done.

7. I am well, glory to God. There's no way of persuading you, when you need a purgative, to take that syrup, the "King of the Medes." It has given me new life, and there's no harm it can cause you. Do not send the accounts by ordinary mail, or even think about doing so, but with the muleteer, even though this means a delay, for nothing would get here.

8. Concerning what you say about your interior life, the greater the disturbance the less attention you should pay to it, for it clearly proceeds from a weak imagination and bad humor; and since the devil sees this, he adds his bit. But have no fear, for St. Paul says that God will not permit us to be tempted beyond what we can bear.[16] And even though it may seem that you give consent, it's not so; rather, you will benefit from all of this. Continue with your cure, for love of God, and try to eat well, and don't remain alone thinking about nothing. Seek some diversion inasmuch as you can and however possible. I would like to be there, for there's much I would talk about for your entertainment.

9. How is it that you didn't write me about the trials of Don Francisco?[17] I would have written him, for I owe him a great deal. When you see the countess of Osorno,[18] give her my regards, and regards also to my María de la Cruz, Casilda, and Dorotea, and to the subprioress and her sister.[19] I don't know what should be done about that blind novice. I tell you it's a heavy hardship.

10. Indeed, Prádonos[20] is a good friend. You do well to speak with him, even though they are now going to change the supe-

rior. If only they'd send Padre Domeneque[21] back! How much I would like that for you. Write soon about how you are, and remain with God. As for the prioress,[22] she has been sorry about your illness. We are all praying to His Majesty for you. When you write to Fray Domingo[23] always give him my regards; and let me know how he is.

Today is All Souls day

I remain yours,

Teresa of Jesus

---

1. Although this Catalina was a friend and an admirer of María Bautista, nothing further is known for certain.
2. Lorenzo de Cepeda.
3. Jerónimo Gracián, visitator of the Carmelites in Andalusia.
4. The Andalusians.
5. A probable reference to Fray Diego de Buenaventura, visitator for the Franciscans in Andalusia.
6. Gaspar de Quiroga, Bishop of Cuenca and Grand Inquisitor, had been named Archbishop of Toledo after the death of Bartolomé de Carranza.
7. Diego de Covarrubias y Leiva was the bishop of Segovia, and Nicolás Ormaneto was the nuncio. Both of these men died within the next year.
8. Don Juan of Austria, the natural son of Charles V, was sent to the Netherlands as a conciliator. After dyeing his hair and beard, he left Valladolid as the valet of Octavio Gonzaga.
9. The Dominican who had been visitator of the Carmelites in Castile.
10. Another Dominican, Padre Domingo Báñez.
11. The son of Teresa's cousin, Francisco de Cepeda.
12. The bishop of Avila's sister, a friend and benefactor.
13. Estefanía de los Apóstoles (cf. F. 11.1).
14. Juliana de la Magdalena was one of the six Carmelite daughters of Nicolás Gutiérrez who was a great help to Teresa in the Salamancan foundation (cf. F. 19.9).
15. Teresa wrote an edifying account of Beatriz's life and death in chapter 12 of the *Foundations*.
16. 1 Cor 10:13.

17. Don Francisco de Salcedo who was undergoing a painful lawsuit in the Valladolid court.
18. Doña María de Velasco y Aragón.
19. María de la Cruz, one of the first nuns of the foundation in Avila, Casilda de Padilla, and Dorotea de la Cruz. The subprioress was Antonia del Espíritu Santo and her sister was Ana de San José (Henao).
20. The Jesuit Juan Prádanos, a former confessor of Teresa's (cf L. 24.4–8).
21. Pedro Domenech had been a Jesuit confessor to Teresa in Toledo.
22. The prioress of Seville, María de San José.
23. Domingo Báñez.

144. To Padre Ambrosio Mariano, Madrid

Toledo, 3 November 1576

(Autograph: DCN Medina de Rioseco [Valladolid])

Valdemoro, seeking a favor from Teresa, insists on his desire to be friends with her. Although she will write a few words of recommendation for Valdemoro's expelled brother, she cautions Mariano about accepting him among the discalced friars.

For *mi padre*, Doctor Fray Mariano de San Benito.

1. Jesus be with your reverence. Today the good Valdemoro[1] was here, and I believe he is telling the truth when he speaks about our being friends, for that is what suits his purposes at present. He speaks to me a lot about St. Paul's persecution of the Christians and of what he did afterward. Were he to do for God one tenth of what St. Paul did we would forgive him for both the past and the future. He tells me he is going to ask you to accept his brother.[2]

2. Certainly, if what he says is true, and in view of your need for preachers, it would be to your advantage to have him. But I fear that since our *padre*[3] in his visitations sends away those who come from other orders, he would not hear of admitting

this person into his own order. What I can do in exchange for the friendship is pray for him. You can judge up there what would be the most fitting thing to do.

3. We are praying hard for the sanctification of those lords. May God bring this about according to whatever need he sees. I am worried about the trials of our good Padre Padilla.[4] The devil will not give up waging war against works as great as those he's doing. May God grant him fortitude and health, and may he make you and Padre Maestro[5] very holy.

4. I haven't learned anything new about the business affairs. I think you would learn about them there first. Tomorrow I will be giving Valdemoro, who is going to Madrid, a letter addressed to you. If in it I make a request in favor of his brother, my ultimate desire is that you do what renders the most service to God.

These little friars are like saints.[6] Seeing souls like this is a great consolation, and gives one strength to suffer the trials that could come upon us.

It is 3 November.

Your reverence's,

Teresa of Jesus

---

1. Alonso Valdemoro was prior of the Carmelites of the observance in Avila (cf. Ltr 133.1).
2. His brother was a former Dominican who had now been expelled from the Carmelites of the observance. But he was being presented to Teresa as a very holy man and a great preacher.
3. Jerónimo Gracián.
4. Juan Calvo de Padilla, who on account of his unofficial zeal for the reform of religious orders was denounced to the Inquisition.
5. Probably Juan de Jesús Roca.
6. These were young, discalced Carmelites on their way from La Peñuela to the student house in Alcalá.

145. To Padre Jerónimo Gracián, Seville

Toledo, 4 November 1576

Teresa is writing many letters to Gracián, but only a few seem to arrive. She now sends word about the dispensation for Casilda and the suspicious visit she had from Valdemoro. Her situation will be a perplexing one if the nuncio, Ormaneto, dies. But she nonetheless feels a great inner freedom.

1. Jesus. May the grace of the Holy Spirit be always with your paternity. During these past days I have written several times. Please God the letters will arrive. It pains me to see how many I write and how few you tell me you receive.

2. Today they brought me those from Valladolid. They tell me the permission for Casilda[1] to make profession arrived from Rome and that she is overjoyed. I don't think you should put off giving your permission so as to wait until you can give her the veil, for we don't know what is going to happen in this life, and the surest course is the safest. So, for goodness' sake, I ask you to send your written permission at once by different routes, so that that little angel won't pine away, for the waiting is very costly to her. You will have already been told, or will be told, that the one to whom Casilda entrusted her report was Fray Domingo.[2] However, if I have the time I will read the letters. If what I said is not included, I will send my report to you.

3. You should know that Perucho[3] was here two days ago. He says that St. Paul persecuted the Christians and that still God touched his heart and that he can do the same for him making him turn over a new leaf. I think he will continue as long as it's convenient for him.

He's absolutely certain that Paul will come as visitator against them.[4] He says he will be the first to give him a good welcome, that he has a brother whom the night owls[5] expelled, a great saint and preacher, indeed without a fault, who was previously a Dominican; he wants him to join the eagles.[6] If all this is true, it wouldn't do us any harm to take him, since we need preachers. The bad part is that it all seems to me to be a fable. Oh, what a great friend I have in him! God deliver us.

4. The one who is giving the property for the monastery would like them to say a Mass for him once a week, and he will provide for the construction of six nice cells. I told him you would not agree to this. I believe he will be content with less and even perhaps with nothing.

5. I am afraid of our losing Methuselah.[7] Tell me what Angela[8] ought to do if this should happen, for she will then be feeling scruples over obedience in regard to which monastery she should be living in. I see clearly that the one is in an out-of-the-way place and that Laurencia[9] will be much worse off than where she is now, at least as regards her health. But it is really the place where her presence is most needed, so no attention should be paid to what pleases her, for on this earth it would be a mistake to take that into account. Well, her greatest happiness would lie in being near her confessor Paul, and there are more possibilities down there—except for building a monastery.[10] Where she is now is even worse than being in Avila as far as dealing with business matters goes. Whatever may be your decision, will you let her know it. If something were to happen and here they told her to go elsewhere, she would not be able to wait for your answer; and she would regret that very much.

6. Also consider if in the designation or choosing of a place for her, it would be fitting to take into account the monastery specified by the previous visitator,[11] for apart from the need for her presence down there, it might be more perfect for her to go to that specified place than to decide on one by herself. So consider carefully, *padre*, what may be the suitable thing to do in this regard. For whether we make a mistake or do what is right the matter will be public. I don't think it will be long before we will have another Methuselah;[12] but maybe it will be.

7. Oh, God help me! What great freedom this woman has in all that takes place. It doesn't seem that anything bad can happen to her or to her Paul.[13] The words of Joseph[14] are powerful, for they can produce results like this. But what learning and eloquence Paul has! It's something to praise God for. May you recommend all this to him, and answer me, for heaven's sake, for nothing is lost in following your counsel, and much could be lost in following other opinions. Let us pray hard for Methuselah and for the great angel,[15] about whom I feel the most distress without my knowing why. May His Majesty give him health and preserve you for many years with great holiness, amen, amen.

Today is 4 November.

Your paternity's unworthy subject and true daughter.

Teresa of Jesus

---

1. Casilda de Padilla received a canonical dispensation from Rome to make profession at age 15 (cf. F. 10–11). Yet, later, during Teresa's lifetime (1581), Casilda transferred from the Carmelites to the Franciscans.
2. Domingo Báñez, who had intervened in favor of Casilda's entering Carmel at age 11.
3. Alonso de Valdemoro.
4. He suspected that Gracián would extend his visitation to include the Carmelites in Castile.
5. The Carmelites of the observance.
6. The discalced Carmelite friars (cf. Ltr. 144.1).
7. Nicolás Ormaneto, the nuncio.
8. Teresa herself. Were Ormaneto to die and Gracián's jurisdiction to come to an end as a result, Teresa would be in a perplexing situation: the Father General had ordered her to remain in a monastery in Castile; the Dominican visitator Fernández had made her a member of the community in Salamanca; and Gracián had given her orders to stay in Malagón until the construction of the monastery there was finished.
9. Another code name Teresa used for herself.
10. Paul is Gracián and the monastery down there is Malagón.

11. Pedro Fernández.
12. A new nuncio.
13. Gracián.
14. Jesus Christ.
15. The Grand Inquisitor, Gaspar de Quiroga.

146. To María de San José, Seville

Toledo, 8 November 1576

(Autograph: DCN, Moncalieri [Turin])

In a quick reply to a letter that had just arrived, Teresa gives her opinion about postulants, dowries, and other financial matters. She suggests a plan for concealing her correspondence with Gracián.

For Mother Prioress, María de San José.

1. Jesus be with your reverence. I don't have time to say all that I would like. Today the muleteer gave me your message. The longer your letters are the happier they make me. I have received so many letters today that there isn't even time to write this, nor have I had time to read the sisters' letters. Give them my best regards.

2. I already wrote you to tell you to accept Garciálvarez's sisters.[1] It seems to me that my letter should have arrived. If they are so good, there is no reason for waiting. I am distressed that you are taking in so many nuns without any improvement in your financial picture.[2] Try at least to get those 300 ducats that you are obliged to pay this year, for I assure you it bothers my conscience that you do not give poor Antonio Ruiz[3] his money. He needs this for food for himself and for his livestock in Malagón. I'm already trying to find someone to help him out with more—and this is my brother,[4] although he will also benefit from so doing—for I see that he has so little to count on there.

3. Even were the postulant recommended by Padre Nicolao not so perfect, I wouldn't send her away. Give him my regards and tell him that his cousin[5] came to see me and sent an alms.

4. As for Pablo,[6] I don't know what to say, for I still haven't understood well—until I read the letter again—why there is such a hurry before the year is up. If they give you 1500 ducats besides what they owe you for this year, give up the inheritance gladly. For these inheritances are never good for us because they end up amounting to nothing. And don't accept the inheritance, but he must take responsibility for that part which they are giving for the house. Don't let it enter your mind to take the inheritance. Say that you can't, that you are not allowed to have an income. Well, you shouldn't be writing me about these things; consider down there what's best for you to do. I wouldn't want anything to be withdrawn from that dowry or from Beatriz's,[7] but that the entire sum be given together. Otherwise I don't know how you can carry on with all that you have to pay every year, and instead of getting out of difficulties, you will lose a great deal. As for the lay sister, I will write to Valladolid to vouch for her and then write you again soon.

I am well.

The date is 8 November

5. I will put the letters for our *padre* in an envelope without an address and with your name on it and two or three crosses; better two, or one, since the letters are numerous. And ask him not to address his letters to me but let you address them and mark them with the same sign. Doing this will conceal them better and make for a better plan than the one I had suggested. Please God you are speaking the truth when you say you are well, and remain with him.

Yours,

Teresa of Jesus

6. I have written you that your letters were given to my brother, and he was delighted with them. He is well, and the prioress of St. Joseph's remains the same.

---

1. Two cousins and a niece were planning to enter the Carmel in Seville.
2. Receiving postulants without a dowry would not help solve the financial problems weighing on the community.
3. A friend of Teresa's, Antonio Ruiz, accompanied her on her trip from Seville to Malagón. Though not well-off, he had lent money to the nuns in Seville.
4. Lorenzo De Cepeda.
5. Francisco Doria.
6. Pablo Matías wanted his daughter, Bernarda de San José, who was still a novice in Seville, to renounce her possessions before the time for her profession, and her dowry as well. He instead made promises of what he would contribute in the future.
7. Beatriz de la Madre de Dios.

147. To Padre Jerónimo Gracián, Seville

Toledo, 11 November 1576

Teresa has heard from Gracián and from the nuns in Seville. She gives him some counsels and envies the nuns who are close to him. In concluding she explains the matter of Doña Elena's dowry and plan for an endowment.

1. Jesus. The grace of the Holy Spirit be with your paternity. Last week while we were within the octave of All Saints, I wrote to you of how I rejoiced in receiving your letter, even though it was short, which was the last that I received. Regarding what you mentioned about writing to Rome, please God the result will be positive and that no other opinions will stand in the way.[1]

2. I also mentioned how delighted I was with the letters you wrote to Padre Mariano[2] which he sent me at my request. It's a story that made me give God much praise. I don't know how

you are able to think up such ingenious tricks. May he be blessed who gives you such ability, for it seems to be his work. So, you must always consider carefully the favor God bestows on you and not go about trusting in yourself. I tell you that Buenaventura[3] was so confident in himself that everything seemed easy (which scared me when I heard about it), yet it didn't do him any good.

3. This great God of Israel wants to be praised in his creatures. Thus we need to seek, as you do, what is for his honor and glory and be as diligent as we can not to seek any for ourselves. His Majesty will take care of us as he sees is fitting. What behooves us is that we understand our lowliness and that in that lowliness his grandeur be exalted. But how foolish I am, and how you will laugh, *mi padre*, when you read this! May God pardon those butterflies[4] who enjoy so peacefully what I could not enjoy there except through much hardship. I can't help envying them, but it is a great joy for me that they are so diligently seeking to provide some relief[5] for Paul, and so inconspicuously.

4. I have already written you many foolish counsels. If you wanted to get even with me, you would have to stop giving me the relief I find in your being able to get some relief for yourself, for you need it so badly in the midst of such great hardship. But my Paul[6] has more virtue than this, and understands me better than before. That there be no occasion for failing in this understanding, I ask that you refuse to be my chaplain except for this purpose. This is so, for I tell you that if I had suffered all the trials involved in this foundation for no other reason, I would consider it to have been well worthwhile. And again it makes me praise the Lord that he granted me the favor of your having a place there where you can get your breath without being with seculars. Those sisters[7] give me great pleasure, and you do me a great favor, by having them write with such detail, for they say you have given them orders to do so. It is a consolation for me to see that you don't forget me.

5. Doña Elena[8] has combined her daughter's share of the inheritance with what she will bring as a dowry if she enters. And she says that the amount should be sufficient for accepting herself, two other nuns, and two lay sisters, and that after the work on the house is completed the remainder should be used for a pious foundation like that of Alba.[9] The truth though is that she submits entirely to what Padre Baltasar Alvarez,[10] you, and I decide. It was he who sent me this information, for he didn't want to respond before finding out what I would say. I paid careful attention to what I have seen as your will and so, after much reflection and discussion, I gave this enclosed response.[11] If it doesn't seem right to you, let me know. Notice that I do not want to see the houses that were founded in poverty having an income.

May God keep watch over you.

Your unworthy daughter and servant,

Teresa of Jesus

---

1. Teresa had wanted Gracián to write to the general of the Carmelite order in Rome about the decision of the discalced friars' chapter at Almodóvar in September to seek to become a separate province.
2. Ambrosio Mariano de San Benito, the discalced friar, had been living in Madrid.
3. Diego de Buenaventura, the visitator of the Franciscans in Andalusia.
4. A code name for the discalced Carmelite nuns in Seville.
5. An allusion to the meals she had recommended they discretely provide for him.
6. Gracián.
7. The Carmelite nuns in Seville.
8. Elena de Quiroga who will become a Carmelite nun. Her daughter was Jerónima de la Encarnación (Villarroel).
9. Their first desire had been to found a school for girls in Medina del Campo under the care of the discalced Carmelite nuns. Since no agreement could be worked out, they decided on a pious foundation providing for Mass and Vespers to be sung on the feast days of the Blessed Virgin Mary.

10 The Jesuit who had been Teresa's confessor at the Incarnation and now living in Medina.

11. A copy of her response to Doña Elena, which has been lost.

148. To Madre María de San José, Seville
Toledo, 11 November 1576

(Autograph: DCN, Valladolid)

Teresa reveals her concern about Madre María's health, about Gracián and her correspondence with him, and about the financial problems and debts of the community in Seville.

For Mother Prioress, María de San José.

1. Jesus be with you reverence. Always include on a small piece of paper a list of the things you want me to answer. Your letters are long—although they don't seem so, because of the joy they give me; but if when in a hurry I have to read them all over in order to answer them, they do seem long.

2. I wrote you two, three, or four days ago that I would put two crosses on the letters for our *padre* but with your address. Let me know when you receive this message because I will not start doing this until then.

3. I tell you that I am very sorry about your fever. Why do you tell me that you are well? I'm bothered by that. But take care to see if it isn't caused by amenorrhea, and do something about it. Don't let it take root. I strongly suspect that it leaves you at times; this consoles me. I suggest you apply some ointments or things to mitigate the fever, and don't fail to tell the doctor. I think you usually have yourself bled every year. Perhaps this would benefit you, as the subprioress[1] says. What I'm telling you is not to stay in the state you are in, waiting until it will be too late for a remedy. May God make you well.

4. I haven't heard anything from Malagón for days. I'm worried, and the doctors don't give me any hope for the prioress'[2] return to health. All the signs and symptoms point to tuberculosis. God is life, and he can give it. Always keep praying for this—also for a person to whom I owe a great deal—and tell everyone to do so, and give them my regards, for their letters are a delight to me. I don't know if I will have a chance to answer them.

5. I tell you that I greatly envy all of you for the happy and peaceful way in which you enjoy the presence of our *padre*.[3] I don't deserve such repose, and so I have no reason to complain. I am very glad that you have this relief, for if you didn't I don't know how you would be able to endure everything else. Nonetheless, I tell you to give orders to the subprioress in my name to subtract all the expenses from the forty ducats owed to St. Joseph's, and don't do otherwise, for you would be undergoing a loss. Consider what you spend as being taken care of here, and deduct from the debt whatever you spend on him. I laugh to myself thinking of how the good subprioress will include everything in the accounting, even the water.[4] But she will be doing well, for that's what I want, except for the little gifts given as alms. I will become angry if you do otherwise.

6. You never tell me who his companion[5] is. That's the only worry I have now, for I am very happy everything is going so well, without anyone's knowing about it. I wouldn't want it to be known in Los Remedios where he is eating, for that would open the door to what cannot be allowed for another superior. Believe me it's necessary to consider the future so that we don't have to answer to God for something we ourselves have started.

7. I am concerned to see how those nuns you are taking in are not of any help to you. Padre Garciálvarez will have received by now the letter in which I say that his relatives[6] should be accepted. And I have written one to you that you should try to have them bring some money to help pay the interest, for

that inheritance must not be worth anything. I wouldn't want you to wait until you don't know where to turn next, but that you provide for yourself before discovering that you are in water over your head. I accepted a nun in Salamanca who, they told me, was bringing a dowry from which I could have sent 300 ducats to Malagón to pay what you owe them and pay the hundred to Asensio Galiano,[7] but she has not come. Pray that God will bring her to us. I tell you that you owe me a great deal for my desire to see you free of worry.

8. Why don't you try to give that money from Juana de la Cruz[8] at once so as not to be so burdened with debt? Consider how this is not something to neglect. Try to get Anegas[9] to bring what you need to pay Antonio Ruiz,[10] for as I have mentioned you are obliged in conscience to give him what you owe him considering his present need.

9. As for Pablo, I reread what concerned him.[11] You mustn't let him think that you want his daughter, but that he should give up trying to have her enter. And realize that this is better for many reasons, for these business people have a lot of money one day, and the next day they lose it all. How much more so since parents look after those who are close to them, and little is left over. What is more fitting is that he pay you all that he still owes you for the house, if it amounts to 1500 ducats, and don't accept an inheritance or agree on a lesser amount. If you can get more from him, get it. Try to find someone who will tell him not to upset his children by leaving their inheritance to a monastery. Even if he gave 2,000 ducats, it would not be a lot.

10. They say that the mother of the Portuguese girl[12] could give the dowry. I think that would be worth more than the others. Well, you will not be in want. At the moment you least expect, God will send you someone who will bring more than you want. It wouldn't be bad if that chaplain were to take responsibility for the major chapel. Don't fail to send him some

gifts to show your gratitude, even though there be no occasion for doing so.

11. Before I forget, you ought to know that I learned here of some mortifications that are being performed in Malagón. The prioress will suddenly give an order that a sister be slapped by another. They got this notion from here. It seems the devil is teaching them under the guise of perfection to put souls in danger of offending God. By no means should you command or consent that any nun give another a slap (they also say pinches are given). Do not guide the nuns with the rigor you saw at Malagón, for they are not slaves. Mortification should be used only for one's growth. I tell you, my daughter, that it's necessary that you be very careful about what these little prioresses dream up. The things that I am now finding out! How this afflicts me! May God make you a saint, amen.

12. My brother is well, and Teresa too.[13] The letter you wrote him in which you spoke of the four *reales* was not received; all the other letters were. He is delighted with them, and cherishes them more than the ones he gets from here.

Today is 11 November, and I am yours,

Teresa of Jesus

13. Try to get our *padre* to respond to the business matters I am writing him about in the enclosed letter. I mean that you insist with him that he not forget.

---

1. María del Espíritu Santo.
2. Brianda de San José.
3. Jerónimo Gracián.
4. Cf. Ltr. 137.5.
5. Andrés de los Santos.
6. The relatives were probably Jerónima de la Madre de Dios (Sotomayor), Inés de San Eliseo, and María de San Pablo (Morales). The three made their professions in the years 1578 and 1579.
7. A contractor from Medina del Campo, a friend and benefactor of Teresa's.

8. Juana de la Cruz (Gómez), still a novice.
9. Mariana de los Santos (actually Vanegas, not Anegas).
10. A good friend of Teresa's, a dealer in livestock who was short of money at the time.
11. This refers to the complicated matter of the dowry for his daughter, Bernarda de San José.
12. Blanca de Jesús María.
13. Her brother Lorenzo and his daughter Teresa.

149. To Padre Jerónimo Gracián, Seville

Toledo, November 1576

Surrounded by so many enemies and spies, Gracián was a victim of calumnies. Teresa warns him about his pastoral intervention in the delicate case of a woman of bad repute.

1. In a way, even though it deeply grieved me, it caused me profound devotion to observe, on the other hand, the tact you are using amid so many calumnies. I tell you, *padre*, God loves you very much and you are doing well in your imitation of him. Rejoice since he is giving you what you ask of him, which are trials, for which he will repay you because he is just. May he be blessed forever.

2. In what regards that girl or woman, I am convinced that it is due not so much to melancholy as to the devil. He is the one putting the woman up to those lies. He is trying to see if he can fool you in some way, now that he has fooled her. So you must proceed with great discretion in this matter and by no means go to her house. May what happened to Santa Marina (I believe it was) not happen to you, for they claimed a child was hers, and she suffered much.[1] Now is not the time for you to be suffering in a matter like this. In my poor opinion you should set this matter aside, for there are others who might win over this soul, and there are many others toward whom you can be helpful.

3. Remember, *padre*, that if she didn't give you that letter under the seal of confession or in confession, it is a matter for the Inquisition, and the devil has a thousand snares. I have learned that someone else died in the Inquisition prison for the same reason. Truly I don't believe she gave the letter to the devil—for he wouldn't have returned it so quickly—or all that she says. But I believe she must be lying in some way—God forgive me—and enjoys seeing you. Perhaps I am calumniating her, but I would like to see you far away from where she is so that you can more easily protect yourself.

4. How malicious I am! But everything is necessary in this life. Don't try to straighten out a matter that's been going on for four months. Be careful, it's very dangerous. Let them fend for themselves. If there is anything to accuse her of in this regard (I mean outside of confession), be careful, because I fear there will be more publicity and they will blame you afterward, saying that you knew about it and were silent. But I'm aware that my saying this is foolish because you already know it....

1. An allusion to the legend of Santa Marina who lived a solitary life disguised as a monk. When accused of being the father of a child, she bore the calumny in silence. Only after her death was the truth discovered.

150. To Padre Jerónimo Gracián

Toledo, 19 November 1576

Teresa complains of Padre Juan de Jesus' method of making visitations of the friars and nuns. She is interested in the possibility of a foundation for her nuns in Granada, and feels misunderstood by Padre Olea.

1. Jesus be with your paternity. Now see the tiresome decrees made by Padre Juan de Jesús.[1] It seems to me he is just repeating what's in your constitutions. I don't know for what

purpose. This is what my nuns fear, that some burdensome prelates will come along and crush them. Laying on heavy burdens accomplishes nothing. It's strange how visitators think they haven't made a visitation unless they have set down some decrees. If the friars were not to have recreation on the days in which communion is received, then those who say Mass daily would never have recreation. And if priests don't observe such a rule, why should the other poor friars have to?[2]

2. He writes me that since he had never visited that house,[3] all these things were necessary, and that must be so. In some matters he must have had to intervene. Still, I felt worn out just from reading the decrees. What would happen if I were obliged to observe them? Believe me, our rule doesn't bear up under rigorous people, for it is rigorous enough.

3. Salazar[4] is going to Granada, something the archbishop arranged, who is a great friend of his. He has a great desire that a house of our nuns be founded there,[5] and this would not displease me. Even if I didn't go, it could be done. But first I would want the foundation to be acceptable to Cyril,[6] for I don't know if visitators can give permission for the foundation of houses of nuns as they can for friars. If only the Franciscans don't get there ahead of us as they did in Burgos.

4. You ought to know that Santelmo[7] is badly annoyed with me on account of the nun who has now left, but in conscience I couldn't have done otherwise, nor could you have done anything. Everything possible was done in this matter, and when there is question of pleasing God, the world can crumble. I have no regrets, nor should you. We'll never gain anything good from going against the will of our Good. I assure you that even if she had been my Paul's[8] sister—which would be the highest recommendation—I could not have done any more. He just refused to listen to reason. He is annoyed with me because I believe my nuns speak the truth. He thinks the prioress is partial and that his candidate was falsely accused about every-

thing. He has arranged for her to enter a monastery in Talavera with others from Madrid, and so he sent for her.

5. God deliver us from having a need for creatures. And may it please him to help us see clearly without any other need than for him. San Telmo says that I have done this because I don't need him now, and that he has been told I am a crafty one. Notice that I needed him most when we were considering sending his candidate away, and how truly misunderstood I was. May it please the Lord that I understand how to do his will always. Amen

Today is 19 November.

Your unworthy servant and subject,

Teresa of Jesus

---

1. Juan de Jesús Roca had been appointed in the chapter of Almodóvar the promoter of observance and has informed Teresa of his visitations.
2. Her objection covers two points: the suppression of recreation on days in which communion is received, and the making of laws only for non-priests.
3. Probably either Altomira or La Roda, houses for the friars, which were not yet visited by Gracián.
4. The Jesuit Gaspar de Salazar, a friend of Teresa's and of the Archbishop of Granada, Juan Méndez de Salvatierra.
5. A foundation for discalced Carmelite nuns was made in Granada in 1581 by St. John of the Cross and Anne of Jesus.
6. A code name for Gracián.
7. A code name for the Jesuit Francisco Olea.
8. Gracián.

151. To Madre María de San José, Seville

Toledo, 19 November 1576

(Autograph: DCN, Valladolid)

In a humorous vein Teresa notices that María de San José affects ignorance in writing to her, and erudition in writing to

Mariano. She responds to many matters and comments on others that cross her mind, showing special concern for the welfare of Gracián.

For Madre María de San José, prioress in Seville.

1. Jesus. May the Holy Spirit be with you, my daughter. I received your letter written on 3 November. I tell you that your letters never tire me but give me rest from other tiring things. I was amused that you spelled out the date. Please God you didn't do so to avoid humbling yourself by putting it down in numbers.[1]

2. Before I forget, the letter to Padre Mariano is very good, if it were not for that Latin.[2] God deliver all my daughters from presuming to be Latinists. May you never try doing so again or permit other nuns to try. I desire much more that you dare to appear simple, which is very characteristic of saints, rather than so eloquent. This is what you get for sending me your letters open. But now since you have gone to confession to our *padre*, you will be more mortified. Tell him that I almost made a general confession the other day to the one I mentioned, and I didn't experience a twentieth of the sorrow I experienced when I had to confess to him. See what an ugly temptation this is![3]

3. Pray for my present confessor[4] who has been a great consolation to me, for it is no small matter for me to be satisfied in this regard. Oh, how well you acted in not calling on the confessor who tormented me so much down there! I wasn't happy in that place with anything. If our *padre* was a source of happiness, you well know how many anxieties went along with it. And the happiness that you could have given me, if you had so wished, because I find your company delightful, you refused to offer. I am glad that you now understand my affection. As for the other one from Caravaca,[5] may God forgive her, she is sorry now also. Such is the power that truth has.

4. Today she sent me a habit made of coarse wool and it's the most suited to our purposes that I've worn—very light. I was deeply grateful to her, for my other one was too worn out to protect me from the cold. And they themselves made the material for the undertunics, although here there is no mention at all of undertunics during the whole summer, and they do much fasting. Now I am beginning to be a nun. Pray that this will last.

5. I sent word to my brother that you have the money. He'll send the muleteer from Avila to get it. You do well not to send it without a letter from him. Take care to remind our *padre* to take up the matter with the duke[6] that he mentioned to me. With his having so much business to attend to and being so alone, I don't know where he finds the energy, if not—through a miracle—from God. I don't think it even entered my mind to say that he not eat there at the monastery, for I see that the need is great. I only say that outside meal times he not go there often, lest this be noticed and he be prevented from ever going there. Rather you are doing me a great favor by the diligence you use to provide for his comfort. I will never be able to repay you. Tell this to the sisters, for also my Gabriela[7] was happy to tell me about this in her letter. Give my regards to her and to all the sisters and all my friends. Give my special greetings to Padre Antonio de Jesús.[8] We are praying that he will benefit from the treatment he is undergoing. I have been sorry for him and so has the prioress.[9] Also give my regards to Fray Gregorio and Fray Bartolomé.[10]

6. The prioress of Malagón[11] is even worse than she usually is. Yet I am somewhat consoled, for I'm told that the source of the pain is not in the lungs and that she does not have tuberculosis. And Ana de la Madre de Dios,[12] the nun who is here, says that she was in that same condition and that she got well. God can do it. I don't know what to say about all the trials that God has given them there. Besides the illnesses they are destitute; they have neither wheat nor money but a world of debts. Please

God the 400 ducats that Salamanca owes them, and were reserved for this house— for I already spoke to our *padre* about it—will be enough to take care of the situation. I have already sent a part of the amount. Their expenses have been high and of many kinds. For this reason I would not want the prioresses of houses having an income[13] to be very prodigal, nor any of the others either, for they will end up by losing everything.

7. The whole burden lies on poor Beatriz,[14] the only one who is well. And she has been entrusted by the prioress with charge of the house. For want of good men, as they say....[15] I am very happy that you are not in want of them there. Don't be foolish in not noting the cost of postage and everything else I tell you to note. You would be losing so much, and it's foolishness. I am sorry that his companion is Fray Andrés,[16] for I don't believe he knows how to keep quiet, and I'm even more sorry that he eats at El Carmen.[17] For love of God tell him to be careful, and he would be tempting God to go elsewhere than Los Remedios on leaving there. May God watch over you and all the nuns and make you saints, for I have many more letters to write.

Today is 19 November

Yours,

Teresa of Jesus

8. Turn over. I have already mentioned that I received the letters among which were those from the Indies and Avila. I would like to know who gave them to you, so as to respond, and when the armada is leaving.

9. I am delighted that you bear poverty so well and that God so provides for your needs. May he be blessed forever. You did very well to give the tunics to our *padre*, for I have no need of them. What we all need most is that you not allow him to eat with those people, and that he be on his guard, for God is doing us such a favor by giving him health in the midst of so many trials. With regard to using linen and wool mixed together, I

would prefer that you wear linen when necessary. Otherwise you would be opening the door to never observing the constitutions well. The material you would end up with would be almost as hot, and you would be observing neither one rule nor the other, and the custom will have begun.

10. I am troubled by what you say about how the rule stating that stockings be made of coarse cloth or rough tow is not observed. Tell our *padre* some time that where the rule speaks of stockings no indication should be given about the material other than that it be poor, and let me know what he says; or better, that nothing be said at all about the material, but that it simply mention stockings. And don't forget. Get him to delay his visitation of the province as much as you can, until it is seen where some things will end up. Have you noticed how charming his letter to Teresita is?[18] There is no end to the talk about her and her virtue. Julián[19] speaks wonders of her, which is no small matter. Read the letter that Isabel[20] wrote to his paternity.

---

1. María de San José knew how to write Arabic numerals but is not doing so, perhaps out of false humility.
2. María de San José sent her letter to Ambrosio Mariano de San Benito without sealing it so that Teresa could read it.
3. Teresa continues to speak in jest. When she was in Seville, Gracián ordered her to make a general confession which proved to be a burdensome mortification for her. On the other hand, María de San José had done the same without any difficulty.
4. The canon Alonso Velázquez.
5. The prioress of Caravaca, Ana de San Alberto, who had previously gone with Teresa for the foundation in Beas and Seville. As with María de San José, she began to appreciate Teresa's affection only after their separation.
6. Probably, the Duke of Alba, Fernando Alvarez de Toledo.
7. Leonor de San Gabriel, the community nurse.
8. Antonio de Jesús (Heredia) was the prior of Los Remedios, the monastery of the discalced Carmelite friars in Seville
9. The prioress of Toledo, Ana de los Angeles.
10. Gregorio Nacianceno and Bartolomé de Jesús.

11. Brianda de San José.
12. Ana de la Madre de Dios with whom Teresa became acquainted in the house of Luisa de la Cerda in Toledo; she was widowed at the age of 21.
13. Monasteries that were endowed and thus had to live on a fixed income.
14. Beatriz de Jesús (Cepeda y Ocampo) was appointed vicaress of Malagón by Madre Brianda.
15. The Spanish proverb is "For want of good men, my husband is mayor."
16. Fray Andrés de los Santos was a lay brother whom Padre Gracián invested with the habit at Los Remedios and was now appointed to accompany him on his travels. Teresa's worries about Gracián's meals were well founded. Gracián wrote in *Peregrinación de Anastasio, dialogo 1*, of his fears about the food he was given and of how he took care to eat only boiled eggs served in their shells lest he be poisoned.
17. El Carmen was the monastery for the Carmelite friars of the observance in Seville, and Los Remedios for the discalced Carmelite friars in Seville.
18. Evidently a letter from Gracián to Teresita, Teresa's niece postulant in Avila, was unsealed and read by both María de San José and Teresa.
19. Julián de Avila, the chaplain of the discalced nuns in Avila.
20. Little Isabel Dantisco, eight years old, was residing in the Carmel of Toledo at Teresa's side. She wrote the letter mentioned.

152. To Madre María de San José, Seville

Toledo, 26 November 1576

(Autograph: DCN, Valladolid)

Teresa responds and comments on matters in the letters she has so far received: the two discalced nuns going to Peterna to reform a community there; the troubles with Garciálvarez; the aspirants to the monastery in Seville; the rumors of her being sent to the Americas. She desires more detailed information about Gracián.

1. Jesus be with you, my daughter. On the feast of the Presentation of Our Lady[1] two letters of yours were delivered to me along with those from our *padre*.[2] Never fail to tell me something just because you think his paternity is telling me about it, for in fact he doesn't, and I am surprised that he writes to me at all with everything else he has to do. The letters you sent by way of Madrid, which contain the memorandum or note that tells about the commotion that has taken place, have not arrived. I don't think any of my letters were lost except the first packet where I told you about my Isabelita[3] having received the habit and the happy moments I spent with her mother.[4] Since there was also a letter there from the prioress[5] and the sisters that presented some questions to our *padre*, and he has not answered, I think they were lost. Let me know through the next mail carrier. I mentioned that when I laughingly asked Isabelita if she were married, she answered very seriously that she was. I asked her with whom, and she answered at once, "with our Lord Jesus Christ."

2. I became very envious of those who went to Paterna,[6] and it wasn't because they went with our *padre*. When I saw that their going there meant suffering, I forgot about the rest. Please God it will be a beginning for how he may use us. There are so few[7] down there that I don't think they will suffer much, except from hunger, for I am told they don't have enough food to eat. May God be with them, for we have urgently begged him about this up here. Send them this letter through a very reliable messenger, and send me any of theirs you have so that I may see how things are going. Always write and encourage and counsel them. It's a harsh trial to be so alone. In no way do I think they should sing anything until their number increases,[8] for this would bring discredit on all. I am delighted

that Garciálvarez's aspirants[9] have good voices. You ought to accept them with whatever they bring because you are few in number.

3. I am astounded by the absurdity of allowing the confessor to bring along with him any other confessor he wants.[10] What a nice custom that would become! Since I have not seen the note from our *padre*, I cannot say anything. I had thought of writing to Garciálvarez to ask him that when he needs counsel he should not go to spiritual masters but search out some truly learned men, for these latter have rescued me from many troubles. I am not surprised about the sufferings of which you speak, for I have suffered much because they told me the devil was behind my experiences. So that you may see what I write to him,[11] I will send the letter unsealed and you can send it to the prior of Las Cuevas.[12] If you can speak to Acosta,[13] I think that will be better. Read that letter and send it to him.

4. It would be no small blessing if the rector[14] there would agree to take you under his care, and so he would be a great help in many matters. But the fathers of the Society want to be obeyed, and so you have to do so. Even though sometimes what they say may not be to our liking, it's worth putting up with for the sake of the importance of having them with us. Think up questions to ask them, for they like to answer questions. And they are right in wanting to do well whatever they undertake. And they do so whenever they undertake a charge like this. In that chaos,[15] this is something that takes on great importance, for when our *padre* leaves, you will be very much alone.

5. It never crossed my mind to want you to accept Nicolao's aspirant[16] for any other reason than that I think you have a great need of money. If the 1,000 ducats from the relatives of Garciálvarez were in currency, it would be all right. It is good that they have to wait, although you shouldn't fail to accept them for reasons of money, in my opinion.

6. I was amused by the motive for which they are sending me to the Indies.[17] May God pardon them. The best thing they can do is say so many things all at once that no one will believe them. I have already written you not to send the money to my brother[18] until he writes to you. Try to get our *padre* to do what Acosta tells him with respect to the one who will be appointed the next rector of the Society, which will be soon. I entreated Salazar[19]—for he was here and is going to Granada and says he may possibly go to Seville—to speak to the provincial[20] down there. If he should come, be very gracious to him and speak to him about whatever you might wish. You can do so for he is a real gentleman.

7. The prioress of Malagón[21] is better, glory to God, and I am much more confident about her health, for a doctor has told me that if the lesion is not in the lungs she will live. May God provide since he sees our need. Don't fail to pray for this. Recommend me to the prayers of all the nuns, and remain with the Lord, for I have many letters to write. On another day I will write the prior of Las Cuevas, for I am delighted about the improvement in his health. May God preserve him for us; and may he preserve you, too, my daughter, for you never tell me that you are well.[22] That worries me. Give Delgado[23] and all the others my best.

Today is 26 November.

Your servant,

Teresa of Jesus

8. Always let me know how Padre Fray Antonio is. Regards to him, to Fray Gregorio and Fray Bartolomé.[24] I give much praise to our Lord upon seeing what our *padre* is doing. May God be pleased to give him health. I hope in God that my daughters will fulfill their duties well.

---

1. 21 November 1576
2. Jerónimo Gracián.

3. Gracián's sister Isabel Dantisco, 8 years old at the time.
4. Juana Dantisco.
5. Ana de los Angeles, prioress in Toledo.
6. A place near Seville where there was a monastery of Carmelite nuns of the observance. The two nuns who were sent as reformers were Isabel de San Francisco as prioress and Isabel de San Jerónimo.
7. There was a small number of nuns in Paterna. In the visitation made ten years before, there were twelve nuns. The mission of the discalced nuns there proved unsuccessful.
8. She is referring to the choral chant that the discalced nuns would have to introduce or seek to improve.
9. Garciálvarez was confessor to the nuns in Seville and sponsoring these aspirants.
10. This has to do with the commotion she referred to in no. 1. Garciálvarez began to interfere in the life of the community and oppose the prioress, María de San José. He would bring other priests with him to help him with his work as confessor. Through an intervention by the Dominican Pedro Fernández and Nicolás Doria, still a diocesan priest, it was recommended that he be dismissed. His dismissal led to further problems down the line.
11. Gracián and Teresa, at this point, wanted to appoint four or five confessors for each monastery with whom the nuns could consult, and they did not want the prioress to allow others to be called in.
12. The Carthusian Hernando de Pantoja.
13. Diego de Acosta, a Jesuit in Seville.
14. The rector of the Jesuits in Seville, Francisco Arias.
15. Seville was by the standards of the time a large bustling metropolis.
16. Nicolás Doria had recommended an aspirant to the discalced Carmelite nuns.
17. The rumor had spread in Seville that the superiors of the order were going to send Teresa to the Americas.
18. The money the Seville community owed her brother Lorenzo.
19. Gaspar de Salazar, a Jesuit and old friend of Teresa's.
20. The provincial of the Jesuits in Andalusia at the time was Pedro Bernal.
21. Brianda de San José.
22. She is alluding to María de San José's reticence about her health.
23. Inés Delgado.

24. The three were discalced Carmelites living at Los Remdios in Seville: Antonio de Jesús (Heredia), Gregorio Nacianceno, and Bartolomé de Jesús.

153. To Don Luis de Cepeda, Torrijos

Toledo, 26 November 1576

(Autograph: Madres Comendadoras de Santiago, Toledo)

Luis de Cepeda is Teresa's second cousin. He was a spiritual man, generous in helping out financially his sister at the Incarnation and also Teresa herself. Three of his sisters were Carmelites and one brother was a member of St. Peter of Alcántara's reformed Franciscans.

To the very magnificent Señor Luis de Cepeda, my lord, in Torrijos.

1. Jesus. The grace of the Holy Spirit be always with your honor, amen. I received your letters and the four ducats. They will be delivered this week. May the Lord reward you for the care you take of our sister at the Incarnation, who is the one most in need.[1] Because of the prioress's illness, Sister Beatriz de Jesús is now in charge of governing the house in Malagón, and she is very busy. She is doing extremely well, glory to God, for I didn't think she was capable of so much.

2. You shouldn't be surprised that you are not able to be very recollected in the midst of so many difficulties. That would be impossible. If you return to your good rule of life when they pass, I will be content. Please God that all goes very well with you, but do not be concerned about having more or having less, for even if a great deal is left for you, everything will soon come to an end. Ask the ladies there to remember me in their prayers; the prioress[2] asks for yours.

Today is 25 November.

Your honor's unworthy servant,

Teresa of Jesus

1. Luis de Cepeda had a sister, María de Cepeda, at the Incarnation in Avila. Beatriz de Jesús in Malagón was also his sister. The prioress in Malagón, Brianda de San José, was chronically ill.
2. The prioress in Toledo, Ana de los Angeles.

154. To Jerónimo Gracián, Seville

Toledo, End of November 1576

(Autograph: Sacristía Santísimo Cristo de San Ginés, Madrid)

A number of letters from Gracián have arrived, and Teresa comments on several items, marveling at all he is doing. She finds it hard to accept Gracián's decision to beg for his food while on his travels. The nuncio's health has improved, but either way Teresa feels calm and a deep inner certitude about a successful outcome for her new Carmels.

1 Jesús. The grace of the Holy Spirit be always with your paternity, and may he keep you, *mi padre*, for many years, amen. I tell you that if God hadn't given me understanding that all the good we do comes from his hand and how little we ourselves can do, it wouldn't be unusual for me to experience a bit of vainglory over all that you are doing. May God's name be ever blessed and praised forever, amen. The things that are happening are stupefying enough, but that you proceed with so much peace is what makes me marvel, and that you turn enemies into friends and make them the authors or, to put it better, the executors of your plans.

2. The choice of Padre Evangelista[1] pleased me. For goodness' sake give him my regards and thank Paul[2] for the recreation he afforded us with his poems and the letter for Teresa.[3]

I rejoiced that the matter concerning the cicadas[4] was not true and that the butterflies[5] went there. I hope in God that this will prove to have been very beneficial and I believe the number is sufficient for that place. They are the objects of much envy, for when it comes to suffering we all have great desires; may God help us to put our desires into practice.

3. It would have been a real trial had the spirit of that house been a bad one. Now you can see how much the spiritual people in that region are to be pitied. May God be blessed that you were there during the uproar. What would the poor things have done! Nonetheless, they are fortunate since they are already benefiting from something, and what you write about the archbishop's visitator[6] I consider very important. This house will do nothing but great good, for it has cost us dearly. I don't think Paul[7] is suffering anything in comparison with the fear he suffered on account of the angels.[8]

4. I was very much amused to learn about your begging, but you haven't ever told me who your companion[9] is. You say you were sending the letter to Peralta[10] in the packets, but it didn't come. They did not give me the one that you addressed to Padre Mariano,[11] nor has he written a word to me. It's been a long time since he has written me. He sent me a letter from you today without writing. Perhaps he has kept the one I'm speaking of and Garciálvarez's document.[12] He also sent me one or two letters by way of Segovia. I thought they were from you, although the addresses were not in your handwriting. Afterward I saw that they were not from you. The news around here is that Methuselah[13] has much improved, glory to God, and no longer has a fever. It's strange the way I feel, for nothing that happens can trouble me, so deeply rooted is the feeling of certitude about a successful outcome.[14]

5. On the feast of the Presentation,[15] I received two letters from you; afterward a very brief one that came with another for Doña Luisa de la Cerda, who is more than just a little happy

over it! In one of these packets the permission for Casilda[16] came. I've already sent it on.

6. Oh, how eagerly, according to what I'm told, would Angela[17] have prepared food for Paul[18] when he experienced that hunger of which he speaks! I don't know why he looks for more trials than God gives him by going about begging.[19] It seems he has seven souls so that when one life comes to an end, there will be another. Scold him, for goodness' sake, and thank him on my behalf for the favor he shows me in taking so much care to write to me. May it be for the love of God.

Teresa of Jesus

What is happening now, although I believe Esperanza[20] will have mentioned it....

---

1. Juan Evangelista, a Carmelite friar appointed by Gracián as prior of El Carmen in Seville and vicar provincial of Andalusia.
2. Gracián.
3. Teresa (Teresita) de Cepeda.
4. The Carmelite nuns of the observance in Paterna who had been calumniated.
5. The two discalced Carmelite nuns who had been sent from Seville to Paterna.
6. The archbishop, Cristóbal de Rojas had appointed a visitator for the monasteries of nuns in Seville.
7. Gracián.
8. The inquisitors. She is alluding to the anxieties Gracián suffered when the Inquisition investigated Teresa and the other discalced nuns in Seville.
9. Gracián, as was the rule, had to have a friar companion with him on his journeys.
10. Code name for Jerónimo Tostado.
11. Ambrosio Mariano de San Benito who was residing in Madrid.
12. The chaplain of the discalced Carmelite nuns in Seville. The document contained a statement by Garciálvarez about outside confessors.
13. The nuncio, Nicolás Ormaneto.

14. She is referring to the survival of the discalced Carmelite way of life.
15. 21 November.
16. The permission for the profession of Casilda de Padilla in Valladolid.
17. Teresa herself.
18. Gracián.
19. Gracián had decided to beg for his meals while on his journeys.
20. Perhaps a code name for the Jesuit Gaspar de Salazar. The rest of the postscript is missing.

155. To Padre Jerónimo Gracián, Seville

Toledo, End of November(?) 1576

1. I sent a letter last week through the mail carrier from here in which I answered Paul concerning the scapular of the tongues.[1] In speaking about it to Joseph, I was told to inform him that he has many enemies visible and invisible, that he should be careful. For this reason, I would not want him to trust so much in the Egyptians—you tell him that—or in the night owls.

1. Gracián has himself explained the meaning of this fragment. When making a visitation of the Carmelite nuns in Paterna, he discovered that a friar had calumniated three of them. As a punishment the friar had to wear a scapular with colored tongues sewn to it as prescribed for faults of this kind in the constitutions of Vienna 1499. These same three nuns were later instigated to bear false witness against Gracián to the nuncio Sega (cf. *Peregrinación de Anastasio*, MHCT 19:310–332). The code names are as follows: Paul (Gracián), Joseph (our Lord), the Egyptians (the Carmelites of the observance in Andalusia), the night owls (the Carmelite nuns of the observance in Paterna).

156. To Don Diego de Guzmán y Cepeda, Avila

Toledo, End of November 1576

(Autograph: DCN, St. Joseph's, Avila)

In this letter of sympathy Teresa seeks to console her nephew, Diego de Guzmán, the son of her older sister, whose wife has died. He had been married since 1564. At various times Teresa had turned to him for his services and help.

1. The grace of the Holy Spirit be with your honor and give you the comfort that is necessary for what seems to us at this moment in time to be so great a loss. But the Lord who has willed this and loves us more than we do ourselves will make us understand in due time that he has brought about the greatest good possible for my cousin[1] and for all of us who wish her well, for he always calls souls to himself when they are in the best condition to respond.

2. You ought not think of having a long life, for everything that finishes so quickly is short. But consider that your loneliness may not last long and entrust yourself completely into God's hands, for His Majesty will do what is most fitting. It is a great consolation to see a death that allows us to have such assurance that she will live forever. And have the belief that if the Lord now takes her to himself, it is so that you and your daughters[2] will have more help since she is in the presence of God.

3. May His Majesty hear us, for we have prayed much for her, and enable you to be resigned to whatever he does and give you the light to understand how short-lived the enjoyments and troubles of this life are.

4. I'm sending two melons that I've found, but they're not as good as I would like them to be.

Your honor's unworthy servant,

Teresa of Jesus

---

1. Doña Jerónima Tapia, Diego's wife, was Teresa's cousin.
2. Doña Catalina de Guzmán and another daughter who died shortly after her mother did.

157. To Padre Jerónimo Gracián, Seville

Toledo, Beginning of December 1576

Though only a child of eight years, Isabel was given the Carmelite habit in mid-November and considered herself a cloistered nun. She made her profession at age 16, taking the name Isabel de Jesús.

1. ...Our Isabel is like an angel. The disposition and happiness of this creature are something to praise God for. Today the doctor happened to pass by a room where she was, for he usually doesn't go that way. Since she saw that he had seen her, even though she tried hard to take flight, she began to cry thinking she was excommunicated and that she deserved to be expelled from the house. We all had a good laugh about this and love her dearly, and with reason....

158. To Madre María de San José, Seville

Toledo, 3 December 1576

(Autograph: DCN, Calahorra [Logroño])

Teresa was receiving fewer letters from Madre María than she was sending her, and there were many things she was eager to know about: Gracián's activities, the nuns in Paterna, the Jesuits in Seville, and so on. Teresa continues, nonetheless, to send news from Castile.

1. Jesus. The grace of the Holy Spirit be with your reverence, my daughter. Not long ago I answered your letters, which are not as many as mine to you. You have never written about the procedure our *padre*[1] follows in making a visitation. Would you be kind enough to do this for me. Please God it is being carried out according to the plan that our *padre* says is used by the archbishop's visitator and by himself for his nuns;[2] this

would be most beneficial. Considering his earnest zeal, it would be impossible for His Majesty not to help him.

2. I greatly desire to know how my nuns in Paterna[3] are doing. I believe they must be doing very well, and considering the news our *padre* will give you that Tostado[4] is not going to be allowed to proceed, the reform promoted by the discalced nuns will not stop with this monastery alone. May God watch over our *padre*, for it seems miraculous the way things are going.

3. I was very pleased with the statement[5] written by our *padre* concerning Garciálvarez, for there is nothing else that would have to be added to it. I haven't heard who was appointed rector.[6] Please God he will be of the same mind as Padre Acosta.[7] Since I wrote to you about this previously, I will not speak of it now or add anything, nor would I know what to say.

4. I didn't hear anything more about the prioress of Malagón[8] since I last wrote, for they told me then that she had improved. Nor have I heard anything about Antonio Ruiz[9] who had another relapse, but I believe that had he died I would have heard by now.

5. My best regards to all those daughters of mine, and remain with God, for I have nothing more to say. I'm enclosing this letter that you may have news about your Teresa[10] and pray for her. May His Majesty watch over you.

6. Alberta[11] has written to Doña Luisa and sent her a cross. I haven't written to her yet—it's amazing how she delights in any little attention from her nuns—nor to Doña Guiomar[12] who is now married. Don't be a thankless one, and remain with God.

Today is 3 December 1576

Your servant,

Teresa of Jesus

1. Jerónimo Gracián.
2. The Archbishop of Seville, Don Cristóbal de Rojas, appointed a visitator for the nuns of his diocese requiring that he follow the plan employed by Gracián.
3. The two discalced nuns who went as reformers to the monastery of the Carmelite nuns of the observance in Paterna.
4. Jerónimo Tostado was appointed visitator for the Carmelite order in Spain, but the king did not approve of this appointment.
5. This was a document in which Gracián put restrictions on Garciálvarez for stepping outside his authority in dealing with the discalced Carmelite nuns in Seville.
6. Rector of the Jesuits in Seville.
7. Diego de Acosta, a Jesuit living in Seville.
8. Brianda de San José.
9. Antonio Ruiz, Teresa's good friend in Malagón.
10. Teresa's niece in the Carmel in Avila.
11. Ana de San Alberto, who was the prioress in Caravaca. She had sent a cross to Luisa de la Cerda, founding benefactress of Malagón, from Caravaca.
12. Doña Guiomar Pardo de Tavera, the daughter of Doña Luisa, was known by María de San José because the latter had served in the household of Doña Luisa in Toledo.

159. To Padre Jerónimo Gracián, Seville

Toledo, 7 December 1576

(Autograph fragment: DCN, Parma [Italy])

Teresa is happy to be receiving frequent letters from Gracián, and from others giving her news about him. She urges him to pay a visit to the inquisitor and sends news about Tostado and about a possible foundation near Burgos. Lamenting the calumnies against both Gracián and the nuns in

Paterna, she also warns him to watch what he eats in the monasteries of the observance.

1. Jesus be with you, *mi padre*. Each time I see letters arriving from your paternity, and how frequently they are coming, I would like to kiss your hands to thank you for having permitted me to remain in this place, for I don't know what I would have done without the relief of living here. May God be blessed for everything. Last Friday I answered some letters from you. Now I've received some more, the ones you wrote from Paterna and Trigueros. The later one was full of worries, and with every reason.

2. Despite all your motives for remaining there, I wish that after you have visited those marquises you would go to see the "angel,"[1] since the letter from him is so insistent, even though it would mean a hardship for you. For even if he is mistaken, these matters are difficult to deal with by letter, and we owe him so much. It seems that God has placed him there for our help, for error itself will turn to our benefit if we follow his opinion. Be careful, *mi padre*, for the love of God, not to displease him, for down there you are deprived of good counsel, and you would cause me much disturbance.

3. I am disturbed also to learn from the prioress how that "saint" is not carrying out the duties of his office[2] well, and even more disturbed by his lack of courage. For love of God, tell him in a way that he will understand that justice will be rendered to him as well as to others.

4. I'm writing this in such a hurry that I am not going to be able to say all that I would like. I was forced to receive a visitor just when I was about to begin this letter, and now it is late at night, and the muleteer is going to deliver it. Since he is so reliable I don't want to miss telling you again what I've already written to you—that is, that the Royal Council has stipulated that Tostado[3] is not to make a visitation of the four provinces.

The one who wrote us about this has seen this ordinance, and his letter was read to me. However, I don't consider the one who read it to be very trustworthy. But I think he was in this case, and I don't think he had any reason for lying. Whatever the case, I hope in God that everything will go well, for the Lord is turning Paul into an enchanter.

5. If I had no other reason to serve the Lord than this, I would consider it a sufficient one. Certainly the way things are unfolding is admirable. You ought to know that for some time Esperanza[4] has not been praising Paul to me, and now he wrote to speak wonders about him and wants me to give him my blessing. What will he do when he learns about how things have been dealt with at Paterna?[5] Indeed, I marvel to see how the Lord is intermingling sorrows with joys, for this is the strait path along which his plans are brought about.

Teresa of Jesus

6. You should know, *padre*, that in a certain manner it is a delight for me when you tell me about your trials, although the matter of the calumny[6] offended me deeply, not on account of what regarded you but on account of the nuns. Since the perpetrators are not finding anyone to be a witness, they are looking for someone who they think will not talk, but she will know how to defend herself, as well as her son Eliseo,[7] better than anyone else in the world.

7. Yesterday a father from the Society wrote me, as well as did a lady from Aguilar del Campo, a nice town thirteen leagues from Burgos. She is a sixty-year-old widow with no children. She has had a serious illness and, desiring to do a good work with her estate (which amounts to 600 ducats in income and a good house and garden), she was told about these monasteries. This appealed to her so much that in her will she left everything for this purpose. Well, she continued to live, but still has a great desire to found a monastery, and so she wrote to me asking that I give a reply. It seems to me to be far away, although perhaps God desires that this be done.[8]

8. Also, in Burgos there are so many women who desire to enter that it is a pity there is no place for them to do so. Well, I will not discourage her but simply reply that I will seek more information about the locality and everything else until I see what you will ordain and if with your brief[9] you can accept monasteries of nuns. For although I cannot go, you could send others. Don't forget to tell me what you decide to have me do in this regard.

9. I have someone in Burgos who can provide me with information. If she gives everything (which she will), it will easily amount to 9,000 ducats, and more with the houses added in, and the distance from Valladolid is not too great. It must be very cold there, but this lady says they have good hedges to protect themselves from it.

10. Oh, *mi padre*, how I would like to share with you those worries, and how well you do to complain to the one who becomes so afflicted over your sufferings. And how it pleases me to see you so close to the cicadas.[10] The result there should be most fruitful. I hope in God that he will provide for them in their poverty. I want to tell you that San Francisco[11] wrote me a letter that made a great deal of sense. May God be with them. Their affection for Paul[12] pleased me very much, and I rejoice—although not as much—that he loves them. I already love the nuns in Seville and I love them more each day for the care they take of the one whom I myself would like to be taking care of and serving. May God be praised that he gives you such good health. Be on guard, for love of God, about what you eat in those monasteries. I am well and happy to have such frequent news of you. May His Majesty watch over you and make you as holy as I beg him to, amen.

Today is the eve of our Lady's Conception.

Your paternity's unworthy daughter,

Teresa of Jesus

1. The inquisitor, probably Gaspar de Quiroga. She very much wanted Gracián to visit him.
2. Antonio de Jesús (Heredia), the prior of the discalced friars of Los Remedios in Seville. The prioress of the discalced nuns in Seville was María de San José.
3. The visitator, Jerónimo Tostado, appointed by the Carmelite order.
4. Probably the Jesuit Gaspar de Salazar.
5. An allusion to the satisfactory solution to the initial difficulties in the reform of the Carmelite nuns of Paterna.
6. In his visitation Gracián discovered that a friar had given false testimony against three of the nuns, which was repeated all over Seville.
7. Gracián.
8. Actually, this foundation never came about.
9. A brief (3 August 1575) from the nuncio Ormaneto authorizing him to be visitator to the Carmelites.
10. The Carmelite nuns in Paterna.
11. Isabel de San Francisco, one of the discalced Carmelite nuns in Seville charged with the reform of the Carmelite nuns in Paterna.
12. Gracián.

160. To Madre María de San José, Seville

Toledo, 7 December 1576

(Autograph: DCN, Valladolid)

Teresa has received a number of letters on which she comments. There are allusions to the calumnies being spread against Gracián and the discalced nuns who were in Paterna. She has acquired statues of our Lady and St. Joseph for the nuns in Caravaca.

For Madre María de San José, prioress of Seville.

1. Jesus be with your reverence. Today, the vigil of the Immaculate Conception, the muleteer sent me your letters and is in a hurry for the reply. So, you will have to forgive me, daughter, if this is so short, for I wouldn't in any way want to be short

with you, for whom my affection is great—I certainly love you much. And now I am so obliged because of the care you take to provide our *padre*[1] with every comfort, as he tells me; thus my love for you has even grown greater. And I am happy that you are doing this with such prudence, for I believe that neither now nor ever will there be another with whom we can deal in this way. Since the Lord chose him for these beginning stages, which are exceptional, I don't think there will be another like him. All that which serves to open doors will end up in something worse than can be imagined when superiors are not like him. But neither will there be so much need for caution, because now, as in a time of war, we need to proceed with more care. May God reward you, my daughter, for the care you take with your letters, which are a source of life for me.

2. This week I received all three that you said you had written. And even though they came all together, they are more than welcome. I was much moved by the letter from San Francisco,[2] which is good enough to be published. What our *padre* is doing seems unbelievable. Blessed be God who gave him so much talent. I would like to have great talent so as to be able to give the Lord due thanks for the favors he grants us and for what he has done in giving our *padre* to us for a father.

3. I see from here, my daughter, the trial and loneliness you are all going through. Please God, the illness of Mother Subprioress[3] will not be serious; I would be sorry even on account of the increased burden it would be for you. I was most happy that you benefited from the bloodletting. If that doctor has understood you, I wouldn't want any other to be taking care of you.

4. Today they brought me the enclosed letter from the prioress of Malagón.[4] For some time now she has not got worse. Everything I can do for her health and happiness, I do. For apart from all that I owe her, her health is very important to me. But

yours is much more so, believe me without a doubt. You can imagine from this how much I want you to be well!

5. From the enclosed note you will see that Mariano[5] received your letter. I've already written you about the one he refers to from my brother,[6] for I think I tore that one up with some other letters. It was still open, and that must be what happened. I was very upset and made a great effort to find it, for it was a wonderful letter. Now he has written me to tell me he has sent you a letter with the muleteer from Avila. Thus, I'll say nothing about him except that his soul is making good progress in prayer and that he gives away a great deal in alms. Pray always for him and for me as well, and remain with God, my daughter.

6. I was much more upset to learn that the prior[7] there is not carrying out his office well than about his pusillanimity. Our *padre* ought also to frighten him by pointing out what is wrong with him, which he will do, as is his custom. My regards to all, and to Fray Gregorio[8] especially, and to Nicolao[9] if he hasn't left, and to those daughters of mine.[10] My greetings to Gabriela[11] for her letters and to the subprioress. Oh if I could give you some of the extra nuns from up here! But God will provide them for you. I've already asked about the fleet.[12] I well understand the burden that you have there, for I am worried about it, but I hope that God will take care of everything and that your health will last. May His Majesty watch over you and make you very holy, amen.

7. I am delighted that you are beginning to recognize what you have there in our *padre*. I was aware of this already in Beas. Some letters from down there and from Caravaca arrived today. I am enclosing the one from Caravaca so that our *padre* may read it, and you also. Return it to me with this same muleteer, for I need it because of what it says about the dowries. In the letter written to the prioress[13] she complains much about you.

8. Now I must send to Caravaca a statue of our Lady that I got for them. It's large and beautiful, and not yet attired. And they are making one of St. Joseph for me that won't cost the nuns anything.[14] You are carrying out your office very well, and you did more than very well to inform me about the pinching, the pathetic customs left over from the Incarnation.[15]

Today is—I've already told you.

Yours,

Teresa of Jesus

9. Our *padre* answered me very well about everything and sent the official permissions I asked for. Kiss his hands for me.

---

1. Jerónimo Gracián.
2. Isabel de San Francisco who was temporarily prioress for the Carmelite nuns of the observance in Paterna. The letter was probably forwarded by María de San José.
3. The subprioress in Seville, María del Espíritu Santo.
4. Brianda de San José who was chronically ill.
5. Ambrosio Mariano de San Benito, who was living at the time in Madrid and to whom Teresa had forwarded a letter from María de San José.
6. Lorenzo de Cepeda.
7. Antonio de Jesús, who was prior of the discalced friars in Seville, was remiss in his duties and a rival of Gracián's.
8. Gregorio Nacianceno.
9. Nicolás Doria, who may have by then departed for Castile.
10. The discalced Carmelite nuns in Seville.
11. Leonor de San Gabriel.
12. When it will set sail for America (cf Ltr. 151.8).
13. The prioress of Caravaca (Ana de San Alberto) wrote to the prioress in Toledo (Ana de los Angeles).
14. These statues are still venerated in the monastery in Caravaca.
15. Cf. Ltr. 148.11.

161. To Padre Ambrosio Mariano, Madrid

Toledo, 12 December 1576

Teresa discusses the reform of the Carmelites in Paterna by her discalced nuns, the document being prepared as a result of the chapter in Almodóvar in September, and Mariano's opinions about certain austerities among the discalced friars.

1. Jesus be with your reverence. I received the packet of letters which included the one from the prioress of Paterna.[1] The many others you mention will perhaps come tomorrow, which is Thursday. They are safe being sent by this route—they won't be lost. I was delighted with the ones that have arrived, and also the one from you. May God be blessed for everything.

2. Oh, *padre*, what joy comes to my heart when I see someone from this order—where God has been so offended—promoting something that is for his honor and glory, and preventing some sins! Yet I feel distressed and envious to see what little use I am in this matter. I would embrace trials and dangers if I could have a share in the spoils of those who are in the midst of them. Sometimes, since I am so wretched, I rejoice to have this calm for myself here. And when I receive news about the trials they are going through down there, I feel undone and I envy the nuns in Paterna. I am overjoyed that God is beginning to make use of the discalced nuns, for often, when I see souls so courageous in these houses, I think that it would not be possible for God to give them so much without a reason. Even if this amounts to no more than their having lived in that monastery—for, after all, they avoided any offense against God there—I am most happy. And how much more so in that I hope in His Majesty their presence there will be most beneficial.

3. Don't forget to include in the document[2] for the friars the authority also to give permission for the foundation of houses

for nuns. You ought to know that my confessor here is Doctor Velázquez,[3] who is a canon of this church and a most learned servant of God—you can easily check this out. He can't accept the idea that no more monasteries for nuns are to be founded, and he ordered me that through Señora Doña Luisa, by way of the ambassador, I try to obtain permission from the general, and if not from him from the pope.[4] He says they should say that our monasteries are mirrors for Spain and that he will provide a draft of the letter.[5] I am informing you about a foundation that is being offered to us.[6] Please answer me on these two matters.

4. I have been greatly consoled by this note you sent me—May God reward you—although your words were about something already fixed deeply in my heart. How is it that you say nothing about Fray Baltasar?[7] Give my regards to all.

5. I have to laugh that Padre Fray Juan de Jesús says I want you all to go barefoot, for I am the one who always opposed this to Padre Fray Antonio. He would have found out that he was mistaken had he asked me.[8] My intention was to attract people of talent, for they would be frightened away by a lot of austerity. What was set down was only so as to distinguish ourselves from the other Carmelites. It could be that I said their feet would be just as cold as when bare.

6. I said something similar when we were talking about how bad it looked for friars to be going around barefoot on good mules; the two don't fit together.[9] Mules shouldn't be permitted except for long journeys or in great need. Some young friars came here traveling by donkey when the distance was short and they could have walked. And so I repeat it doesn't look right for these young discalced friars to be traveling on mules and with saddles. That they go about barefoot never entered my mind; there are already too many doing so. Advise them not to do so but to follow the custom. Write about this to our *padre*.[10]

7. What I have insisted on with him is that the friars be given good meals. I am well aware of what you say, and it often saddens me—and even yesterday, or today, before I saw your letter I was sad. It seemed to me on observing the way they treat themselves that within no more than a couple of days everything could fall apart. I turned to God for comfort, for he who started this work will set everything right, and so I was delighted that you share this opinion.

8. The other thing I urged that he impose is manual work, even if it is no more than making baskets or something, and that this be done during the recreation hour if there is no other time. This is most important where there are no studies. Understand, *padre*, that I am fond of strictness in the practice of virtue but not of austerity, as you see in our houses of nuns. This is perhaps so because I am not very penitential. I praise our Lord greatly because he gives you so much light in matters of such importance. It is great to desire his honor and glory in everything. May it please His Majesty to give us the grace to die a thousand deaths for this, amen, amen. Today is Wednesday 12 December.

Your reverence's unworthy servant,

Teresa of Jesus

9. You are being very charitable in sending me those letters, for our *padre* writes only very briefly when he writes me. I am not surprised by this, and I even beg him to do so. Well, I praise the Lord when I read them, and you should too because you were the initiator of that work.[11] Don't fail to speak often with the archdeacon.[12] We also have with us the dean[13] and the other canons. I am already making new friends.

---

1. Isabel de San Francisco.
2. The juridical document that was being prepared so as to normalize the situation of the discalced Carmelites.
3. Alonso Velázquez who later became the bishop of Osma.

4. Doña Luisa de la Cerda was related by marriage to the king's ambassador to Rome, Juan de Zuñiga. The general was Giovanni Battista Rossi, and the pope, Gregory XIII.
5. That is, those peering into these mirrors would see reflected images of what the lives of nuns ought to be.
6. Cf. Ltr. 162.7.
7. Baltasar de Jesús (Nieto).
8. The constitutions of 1576 for the discalced friars stipulated that they go about either barefoot or with sandals made of hemp. Teresa preferred the latter practice, which was accepted in the constitutions of 1581.
9. Travel by mule was a higher class form of travel than by foot or donkey. The bare feet were to represent poverty.
10. Jerónimo Gracián.
11. The foundations of the discalced Carmelites in Seville.
12. The Archdeacon of Toledo, Don Francisco de Avila.
13. Diego de Castilla.

162. To Padre Jerónimo Gracián, Seville

Toledo, 13 December 1576

(Autograph: DCN, Alcalá de Henares)

Expressing her gratitude and happiness with the letters she has received from Gracián, Teresa then goes on to discuss many matters: the reform of Paterna; a new foundation and how to obtain permission for it; Gracián's visitation in Andalusia; the possibility of a separate province for the discalced friars and nuns; the lawsuit in Beas; the illness of the prioress in Seville; and the personality of little Isabel. She has a high esteem for the spiritual value of the life of prayer lived by her nuns.

1. Jesus be with your paternity, *mi padre*. Oh, what a good day I had today, for Padre Mariano has sent me all your letters! There's no need for you to tell him to do so, for he does it in response to my request. And even though they arrive late, they

are a great consolation to me. But still you do me a great charity when you write telling me the substance of what is going on; for as I say those other letters arrive late, although when he receives one for me, he sends it on at once. We are very good friends.

2. I was moved to praise the Lord for the manner and grace and, above all, perfection with which you write. Oh, *mi padre*, what majesty lies in your words when you write about perfection and what consolation they bring to my soul! Even if we were not faithful to God for the good that comes from this, but were so only on account of the authority he confers on others (and the greater the authority the more faithful), our gain would be most great. It seems clear that you are on good terms with His Majesty. May He be blessed for everything, for he grants me so many favors and gives you so much light and strength. I will never be able to serve him enough.

3. The letter you wrote me from Trigueros about Tostado[1] was excellent, and you did well to tear up those that were delivered to you with requests. Well, *mi padre*, God is helping you and teaching you with all clarity, as they say. Have no fear of failing in your great undertaking. Oh, how I envy you and Padre Fray Antonio[2] because of the sins you prevent, and here I am with only desires!

4. Let me know on what grounds the accusation was made against the nun who is a virgin and bearing a child. I think a charge like that is the greatest stupidity.[3] But none could match the one you wrote me about the other day. Do you think it is a small favor the Lord grants you to be able to bear these things the way you do? I tell you he is repaying you for the services you are rendering him down there. This will not be your only reward.

5. I am frightened by all the adversity, especially about the Masses, for I went to the choir to ask God's help for those souls. It isn't possible that God would allow so much evil to increase, now that he has begun to reveal it. Every day I am learning

more about the fruit of prayer and the value before God of a soul that for God's honor alone seeks help for others. Believe me, *mi padre*, I think the desire is being accomplished for which these monasteries were founded, which was to pray to God to help those who struggle for his honor and service, since we women count for nothing. When I consider the perfection of these nuns, I am not surprised by what they obtain from God.

6. I was delighted to see the letter that the prioress of Paterna[4] wrote you and the skill God gives you in everything. I hope in God the nuns will do much good, and I felt a great desire that these foundations continue to be made. I've already written to you about one, concerning which the prioress in Medina[5] writes in the enclosed letter. It's not 1,000 ducats that she is giving but 600. It could be, now, that the donor is keeping the rest. I discussed this matter with Doctor Velázquez because I had a scruple about dealing with it against the general's will.[6] He insisted that I try to get Doña Luisa to write to the ambassador[7] and ask him to obtain permission from the general. He offered to give the information that needed to be presented and said that if the general doesn't give it, permission should be sought from the pope, informing him that these houses are mirrors for Spain. This is what I am planning to do unless you think otherwise.

7. I answered requesting that they write me again about the way in which this money was given. I have already written to Maestro Ripalda,[8] who is now rector in Burgos and a great friend of mine from the Society, that he inquire for me and let me know, and that I would send someone there, if fitting, to see the place and begin the negotiations. So, if it seems all right to you, Antonio Gaytán and Julián de Avila[9] could go when the good weather comes. You can send them the authorization and they will be able to make the foundation as they did in Caravaca without my having to go. Even if more nuns are taken for the purpose of reforming other houses, there are enough

to go around as long as the number in the houses is small, as is the case down there. In others, where the nuns are more numerous, I think more than two should go, and even down there I do not regret their letting a lay sister go,[10] for they have them, and what truly fine ones!

8. I am certain that no remedy exists for monasteries of nuns if there is not someone behind the doors to watch over them. The Incarnation is now something to praise God for.[11] Oh, what a desire I have to see all of the nuns free from the jurisdiction of the calced friars. I will dedicate my life to our being made a separate province, because all the harm comes from our not being separate, and there is no remedy. For although other monasteries are relaxed, they are not so to such an extreme. I mean those subject to the friars, for it's a terrible thing with those subject to the ordinaries. And if superiors realized what their responsibilities are and took the care that you do, matters would go otherwise. And it would be no small mercy from God that there be so many prayers offered by good souls for his church.

9. I think what you say about the habits is very good, and one year from now you can give them to all the nuns.[12] Once it's done, it's done, for all the clamor lasts for only a few days. And if some are punished the others will remain silent, for women on the whole are timid. Those novices should not remain there, for goodness' sake, for they would have such a bad beginning. It's very important that we have success with this monastery, for it is the first. I tell you that if you think they are your friends they are repaying you with their deeds.[13]

10. I approve of the severity used by our Padre Fray Antonio.[14] Understand, then, that with some it would not be harmful to so act, and this is very important, for I know them. Perhaps more than one sin of the tongue will be avoided and they will even become more submissive. Gentleness must be accompanied by severity—this is the way God leads us—and for those very determined individuals there is no other remedy.

And I repeat that those poor discalced nuns are very much alone, for if one of them gets sick it will be a severe trial. God will give them health since he sees the need.

11. All your daughters here are doing well, except for those in Beas who are being killed by lawsuits.[15] But it is no serious thing that they suffer something, since the foundation was made without much trouble. I will never have better days than those I had there with my Paul.[16] I was pleased that he wrote me as "your dear son"; and how quickly I said (being alone), "He is right!" I was delighted to hear it, and I would be even more delighted if matters down there proceeded so well that he could return to care for matters up here which I hope will be entrusted to his care.[17]

12. I am distressed over the sickness of the prioress[18] there, for it would be hard to find another one like her for that post. Make sure she gets good care and that she takes something for that continual fever. Oh, how well I get on with my confessor![19] To make me do some penance he obliges me to eat more every day than I usually do and to pamper myself.

13. My Isabel[20] is here. She asks how you can joke with her so much as not to answer her. I gave her a little melon; and she told me it was very cold, that it deafens her throat.[21] I tell you she uses the most delightful expressions, and she's always happy, with a gentle disposition that reminds me very much of *mi padre*.[22] May God watch over him much more than me, amen, amen.

Your Reverence's daughter,

Teresa of Jesus

14. You should know that the nuns down there have a strange fear of the prioress, and also the custom of never saying anything precise to their superiors. The students who serve them must be watched. May God keep you.[23]

---

1. Jerónimo Tostado.

2. Antonio de Jesús Heredia.
3. She is alluding to a gross calumny against the nuns in Paterna.
4. Isabel de San Francisco who was brought there from the Carmel in Seville.
5. Inés de Jesús (Tapia). She is alluding to the projected foundation in Aguilar de Campo (cf. Ltr. 159.7).
6. Alonso Velázquez. She has scruples about planning new foundations with authorization from Gracián (whose powers are doubtful in this matter) against the desires of the general of the order (Giovanni Battista Rossi).
7. Luisa de la Cerda (cf. Ltr. 161.3).
8. Jerónimo Ripalda.
9. These two had been commissioned before to make the foundation in Caravaca (cf. F. 27.4).
10. Letting Margarita de la Concepción go to Paterna.
11. The Incarnation in Avila where St. John of the Cross was at the time confessor.
12. Gracián had imposed on the nuns in Paterna a reform of their religious habit consisting in the use of a poorer, coarse material.
13. She is using irony, for they were a trial to Gracián.
14. Antonio de Jesús Heredia; tending to be easy going, he would have sudden fits of severity.
15. They were being sued for having made a window in the wall between the parish and the church so that they could hear the sermons.
16. Jerónimo Gracián.
17. She is hoping that the reform in Castile will be placed in the hands of Gracián.
18. María de San José.
19. Antonio Velázquez.
20. Isabel Dantisco, Gracián's little sister.
21. Being only eight years old, she was probably trying to say that it made her throat numb.
22. Gracián.
23. The postscript is not present in the autograph.

163. To Madre María de San José, Seville

Toledo, 13 December 1576

(Autograph: DCN, Valladolid)

Teresa responds to a previous letter that brought news about the illness of Madre María (for which she prescribes a remedy) and the sudden death of an elderly woman who helped the nuns as portress. She also comments on the nuns' efforts to obtain water, and replies concerning the address of her brother in South America.

For Mother María de San José, Carmelite prioress.

1. Jesus. May the Holy Spirit be with your reverence, my daughter. Until you write that your fever is gone, I will be worried about you. Be careful that it doesn't turn into jaundice, which can happen where there is anemia. Although there was hardly ever any occasion for me to contract this illness, I have suffered much from it. The cure consisted of some aromatic fumigations with vetch and coriander leaves and egg shells and a little oil and a little bit of rosemary and a little lavender, which I inhaled while lying in bed. I assure you that I recovered. This is only for you; I think it would be good if you tried it sometime. I once suffered from fevers for eight months, and with this remedy they went away.

2. I do not tire of thanking God that little Blase was there on the night the good old woman died.[1] May the Lord take her to himself, as we have begged him here. I don't think there will be any need to console her sister or niece. Give them my regards and tell them they are right in being happy that she has gone to enjoy God. But Beatriz[2] must not be desiring the same, for she should be careful that she doesn't commit a sin with such foolishness. You did me a great favor by writing such a detailed account of all this, and I rejoice that you have received so good an inheritance. It doesn't seem to me that the devil

has afflicted you down there with the pusillanimity he did me, for now I see that it was he; up here I have returned to the way I felt before. What is this that the good prior of Las Cuevas is writing to Padre Mariano that he try to get a trickle of water for you?[3] I don't know how he could succeed, although it would certainly make me very happy. He puts as much effort into the matter as he would if it were for himself. Blessed be God that he is in good health; I'm going to write to him.

3. Many regards to all the nuns, and to my Gabriela,[4] for her letters are a delight to me. Let me know whether she is a good turn sister, and don't forget to give my greetings to Delgada,[5] and tell me whether Fray Bartolomé de Aguilar[6] is well. I don't know how you can be sick since you have our *padre*[7] there. Each day God gives with both…,etc.[8]

4. Peru is where my brother[9] is, although by now I believe he has moved further on. I will find out from Lorenzo.[10] But in regard to what you have to do down there, remember that he doesn't have an established residence, because he is not yet married, and he is in a place one day, and gone the next, as they say. I sent your letter to my brother, Lorenzo. If you have told him what country this man of whom you speak is from, perhaps he will know to whom you can recommend him. Try to find out about this and write to me when you do.

5. It would be only right to pay for the house with Beatriz's dowry,[11] for she played a part, I believe, in our being sent down there. Always tell Gabriela to keep me informed on how things are going in Paterna so that you don't have to tire yourself. It's no surprise that they have little peace. Ask *mi padre* if it wouldn't be good for Margarita[12] to go there and join them, for she would certainly have the courage. It seems to me they are very isolated, and I think she could make profession (although I don't remember when she received the habit). If one of the two sisters were to become sick it would be a rough situation, and you are not in want of lay sisters. May God be with you, amen.

Today is the feast of St. Lucy.

Yours,

Teresa of Jesus

6. From the enclosed letter you will see how the prioress of Malagón[13] is doing; it is from her doctor.

7. Read the two other enclosed letters. So that you don't do what I am advising San Francisco,[14] I'm sending them to you open; close them. If Father Prior[15] gives you any pictures for me, don't take any of them for yourself; he will give you as many as you want down there.

---

1. Little Blase is the boy who served in the sacristy of the Carmel in Seville. The "good old woman" was Juana de la Cruz's sister, who did volunteer work as portress for the nuns in Seville.
2. Beatriz de la Madre de Dios was her niece.
3. The nuns in Seville were unable to get their neighbors, the Franciscan friars, to allow them to tap their water. Now the Carthusian prior is trying to get Padre Ambrosio Mariano, who has connections in Madrid, to intercede for them.
4. Leonor de San Gabriel.
5. Inés Delgado.
6. A Dominican friend of Teresa's in Seville.
7. Jerónimo Gracián.
8. She just begins the Spanish proverb: "Each day God gives with both hands, but we don't know how to benefit."
9. Agustín de Ahumada. He went on to Chile where he became governor of Quijos in 1579.
10. Lorenzo de Cepeda, who was in Avila.
11. Beatriz de la Madre de Dios, whose story Teresa tells in *Foundations*, 26.3–15.
12. Margarita de la Concepción. She made her profession on 1 January 1577 and did in fact go to Paterna.
13. Brianda de San José.
14. Isabel de San Francisco, the prioress in Paterna.
15. Hernando de Pantoja, the prior of the Carthusians.

164. To Madre María Bautista, Valladolid

Toledo, Middle of December 1576

Preparations are being made in Valladolid for the profession of the young Casilda de Padilla, a vocation opposed by the family, who were from the Castilian nobility. Now trouble arose over money and the dowry from other interested parties. Teresa gives counsel, but then leaves everything to María Bautista's judgment and the advice of others. Only a fragment remains and the authenticity of the text is uncertain.

1. ...I will be happy if she leaves it to him as she did the rest. Be careful how you speak to her[1] about all this that I am writing to you, for she will tell her mother,[2] and this will look bad after the letter I've written to Don Pedro.[3] You can easily tell her that she should leave it to his conscience; otherwise I would not interfere in the matter, as is true.

2. I am amused that Doctor Velázquez[4] thinks that Don Pedro should not take it upon his conscience, while as usual there will be someone to tell Don Pedro that he can do so. Those who think the fathers of the Society are being moved by their own interests are so displeased that they have thought it good for him to act in this way. Don Pedro is more considerate of my reputation than you because he is delivering me from getting involved. May God pardon and watch over you for me and give you many happy years.

3. I am always concerned that you not displease Señora Doña María.

4. We are doing well. I sent your letter to Father Provincial[5] in which you say that Doña María now wants her to renounce her possessions in favor of the house.[6] I don't know what to say about this world, for where there is a question of self-interest there is no holiness, and this makes me want to abhor everything in it. I don't know why you are getting a Theatine[7]

mixed up in all this (for Catalina tells me that Mercado is one),[8] since you know their own interests are at stake. Prádano[9] has pleased me very much; I believe he is a man of great perfection. May God give perfection to us also, and to them their money.

5. My regards to all and especially to Casilda, and hurry on with her profession. Don't delay any longer, for it's enough to kill her. I will send your letter to Father Provincial. I well imagined that Doña María was waiting for those from Don Pedro for the sake of her own business affairs. This displeased me very much. Do you think I told him about it? I don't think so; saying yes would make me feel a scruple. After all, since you have a superior, I believe it would be better for you not to renounce anything until you get his opinion. So don't pay attention to what I have said other than to draw light about what would be more fitting. I would not want to impose this on you, for you have enough trials. Write about it all to Padre Maestro,[10] and through Arellano,[11] the Dominican, you could let me know whether she is calm. Señora Doña María[12] will have him come....

---

1. Casilda de Padilla, who will make profession in Valladolid with the name Casilda de la Concepción (cf. F. 11).
2. María de Acuña, Casilda's mother.
3. Pedro Manrique, Casilda's uncle, first a canon in Toledo and now a Jesuit.
4. Alonso Velázquez, a canon in Toledo and confessor to Teresa.
5. Juan Suárez, the Jesuit provincial.
6. Doña María came to agree that her daughter Casilda renounce her inheritance in favor of the Carmel in Valladolid.
7. Jesuits at that time were often called Theatines.
8. Catalina de Tolosa from Burgos; Mercado was probably a Jesuit.
9. The Jesuit Juan de Prádonos (cf. L. 24.4–5).
10. The Dominican, Domingo Báñez.
11. Unknown; possibly Juan de Orellana.
12. Probably María de Mendoza.

165. To Diego Ortiz (?), Toledo

Toledo, 16 December 1576

(Autograph: DCN, Toledo)

This letter seems to be addressed to Diego Ortiz who had written Teresa about his fears and scruples. He was sending her a statue of St. Joseph.

1. Jesus be with your honor, and may he repay you for the consolation you give me in so many ways. Indeed, there are things in the writing you sent that I have never heard or even thought of.[1] May God be blessed for everything. That there be matter for confession in these things or in the fact of your coming here seems to me to arise from a scruple rather than virtue. You displease me very much for this. But you have to have some fault, since, after all, you are a son of Adam.

2. I was greatly consoled that my father St. Joseph will arrive so soon[2] and that you are so devoted to him. The sisters there[3] will be very happy, for they are like strangers in that place and far from anyone who could console them, although I certainly believe that the true consolation is really close to them. In charity, would you take the measurements of the length and width, and this has to be done at once so that the box can be made tomorrow, for they cannot do so Tuesday since it is a feast day, and on Wednesday morning the wagons leave.

3. It's no small thing for me to have to give up so soon the statue of our Lady. I will feel extremely lonely without it. So, in charity, you can provide a remedy for me by sending the one you are going to give me for Christmas. With all our hearts we will beseech the Lord to give Christmas gifts to you and those

gentlemen. Give them my respects and may you remain with God.

Your unworthy servant,

Teresa of Jesus

4. The three foundresses will make their profession on New Year's Day,[4] and it will be a consolation for them to have the statues there.

---

1. Antonio de San José, an early editor, thinks he was having doubts about whether Teresa was pleased with his visits or whether he was just wasting her time. And perhaps he also mentioned that they should both go to confession and that they would do better to be more retiring.
2. A statue of St. Joseph.
3. The Carmelite nuns in Caravaca for whom the statue is destined.
4. The foundresses of the Carmel in Caravaca were Francisca de San José, Francisca de la Cruz, and Francisca de la Madre de Dios. They did not make profession on that day.

166. To Madre Brianda de San José, Malagón

Toledo, 18 December 1576

(Autograph: DCN, Loeches [Madrid])

Madre Brianda, the prioress in Malagón, continues to be very sick. Beatriz de Jesús is taking her place as superior of the house. The community is in need of a larger house. Mentioning the problem over Casilda de Padilla's dowry, Teresa shows that she prefers not to become involved in the matter. She is in good health. The autograph is torn and parts are missing.

1. May the Holy Spirit be with your reverence, my daughter, and give you his intense love this Christmas so that you do not feel your illness so much. May God be blessed, for many will think they are having a very good Christmas with health and

happiness and well-being, whereas on the day when they will have to render an account to God they will see that it was badly spent. You need not be disturbed about such matters, for in that bed you are gaining glory upon glory.

2. It is a good thing that you are not worse in such trying weather. Do not be surprised by your weakness, for you have been sick a long time. The cough must have come from some cold draft you may have been in, but without knowing for certain the cause, nothing can be prescribed for you here. It's better if the doctors there prescribe for you.

3. About the nun, I have no aspirant to send you, but in seeing your need I wondered if it wouldn't be better to send one from Medina who they assure me is very good. But, since you say that you can get along with those 100 ducats, it's better not to take anyone until you have a house.[1]

4. I'm amazed that they order you to get up in weather like this. For goodness' sake don't do so—it would be enough to kill you—until the weather gets better; but not now, for it's even dangerous for those who are big and healthy....

5. My greetings to...and that I am letting her know that there is quite an uproar because Sister Casilda[2] is renouncing her possessions. Don Pedro[3] has written me about this. Doctor Velázquez,[4] who is my confessor, says that they cannot make her go against her will. Well, I have left it to Don Pedro's conscience. I don't know where it will all end up. They want to give her 500 ducats and the cost of her veil—what an expense that is, so great that it has to be mentioned![5]—but they do not want to give it now. Surely, this angel owes but little to her mother. On account of the child's distress, which is great, I would like to see the whole matter concluded. And so I wrote to her asking her not to worry even if they don't give her anything.

6. Beatriz[6] writes that she is better now and suffers no more. Since she sees you want her to be well, she thinks she is well

even though she may be sick. I've never seen anything like it, as the poor licentiate[7] says...I am fine. May it please the Lord that you, my daughter, will be well very soon, amen.

7. Beatriz's trousseau according to the list they sent me amounts to practically nothing.[8] I told them to send it by way of Antonio Ruiz[9] at least the blankets and two sheets and some drapery. I think the cost to do so will amount to more than the things are worth. I will pay for it here if you want. Her sister[10] sent to ask for the mattresses and some other little things....

---

1. They are waiting for Luisa de La Cerda to provide an adequate house for the nuns.
2. A brief from Rome allowed Casilda de Padilla to make profession before the required age of seventeen.
3. Don Pedro Manrique de Padilla, a canon in Toledo, Casilda's paternal uncle.
4. Alonso Velázquez, a canon in Toledo and future bishop of Osma.
5. The family was very wealthy and so the irony. In the end they didn't even give the 500 ducats.
6. Beatriz de Jesús (Cepeda y Ocampo), Teresa's cousin, who was acting superior during Madre Brianda's illness.
7. Probably the chaplain at Malagón, Gaspar de Villanueva.
8. Beatriz had joined Teresa's reform from the Incarnation, and this was all she brought with her from that monastery.
9. A merchant friend of Teresa's in Malagón.
10. María de Cepeda was a nun at the Incarnation in Avila who after having joined Teresa's reform had to return for reasons of health.

167. To Madre María de San José, Seville

Toledo, 27 December 1576

(Autograph: Parroquia de Budia, Guadalajara)

A quick letter that Teresa writes at two o'clock in the morning right after Christmas to express her gratitude for letters received and to send some greetings. She was not feeling well for some days before Christmas.

1. Jesus be with you, my daughter. The clock will soon strike two, and so I can't be long, I mean two o'clock in the night. For this reason I can't write to the good Nicolao;[1] wish him a happy New Year. Today, his cousin's wife[2] was here. That man who wants to found a monastery is always in the same frame of mind. He persists with his good desire, but since the business in Madrid that would allow it is not concluded and Padre Mariano[3] is not coming here, things remain the same.

2. I am delighted that you have received such a good nun. Give my regards to her and to all the sisters. I was also delighted with the letters from my brother[4] that you sent me. What makes me sorry is that you don't say anything about your health; may God grant you the health I desire for you. He does us a great favor by giving it to our *padre*.[5] May he be forever blessed.

3. The muleteer brought me your letters for Malagón. I don't know if he brought the money. It would have been really foolish not to accept what my brother is giving you—would that it had been more. It will be kind of you if you send me the sweets you mentioned if they are especially good, for I would like to have them for a particular need.

4. I am well, although the days before Christmas I was somewhat down and got worn out from too many business matters. Despite it all, I did not break the Advent observance. Give my regards to all the people you think you should, especially to Padre Antonio de Jesús,[6] and ask him if has made a vow not to answer me. Greetings to Fray Gregorio.[7] I am very happy that you have enough to make your annual payment.[8] God will provide the rest. May His Majesty watch over you, for I have been wanting to see a letter from you.

Today is the feast of St. John the Evangelist.

Your reverence's,

Teresa of Jesus

---

1. Nicolás Doria.
2. Probably Francisco Doria's wife who was living in Toledo.
3. Ambrosio Mariano de San Benito, who was in Madrid.
4. Lorenzo de Cepeda.
5. Jerónimo Gracián.
6. Antonio de Jesús (Heredia) was prior of the discalced monastery (Los Remedios) in Seville.
7. Gregorio Nacianceno.
8. The annual payment that had to be made on the monastery debt.

168. To Don Diego de Guzmán y Cepeda, Avila

Toledo, December, 1576

Teresa asks for help in finding a house for her brother Pedro, who has recently returned from America, and offers sympathy to Diego at the recent deaths of his wife and daughter.

❖❖❖❖

1. Jesus. The grace of the Holy Spirit be with your honor. This is a letter Señor Ahumada[1] wrote me. I am sending it to you that you may see what he is here asking of you and not fail to do it in time. And, lest you forget because of your present grief, tell Señora Magdalena[2] at once, so that she may take care of the matter. It would be a regrettable thing to rent the house when not needed, or to give it up when needed. Give her my best wishes, and tell her also to let me know how she is doing.

2. It seems to me that our Lord wanted to bring that little angel to be with her mother in heaven.[3] May he be blessed for everything, for as I've been told, the poor little one was always

sick. God has granted a great favor to us all, and to you especially by giving you so many people up there to help you bear the trials of this life. May it please His Majesty to watch over Doña Catalina,[4] and may he always guide you by the hand, amen.

Your unworthy servant,

Teresa of Jesus

---

1. Pedro de Ahumada, Teresa's brother.
2. Magdalena de Guzmán, Diego's sister.
3. Both Diego's wife and daughter had recently died.
4. Catalina de Guzmán, another daughter of Diego's.

169. To Padre Jerónimo Gracián, Seville

Toledo, End of December 1576

Isabel is Gracián's little sister. She received the Carmelite habit in Toledo when only eight years old.

1. My Isabel is getting better every day. When I go to recreation, which is not often, she sets aside her needlework and begins to sing:

Mother Foundress
Is coming to recreation;
Let's all dance and sing
And clap our hands in jubilation.

2. But this is for a moment. Outside the time of recreation she remains in her hermitage so absorbed with the Infant Jesus, the shepherds, her work, and her thoughts (which she tells me about) that it is something to praise the Lord for. She sends her regards, and prays for you. And she desires to see you, but not Señora Juana[1] or anyone, for she says they are of the world.

She is for me a delight, but all this writing leaves me little time to enjoy it....

1. Juana Dantisco, Isabel's and Gracián's mother.

170. To Padre Jerónimo Gracián, Seville

Toledo, Around December 1576

Teresa refers again to Padre Antonio's jealousy. (Cf. Ltr. 138.2).

1. I am happy that Padre Fray Antonio[1] is not with you, for according to what they tell me, when he sees so many letters of mine and none for him, he becomes disturbed. O Jesus, what a wonderful thing it is for two souls to understand each other, for they neither lack something to say, nor grow tired.

1. Antonio de Jesús (Heredia).

171. To Lorenzo de Cepeda, Avila

Toledo, Christmas Season 1576–77

(Autograph fragment: Discalced Trinitarian Nuns, Madrid)

We don't know whether this represents a short note or a postscript to a lost letter. It accompanied a little song Teresa sent to Lorenzo.

...is a little song for Fray John of the Cross they sent me from the Incarnation. Tell him that I told you I greatly enjoyed it. I would like Francisco to sing it for you.[1]

1. The persons alluded to are St. John of the Cross and Lorenzo's son Francisco. The Incarnation is the name of the Carmelite monastery of nuns in Avila.

Letters 172–224 (1577)

172. To Don Lorenzo de Cepeda, Avila

Toledo, 2 January 1577

Written during the Christmas feast days, this letter reflects the spirit of those days of gift giving in which the nuns composed verses for one another. Teresa, as Lorenzo's spiritual director, replies to the questions he had put to her. She asks him to send her a chest, which contains some of her important papers, and for some information for the nuncio. Comments are made about some responses submitted for her Satirical Critique.

1. Jesus be with your honor. Serna[1] allows me so little time that I did not want to go on at length, but when I begin writing to you—and since Serna comes so seldom—I need time.

2. Do not read the letters I write to Francisco,[2] for I fear that he is somewhat melancholic and is doing a lot by being open with me. Perhaps God gives him those scruples to detach him from other things. Fortunately, for his good, he is able to believe me.

3. Clearly, I didn't send the paper, although I was wrong in not telling you. I gave it to a sister to copy, and I have not been able to find it. Until they send another copy from Seville, there is no way I can send it to you.[3]

4. I think by now they will have given you a letter I sent by way of Madrid, but in case it has been lost I will have to repeat what I said there. I regret having to spend time doing so. First, look over that house you have rented belonging to Hernán Alvarez de Peralta. I think I have heard it mentioned that in one of the rooms the walls are ready to cave in. Be very careful.

5. Second, send the small chest and any other of my papers that may have been in the bundles, for it seems to me there was a bag containing papers. Have them sent to me well sewn. If Doña Quiteria[4] through Serna sends a parcel that she needs to send, they will easily fit inside. Add my seal also, for I can't bear using this seal with the skull. I prefer the one with the monogram of him whom I would like to have engraved on my heart as had St. Ignatius.[5] Don't let anyone open the chest, unless it's yourself, for I think the writing on prayer[6] is in there, and don't tell anyone what you find in it. Be on guard, for I don't give you permission to do this, nor would it be fitting. Even though it may seem to you that this would render service to God, I forbid it because of other disadvantages that would result. Enough said, for were I to learn that you tell someone, I would never let you read anything again.

6. The nuncio[7] has asked me to send him copies of the patent letters authorizing me to found these houses, and an account of how many there are, and where, and how many nuns, and from where, their age, and how many I think have the qualities for being prioress. The lists of these things are in the chest, or maybe in the bag. Well, I need everything that is there. They say he wants it so as to set up the province.[8] I fear, instead, that he may want our nuns to reform other monasteries, for he has spoken of this previously, and such a thing would not be good for us, except for monasteries of our order. Tell this to the subprioress, and tell her to send me the names of those who are in that house, the ages of those who are there now, and how long they have been nuns. This should be done

with good handwriting in a small notebook, and signed with her name.

7. Now it occurs to me that I am prioress there and that I can do it, and so it is not necessary that she sign it but only send me the information, even if in her handwriting, for I can copy it. There is no reason for the nuns to know about this. You take care of how this is to be sent so that the papers aren't in danger of getting wet, and send the key.[9]

8. That which I said is in the book is in the one where I treat of the *Paternoster*. There you will find much about the prayer you are experiencing, although not to the extent in which it is explained in the other book. It seems to me it is found in the section on *Adveniat regnum tuum*.[10] Read it again, at least the part on the *Paternoster*. Perhaps you will find something that satisfies you.

9. Before I forget, how could you make a vow without telling me? That's a nice kind of obedience![11] This troubled me, although your determination pleased me. But what you did seemed to be dangerous. Inquire about this, for that which is a venial sin could become a mortal sin on account of the promise. I will also ask my confessor who is a most learned man. And it seems to me foolish, for what I promised carried with it certain conditions.[12] I would not dare promise what you did, for I know that even the apostles committed venial sins. Only our Lady was free from them. I am sure that God accepted your intention, but it would seem to me wise for you to have the vow commuted at once for something else. If it can be done by means of a bull, do so immediately. This jubilee year would be a good occasion for doing so.[13] God deliver us from committing ourselves to something in which it is so easy to fail without our hardly even being aware of it. If God hasn't charged you with a greater fault, it is because he knows our nature well. In my opinion you should correct this situation at once, and don't make any more vows, for it's a dangerous thing. It doesn't seem to me to be inappropriate to speak at times about

your prayer with your confessors, for, after all, they are close at hand and they can give you better counsel about everything, and nothing would be lost.

10. Your being sorry that you have bought La Serna is the work of the devil who doesn't want you to be grateful to God for the favor he granted you in this regard, which was great.[14] Be convinced that it is the best you could do from many viewpoints, and you are providing your children with something more than property, which is honor. Nobody hears about your purchase without thinking that you were most fortunate. And do you think there is no work in collecting rent? You would be spending all your time in property seizures. Consider this a temptation; don't pay any heed to it, but praise God for what you bought, and don't think that if you had more time your prayer would go better. Make no mistake about this, for time well spent, like looking after your children's property, does not hurt prayer. God often gives more in a short moment than in a long time. His works are not measured by time.

11. Try, then, after these feast days are over to devote some time to getting all the records in suitable order. And what you spend on La Serna will be well spent, and when summer comes you will be happy to go and spend some days there. Jacob did not become less a saint for tending his flock, nor Abraham, nor St. Joachim. When we try to avoid work, everything tires us. That's the way it goes for me, and for this reason God wills that I be always loaded down with many things to do. Discuss all these things with Francisco de Salcedo, for in these temporal matters I willingly let him stand in my stead.[15]

12. It is a great favor from God that you tire of what others find restful, but not for this reason should you renounce it. We have to serve God as he wishes and not as we wish. The livestock business is what in my opinion you can disregard. For this reason I am somewhat happy that you have given up the business with Antonio Ruiz that was based on profit.[16] For even in the eyes of the world one suffers some little loss through

such dealings. I think it would be better for you to be moderate in almsgiving, for God has given you food and what you need to give alms, but not a lot. I do not call what you want to do at La Serna the livestock business, for it is something very good; it is not what I call a business. I've already told you that in all these matters you should follow the opinion of Francisco de Salcedo, and you will no longer have such ideas. And always give my best regards to him and anyone else you choose, and to Pedro de Ahumada[17] to whom I would like to have time to write so that he might answer, for his letters are a delight to me.

13. Tell Teresa[18] not to fear that I love anyone as much as I do her and that she should distribute the holy pictures, except those I put aside for myself, and that she give some to her brothers. I long to see her. I was moved by what you wrote about her to Seville. They sent me your letters, which filled the sisters with joy when I read them in recreation, and me too. Whoever would take away gallantry from my brother would be taking away his life. Everything seems to him good, since his gallantry is put into practice for saints, for I believe these nuns are saints. In every instance they put me to shame.

14. We had a great feast yesterday for the Holy Name of Jesus;[19] may God reward you. I don't know what to send you for all you do for me except these carols I composed, for my confessor[20] gave me orders to bring some happiness to the sisters. I spent the past evenings with them, and I didn't know how to bring them joy except with these. They have a delightful sound—it would be nice if Francisquito[21] could sing them. See if I'm not making good progress! Nonetheless, the Lord has granted me many favors during these days.

15. I am amazed by those he is granting you. May he be blessed forever. I understand why devotion is desired, which is good. It is one thing to desire it and another to ask for it. But I believe that what you are doing is the best. Leave it all to God and leave your interests in his hands. He knows what is fitting

for us, but always strive to journey along the path I wrote you about. Realize that it is more important than you think.

16. It wouldn't be bad when at times you wake up with those impulses of love of God to sit up in bed for a while; always being careful though that you get the sleep your head needs (for unawares you could end up incapable of prayer). And be careful and try not to suffer much cold, for the cold is not good for the pains in your side. I don't know why you want those terrors and fears, for God is leading you by love. They were necessary back then. Don't think it is always the devil who impedes prayer, for God in his mercy sometimes takes it away. And I am inclined to say that this is almost as great a favor as when he bestows much prayer; and this for many reasons that I do not have time to tell you now. The prayer God gives you is incomparably greater than thinking about hell, and you wouldn't be able to do so even if you desired. And don't desire to do so, for there is no reason for it.

17. Some of the responses of the sisters[22] made me laugh. Others were excellent, for they gave me light on the subject, for don't think that I know the meaning. I didn't do any more than mention to you haphazardly what I will speak to you about the next time I see you, God willing.

18. I was amused by good Francisco de Salcedo's response. His humility is in a sense strange. God so leads him with fear that it could even seem to him wrong to speak of these matters in this way.[23] We have to accommodate ourselves to what we see in souls. I tell you he is a holy man, but God is not leading him along the road he is leading you. Indeed, he is leading him as he does the strong, and us as he does the weak. The response was long for someone of Francisco's temperament.

19. I just now read your letter again. I hadn't understood that you wanted to get up during the night, as you say, but thought you just wanted to sit up in the bed. I thought that was already a lot, for it is important not to go without sleep. In no way should

you get up no matter how much fervor you feel, and even less so if you can sleep. Don't be afraid of sleep. If you could hear what Fray Peter of Alcantara said in this regard, you wouldn't be afraid of going to sleep, even if you had become wide awake.

20. Your letters do not tire me, for they console me greatly, and I would be consoled if I were able to write more frequently. But I have so much correspondence that I cannot write more often, and even tonight my prayer has been impeded by this work. This doesn't cause me any scruple, only regret at not having time. God gives it to us that we might always spend it in his service, amen.

21. Different kinds of fish in this town are so scarce that it is a pity for the sisters, and so I was delighted with those sea bream. I think considering the weather they could have been sent without bread.[24] If you manage to have some when Serna comes, or some fresh sardines, give the subprioress the means for sending them, for her package was very well wrapped. This is a terrible place for having to go without eating meat, for there is never even a fresh egg around. Nonetheless, I was thinking today that I haven't felt so well in years, and I am keeping all the observance that the other nuns do, which is a great consolation for me.[25]

22. The enclosed verses that are not in my handwriting are not my work, but they seem to me good for Francisco. In the way the nuns at St. Joseph's compose theirs, one of the sisters here did these. During these Christmas festivities we did a lot of this in recreation. Today is the second day of the year.

Your honor's unworthy servant,

Teresa of Jesus

23. I thought that you would send us your carol, for these have neither rhyme nor reason to them, and the sisters sing everything. I now recall one that I once composed while in deep prayer, and it seemed I entered into even greater quiet.

Here it is, but I don't remember if the verses went just like this. See how even from here I want to provide you with some recreation.

Oh Beauty exceeding
All other beauties!
Paining, but You wound not,
Free of pain You destroy
The love of creatures.

Oh, knot that binds
Two so different,
Why do You become unbound
For when held fast You strengthen
Making injuries seem good.

You bind the one without being
With Being unending;
Finish, without finishing,
You love, without having to love,
Magnify our nothingness.

24. I don't remember any more. What a brain for a foundress! But I tell you I thought I had a great one when I composed this. God forgive you for making me waste time, but I think these stanzas will touch you and inspire you with devotion, but don't tell anyone. Doña Guiomar[26] and I were together at that time. Give her my regards.

---

1. Serna is probably one of Lorenzo's servants.
2. Francisco is Lorenzo's oldest son.
3. This paper written by Gracián was meant for Garciálvarez, the chaplain for the Carmel in Seville, limiting his powers as confessor. María de San José sent it to Teresa from Seville. It is of interest to Lorenzo because of his close ties with the nuns in Seville.

4. A Carmelite nun who was several times prioress at the monastery of the Incarnation in Avila.
5. According to legend, the letters IHS were found impressed in gold on St. Ignatius of Antioch's heart after his martyrdom.
6. Probably an allusion to some of the *Spiritual Testimonies*.
7. Nicolás Ormaneto wanted the patent letters from the Carmelite general Giovanni Rossi authorizing her to make foundations.
8. The nuncio was thinking of forming a province of the houses founded by Teresa.
9. The key to the small chest.
10. *The Way of Perfection* is the book where she reflects on the Our Father and in chaps 30–31 deals with the prayer of quiet. The other book is *The Book of Her Life*, where she treats of the prayer of quiet in chaps 14–15.
11. Lorenzo had taken Teresa as his spiritual director and promised obedience to her. Now, without consulting her, he has made a vow of doing always the more perfect thing.
12. Teresa had made a "vow of perfection," but with certain conditions that her brother hadn't taken into consideration. Her confessor was Alonso Velázquez.
13. The privileges of the Holy Year of 1570–71 were extended to the entire Catholic world by Gregory XIII for the year 1576.
14. La Serna, about three miles from Avila, was a property purchased by Lorenzo. Now he was thinking of selling it to be free of administrative responsibilities and have more time for prayer.
15. Francisco de Salcedo was a friend of Teresa's of whom she speaks in her *Life*, and who had since become a priest after his wife's death.
16. Antonio Ruiz was in the livestock business.
17. One of Teresa's brothers.
18. Lorenzo's daughter, living with the nuns in the Carmel of Avila.
19. On the first day of the year, the feast of the Circumcision, they celebrated the Holy Name of Jesus.
20. Alonso Velázquez.
21. Lorenzo's oldest son, Francisco de Cepeda, who was then seventeen.
22. She is referring to the answers given to the words "Seek yourself in Me" of which she wrote a satirical critique according to the custom of the time (see "A Satirical Critique" in vol. 3 of her Collected Works, pp. 357–62).

23. He questioned the humorous way in which the critique of the answers was to be made.
24. To keep the fish fresh in those days it was wrapped in slices of bread.
25. She kept the Advent fast and abstinence.
26. Guiomar de Ulloa. They were together a good deal during the years 1558–62.

173. To Madre María de San José, Seville

Toledo, 3 January 1577

The spirit of Christmas is still with Teresa as she expresses her desire to keep in close touch with those living in Seville. She shows her loving concern about the health of the prioresses of Seville and Malagón. After sending regards to different friars and nuns, she mentions the spiritual progress her brother is making.

1. Jesus be with your reverence, my daughter. You must have experienced a happy Christmas since you have *mi padre*[1] there, for I would too, and happy New Year. It seems that things down there are not going to end so quickly, and I am already feeling anguish over the loneliness his absence causes us up here. Oh what freezing cold we're having! It is not much different than in Avila. Nonetheless, I am well, although I am longing to receive a letter from down there because it seems a long time since I have received any. The mail is as slow in getting up to us as it is in getting down to you. Truly, everything seems slow to one with longings.

2. From your note at the top of your letter I see that you are feeling better since you have been bled; what I want to know is whether the fever has gone away. I was happy to receive your letter and would be much happier to see you. I would be particularly happy now, for I feel that we are very close friends, for there are few others with whom I would enjoy speaking about any number of things. You certainly please me, and so I

rejoice to see from your letters that you have come to understand,[2] and that if it pleases God we see each other again you wouldn't be foolish, for you have come to know how I love you, and so I feel much tender compassion for you in your illness.

3. As for the illness of Mother Prioress of Malagón,[3] no one understands it. They say she is somewhat better, but the high fever doesn't go away, nor can she get up. I so much wish she could get well enough to be brought here. Don't fail to pray much for her. Since I know I don't have to insist on this with you, I don't repeat it every time.

4. Don't you notice that every time I write to *mi padre*, I find pleasure in writing you, however busy I am? Well, I tell you that I myself am surprised at this. And I should write to my Gabriela[4] sometimes! My best regards to her, and to Beatriz,[5] and to her mother and to all the nuns.

5. I am writing to *mi padre* that it is very important, since they need nuns at Paterna—I mean lay sisters—that he send some of ours, for these would be a help to the other nuns who I assure you are few in number.[6] Send them my regards, and always let me know how they are doing. Fray Ambrosio[7] told me how good our *padre's* health is. I felt very grateful to you, for I think a major part of this is due to your care for him. Blessed be God who grants us so many favors. Many regards to Padre Fray Antonio.[8] Since he never answers me, I don't write to him. Insofar as possible try not to let him know about all the letters I write; tell *mi padre* not to say anything to him about them. My regards to Garciálvarez and anyone else you happen to see. It has just occurred to me to ask what you did for early Christmas morning.[9] Let me know, and remain with God. May His Majesty make you a saint, as I beg of him.

It is the third day of January.

6. My brother[10] wrote me yesterday. The freezing cold isn't doing him any harm. The favors he is receiving in prayer are

something to praise God for. He attributes them to the prayers of the discalced nuns. He is making much progress and doing good for all of us. Do not forget him.

Yours,

Teresa of Jesus

Turn the page.

7. I gave the paper from our *padre*,[11] the one he wrote to Garciálvarez, to a sister to copy, for it is excellent for every house and for Avila. It seems the devil made it disappear. Anyway, send me another like it in good script, and don't forget.

---

1. Jerónimo Gracián.
2. María de San José regretted her not having appreciated Teresa's presence enough when they were together in Seville.
3. Brianda de San José.
4. Leonor de San Gabriel.
5. Beatriz de la Madre de Dios; her mother is Juana de la Cruz.
6. Only two discalced nuns were living with the community of Carmelite nuns in Paterna; they had been sent there to reform it.
7. Ambrosio de San Pedro, a discalced friar who had come from Seville.
8. Antonio de Jesús (Heredia) who paid little regard to Teresa's requests.
9. In the Seville Carmel it was the custom to celebrate the early dawn of Christmas with special festivity.
10. Lorenzo de Cepeda, who is in Avila.
11. The paper written by Gracián limiting the powers of the confessor at the Carmel in Seville.

174. To Padre Jerónimo Gracián

Toledo, 9 January 1577

She rejoices that Gracián's health has improved and urges him not to overwork. She insists on the need for good confessors in the work of reform, which cannot be brought about through force. The final part refers in a veiled way to the vow of obedience she made to Gracián.

1. Jesus. The grace of the Holy Spirit be with your paternity, *mi padre*. Oh, how many blessings this old daughter of yours begged for you on reception of this letter that Padre Mariano[1] sent me today, 9 January. On the vigil of the Epiphany I had received the letter that came with the commission for Caravaca,[2] which it was my delight to be able to send on, within two days, with a very reliable messenger. Your letter, despite your effort to soften the news of your illness, distressed me greatly. Blessed be God for granting me the wonderful favor of restoring you to health. Then I wrote to those monasteries I could asking for prayers for you. I will have to write again to give them the good news, having no other way to inform them. What a blessing it was that this other letter arrived so quickly. Every day I feel a greater obligation to you for the care you take to bring me joy; so I hope that God will reward you.

2. I tell you I was most pleased that now, as though you had no other responsibilities, you are dedicating yourself to the confessional. It seems to me to be something supernaturally inspired. Nonetheless, we must not seek miracles from God, and it's necessary that you realize you are not made of iron, and that many in the Society[3] have ruined themselves through overwork. For days I have been weeping over what you tell me about the perdition of those souls who entered religious life in order to serve God. It would benefit them greatly to be given good confessors. If in those monasteries to which the discalced nuns are sent[4] you do not provide help of this kind, I fear for the fruitfulness of the effort. Oppressing them with exterior practices and not providing someone to help them interiorly would be like burdening them with a heavy trial. I had this problem at the Incarnation until the discalced friars came.[5]

3. Since you want to do this work only to help souls, then do so by finding someone who can guide them, and give orders that if there is a monastery of friars nearby, none of them be allowed to go and disturb these souls. I think Millán[6] is in Antequera; perhaps he would be good. At least his letters that you send me are truly refreshing. May the Lord be pleased to direct everything well.

4. Oh, how happy it makes me to see the perfect way in which you write to Esperanza.[7] For when dealing with letters that will be shown around, it is good that they be written in this way, even for your own sake. And how absolutely right you are in what you say about the reform, that souls are not to be conquered like bodies by force of arms. May God keep you, for you make me very happy. For my prayers for you to be efficacious, I would want to be very good—I mean so that my supplications might be heard. In my desires and purposes I never find that I am cowardly, glory be to God, except when it comes to Paul.[8]

5. Oh, what delight Angela[9] found in the sentiment he manifested on a page written after a letter he sent! She says she would like to kiss his hands repeatedly and wants to tell you to be at ease, for the matchmaker[10] was so qualified and made the knot so tight that it will be taken away only when life ends. And after death the knot will be even tighter, for the foolish striving for perfection will not be so excessive and the remembrance of you will rather help her praise the Lord. Her former freedom in fact kept her at war.[11] Now the submission in which she lives is far better and more pleasing to God, for she finds someone who helps her bring to the Lord souls who will praise him. And this is such a great consolation and joy that I share in it in large measure. May he be blessed forever.

Your paternity's unworthy daughter and subject,

Teresa of Jesus

---

1. Ambrosio Mariano de San Benito who is in Madrid.

2. This contained the provisions that allowed the nuns in Caravaca to conduct a lawsuit.
3. The Jesuits.
4. They were sent there for the purpose of reforming the communities.
5. St. John of the Cross was one of the friars who helped Teresa in this way.
6. A Carmelite friar of the observance.
7. It remains uncertain whom she is referring to by this code name.
8. Gracián.
9. A code name for herself.
10. Christ.
11. She seems to be referring to what she describes in her *Spiritual Testimonies,* 56. 1–3.

175. To Madre María de San José, Seville

Toledo, 9 January 1577

(Autograph: DCN, Valladolid)

Teresa responds to good news about the financial situation in the Seville Carmel, recommends Fray Bartolomé, and comments on the carols that were sent and Madre María's being almost provincial. She draws some comparisons between Teresa de Cepeda and Isabel Dantisco. She also gives her opinion about the material to be used for the nuns' habits.

For Madre María de San José, prioress.

1. Jesus be with you, my daughter. Before I forget, how is it that you never tell me anything about Padre Fray Bartolomé de Aguilar, the Dominican? I tell you, we owe him a great deal, for all the things he said were bad about that other house we bought were the reason for our having left it. As often as I think of the kind of life you would have had to live there, I can't thank God enough. May he be praised in everything. Be convinced that Fray Bartolomé is very good and that for matters

concerning religious life he has more experience than others. I wouldn't want you to forget to call for him at times. He is a very good friend and well informed, and a monastery has nothing to lose by having persons like him to speak with. Here is a letter I've written him; please send it on.

2. Before I forget, I liked the note you sent me about the alms that were received and your estimation of how much you have earned. Please God what you say is true, for I would be delighted. But you're a fox, and I fear you are using some ruse as you do in regard to your health in order to please me.

3. Our prioress in Malagón[1] remains the same. I have repeatedly asked our *padre*[2] if water from Loja[3] brought this far would help, for we could send for it; remind him of this. Today I have sent him a letter through a priest who was going down there to see him only on business. I was delighted to have that opportunity and so I am not writing to him now. You do me a great favor by sending me his letters, but be assured that even if there are no letters from him, those from you are most welcome—have no fears about that.

4. I have already sent your package to Doña Juana de Antisco.[4] There hasn't been time yet for me to receive an answer. For persons like her, it doesn't matter even if you have to spend something from the monastery, especially since we are not in need the way we were in the beginning. For when there is need, you are more obligated to your daughters.

5. Oh, how vain you will become now that you are almost provincial.[5] And how it amused me that you said with such indifference, "Here are some carols from the nuns," when you were probably the one behind them.[6] I don't think it would be bad for me to tell you—since you say that nobody there tells you anything—to be careful not to yield to vanity. At least it appears evident you don't want to say or do anything foolish. Please God your intention will always be to serve him, for there is nothing wrong in all this. I am laughing to myself to see how burdened I am with correspondence and yet spend time writ-

ing about trivia. I will easily pardon you for boasting of knowing how to guide the one with the gold ingots[7] if you in fact succeed, for I have a strong desire to see you without worry. Yet my brother is advancing so much in virtue he would willingly come to your aid in all your needs.

6. It's gracious of you not to want there to be any other like Teresa.[8] But you should know, certainly, that if my Bela[9] does not have the natural and supernatural grace of the other (for we have truly seen some of the things God was bringing about in her), she has more intelligence, talent, and gentleness, so that you can get her to do whatever you wish. It's extraordinary the talent this child has, for with some drab little shepherds and some little nuns and a statue of our Lady belonging to her, there isn't a feast in which she doesn't create something with these in her hermitage or at recreation, along with some verses for which she provides a lovely tune, all of which leave us amazed. I have only one problem: I don't know how to correct the way she holds her mouth, for she keeps it very tight and has a laugh that is extremely cold, and she always goes around laughing. Sometimes I make her open her mouth, at other times close it, and at other times tell her not to laugh. She says it's not her fault but her mouth's, and she's right. Whoever has seen the charm of Teresa, physical and otherwise, must notice the difference more—and here they do—although I do not manifest my own view; I'm only telling you this in secret. Don't say anything to anyone, but I would like you to know the trouble I'm going to in order that she correct the way she holds her mouth. I think that when she's older, it won't look so cold, and at least her words are not cold.

7. That is my picture of your girls so that you don't think I am lying when telling you how one is better than the other. I've done so that you may have a laugh. Have no fear that I will dispense you from all the work I give you in receiving and sending letters.

8. Most pleasing to me were the verses that arrived from down there. I sent the first ones to my brother and some of the others, for they were not all of equal merit. I think you could show them to the old saint,[10] telling him that this is how you spend your recreation, always speaking the language of perfection, and it is right to provide some diversion for the one to whom you owe so much. All that charity of his amazes me.

9. You ought to know that some adversity is being prepared for Padre Garciálvarez,[11] for they say that he is educating you in pride; tell him this. Now the nuns in Avila are anxious about what they will write you, for my brother told them you had sent him the letter so that they would respond. You should know that no one here wears, or has worn, worsted cloth except me, for even now with all the freezing cold, I have not been able to do otherwise—I have a great fear of the pain in my kidneys. So much has been mentioned to me about what I'm doing that I have a scruple about it. And since our *padre* took away my old habit, which was made of coarse wool, I don't know what to do. May God pardon him. Nonetheless, I say that because of the heat down there you couldn't wear anything but underskirts of light material, but not the same for the habit. The other matters little. Until they bring me what my holy prior is sending me, I don't know what to write him about, because I cannot say that I received it. I must write him a letter that I can send with the muleteer.

10. O Jesus, how obliged I am to him for what he does for you. How we laughed over Gabriela's[12] letter, and how we were filled with devotion on hearing of the diligence of our saints and also the mortification of good Garciálvarez. I pray earnestly for them. Give my regards to him and to all the nuns, for I would like to write to each one, so much do I love them. Certainly, I have an especially great love for each sister; I don't know why. My regards to the Portuguese nun's mother,[13] and to Delgada.[14] How come you never mention Bernarda López?[15] Read the enclosed letter for Paterna,[16] and if it doesn't sound

right you can make your emendations as the superior of that house. You have an advantage over me in knowing what would be the appropriate thing to say. God reward you for what you do for them—I mean this—for it gives me much consolation. It's a pity I don't know how to end when I write. Please God you will not gain the habit of charming others, as our *padre* has. May God charm you and transport you into himself, amen, amen.

Your reverence's servant,

Teresa of Jesus

11. Open this letter to the prioress of Paterna and read it, for I sealed it by mistake. And read the one for the prior of Las Cuevas to whom I have written again—although in such a hurry that I don't know what I said—and seal it.

---

1. Brianda de San José, whose illness was continuing.
2. Jerónimo Gracián.
3. Loja was an Andalusian city about 24 miles from Granada that had become famous for the healing qualities of its water.
4. Gracián's mother.
5. Gracián, who had to be absent from Seville for a time, gave María de San José the power to intervene in the monastery in Paterna.
6. The carols had been composed for the Christmas festivities that had just passed.
7. A Sevillian aspirant was promising to bring bars of gold worth 6,000 ducats as a dowry, which would have been a financial boon for the needy monastery, but the whole plan fell through.
8. Teresa's niece, a Carmelite aspirant at St. Joseph's in Avila, ten years old at the time.
9. Isabel Dantisco, Gracián's sister, eight years old and living in the Carmel of Toledo.
10. Hernando de Pantoja, the prior of the Carthusians at Las Cuevas.
11. Garciálvarez was the nuns' confessor in Seville. Teresa, in jest here, is probably referring to the austerity in dress that he was inculcating for the nuns.
12. Leonor de San Gabriel.

13. The Portuguese nun was Blanca de Jesús. Her mother, Doña Leonor Valera.
14. Inés Delgado, a benefactor.
15. The Carmelite daughter of Andrés López, Juana de San Bernardo.
16. A letter addressed probably to the prioress of Paterna, Isabel de San Francisco.

176. To Padre Ambrosio Mariano, Madrid

Toledo, Middle of January 1577

(Autograph fragment: Rome Generalate, O.C.D.)

Mariano was living in the Carmel of Madrid with the friars of the observance and had become sick. Teresa is now happy because he has recovered and also because in Toledo they have an archbishop after the see had been vacant for seventeen years on account of the process against its archbishop, Cardinal Bartolomé de Carranza. Her main purpose in writing the letter is to warn Mariano that the delicate matter of a foundation for discalced friars has been entrusted to two untrustworthy friars.

1. Jesus be with your reverence. Oh, how happy it made me to learn that you are well! May God be blessed forever, for in these past days I have been troubled about your health. Take care of yourself, for the love of God, for if you are well everything will work out all right. Indeed, when I see you sick or with some suffering, I understand how much I love you in the Lord.

2. Before I forget, don't in any way try to have Nicolao[1] come up here—that would be very unfortunate for the nuns in Seville—until that widow[2] has entered down there. The prioress has been writing me about how the devil is trying to block her entrance and how Nicolao is carefully dealing with this matter. Although she has a keen desire to enter, others are making her doubtful. You must realize how important this is to

the nuns, since with her dowry they could pay off their debt on the house.

3. I am very delighted with the good archbishop God has given us here.[3] I don't worry about that gossip of the friars; it will end up like their other calumnies:[4] they have found a man who longs to undergo such things.

4. As soon as I received your letter, I sent the archdeacon[5] his. I don't think he will do anything, and I would like us to stop bothering him. Since we now have an archbishop, I have thought we could perhaps get him to speak to the chapter since the matter has already become public.[6]

5. If Tostado[7] is being dealt with the way you say, don't be afraid that the friars will be an obstacle to it any more. I am delighted that you are going to see Señora Doña Luisa,[8] for we owe her a great deal in every way. She wrote to me saying she thought you were going to come to see her. The archdeacon said he would try to get them to answer the letter promptly and that he would come to see me. I will take care of the matter, for during these past days I haven't been able to attend to business affairs.

6. I did not dare express myself so openly in previous letters. Now that you are well, I want you to know that I can't wait to take the matter out of the hands of those blessed friars to whom Padre Juan Díaz[9] entrusted it, for Maestro Córdoba[10] is a cousin of Padre Valdemoro, and the other is a friend of both the prior and the provincial,[11] who believe everything that is told to them, which is not little. I truly believe that they were not, in their minds, deceptive, for they are both well-meaning men. But when it seems that one might be proceeding unjustly, one doesn't have much enthusiasm. From what we can figure out, our *padre*[12] will now be in Granada. The prioress[13] of Seville informed me that the archbishop[14] has sent word asking him to return to Seville; I don't know any more.

7. Thank Nicolao for what he is doing for the nuns. And for goodness' sake let him be if God calls him to more important matters than those of the archbishop, for God will provide someone else, although I certainly regret any trouble this would cause the archbishop; and that is how it should be, for we owe him a great deal. For some days I have been certain that the Grand Inquisitor[15] would be the archbishop here; this is fortunate for us, and even if in some things it seems he is not so....

1. Nicolás Doria who planned to join the discalced Carmelites, which he did at the end of March.
2. This wealthy widow never did enter the Carmel.
3. The new Archbishop of Toledo, Gaspar de Quiroga.
4. She is alluding to the first wave of calumnies against Gracián, who coveted sufferings for Christ.
5. The Archdeacon of Toledo was Francisco de Avila.
6. It seems there was a secret project underway for a foundation of discalced Carmelite friars in Toledo.
7. Jerónimo Tostado, visitator and vicar general for the Carmelites in Spain.
8. Luisa de la Cerda.
9. He was a priest and disciple of St. John of Avila and Mariano's friend and adviser.
10. A Carmelite friar of the observance from Castile.
11. Alonso Valdemoro was prior of the Carmelites in Avila. The prior of the Carmelites in Toledo was Alonso Maldonado, and the provincial of the Carmelites in Castile was Juan Gutiérrez de la Magdalena, familiar names in the story of St. John of the Cross's imprisonment.
12. Gracián.
13. María de San José.
14. Don Cristóbal de Rojas.
15. The Grand Inquisitor was Don Gaspar de Quiroga, who had a niece in the Carmel of Medina del Campo, Jerónima de la Encarnación. María de San José testified that Teresa had a presentiment that Quiroga would be named Archbishop of Toledo many years before he was.

177. To Lorenzo de Cepeda, Avila

Toledo, 17 January 1577

Teresa answers Lorenzo's questions about prayer and gives him advice regarding his contemplative experiences. In doing so, she manifests something about her own extraordinary experiences at the time and speaks of her secret writings. She also gives attention to the more ordinary things of life: sardines, sweets, money, repairs on a house, health remedies, and a hand warmer.

1. Jesus be with your honor. I already mentioned in the letter sent through the mail carrier from Alba that the sardines arrived in good condition and the sweets at a good time, although I would have preferred that you had kept the best for yourself. May God reward you. Now don't send me anything else, for when I want something I'll ask for it. Congratulations for having moved to our area. Nevertheless look over carefully the room I mentioned, for if repairs are not made it will be dangerous; it was in such a state that the danger was great. Anyway, be careful.[1]

2. With respect to the secret[2] in my regard, I don't mean that you should feel obliged under pain of sin, for I am very much opposed to that sort of thing and one can slip if not careful. It's enough that you know it would cause me distress. As for the promise, my confessor[3] has told me that it was not valid, which made me very happy, for I was worried about it. I also told him about the obedience you promised to me, which seemed to me inopportune. He says that obedience is good, but that you shouldn't promise it to me or to anyone else. And so I don't want you to do so, and even without the promise I accept your wish only reluctantly. I do so for the sake of your consolation on the condition that you don't make a promise of it to anyone. I rejoiced that you feel that Fray John understands you, for he has experience. And even Francisco has a little, but

not of what God is granting you. May he be blessed forever without end. With both of them you are now well cared for.[4]

3. How good God is! It seems to me he wants to show his greatness by raising up miserable people, and with so many favors, for I don't know any who are more wretched than the two of us. You ought to know that for more than eight days I have been in such a state that were it to last I would not be able to attend to so many business matters. From the time before I last wrote you, I've begun to have raptures again, and this distresses me because they happen in public sometimes. One came upon me at Matins. Trying to resist them doesn't help, nor can they be disguised. I'm so terribly embarrassed that I want to hide I don't know where. I plead with God not to let this happen to me in public. Beg this of God for me, because there are many disadvantages to experiencing them, and it doesn't seem to me that the prayer is better. I've been going around these days as though I were partially drunk; at least I am well aware that the soul is in a good place. Since the faculties are not free, it is a difficult thing to have to attend to more than what the soul wishes.

4. Prior to this, for about eight days I often found it impossible even to have a good thought, but was left in extreme aridity. In a certain way this highly pleased me, for I had spent some other days before those like the ones I am having now, and it is a great pleasure to see so clearly the little that we can do of ourselves. May he be blessed who can do everything, amen. I have said a great deal. The rest is not meant to be written or even spoken. It's good that we praise the Lord, each for the other; at least you should do so for me, for I am incapable of giving him the thanks I owe him, and so I need much help.

5. As for what you told me you experienced, I don't know what to say, for it is certainly beyond what you can understand and the beginning of many blessings, if you do not lose them through your own fault. I have already passed through this kind

of prayer, and the soul afterward usually finds rest, and sometimes undertakes some penances. Especially, if the impulse is very strong, it doesn't seem the soul can endure it without doing something for God. It is a touch of love that is given to the soul in which you will understand, if it goes on increasing, what you say you do not understand in the poem;[5] for it is a great affliction and pain that comes without one's knowing how, and most delightful. And although, as a matter of fact, it is a wound caused by the love of God in the soul, one doesn't know where it comes from or how, or whether it is a wound or what it is, but it feels this delightful pain that makes it complain, and so it says:

Sin herir, dolor hacéis
y sin dolor deshacéis
el amor de las criaturas[6]

6. For when the soul is truly touched by this love of God, the love it has for creatures is taken away without any pain, I mean in such a way that the soul is no longer attached to any love. This doesn't come about without this love of God, for whatever regards creatures, if we love them greatly, causes pain; and separation from them causes much more. As God takes hold of a soul, he gives it dominion over all creatures. And even if that presence and delight is taken away (which is what you are complaining of), as if nothing had been experienced in the bodily senses, to which God wanted to give some share in the soul's joy, God doesn't abandon it. Neither does he fail to leave it enriched with favors, as is seen by the effects afterward with the passing of time.

7. As for the lascivious feelings that you tell me about, don't pay any attention to them. For although I have never experienced this—for God in his goodness has always delivered me from those passions—I think it must happen because the delight of the soul is so great that it arouses these natural feelings. They will die away with the help of God if you pay no attention to them. Other people have spoken to me about this.

8. The shaking will also go away, for since it is something new the soul grows frightened, and it has reason to be frightened. As the experience repeats itself you will become more capable of receiving favors. Do all that you can to resist this shaking and any exterior thing so that none of this becomes a habit, for it is a hindrance more than a help.

9. As for the heat you say you feel, it has little importance; it could be somewhat harmful to one's health if excessive, but it will also perhaps go away as will the shaking. These things, in my opinion, have to do with one's physical constitution. Since you have a sanguine temperament, the intense movement of the spirit along with one's natural heat, which is gathered in the superior part and touches the heart, can give rise to this. But, as I say, the quality of the prayer isn't any greater on this account.

10. I think I've answered what you said about "feeling afterward as though nothing happened."[7] I think it may be St. Augustine who says that the spirit of God passes without leaving a trace just as an arrow passes through the air without leaving one. Now I recall that I answered this question. A huge amount of mail has arrived since I received your letters, and I still have many letters to write so that I don't have much time for this one.

11. At other times the soul is left in such a condition that it cannot return to itself for many days, but it seems like the sun that cannot be seen although its rays can be felt. So the soul seems to have its seat far off somewhere, and it animates the body, not being in it, since one or other of its faculties is suspended.

12. You are doing very well with your style of meditation, glory to God; I mean when you don't have the prayer of quiet. I don't know if I have answered everything; I always reread your letters, which requires a bit of time, and now I haven't had time to reread your last one except in bits and pieces. You shouldn't make the effort to read over those you send me. I never reread

mine. If some word is missing, put it in, and I will do the same here with yours. The meaning is at once clear, and it is a waste of time to reread them unnecessarily.

13. For those days when you are unable to be recollected during the time of prayer, or have a desire to do something for the Lord, I am sending you this hairshirt, for it is a great help in awakening love, provided that you don't wear it when fully dressed or when sleeping. You can wear it anywhere on the body and adjust it so that you feel discomfort.

14. I am fearful of doing this, for you are so sanguine that anything could alter your blood. But doing something for God (even a trifle like this) when one has this love brings about so much happiness that I wouldn't want us to neglect trying it. When winter is over, you will do some other little thing, for I am not forgetting you. Write to let me know how you are faring with this trinket. I tell you that whatever may be the punishment we desire to impose on ourselves, it does become a trinket when we remember what our Lord suffered. I am laughing to myself to think how you send me sweets, presents, and money, and I send you hairshirts.

15. Give my regards to Aranda.[8] Tell him to throw some of these enclosed pastilles around your room or close to the brazier, for they are very healthy and pure, and were given to me by the discalced nuns, who don't use anything out of the ordinary. However mortified you want to be, you can use them. They are excellent for rheumatism and headaches. Would you have this little package delivered to Doña María de Cepeda at the Incarnation.[9]

16. You should know that everything is agreed on for a very good nun to enter the monastery in Seville. She has 6,000 ducats free of any ties, and before entering she has given some gold ingots worth two thousand. She insists so much that they begin to pay for the house with them that the prioress is doing so and has written me that she will pay three thousand now. This made me very happy for they were carrying a great bur-

den. Well, as soon as the nun makes profession, the prioress will pay off everything, and perhaps even before. Pray for this and give God thanks, for in this way the work you began is coming to its conclusion.[10]

17. Our Father Visitator[11] is busy organizing different things; he is well and making his visitation of the houses. It is amazing how calm the province is and how they love him. The prayers are having their good effect, as well as the virtue and talents God gives him.

18. May God be with you and keep you, for I don't know how to stop when I speak to you. All send their best regards, and I do too. Give Francisco de Salcedo my best. You are right to be fond of him, for he is a holy man. My health is very good.

Today is 17 January.

Your honor's unworthy servant,

Teresa of Jesus

19. I wrote to the bishop to ask him to send the book,[12] for perhaps I will be stirred to finish it by writing about what the Lord has given me since. Or another large one could be written, if the Lord should desire that I be able to express myself; and if I can't, there would be no great loss.

20. There were some little things belonging to Teresa in the small chest;[13] I'm sending them back. The little round brazier[14] is for Pedro de Ahumada,[15] for since he spends much time in church, his hands must get cold. I don't need any money now. May our Lord reward you for your care and watch over you for me, amen. You can entrust the matter about the money to the prioress of Valladolid, for she will take care of it very well. She knows a merchant who is a great friend of the house, and a friend of mine and a good Christian.[16]

---

1. She is referring to Peralta's house, near the discalced Carmelite nuns in Avila, which Lorenzo had bought.

2. A reference to the contents of her *Life* and other private writings about her spiritual life.
3. Alonso Velázquez.
4. The two are St. John of the Cross and Francisco de Salcedo.
5. Lorenzo did not understand the first stanza of the poem Teresa had sent him "Oh Exceeding Beauty": Oh Beauty exceeding/All other beauties!/Paining, but You wound not/Free of pain You destroy/The love of creatures (see P. 6).
6. Without wounding you cause pain, and without pain you wear away the love of creatures.
7. She answered this indirectly in no. 6.
8. Jerónimo de Aranda, Lorenzo's servant.
9. María de Cepeda, Teresa's cousin, was a nun and ill at the Incarnation in Avila.
10. She is alluding to Lorenzo's generosity in financing the foundation in Seville.
11. Jerónimo Gracián.
12. The bishop was Don Alvaro de Mendoza, and the book was a copy of her *Life*.
13. This little chest was sent back from Avila at Teresa's request (cf. Ltr. 172.5).
14. These braziers were made small enough to be held in the hands to keep them warm.
15. Teresa's brother.
16. The prioress of Valladolid was her cousin María Bautista. The merchant was Agustín de Vitoria, who will later help Teresa with the foundation in Palencia.

178. To María de San José, Seville

Toledo, 17 January 1577

(Autograph: DCN, Bologna, Italy)

Teresa expresses her joy at the prospect of the wealthy aspirant entering the Carmel of Seville. She also gives practical advice for the nuns at Paterna on bringing about reform. She is exhausted from writing letters.

1. Jesus be with your reverence. Oh, my daughter, what a letter you sent me, filled with good news, as regards both your health and the nun who will render us so good a service as to pay for the house! Please God there will be no mishap. I pray for this urgently, for it would give me the greatest happiness to see you freed from the burden of debt. If she enters, help her along, for the love of God; she truly deserves it. I really wish I had more time so that I could write a long letter; but I wrote today to Avila and Madrid and elsewhere, and my head is in a terrible condition. I received your letters, the ones you mentioned. One that I wrote to Father Prior[1] of Las Cuevas—which I sent unsealed so that you could read it—must have got lost, for you say nothing about it. You must all feel lonely without our good *padre* there.[2]

2. Tell Señor Garciálvarez[3] that he must be a father now more than ever. I am delighted that his relative[4] has entered. Give her my best regards, and also send this letter to the nuns in Paterna[5] (for I have so great a desire to write to them) so that they will know that I am well and was delighted with their letter and delighted to know that Margarita[6] is going there and also a confessor. They shouldn't be surprised that those nuns do not become like us at once. To think they should would be foolish. Nor should they place so much stress on silence and other things that in themselves are not sinful. By taking away from people something they are accustomed to, you make them sin more. Time is needed so that God may do his work and you not exasperate them. We are praying very much for them here.

3. It is wrong for the prioress to allow them to insult her, unless she can do so by pretending that she didn't understand what was said.[7] Those who govern must know that, save for

matters concerning the enclosure, God will do the rest, and they should proceed with great gentleness. May he be with you, my daughter, and watch over you and all the other nuns. Give them my regards.

4. Tell the prioress of Paterna[8] to send me news of how they are. In all her letters she pays no more attention to San Jerónimo[9] (who may be the more efficient of the two) than if she were not there. And tell San Jerónimo to write to me; and both of them to put their trust in God so that they may succeed in everything, and that they shouldn't think they can do anything of themselves.

5. I am well. Mother Prioress of Malagón[10] is as usual. Let me know if our *padre*[11] took money for the trip, for it was my understanding that he didn't. Send him this letter, please, and do so with great caution taking care that it get to him quickly; but the carrier should be trustworthy. I am truly sorry about the departure of the public attorney.[12] It seems God wants us to know that it is he alone who does everything. Give my regards to the Carmelite prior[13] and to good Fray Gregorio,[14] and tell him to write me.

Today is 17 January. I am

Your reverence's servant,

Teresa of Jesus

6. I liked your Matins. I believe it must have gone well, for the Lord always helps at the time of greatest need. Don't fail to write me, even though our *padre* isn't there. I won't write so often, but that's because of the cost of the postage.

---

1. Hernando de Pantoja.
2. Jerónimo Gracián was absent from Seville at the time.
3. He was the confessor for the discalced Carmelite nuns in Seville.
4. Garciálvarez helped more than one relative enter Carmel.
5. The discalced Carmelite nuns who were living among the nuns of the observance in Paterna.

6. Margarita who had just made her profession on 1 January was going to Paterna to help out the others.
7. She is alluding to the rude language the nuns used toward the prioress.
8. Isabel de San Francisco.
9. Isabel de San Jerónimo.
10. Brianda de San José.
11. Jerónimo Gracián.
12. Francisco de Arganda.
13. The Carmelites of the observance whose prior was Juan Evangelista, appointed by Gracián.
14. Gregorio Nacianceno, at the discalced monastery of Los Remedios in Seville.

179. To Madre María Bautista, Valladolid

Toledo, 21 January 1577

Here Teresa rejoices over Casilda's profession and the pope's dispensation, but she is very tired. Gifted candidates should be accepted without concern over the dowry. Plans are in progress for a new foundation.

1. Jesus be with you, my daughter. My congratulations to you and your daughter on the occasion of her taking the veil.[1] May it please God that you have the joy of her presence for many years and that you both serve him with the holiness that I have begged of him during these days, amen.

2. I would love to write a long letter to answer yours, and certainly I now have the opportunity, but it could do me great harm, for I am very tired. I already had the thought of not writing until I had more time, but I am doing this so that you will know I have received all your letters. They are arriving here very safely. I am not sending the pope's dispensation,[2] for it is in Latin and I have not yet found anyone to translate it for me. I will send it to you later. They gave it to me yesterday, the feast

of St. Sebastian. It inspired the sisters with much devotion, and me as well. May God be blessed, for thus everything has been concluded. The fact that Señora Doña María[3] is happy makes me so as well, very much so. Give her my very best wishes, and a good embrace to my Casilda; how I would love to do so personally. It would have given me great joy to be there. You did well to pay great attention to the friars; that must have added more solemnity to the ceremony.

3. In regard to what you say about the other nun's[4] dowry, you told me that it would be necessary to take out fifty ducats for the trip. I asked you that if this were so, why you said the dowry would be six hundred ducats. Don't specify any amount. I don't remember about the trousseau. If she is all they say she is, it makes no difference if what she brings doesn't amount to much. For I tell you that we really need talented nuns. Be assured that she will bring what she has. You already know that if the nuns are very suited for us, we don't have to be so concerned about the dowry. Her mistress is saddened to death that they are taking her away, from what I have been told. And this must be true, so she will not give her much help. Her master has been well informed that it must be restored to him if she does not live up to what he says of her. I have been so insistent about taking this nun that I have wondered if it were not a temptation.

4. Read the enclosed letter, close and seal it, and entrust it to Agustín de Vitoria,[5] or to someone you are sure will deliver it promptly, for it is not possible to pay the portage and it must be delivered safely.

5. Father Visitator[6] is so avid about your taking that house that as soon as you are in agreement, I will send Antonio Gaytán.[7] He has been commissioned by the visitator to sign the deeds. Once this is decided, a way will be provided for dealing with that woman, for she is old and very sick, and something must be done because the need of souls there is great. May God direct the matter and watch over you, for you have

carried out your affairs well. May he be blessed who does it all, for you[8] are very wretched.

Today is 21 January.

Your servant,

Teresa of Jesus

---

1. Casilda de Padilla who made profession on 13 January.
2. Casilda needed a dispensation from the required age in order to make profession when only fourteen.
3. María de Acuña, Casilda's mother.
4. This person has not been identified.
5. A merchant friend who accompanied Teresa on her trip to Soria (F. 29.9) and had a daughter in the Carmel of Valladolid.
6. Jerónimo Gracián. She is referring to a foundation in Aguilar de Campo, which never materialized.
7. A friend of Teresa's from Alba de Tormes.
8. These words were written with an affectionate irony.

180. To Madre María de San José, Avila

Toledo, 26 January 1577

(Autograph: DCN, Valladolid)

Teresa expresses gratitude for the many things that the prioress in Seville has sent: an agnusdei, courbaril resin, balsam, brinquinillos, potatoes, oranges, and sweets. She sends some important mail for Gracián and gives instructions that it be delivered to him quickly and safely. Also sends news about Malagón.

For my daughter, Mother Prioress of St. Joseph's in Seville.

1. Jesus. May the Holy Spirit be with your reverence, my daughter. And I tell you that up here I could still add to the praises you bestow on our *padre*,[1] and with the greatest sincerity. I don't know what it is that induces me to love you so

much. I am now beginning to believe that you are reciprocating. May it please the Lord that this will be shown by our praying earnestly for each other.

2. Yesterday, the feast of the Conversion of St. Paul, the muleteer brought me your letters and money and all the rest. Everything was so beautifully wrapped that it was a pleasure to behold, and so everything arrived safely. May God reward you for the happiness you gave me because of what you sent to our *padre*'s mother.[2] No one thus far has done so much, and he is very happy. Why shouldn't I love you so greatly, for you do nothing but please me? I only coveted somewhat the *agnusdei*,[3] for I had been desiring these past days something to give to the administrator,[4] who doesn't fail to come to my help whenever I need something. He has worked especially hard for the house in Malagón, and will continue to do so. That house is undergoing such a dry spell that, given my nature, it is a great trial for me. In every house there is some little portion of the cross, but I do not regret it.

3. God has granted me such a favor by alleviating the worries of your house and allowing everything to go so well that I have nothing to complain about. It is especially good that you give me hope that you can pay part of the debt, for when I think of your having to pay more than a ducat a day, I cannot help but be troubled. Such disturbance is beneficial because it makes me pray that God will lift the burden from you. May it please His Majesty at least to lighten it, amen.

4. To return to the *agnusdei*, because of the one to whom it was destined, I did not want to fail to send it, for it gave value to the rest, which looked nice. Here we took some of the balsam, since Isabelita[5] told us they have a lot of it there, and three *brinquinillos*[6] so that you don't think my Isabelita is the daughter of a bad mother who will give her nothing; those that are being sent are enough. May God reward you, my daughter, amen, amen, amen. And for the potatoes, which arrived in good condition right at the very time when I have no desire to eat! And the oranges gladdened the hearts of some of the sick nuns, although they are not seriously sick. Everything else is very good, and the sweets as well, and there are many.

5. Doña Luisa[7] was here today, and I gave her some. Had I known that she would prize them so highly, I would have sent them to her in your name, for she is made happy by any little thing at all, but it seems better to us not to give much to these ladies. My brother[8] sent me the best box from those you sent him. I am glad that this didn't cost you anything. You can, then, when you think it is appropriate, ask for something for some person you consider worthy, or if you are given a gift, say that you are accepting it for so and so or some specific person; then you would not be giving away what belongs to the monastery.

6. I had not sent the prioress[9] of Malagón any of the sweets my brother sent me because of the high fever she has; they would kill her. And I wouldn't want you to send her any gift that would worsen her fever. But it would be very good if you sent her other things, such as sweet oranges, for she suffers from nausea, and other items suitable for a sick person. I would like so much to bring her here. Now I am hoping to get water from Loja. I have written to our *padre* to let us know if he stops there, for I will send someone to get it. I think she is being well cared for, for I insist very much on that. What she most prefers now are *mantequillas*.[10]

7. I would like to respond at length to your letters, for I have received them all, but the muleteer is leaving tomorrow and you can see all the correspondence I am including for our *padre*. I apologize for the cost of the portage, but this is something so important that it is necessary to have a good carrier. And you, too, should get Padre Fray Gregorio[11] and ask him for me to send the letters quickly with some trustworthy person—Diego[12] if he is there—for out of love for me he will do so gladly. If the person is not trustworthy or not going immediately, they shouldn't be given to anyone, for I wouldn't dare send some of the letters unless the carrier were very safe.

8. The orders sent me by the general while I was down there[13] have also been seen here. They forbid not only me but all the nuns to go out, so that the nuns cannot leave their monasteries to be prioresses or for any other reason. And if our *padre*'s commission were to end, everything would be destroyed. For although we are subject to the discalced friars, being so is not enough unless as commissary our *padre* declares we have this permission. His statement is sufficient for me and for the nuns, but at any moment something could happen to change this.

9. So, make every effort, for goodness' sake. And whoever is the carrier should wait for our *padre* to prepare the statement, which won't take much time, and bring it back to you. And if you can't send it with the muleteer, paying well for the portage, don't send it. Tell our *padre* that I told you to have him send it to you. It's strange how stupid we have been. The administrator has examined it, who is a great legal scholar, and Doctor Velázquez.[14] They both say this can be done and are sending instructions.[15] May God do what is most suited for his service, for they are ordering me to get this in a hurry, and so I am doing it.

10. It's lucky you didn't give the money to Antonio Ruiz,[16] for the manager[17] who was to bring it is here. I had already told the one who is in charge of paying the portage for me to give

the twenty reales so that we don't get in debt over trifles; but he will do what you say. We also took a little of the courbaril resin. I had wanted to write and ask you to send some, for some pastilles may be made from it with rose-colored sugar that are very helpful for my rheumatism. There is still a lot left over. Next Tuesday they will deliver the package with care.

11. I was especially delighted to learn that you are well. Be careful that you don't start acting as though you are healthy. We don't want to begin worrying again, for you made me go through some anxious moments. My regards to the subprioress,[18] to all the nuns, and to everyone. I will write soon through the mail carrier. No more now except that Casilda[19] has made her profession.

May God keep you, my daughter, and make you holy, amen.

Your reverence's servant,

Teresa of Jesus

Greetings to Garciálvarez and his cousin,[20] and to all.

---

1. Jerónimo Gracián.
2. Juana Dantisco, Gracián's mother.
3. A small wax disk with the image of a lamb, blessed by the pope in special ceremonies that took place every seven years.
4. Luisa de la Cerda's administrator, Juan Huidobro de Miranda.
5. Isabel Dantisco who lived with the community in Toledo.
6. These were delicate sweets popular especially in Portugal.
7. Luisa de la Cerda.
8. Lorenzo de Cepeda to whom María de San José had also sent sweets.
9. Brianda de San José.
10. Pastries made from sugar, butter, and eggs.
11. Gregorio Nacianceno, a discalced Carmelite at Los Remedios in Seville.
12. A letter carrier with this name known by Teresa.
13. Giovanni Battista Rossi was the general. The orders given to Teresa represented a decision made by either the general definitory or the general chapter of the order held in Piacenza in June 1575.

14. Alonso Velázquez, Teresa's confessor in Toledo.
15. The instructions suggested the manner in which Gracián by his powers as apostolic commissary could modify the orders given by the general.
16. A friend of Teresa's who was a resident in Malagón.
17. Probably Luisa de la Cerda's administrator, Juan Huidobro de Miranda.
18. The subprioress in Seville was María del Espíritu Santo.
19. Casilda de Padilla who had made profession in Valladolid on 13 January.
20. Garciálvarez's cousin was a novice, Jerónima de la Madre de Dios.

181. To Padre Ambrosio Mariano de San Benito, Madrid

Toledo, 6 February 1577

(Autograph: Vatican, Secretary of State)

Mariano seemed on the surface to be tough, but down deep he tended to be naive and fearful (not without reason). Teresa gives him the latest news about Gracián, Tostado, Fernández, and the nuncio. She gives some practical advice about how to proceed in Madrid and presents him with some tasks to carry out for her in that city.

1. Jesus. The grace of the Holy Spirit be with your reverence, *mi padre*, amen. For goodness' sake, don't use señora in the title when addressing me, for that's not our way of speaking.[1] What a great pity those stabbings in Andalusia are.[2]

2. Our *padre*[3] isn't writing anything to me except that he is well, although at times he does suffer some ailments. The waters from the spring at Antequera will cure him. I just don't understand this business of Padre Fray Buenaventura,[4] because I think you wrote to me that they had taken away his authority. If they have taken it away, how, unless they have given it back to him, can he send to have friars arrested? God has granted us a great favor in that our *padre* has carried out matters with so much peace. And as long as no one stops him short, he will

bring everything to a better conclusion, which is what I hope for in the Lord.

3. *Padre*, don't become distressed over the arrival of Tostado. Leave matters to our Lord, for this is his work and he will draw out much good from it all. It doesn't cause me any grief, because I see that all our affairs seem to be going upstream and they are going better than those that seem to be flowing with the current, because God is showing his power. What seems hardest is that he is coming just when the nuncio is departing,[5] for the commission of our *padre*[6] will then come to an end.

4. You should know that the nuncio sent for Tostado[7] some days ago, and the friars here, those of the cloth,[8] are surprised because of his delay in coming. I think they will send a messenger if they haven't done so already. They say their mistake lay in not having sent someone whose sole mission would have been to summon him.

5. All right, let him come, and we will see how this venture will end up. If the king remains as steadfast as he was, and the others, too,[9] his coming will have little impact. And should they change their opinion, this will be for the best; don't worry, *mi padre*. My counsel is that you should remain in the house that they gave you there; give up looking for property.[10] I can't bear those negotiations and setting aside the certain for the doubtful, for time is followed by more time.

6. Remain where you are for now. I believe it would have been better to have made a foundation for nuns than to negotiate for something for the friars better than what they would construct for themselves; have no doubt about it. I already saw the truth of this in Madrid during the eight days that I was there.[11] Let's not get overwhelmed, for these are serious matters and, as you say, the best thing about them is the persecution. And since nothing is achieved without it, all is going well for now.

7. I am delighted that our *padre* is not in Seville[12] and, as you say, it would be better if he came closer to us up here, although there is a house of discalced friars in Granada[13] where he could stay. But still, if his commission ends and Padre Tostado keeps his power, it would be good if they did not meet. Those who are here say only that Tostado must go directly to Madrid; that is the command the nuncio gave. They say that it is true he was given the royal ordinance,[14] but that the royal council has reconsidered the matter and changed their opinion.

8. Yesterday Pedro González[15] told me that he saw in a letter from Rome that another nuncio has been named.[16] I believe, *padre*, that he will come thoroughly forewarned against us; but if God is with us, etc.[17]

9. Padre Maestro Fray Pedro Fernández[18] is here. He has come to see me. I believe a month will go by before he goes to Madrid. Be sure, *padre*, he will not go against the *acts*[19] of the apostolic visitators. As for Padre Tostado, serve and obey him; but not in something contrary to the *acts*, for that would destroy us.[20] Therefore if he comes, however gentle you may be, you should remain firm on this point. This won't matter to our Father General[21] as long as we are under obedience to him. If the *acts* are observed—as they will be—it would be life-giving to us if Tostado took over the reform. May it do him much good! I am afraid, *mi padre*, that God will not do us this favor! May it please His Majesty to guide things for His greater service, and may whatever comes come.

10. I am sending a request for Juan Díaz[22] to do me the favor of attending to a business matter in Caravaca. You will see what it is because I am sending the report and the letters of recommendation for the Bishop of Cartagena.[23] I don't think it would be a bad idea for you to beseech the duchess[24] for me to send a servant to recommend the matter to him also. For it is said that he is very devoted to her ladyship. I don't know how to express in words the affliction those sisters are going

through, and they are so far away. Seeing the occupations....Don't fail to help them for the love of God.

May His Majesty be with you always, amen.

Today is 6 February. My regards to Father Prior.[25]

Your reverence's unworthy servant,

Teresa of Jesus

1. Mariano has done this before (cf. Ltr. 133).
2. She is referring to some violent actions among the friars on account of efforts to reform them.
3. Jerónimo Gracián.
4. Diego Buenaventura was the Franciscan visitator for his order in Andalusia.
5. Nicolás Ormaneto. His departure from Spain was a false rumor.
6. Jerónimo Gracián.
7. Jerónimo Tostado, appointed visitator of the Spanish Carmels, would arrive in Spain in mid-May, 1577.
8. The Carmelites of the observance.
9. She is referring to the other members of the royal council.
10. Mariano was living in a small temporary house in Madrid with the hope of establishing a foundation for the discalced Carmelite friars in Madrid.
11. She had spent some days in Madrid at the beginning of 1569 (cf. F. 17.5).
12. Gracián at the time was making his visitation of Andalusian monasteries outside Seville.
13. A monastery had been founded there in 1573.
14. An ordinance from the royal council was issued in December 1576 to impede Tostado from exercising his faculties as visitator in Castile. The rumor was spreading that they had changed their minds.
15. A canon and treasurer of the cathedral in Toledo. It was he who later provided refuge for St. John of the Cross when he escaped from prison.
16. This was another false rumor.
17. Cf. Romans 8:31.
18. The Dominican Pedro Fernández was appointed visitator of the Carmelites in Castile in 1569.

19. The decisions made by the apostolic visitators (Pedro Fernández, Francisco Vargas, and Jerónimo Gracián).
20. Teresa had to qualify this statement shortly afterward (cf. Ltr. 183.4).
21. Giovanni Battista Rossi.
22. A priest and friend of Mariano's in Madrid.
23. Gómez Zapata was then staying in Madrid. The monastery of Teresa's nuns in Caravaca still needed the permission of the bishop. The community ran the risk of having to go without Mass.
24. Either the Duchess of Osuna or the Duchess of Frías, both of whom were residing in Madrid.
25. The prior of the Carmelites of the observance in Madrid, Francisco Ximénez.

182. To Don Lorenzo de Cepeda, Avila

Toledo, 10 February 1577

Teresa has been seriously exhausted and the doctor has warned her not to continue writing letters past midnight and to get the help of a secretary. She continues in her role as spiritual director to Lorenzo. She speaks as well of the Satirical Critique, *Tostado, and problems in Caravaca.*

1. Jesus be with your honor. I have now recovered from the exhaustion of the other day. Since I thought I had too much bile and fearing that my condition would hinder me from observing the Lenten fast, I took a purgative. That day there were so many letters and business matters to attend to that I kept writing letters until two in the morning. This did my head so much harm that I believe the experience has been for my benefit because the doctor has given me orders never to go on writing after midnight, and that sometimes I should get someone else to write my letters.[1]

2. And certainly the work of letter-writing has gone to excess this winter. And I am very much to blame because I sacrificed sleep so as not to have my morning disturbed, and since I did my writing after the vomiting everything worked together

in doing me harm. On the day in which I took the purgative I became especially sick, but it seems I am getting better. So you needn't be disturbed, for I am taking good care of myself. I have mentioned this so that you will know why it will be, sometimes, that a letter for you is not in my handwriting or is shorter in length.

3. I am pampering myself as much as I can, and so I was annoyed with what you sent me, for I prefer that you eat them yourself. Sweets are not for me, although I did eat some and will eat the rest. But don't do this again for it displeases me greatly. Isn't it enough that I never send you any delicacies?

4. I don't know what *patrenostres*[2] those are that you say when taking the discipline, for I never told you anything like that. Read my letter again, and you will see what I said; and don't take the discipline any more than is mentioned there. In no way should it be taken more than twice a week. In Lent you may wear the hairshirt once a week provided that you remove it if you see it is doing you harm. Since you are so sanguine, I fear very much your doing this. And since taking the discipline can be bad for the eyesight, I don't agree to your taking it any more often. Also it is a greater penance to practice moderation after having begun, which amounts to breaking the will. You must let me know if the hairshirt makes you feel ill when you wear it.

5. That calm prayer you mention is the prayer of quiet which is described in that little book.[3] As for those sensual stirrings, so that you be tried in every way, as I told you, I see clearly that this is not a matter of importance and that the best thing you can do is to pay no attention to them. Once a very learned man told me that a man came to him extremely distressed because every time he received communion a terribly lascivious mood came over him (much worse than your experience) and that he had been ordered not to receive communion more than once a year, which was enough to fulfill his obligation. And this learned man, although he was not a spiritual person,

understood the weakness and told him that he should pay no attention to it and receive communion every eight days. And the trouble went away when the man lost the fear of it. So, you shouldn't pay any attention to this.

6. You can speak with Julián de Avila about anything, for he is very good.[4] He tells me he gets along well with you, and that makes me happy. Go to see him from time to time, and when you want to do some favor for him, give him an alms, for he is very poor and detached from riches, in my opinion. He is one of the better priests there, and it is good to have conversations like this, for everything doesn't have to be prayer.

7. As for sleep, I tell you and command you that it not be less than six hours. Consider how necessary it is for us who are older to take care of these bodies so that they do not tear down the spirit, which is a terrible trial. You wouldn't believe the displeasure I feel these days, for I don't dare pray or read, although, as I say, I am now feeling better. But I have learned my lesson, I'm telling you. So, do what you are told; this is how you will fulfill your duties to God. How foolish it is to think that this is like the prayer that did not allow me to sleep! There is no likeness between them, for I tried much harder to sleep than to stay awake.

8. Certainly I fervently praise the Lord for the favors he grants you and for the effects that follow. You can see how great they are by the virtues you are given, which you would not have been able to acquire even after much effort. You should know that the weakness of the head doesn't depend on eating or drinking; do what I tell you. The Lord is doing me a great favor by giving you such good health. May it please His Majesty to give you many years to spend in his service.

9. This fear that you mention, I think certainly must come from the fact that your spirit senses the evil spirit, and although you do not see it with your bodily eyes, the soul must see or feel it. Keep holy water nearby, for there is nothing that has so much power to make him take flight. It has often helped me.[5]

Some did not stop at causing fear, but tormented me greatly; this is for you alone. But if the holy water does not get sprinkled on him, he will not flee, and so it is necessary to sprinkle it all around.

10. Don't think your sleeping so well is a small favor from God, for it is a very great one. And I repeat, don't try to go without sleep; this is not the time for that.

11. It seems to me to be the sign of great charity to desire to take trials for yourself and to give delight to others, and it is a great favor from God that you can even think about doing this. But, on the other hand, it is great foolishness and a lack of humility to imagine that you could possess the virtues Francisco de Salcedo has, or those that God has given you, without prayer. Believe me and let the Lord of the vineyard work, for he knows what each one needs. I have never asked him for interior trials, although he has given me many and truly heavy ones in this life. One's natural constitution and humors have a large part to play in these afflictions. I am glad you are getting to understand the temperament of that saint,[6] for I would like you to be tolerant of his disposition.

12. You should know that I foresaw the effect the judgment would have on him and that he would feel hurt, but it wasn't possible to answer in a serious vein.[7] And if you saw my answer, I didn't fail to praise some of the things he said. Regarding my answer to your response, I couldn't have said anything else without lying. I tell you definitely that my head was in such a condition that I don't even know how I said what I did. That day the business matters and letters had so piled up that it seemed, as it does sometimes, that the devil had done this. And my night was a bad one, for the purgative did me harm. And it was a miracle that I didn't send a letter I had written to Padre Gracián's mother to the Bishop of Cartagena, for I had put it in the envelope addressed to him; I can't thank God enough.[8] I was writing to the bishop about what was happening between the nuns of Caravaca and the vicar general, whom

I have never seen. It seems to be a crazy thing; he's forbidden Mass to be said for them.[9] Now this has been taken care of, and the rest I think will turn out all right, which is that he accept the monastery. He can't do otherwise. Enclosed with mine were some other letters of recommendation. See what could have happened, along with my departure from here!

13. We still have fear of this Tostado, who is returning to Madrid.[10] Pray for this. Read the enclosed letter from the prioress in Seville. I was delighted with the one she sent me from you, and the one you wrote to the sisters, which certainly is charming. They all kiss your hands many times, for they were delighted with your letter, and especially my companion. She is the one who is fifty years old and came with us from Malagón. She is extremely good and most wise. At least she is extremely good in watching out for my well-being and shows great concern for me.[11]

14. The prioress of Valladolid wrote me about how everything that could be done in the matter was being done, for Pedro de Ahumada was there.[12] I believe that the merchant[13] who is in charge of the affair will do well. My regards to him and to my little boys,[14] especially Francisco, for I long to see them. You did well in letting the servant girl go, even though there was no occasion to do so, for they don't do anything but get in each other's way when there are so many. Greetings to Doña Juana, Pedro Alvarez,[15] and to all. You should know that my head is much better now than when I began this letter. I don't know if this is not caused by the delight I find in speaking with you.

15. Today Doctor Velázquez[16] was here, who is my confessor. I spoke to him about what you tell me regarding the silver and the tapestries you want to give up, for I didn't want you to fail to advance in the service of God because of my not helping you. There are cases in which I do not trust my opinion, although in this matter his opinion was the same as mine. He says that these things don't have significance as long as you

strive to see how little they matter and are detached from them, and that it is reasonable to have a home appropriately furnished since you have sons whom you will have to marry off. So for now be patient, for God usually always provides the occasion for carrying out good desires, and he will do so for you. May God keep you and make you very holy, amen.

It is 10 February.

Your honor's servant,

Teresa of Jesus

---

1. In the months that follow she will use a secretary to help with her correspondence.
2. Teresa's Spanish adaptation of the plural of Pater Noster.
3. *The Way of Perfection*. It seems Lorenzo had a copy for his use and study.
4. Julián de Avila was the chaplain at St. Joseph's in Avila. He accompanied Teresa on many of her foundations.
5. Cf. L. 31.
6. Francisco de Salcedo.
7. She is referring to the humorous critique she wrote on Francisco de Salcedo's answer to the question about the words "Seek Yourself in Me" (See *A Satirical Critique* in The Collected Works of St. Teresa of Avila, vol. 3, pp. 359–62.)
8. Both were in Madrid and after addressing the envelopes, she put the letters in the wrong envelopes. It was the night in which she got sick after staying up until two in the morning writing letters. The Bishop of Cartagena was Gómez Zapata; Gracián's mother, Juana Dantisco.
9. The foundation was made with the permission of the council of the Order of Knights by command of King Philip II and also with the permission of the Carmelite provincial, Angel de Salazar. Not happy about this, the vicar of the diocese, Andrés Hernández, gave permission for Mass until carnival time only, and then withdrew it.
10. Jerónimo Tostado. The royal council opposed his appointment (1576–77), so he went to Portugal to carry out his mission. He returned to Madrid in November 1577.
11. Ginesa de la Concepción (Guevara). A widow, she entered the Carmel in Malagón as a lay sister. She was one of those lay sisters who took loving care of Teresa during her final years.

12. The prioress of Valladolid was her cousin María Bautista; Pedro de Ahumada was her brother.
13. Agustín de Vitoria.
14. Lorenzo's sons.
15. Doña Juana was Teresa's younger sister; Pedro Alvarez Cimbrón was Lorenzo's friend and adviser.
16. Alonso Velázquez, a canon in Toledo.

183. To Padre Ambrosio Mariano de San Benito, Madrid
Toledo, 16 February 1577

(Autograph: DCN, Clamart, Seine [France])

Teresa is distressed about Mariano's illness and wants to be kept informed. Rumors about the nuncio and Tostado continue. She has consulted Pedro Fernández, the former Dominican visitator. The discalced friars need a Cardinal Protector. She is sending some letters that must be delivered very secretly.

1. Jesus. The grace of the Holy Spirit be with your reverence, *mi padre*. I'm not surprised that you are sick, but rather that you are alive after what you must have undergone there both interiorly and exteriorly. I felt infinitely distressed when they told me you were in bed because I know you. Since the illness is not dangerous, although painful, I was very much consoled. I was wondering if you hadn't caught some cold since you travel about so much. Let me know in a detailed way how you are, for love of God—for even if it is in the handwriting of Padre Miseria,[1] I will be happy—and whether you need anything. And let nothing cause you distress, for whenever things seem to be going well I am usually less happy than I am now. You already know that the Lord wants us to see that it is His Majesty who does what is good for us. That we come to understand this better and know that the work is his, he

usually permits a thousand setbacks. It is then that everything turns out best.

2. I am told nothing about Padre Padilla,[2] which troubles me, nor does he write to me. I would like him to be healthy so that he could care for you. Since Padre Baltasar[3] has to leave, may it please the Lord that you recover your health quickly. I am writing to those fathers about what was done and what I think about it. This messenger has no other task to carry out.

3. You know, *mi padre*, I have considered how much we will miss the good nuncio,[4] for, after all, he is a servant of God. His departure would trouble me deeply, and I think that what remains to be done is due to the fact that his hands are tied more than we think. I have a great fear that while negotiations are going on in Rome they will have trouble, for there is someone there continually trying to keep things tied up. I recall that the good Nicolao[5] said, when he passed through here, that the discalced friars would have to get a Cardinal Protector. Today I spoke with a relative, who seems honest, who told me that he knows a prudent person in the curia in Rome who if we paid him would do all that we want. I at once told him that I wanted to have someone there who could discuss matters with our Father General.[6] See if it would be good for the ambassador[7] to petition him in favor of the discalced friars.

4. You should know that Padre Fray Pedro Fernández[8] was here. He says that if Tostado[9] does not have power over the visitators, the *acts*[10] remain in force. But he says that if he does, we have only to be silent and obey, for he thinks that the commissaries cannot set up provinces and appoint definitors if they do not receive more authority than they have had.[11] So it is good that we look for help elsewhere. May God help us, for he will do everything, and in his mercy restore you to health quickly, as we are all begging him.

This messenger is not going to Madrid for any other purpose than to see what they want done and to get news about you.

5. Please tell Padre Juan Díaz[12] to deliver these letters to Padre Olea,[13] for they are very important to me, or send for him and give them to him very secretly if you cannot get them to him in another way.

Today is 16 February.

Your Reverence's unworthy servant,

Teresa of Jesus

1. Fray Juan de la Miseria, who was not a priest even though she calls him padre.
2. Juan Calvo de Padilla, the zealous reformer who had recently fallen into disgrace for having dared to sign Ormaneto's name to some documents without the latter's knowledge.
3. Baltasar de Jesús (Nieto).
4. Nicolás Ormaneto. He himself told Mariano about the rumor that he was going to be replaced.
5. Nicolás Doria.
6. Giovanni Battista Rossi.
7. The king's ambassador to Rome was Juan de Zúñiga.
8. The former Dominican visitator of the Carmelites in Castile.
9. Jerónimo Tostado.
10. The decisions made by former visitators.
11. Gracián was an apostolic commissary named by the nuncio.
12. Juan Díaz residing in Madrid belonged to a group of followers of St. John of Avila.
13. Francisco de Olea, a Jesuit.

184. To Padre Ambrosio Mariano de San Benito, Madrid

Toledo, 18 February 1577

(Autograph: Colegio S. Estanislao, Miraflores del Palo [Malaga])

The project of founding a house of discalced Carmelite friars in Madrid is meeting with many difficulties. The permission must come from the Archbishop of Toledo who is in Madrid at the time. A written opinion from the prior of the Carmelites of the observance was required but had not arrived. However, the Carmelite Maestro Córdoba makes it clear that the prior is adamantly opposed to the foundation. Padre Diego Pérez is helping Teresa with these problems as intercessor and messenger.

1. Jesus be with your reverence. Since I was waiting for a letter from the Carmelite prior,[1] I mean an answer from him, I had not sent a mail carrier. And that was fortunate because the one who is carrying this is Señor Diego Pérez.[2] I praised the Lord to see him free. It really seems that he is an authentic servant of God, for our Lord has tried him in suffering. It's a pity to see the condition the world is in.

2. If a letter from Señora Doña Luisa de la Cerda[3] is necessary for your negotiations, you should know that she is not here but in Paracuellos,[4] near Madrid, three leagues from there. This *padre* pleased me very much; he must have a great talent for every kind of good.

3. The Carmelite prior's decision, according to what Maestro Córdoba[5] said, in the presence of Señor Diego Pérez, is that until he sees the permission for the foundation of the monastery given in the handwriting of our most Reverend Father General[6] he will do everything he can to oppose it. He says that there is no reformer and that the nuncio[7] can do nothing except by means of one. And he is so convinced of this and that the discalced friars are acting against obedience, since they are not obliged to follow the visitators but their general, that it would have been useless for me to have said anything to the contrary. Diego Pérez could not even persuade him. He says also that the king, having seen how the discalced friars are living in disobedience, has given the command that his ordinance[8] coming through the royal council be issued.

4. I tell you that it is something for which to praise God, the way those fathers[9] carry on their affairs. I was quick to believe their assertion that they had a new brief, but it is the one from

the general chapter[10] given a year and a half ago. Maestro Córdoba saw it today. I think he is a cousin of Padre Fray Alonso Hernández,[11] and I don't know why—since he has it there—he doesn't inform them how matters stand.

5. If the prior's response to his lordship should arrive before this letter goes out, I'll send it along also; otherwise, let me know if I should send it to the archdeacon.[12] But until the king's orders are nullified, it is useless; once they are, quick action will be necessary. Let us avoid tiring others. Padre Diego Pérez could tell his lordship the prior's answer since he has heard it. I don't think the archdeacon could answer so quickly, and it's better that his lordship be informed. Please God your health is better, for I am very worried about you.

Today is 18 February.

Your reverence's unworthy servant,

Teresa of Jesus

---

1. The Carmelite prior in Toledo was Fernando Maldonado. Teresa was waiting for an answer that she could send to the Archbishop of Toledo, who was in Madrid.
2. Diego Pérez de Valdivia, a disciple of St. John of Avila, was calumniated before the Inquisition of Córdoba, and now freed from prison.
3. The noblewoman from Toledo who was Teresa's friend and benefactor (cf. L. 34).
4. Paracuellas de Jarama, where Teresa had wanted the monastery in Malagón to be.
5. A Castilian Carmelite of the observance.
6. Giovanni Battista Rossi.
7. Nicolás Ormaneto.
8. She is referring to a document of the royal council unfavorable to the discalced friars. The document has not been found.
9. The Carmelite friars of the observance.
10. The general chapter in Piacenza which was held in May, 1575.
11. A Carmelite of the observance who had recently been vicar of the monastery in Avila.
12. Francisco de Avila, the Archdeacon of Toledo.

185. To Don Lorenzo de Cepeda, Avila

Toledo, 27–28 February 1577

Lorenzo had written Teresa in concern about her health, but he also took the opportunity to seek further spiritual guidance. She responds assuring him that she is better and giving him the guidance he seeks. Some of the other topics deal with their relatives, the Inquisition, Tostado, and the goodness of some of the prioresses toward her.

1. Jesus be with your honor. Before I forget, as I have at other times, tell Francisco[1] to send me some well-cut pens. There aren't any good ones around here, they are a nuisance and make my task harder. Never prevent him from writing to me, for perhaps he may have a need to. He is satisfied with a few words for an answer and they don't cost me anything.

2. I think this illness will end up serving a good purpose, for I am beginning to get accustomed to having another do my writing for me. I could have already done so in matters of little importance; I will continue doing this now.[2] I am much better, for I have taken some pills. I think it did me harm to start fasting during Lent, for it wasn't only my head but my heart as well that was affected. The heart is much better, and even the head has improved the last couple of days, for that is what caused the most pain—which wasn't little. I was afraid I might become incapacitated for everything. It would have been a serious imprudence to try to practice prayer. And our Lord sees clearly the harm this would have done me. I don't experience any more supernatural recollection. It is as though I had never received any, which truly surprises me, for it wasn't possible for me to resist.[3] Don't be troubled, for little by little my head will become stronger. I take all the care of myself that I see is necessary, and even a little more than is the custom here. Otherwise I wouldn't be able to practice prayer.

3. I have a strong desire to get well. My illness is at a cost to you. For this reason I think my desire is good. I am in such a condition that I need to get better so as not to be a burden. Since mutton does not agree with me, I always have to eat fowl. The root of the whole problem is weakness from my having fasted since the feast of the Exaltation of the Cross in September along with all my work and at my age.[4] Well, to see myself capable of so little is bothersome, for this body of mine has always done me harm and prevented me from good. I'm not so bad off that I cannot write to you myself. I will not inflict this mortification on you for now, which would be a great one judging from myself.

4. As regards the mortification of not being able to use the hairshirt, you will have to pardon me for imposing it on you, for you must not be doing what you choose to do. You should know that the discipline ought to be taken for only a short duration. In that way, you feel it more and it is less likely to do harm. Don't hit yourself too hard; this won't matter even though you may think it is a great imperfection. That you might do something of what you would wish, I am sending you this hairshirt you can wear on two days during the week, by which I mean from the time you get up until you go to bed; don't wear it while sleeping. I was amused by the precision with which you count the days. This is a new practice, and I don't believe the discalced Carmelite nuns have attained to such resourcefulness. See that you never wear the other one; store it away for now.

5. I am sending one to Teresa[5] and also a discipline that she requested of me, a very hard one. Have it sent to her with my best regards. Julián de Avila[6] in writing me has many good things to say about her, which moves me to praise the Lord. May he guide her always, for he has granted a great favor to her, and to us who love her dearly.

6. In a certain way I had desired that you experience some aridity during these days, and so I was delighted when I saw

your letter, although what you mentioned cannot be called aridity. Think that what you experience is beneficial for many reasons. If this hairshirt fits all around the waist, place a little linen cloth between it and the stomach. And be careful so that if you feel any discomfort around the kidneys you do not wear it or take the discipline, for you will suffer harm. God desires your health more than your penance, and that you obey. Remember about Saul, and don't do otherwise.[7] You will be doing no small thing if you learn how to put up with that person's disposition, for I hold that the source of all those troubles and sorrows is melancholy, which has a tight control on him.[8] So, there is no fault or anything for us to be surprised about; we should praise the Lord that he does not give us this torment.

7. Take great care not to give up sleep and to eat enough at your collation, for with your desire to do something for God you will not notice anything until the harm is done. And I tell you that I had to learn my lesson for the sake of myself and others.[9] In a certain sense the daily use of the hairshirt is less of a burden because through habit the novelty of which you speak wears off. You shouldn't tighten it around the shoulders the way you usually do. Be careful that none of these things do you any harm. God is granting you a great favor by your being able to bear so well the lack of prayer, for this is a sign that you are resigned to his will. This I believe is the greatest good that prayer brings about.

8. There is good news about my papers. The Grand Inquisitor himself read them, which is something new—he must have heard some praise of them—and told Doña Luisa that they contained nothing the Inquisition would have to deal with, and that there were good things in them rather than bad.[10] And he asked her why I hadn't founded a monastery in Madrid. He is very favorable toward the discalced friars. He is the one who has now been made archbishop of Toledo. I believe Doña Luisa went to see him there where he is, and recommended this matter strongly, for they are great friends, and she wrote to me

about it. She will be coming soon and I will find out the rest.[11] You may tell this to the bishop, the subprioress, and Isabel de San Pablo (in secret, so that they don't tell anyone but pray for this matter),[12] and to no other person. This is very good news. My stay here has been beneficial for everything, except for my head because I have had more letters to write than elsewhere.

9. In the letter from the prioress you will see how they have paid half of the amount on the house, without touching the dowry of Beatriz and her mother.[13] They will soon pay everything with the Lord's help. I was delighted with it, as also with that letter from Agustín and to know that he is not going down there.[14] I was sorry that you had already sent a letter without mine. I will have one from the Marchioness of Villena for the viceroy—she is his beloved niece—when they can be sent safely. It grieves me to see him still involved in these things.[15] Pray for him, which is what I am doing.

10. Regarding what you say about holy water, I don't know the reason but only what I experience.[16] I have mentioned this to some learned men and they did not object to it. It's enough that the church uses it, as you say.

Despite all the difficulties that the nun reformers are having, many sins are being prevented by them.[17]

11. There is a lot of truth in what Francisco de Salcedo says regarding Señora Ospedal—at least that in this instance I am like her.[18] Give my best regards to him, and to Pedro de Ahumada also. I do not want to write any more except that you look to see if you could give Juan de Ovalle[19] what he needs to buy some sheep. This would be most helpful to him and a great act of charity, if you can do it without a loss to yourself.

12. I have changed pens so often in this letter that my handwriting will seem worse than usual; it is due to this and not to my being sick. I wrote this yesterday, and today when I got up

I felt better, glory to God. The fear of remaining incapacitated is worse than the illness.

13. My companion has been charming in her words about the stone paver.[20] She told me such wonderful things about him that I told her to write to you. Nonetheless, I think that since the prioress says he is reputable, she ought to know. I don't think he would do a bad job, seeing that she knows both workers; although I always thought that Vitoria would be best suited.[21] Please God the work will be done well, and may he keep you, as I beg him, for his service, amen. Today is 28 February.

14. Father Visitator is well. Now Tostado is returning, according to what they say. From the way all these affairs of ours are going one learns what the world is, for it seems to be nothing but a farce.[22] Nonetheless, I long to see him freed of all those affairs. May the Lord do as he sees is necessary. The prioress and all the nuns send their regards. The prioress of Seville pampers me as does also the prioress of Salamanca. And even those of Beas and Caravaca have not failed to do what they can; in short, they show their concern.[23]

15. I would like to be near you so that you could see all of this, and also, that I could have the pleasure of sending some of it to you. Even just now some very tasty shad arrived from Seville wrapped in bread. I was delighted for there is a great scarcity of fish in this town. Seeing the affection with which they do it is what pleases me.

Your honor's unworthy servant,

Teresa of Jesus

---

1. Francisco de Cepeda, Lorenzo's son.
2. In fact, she continued writing almost all her letters by herself.
3. She is referring to the ecstasies she was beginning to experience in public again some days previous to this (cf. Ltr. 177.3).

4. The monastic fast, observed also in the Carmelite order, began with the feast of the Triumph of the Cross (14 September) and ended on Easter. She was close to 62 years old.
5. Lorenzo's daughter, living in the monastery of St. Joseph's in Avila.
6. The chaplain for the discalced nuns in Avila.
7. She is alluding to 1 Sam 15:22: "Obedience is better than sacrifice and submission than the fat of rams."
8. This person is their brother Pedro de Ahumada.
9. From her own excessive work and penance she almost became incapable of doing anything.
10. The "papers" were the autograph of her *Life*. The manuscript had been in the possession of the Inquisition since 1575. The Grand Inquisitor was Gaspar de Quiroga. Doña Luisa de la Cerda was Teresa's friend and benefactor from Toledo.
11. Actually the Inquisition did not return Teresa's manuscript to her.
12. The bishop is Don Alvaro de Mendoza. It was he who had to send the autograph of Teresa's *Life* to the Inquisition. The subprioress at the Carmel was María de San Jerónimo. Isabel de San Pablo was also a nun at St. Joseph's in Avila, the daughter of Teresa's cousin Francisco de Cepeda.
13. The prioress was María de San José of Seville. Teresa was interested in paying off the debt on the monastery in Seville without touching the dowries of Beatriz de la Madre de Dios and her mother, Juana de la Cruz.
14. Agustín de Ahumada, Teresa's brother, lived in America. The Marchioness of Villena, Juana Lucas de Toledo, was a niece of the Viceroy of Peru, Francisco de Toledo, under whose rule Agustín was subject.
15. Agustín de Ahumada with his fiery and warlike temperament was a cause of anxiety for Teresa; she feared for his eternal salvation.
16. Cf. L. 31.2,4,6,9,10.
17. Some of the discalced Carmelite nuns from Seville, through Gracián's initiative, were engaged in reforming a monastery of nuns at Paterna.
18. It seems Francisco de Salcedo had compared Teresa to his housekeeper, Señora Ospedal, and Lorenzo mentioned this to his sister.
19. Teresa's brother-in-law.
20. Nothing is known of him.
21. Her companion is Ginesa de la Concepción, the lay sister who was helping her. The prioress was María Bautista of Valladolid. Vitoria is

Agustín de Vitoria, a merchant from Valladolid, to whom Lorenzo's financial affairs were entrusted.

22. The visitator appointed by the nuncio, Ormaneto, was Jerónimo Gracián. Jerónimo Tostado, appointed visitator at the Carmelite general chapter of Piacenza (1575), is returning from Portugal.
23. Five prioresses who show concern for Teresa's health are Ana de los Angeles (Toledo), María de San José (Seville), Ana de la Encarnación (Salamanca), Anne of Jesus (Beas), and Ana de San Alberto (Caravaca).

186. To Madre María de San José, Seville

Toledo, 28 February 1577

(Autograph: DCN, Valladolid)

At the beginning of February Teresa had become completely exhausted from too much work and incapable of doing any more letter-writing. The prioress of Seville had heard about her condition and sent her many gifts along with good news about their financial situation. She also communicated some unpleasant news about some calumnies and one of the nun's indiscretions. Teresa, now feeling better, comments on all of this.

For Mother Prioress of San José in Seville.

1. Jesus be with you, my daughter. Because of the illness described on the enclosed piece of paper,[1] I have not been writing to you, waiting until I felt better so as not to cause you any grief. Although I am much better, I can still do only a little writing; otherwise I immediately feel the harm it does me. But in comparison with how I was a short time ago, the improvement is great, glory to God. May he repay you for the good news you sent me, for I tell you it truly was good news for me, at least regarding the house. What a relief it is to see you free of debt. I have prayed hard for this here, and so will gladly tell about the good news.

2. May God be pleased to hear my prayer, for now with your riches, the office entrusted to you, and the fact that everything is going so well, you will need much help in order to be humble. It seems to me that God is doing this through the favors he is granting you. May he be forever blessed, for you can be very sure that it is he who is bestowing them on you.

3. Would that I could feel the same about San Jerónimo.[2] This woman really makes me suffer. Believe me, she should not have separated herself from me or gone where she could be in fear. Please God the devil will not cause us any trouble, or we will have our hands full. You should advise the prioress[3]— until my letter arrives—not to allow her to write a word and to tell her that I think she has become the prey of a very bad humor, and that if this is not so, the matter becomes worse. Since the muleteer is leaving next Monday, at which time I will send a long letter, I am not saying anything more here.

4. God help me, how rich you are! These nuns are amazed at what you sent me. The food arrived ready to eat, and all the rest was beautiful, especially the reliquaries. The large one will be better for Señora Doña Luisa.[4] We have fixed it very nicely, for it arrived with the glass broken, and we have put in new glass and made a solid base for it. I will say more about this when I write at length later. Remain with God.

5. I was most displeased that our *padre*[5] refuted the things said against us, especially the very indecent things, for they are foolish. The best thing to do is to laugh at them, and let the matter pass. As for me, in a certain way, these things please me.

I am most happy about your health. May God keep you for me, and all the nuns, amen. Pray for me.

6. Because this letter will perhaps go first, I didn't want to neglect writing by this means. I will write to Mother Subprioress,[6] because her complaints amused me. The prior-

ess in Malagón[7] is doing very badly. Today is the last day of February.

Your reverence's unworthy servant ,

Teresa of Jesus

7. For some days I have been holding on to the reply from our *padre's* mother.[8] It will go out on Monday. She also wrote to me at length about the joy you brought her.

---

1. This was probably an account of Teresa's illness done by one of the nuns in Toledo.
2. Isabel de San Jerónimo, the second of the discalced nuns who went to reform the monastery in Paterna, was psychologically unsuited to the task.
3. Isabel de San Francisco.
4. Luisa de la Cerda, who shared in the gifts from Seville.
5. Jerónimo Gracián had become the object of coarse calumnies because of his seeking to reform the monastery of nuns at Paterna.
6. The subprioress in Seville was María del Espíritu Santo.
7. Brianda de San José.
8. Juana Dantisco, Gracián's mother.

187. To Padre Ambrosio Mariano de San Benito, Madrid

Toledo, 28 February 1577

Teresa gives advice to Mariano urging him to obey the nuncio, keep his temper in check, and not go directly to the king with his requests. She informs him about the calumnies in Andalusia and her own recent illness.

1. Jesus be with your reverence, *mi padre*. Today Señor Don Teutonio,[1] who is in Madrid, wrote me that the nuncio[2] is not going to leave. If this is true—unless you stay in Alcalá under the pretext of being ill—you must in no way give the impression that you are disobedient.[3]

2. You should know, *padre*, from what I understand, that these fathers[4] would now like to be our friends; and until we see what God ordains, it is good to be compliant, as you have been. Certainly I do not cast blame on the nuncio, but the devil's battery is of the kind that nothing would surprise me. You shouldn't fear that no one will dare defend you, for the Lord is your keeper. Since up to the present he has granted us the favor of helping you hold your temper in check, may you continue doing so. Let this be your cross for now, certainly no small one. If the Lord had not helped you in a special way, I don't believe you would have been able to put up with so much.

3. As for the Council's response,[5] there is nothing to hope for. Don't you see that these are all polite words? What need is there to have this directive sent from here so that it can be annulled, since they have a copy of it there and know that it is authentic? Now is not the time. Let us wait a little, for the Lord knows what it is he is doing better than we know what it is we want.

4. What do you think of how they make us appear in this piece of writing? I don't know why one tries to refute these things. Our *padre*[6] is making a mistake, for this is something utterly base. For the love of God, don't show it to anyone, for they would think it imprudent to pay any attention to such foolishness or talk about it. I think it would be very imperfect to do anything about it, except laugh.[7]

5. You should know, *mi padre*, that my heavy correspondence and many other duties that I tried to handle all alone have caused a noise and weakness in my head.[8] And I have been given orders that unless it's very necessary I should not be writing letters in my own hand, and so I will not be long. I only say that as regards what you said you want to procure from the king, don't think about doing it until you have considered it most carefully, for in my opinion we would lose much

of our credibility. God will do what is necessary by another means. May he watch over you for me.

Your reverence's servant,

Teresa of Jesus

---

1. Teutonio de Braganza, the future Archbishop of Ebora.
2. Nicolás Ormaneto. It had been rumored that he was going to be relieved of his office.
3. Mariano was living outside the monastery because he wanted to have more freedom to deal with the business of the discalced friars. The nuncio had disapproved of this.
4. The Carmelites of the observance.
5. The answer to a petition probably made by the discalced friars that the directive issued against them be withdrawn (cf. Ltr. 184.3).
6. Jerónimo Gracián who is carrying out his commission as visitator of the Carmelites in Andalusia.
7. She is referring to calumnies uttered against the discalced Carmelites in Andalusia.
8. Only now does she inform Mariano of the illness she has suffered from overwork and that she must not be writing letters.

188. To María de San José, Seville

Toledo, 1–2 March 1577

Though not yet well enough to be writing her own letters, Teresa dispenses herself and sends a four-page letter in her own hand to María de San José. After receiving many gifts from Seville she is anxious to express her gratitude. Also there is an urgent matter concerning one of the discalced nuns in Paterna who was publicly manifesting some unusual prayer experiences. Such publicity could incur criticism for the nuns and trouble with the Inquisition. Finally, she sends along her little work A Satirical Critique *together with the writings that were the object of her satire.*

For Mother Prioress of San José in Seville.

1. Jesus. The grace of the Holy Spirit be with your reverence, my daughter. After so much good news and the many gifts you have sent me, I have every reason to write a long letter; at least doing this would make me very happy. But I wrote you yesterday and the labor this winter of letter-writing has so weakened my head that I have been truly sick.[1] I am much better, but nevertheless, I almost never write in my own hand, for they say I must not do so if I want to recover completely.

2. Oh, how delighted I was with the beautiful things you sent me through the administrator.[2] You wouldn't believe how much work he takes on for the monastery in Malagón and how ready he is to help me. And don't think it takes little effort to keep the construction work going well, for there are a thousand things that have to be attended to with the workmen. I gave him the small reliquary. Both are very lovely, but the large one is still better; especially the way it was embellished here, for it arrived with the glass broken as I wrote you.[3] New glass was put in that looks very nice. The base was twisted, so we had an iron one cast. This should have been done in the first place. I also gave him the jar, I mean the little cup, which was the most charming I've ever seen. Don't think that because I have to wear a habit of finer material, things have got so bad that I need to drink from something as nice as that! I also gave him the bottle just as it was. He greatly appreciated this. He is a man of integrity. Well, from down there you have helped your house in Malagón.[4] They wouldn't let me give away the orange-flower water, because it gives life to the prioress[5] and is beneficial for me too, and we didn't have any. Ask for some,

on my part, from the mother of the Portuguese nun[6] and have it sent to us. Do this out of charity—that is the condition.

3. Oh, how happy I am that you have paid off the debt on the house. But until that nun is professed we ought not rejoice too much. It is true, though, that if that should not happen, God will provide in another way. Pray hard that he might be pleased to take away this trouble I have with my head. Today, by the mail carrier, I sent you an account of what in part brought it on.[7]

4. Your manner of prayer makes me happy. Recognizing that you have it and that God is doing you a favor is not a lack of humility since you understand that it is not your doing but his. That is how we know that the prayer is from God. I greatly praise him that you are faring so well, and I will try to give him joyful thanks as you ask me. Ask God that I might be the kind of person whose prayers he will answer.

5. In regard to Beatriz,[8] her prayer is good, but insofar as possible avoid paying attention to these things in conversations or any other way. You know this depends very much on the prioress. San Jerónimo[9] did not speak of that here, because the prioress[10] immediately interrupted and scolded her, and so she kept quiet. And you saw that when I was there she never carried on in this way. I don't know whether we were wrong in letting her leave our midst.[11] Please God things will turn out well.

6. Think what would have happened if the others rather than the prioress had found the page![12] May God pardon the one who has told her to write. Our *padre*[13] would like me to write to her in a severe manner with respect to this. Read the enclosed letter that I am writing her, and if it seems all right to you, send it to her. You are doing extremely well in not allowing anyone to talk about it to others. The prioress in Beas[14] writes me that the nuns speak only of their sins with their confessor and that they are all finished within a half hour. She tells me that it should be like this everywhere, that they are all very

much at peace, and that they have a great love for their prioress in whom they confide. Since I have some experience in this matter, you could ask them why they don't write to me but go and ask someone who perhaps doesn't have as much I do. And in a matter like this it would be fitting more than in any other. And tell San Francisco[15] to make her eat meat after Lent is over and not let her fast.

7. I would like to know what she means when, without explaining, she speaks of the great force that God uses over her. What a trial it is that she now goes around weeping all the time in front of others and is seen as ready to write at any moment. Get what she wrote and send it to me. And remove any hope she has of speaking about this with anyone other than our *padre*, because those conversations have ruined her. Be aware that this language is understood there less than you think. However if it is used in confession and with Padre Acosta[16] no harm can come. But I know well that it is less fitting for her than for anyone. It is a good thing the order was given that in Paterna more leeway could be allowed to the nuns, although it would have been better if from the start they had required only what was obligatory.[17] In these matters of reform, if the nuns obtain something by shouting, it seems to them at once that they will obtain everything else in the same way. You did very well in advising them to live in community.

8. I have not given the letters or reliquary to Doña Luisa[18] because she was away and returned the day before yesterday. I am waiting for all the visits to die down. Pray for her and for Doña Guiomar,[19] for they have many trials.

9. Since I am not writing this letter all at once, I don't know whether I may have forgotten to answer any of the things you asked about. Since these bolts I am sending are similar to the ones that are here on the grille in the choir, I don't think it's necessary that they be more attractive, although I suppose you won't be satisfied with them. But do as they do here, for the nuns here don't consider themselves less refined than you,

and a little bolt is better than something else, for I don't know what kind of locks you want. The crucifixes are being made. I believe they will cost a ducat.

10. All the nuns ask for your prayers, and Isabel[20] was delighted with the sweets and the coarse woolen cloth. May God reward you. As for myself, I have plenty of clothes. Do you think it doesn't sadden me to have nothing to send you? It certainly does. But the barrenness of this region is incredible except for the quinces when they are in season, and even then, the quinces down there are much better. The nuns were delighted with the spices and the *catamaca*.[21] They didn't allow me to send any to anyone—I very much would have liked to—for many have great need for it.

11. Enclosed are the responses[22] to the question I posed to my brother. The respondents had decided to submit their answers to the judgment of the nuns at St. Joseph's in Avila. The bishop[23] was present and told them to send the answers to me so that I might judge them, just when my head was in too miserable a state even to read them. Show them to Father Prior and to Nicolao,[24] but you must explain to them what was being done, and don't let them read the judgments before reading the answers they submitted. And if you can, send them back so that our *padre* can enjoy them—for that is why they sent them to me from Avila—even though this may not be along the muleteer's way.

12. I am sending you this letter that my brother[25] wrote me (he writes many about the favors that God grants him and this one was near at hand). I think it will make you happy since you are fond of him. Tear it up right away, and remain with God, for I'll never end this and writing is bad for me. May His Majesty make you a saint.

13. Now they have just given me a letter written by our *padre* from Málaga fifteen days ago, I mean from tomorrow. He is well, glory to God. Today is 2 March.

My regards to all, and let me know about Fray Bartolomé's[26] health.

Your reverence's servant,

Teresa of Jesus

14. Be grateful that I wrote this out myself, for I haven't been writing my own letters even to St. Joseph's in Avila.[27] Yesterday I wrote to you and to our *padre* through the mail carrier. Thus, I'm not doing so now.

---

1. She had been suffering for about a month from an illness that was brought on through overwork.
2. Luisa de la Cerda's administrator, Juan Huidobro de Miranda.
3. In Ltr. 186.4.
4. María de San José had made her profession in Malagón.
5. Ana de los Angeles.
6. The Portuguese nun was Blanca de Jesús María; her mother was Leonor de Valera.
7. See Ltr. 186.1.
8. Beatriz de la Madre de Dios, a nun in the Seville Carmel.
9. Isabel de San Jerónimo, one of the three who went to help reform the community in Paterna. She and Beatriz showed a certain lack of balance in their prayer experiences.
10. One of the prioresses in Castile before Isabel de San Jerónimo went south to Andalusia.
11. She went with the group to Paterna.
12. One of her confessors told Isabel to write down her experiences in prayer. One of her pages was mislaid and fortunately landed in the hands of the prioress in Paterna, Isabel de San Francisco.
13. Jerónimo Gracián.
14. Anne of Jesus; it was she for whom St. John of the Cross wrote his commentary on *The Spiritual Canticle.*
15. Isabel de San Francisco was the prioress in Paterna.
16. The Jesuit Diego de Acosta.
17. It seems those discalced nuns who went to reform the community in Paterna started out by demanding more than what the nuns were obliged to by their constitutions.

18. Luisa de la Cerda.
19. Guiomar Pardo, Doña Luisa's daughter.
20. Isabelita Dantisco, Gracián's young sister living in the Carmel in Toledo.
21. She wrote *catamaca* instead of *tacamaca*. It was a resin that was used as a sedative.
22. These were the answers to the question about the meaning of the words "Seek Yourself in Me" (See SC. intro.)
23. The Bishop of Avila, Don Alvaro de Mendoza.
24. The prior of the Discalced friars in Seville, Antonio de Jesús, and Nicolás Doria.
25. Lorenzo de Cepeda.
26. Bartolomé de Jesús, one of the discalced friars in Seville.
27. What follows was written on the outside next to the address.

189. To Padre Ambrosio Mariano de San Benito, Madrid

Toledo, 15 March 1577

With little hope of receiving permission quickly for his proposed foundation in Madrid, Mariano moved out of the monastery of the Carmelites of the observance and was living in the homes of his secular friends. Teresa is not happy with this arrangement, and also fears his propensity to anger and arrogance. She has some firm words for him.

1. Jesus be with your reverence, my *padre*. I don't know why you neglected to write to me through this muleteer and acknowledge that you have received the answer from the Council which I sent you last Thursday. I would like to know how you can be in that city without living with the friars, I mean in the Carmelite monastery, since the nuncio[1] has insisted so much on this. It's only right that we not displease him in anything; it would not be fitting for us to do so. I would very much like to speak with you because there are things that can be spoken but not written.

2. Up until now with the expectation of having a house there, any arrangement seemed acceptable. But believe me, *padre*, so prolonged a stay, and with four discalced friars, doesn't seem right to anyone, and it attracts attention, and not just the attention of the friars of the cloth,[2] which we don't have to be concerned about. But I would not want us to provide the slightest occasion for criticism by doing anything that would give the appearance of non-compliance. Pay no attention to the fact that the marquis[3] tells you the nuncio would not be displeased.

3. I also beg you to speak with great caution, whether you have any complaints about the nuncio or not. Because of your frankness—with which I am familiar—I fear that you are careless about this; please God nothing will reach his ears. You must realize that all the devils are waging war against us, and that it is necessary to look for support only from God. This we do by obeying and suffering, and then he will take over.

4. I would think it very fitting that when Passion Sunday comes you and the other discalced friars go to your monastery in Pastrana or Alcalá, for it isn't the appropriate time for carrying on business.[4] If there is some business to be attended to, it's enough that the licentiate Padilla[5] be there to take care of it as he has always been. Days such as these are not the time for religious to be outside their monasteries. It wouldn't look good to anyone, much less to the nuncio who is so retiring. It would be very consoling to me if you did this. Think it over carefully and realize that it is the appropriate thing to do. Otherwise you will have to live with the friars of the cloth, which I think would be worse.

5. Be very careful not to talk with the archbishop.[6] Once he is informed, it isn't fitting for you to insist even if you have the opportunity to speak with him. He has accepted responsibility for the matter. After this, the best way to carry on the business is to be silent and speak with God.

6. This letter has been written after much reflection and with more than one reason, all of which I cannot go into. But I see

that it is very advisable for you to do what I am asking. No harm could come to us from your doing so and a great deal if you do not do so. When we see that something is right, there is no reason to delay. Our Lord gives us many opportunities in which to merit, and I am aware of those you have had and do have, for I am amazed by how you have controlled your temper. But now prudence is necessary and God is giving it to you as he did in that matter with the bishop. May he be blessed forever, for in the end he will favor his work.

7. They say that Tostado[7] is coming by way of Andalusia. God be with him whatever may happen. I think it will be better to have to contend with him than with the one we have had to contend with up until now. May God give us light, and may he watch over you and those fathers who are with you. I am a little better.

Today is 15 March.

Yours,

Teresa of Jesus

---

1. Nicolás Ormaneto. He wanted Mariano to reside in a monastery while negotiating in Madrid for a foundation for discalced Carmelite friars there.
2. The Carmelites of the observance.
3. The Marquis of Mondejar, Luis Hurtado de Mendoza, who was also the Count of Montilla and a good friend of Mariano's.
4. She wanted them to spend Holy Week in their monastery.
5. Juan Calvo de Padilla.
6. The archbishop of Toledo, Gaspar de Quiroga; it was from him that he had to obtain the permission for founding a monastery in Madrid.
7. Jerónimo Tostado. The nuncio did not want him to choose Andalusia as the place in which to begin the visitation.

190. To Madre María de San José, Seville

Toledo, 9 April 1577

(Autograph: DCN, Valladolid)

She tells about the crucifixes she is sending; her grief over the death of a lay sister in Toledo; and her joy that Nicolás Doria has joined the discalced Carmelites. She wants to send her Way of Perfection *to the Carthusian prior.*

For Mother Prioress of San José of the Carmel in Seville.

1. Jesus be with your reverence, my daughter. I have written you a letter through the mail carrier. I believe it will arrive sooner than this one. Now I am sending off the crucifixes, which are no better or worse than the others. They only cost nine reales apiece, and I even think a *cuartillo*[1] less. I have been told that they couldn't have been made for anything lower than a ducat. You will have to get a turner to make the holes. Since they brought them during the Easter feast days I wasn't able to have this done, so I'm sending them as they are. It's more convenient. The crosses are made from ebony wood. They are not expensive, so I would have liked to send you even more.

2. I long for news about good Bernarda.[2] I have already written to you of how God took a sister[3] from this house to himself, which caused me deep grief.

3. In regard to your speaking to Garciálvarez[4] about your prayer, there is no reason to stop, for there is nothing in it that needs correcting. And this is true also for those who proceed as you do. It would seem strange for you to desist, especially since this would not conform to what our Father Visitator[5] requests. Give him my best regards.

4. Oh, how I would like to send my little book to the prior of Las Cuevas,[6] who has asked for it. We owe him so much that I would like to please him in this way. And it wouldn't harm

Garciálvarez to learn something about our procedure, especially in prayer. If the book were there I would give it to the prior, for we have no way of compensating this saint in the way he deserves, other than by doing what he asks of us. Perhaps this will be possible one day. It has been such a busy day for me that I cannot go on at greater length.

5. I have already written informing you that I received what the muleteer brought, although it didn't arrive in good condition. This is not a good time to send such things, because of the heat. Don't send me anything but the orange-flower water, for the flask broke. And if you can find any, send some crystallized orange blossoms, dry, and sprinkled with sugar, for I will pay for their cost. Otherwise send the sweets. But I prefer the orange blossoms, whatever the price, even if only a small quantity.

6. I've already told you that one of our nuns has gone to heaven, and about the trials we have had, and how delighted I am with the entrance of Nicolao.[7] I greatly appreciate your solicitude for the nuns in Paterna, for they write to me about it. I think it was God's providence that someone with your charity and talents remained down there for the good of us all. I hope that these good qualities he will greatly increase in you.

7. I don't think I will be able to write to Father Prior of Las Cuevas. I'll do so another day. Don't let him know about these letters. My regards to all the nuns, especially Gabriela,[8] to whom I would like to write. Oh, how I long to see that widow inside the monastery and professed.[9] May God bring this about, and watch over you, amen. I also sent you a letter of Doña Luisa's.[10] It's the last day of Easter.

Your unworthy servant,

Teresa of Jesus

8. You should know that the brother of San Francisco[11] was dismissed from the Society of Jesus, for which I was sorry. I didn't dare write to her lest I cause her grief, but perhaps it

would be better for her to learn of it from us. You will see from the enclosed page that I sought to have assurance of this through a friend of his in the Society who is in Salamanca; it contains what the prioress[12] wrote me. I am happy that he has enough to eat. Perhaps he will be better off, even for God's service. If you think it wise, tell her, and send her these lines along with mine.

9 Padre Fray Bartolomé de Aguilar[13] says that he would willingly speak to your community more often, but that he hasn't been asked, and that since he is subject to his superior he needs to be asked. Don't fail to invite him to preach some sermons, and invite him to visit you, for he is very good. You can certainly read the letters. Why not?[14]

---

1. An old coin worth a fourth of a real.
2. Bernarda de San José (Matías) in the monastery in Seville. She had already died.
3. She is probably referring to Catalina de San Miguel.
4. The confessor at the monastery in Seville got involved in questions concerning the prayer of some nuns in the community who were not too balanced.
5. Jerónimo Gracián.
6. The Carthusian Hernando de Pantoja. The "little book" was the *Way of Perfection*. Her brother Lorenzo de Cepeda was reading it at this time.
7. Nicolás Doria, an ordained priest who had entered the discalced Carmelite friars on 24 March 1577.
8. Leonor de San Gabriel.
9. It doesn't seem she ever did enter.
10. Luisa de la Cerda.
11. Isabel de San Francisco, who was the prioress in Paterna.
12. Ana de la Encarnación, the prioress in Salamanca.
13. A Dominican priest.
14. This whole section in no. 9 was written outside on the envelope.

191. To Padre Ambrosio Mariano, Madrid

Toledo, Middle of April 1577

(Autograph: DCN, Segovia)

She feels somewhat better after having been bled. With much relief that Mariano has consented to submit to the nuncio and live in a monastery with the Carmelites of the observance, she cautions him to be careful with his words. Tostado has not received permission from the royal council to begin his visitation.

1. Jesus be with your reverence. Oh, how I would like to make this a long letter! For your letter brought me great joy. But I was bled yesterday and they've ordered me to be bled again today. This has hindered me from writing. I didn't think the mail carrier was going to leave so soon, and he is rushing me. The bloodletting has restored life to my head. I will soon be well, if God so wills.

2. What made me so happy is that you are going to live with the friars,[1] since you have to stay in Madrid. But be careful, *padre*, for they will weigh all your words. For love of God, be cautious and not so candid. I truly believe what they say about Tostado,[2] for if he is prudent he will not come until he receives the consent of the one you mention. Thus, he wants to obtain it with your help.[3] I've never seen anything so charming. Now I have received the letters that you told me you had sent, and yesterday that one from our *padre*.[4]

3. As regards Padre Fray Baltasar,[5] certainly I have written to him, and more than once. As long as you live with the friars, you will be doing very well to stay in Madrid. Continue to please the nuncio as you are now doing, for after all he is our superior, and everyone appreciates obedience.

There's no more time.

Yours,

Teresa of Jesus

1. In the monastery of the Carmelites of the observance in Madrid (cf. Ltr. 189.2,4).
2. Jerónimo Tostado (cf. Ltr. 189.7).
3. Jerónimo Tostado had not received permission from the royal council to carry out his visitation and was now, it seems, trying to obtain it through Mariano, who was a good friend of the king's.
4. Jerónimo Gracián in Andalusia.
5. Baltasar de Jesús (Nieto) who paid less attention to Teresa than even Mariano did.

192. To Padre Ambrosio Mariano de San Benito, Madrid

Toledo, April–May 1577

(Autograph: DCN in Créteil, Seine [France])

Gracián has sent a letter by way of Malagón urging the nuncio to take a certain action. Teresa forwards it to Mariano after recommending patience to Gracián.

1. Jesus. The grace of the Holy Spirit be with your reverence. Yesterday Padre Fray Francisco de la Concepción[1] arrived, who has been staying in Malagón. From the enclosed letter that our *padre*[2] has written, you will see what a hurry he is in to receive a reply.

2. Juanico[3] came beforehand and told me to expect Padre Fray Francisco who would be coming soon with Mother Prioress from Malagón.[4] She has come to see if the doctors here might be able to cure her illness, for she has improved enough to travel, which is no small thing. A nun[5] from here who is very good went in the meantime to preside at Malagón.

3. It seemed to me that it would not be good to send Fray Francisco to Madrid to wait for a message lest there be too many friars there bothering those blessed men.[6] It's better that he wait here or in Malagón. If you order otherwise, he will go. But it's preferable that you make him stay here and send the message to him here, for this young messenger is trustworthy.

4. Our *padre* is right. But now I see that you can do no more, and so I wrote to him yesterday that I already knew that it would be almost useless to try to get Methuselah[7] to hurry. Nevertheless. do all that you can, for goodness' sake, and write to me at length.

5. What do you think of the trial Señora Doña Luisa is undergoing?[8] She and her daughter are very distressed. Pray for them, and remain with God, for I am very busy.

Your reverence's servant,

Teresa of Jesus

6. My regards to Padre Padilla.[9] The trials, as you know, have caused him so much suffering and left him in so painful a situation that he can be trusted to rise above this other affliction.

---

1. He was the confessor at the Carmel in Malagón.
2. Jerónimo Gracián. On 6 April he had sent a report to Ormaneto, the nuncio, on what he had accomplished in his visitation of the Carmelites in Andalusia. It was to be followed by another more extensive report.
3. One of Teresa's messengers.
4. Brianda de San José who had been seriously ill.
5. Ana de la Madre de Dios became the vicaress at Malagón.
6. The Carmelite friars of the observance who gave lodging to the discalced friars who were in Madrid.
7. Code name for Nicolás Ormaneto.
8. Luisa de la Cerda's daughter, Guiomar de Pardo de Tavera had become a widow after only a year of marriage to Juan Pardo de Zuñiga.
9. This postscript was written in the margin.

193. To Madre María de San José, Seville

Toledo, 6 May 1577

(Autograph: DCN, Valladolid)

Gifts arrived from Seville as well as news that an angelic novice had died. Teresa gives her opinion and counsel on several matters she had been asked about. Gracián will soon be in Toledo, and the seriously ill prioress of Malagón is now Teresa's companion in Toledo.

For Mother Prioress, María de San José

1. Jesus be with your reverence and reward you for so many nice gifts. Everything arrived safely and in good condition. I'll be writing more about this through the muleteer. Here I'll mention what is important.

2. I have felt envious of that angel.[1] May God be praised that she was worthy to enjoy him so quickly, for I certainly do not doubt this. As for the rest, be assured that it was plain madness. Don't pay any attention to them or say anything about them, nor of what Beatriz[2] said. I have greatly prized her charity. Give her my regards and thank her for me as well as her mother,[3] and give my regards to all.

3. I am worried about that fever of yours and the subprioress's[4] illness. Blessed be God who so wants to put us to the test this year and give you so many trials at the same time. And the worst is the poor health, for when one is in good health everything is bearable. Let me know as soon as possible how you are doing with your fever and also how the subprioress is. Please God the illness will not be as long-lasting as usual, for you are so few in number that I don't know how you will be able to get along. May God provide as he can, for I am worried.

4. In what you say about the burial, be assured that you did very well.[5] Here we bury the nuns within the cloister, and so I must get our *padre*[6] to make this a rule. The other practice is for nuns who are not bound to enclosure. Thus Padre Garciálvarez[7]— give him my regards—was perfectly right, as he was also in holding that a priest may enter the enclosure for a reason like this.[8] But no, it would be better in this regard that the priest be always Padre Garciálvarez. The monastery of the friars is so far away that I don't see how this could be done. I think Padre Garciálvarez is preferable since he is the nuns' ordinary confessor. I will take this matter up now with our *padre* and send you a license, for I will see him, God willing, before Pentecost. The nuncio[9] has already sent for him, and it seems the negotiations are going well. Imagine how happy I am. He has gone to Caravaca and Beas.

5. I am sending you this letter from Alberta[10] so that you will know how they are doing. We are still not finished with that monastery. Pray for them and for the nuns in Beas who are a cause of distress for me because of their lawsuits.

6. Yesterday I received your letter and found someone at once with whom to send it to our *padre*. While he is here I will repay you for the care you have taken in delivering mine to him. Accept the lay sister;[11] please God she will be sufficient for you. I already told our *padre* that I would write you to accept her.

7. Regarding the renunciation of property of good Bernarda, keep in mind that since her parents are alive, the monastery does not receive the inheritance because it is the parents who are the heirs. If they had died before she did, the monastery would receive the inheritance. This is certain for I have consulted learned experts. Parents and grandparents are heirs by right. In their absence, the inheritance goes to the monastery. Their obligation is to give her a dowry, and if by chance they do not know this, they will praise God for the agreement you wish to come to with them. If they at least give the equivalent

of what they promised in the guaranty to pay, it would be an excellent thing. See what you can do down there in this regard, for it would not be fitting for them to fail to give some dowry.

8. Padre Nicolao[12] will know what the best thing to do is. Many regards to him, and to Padre Fray Gregorio[13] as well, and anyone else you see, and remain with God. Although for some days my head has been much better, there is never a day in which I do not experience much noise in my head and it's very painful for me to write.

9. Mother Prioress from Malagón[14] will be good company for me, but it grieves me to see her so ill without any hope of recovery, although there is great improvement. She eats better and is able to get up. But since the fever does not go away, we cannot pay too much attention to that, according to the doctor. God can do all things, and he could grant us this favor. Pray much that he do so. Since she is writing to you, I will say no more about her.

Today is 6 May.

Your unworthy servant,

Teresa of Jesus

10. Give my special regards to Gabriela.[15] I thoroughly enjoyed her letter and am happy that she is in good health. May God give this to all of you, as he can, amen, amen.

---

1. Bernarda de San José, a novice in Seville.
2. Beatriz de la Madre de Dios, who was not well balanced.
3. Beatriz's mother was Juana de la Cruz, also a nun in the Carmel of Seville.
4. María del Espíritu Santo.
5. She had resisted pressures from outside to have Bernarda buried in the church.
6. Jerónimo Gracián.
7. Confessor to the community.

8. He entered to administer the sacraments to Sr. Bernarda both in her illness and for her burial.
9. Nicolás Ormaneto.
10. Ana de San Alberto, prioress of Caravaca.
11. Juana de San Bernardo.
12. Nicolás Doria, now a discalced Carmelite novice at Los Remedios in Seville.
13. Gregorio Nacianceno.
14. Brianda de San José, so seriously ill, had now transferred to Toledo for better care.
15. Leonor de San Gabriel.

194. To Padre Ambrosio Mariano de San Benito, Madrid
Toledo, 9 may 1577

(Autograph: DCN: Clamart, Seine [France])

Having taken Teresa's advice, Mariano was residing with the Carmelites of the observance in Madrid. Teresa now cautions him further about some of his actions and friendships. The condition of her head is still bad and she writes only with difficulty. She concludes with some clarifications about the foundation in Caravaca.

For Padre Doctor Fray Mariano de San Benito in Madrid. Hand delivered.

1. Jesus be with your reverence and repay you for the good news you sent me; it seems to be in our favor for many reasons. The messenger boy left at once.[1] May God direct everything for his own greater glory. This is what we are all aiming for and nothing else.

2. I am delighted that you are getting along so well with those fathers,[2] except that they do not fail to create difficulties. I have been told that Padre Fray Angel[3] wrote to the Bishop of Salamanca not to give permission for the foundation and that

they initiated a lawsuit as they did here, no more nor less.[4] O *mi padre*! How poorly these negotiations are being handled. The foundation could have been already made had they known how to go about it properly. But things have only served to hurt the reputation of the discalced friars. Be assured that to take action at the wrong time never turns out well. On the other hand, I think what happened is part of God's plan and a great mystery. It will be revealed to us. If what you tell me gets done, everything will be settled. God reward you for the esteem you show for my opinion; may he be pleased that this continue. It seems to me you are receiving good advice where you are and that it's not necessary that you pay much heed to what I say. It is a great consolation to me that the negotiations are in such good hands. May he who does this be blessed, amen.

3. Why don't you ever say anything about Fray Baltasar?[5] I don't know where he is. Give him my regards, and regards to Padre Padilla and Padre Juan Díaz.[6] The prioress here and Brianda from Malagón ask for your prayers.[7] After the latter came here she improved, but tonight she is worse. There is some hope that she will live. May God preserve her, and watch over you.

4. Take care, *padre*, to be on your guard, and don't grow careless about anything, for the friendships shown to you could be feigned. The true friend to whom we must pay heed is God, and if we try always to do his will there is nothing to fear. I would love to know what that response[8] is, and I also wish that you and Father Master[9] could stay in a place where you would be truly welcome. There is no lack of the cross in this life, however much we may do to escape it, if we belong to the party of the Crucified One.

5. In regard to Antonio Muñoz,[10] he is mistaken, for Doña Catalina de Otálora[11] is not one of our nuns, nor was she ever, but she is a widow who helped that foundation. But I don't believe she is there now, nor do I know her, nor would it be compatible with my religious profession to get involved with

that matter. You may tell him this. In fact, I have felt a scruple about what I asked you in this respect. Since I do not know that gentleman well—between you and me, although he is a close relative of hers, I've only seen him once—I don't know what task would suit his soul. So I beg you not to pay any attention to my opinion in this matter, but act in accord with what you observe in his personality.

6. Don't say anything about this to him lest he become distressed, for I pity him. But give him my regards and say that I am not writing to him because of the bad condition my head is in, for it is still in a bad state. Tell him that I wrote to his wife, Doña Beatriz[12] today and that the señora of whom he speaks is not a nun.

May God watch over you, for we need you, amen.

Today is 9 May.

Your reverence's unworthy servant,

Teresa of Jesus

---

1. Probably Juanico.
2. The Carmelites of the observance in Madrid. It was Teresa who urged that he reside with them while in Madrid.
3. Angel de Salazar, the former Carmelite provincial of Castile.
4. The bishop was Francisco Soto y Salazar. The discalced friars wanted to found a college in Salamanca for their students.
5. Baltasar de Jesús (Nieto). Since he was known to be given to intrigue, Teresa was worried about his presence in Madrid, while Mariano was saying nothing about him.
6. Juan Calvo de Padilla and Juan Díaz were priests and friends of hers in Madrid.
7. The prioress of Toledo was Ana de Los Angeles. Brianda de San José, the prioress of Malagón, had come to Toledo seriously ill.
8. She is probably referring to the response Gracián was awaiting from the nuncio.
9. Juan de Jesús Roca.
10. He was a relative of the deceased husband of Catalina de Otálora.

11. She helped with the foundation of the Carmel in Caravaca and allowed three young aspirants to live in her house until the foundation was made (cf. F. 27.1–4).
12. Antonio Muñoz's wife.

195. To Madre María de San José, Seville

Toledo, 15 May 1577

(Autograph: DCN, Valladolid)

Many gifts have arrived from Seville. Expressing her great gratitude for them, Teresa expands on some of the topics she spoke of in a previous letter to Madre María.

For Mother Prioress of Seville.

1. Jesus. The grace of the Holy Spirit be with you, my daughter. I would much rather know that you are in good health than have all the gifts you are sending, although they are worthy of a queen. May our Lord reward you. The orange-flower water is nice, and there's an ample amount of it. It came just at the right time. I'm infinitely grateful. And the corporals are exquisitely done. It seems God inspired you because the prioress of Segovia[1] has sent me a pall.[2] When I was there, if I recall, I asked her to make one for me. It is all chain stitched with tiny pearls and garnets. They say the handwork alone is worth thirty ducats. And now we have the corporals made by Beatriz[3] with the little cross—more of them could have been added to fill up the box. The corporals are so lovely that I prefer them to everything else. The water arrived in good condition and now we have enough. It must have been you, as usual, who did the packing, for the things were well arranged.

2. I would want nothing more than to repay you in some way for what you sent me, for after all the gifts were a gesture of love. I have never in my life seen a place as dry as this when

it comes to anything that tastes good. After my return from Seville, it seems to be even more sterile.

3. I have given orders here that the bill I owe for one hundred ducats to Asensio Galiano[4] be paid now in Seville. I don't know if you remember that fifty ducats went to Mariano[5] for the expenses of preparing that house for our arrival, and the other fifty were spent for the rent. For since Asensio has died, I have taken care to pay it, and I will not rest until I see you free of all these worries. The trials the Lord is giving you are enough. I am truly distressed over your illness and that of the subprioress,[6] coming now at the beginning of summer. May God provide a remedy because I don't know what you are going to do.

4. I have already written by the mail carrier that you should take the lay sister[7] and that the body of that little saint[8] remain where it is, in the choir, for we must be buried within the enclosure and not in the church. I also wrote that since this saint's mother and father are living they become the heirs, even if she renounced these goods in favor of the monastery. If they had died before her, the monastery would have been the beneficiary. But they are obliged to give a suitable dowry. So, work things out as best you can. If he gave over the amount established in the guaranty, that would be great.[9] But don't be having scruples about perfection, for however much we do they will say we are covetous. Well, you will have to follow whatever orders our *padre*[10] gives. Write to him, and take good care of yourself, for me and for love of God.

5. I feel very sorry for Madre Brianda,[11] although it seems she is better since she came. I greatly enjoy her company. Since she will be writing, according to what she has told me, I will say no more about her.

6. You will already have learned that the nuncio has sent for our *padre*.[12] The negotiations seem to be going well. Pray for him. May His Majesty watch over you for me and make you very holy. I have been envious of the good Bernarda. We have

prayed very much for her in these houses, although I don't believe she has need of it. Today is the vigil of the Ascension.

Yours,

Teresa of Jesus

7. My regards to Mother Subprioress and to Gabriela.[13] Send me the recipe for the syrup that Sister Teresa was taking, for her father is asking for it.[14] Don't in any way forget; it's what she took habitually during the day.

---

1. Isabel de Santo Domingo.
2. The word could refer either to a pall or to the veil that was used to cover a ciborium.
3. Beatriz de la Madre de Dios in Seville.
4. A contractor from Medina del Campo and friend of Teresa's.
5. Ambrosio Mariano de San Benito who was in charge of the preparations for the foundation in Seville.
6. María del Espíritu Santo in Seville.
7. In Ltr. 193.6.
8. Bernarda de San José; cf. Ltr. 193.2,4.
9. Bernarda's father, Pablo Matías, had been a guarantor along with Teresa's brother Lorenzo de Cepeda for the purchase of the house in Seville.
10. Jerónimo Gracián.
11. Brianda de San José who had come from Malagón because of her illness.
12. Nicolás Ormaneto had requested that Gracián come to see him in Madrid.
13. Leonor de San Gabriel.
14. Teresa's niece who was now a novice at St. Joseph's in Avila. Her father was Lorenzo de Cepeda.

196. To Madre María de San José, Seville

Toledo, 28 may 1577

(Original and Autograph: DCN, Valladolid)

Both Gracián and Tostado have passed through Toledo on their way to Madrid. It is a precarious moment for the stability of Teresa's foundations and ideal; she begs for prayers. They have been unable to find a buyer for the cloth Madre María has sent for them to sell.

For Mother Prioress in Seville.

1. Jesus. The grace of the Holy Spirit be always with your reverence, my daughter, and I hope he gave you as joyous a Pentecost as I desired for you. Here we had a happy time with the arrival of our *padre*,[1] who is on his way to Madrid, having been sent for by the nuncio.[2] He looks healthy and well fed, blessed be God. You should know that it is necessary now to pray much for the affairs of the order and with great n ...[3] and care, for the need is serious.

2. Tostado[4] is already in Madrid. Four or five days ago he passed through here in such haste that he stayed no longer than three or four hours. Please the Lord that in everything he will do what is for God's greater honor and glory, for we desire nothing else. Pray that my head will get better for it is still in bad condition.

3. We have had poor luck with your cloth. They have shown it to half the houses and monasteries in Toledo but have not been able to sell it. Everybody thinks that four reales is too much to ask for it, but our conscience would not allow us to let it go for less. I don't know what we should do about it. Decide what you would like to do. May our Lord be with you.

The last day of Pentecost.

4. Our *padre* is not here today, for he is preaching at the place where his sister is.[5] He will not be able to write, because the mail carrier is departing.

5. I long to know how you and all the nuns are; some time has gone by since I've received a letter from you. May God watch over you for me. Madre Brianda[6] is very sick and asks for prayers. I beg prayers from all of you and from Fray Gregorio,[7] for now is the time in which we need the prayers of everyone.

6. Send this letter to him right away, and let everyone be on the watch because with the help of the Lord we shall see something good come about, or the opposite will happen. Never was there so much need for prayer. May God keep you.

Your reverence's,

Teresa of Jesus

---

1. Jerónimo Gracián.
2. Nicolás Ormaneto, who was now ill.
3. Teresa's secretary probably missed what was dictated here.
4. Jerónimo Tostado was the visitator of the Carmelite order appointed by the general.
5. Juana Dantisco was in attendance at a school for young ladies of the nobility. From the beginning of this paragraph to the end, the letter is in Teresa's hand.
6. Brianda de San José.
7. Gregorio Nacianceno, a discalced Carmelite at Los Remedios in Seville.

197. To Padre Jerónimo Gracián, Madrid

Toledo, 13 June 1577

Having found joy in Gracián's letters, Teresa writes hastily. Baltasar de Jesús informs her of tensions over the foundation in Madrid. She asks Gracián to strive to settle the matter about the tax still owed by the community of her nuns in Seville.

For Our Padre Maestro Gracián, Commissary Apostolic and Carmelite Visitator. In Madrid.

1. Jesus be with your paternity. Yesterday I received your letters. With the joy they brought me, I was repaid by the Lord for the pain caused me by the other letters, which were delivered by the same mail carrier who is going to deliver this letter. The nuns at the turn hadn't understood that he would return so quickly, and so there's no time for me to write at length.

2. I don't have time to write to Señora Doña Juana. Please God Señor Gracián's illness is not serious, for I was sorry to hear of it.[1]

3. Today, the octave day of the feast of the Most Blessed Sacrament, Padre Fray Baltasar preached here. He says that in the house where he is residing the other friars are very disturbed about the foundation we are trying to make in Madrid.[2] The matter about the excommunication frightened me.[3]

4. I believe I will have to make use of a private messenger to send you the contracts for your signature, for I think they will be ready today.

5. My brother kisses your hands and asks me to tell you how necessary it is that you carry on very diligently in regard to the lawsuit over the excise.[4] Give money to the procurator to send to the appropriate person so that the process can be concluded quickly and finished before August. This is necessary because of the grave hardship of which I spoke to you.

6. I was extremely pleased that your friend Elías[5] is beginning to understand the reason. You should know that I went to much trouble there so that the prosecutor[6] would understand her and I sent him word to tell you not to go, and I was suc-

cessful. I don't know whether they gave you the letters. I cannot say more.

Your paternity's unworthy servant,

Teresa of Jesus

---

1. Juana Dantisco and Diego Gracián de Alderete were Padre Gracián's parents.
2. Baltasar de Jesús (Nieto) was residing at the monastery of the Carmelite friars in Toledo. They were upset about the discalced friars' plans for a foundation in Madrid.
3. It is not known with certainty what excommunication Teresa is referring to here.
4. Lorenzo de Cepeda had come from Avila. The tax was a burden imposed on the Carmelite nuns in Seville because of a mistake in the contract that was agreed to at the time of the foundation.
5. Juan Evangelista in Seville.
6. Francisco de Arganda was the prosecutor for the Inquisition of Seville. She is probably referring to the woman mentioned in Ltr. 149.2.

198. To Madre María de San José, Seville

Toledo, 28 June 1577

(Autograph and Original: DCN, Valladolid)

She refers to the illnesses of other nuns and to her own. Her brother Lorenzo is in Toledo. She gives advice about accepting some postulants, Madre María's plan to move, the nuns in Paterna, the mitigation of certain austerities, and the need to borrow money to buy food.

For Mother Prioress in Seville.

1. Jesus. The grace of the Holy Spirit be in your reverence's soul, my daughter. I am deeply sorry that you have so many trials and that the fevers are continuing. But whoever wants to be a saint must suffer more.

2. Our *padre*[1] sent me your letter written to him on the 10th of this month. My head is in a miserable state, and all of these days I've been worried about both your health and Mother Subprioress's,[2] for I am very sorry about your illness. Madre Brianda[3] is better at times and then her sickness returns.

3. As for my head,[4] there has been some improvement in that some of the weakness is gone. I can write and use it more than usual. But the noise continues and is most unpleasant, and so I use a secretary, except for secret matters or when I am obliged for reasons of courtesy to write the letter myself. So, be patient in this regard as in all else.

4. I had written up to this point when my brother[5] arrived. He sends you his best regards. I don't know if he will write to you. I mean Lorenzo. He is well, glory to God. He is going to Madrid on business. Oh, how sorry he has felt about your trials. I assure you that God truly wants you to be very holy. Take courage, for this period will be followed by another and you will be glad to have suffered.

5. As to whether the little slave girl should enter, by no means oppose it, for at the beginning in making these foundations many things are done that lie outside the general norm. You don't have to talk with her about perfection. It is enough that she serve well. The rest doesn't matter much for a lay sister. She could go her whole life without making profession if she is not meant for it. Her sister's situation is worse, but don't fail to receive her either and beg God to make her good. Don't be demanding with either of them as regards perfection. It's enough for them to carry out well the essentials. They owe you much and you rescued them out of great difficulty.[6] Something has to be suffered. It is always this way in the beginning; it cannot be otherwise.

6. That other nun, if she is so good, take her. There's need for many nuns to replace those that die. The nuns go to heaven; don't grieve. I already see how you miss the good subprioress.

We will try to get those in Paterna to return, once matters are settled.

7. Oh, what a letter I wrote you and Padre Fray Gregorio![7] Please God it will reach you. How I took you to task regarding your plan to move! I don't understand how you could even begin to speak about such a foolish thing.[8]

8. Regards to him and to all my friends and my daughters. My brother has just arrived and I don't want to keep him waiting. May God watch over you carefully, for your illness grieves me more than anything. For goodness' sake take care of yourself and also my Gabriela.[9] You should all wear linen and forget about austerity at a time when you are in such need. Here there is much sickness. My regards to all the nuns. May God preserve you for me, for I don't know how I can love you so much. Brianda sends her regards to you. Despite her illness, she is very good company for me. Today is 28 June.

9. Try to borrow money for food, for you can pay it back later. Don't go hungry, for that grieves me very much. We also try to do that here, and afterward God provides.

Your reverence's,

Teresa of Jesus

---

1. Jerónimo Gracián.
2. María del Espíritu Santo.
3. The prioress of Malagón, residing while ill in Toledo.
4. She had been suffering from this infirmity in her head since 6 February. What follows is in her own hand.
5. Lorenzo de Cepeda. He was passing through Toledo from Avila on his way to Madrid.
6. There is no record that this slave girl or her sister ever actually entered.
7. Gregorio Nacianceno.
8. She is referring to María de San José's plan to move the community to a different location in Seville, which was actually carried out eight years later.

9. Leonor de San Gabriel.

199. To Padre Jerónimo Gracián

Toledo/Avila, July 1577(?)

This fragment shows that in making her foundations, Teresa had to be flexible and adapt to the circumstances (cf. Ltrs. 198.5; 200.3).

✣✣✣✣

1. Do you think, *mi padre*, that in the houses I founded I had to adjust to only a few things that I didn't like? No, there were many things. One has to suffer something in order to accommodate a need like this.

200. To Madre Ana de San Alberto, Caravaca

Toledo, 2 July 1577

(Autograph and Original: DCN, Caravaca)

Madre Ana is the prioress sent to make the foundation in Caravaca. She has written to consult Teresa on several matters (nuns, professions, clothing, illness, money, and a problem with the bishop). Teresa mentions the death of Ormaneto. Her head is still bothering her.

✣✣✣✣

For Madre Ana de San Alberto

1. Jesus be with your reverence, my daughter. It was most consoling to know that the house is so cool and that you will not have to suffer as you did a year ago. It would be a real delight for me, if it pleased God, to spend some days down there with you. I would have fewer letters and business matters to attend to and be near the little ducks and the water, which must make you feel like hermits. I don't deserve this, but I am very happy that you can enjoy it for me.

2. You should know that I never thought I loved you so much, for I have a great desire to see you. Perhaps God will so ordain. I pray very much for you and have the satisfaction of knowing that he will assist you in everything. I have no worries about your helping those souls to attain a high perfection. But you must realize you cannot treat all the nuns alike. That sister to whom our *padre* gave the habit should be treated like someone who is sick; no demands should be made of her that require much perfection. It's enough that she does the best she can, as they say, and avoids offending God.[1]

3. There is much to suffer everywhere, especially when beginning, for until a house is established we take in all the nuns we can, if they have the money, so as to supply for the needs of the others. Especially in this case it was right to take her for she contributed to the start of the foundation. Bear with her, my daughter, as best you can. If her soul is in a good state, consider how she is a dwelling place of God.[2]

4. I praise him every time he sends some joy to our *padre*. So that you will do this, I tell you that our *padre* said you were one of the best prioresses. Since you are so alone,[3] His Majesty helps you. Regarding the money you owe Malagón, don't worry about it. It's enough that you send it when you can.

5. Our *padre* is well, glory to God. But he has many trials, for, as you know, the nuncio[4] died and Tostado, who is the vicar general sent by our Most Reverend Padre,[5] is in Madrid. Although the king until now has not wanted him to carry on any visitations, we don't know how things will end up.

6. Our *padre's* commission[6] has not ended even though the nuncio is dead, and so he is still visitator. I believe he is in Pastrana now. Much prayer is necessary so that what is for the greater service of God will be done. We are praying much here and have held processions. Don't neglect to do this, for the need is now great, although it appears that everything will turn out all right.

7. Despite all his troubles our *padre* has not failed to attend to the affairs of your house and has spoken twice with the bishop,[7] who received him very graciously. He said he would do all that was required and he wrote himself to that lady.[8] He sent me a letter here last week, but he was waiting for I don't know what. Our *padre* is very happy and he says that everything will be done well. Don't worry if there is a little delay, for I assure you things were done with great care. The income has been satisfactory. Don't be disturbed, for everything will be done promptly.

8. If you are happy with the postulants—I mean, the elderly woman's daughters[9]— you don't have to do anything else than admit them to profession, even though they may have some infirmities, for there is no woman without them. The problem with my head is a little better, although I cannot write myself. I don't write to any monastery except through a secretary, unless in regard to something special, and thus I will finish this one myself.

9. What shall I say of the commotion caused by our illnesses, especially in Seville. The enclosed letter will inform you about them. I am sorry about Encarnación,[10] although those are infirmities that diminish as one grows older. Give her and everyone else my best regards, especially the subprioress and the foundresses.[11]

10. The presider in Malagón is Ana de la Madre de Dios. She is a very good religious and carries out her office well without deviating one iota from the *Constitutions*. In Seville they have many trials. The subprioress[12] has been annointed, and the prioress[13] has a continuing fever. So this is not the time to ask them for something. Remember that they bore the cost of your expenses from Seville. They are going to receive some postulants and they will pay you.

11. As for the fish you want to give us, that's a joke unless you find a way to ship it, for it would cost a lot to do that. Regarding the cloth underskirts of which our *padre* speaks, if you are

unable to buy others for everyone at once, dispose of the cloth ones little by little until they are all gone. Sell them for as much as you can.

12. Be very gracious in everything with Doña Catalina de Otálora[14] and strive to satisfy her. You know what we owe her, and ingratitude makes a bad impression. If she writes to one of the nuns, give the nun the letter and have her answer it. May our Lord make you very holy.

Madre Brianda[15] sends her regards. Her condition is the same, which is bad.

Today is 2 July.

Your mother and sister are well.

Your reverence's unworthy servant,

Teresa of Jesus

---

1. Francisca de la Madre de Dios (Sahojosa) had been invested in the habit by Jerónimo Gracián. She was one of the three young women living a recollected life in Catalina de Otálora's house in the hope that Teresa would make one of her foundations in Caravaca. At the last minute she abandoned the group, but now had returned asking for the habit. Her health was not strong and she had a propensity toward melancholy (cf. F. 27.3,4).
2. Teresa at this time was working on *The Interior Castle*.
3. Caravaca was far away from the other foundations.
4. Nicolás Ormaneto died on 18 June.
5. Jerónimo Tostado was the visitator appointed by the Carmelite general, Giovanni Battista Rossi.
6. The powers of visitator received from the nuncio Ormaneto.
7. The Bishop of Cartagena, Gómez Zapata, to whom Teresa had recourse in a litigation regarding the abnormal situation of the monastery in Caravaca, which was founded with a license from the council of the Order of Knights but without the bishop's permission.
8. The Duchess of Osuna or perhaps the Duchess of Frías.
9. Inés de Jesús and Ursula de San Angelo, daughters of Martín Robles and Catalina Cuello.
10. Ana de la Encarnación (Arbizo).

11. The subprioress was Barbara del Espíritu Santo; the foundresses were Francisca de la Cruz (Cuéllar), Francisca de San José (Tauste), and Francisca de la Madre de Dios (Sahojosa).
12. María del Espíritu Santo.
13. María de San José.
14. She was the widow and benefactor of the discalced nuns, who welcomed the founders into her home (cf. F. 27.1).
15. Brianda de San José.

201. To Gaspar de Villanueva, Malagón

Toledo, 2 July 1577

This confessor and chaplain for the discalced Carmelite nuns in Malagón had not acted prudently with respect to some disturbances and irregularities within the community. Teresa had arranged for a discalced friar to substitute for him. She now politely suggests that he give up his work with her nuns.

To the Very Magnificent and Reverend Señor Licentiate Villanueva.

1. Jesus. The grace of the Holy Spirit be with your honor. Your letters brought me much distress. To think that in one of these houses things are worse than they are in any of the houses of calced nuns in Andalusia is like a death to me. I have had little luck with that house in Malagón. I don't know what terrible things the presider[1] is doing to them that they should behave in the way you say they do in your letter to Mother Prioress.[2] That which a superior like our *padre*[3] said to them should have been enough to smooth things over. Their lack of intelligence is clearly evident and I cannot fail to blame you, for I know that you can do so much with them. If you had done what you did when they were tempted to rise up against Madre Brianda, things would be different.

2. What they will gain from all of this is that they will not see her again, even if God restores her to health, and will be left

without your assistance, for this is the way God pays those who serve him badly. And you will see where such contentious people end up who are so troublesome a trial to me, and I beg you to tell this to Beatriz.[4] My feelings toward her are such that I wouldn't even want to hear her name mentioned. I ask you to tell her that if she starts to oppose the presider or object to anything that is done in the house and I learn about it, she will pay dearly. Out of love for God, teach the nuns, as you have always done, to embrace the Lord if they want to have peace and not be going about so disturbed. Do you fear that there are others like Ana de Jesús?[5] Indeed, I would rather see them worse than she has been than disobedient. The sight of one of them offending God makes me lose all patience, and the Lord gives me very much patience in everything else.

3. As for the possibility of Ana de Jesús receiving communion, it is certain that she can, for the case has been carefully studied. Now that she is able to, let things stand for a month to see how it goes. In this regard, refer to what Mother Prioress writes to you. Your not having been informed was a great mistake. You did well to give her communion since you had no further knowledge.

4. As for the curate, this is why I was fearful about Fray Francisco's[6] departure, for not even the provincial[7] wants them to confess always with the same confessor; nor does this seem good to me. I have already told you this. I regret the long conversations with the confessor. I will inform him of this because it is something to be careful about.

5. The presider told me that in a certain matter you were not in much agreement with her. She led me to think that you do not believe she is dealing openly with you. Her not being open with you seems wrong to me. I am going to write to her about this and other things in such a way that she will not know that you have written anything to me. It would be good if you spoke to her plainly and complain about how she acted with Ana de Jesús. If you do not disentangle what the devil has be-

gun to put together, things will go from bad to worse and you will be unable to bear them with peace of soul. Although it will be distressing to me that you are leaving, I believe you are more obliged to preserve your own tranquillity than to do me a favor.[8] May the Lord grant us tranquillity, as he can, amen.

I kiss the hands of those lords many times.

They say that even though the nuncio died,[9] our *padre's* commission has not ceased and that he is still visitator. In certain respects I am very sorry about this.

Your unworthy servant,

Teresa of Jesus

---

1. Ana de la Madre de Dios who was sent there from Toledo.
2. The prioress of Malagón, Brianda de San José, who was residing in Toledo on account of her illness.
3. Jerónimo Gracián.
4. Beatriz de Jesús (Cepeda y Ocampo), Teresa's cousin.
5. Ana de Jesús (Contreras), who was mentally ill.
6. Francisco de la Concepción (Espinel), who had been sent to Malagón as confessor and now returned to his monastery.
7. Jerónimo Gracián.
8. Teresa's delicate way of letting him know he need no longer stay on at Malagón.
9. The nuncio, Nicolás Ormaneto, who had given Gracián the powers of a visitator of the Carmelite order in Spain.

202. To Madre María de San José, Seville

Toledo, 11 July 1577

(Autograph: DCN, Valladolid)

Madre María has again sent gifts, among which were some coconuts. She was having a number of difficulties: her own poor health, a nun gravely ill, a melancholic aspirant proposed to the community by the archbishop, and some other problematic candidates. Teresa gives advice and sympathizes with her.

❧❧❧❧

For Mother Prioress, María de San José

1. Jesus be with you, my daughter. By the fact that you tell me you are somewhat better, it seems I am capable of bearing everything willingly. May it please the Lord that you continue to improve and may he repay the doctor, for I am dutifully grateful to him.

2. It's amazing that the subprioress[1] is still alive. He who made her can easily give her health, for he gave her being from nothing. He is truly exercising her in suffering as he is all of you. Enduring something like this makes one ready for anything, even going to Guinea[2] or beyond. Nonetheless, I would like to see it over with, for it causes me much grief.

3. Since I told Madre Brianda[3] to write about what is happening here, I will only mention the things I need to. Neither the pictures intended for Doña Luisa nor the letter arrived,[4] nor did you mention whether you received the cloth and the crucifixes.[5] Let me know in the next letter and pray for Brianda, for I am happy to see her so much better.

4. Accept the nun gladly,[6] for the dowry you say she has is not a bad one. I wish that that widow had already entered. The other day I wrote to you to take the little black girl gladly, for she will not do you any harm, and her sister as well.[7] Neither did you mention whether you received that letter. I was sorry about Garciálvarez's[8] illness. Don't forget to tell me how he is and whether your improvement is continuing. I received the coconuts; and they are something to behold. I will send them to Doña Luisa. The one for me is beautifully decorated. Our *padre*[9] says he will break it open tomorrow.

5. Regarding Paterna, he says not to talk about it until he goes there—we spoke to him a lot about that today—for ev-

eryone would be disturbed at the thought that he is not the visitator,[10] and he is right.

6. May God repay you for all the gifts you give me—you must dream of being a queen—and for even sending the portage. For goodness' sake take care of yourself and take it easy, for I would be receiving a great gift by your doing that. The sisters were delighted to see the coconut, and I too. May he be blessed who created it, for it is certainly something to behold. It pleased me how with all your trials you have the vitality to think of things like this. The Lord well knows whom he gives trials to.

7. Just now I have spoken to our *padre* about the aspirant proposed by the archbishop.[11] I am very displeased to see how persistent they are in their entreaties while he does not favor it. Our *padre* says that he thinks she is a melancholic *beata*—and with such we should have learned our lesson—and it would be worse to send her away afterward. Try to speak to her a few times to see what she is like. And if you see that she is not for us, it wouldn't seem to me a bad idea for Padre Nicolao[12] to speak to the archbishop and tell him about the bad luck we have with these *beatas*; or try to delay the decision.

8. It has been a long while since I wrote the enclosed letter to Fray Gregorio[13] and sent it to our *padre* to send on to him, and now he returned it to me. It's dated, but don't fail to read it so that the foolish temptation you've had to leave the house you are in doesn't return. I am sorry about the great trial you will have with that sister, and I pity the poor little soul for what she suffers. May God provide a remedy. Give everyone my regards. It would be a great consolation for me to see you, for I find few nuns so pleasing to me, and I love you greatly. The Lord can do all.

9. Best regards to Padre Garciálvarez and to Beatriz, her mother[14] and the others, to whom I say that they need to be very perfect. The reason is that the Lord is beginning this foundation with them and has deprived them of their support.[15] I

don't know how you are able to manage everything. It's true that it would have been worse for you if you had to deal with calced nuns as was the case elsewhere.[16] For, after all, your nuns will follow the path you point out to them. The worse thing is that you have to undergo everything with poor health. My experience is that when one's health is good, everything is bearable. May God grant it to you, my daughter, as I desire and beg of him, amen.

Today is 11 July.

Your reverence's,

Teresa of Jesus

10. Since our *padre* was here, he opened the package and gave me the letters, but kept the pictures and must have forgotten. I accidently found this out today, for he and Padre Antonio[17] were arguing over them. I saw two and they were beautiful.

---

1. María del Espíritu Santo, the subprioress in Seville.
2. Like going off to the land of the Moors (cf. L. 1.4).
3. Brianda de San José, residing in Toledo because of illness.
4. They had come; see no. 10 of this letter. Doña Luisa de la Cerda.
5. Cf. Ltr. 196.3 and Ltr. 190.1.
6. Cf. Ltr. 198.6.
7. Cf Ltr. 198.5.
8. The confessor of the discalced nuns in Seville.
9. Jerónimo Gracián.
10. Doubts had arisen whether or not Gracián's faculties continued in force after the death of the nuncio.
11. Don Cristóbal de Rojas, the Archbishop of Seville and friend of Teresa's.
12. Nicolás Doria, a novice with the discalced Carmelite friars at Los Remedios.
13. Gregorio Nacianceno at Los Remedios, who was considering along with Madre María the possibility of moving to a new house.

14. Beatriz de la Madre de Dios (Chaves) and her mother, Juana de la Cruz.
15. Padre Gracián who had been a support to the community.
16. Many nuns from the monastery of the Incarnation in Avila joined Teresa's first communities.
17. Antonio de Jesús (Heredia), prior at Los Remedios in Seville.

203. To Roque de Huerta, Madrid

14 July 1577

(Autograph: DCN, Antequera [Málaga])

Roque de Huerta, residing in Madrid, was a friend of the Gracián family and a trustworthy person through whom Teresa's correspondence could be sent. She was now entering a difficult period which required secrecy, especially in her correspondence with Gracián.

1. Jesús. May the Holy Spirit be with your honor. Our *padre*, Master Fray Jerónimo Gracián,[1] spoke to me of his fondness for you and how much he trusts that without trouble you will do everything you can to help me; and that is no small thing since I have so many business matters to take care of. And so from now on I will turn to you with the letters destined for our *padre*, which is what matters the most to me. But this must be on the condition that you contribute no more than the effort involved, and in all simplicity we will take care of the postage; otherwise I would not want to accept your favor.

2. If there is any way in which I can be of assistance to you, I will do so gladly if I can. I beg you to send these letters to the parties they are addressed to.

Today is 14 July.

Your honor's unworthy servant,

Teresa of Jesus

1. Gracián during this period had been in both Toledo and Madrid. The nuncio Ormaneto had been dead for a month. Gracián's position was uncertain, and opposition to Teresa's undertaking was about to intensify.

204. To Padre Jeronimo Gracián, Madrid(?)

Toledo/Avila, July 1577(?)

(Autograph: Diocesan Museum, Cathedral of Valladolid)

She warns against allowing situations that would give rise to small-town gossip.

1. ...If some friar should have to stay there,[1] your paternity ought to advise him strongly not to spend much time talking to the nuns. Look, *mi padre*, this is very necessary. And I wouldn't even want the licentiate[2] to do so, for even though he is so good, such goodness can give rise to bad judgments in people with malicious minds, especially in small towns, and everywhere else as well.

2. Believe me, the more you see that your daughters are cut off from such very special relationships, even though they are very holy ones, the better it is, even for the peace of the house. And I wouldn't want this to be forgotten....

1. Malagón (cf. Ltr. 201).
2. Gaspar de Villanueva, the chaplain for the Carmelite nuns in Malagón.

205. To Padre Jeronimo Gracián, Seville

Toledo, July/August 1577(?)

Teresa seeks permission to admit Gaytán's eight-year-old daughter into the Carmel of Alba.

1. ...Antonio Gaytán has been here.[1] He came to ask if his daughter could be received in Alba.[2] She must be about the same age as my Isabelita. The nuns[3] write me that she is especially amiable. Her father will provide food and afterward give all her disposable possessions, which they say amount to six or seven hundred ducats and even more. And what he does for that house[4] and for the order is priceless.

2. I beg you not to fail to send me the permission, in your charity—and quickly. I tell you these little angels[5] edify us and are refreshing. With no more than one in each house, I don't see any obstacle but a benefit....

---

1. He was a widower and resident in Alba de Tormes.
2. Mariana Gaytán was eight years old, Isabelita Gracián, nine.
3. The discalced Carmelite nuns in Alba de Tormes.
4. The monastery of nuns in Alba de Tormes.
5. The children that had been admitted into her Carmels and mentioned by Teresa were four in number: Teresita de Cepeda, Isabelita Gracián, Casilda de Padilla, and Mariana Gaytán.

206. To Don Alvaro de Mendoza, Olmedo

Avila, Beginning of August 1577

(Autograph: Diocesan Museum, Cathedral of Valladolid)

Because the bishop of Avila had been named bishop of Palencia, Teresa had asked him to allow the jurisdiction of the discalced nuns at St. Joseph's in Avila to pass to the Carmelite order and she now thanks him for having granted her request. Gracián, with Teresa, had gone to receive the obedience of the nuns there and visit the community. This letter was written a few days later. She agrees to intervene concerning a marriage of Don Alvaro's niece and begs that a benefice be given to her friend, Gaspar Daza.

⁂

To the Most Illustrious and Most Reverend Señor Don Alvaro de Mendoza, Bishop of Avila, my lord, in Olmedo.

1. Jesus. May the grace of the Holy Spirit be always with your lordship, amen. I have recovered from the illness I had, although not from the noise in my head, which always torments me. But just to know you are in good health I would willingly suffer greater ills.

2. I kiss your lordship's hands many times for the favor you show me by your letters, which are a great consolation for us. The nuns have also received their letters, and they have come and shown them to me feeling highly favored, and rightly so.

3. If you had seen how necessary it was for a visitation to be made by someone who knew how to explain the constitutions, and was also familiar with them through practice,[1] I think you would have been very happy. And you would have realized what a great service you rendered to our Lord and all the good you did for this house by not leaving it under the power of someone incapable of recognizing the way in which the devil could begin to meddle, and indeed had begun to do so. Thus far no one was at fault since their intentions were all good. Indeed, I cannot thank God enough.[2]

4. As for our needs, we will not suffer from any want. If in some need the bishop will not help the house,[3] you should not be disturbed. The monasteries can come to the help of each other, which is better than their relying on someone who doesn't show the love for us that you have shown throughout your entire life. If only we had you here and could enjoy your presence—and this is what makes us sad. As for the rest, it

seems we have made no changes, for we are as always your subjects. And all the superiors will also be, especially Padre Gracián, who seems to have caught the love that we have for you.

5. Today I sent him your letter, for he is not here. He went to Alcalá to dispatch those who are going to Rome.[4] The sisters have been very happy with him. Indeed, he is a great servant of God. But for them it is also a real help to see that in everything he follows what you have set down.

6. In regard to that lady, I will try to do what you ask, if the occasion arises, for the person who informed me does not usually come to this house. But from what could be gathered the matter has nothing to do with a wedding. After reading your letter, I wonder if, in fact, it is about a wedding that someone was trying to prevent. I don't think, though, that the one with whom I spoke is zealous for anything else than God and the common good. May His Majesty guide matters for his greater service since things have already reached such a point that even if you do not so wish you will be involved. I am greatly consoled that you are free enough not to feel disturbed. Consider whether it wouldn't be good to warn the abbess[5] and to show that you are very displeased with the party who intervened to see if that wouldn't be of some help. I tell you this was strongly recommended to me.[6]

7 As for the matter concerning Maestro Daza,[7] I don't know what to say, so great is my desire that you do something for him, for I see his good will toward you. Even if what you do amounts to little, I would be happy. He is so devoted to you, he says, that if he thought you found him bothersome by his asking for such favors he wouldn't stop serving you but try never to ask you for any favors. Since his devotion to you is so great and he sees that you are doing favors for others and have done so in the past, he is a little upset and thinks he is one of the unlucky ones.

8. With regard to the canonry, he is writing to you himself to explain. If he could be certain that you would favor him if some vacancy were to arise before you leave, he would be happy. And I would be happy because I believe this would be pleasing to God and to everyone—and truly you owe it to him. Please God this will be possible so that you will leave everyone satisfied. Even if it means something less than a canonry, I think he would accept it gladly. Well, not everyone has the detached love for you that your discalced nuns do, for all we want is that you love us and that God preserve you for us very many years.

9. My brother[8] readily shares these sentiments. He is now in the parlor. He kisses your hands many times; and Teresa,[9] your feet. We are all embarrassed that you ask again for prayers, for we would be offended to think that you do not know we are always praying for you. They are in a hurry for this letter, so I cannot go on any longer. I think that if you tell Maestro Daza that if a vacancy arises you will give it to him, he will be content.

Your lordship's unworthy servant and subject,

Teresa of Jesus

1. She is referring to the visitation of St. Joseph's in Avila made by Gracián when the community passed from the jurisdiction of the bishop to that of the order.
2. She cannot thank God enough for the transfer of the jurisdiction of the discalced nuns in Avila to the order.
3. The new bishop of Avila.
4. The chapter of discalced friars in Almodóvar del Campo (September 1576) decided—and this was Teresa's urgent wish as well—to send two discalced friars to Rome to plead their case, but the two (Pedro de los Angeles and Juan de San Diego) never actually left until the end of 1578.
5. Doña Quixada de Mendoza, the abbess of Las Huelgas in Valladolid, a cousin of Don Alvaro's.
6. This obscure paragraph concerns the marriage of Don Alvaro's niece.

7. Gaspar Daza, one of the priests for whom Teresa's *Life* was intended, was seeking a benefice from Don Alvaro and had asked Teresa to intercede.
8. Lorenzo de Cepeda.
9. Lorenzo's daughter.

207. To Don Alvaro de Mendoza, Olmedo

Avila, 6 September 1577

She expresses her happiness at the marriage of Don Alvaro's niece, about which the bishop was worried lest she be too young. Assuring him of her prayers for his sister, who was ill, she also expresses her gratitude for the charity in alms that Don Alvaro had ordinarily shown to the discalced nuns in Avila.

1. Jesus be always with your lordship. The marriage of Señora Doña María[1] made me very happy. Truly, despite my great joy, I could not completely believe it was happening. So it was a real relief for me to learn of it from your letter. May God be blessed for such a great favor, since these past days I have been anxious and worried longing to see you free of such a great concern. And it came about at so little cost to you, for I've been told that it is quite an honorable marriage. As for the rest, not everything can be perfect; it would have been much more troublesome had he been very young. Wives are treated much better by someone who is mature in age. This would be particularly true in the case of a wife who has as many reasons to be loved as she has. May it please the Lord that they have a happy life together, for I don't know what else could have given me so much pleasure at this time.

2. I have been distressed about Señora Doña María's[2] illness. Please God, it will not be as serious as it usually is. Here we are taking more care than usual to pray for her.

3. May our Lord reward you for the alms. It came just at the right time, for we had no one to turn to, although I wasn't too

worried. Francisco de Salcedo was more anxious than we were, for we always trust in God. The other day he told me that he wanted to write to you and only say in the letter, "Lord, we have no bread."[3] I did not allow him, for my desire to see you free of debts is such that I would rather we suffer want than be the cause of an increase in your expenses. But since God gives you so much charity, I hope that His Majesty will provide for you in other ways. May he be pleased to preserve you for many years and bring me to a place where I might enjoy your company.

4. Padre Gracián is determined not to allow me to go to the Incarnation. But it is God whom I fear, even though nothing would be worse for us at present.[4] I am delighted that you are being careful about your most generous nature and avoiding occasions like the festival.[5] May it please God that this will be for your good and may he watch over you more than me.

Today is 6 September.

Your lordship's unworthy servant and subject,

Teresa of Jesus

5. Teresa[6] kisses your hands and is doing what you ordered her to do; she would gladly go with you.

---

1. Don Alvaro's niece, Doña María Sarmiento y Pimental, was the daughter of María de Mendoza and Francisco de los Cobos. She married Gonzalo Fernández de Córdoba, the Duke of Sessa.
2. Don Alvaro's sister, María de Mendoza.
3. Don Alvaro usually provided bread for the community, as he did afterward with the community in Palencia (cf. F. 29.11).
4. Although the term of the prioress at the Incarnation had not yet expired, Teresa was being considered as a likely possibility to be the next prioress.
5. The festival days in Palencia took place at the beginning of September. It was a time when the rich made a display of their wealth.
6. Teresa's niece.

208. To the King Don Philip II, Madrid

Avila, 18 September 1577

This letter was motivated by a libelous document being circulated against Gracián and the discalced nuns. It was the work of the notorious Baltasar de Nieto and signed by a lay brother, Miguel de la Columna, who had accompanied Gracián in his travels as visitator. In it Gracián is accused of grossly immoral conduct at some of the Carmels. Tomás Gracián, secretary to the king, wrote a defense of his brother and presented it along with Teresa's letter to Philip II. By the end of the month, the confused Miguel de la Columna retracted what was contained in the letter he had signed.

1. Jesus. The grace of the Holy Spirit be always with your majesty, amen. News has reached me that a memorandum was delivered to your majesty against Padre Maestro Gracián. I am astonished at the intrigues of the devil and these calced fathers. They're not satisfied with defaming this servant of God (for he truly is and has so edified us that the monasteries he has visited[1] always write to me about how he has left them with a new spirit), but they are striving now to discredit these monasteries where God is so well served. For this purpose they have made use of two discalced friars.[2] The one had been a servant in these monasteries before becoming a friar and did things that made it obvious he often lacked good judgment. The friars of the cloth[3] have availed themselves of this discalced friar and others antagonistic toward Padre Maestro Gracián—for he is the one who must punish them—and had them sign things that were absurd. I would laugh at what is said about the discalced nuns if I didn't fear the harm the devil can do with it, for in our communities such things would be horrendous.

2. For love of God I beg your majesty not to allow such infamous testimony to be presented to tribunals. The world is such

that some suspicion can remain—however well the opposite is proven—if we provide the opportunity. It is not helpful for the general reform that aspersions be cast on an order that by the goodness of God has been so well reformed. Your Majesty could, if you care to, acquaint yourself with this reality through some testimonies that were gathered by order of Padre Gracián. They concern certain facts about these monasteries taken from some serious and saintly persons who have dealings with these nuns.

3. Since the motives of those who wrote the memorandum can be investigated, consider, your majesty, for love of our Lord, that this matter is something concerning God's honor and glory. If those of the cloth see that you are paying attention to their testimonies, they will accuse the visitator of heresy to prevent any further visitations, and where there is little fear of God this will be easy to prove.

4. I feel sorry for all that this servant of God suffers, despite the rectitude and perfection with which he proceeds in everything. This obliges me to beg your majesty to favor him or give orders that he be removed from this situation so full of perils, for he is the son of parents who are in your majesty's service,[4] besides his own good qualities. Truly, I think he is a man sent by God and his Blessed Mother. His devotion to her—and it is great—is what led him to the order and to helping me.[5] For more than seventeen years I suffered alone from these fathers of the cloth, and I no longer knew how to bear it; my own weak efforts were insufficient.

5. I beg your majesty to pardon me for being so lengthy. The great love I bear you has made me bold and I reflect that since the Lord puts up with my indiscreet complaints, you will also.

6. May it please him to hear all the prayers of the discalced friars and nuns that he preserve your majesty for many years, for we have no other support on earth.

Written in St. Joseph's in Avila on 13 September 1577.

Your majesty's unworthy servant and subject,

Teresa of Jesus

7. I suspect that since Tostado[6] will remain in his present position, the visitation will be of no benefit, but rather very harmful, especially since that preacher[7] who was previously a calced friar, and about whose life I beg your majesty to inquire, has linked up with him. And if it is necessary, all of us discalced nuns will swear that we never heard Padre Gracián speak a word—nor did we see anything in him—that was not edifying. And he was so extremely cautious about not entering the enclosure of the monasteries that even in conducting the chapters, when entering would seem unavoidable, he usually did so at the grille.[8]

---

1. She is referring to his canonical visitations.
2. The two discalced Carmelite friars were the lay brother Miguel de la Columna and Padre Baltasar de Nieto.
3. She is referring to the Carmelites of the observance.
4. Gracián was the son of Diego de Alderete, the king's secretary.
5. She speaks of his devotion to our Lady and how this led him to Carmel in her *Foundations*, 23.4–6.
6. Jerónimo Tostado, appointed visitator for the Carmelites in Spain at the general chapter.
7. Baltasar de Jesús (Nieto).
8. These chapters were meetings of the entire community called by Gracián during his canonical visitations for the correction of faults. It was customary for visitators to enter the enclosure on occasions like this.

209. To Roque de Huerta, Madrid
Avila, 7 October 1577

(Autogaph: Discalced Trinitarian Nuns, Madrid)

Roque de Huerta, residing in Madrid, was a friend of the Gracián family. Recommended by Padre Gracián he was especially suited for seeing to a safe delivery of Teresa's correspondence during this difficult period of intrigue.

To the very magnificent Señor Roque de Huerta, chief forest guard of his majesty, Madrid.

1. Jesus be with your honor always. Since these letters are of the greatest importance they are being sent with a much higher portage. I beg you to have them sent with the usual caution and quickly. If you cannot find a safe and trustworthy person, engage a private messenger and our *padre*[1] will pay for it.

2. There are two packs of letters, for we had already sent one when another business matter arose, and this mail carrier would in no way let us add the later ones to the earlier ones, so it was necessary to make another pack. May the Lord guide them as the need requires, and may he watch over you for his greater service.

Written on 7 October.

Your unworthy servant,

Teresa of Jesus

3. Let me know, for the love of the Lord, if there is anything new about the business matters, and pay a good portage.

4. It is very important that both packs of letters be delivered together to our *padre* and with all possible haste, as I have said.

---

1. Jerónimo Gracián.

210. To Don Juan de Ovalle, Alba de Tormes

Avila, 20 October 1577

(Autograph: Parish of San Juan, Avila)

Teresa's brother-in-law needs a favor from the Archbishop of Toledo, who has just arrived in Toledo. Teresa writes at night in haste to inform him of his chance to travel there and speak to the archbishop. Having returned to Avila in July, Teresa now is pained over the situation of the nuns at the Incarnation.

1. Jesus be with your honor. Yesterday evening I received a letter from our Padre Gracián in which he tells me that the papal bulls for the Archbishop of Toledo have arrived. He believes the archbishop is already in Toledo, and that if he is there, he will be there in order to take possession[1] of his see. Just now I have found this man, which I consider most fortunate. He says he will deliver the letter on Tuesday by noon. Today is Sunday, 19 October, I believe.[2]

2. Since it is now so late into the night, I am saying no more, nor did I let my brother know about this messenger, for I don't believe he would have anything to ask of you. I gave the messenger three *reales* and I will give him another two here. When he is there give him two for his return, for we agreed on seven. I have some scruple about paying him everything here until I ask advice. Oh, what a trial these restraints of our poverty are! May it please the Lord—since I can't do anything—to provide for you in some other way, as he can.

3. I will have my letter ready so that you will not have to delay here, for it will be important for you to find the archbishop in Toledo.[3] Yesterday I wrote again to Señora Doña Luisa that she not forget and to the prioress[4] to keep reminding her. God willing, all these efforts and favors should be enough. Choose an animal that travels well and not some poor beast that's going to wear you out.

4. The nuns[5] are without Mass, and there is nothing new, not even with regard to the other business matters, although they are proceeding well. Tell the prioress[6] about this messenger in case she may want to write to me.

5. My sister may consider this as written for her too, and give my regards to Beatriz.[7] Had we been seers,[8] you could have left in time for Toledo by leaving from here, although the season is still good for travel. May the Lord take care of things, and since it's so late I'll say no more.

Your honor's unworthy servant,

Teresa of Jesus

1. In the letter Gracián mentioned that the Archbishop of Toledo, Gaspar de Quiroga, was to receive the pallium on 20 October 1577.
2. It was actually 20 October.
3. She plans to write a letter of recommendation to the archbishop for her brother-in-law.
4. She asked Doña Luisa de la Cerda to intercede in his favor. The prioress was Ana de los Angeles.
5. The Carmelite nuns at the Incarnation were excommunicated because they had voted for Teresa for prioress even though forbidden to do so by their provincial.
6. Juana del Espíritu Santo, prioress at the Carmel of Alba de Tormes.
7. Her sister was Juana de Ahumada; Beatriz was Juan de Ovalle's daughter.
8. Juan de Ovalle had just been in Avila.

211. To Madre María de San José, Seville

Avila, 22 October 1577

(Original and Autograph: DCN, Valladolid)

The new nuncio, Felipe Sega, resistant to Teresa and her endeavor, has arrived in Madrid. Libelous statements against Gracián had been circulated and sent to the king, but the calumniators were made to retract. Yet the false reports against Gracián, María de San José, and the discalced nuns keep reappearing. Many nuns at the Incarnation in Avila have been excommunicated for electing Teresa as prioress against the provincial's orders.

For Mother Prioress in Seville.

1. Jesus be always with your reverence, my daughter. Last month I wrote to you by way of a muleteer from this city, and my brother[1] also wrote. In the letter I mentioned that our business matters had gotten complicated. You will have learned this from Padre Fray Gregorio[2] in a more complete way than I could have then put in writing. Now, God be blessed, they are proceeding very well, better each day. Our *padre*[3] is well, and he still retains his commission, although I would very much like to see him liberated from those people.[4] They make up so many things that it would be impossible to put them all in writing. But the good part is that everything ends up raining down on their own backs and turns out to our benefit.

2. You will have already learned how Fray Miguel and Fray Baltasar[5] retracted. Fray Miguel swears that he wrote nothing in the memorandum and that they made him sign it, with force and threats. He said this and other things in the presence of witnesses and a notary, and before the Blessed Sacrament.[6] The king[7] understood that this is evil and so they do nothing but harm themselves. My head is in a wretched state. Pray for me and for these brothers that God will enlighten them for the salvation of their souls.

3. I tell you that what is going on at the Incarnation[8] is of a kind, I think, never before seen. By orders of Tostado[9] the provincial[10] of the calced friars came here fifteen days ago for the election with threats of great censures and excommunications for anyone who might cast a vote for me. Despite this, they paid no heed, and as though he had said nothing to them at all, fifty-five nuns voted for me. As each vote for me was given to him, he excommunicated the nun, and he cursed and

pounded and beat the ballots with his fist and burned them. He has left the nuns excommunicated for fifteen days now without their being allowed to hear Mass or enter the choir, even when the Divine Office is being said. And they cannot speak to anyone, not even their own confessors or parents. And what is most amusing is that the day after this pounding election the provincial returned and called them together for an election, but they answered that there was no need for another election because they had already had one. And seeing this he excommunicated them again and called the remaining nuns, which numbered forty-four, and had them elect another prioress[11] and sent the result to Tostado for confirmation.

4. Now she has been confirmed in office, but the others are holding fast and say they will not obey her except as a vicaress. Learned men say that the nuns are not excommunicated and that the friars are acting contrary to the Council[12] in confirming a prioress who received an insufficient number of votes. The other nuns sent word to Tostado that they want me for prioress. His answer was no; if I wanted, I could go there to live in seclusion[13] but it would be inadmissable for me to go as prioress. I don't know where it will all end up.

5. This, in sum, is what is happening now, for all are stunned to see something like this which offends everyone. I would gladly pardon the nuns if they would leave me in peace, for I have no desire to find myself in that Babylon[14]—and even less so because of my poor health. And it gets even worse when I'm in that house. May God do what serves him most and free me from them.

6. Teresa[15] is well and sends you her regards. She is a lovely child and has grown a great deal. Pray for her that God may make her his servant. Let me know whether the widow[16] has entered—as has been my wish—and whether her sister has returned to the Indies.

7. I have felt a longing to speak to you about many things, which would be consoling for me. But some day I will have more time and a safer messenger than the one who is going to bring this. Señora Doña Luisa is a great help and favors us in every way. Pray for her and for the archbishop of Toledo, and don't ever forget the king.[17]

---

1. Lorenzo de Cepeda.
2. Gregorio Nacianceno, in Seville.
3. Jerónimo Gracián was commissioned as visitator and apostolic commissary.
4. The calced Carmelite friars in Andalusia.
5. Fray Miguel de la Columna, a lay brother; Baltasar de Jesús (Nieto).
6. For the texts of the retractions see MHCT 1:390–91; 393–99; 406–15.
7. Philip II.
8. Teresa's former monastery of the Incarnation in Avila.
9. Jerónimo Tostado, visitator of the Carmelites in Spain.
10. The provincial of the Carmelites in Castile was Juan Gutiérrez de la Magdalena.
11. Doña Ana de Toledo who obtained 34 votes.
12. The Council of Trent in Session 25, chap 6. The nuns remained excommunicated for about two months.
13. This reflects the orders she received from the general chapter of Piacenza to retire to a monastery in Castile and not leave it.
14. The monastery of the Incarnation.
15. Teresita de Ahumada, her niece.
16. Doña Ana de Vaena.
17. Doña Luisa de la Cerda; Gaspar de Quiroga, and Philip II.

212. To Roque de Huerta, Madrid

Avila, 22 October(?) (1577)

(Autograph: DCN, Cracow, Poland)

Teresa has been elected prioress at the Incarnation, but the election has been annulled by the provincial, and the nuns who voted for her have been excommunicated. She is now writing to seek help for them through influential friends. The autograph is badly damaged.

To the very magnificent Roque de Huerta, chief forest guard of his majesty. Trinidad, in Madrid.

1. May the Holy Spirit be with your honor. Since I wrote at length through Diego Hernández[1] two days ago, I believe, and the carrier of this letter is waiting, I will not be long. I am not writing to our *padre*,[2] because I did so at that time.

2. I have a great desire to know what is happening with the poor nuns at the Incarnation....It is something that will soon be found out.

3. You should know that the one whom they made prioress[3] at the Incarnation has been anointed. And I feel sorry about the new trials that those poor nuns are suffering; over fifty of them have been deprived of active and passive voice,[4] and as usual it is the provincial[5] who will appoint the prioress, with only the votes of the other nuns.[6] And perhaps the result will be worse than what they are seeking. Oh, how they need our good friend Padilla![7] For if there were someone who....

4. I also wrote to the Duchess of Alba....[8]

Your honor's unworthy servant,

Teresa of Jesus

5. I received the letters that Diego Hernández brought and was greatly comforted by them. I made use of him to respond to you and to our *padre*. I believe everything is already there by now. Don't forget to inform Isabel López's relative.[9]...to see if there can't be some way to help these poor souls.

---

1. A young trustworthy mail carrier.
2. Jerónimo Gracián.
3. Doña Ana de Toledo.

4. They were deprived of their right to vote or be elected during chapter meetings.
5. Juan Gutiérrez de la Magdalena.
6. The nuns who had followed the provincial's orders not to vote for Teresa.
7. Juan Calvo de Padilla, who was committed to the work of the reform of religious life.
8. María Enríquez de Toledo, to whom a letter was written signed by twenty nuns from the Incarnation asking for help against the provincial.
9. Perhaps Juan López de Velasco, a secretary to the king, Philip II.

213. To Padre Jerónimo Gracián

Avila, October 1577 (?)

This seems to have been written at the time Gracián had withdrawn to live a quieter life of prayer in Pastrana after his task as visitator was over.

I tell you that Joseph[1] is right in letting him sleep. I am delighted, for from the time you left I begged for this with insistent prayers since it seems to me something necessary. And I almost believe that he is doing it for me—in fact I do believe it—since I begged for this so fervently. At least with that sleep the work will be bearable. Nonetheless, it seems to me that you are allowing yourself very little, for if you are going to Matins and getting up early, I don't know how you are getting enough sleep.[2]

1. Code for Jesus Christ.
2. Matins began at midnight and lasted for one hour. At five in the morning he had to be in choir again.

214. To Padre Jerónimo Gracián

Avila, November 1577

Gracián used to confide everything about his interior life to Teresa and at one point he made the same promise as Teresa did of always seeking to do whatever is the most pleasing to God. She here expresses her feelings about the promise he made.

1. I take it as a very great favor from God that in the midst of so many storms Paul[1] has the strength to make such great decisions. Just one hour of these troubles a month would be too much, for they present so many occasions for taking away one's peace. Glory be to the One who gives it.

2. If you carry out that promise, I will need nothing more for my consolation, for all other trials will finally come to an end. And if they did not, it would matter little. Tell him[2] that I must keep that written document so as to remind him of its words should he not have it.

3. His willingness came just at the right time because of the fears I experience. My great anxiety is that Paul might stray in some way from the will of God. In this regard Joseph[3] has greatly reassured Angela[4] that he is doing well and continuing to merit more and more.

---

1. Gracián.
2. That is, Gracián should tell himself (Paul).
3. Jesus Christ.
4. Teresa.

215. To Rodrigo de Aranda, Madrid

Avila, 10 November 1577

This letter seems to be intended for Rodrigo de Aranda, a relative of Gonzalo de Aranda's who was helpful to Teresa in the founding of St. Joseph's in Avila. While Rodrigo is still in Madrid, Teresa seeks his help for the cause of the nuns of the Incarnation who are still excommunicated. She is deeply pained by the whole event.

To the very magnificent and reverend Señor Rodrigo de Aranda, in Madrid.

1. Jesús. May the Holy Spirit be with your honor, and may the Lord repay you, *mi padre*, for the consolation your letters give me. The favorable sentence given in the litigation[1] has been a tremendous one for me. I thanked our Lord abundantly. I don't know if finding so much pleasure in a temporal matter speaks of much perfection. I believe your joy must have been very great and that I can extend congratulations to you, and so I do. Your absence at a time like this has made us feel alone. God willing, things will be smoothed over so that we won't need any favor from my lady, the marchioness,[2] or any of your zealous efforts.

2. You should know, *mi padre*, that the nuns are in a situation that pains me very much—I mean the nuns at the Incarnation.[3] I strongly desire that they obey the present prioress as prioress; they do obey her but only as vicaress. Perhaps they are mistaken, but it seems to them that the well-being of that house depends on what has been done and that it will be destroyed because the friars will be going back there.[4] So they say they want to wait as long as they can. For goodness' sake, would you find out if there is any way in which Tostado[5] or the provincial[6] could absolve them, or if the nuncio[7] could intervene, for nothing is being done in the tribunal about it. If this situation were to go on for a long time, it would be hard to manage.

3. Would you speak about it also to Señor Licentiate Padilla[8] and, if appropriate, write to Padre Julián de Avila,[9] who is very influential with them, to see if perhaps he could get them to

obey Doña Ana.[10] For since the nuns know I don't want to go there, they pay little attention to what I say.

4. I beg my lady the marchioness to help in this matter in any way she can. If I saw the nuns were pacified, I would be greatly consoled. I am not writing to Señor Licentiate Padilla so as not to tire him, for he has trials enough; but I greatly desire to know what is happening concerning Tostado. Read these details about the nuns to the licentiate, I beg you, for things cannot go on as such and should have been resolved already. It is a great disturbance, and offenses against God will not be lacking.

5. May His Majesty watch over you. Your daughters[11] commend themselves to your prayers.

Today is the vigil of St. Martin.

6. If after you have inquired into everything—and after you have spoken with Señor Licentiate Padilla—you cannot find a messenger who will come immediately, my lady the marchioness will send you one of hers. And if you see that doing that would prove troublesome, then hire a messenger and we will pay the expense here. It wouldn't do to prolong the waiting beyond next week; otherwise, as you can see in Fray Juan's[12] enclosed note, the house will be in turmoil. And if you should hire a messenger, let Señor Licentiate Padilla and Señor Roque de Huerta[13] know, for perhaps they may have some letters from our *padre*[14] to send us.

May the Lord direct everything, for these things are painful to me, and may he watch over you.

Today is the vigil of St. Martin's feast.

Your honor's unworthy servant,

Teresa of Jesus

7. I am writing to the licentiate Señor Padilla, and so you need not speak of anything more than about how to proceed,

for matters are such that there is no time for delay. Show him the enclosed note.[15]

---

1. This litigation was different from that concerning the nuns at the Incarnation.
2. The Marchioness of Elche, Juana de Braganza, a relative of Teutonio de Braganza.
3. The nuns were excommunicated by the provincial on 7 October for having gone against his orders not to vote for Teresa. They appealed to the Royal Council against the provincial and were waiting for a judgment.
4. The nuncio, Nicolás Ormaneto, had forbidden the Carmelite friars of the observance to go to the Incarnation after they had imprisoned St. John of the Cross the first time, in January 1576.
5. Jerónimo Tostado, the general visitator for the Carmelite order in Spain.
6. Juan Gutiérrez de la Magdalena, provincial of the Carmelites in Castile.
7. The new nuncio, Felipe Sega.
8. Juan Calvo de Padilla.
9. The chaplain at St. Joseph's in Avila, where Teresa was now residing.
10. Ana de Toledo, who was elected by a minority and confirmed as prioress by the provincial.
11. The nuns at St. Joseph's.
12. St. John of the Cross, who at the time was confessor to the nuns at the Incarnation and residing in a little house next to the monastery
13. Teresa's loyal friend, the king's chief forest guard.
14. Jerónimo Gracián.
15. The note from John of the Cross.

216. To Padre Jerónimo Gracián, Pastrana/Alcalá (?)

Avila, December 1577 (?)

These two fragments may belong to different letters. They seem to belong to the period in which Gracián was waiting for a decision from the new nuncio, Felipe Sega, and living an intensely ascetical life.

1. I praise our Lord highly that he is giving you this quiet and the desire to please him in everything, and that he enlightens you at times with such delightful understanding. This is all the work of his great mercy. Well, His Majesty must give the help that matches the trials, and since they are great, so also are the favors. May his name be blessed forever.

2. I tell you, *mi padre*, that it would be good for you to get your sleep. Realize that you have a great deal of work, and the tiredness is not felt until the head gets into such a condition that there is no remedy, and you already know how important your health is. In this matter follow the opinion of another, out of love of God, and when it is time to sleep set aside your projects, however necessary, and your prayer. Consider doing me this favor. When he sees this fervor of spirit, the devil often presents things as of great importance for God's service so that the good he cannot cut short by one extreme he does by another.

217. To Padre Jerónimo Gracián

Avila, December 1577 (?)

Teresa urges Gracián not to give up prayer time for the sake of his business matters.

I just read again the letter from Paul[1] in which he says he is giving up sleep so as to work on his projects. And I think he says this in reference to his absorption in prayer. He shouldn't get into the habit of abandoning so great a treasure—tell him this—unless it involves giving up the sleep that the body needs. For the blessings the Lord gives in prayer are most remarkable, and I am not surprised that the devil would like to take them away. And since this favor cannot be received whenever one wants, it must be prized when God gives it. In a moment His Majesty will present to us better plans for serving him—apart from so great a gain—than the intellect could ever search out. And believe me, what I'm saying is the truth—unless there is question of some important business matter that has to be concluded at the moment—even if then the sleep does not come because of worries. And if sleep does come, there will be other times for thinking about what the fitting thing to do is. A book I once read says that if we leave God when he wants to be with us, we will not find him when we want to be with him.

1. Gracián.

218. To the King Don Philip II

Avila, 4 December 1577

During the previous night, Fray John of the Cross was taken prisoner and no one knows his whereabouts. The city is scandalized; Teresa worries for his life. The situation is aggravated by the on-going oppression of the nuns at the Incarnation. Fray John of the Cross is a saint "and has been one all his life."

1. The grace of the Holy Spirit be with your majesty, amen. I strongly believe that our Lady has chosen you to protect and help her order. So, I cannot fail to have recourse to you regarding her affairs. For the love of our Lord, I beg you to pardon me for so much boldness.

2. I am sure your majesty has received news of how the nuns at the Incarnation tried to have me go there,[1] thinking they would have some means to free themselves from the friars, who are certainly a great hindrance to the recollection and religious observance of the nuns. And the friars are en-

tirely at fault for the lack of observance previously present in that house. The nuns are very much mistaken in their desire that I go there, for as long as they are subject to the friars as confessors and visitators, I would be of no help—at least not of any lasting help. I always said this to the Dominican visitator,[2] and he understood it well.

3. Since God allowed that situation to exist, I tried to provide a remedy and placed a discalced friar[3] in a house next to them, along with a companion friar.[4] He is so great a servant of our Lord that the nuns are truly edified, and this city is amazed by the remarkable amount of good he has done there, and so they consider him a saint; and in my opinion he is one and has been one all his life.

4. When the previous nuncio[5] through a long report sent him by the inhabitants of the city was informed of the things that were happening and of the harm that the friars of the cloth were doing, he gave orders under pain of excommunication that the confessors be restored to their house (for the calced friars had driven them from the city heaping abuse on them and giving much scandal to everyone). And he also ordered that no friar of the cloth under pain of excommunication go to the Incarnation for business purposes, to say Mass, or hear confessions, but only the discalced friars and secular clergy. As a result, the house was in a good state until the nuncio died. Then the calced friars returned—and so too the disturbance—without demonstrating the grounds on which they could do so.

5. And now a friar[6] who came to absolve the nuns caused such a disturbance without any concern for what is reasonable and just that the nuns are deeply afflicted and still bound by the same penalties as before, according to what I have been told. And worst of all he has taken from them their confessors.[7] They say that he has been made vicar provincial, and this must be true because he is more capable than the others of making martyrs. And he is holding these confessors captive

in his monastery after having forced his way into their cells and confiscating their papers.

6. The whole city is truly scandalized. He is not a prelate nor did he show any evidence of the authority on which these things were done, for these confessors are subject to the apostolic commissary.[8] Those friars dared so much, even though this city is so close to where your majesty resides, that it doesn't seem they fear either justice or God. I feel very sad to see these confessors in the hands of those friars who for some days have been desiring to seize hold of them. I would consider the confessors better off if they were held by the Moors, who perhaps would show more compassion. And this one friar[9] who is so great a servant of God is so weak from all that he has suffered that I fear for his life.

7. I beg your majesty for the love of our Lord to issue orders for them to set him free at once and that these poor discalced friars not be subjected to so much suffering by the friars of the cloth. The former do no more than suffer and keep silent and gain a great deal. But the people are scandalized by what is being done to them. This past summer in Toledo, without any reason, the same superior took as prisoner Fray Antonio de Jesús—a holy and blessed man, who was the first discalced friar.[10] They go about saying that with orders from Tostado[11] they will destroy them all. May God be blessed! Those who were to be the means of removing offenses against God have become the cause of so many sins. And each day matters will get worse if your majesty does not provide us with some help. Otherwise, I don't know where things will end up, because we have no other help on earth.

8. May it please our Lord that for our sakes you live many years. I hope in him that he will grant us this favor. He is so alone, for there are few who look after his honor. All these servants of your majesty's, and I, ask this of him continually.

Dated in St. Joseph's in Avila, 4 December 1577.

Your majesty's unworthy servant and subject,

Teresa of Jesus, Carmelite

1. Teresa had been prioress at the Incarnation 1571–74. The nuns attempted to elect her again on 7 October.
2. Pedro Fernández, who had appointed her prioress at the Incarnation.
3. St. John of the Cross.
4. Germán de San Matías.
5. Nicolás Ormaneto who died 18 June 1577.
6. Hernando Maldonado, prior of the monastery in Toledo. He went there for the purpose of absolving those who voted for Teresa from the excommunication imposed on them.
7. The confessors were John of the Cross and Germán de San Matías.
8. Jerónimo Gracián.
9. John of the Cross.
10. Hernando Maldonado was the superior. Antonio de Jesús (Heredia), one of the first two friars to become discalced (the other being John of the Cross), had accompanied Teresa and Gracián on their recent trip from Toledo to Avila. On his return, Antonio was ordered by Maldonado to remain sequestered in Toledo.
11. Jerónimo Tostado.

219. To Padre Gaspar de Salazar, Granada

Avila, 7 December 1577

Teresa gives an account here of some of the sad events that have been taking place, the excommunication of the nuns at the Incarnation and the libelous accusations made to the king against Gracián and the nuns. She feels deep calm in the midst of it all and has completed a new book, although the problem with noise in her head continues.

To the very magnificent and most reverend lord and *padre*

mio, in Granada.

1. Jesus. May the Holy Spirit be with your honor, *mi padre*. Today, the vigil of the Conception, I received a letter from you. May the Lord repay you for the consolation it gave me. This was necessary, for you should know that for more than three months, it seems, hosts of demons have joined against the discalced friars and nuns. They have stirred up so many persecutions and calumnies against us nuns as well as Padre Gracián, and these are so hard to stomach, that all we can do is take refuge in God. As a result, I believe he has heard our prayer, for the nuns are, after all, good souls. Those who sent memoranda to the king have retracted their words about the lovely exploits they attributed to us.[1] The truth is a great thing and these sisters above all rejoice in it. As for me, it matters little. I've grown used to such things, and it's not surprising that they leave me untouched.

2. Now, to top things off, the nuns at the Incarnation have agreed to vote for me for prioress, and though I received fourteen or fifteen more votes than needed, the friars so conspired that another nun who had fewer votes was elected and confirmed.[2] And the friars would have done me a great favor, provided everything had proceeded peacefully.

3. Since the nuns did not want to obey the newly-confirmed prioress except as vicaress, they were all excommunicated—more than fifty of them. Although in fact, according to learned men, they were not really excommunicated, they have nonetheless had to undergo two months without being able to attend Mass or speak to their confessors,[3] and they are in anguish. Although the nuncio[4] has now given orders for them to be absolved, they are still in the same situation. Just think, what a life it is, to see all of this going on!

4. The case has now gone to the royal council. Although it is very troubling to see this, it's much preferable to my having to go there. Pray for me, for goodness' sake, for until we become

a separate province[5] I don't think we will ever have peace. The devil is trying to prevent this as much as he can.

5. Oh, if I could only speak to you to give you an account of so many things. What is happening and has happened is such a story that I don't know where it will end. When there is some news, I will write to you at length, for they tell me the letters are being delivered safely. It would have been a great help for me to know that you had such a friend in Madrid, but perhaps I still may look to benefit from his help.

6. I wrote to you at length from Toledo. You didn't tell me whether you received the letter. It wouldn't be surprising—with my luck—that you went there, now that I am here. Indeed, it would have meant a little comfort for my soul!

7. Peralta is very grateful to Carillo for what has been done for his relative,[6] not because of concern for her, but because he ascertains that in everything his will is being done. If you should see him, tell him this and that, after all, in no friend does he find so much loyalty.

8. It truly seems that he arranged this friendship. Inform him that the matter written about from Toledo to that person was never resolved successfully. It is known for sure that the jewel is in his hands and that he praises it highly.[7] So until he tires of it he will not give it over. He said that he wants to examine it carefully. It is said that if Señor Carillo[8] were to come here he would see another[9] which—insofar as one can tell—has many advantages over the previous one. It deals with nothing else but who He is; and it does so with more exquisite enameling and decoration. The jeweler did not know as much at that time, and the gold is of a finer quality, although the precious stones do not stand out as they did in the previous piece.[10] It was done by order of the glassmaker,[11] and that is evident according to what they say.

9. I don't know what got me into writing so much at length. I have always been fond of reaching my goal even when it's at

a cost to me. Since he is a friend of yours, you will not tire of delivering these messages.

10. It is said also that one has not written to you through that person, because it would have been only a matter of courtesy and nothing more. Always tell whether you are in good health. I am happy to see that you are almost free of worry. That is not the case with me, but not knowing how, I am at peace and—glory to God—nothing takes it away from me. This noise in my head is distressing to me, for it is constant.

11. Don't forget to pray for me and this order, for there is great need. May His Majesty keep you as holy as I beg of him, amen.

12. These sisters send many regards. They are very good souls. All of us consider ourselves your daughters, especially I myself.

Your honor's unworthy servant,

Teresa of Jesus

---

1. The memorandum against both Jerónimo Gracián and the nuns was sent by Baltasar de Jesús (Nieto) and Miguel de la Columna.
2. This election took place on 7 October 1577. The nun confirmed as prioress was Ana de Toledo.
3. One of the confessors was John of the Cross who at this point had been taken prisoner.
4. Felipe Sega.
5. Her desire was that the discalced nuns and friars be allowed to form a separate province and thus have their own provincial and the ability to live their life without interference.
6. In the code language here Peralta is Christ; Carillo is Salazar himself; and the relative is Teresa.
7. The matter concerned the denunciation of Teresa's *Book of Her Life* to the Inquisition. Her book is the jewel; and "that person" is the inquisitor, Gaspar de Quiroga.
8. Gaspar de Salazar.
9. The other jewel is *The Interior Castle*, which Teresa had just recently completed (29 November).

10. She is referring to the mystical graces. The precious stones do not stand out as clearly as in the *Life* because in the *Interior Castle* she hides her identity.

11. The glassmaker is Jesus Christ. In her new book she had compared the soul to a castle made of crystal.

220. To Don Juan de Ovalle and Doña Juana de Ahumada, Alba

Avila, 10 December 1577

Teresa is trying to help her brother-in-law but not receiving much assistance from her friends. What has been happening at the Incarnation is distressing for her, especially the capture of John of the Cross.

1. Jesus be with your honors. I don't have time to write. I only want to say that I am being very careful about that business matter.[1] I wrote twice to Señora Doña Luisa, and now I am thinking of writing her again. It seems to me she is slow in responding. Certainly I have done and am doing all that I can. May God do what is best for your salvation, for that is what is important. There is no need to send her anything, for I fear that all may be lost. Rather, I am sorry about what you spent to go to Toledo, without any results that I can see. It wouldn't do any harm to send some gift to her brother,[2] for after all he is the master, and nothing would be lost thereby. They are incapable of doing anything unless they think they are gaining something.

2. All gentlemen spend their winters in the country. I don't know why you are troubled about doing the same. Since you—I mean my sister—will have the company of Señora Doña Beatriz, to whom I send my best regards, I am not concerned.[3] I am no worse than usual, and that's already good.

3. The nuns have been absolved, although they are still as insistent as before and bear a greater trial, for the discalced

friars have been taken away from them. I don't know where it will end up, for it is really distressing to me. Those fathers are carrying on as though out of their minds.[4]

4. My brothers are well. They don't know about this letter, I mean this messenger, unless they found out from elsewhere. Teresa no longer has a fever, but the head cold continues.[5]

May God be always with your honors.

Today is 10 December,

Your unworthy servant,

Teresa of Jesus

---

1. Juan de Ovalle was seeking help from intermediaries to obtain a position.
2. Luisa de la Cerda's brother was Fernando de la Cerda.
3. She wonders why they don't spend the winter in Galinduste as in previous years. It would be cheaper for them. Beatriz was Juana's daughter.
4. The nuns, though absolved from the excommunication, were still insisting on their rights to have Teresa for their prioress. The Carmelites of the observance in Castile had taken away as prisoners the confessors John of the Cross and Germán de San Matías, which explains Teresa's strong language.
5. The two brothers are Lorenzo and Pedro. Teresa is her niece who was residing at St. Joseph's in Avila.

221. To Madre María de San José, Seville

Avila, 10 December 1577

(Autograph and Original: DCN, Valladolid)

Not receiving any letters from Madre María, she has been receiving news through the prior of Las Cuevas. Teresa fears for the three discalced nuns in Paterna. In Avila St. John of the Cross and his companion have been taken prisoners. With the help of a secretary she relates the happenings at the Incarnation. She also questions the nuns' desire to move to another house in Seville. Numbers 1–4 and 10–14 are the autograph parts of the letter.

1. Jesus be with you, my daughter. Oh, how long it's been since I've received a letter from you, and how far away it seems that I am up here. Even were I close, it would have been difficult to write you these past days because of all the turmoil going on, about which you will be informed in this letter. I tell you the Lord has not left me idle. Before I forget, with regard to the *agnusdei*, I would like to see it decorated with pearls. If something pleases you, you don't have to ask me about it, for I am happy if you are. May you enjoy much happiness.

2. I would have wanted that in the midst of those disturbances—for they tell me the province is getting stirred up again—the nuns in Paterna be brought back quickly;[1] this is something I strongly desire. Our *padre*[2] has written me that he wrote telling you to do this, with the consent of the archbishop.[3] Try to obtain it before other hindrances arise.

3. Here they are reminding me to ask you for a little *caraña*[4] because it's very helpful to me. It must be of pure quality. Don't forget, for goodness' sake. You can send it well wrapped to Toledo, for they will send it on to me. Or it's enough to entrust it to the man from here when he returns.

4. Don't fail to be most diligent regarding the nuns in Paterna, for apart from the nuns themselves, I would like this for your sake. I don't know how you've been able to get along without them. Now my companion will tell you the story of our trials.[5]

5. Write and tell me whether you have paid for that house or have any money left and why you are in a hurry to move.[6] Tell me about it all, for the prior of Las Cuevas[7] is writing me about it.

6. You should know that the nuns at the Incarnation have been absolved after almost two months of excommunication in which they underwent much anguish. The king commanded that the nuncio give orders to absolve them. Tostado[8] and his councilors sent a prior from Toledo[9] for this purpose, and he absolved them with so many constrictions that it would take a long time to list them all, and he left them more disturbed and dejected than before. And all of this happened because they did not want the prioress[10] the superiors wanted, but me. And the two discalced friars[11] that had been placed there by the apostolic commissary and the previous nuncio were taken away and imprisoned as though they were criminals. I am terribly distressed and will be so until I see them freed from the power of those people. I would rather see them in the land of the Moors.

7. It is said that on the day they were captured, they were flogged twice. They are receiving the worst treatment possible. Maldonado—the prior of Toledo—took Padre Fray John of the Cross to present him to Tostado. The prior here[12] took Fray Germán to San Pablo de la Moraleja.[13] And when he returned he told the nuns that were on his side that he left that traitor in good hands. They said that blood was coming from his mouth as he was taken away.

8. The nuns are suffering over this, more so than from all their other trials, which are heavy. For goodness' sake pray for them and for those saintly captives, for tomorrow it will be eight days since they were seized. The nuns say they are saints and that in all the years the friars were there they behaved in every way like apostles. I don't know where the crazy ideas of those people are going to end up. May God in his mercy provide the remedy he sees as necessary.

9. Give my best regards to Padre Fray Gregorio.[14] Tell him to have prayers said to God concerning all these trials, for it is a great pity to see what these nuns are suffering; they are martyrs. I am not writing to him, because I did so a short time ago.

The letter for him went along with the one I sent you. My best regards to my Gabriela[15] and to all the nuns. May God be with you all.

Today is 10 December.

10. I can't figure out how you are going to get the money to buy another house, for I don't even remember if the one you are in is paid for. It seems to me you told me the interest has been paid off. But if this postulant doesn't want to become a nun, she will clearly want her money back, especially if her sister gets married.[16] Keep me fully informed about everything, for goodness' sake, for through Padre Padilla the letters arrive safely as long as they are sent to the archbishop. Or send them through our *padre*, and then they arrive sooner than when sent by way of Toledo.

11. If you have so much money, don't forget what you owe my brother.[17] He is paying five hundred ducats interest on a property he bought. It would be a great help to him even if you sent only two hundred ducats, for he has received nothing from the Indies.

12. Let me know also how the uprising in the province is going and whom they made vicar, and give my regards to Padre Evangelista and tell him that God is giving him good opportunities for becoming a saint.[18] Tell me all about your health and give me news about the nuns. And if you don't have time, let my Gabriela write me about it.

13. Many greetings to Beatriz[19] and to Señor Garciálvarez;[20] I was very sorry about his illness. My greetings to all the nuns and to Padre Nicolao.[21] May God watch over you for me.

Your servant,

Teresa of Jesus

14. Be careful to take good care of your health, for now you see how important that is. Perhaps you will move to a house where you will roast alive. Consider the great comfort you have

in the one you now occupy; and it is new. It could be that you will become so stubborn that I will let you buy one. I surely want you to be at peace. But you saw all the boasting about how good the first one was.[22]

---

1. Three discalced nuns from Seville were living in a monastery of Carmelite nuns in Paterna in order to reform it.
2. Jerónimo Gracián.
3. Cristóbal de Rojas, the Archbishop of Seville.
4. An aromatic resin from the Indies having medicinal properties.
5. Teresa actually dictates the rest to her secretary.
6. They were thinking of buying a new house and moving.
7. Hernando de Pantoja.
8. The Carmelite general visitator for Spain, Jerónimo Tostado.
9. Hernando Maldonado.
10. Ana de Toledo.
11. St. John of the Cross and Germán de San Matías.
12. The prior of the Carmelites in Avila, Alonso Valdemoro.
13. A small town between Avila and Medina del Campo where the Carmelite friars had another monastery.
14. Gregorio Nacianceno, a discalced friar at Los Remedios in Seville.
15. Leonor de San Gabriel.
16. Cf. Ltr. 202.4.
17. Her brother Lorenzo had advanced a large sum of money for the foundation.
18. Juan Evangelista had been appointed prior of the Carmelites of the observance in Seville by Gracián in his apostolic visitation. In the uprising he was deposed and a vicar was appointed.
19. Beatriz de la Madre de Dios.
20. He was the community confessor.
21. Nicolás Doria was then a novice with the discalced Carmelites in Seville.
22. An ironic statement about the first house, highly praised by Padre Ambrosio Mariano. The first house would have proved a disaster and fortunately the purchase fell through (cf. F. 25.4–6).

222. To Madre María de San José, Seville
Avila, 19 December 1577

(Original and Autograph: DCN, Valladolid)

Teresa has received letters from different people in Seville and gifts for Christmas. But in Avila things are going badly and she is suffering from it all.

1. Jesus be always with your reverence, my daughter. I received yours, and with it the potatoes, the keg, and seven lemons. Everything arrived in good condition. But the portage cost so much that there is no reason for you to be sending me anything any more; it's a matter of conscience.

2. A little over eight days ago I wrote to you by way of Madrid, and so I will not be long. There is nothing new as regards the business spoken of in that letter and about which we are very distressed. Although it's sixteen days from today that our two friars have been taken captive, we don't know if they have been released, although we trust in God that he will provide a remedy.

3. Since Christmas is now coming and since matters of justice cannot be handled until after the feast of Epiphany, the delay will amount to a long time for those[1] who are suffering, if the matter hasn't been settled yet. And these nuns at the Incarnation[2] are also very distressed, for they are in anguish over so many trials, and more so because these holy confessors have been removed and held under such constraint. For goodness' sake, pray for them all, for what they are suffering is a great pity.

4. I rejoice that you and all the sisters are well and that the good work Bernarda[3] did for us has been discovered. Please God the widow[4] will do what you said about not asking them for money. I wrote to the prior of Las Cuevas[5] when I wrote to you. I sent the letter by way of Madrid, as I said. And since I

don't know if this messenger is dependable, I'm saying no more.

5. My regards to Padre Garciálvarez[6] and to Padre Fray Gregorio,[7] whose letter—with which I was delighted—I am not answering for the reason I mentioned. I will try to see if anyone here knows that rector and have them write to him. Best regards to my Gabriela,[8] whose letter was a delight for me. Regards to all the sisters and give Doña Leonor[9] every best wish from me that you like, and let her know how consoling it is for me to learn of her great charity toward your house. And now that you may know how things stand, the portage for all that you sent me came to twelve *reales*. The package was very loosely bound; I don't know why.

Remain with God; may he give all of you as happy a Christmas as I want you to have.

Today is 19 December.[10]

6. Teresa[11] and all the nuns send their best regards. This head of mine is in a wretched state—I don't know how you have understood it to be otherwise—and so many trials have come together that at times I feel exhausted. I don't know when this letter will reach you or if this is a safe way to send it. My brother[12] is well. Don't forget to remember me to all the nuns, and tell those from Paterna that I enjoyed their songs and that from what we can gather their hopes will soon prove vain and they will see this clearly.[13] I give you permission to tell them all that you wish as coming from me.

Your reverence's unworthy servant,

Teresa of Jesus

7. Note that I am seriously ordering you to obey Gabriela in whatever has to do with the treatment prescribed for you, just as I am ordering her to take care of you, for she sees how important your health is to us.

1. John of the Cross and Germán de San Matías. Actually, John of the Cross was in prison until the following August when he got out only through a perilous escape. Fray Germán was held for several months.
2. The Incarnation in Avila.
3. Teresa is being ironical. Benefactors were giving alms to the nuns through the assistance of Bernarda, a beata in Seville. But Bernarda, wrongly thinking the nuns had enough, distributed the alms to other poor people.
4. There were a number of different widows who had sought to enter the Carmel.
5. Hernando de Pantoja.
6. Confessor for the Carmel in Seville.
7. Gregorio Nacianceno.
8. Leonor de San Gabriel who had served as a nurse for Teresa and was now doing the same for María de San José.
9. Leonor de Valera.
10. The remainder of the letter is in Teresa's handwriting.
11. Her niece Teresita.
12. Lorenzo de Cepeda.
13. The three discalced nuns who had returned from Paterna on 4 December had hopes of taking up again their task which was disrupted by the Carmelites of the observance. Teresa predicts the opposite.

223. To Padre Jerónimo Gracián

Avila, Christmas Eve 1577

This note was written with respect to a letter from the Jesuit Jerónimo Ripalda requesting the foundation of a Teresian Carmel in Burgos.

I will answer that they should wait until summer. I have always desired to found a house there, for it would render great service to God. With such a dowry[1] a house could be bought, for the sisters could be separated at a later time.[2]

1. Ripalda promised a dowry of 5,000 ducats.

2. The sisters would not always have to remain together in the same monastery.

224. To Don Antonio de Soria, Salamanca

(Date Uncertain)

(Autograph: Cathedral in Salamanca)

The addressee is the administrator for Francisco de Fonseca, Lord of Coca and Alaejos. He had sent an alms to Teresa asking for a favor in return.

To the very magnificent Señor Antonio de Soria, my lord.

1. Jesus. May the Holy Spirit be with your honor, amen. I received the one hundred *reales* and the rest of what the carrier of this letter brought. May the Lord preserve for many years the one who sent them and grant my prayer to give him health.

2. The carrier is bringing the bed, and if Señor Sotomayor is there, I beg you to tell him to examine it to see that no damage was done to it. I was present when it was packed in the cart and saw that the work was done carefully. I am sorry that this is such a lamentable place that I could not find what you asked me for anywhere. They took pains to try to find it—as this good man will tell you—and found no more than these three. Please God they will be what you want, for we were unable to make out one part of your letter in which you explain how they should be. Here we call the best kind camlet; any other kind is worthless. Certainly I have been wondering what I could send that you did not already have there, and I don't find anything worthwhile; if I could, it would make me very happy. But it would make me very happy if you informed me of some way I could serve you, without Señor Don Francisco knowing about it.[1]

3. May our Lord ever guide your honor and make you very much his own.

Your servant,

Teresa of Jesus

I am sending seven pieces: two of green damask and five of gold fabric.

---

1. Francisco de Fonseca.

Biographical Sketches

Biographical Sketches

Acosta, Diego de. A Jesuit friend of Teresa's, he had been a professor of theology in Salamanca and, later, provincial in Andalusia. When he was living in Seville, Teresa advised the prioress there to consult him since she considered him a man of good judgment.

Ahumada, Agustín (1527–91). One of Teresa's brothers, he went to Peru with Pedro de La Gasca. After ten years of war, on an expedition to Chile, he returned to Peru. There he became a member of the council of war for the viceroy, Francisco de Toledo. This came about through the mediation of Teresa's friend and spiritual director, García de Toledo, who was advisor to the viceroy. Agustín was the youngest and most restless of Teresa's brothers. He remained unmarried, and Teresa worried about his spiritual condition. At one time she prayed with real daring for his conversion (ST. 16). At one point he had to ask Lorenzo to help his natural daughter, Leonor. At the end of his life, Agustín testified that he had once received a letter from his sister warning him not to accept any office in the Indies if he valued his salvation. He returned to Spain, but later, after Teresa's death, decided to go back to the Indies since he had been offered the governorship of Tucumán. During the voyage there he began to feel deep remorse over his decision to accept the office and fell sick with a fever. A feeling came over him that he had made a mistake by dismissing his sister's advice of some time ago. He died during the voyage, but in great quiet and peace, which he felt was a grace obtained for him by his sister, whose relic he was carrying with him.

Ahumada, Juana de (b. 1528). Younger than Teresa by thirteen years, Teresa's sister Juana was also the youngest in the family. When their father died, Teresa took her to live with her at the Incarnation, since there was ample room in her cell, which was really a suite of rooms. For about nine years she was provided for by her sister with much love. Juana married Juan de Ovalle in 1553. She and her husband helped Teresa with the first foundation in Avila as is explained in the *Life* (33.11). Teresa's opinion of her is revealed in a letter to her brother Lorenzo: "Juana is so honorable and trustworthy that she makes you want to praise God, and she has the soul of an angel" (2.9). Her marriage to Juan de Ovalle, nonetheless, resulted in much suffering for her because of his childish and jealous disposition. Lorenzo had to come to the assistance of the couple because of their financial difficulties. Three of their five children died in infancy.

Ahumada, Pedro de (b. 1521). A neurotic type, difficult to cope with, he was the brother who most tried the patience and goodness of Teresa. He left Spain for the Indies and then also traveled on an expedition to Florida. After his wife's death, he returned to Spain. Because he was unable to support himself, Teresa urged her brother Lorenzo to care for him.

Alba, Duchess of (María Enríquez de Toledo). In 1573, ordered by the king, Teresa had to journey to Alba to visit and console the duchess who had heard the rumors about the king's disapproval of the policies followed by her husband Don Fernando. The duke was soon relieved of his charge as captain general, recalled to Spain, exiled from the court, and confined in Uceda. The duchess of Alba became a close friend of both Teresa and Antonio de Heredia. In her *Interior Castle* (VI.4.8), when trying to tell about the knowledge of God's secrets and grandeurs that God sometimes granted her while she was in ecstasy, Teresa used the analogy of all the precious objects on display in one of the rooms in the duchess's palace. When orders were given that copies of Teresa's *Medita-*

tions on the Song of Songs be burned, the nuns in Alba de Tormes gave their manuscript to the duchess. When the nuns at the Incarnation were excommunicated by the provincial for voting for Teresa as prioress, both they and Teresa wrote for help to the Duchess of Alba. In the last month of her life, Teresa was on her way back from Burgos to Avila to be present for the profession of her niece Teresita. But the Duchess of Alba had asked Antonio de Heredia, who was vicar provincial at the time, to give orders to Teresa to come to Alba because her daughter-in-law was about to give birth and she wanted Teresa to be with her at the time. It was a painful and difficult moment for Teresa to have to accept this obedience. After Teresa's death, Juana de Ahumada gave the duchess the cross of which Teresa speaks in her *Life* (29.7).

Alba, Duke of (Fernando Alvarez de Toledo) (1507–82). The third duke of Alba, he was born in Piedrahita (Avila). When still young he fought against the French in Fuenterrabia. At age twenty-two, he married María Enríquez. Later revealing his talents as a military man in the defense of the coast of Catalán, his genius as a military strategist was recognized. Nonetheless, Charles V warned King Philip II to be careful and curtail any tendency to allow him too much power within the government. In 1567, when the iconoclasts in the Low Countries provoked the anger of Philip II, the Duke of Alba was called from Italy and ordered to quash the insurrection. With 10,000 troops the duke marched confidently on Brussels. But his attempts to repress revolt with brutal efficiency were in the end counterproductive. Deep fissures opened up among the king's policy-makers, prompting the king to write to the duke: "I can easily find you a successor able and faithful enough to bring to an end, through moderation and clemency, a war that you have been unable to bring to an end by arms or by severity." In 1573, he was recalled to Spain because of the king's displeasure with the harsh ways in which he exercised his office. In 1574, his son Don Fadrique attempted to marry Magdalena de Guzmán without the necessary authorization from the king,

Philip II, whose rigidity over questions of marriage among the aristocracy was well known. The king angrily imprisoned both father and son, the former in the castle of Uceda and the later in that of Mota. In January 1579, the duke and duchess with their retinue left Madrid for the tranquillity of house arrest at Uceda. Foreign dignitaries, including the king of France and the pope, pleaded in the duke's favor, but the king in a display of his notorious stubbornness, refused to relent. Don Fernando was frequently visited there and consoled by Gracián. In this predicament, at Uceda, the duke read St. Teresa's *Life*. In 1579 he wrote to the nuncio Sega in favor of the discalced friars and nuns. One time Gracián jokingly suggested to the duchess that Teresa loved the duke more than she did her. Teresa wrote to the duchess with all her exquisite tact in order to calm her and give her assurance of her love and esteem. In 1578, at the death of Don Sebastián, the king of Portugal, Philip II, had to make a difficult choice. When it became clear that a commander for the Portuguese campaign had to be appointed, Philip directly faced the embarrassing prospect of having to choose the Duke of Alba. His councillors were unanimous that only Alba had the necessary reputation and prestige. Philip recalled the duke, whose age was then 73, to active service and engaged him to lead his armies in the conquest of Portugal. Teresa commented disapprovingly, "if this matter is pursued through war, I fear great harm." In 1580 Don Fernando, happy to be given the order and meeting with little effective resistance, carried out the task quickly. He died two years later in Lisbon, assisted in his last moments by Fray Luis de Granada.

Alcántara, Peter St. (1499–1562). Juan Garavito was born in Alcántara in Extremadura and studied at Salamanca either law or philosophy 1511–1515. After finishing his studies, he entered a Franciscan hermitage in Majarretes and became known as Pedro de Alcántara. Ordained in 1524, he soon distinguished himself for his apostolic zeal throughout Spain and Portugal. Frequently appointed guardian (superior), he afterward became provincial in 1538. In 1554 at the age of fifty-five, he received a brief from the Holy See allowing him to live an eremitical life. After two years in this life, he was appointed by the superiors of his order to undertake a reform of the Franciscans. It was he who was able to assure Teresa about her mystical prayer and free her from the many fears that other confessors had stirred in her, as she tells in her *Life* (30.1–7). He went personally to Francisco de Salcedo and Baltasar Alvarez explaining why they had nothing to worry about in her case. He also gave Teresa excellent advise, helping, and strongly encouraging her to make her first foundation (L. 36.20). The Bishop of Avila was convinced by him to accept the new house of nuns under his jurisdiction. Even after his death Peter continued to help Teresa in extraordinary ways (L. 27.19). He was beatified in 1622 and canonized in 1669.

Alvarez, Baltasar (1533–80). Born in Cervera del Rio (Logroño), he entered the Jesuits in 1555 after graduating from Alcalá. He was twenty-six and only one year ordained when he became Teresa's confessor in Avila. He carried out this ministry between the years 1559–65, a crucial stage in Teresa's spiritual journey. During this time, Teresa began to experience her visions, revelations, and woundings of love. Timid in temperament and easily influenced by those around him, he suffered hesitations and doubts, which were a long time in dissipating entirely. Although he tried to assure Teresa, she could clearly see that he was nervous and apprehensive about her. Neither was he much help to her in the midst of all the troubles she had from her superiors and the townspeople at the time of her first foundation. But during the years he was directing Teresa, he was undergoing problems of his own, scruples, doubts, and fears about his spiritual life, prayer, and ability to direct others. Despite his wavering, Teresa thought of him as a saint and one of her best friends. In 1565, he was transferred to Medina del Campo as novice master. In 1573, the provincial of Castile, together with Martín Gutiérrez and Juan Suárez were captured by the Huguenots in the south of France and tortured. Martín Gutiérrez died as a result. Baltasar Alvarez had been left as vice-provincial in Castile, and was forced into frantic efforts to collect 18,000 ducats as ransom money. He was weighed down with worries over the debts incurred. The new general in Rome appointed Juan Suárez as provincial for Castile, and Baltasar Alvarez as rector in Salamanca. Alvarez's arrival in Salamanca filled the Carmelite nuns with hope because they admired his spiritual discernment. But to the great disappointment of Teresa, the provincial Juan Suárez, whom Alvarez had succeeded in ransoming from the Huguenots, paid heed to the accusation that Alvarez was devoting too much care to the nuns in hearing their confessions and began to take action against him. He objected that Alvarez's form of prayer ("learned through his dealings with Madre Teresa and her nuns, in which space is given for the action of God") was suspect. Because of the *alumbrados* the times were precarious for anyone speaking of quiet in prayer. Later, in his visitation in 1577, Diego de Avellaneda would give the coup de grace, when he ordained that "they [the Jesuits] should not waste time on women, especially Carmelite nuns, either in visits or letters, but "gently and efficaciously" get away from them. The decision was a great sorrow for Teresa. But Baltasar Alvarez remained her friend until he died After many other administrative posts, he became provincial of Toledo. He continued throughout his life to support Teresa in her founding new monasteries. While he was in Medina, he began himself to experience infused prayer. But his new mode of prayer gave rise to worries on the part of his superiors. They considered it to be dangerous and foreign to the *Spiritual Exercises* of St. Ignatius of Loyola. They forbade him to continue with this kind of prayer, and he submitted. Although eighteen years younger than Teresa, he died before her at the age forty-seven. When word reached her of his death, she wept for over an hour and no one could console her. When asked why she was weeping that much since she was so detached from the things of the world, she replied: "I am weeping because I know what a great loss this is to the Church of God; and she then went into a rapture for two hours."

Ambrosio Mariano de San Benito (Azzaro) (1510–94). Born in Bitonto, Italy, he was descended from a noble Neapolitan family and gifted with a high intelligence. In his youth he dedicated himself to intense study, receiving a doctorate in both theology and canon law. Backed by these degrees and his recent studies, he took part in the Council of Trent, where he received important commissions to carry out in certain countries in northern Europe. He met with success in these endeavors and won for himself an element of renown. Invited by Queen Catherine of Austria, the wife of Sigismund II of Poland, to serve as major-domo in her palace, he felt actually as though in a prison, and resigned and joined the military. He was later falsely accused of homicide, but refused to defend himself, spending two years in prison until ultimately his innocence was acknowledged. Being informed about his extraordinary knowledge in geometry and hydraulics, Philip II employed him in an engineering project to make the Quadalquivir navigable from Seville to Córdoba. While in Seville, he felt touched by a special grace and decided to renounce the world and withdraw into solitude in Tardó, an isolated spot in the Sierra Morena, where a group of hermits were living a life of extraordinary austerity and penance under the direction of Mateo de la Fuente. He lived there for eight years. In 1568, he was called by Philip II to Aranjuez to direct the construction of a large irrigation canal. After finishing this project, he went to Madrid and received hospitality there in the palace of Doña Leonor Mascareñas. At this time, in June 1569, he met St. Teresa. It was a providential and decisive meeting for the hermit. Teresa invited him to join her, showing him the constitutions that she had written for her nuns. In the morning of the following day, he informed Teresa that he had decided to embrace her reform. What is more, because of the decree of Pius V, which obliged solitaries to enter orders already established, he had been planning to go to Rome with his companion, Juan

Narduch, to obtain from the Holy Father the authorization to live an eremitical life in a solitary place on a property belonging to Prince Ruy Gómez de Silva near Pastrana. Coincidently, Teresa was on her way there to make a foundation of her nuns. One month later, Mariano received the habit of the discalced Carmelite friars and inaugurated the life of the reform there along with Juan de la Miseria and Baltasar de Jesús Nieto. He made his profession the following year, and in 1574, at the urging of Gracián, he was ordained a priest. But he could never detach himself from engineering. As one chronicler put it, he preferred construction to hearing confessions. An admirer of the extraordinary woman penitent, Catalina de Cardona, about whom Teresa wrote a detailed account (see F. 28), he assisted her in her desire to have a monastery of discalced Carmelite friars near her cave in La Roda. Following his inclination to mine under mountains and live underground, he made a passageway so that Catalina could walk in her cave untroubled by cold or heat, with openings for light at intervals. This undertaking depleted funds that had been raised to build a monastery for the friars, and in the end the extensive underground digging weakened the foundations of the friars' monastery, and it collapsed

He did render important services to both Teresa and Gracián, but because of his impulsiveness and rough manner he caused them suffering as well. Teresa pleaded with him to use discretion and moderation and to be more submissive and respectful toward the general's wishes. In his fascination with the penitential life of Catalina de Cardona, he pushed for austerity within the order. At the chapter of Alcalá, in which the discalced Carmelites became a separate province and were able to elect their own provincial, Ambrosio Mariano supported Antonio de Jesús (Heredia) for provincial, as did some other admirers of Catalina de Cardona. Teresa, of course, strongly favored Gracián, whose ideals for the friars were more like her own, and she grew impatient with Mariano. Fortunately for both friars and nuns, Gracián was elected, but by a margin of only one vote. Mariano next founded a monastery for the friars in Lisbon in 1581, but a year later, a little before the Teresa's death, he was called by Philip II to Seville for another construction project. In 1588 and 1590 he was elected to be second councillor to the vicar general, Nicolás Doria. He died in Madrid while serving as prior of the monastery there.

Ana de San Alberto (d. 1624). From the town of Malagón, she entered the Carmel there at its beginning, making her profession in 1569. Teresa usually called her Alberta. She went with Teresa on the foundations in Beas and Seville. In November 1576, under Teresa's direction, she made a new foundation in Caravaca where she was appointed prioress, remaining so for fifteen consecutive years. Teresa urged her to take St. John of the Cross as her director and speak to him as openly as she would to Teresa herself. One letter of John's to her has survived as well as some other fragments from his letters to her.

Anne of Jesus (Ana de Jesús Lobera) (1545–1621). Born in Medina del Campo, she entered St. Joseph's in Avila, but made her profession in Salamanca on 22 October 1571. Teresa brought Anne with her to be prioress for the new foundation in Beas in 1575. In 1582, Anne traveled to Granada, accompanied by St. John of the Cross, to make a foundation for nuns there. It was to her that John dedicated his commentary on the *Spiritual Canticle* (1584). In 1586, after Teresa's death, again accompanied by John of the Cross, she made a foundation in Madrid. While prioress there she enlisted the help of Luis de León to serve as editor for the publication of the works of St. Teresa, which appeared in 1588. Falling into disfavor with Nicolás Doria, the vicar general of the discalced friars and nuns, for having obtained a brief from Sixtus V stating that no one has authority to change or modify the nuns' constitutions (given in Alcalá a year before Teresa's death), Anne was deposed as prioress in Madrid. After Doria died, she was elected prioress in Salamanca in 1596. At the head of five Carmelite nuns from Spain, and in response to the urgent appeals of Pierre de

Bérulle, she made a foundation in Paris in 1604. Accompanying Bl. Anne of St. Bartholomew on the foundation in Pontoise in 1605, she some months later made a foundation in Dijon. But noting that Bérulle held firmly to his jurisdiction over the discalced Carmelite nuns in France and was determined to direct them in accord with his own plans, she went to the Spanish Netherlands at the beginning of 1607. Under the jurisdiction of the discalced Carmelite friars, she made foundations in Brussels (1607), Louvain (1607), and Mons (1608). In 1614, she was struck down by illness and for eight years underwent painful bodily sufferings: soar throats, pleurisy, sciatica, paralyses, dropsy, tumors, and burning throughout her entire body. She died in Brussels. The cause for her beatification was introduced shortly after her death, but did not advance. The diocesan investigation has been transferred to Rome for continued study.

Ana de la Encarnación (Tapia) (d. 1601). A cousin of Teresa's, she was a nun at the Incarnation and went with Teresa on the foundation to Medina del Campo (1567). There her sister, Inés de Jesús, became prioress and she subprioress. In 1570 she went with Teresa on the foundation in Salamanca and became prioress there. In the beginning she had to bear with the constant displeasure of Pedro de la Banda, the owner of the house in which the foundation was made (F. 19.10). She remained in Salamanca and was prioress there for many years.

Antonio de Jesús (Heredia) (1510–1601). Born at Requena in the province of Valencia, he received the Carmelite habit at the age of ten. After his studies at Salamanca, he was ordained a priest at the age of twenty-two. In 1536, he was made prior at La Moraleja and held the office of prior also at Toledo (1561), Avila (1565), and Medina (1567). Having assisted St. Teresa in the organization of the life at St. Joseph's in Avila and with the foundation in Medina del Campo, he offered to follow Teresa's ideal and become a member of the first discalced Carmelite community for friars. This first community, which included St. John of the Cross, was established in the solitude of Duruelo in 1568. He was the superior there and later, too, in Mancera when the new community moved there in 1570. In 1573 the visitator Fernández sent him to be prior of the Carmelites of the observance in Toledo. In 1575, he made a foundation for the discalced friars in Almodóvar del Campo and became its prior. But in November of that year, he traveled with Gracián to Seville to be his adviser in the troublesome visitations the latter had to carry out in Andalusia. Here he became prior of Los Remedios (1576–78), a monastery for discalced Carmelite friars. In 1580, he once more became prior of Mancera. A year later in the election for a provincial among the discalced friars, at their first chapter in Alcalá (1581), he ended up with four votes less than Gracián, who became the first provincial. Antonio was present in Alba de Tormes as vicar provincial assisting St. Teresa in her last illness and death there in 1582. In 1591 he was elected provincial of Andalusia. Although he was learned and a good preacher, he tended to be touchy, quarrelsome, and a bit of a gossip. Not always showing good judgment in the delicate situations preceding the separation of the discalced friars and nuns into a separate province, he showed poor judgment as well in his ascetical practices. Thus, after the chapter in 1581, they had to forbid him to go about barefoot and made him wear hemp sandals like the others. In his relations with Teresa he manifested a jealous immaturity. Although he esteemed her highly, he thought she should prefer him to others who joined her reform after himself. Since she was obliged to write much more to Gracián than to him, she cautioned Gracián to avoid letting him know how often she wrote. Sometimes in his childishness he would refuse to write to her for months, nor would he answer the letters written by her to him, which presumably overflowed with warmth and love and good humor. He never saved any of her letters to him. It was he who as vicar provincial ordered Teresa at the end of her life to go to Alba de Tormes. By doing this he frustrated her avid plans to go to Avila for the profession of her niece Teresita. Teresa died in Alba de Tormes not long after her arrival. Antonio's last years were spent in Granada. He left Granada for Vélez-Málaga in March where he died at the age of 91. His remains are kept there by the discalced Carmelite nuns.

Avila, John of, St. (1500–69). Born in Almodóvar del Campo, John of Avila studied at Salamanca and Alcalá. Called "the apostle of Andalusia," he dedicated himself to a fervent ministry of preaching in Andalusia and strongly influenced the spiritual currents of his day. He is best known for his little work *Audi filia*. In 1561, Don Francisco de Soto, bishop of Salamanca and inquisitor general, passed through Avila. Anxious about not being deceived because of the extraordinary mystical experiences she was undergoing, Teresa arranged to see him and explain her experiences and manner of prayer. After listening to her, he recommended that she write everything down and send it to John of Avila and then abide by his response. Even though other learned men, including Domingo Báñez, had approved *The Book of her Life*, Teresa was not at ease without an opinion from John of Avila, for she had not forgotten Soto's advice. With the help of Luisa de la Cerda, after much insistence with her, and even annoyance over her procrastinations, Teresa managed to get her manuscript into the hands of the revered John of Avila. On 12 September 1568, he sent the manuscript back to her with a lengthy letter of approval. He advised her to continue along her path and give thanks to the Lord who had given her his love and a knowledge of herself. He told her not to pay much attention to her extraordinary experiences although not to make light of them either. He discerned signs that many were from the Lord and held that the others would do her no harm as long as she continued to seek counsel. At last Teresa was able to set aside her anxieties about it. John of Avila died in Montilla (Córdoba). When Teresa received word of his death she wept inconsolably. When those who tried to console her said that he was a saint and that she had nothing to grieve over, she answered that her grief was over the loss his death was for the church and to many souls who found in him their strong support. He was beatified by Leo XIII in 1894 and canonized by Paul VI in 1970.

Avila, Julián de (1527–1605). Born in Avila, he began his studies in philosophy there at Santo Tomás. One day coming home late, he suddenly began to feel fear over the anger his tardiness would stir up in his father, so he decided that instead of going home he would take off and wander about the world. After a couple of years, while living in Córdoba, he started to get homesick and decided to return to Avila. On the way he was thrown from his mule and so wounded by his own sword that he lost consciousness and almost died. After this jolting experience, while meditating on the fragility of life, he decided to become a priest. He confessed to Gaspar Daza in Avila and, with this priest's help, was reconciled with his father. Taking up his studies once more, he was ordained a priest in 1558. Twelve years younger than Teresa, he was always one of the first to come to her help. She knew his limitations, though. He lacked initiative, had little executive ability, and manifested no great depth, yet he faithfully carried out what he was commissioned to do and was much loved by everyone for his charity, patience, amiableness, and sense of humor, although it was admittedly odd. He perhaps got to know Teresa through Gaspar Daza who continued as his confessor. A chaplain of the Bernardine nuns, he was also appointed chaplain for the discalced Carmelite nuns in Avila. As such he became Teresa's steady traveling companion for her first eleven foundations. During the process for the beatification of Teresa, some questions arose about a certain expression used by Teresa in her writings. The pope intervened and asked Julián de Avila to send information about what he thought she meant in the passages in question. The final amplified form turned out to be a biography of Teresa written by Julián de Avila. It is a delightful narrative of the adventures, hazards, and setbacks surrounding Teresa's foundations but mingled with it are some mystical reflections that do not fit the narrative. Because of illnesses that led to his death, he had to cut this work short. He died in Avila and is buried in the Carmelite chapel of St. Joseph's in Avila.

Baltasar de Jesús (Nieto) (1524–90). Born in Zafra (Extremadura) of a Portuguese father and Spanish mother, he entered the Franciscan order in 1563, but then transferred to the Carmelites while his brother was provincial. When stationed in Utrera, Baltasar assaulted the prior, and when corrected by Rossi, the general, he replied with an insolent letter. Later Rossi declared in his account of the visitation in Spain: "When we came to Andalusia, we strongly rebuked these three brothers [the Nieto brothers, Caspar, Baltasar, and Melchor] for their petulant and libidinous conduct by which they had befouled themselves." The most unsavory of the three was Melchor. In 1565, in Ecija, he attacked the visitator Mazzapica, struck him in the face, seized and tore his capuce, and threw him to the ground. Caspar had him put in irons and dispatched to Seville. En route, in Carmona, Baltasar got into the cell where his brother was being detained, provided him with a sword, and helped him escape. For aiding and abetting his brother, Baltasar got three years' exile in Castile or Portugal with a privation of his seniority and vote in the community. In May of 1567, Rossi absolved him from his penance of confinement and restored his active and passive voice provided he would live in the province of Castile. But later because of further difficulties, Rossi expelled him from the order. However, the visitators appointed by the king absolved him from excommunication. Incredibly, he was received among the discalced Carmelites and took the name Baltasar de Jesús. He became prior of Pastrana in 1570, founded the college at Alacalá in 1570, and the monastery in Granada in 1573. But he was then sent back to Pastrana where he continued as prior. Because of his eloquence as a preacher he was esteemed by many and had influential friends. In 1577, he abandoned his priorate in Almodóvar and went to Madrid where he placed himself under Tostado. Composing a letter defamatory of Gracián and the discalced friars, he induced Fray Miguel de la Columna, who was somewhat retarded, to sign it. In the letter he makes the accusation that Gracián in his visitations in Andalusia had the discalced nuns serve him sumptuous meals with turkey and partridge. He asserts further that Gracián entered the nuns' cloister and had the nuns sing and dance for him, and wrote sonnets and romances for the nuns to sing. At Beas, he goes on, a young beautiful nun danced before him dressed up in silk vestments from the sacristy "so that she seemed more a prostitute than a nun." The letter went on to say that some of the houses of the discalced nuns were very lax and followed certain practices that resembled those of the *alumbrados.* Horrified, Teresa wrote a letter to the king in defense of Gracián and her nuns, pointing out how absurd the accusations were. The two discalced friars later retracted. In the end Baltasar, having lost any standing he might have still had in the eyes of others, transferred to Lisbon where he died.

Banda, Pedro de la. The house in Salamanca where the nuns first established themselves was near both a river and the city reservoir. Because of this and the poor condition of the house itself, the health of the community eventually suffered. The nuns found another house owned by Pedro de la Banda, who was described by the chronicler as ill-mannered. The house was from an entailed estate and could not be sold without a royal license. However the vendor gave his word that the nuns could have it even if the license was not given and that they could do their renovations. Pressured to leave the unhealthy house in which they were living, Teresa moved quickly. The little community spent all they had (over 1,000 ducats) turning this new house into a monastery, complete with cloister, cells, refectory, and chapel. She paid for all of this from the dowries of the nuns who had already entered. But after they had moved in, Don Pedro, who had been away, retuned and was furious for what they had done to the house. Teresa decided to let go of the house, but he didn't want that either. What he, or rather his wife, Aldonza Ruiz Maldonado, wanted was money to provide for two daughters. The contract had not required payment of this money until the king's license arrived and was warranted. Don Pedro resorted to a law suit, claiming that the contract was null and void for lack of the royal license. Writing about this three years after the event, Teresa remarked that the purchase had not yet been finalized. In fact it took forty-four years, during which the nuns were twice evicted, before the matter was settled.

Báñez, Domingo (1528–1604). Born in Valladolid, he began his studies in Salamanca in 1543 and entered the Dominicans there (San Esteban) in 1546 where he made his religious profession a year later. He remained in Salamanca, studying philosophy and theology (1547–51) and then teaching these subjects at San Esteban for ten years. In 1561 he was transferred to Santo Tomás in Avila as professor until 1567. During a part of this time in Avila, he was confessor to St. Teresa and the nuns at St. Joseph's. He fearlessly defended Teresa and her work before the irate city council of Avila. In 1565 he took his doctor's degree in the University of Siguenza. In 1567 he became professor of theology at Alcalá. In 1573–77 he was Rector at St. Gregory's in Valladolid, then returned to Salamanca as professor in 1577. In 1577 he won the chair of Prime at Salamanca university, which he held until 1604. He was a preacher and theologian with great prestige, becoming famous for his debates with the Jesuits over the complex question of predestination and free will. According to witnesses, he always had great admiration and respect for Teresa. As official censor for the inquisition, he was given the task of examining Teresa's *Book of her Life,* which had been denounced to that body by the princess of Eboli. He gave the work his approval and defended Teresa's spirit, also pointing out, however, that the work should be kept secret. After Teresa's death, he published in 1584 his magisterial work of theology, a commentary on the Summa of St. Thomas Aquinas. In 1590, he wrote to Nicolás Doria about a controversy that was taking place concerning St. Teresa's constitutions. Since the problem had originated with Anne of Jesus and the nuns at Santa Ana in Madrid, he wrote to Doria, urging him to refrain from any kind of ruthless punishment of the discalced nuns, especially the community at Santa Ana. Báñez died in Medina del Campo.

Beatriz de Jesús (Cepeda y Ocampo) (d. 1607). The daughter of Teresa's cousin, she was a nun at the Incarnation, the one who witnessed Teresa levitate during a conversation with St. John of the Cross when he was confessor there. She joined the discalced nuns in Avila and then went with Teresa to Malagón. Fond of the prioress, Brianda de San José, she took over as superior when the prioress became too sick to continue in her office. At first Teresa doubted her capability, and Beatriz thought as well that it would be too difficult a task. Nonetheless, as things turned out, she did "extremely well," Teresa reported. She accompanied Teresa to the foundation in Villanueva de la Jara, returning with her once the foundation was made. In December 1581, she accompanied St. John of the Cross to Beas and on to Granada for the foundation of nuns there. Later, in 1586, she was chosen for the foundation in Madrid. Ultimately, she was appointed subprioress in Ocaña, which is where she died.

Beatriz de la Madre de Dios (Chaves) (1538–1624). Inspired by the preaching of Gracián, she decided to enter Carmel in Seville and made her profession in 1576. But she was emotionally unstable, no doubt owing to the terrible treatment she had received as a child and young adult. Teresa gives an account of this distressing treatment in her *Foundations* (ch. 26). Beatriz as a nun began to experience false ecstasies and visions. Spending hours in the confessional, she continued going from bad to worse. The confessor, Garciálvarez, dealt with the matter poorly and spoke against the prioress, who was trying to put an end to the long hours in the confessional. When the nuncio Sega placed the discalced friars and nuns under the jurisdiction of the Carmelites of the observance, the provincial of the latter group in Andalusia, Diego de Cárdenas, made an official visitation of the monastery of nuns in Seville, at which many false accusations were made by Beatriz. He misconstrued what was taking place and deposed the prioress, María de San José, appointing, of all people, Beatriz de la Madre de Dios as prioress. Understandably, she lasted hardly a year in office. Teresa, however, always insisted that she be treated with kindness. Beatriz eventually matured and lived a long life, dying at the age of 86.

Braganza, Teutonio de (1530–1602). Son of the Duke of Braganza, Don Teutonio did his studies in Coimbra and Paris. He entered the Society of Jesus in 1549 but later left after a disagreement with St. Ignatius over the removal of Simón Rodríguez, provincial of Portugal. Teresa met him in Salamanca in 1574, and they remained friends for the rest of her life. But he was not as skilled as necessary in carrying out some of the favors Teresa wanted of him. Such was the case with the college for her discalced friars that Teresa wanted in Salamanca. In 1578 he was appointed archbishop of Evora. In his zeal he committed large sums of money to foundations for works of charity and religion. An author of many works, he also helped in the publication of others including St. Teresa's *Way of Perfection*, printed at his expense in 1583.

Brianda de San José (d. 1586). Born in the province of Burgos, she made her profession in Toledo, and then moved to Malagón to become prioress there. When Teresa arrived in Malagón on her return from Seville, she found that Brianda was seriously ill. Thinking the illness, which was thought to be consumption, resulted from the poor condition of the house the nuns were living in, Teresa began strongly urging Luisa de la Cerda to build the new monastery as she had promised. Hoping that the prioress' health would improve in Toledo, Teresa arranged for her to be brought there where she could attend to her care. She once went so far as to describe her as the best nun in the order. As things turned out, Brianda eventually recovered and was twice elected prioress in Toledo, although she died only a few months after the second election.

Cepeda, Francisco de (ca. 1560–1617). The older of the two sons of Teresa's brother Lorenzo. Lorenzo arrived with them in Seville from America in 1575. After two years of college and after some dissolute living and even plans for a marriage, Francisco was deeply moved by his father's death in June 1580. He consequently decided to enter the discalced Carmelite novitiate in Pastrana in October of that year. Nicolás Doria was prior of the novitiate in Pastrana and made little account of Francisco's being Teresa's nephew. He in fact sent him away coldly without allowing him to receive the habit. Gracián had accompanied him to the novitiate, but he was not enthused about the vocation either. Nonetheless, Teresa was saddened over what took place, for she believed he would have made a holy Carmelite. On 8 December of that very year, he married Doña Orofrisia de Mendoza y Castilla, a beautiful young girl not yet fifteen, niece of the Duke of Infantado, but of little wealth. Teresa hadn't learned about the wedding until after it was over. It brought her nothing but trouble. Don Lorenzo had named Teresa the only executor of his will. The mysterious fact that the will appeared torn in half when presented for its execution served as a pretext for some to say that the will was invalid. But the reason behind this protest lay in the fact that Don Lorenzo provided that should Francisco de Cepeda die without an heir, the inheritance was then to be used for the pious works that Teresa knew about, which were mainly that of building a chapel at St. Joseph's in Avila. This clause aggravated Francisco's mother-in-law, Doña Beatriz de Castilla, who brought a lawsuit against Teresa and turned María Bautista against her. When toward the end of her life, Teresa arrived sick in Valladolid on her return from Burgos, Beatriz sent a lawyer to her who treated her very badly. Although Teresa came to an agreement with Francisco for the sake of peace, the latter went from bad to worse financially because of poor administration of his funds. Finding himself without money and without children he returned to America in 1591 in search of a fortune. That same year, his wife sold *La Serna,* the property inherited from Lorenzo, for the same amount at which Don Lorenzo bought it. The amount was not sufficient to pay off all the debts. Entering into the service of the viceroy of Perú, Francisco never managed to better his lot. In 1604, from a Franciscan house in a little town in Ecuador, he wrote to his wife a tender letter of sympathy on the occasion of her mother's death. Francisco died in Quito. His sister Teresita in her testimony for Teresa's canonization cause said that he died a holy death, and that miracles had even been attributed to him.

Cepeda, Jerónimo de (1522–75). One of Teresa's brothers, he went with Lorenzo to America in 1540. Apparently he had fathered a child out of wedlock, which grieved Teresa. She did all she could to help the situation, urging her brother Lorenzo to provide a dowry for Jerónimo's daughter. Partly for reasons of health he decided to return to Spain with Lorenzo in 1575, but died of a malignant fever at Nombre de Dios shortly after embarking from Panama for the return. Teresa wrote that he died like a saint.

Cepeda, Lorenzo de (1519–80). Lorenzo, especially after his return from America, was the brother who helped Teresa most and remained closest to her. In fact, she became his spiritual director. Only nineteen when he left for America, he took part with his brothers Hernando, Jerónimo, Antonio, and perhaps Rodrigo in the battle of Añaquito in 1546, fighting on the side of Charles V. In that encounter Antonio died and Lorenzo was seriously wounded. In 1556 he married a wealthy young girl from the nobility, Juana Fuertes Espinosa. She was eighteen at the time. Holding important offices in Quito, even that of mayor, he turned out to be financially successful. When his wife died in 1567, she left Lorenzo with four living children out of the seven that were born: Francisco, Lorenzo, Esteban, and Teresita. Later with the education of his children in mind, Lorenzo decided to return to Spain. He had spent thirty-four years in the work of conquest and pacification of the Indies. He had engaged in the struggle in company with the viceroy, Blasco Nuñez Vela, against Gonzalo Pizarro. Later, after Vela had been killed, he accompanied the priest Pedro de la Gasca from his entry into Peru until he waged battle against Pizarro. When he was chief magistrate in the cities of Loxa and Zamora, Lorenzo had come to the aid of the cities of Loyola and Vallid under siege by the Indians. On his return trip to Spain, he took along his brothers Pedro and Jerónimo. Jerónimo died on the way back as did also Lorenzo's youngest son, Esteban. Having left Panama in May, the Cepeda's arrived in Spain in August 1575. Great was his surprise when Lorenzo learned that his sister Teresa was in Seville. He then traveled from Seville to Madrid to make a claim that his remuneration had been insufficient and begged that "he might receive more, according to his many and good services, and his quality; and as he had three small children to be brought up in virtue and good customs, he asked to be excused from returning to that land, while still enjoying the income from his holdings there." But his efforts failed and he returned to Seville sick and discouraged. In March 1576, Pedro left with Lorenzo's two nephews and Teresa's brother-in-law, Juan de Ovalle, for Avila. In June, Teresa, together with Lorenzo and his daughter Teresita, Gregorio Nacianceno, and Antonio Ruiz, left for Malagón on the way to Toledo. Since Teresa had to remain in Toledo for a longer time, Lorenzo departed with Teresita for Avila. Shortly afterward, he enrolled his two sons in the College of San Gil, operated by the Jesuits. In October he bought a piece of farm land and woods six kilometers southeast of Avila in a place called *La Serna*. Retiring there with his brother Pedro to devote his final years to the care of the land and a life of prayer, Lorenzo tried to follow a daily schedule similar to that of the Carmelites. He sought spiritual direction from Teresa for his life of prayer and also from St. John of the Cross among others. Becoming one of the victims of the devastating influenza that ravaged Spain in 1580, he died at *La Serna* in June. After

Lorenzo had returned from America, Teresa kept up a correspondence with him in which he sought her counsel and she sought his. He was a generous benefactor of Teresa's helping her with her foundation in Avila and later with the foundation in Seville and with other projects.

Cepeda, Lorenzo de (son) (1562–ca. 1627). Lorenzo's younger son came to Spain with his father in 1575. In 1578, he decided to return to America where his father had sizable estates. He made a formal renunciation of his inheritance in exchange for a transfer of property to him by his father. Leaving an illegitimate daughter in Spain, he then sailed for America in May 1580, a month before his father died. Teresa had told him frankly that though she was very grieved at the offense he had committed against God, she loved the little girl dearly. In fact, Teresa did all that she could to look after the girl's education and welfare. Lorenzo married in America a year later and became materially successful. He had five daughters from this marriage.

Cepeda, María de (b. 1506). The oldest in the family, Teresa's stepsister was cared for by her maternal grandmother after her mother's death when she was hardly a year old. She was the child, it was said, who most resembled her father: austere, meticulous, and somewhat rigid. Having married in 1531, she went to live with her husband Martín Guzmán Barrientos in the town of Castellanos de la Cañada. Teresa stayed with them during the illness she suffered when young. María and her husband showed Teresa much love and affection. Later Teresa came to María's assistance in a lawsuit. A widow by 1561, Maria was sued by her brother-in-law Juan de Ovalle, who tried to bring her to court over an old lawsuit concerning her inheritance. Teresa energetically came to her defense, urging her brother Lorenzo to give orders that of the 1,000 pesos he had sent to his sister Juana (Juan de Ovalle's wife), only 500 would be given to her, and the other 500 given to María, if Juan de Ovalle went ahead and brought María to court. This put an end to the troubles over Don Alonso's estate which caused so much unpleasantness among his offspring and in-laws. Teresa helped María in another more important matter. When Maria's husband died suddenly, Teresa was grieved that he didn't have a chance to go to confession. The Lord then told her in prayer that her sister would also die suddenly and so should be always prepared. Teresa went to visit her sister and exhorted her to frequent the sacraments. María paid attention to Teresa's urgings and underwent a conversion of life. She in fact did die suddenly about five years later (L. 34.19).

Cerda, Luisa de la (d. 1596). Daughter of the second duke of Medinaceli, Luisa de la Cerda in 1537 married Antonio Arias Pardo de Saavedra, nephew of Cardinal Pardo de Talavera and one of the wealthiest and most titled men in Castile. Of his seven children, four were still alive when he died in 1561. His death left his wife so afflicted that the family began to fear for her. Finally, after many other failed attempts to comfort her, the family asked the provincial of the Carmelites to allow Teresa to stay with her in her palace in Toledo. Teresa remained with her for about six months and was able to help free her from the bonds of her affliction, frequent the sacraments, and practice good works. While living in the palace, Teresa was able to observe that nobility and wealth did not free one from the slavery of many human passions. In 1567 Luisa offered to fund a foundation in Malagón if the nuns would pray for her deceased husband. The house that the nuns rented there was poor and inadequate for their needs. Finally on her return from Seville, Teresa insisted that Luisa build them a new monastery, which she had promised to do. The new monastery, the only one of Teresa's houses that was not an adaptation of some already existing house, was built according to Teresa's own specifications and still exists as a Carmel today, as do all of Teresa's foundations. When the foundation of nuns in Toledo was made, Luisa gave them hospitality in her home while they tried to find a house for themselves. They were very poor and met with serious difficulties, but it doesn't seem that Luisa did anything to help them. Teresa wrote in her *Foundations*, "It will seem impossible that though we had stayed in the house of that lady who loved me so much, we had to enter the new foundations in so much poverty (15.13). Nonetheless Teresa continued on good terms with Doña Luisa, sending her little gifts, but also feeling free to ask her for favors when she needed help for herself or someone else. Among these favors was the task Doña Luisa undertook to deliver the precious secret manuscript of Teresa's *Life* to St. John of Avila.

Dantisco, Juana (Gracián's Mother) (1528–1601). Daughter of Juan Danzich, the ambassador of King Segismund I of Poland to the court of Charles V. At the age of twelve, she married Diego Gracián de Alderete. They were married for fifty years and had twenty children. She became a close friend of Teresa's. Two of her daughters, María and Isabel, became discalced Carmelite nuns. She died in Valladolid assisted by her son, Padre Gracián.

Daza, Gaspar (d. 1592). This devout and learned priest was one of the first to receive from Teresa an account of her spiritual experiences and remained her friend throughout her life. However, despite his good intentions, his attempts at directing Teresa, as she explains in her *Life*, only caused her greater fears, especially of the devil. She writes: "He began with a holy determination to guide me as though I were a strong person....When I saw him at once so determined about little things that, as I say, I didn't have the fortitude to give up immediately and so perfectly, I was afflicted. Since I saw he was taking my soul's attachments as something I would have to die to all at once, I realized there was need for much more caution" (L. 23.8). At this time in her life, Daza was not the spiritual director she needed. He thought she could change herself according to his directives. Blessed Anne of St. Bartholomew later reported also that he was incredulous when it came to revelations. Daza was the one commissioned by the bishop to give the habit to the first four discalced Carmelite nuns, establish the enclosure, and reserve the Blessed Sacrament in their little chapel in St. Joseph's on 24 August 1562. He was Julián of Avila's confessor and spiritual director. In the absence of Teresa, who in the beginning was not allowed to live in the new community, he took charge of directing the first novices and giving them the veil. At the time that the Bishop of Avila was appointed to Palencia, Teresa wrote and asked the bishop with wonderful courtesy and tact that he give Gaspar Daza a canonry or some other benefice. Daza, at his own expense, had a side chapel constructed in the chapel of St. Joseph's in Avila that was built after Teresa's death. He died in 1592 and is buried in the floor of this chapel close to the tomb of Julián de Avila.

Doria, Nicolás. See Nicolás (Nicolao) de Jesús María.

Eboli, Princess of (Ana de Mendoza) (1540–92). Born in Cifuentes (Guadalajara), she was the daughter of Diego Hurtado de Mendoza, the prince of Melito. In 1553, at age thirteen, she was promised in marriage to Ruy Gómez de Silva, a close friend of King Philip II, twenty-four years her senior. She bore a total of ten children. Capricious, haughty, and irascible, she was known as well for her physical beauty. With energy and ambition she propelled herself into the social and political life of the court. Sánchez Coello, in a famed portrait of her, painted her with a black patch over her eye, which has given rise to erroneous speculation that she was blind in one eye. When she was eighteen she fell and injured her eye, which created an embarrassing situation for a woman who was both beautiful and vain. Her admirers used to say, "She has only one sun, but it is enough to give light to the whole court of Spain, and the whole world as well." When she heard about Teresa, she wanted to have one of the Teresian Carmels in Pastrana. From the beginning of June to the middle of July 1569, Teresa lived in the princess's palace in Pastrana and suffered much from the princess's many whims. Having insisted on reading Teresa's *Life*, the princess passed it around in the household, turning the book into an object of ridicule. During this time, two houses were founded in Pastrana by Teresa, one for nuns and one for friars. The one for nuns was short-lived. When her husband died in 1573, the princess demanded that she be accepted in Teresa's monastery of nuns, where she received the habit from the notorious Baltasar de Jesús (Nieto). When the prioress had first heard of her plans, she exclaimed: "The princess a nun! That's the end of this house." The difficulties began at once. The princess brought her maids with her and haughtily announced that the only one she ever submitted to in this world was her husband, the prince, and that the prioress was crazy if she thought she would submit to her. One day she decided she would live with one of her maids in a hermitage that was in the garden, but understandably that did not last long and she returned to her palace. Angry about the whole fiasco, she decided to cut off all support to the nuns. In the end, the nuns saw no alternative but to escape from her clutches which they did—the whole community of fourteen nuns—in the middle of the night. Teresa received them with outstretched arms in Segovia in April 1574. The princess reacted by denouncing Teresa's *Life* to the Inquisition. Having emerged from her secluded life in the monastery, the princess entered once more into the ebullient life of the court. Among her close friends was Antonio Pérez. Rumors spread that she was his lover. But her link with Pérez was probably based on political scheming, not passion. In the bitter rivalry that developed between Antonio Pérez and Juan Escobedo, secretary to Don Juan of Austria, she became suspect of having had a role to play in Escobedo's murder. Pérez and Eboli were arrested on the king's orders in July 1579. Confined to the castle of Santorcaz, she was later moved to the family palace at Pastrana, and began to live so recklessly that the king had to intervene, appointing a special council to care for her property. More than once Teresa sent Gracián to visit her at Santorcaz and Pastrana to try to comfort her. She died at the age of 51, refusing to allow the doctor to enter her palace to attend to her.

Fernández, Pedro (1527–80). Born in the small town of Viluestre on the banks of the Duero, he made his profession as a Dominican in the monastery of San Esteban in Salamanca around 1547. An eminent theologian, he was appointed by Philip II to attend the Council of Trent. When elected provincial, he soon became known as the saintly provincial. In August 1569 he was appointed apostolic visitator of the Carmelites in Castile by Pius V. Through his simplicity, tact, and austerity, often making his visitations on foot, he won their esteem. Although at times strict with Teresa, he was always respectful and considerate, for he had a high regard for her. A man of few words and many good works, prudent in his counsels to Teresa, he was strict about the observance and fond of recollection and virtue. After he had sent Teresa back to the Incarnation to serve as prioress, he wrote to the Duchess of Alba of the positive results of her government there, asserting that there is as much calm and peace at the Incarnation as among the ten or twelve discalced nuns in Salamanca, But, he also noted that if Teresa were to leave, they would all go back to the way they were because their foundation was weak. He died at the age of fifty-three shortly after arrival of the brief from Rome that allowed for the separation of the discalced friars and nuns into a separate province.

Galiano, Asensio (d. 1577). One of those who helped Teresa when she made her second foundation in Medina del Campo, he belonged to the middle class. A tax collector for the state, Asensio admired Teresa and her nuns and offered them many valuable services. At one point Doña Elena de Quiroga had promised to help Teresa buy a house adjacent to the nuns' house in Medina so that they could provide for a chapel. Not knowing about this, the nuns had enlisted Asensio's help promising him the patronage of the chapel. But fortunately both parties made their donations anyway. Asensio also helped the nuns financially when they made the foundation in Seville. It seems that Asensio continued living in Medina and that he died in 1577.

Garciálvarez. Coming to know Teresa and her nuns in 1575 when they made their foundation in Seville, he rendered them many important services in the first months. He then served unselfishly as their chaplain and was their confessor for about a year. One time he protected them from being swindled in the purchase of a house. Despite this positive picture, Garciálvarez also had his defects, suffering from scrupulosity, limited intelligence, and a lack of sound judgment. In the spring of 1575, a woman entered the monastery who in the world was renowned for her supposed holiness. Since the way of life in the Carmel was too difficult for her, she had to leave after two or three months. Garciálvarez was her confessor. Wounded in her self-love by this lack of perseverance, she began to spread a series of calumnies throughout the city, with Garciálvarez's approval, about the life of the nuns. When the Inquisition heard of this they came to the monastery with their many coaches in November or December of 1575. After intensive questioning of the nuns, they began to realize that the accusations were a farce. What happened later was more serious, when Garciálvarez's intervention was more direct. In September 1576, Beatriz de la Madre de Dios Chaves made her profession, and in January 1577 Margarita de la Concepción Ballestreros made hers as a lay sister. One day Garciálvarez decided that these two should make a general confession and proceeded to keep them in the confessional all day, sometimes having them both together sometimes separately. These endless confessions went on for two or three months. Garciálvarez believed all the accounts about the irregularities in the monastery with which Beatriz filled his ears. The reputation of the community also began to suffer outside. The prioress, finally, with good counsel, dismissed him as the community's confessor. The situation worsened when the new nuncio Sega published a decree which placed the discalced friars and nuns under the jurisdiction of the provincials of the Carmelites of the observance. The provincial in Andalusia, Diego de Cárdenas, allowed Garciálvarez to return as confessor and then made a canonical visitation of the monastery. He believed the outlandish tales that were the product of Beatriz's unbalanced mind. She claimed that Gracián had undressed in front of the nuns and advised them that they need not confess mortal sins. The majority of nuns, deceived and ignorant of what a visitation is, signed whatever the visitator asked them to sign. As a result, the prioress, María de San José, was deposed and excommunicated. He appointed the source of all the accusations, Beatriz de la Madre de Dios, prioress. She lasted about a year. Then through the intervention of Philip II, Angel de Salazar was named vicar general of the discalced friars and nuns. He deprived Diego Cárdenas of his jurisdiction and, under Teresa's influence, sought to undo the wrong done to the nuns in Seville. He deprived Garciálvarez of his faculties and Beatriz of her office as prioress. He restored active and passive voice to María de San José and appointed the oldest nun as provisional prioress. In June 1580, María de San José was elected prioress again. But what seems strange, Teresa would never place blame on Garciálvarez. Because of the great favors he had done for her in the first months of the foundation, she remained always grateful to him and did not want the nuns to speak against him.

Gaytán, Antonio. When Teresa began to have dealings with him in Alba de Tormes in 1573, he was already a widower and enjoyed a life free from financial worry. Teresa thought highly of him, as is clear from what she reports in her *Foundations* (21.6). Through his friendship with Teresa, he became a fervent Christian. In 1574, he accompanied her on the foundation in Segovia. She also entrusted to him the secret and demanding mission of leading fourteen nuns in their escape from Pastrana and the Princess of Eboli to Segovia. In 1575, he accompanied Teresa on her journey to Beas. While she was there she sent him and Julián de Avila to Caravaca to negotiate for a foundation there. It proved a long, tedious journey for the two in bad weather and on miserable roads. On 18 May they left Beas for another taxing trip, this one with Teresa to Córdoba and finally Seville, where Teresa made her next foundation. There, Antonio had to borrow money to return to Castile. As is evident from Teresa's letters, he approached her as a spiritual director and sought her advice. In the summer of 1577, he asked her if the nuns in Alba de Tormes would receive his daughter, who was still a child only seven years old, as she had done in the case of her niece Teresita and Gracián's little sister, Isabelita. He promised to pay for her sustenance and also a special dowry. Recommending the idea to Gracián, Teresa asked for his permission. She wrote: "I tell you these little angels edify us and are refreshing. With no more than one in each house, I don't see any obstacle but a benefit." At the beginning of 1581, Antonio Gaytán married again. Under the influence of his new wife, it seems, he became remiss in sending what he had promised for the sustenance of his daughter, and the nuns began to fear they would not receive the dowry he had promised to give when the time for her profession came. In 1581 Teresa had to write and urge him to keep to his commitments to the nuns. It seems that in the end he took care of the matter. His daughter, taking the name Mariana de Jesús, made her profession in 1585, and later in Tarazona became novice mistress, subprioress, and prioress. After the death of Teresa, no more mention is made in the chronicles of Antonio Gaytán.

Gracián de la Madre de Dios, Jerónimo. See Jerónimo de la Madre de Dios (Gracián).

Gregorio Nacianceno (1548–99). Born in Villarubia de los Ojos (Ciudad Real) and orphaned at the age of twelve, he studied in Alcalá and was ordained in 1573. Teresa met him in Malagón when she was on her way from Valladolid to make a new foundation in Beas. His two sisters chose to follow Teresa by entering her Carmels. Freed thereby from all family responsibilities, Gregorio accompanied Teresa and her companions on her journey to Beas. While he was there, Gracián invested him in the habit of the discalced Carmelites, changing his name from Gregorio Martínez to Fray Gregorio Nacianceno. Fray Gregorio then went along with Teresa on the journey to Seville. There he made his novitiate at the discalced monastery of Los Remedios. Three months after his profession in April 1576, he was appointed vicar of the house. In June of that year he traveled back with Teresa, her brother Lorenzo, and Teresita to Castile. In addition to being vicar at Los Remedios, he served for a time as novice master there. It was he who as vicar received the vows of Nicolás Doria in 1578. Later, he was named prior of La Roda and then Valladolid. Eventually, in 1585, Gregorio along with St. John of the Cross became one of the members of Doria's *consulta* and in that capacity also held the post of vicar provincial of Old Castile. He continued to hold various posts of responsibility until his death.

With high esteem for Nicolás Doria, he found little worth prizing in Fray John of the Cross. This he showed publicly when John's body, with much ceremony, was brought back to Segovia from Ubeda. In 1594 he appointed Diego Evangelista, the unprincipled friar who had vengefully sought the expulsion of John of the Cross from the order, vicar provincial of Andalusia. In his stance toward Gracián, Gregorio behaved as he did with John. In 1597 he became prior in Madrid and died there in December 1599.

Hernández, Pablo (b. 1528). Born at Santiago de Compostela, he became a Jesuit and later a consultor for the Inquisition. Becoming a member of the Jesuit community in Toledo in 1568, he helped Teresa make her foundation there that same year. They became good friends and he continued to use his influence to help her. Because of his grave demeanor, she gave him the nickname "eternal father."

Inés de Jesús (Tapia) (d. 1601). She and her sister, Ana de la Encarnación, were Teresa's cousins and belonged to the community of the Incarnation in Avila. She helped Teresa in the foundation of St. Joseph's in Avila and was present when the first four discalced nuns received the habit. Accompanying Teresa on the foundation in Medina del Campo, she was named prioress of that new community, but remained a calced nun. At one point she was removed from her office of prioress and sent to the new foundation in Alba de Tormes, but subsequently she returned to her post in Medina. Not until 1581 did she renounce the mitigated rule and become a discalced Carmelite. In that same year, she joined Teresa for the foundation in Palencia where she was elected prioress. In 1588, she went on the foundation in Zaragosa, later returning again to Medina. She died on the same day as her sister Ana, 22 April 1601. Teresa was particularly attached to her and placed great confidence in her. Her remains are buried next to those of St. John of the Cross's mother (Catalina Alvarez) in Medina del Campo.

Isabel de Jesús (Isabelita Dantisco or Gracián) ((1568–1639). Gracián's little sister, she entered the Carmel of Toledo at the age of seven. There she received the habit from Teresa herself in 1576. She made her profession at the age sixteen. Teresa spoke of her with much affection and used to call her "la mi Bela." In 1586, two years after her profession she was made subprioress in a new foundation in Cuerva where she lived until her death at the age of seventy-one. She suffered her brother's expulsion from the order with resignation, as also her last eighteen years of blindness.

Isabel de Santo Domingo (Ortega) (1537–1623). Born in Cardeñosa (Avila), she lost her mother at the age of four and her father when fourteen. Her uncle in Avila then cared for her. Becoming a penitent of St. Peter of Alcántara's, she was introduced by him to Teresa. Entering St. Joseph's in Avila in October 1563, she received the habit the next year and made profession in October 1565. Gifted with great piety, much common sense, and unusual talent, she was esteemed by Teresa, who considered her counsel on many occasions to be indispensable. For many years and in many matters, she served as

Teresa's right arm. It was said, perhaps with exaggeration, that she helped Teresa more than any of the other nuns. She went with her to make the foundation in Toledo and remained there as prioress. After a few months, she received the difficult task of prioress in Pastrana, where the Princess of Eboli reigned. Later, once the escape from Pastrana was achieved, she became prioress in Segovia. After Teresa's death, she made a foundation in Zaragoza in 1588, and in 1598 became the first prioress in Ocaña. Before her triennium was completed, she was called to return to Segovia to help that community out of its financial difficulties. In 1604, she returned to St. Joseph's in Avila and lived there—as prioress from 1606–10—until her death.

Jerónimo de la Madre de Dios (Gracián) (1545–1614). Although Gracián was not the first discalced Carmelite friar, Teresa saw him as ideal, one sent by God just at the right moment for the renewal of the observance of the primitive rule (F. 23). He represented for her both its salvation and the future of the discalced friars. Born in Valladolid on 6 June 1545, he was one of the twenty offspring of Diego Gracián Alderete and Juana Dantisco. His father was secretary for both the emperor Charles V and the king Philip II. His grandfather on his mother's side, Juan Dantisco, was ambassador to the Spanish court for Sigismund I of Poland. Jerónimo Gracián began his studies at age six with private tutors. When he was fourteen the family had to move to Toledo. His father wanted him to prepare for a career as secretary to the court and carry on in the family tradition. But Gracián desired to go on for university studies. The family had to raise the money from benefactors for this venture, among whom was Philip II himself. Beginning his studies at the University of Alcalá in 1560 at age fifteen, Gracián received his bachelor of arts degree in 1563, and a year later his masters degree. After finishing his studies in the arts, he registered in the school of theology finishing in 1568. He then went on for a four-year doctorate course in theology. In 1572, with only one remaining test to undergo for the doctorate, when at the very point of receiving what many ambitioned but only a few achieved, he oddly abandoned everything. During his studies for the doctorate, in 1571, he was ordained to the priesthood.

At this time he became friendly with the Jesuits and was thinking seriously of joining them. One day, on the feast of St. Francis in 1571, he went to celebrate Mass for the Franciscan nuns, but by mistake went to the discalced Carmelite nuns in Alcalá, a community founded not by Teresa but by María de Jesús (cf. L. 35.1–2). Presuming they were Franciscans, he preached on St. Francis. After Mass the foundress spoke to him, explained the difference, and gave him a copy of Teresa's constitutions. He grew enthused about them and actually wrote to Teresa without ever having met her. These incidents led to his study of the Carmelite order. Subsequently, at the age of twenty-seven, he entered the novitiate of the discalced Carmelites in Pastrana. It was a bad year to enter the novitiate in Pastrana. It was precisely the time when the novice master was introducing a number of absurd ascetical practices. Teresa once remarked that Gracián had learned how to govern by way of contrast, treating others just the opposite of the way he was treated in Pastrana. Despite his being only a novice, at Teresa's request, he preached and gave spiritual direction to her nuns in Pastrana.

A few months after his profession on 25 April 1573, he was named by Fancisco Vargas as visitator of the Carmelites of the observance in Andalusia. Vargas delegated his own powers to Gracián. Before a year was up, Vargas named him vicar provincial of all the Carmelites in Andalusia. In view of the difficulties that arose regarding the legality of this appointment, the pope's nuncio to Spain, Nicolás Ormaneto, on 22 September 1574, named Vargas and Gracián visitators *in solidum,* thus responding to the revocation obtained by the general of the order on 13 August 1574. But the chapter of Piacenza in May–

June of 1575 was to cause further difficulties for the discalced friars and nuns.

At this same time, in the spring of 1575, Gracián, in Beas, finally met Teresa. From a theological and spiritual point of view, this was the most decisive meeting in the history of the Teresian Carmel after her meeting with St. John of the Cross in Medina del Campo. Something that happened to Fray John of the Cross now happened to Gracián: a direct communication of the Teresian charism. Gracián from then on found a spiritual support in Teresa for all the burdens that had been laid on him. Impressed by his learning and his access to the king, Teresa was, above all, highly impressed by his spirituality and his gentle mode of governing. At this first meeting the affinity between them became clear almost instantaneously. They concurred in all their points of view. Gracián says: "We commented on all matters of the order, both past and present and on what was necessary to foresee for the future. Both were euphoric after the meeting. The two were adaptable, had a gift for getting on well with people, and open to broad horizons. Shortly after meeting him, wanting to do something more in the service of the Lord, Teresa made a vow of obedience to Gracián in honor of the Holy Spirit for a wonderful favor received on the vigil of the feast of Pentecost (ST. 35 & 36). After this, Gracián, in turn, made a decision to consult Teresa in all matters. This wise practice resulted in his being criticized and even calumniated for taking up business matters with a woman and letting himself be ruled by one.

Countering the chapter of Piacenza, Ormaneto enlarged the faculties of Gracián on 3 August 1575, naming him commissary and reformer of the Andalusian Carmel and of the discalced friars and nuns of Castile. Gracián's work turned out to be decisive for the advance of the Teresian Carmel. Nonetheless, the persecutions, calumnies, and Carmelite family struggles ended in his being deposed by the new nuncio, Felipe Sega, and his being confined in a monastery in Alcalá. In October 1578, the discalced friars and nuns were put under the jurisdiction of the provincials of the Carmelites of the observance. Since this move created further conflicts and even public scandals, the king intervened and appointed a commission to deal with the whole matter. This commission, on 1 April 1579, placed Angel de Salazar, a former provincial of the observant Carmelites in Castile, in charge of the discalced friars and nuns. He was, in Gracián's view, a gentle and discreet man whose main concern was to console the afflicted and promote peace. Salazar then named Gracián commissary and visitator of the discalced friars and nuns in Andalusia. Finally, through the intervention of Philip II, Gregory XIII, in the brief *Pia consideratione* (22 June 1580), allowed the discalced Carmelites to form a separate province, which in Teresa's words "was all that we were desiring for the sake of our peace and tranquility."

On 4 March 1581, in the chapter of Alcalá, Gracián was elected the first provincial of the Teresian Carmel. But not all were in favor of Gracián, and the vote was anything but unanimous. At the end of her life Teresa herself warned Gracián against being arbitrary and authoritarian. He governed until 1585, attending to the organizational and juridical needs of the new province, extending the discalced friars' presence outside of Spain and opening the first mission in Africa. He was forty years old at the time, and had been superior for as many years as he was a professed religious. Not all the friars shared Teresa's judgment of Gracián as "the one who was best able to bring about a union between religious perfection and gentleness." On finishing his provincialate, Gracián presented to the chapter of Lisbon (May 1585) a detailed defense of his government. According to the opposition, he had been too soft, should have given fewer dispensations, and done more to correct abuses in the strict observance. It seems there were always those who wanted him to do more punishing and threatening. Gracián proposed Nicolás Doria as his successor. Doria had been in Genoa during the previous three years. He was accepted and Gracián was elected as his first councillor. When the chapter continued in Pastrana, Gracián was elected vicar provincial of Portugal.

At the end of 1586, Gracián published a work zealously promoting the missions, which marked the beginning of trouble with the new provincial. He was ordered to withdraw the book from publication. Furthermore, Gracián had begun to oppose the new form of government devised by Doria at the end of 1585, called the *consulta*. This was to be a government consisting of a body of five members who would decide matters by vote. He also supported those nuns who opposed changes in Teresa's constitutions. The result was a plan to send Gracián to Mexico to serve there as vicar. While Gracián was in Seville preparing to go to Mexico, orders came from the religious authorities in Portugal, commissioning him to make some visitations in Portugal. There was fear that the English would invade, and it was rumored among Castilians that the Carmelite prior in Lisbon, Padre Antonio Calderón, was an Antonista hiding arquebuses and making plans for betrayal. Gracián's task was to find the friars favoring the revolution, calm them down, and urge them to stay out of politics. This new commission, of course, prevented his going to Mexico. In 1588, Doria obtained the authority to be a vicar general of the discalced friars and nuns. In the meanwhile Gracián was carrying out his assignment as visitator of the Carmelites of the observance in Portugal.

When the nuns obtained a brief from Sixtus V confirming their desire that the constitutions of St. Teresa not be changed, it was seen as opposition to Doria's government. Gracián was reputed to have given his strong support to the nuns. After he finished his two-year visitation in Portugal, the time seemed ripe for Gracián's brethren to begin a process against him. He was imprisoned in the monastery of San Hermengildo in Madrid and forbidden to write any letters without permission from Doria. The investigations and interrogations went on for six months. On 17 February 1592, the sentence was pronounced against Gracián. He was declared incorrigible, ordered to remove the habit of the discalced Carmelite friars, and expelled for sowing discord and opposition to the superiors.

After much reflection and counsel from others, Gracián decided to defend himself and take his case to the supreme authorities in Rome. Traveling in the habit of a hermit and as a pilgrim, he did so with the determination to defend the good name of the nuns as well. He was forty-seven at the time. By June 1592, he was in Rome only to find that the ambassador of the king had taken Doria's side, favoring the more austere elements of religious life. Gracián could do no more than give Pope Clement VIII his side of the story and leave the matter in the hands of God. After doing so, he went on to Naples, but the viceroy there rejected him, so he was forced to go to Sicily where the Countess of Olivares received him warmly. Gracián carried on an intense apostolic activity throughout Sicily, even giving courses in Scripture in Palermo. While he was immersed in these activities, the decision of Rome reached him. It could hardly have been more discouraging. He was forbidden to enter any monastery of the order again and advised to take the habit of the discalced Augustinians. Hoping to get a reversal of the decision, he took a boat for Rome. But it was captured by Turks. Gracián was stripped and chained and his feet branded. As he himself wrote, his habit was now his birthday suit (*aquel habito en que nací)*, and he had to work at the oars in the galleys. The ship went about its pillaging throughout the month of October and then landed in Tunis in November.

Gracián was held captive for two interminable years in the midst of indescribable suffering and hardship. While held bound by four twenty-five-pound iron weights in a dark and fetid dungeon, he began a correspondence with his friends trying to raise money for his ransom. After a first amount of money arrived, he was allowed more freedom of movement so that he could preach and hear confessions among the hundreds of Christian prisoners. In 1594–95, he worked intensely in this ministry, also saying Mass daily. By the beginning of August 1595, he was able to leave Africa and captivity behind him.

From Genoa he wrote to the general in Spain, Elías de San Martín, asking once more to be readmitted into the order, but he received no answer. While waiting for a response, he spent his time working for captives in Africa, trying to raise money for them and to interest the authorities in helping them. In mid-October, he went to Rome to plead his case. While in Rome he also devoted his time to preaching, spiritual direction, working on behalf of the poor captives in Africa, and, what comes as no surprise, promoting the cause for beatification of St. Teresa. In this latter regard, he found more enthusiasm for Teresa's cause in Italy than he did in Spain.

On 16 March 1596, he received a pontifical brief absolving him from any penalties and censures he may have incurred and authorizing him to return to the discalced Carmelites. The superiors were told to receive him and treat him kindly and give him all the privileges. Because of the hard opposition to him in Spain, it was recommended that he remain in Italy. There he was warmly received by the vicar general of the Carmelites of the observance who granted him permission to live among them and wear the discalced habit.

Not long after this, he was named by Cardinal Daza an official theologian of the Holy Office. Gracián then took up lodging in the cardinal's house. He also continued his work on the cause of St. Teresa and initiated as well procedures for a foundation of her nuns in Rome. Continuing his efforts to raise money to help ransom other captives, he even promoted this cause for the ransom of captives in front of Clement VIII.

In 1600 the discalced Carmelites divided into two congregations, one Spanish (St. Joseph) and the other Italian (St. Elías). Known in Rome for his experience in Moslem lands,

Gracián was commissioned to preach to captive Christians in Morocco during the jubilee year. In order to do this, he had to go to the royal court in Madrid for his official papers. What was to be a short journey to Spain turned into a six-year stay. He carried out his preaching in Morocco for about seven months and then returned to Madrid in 1602, where in writing to Rome that his mission was over, he offered to go to Ethiopia. In the meantime, he undertook an apostolate in Spain, preaching at times as many as four sermons a day. He also continued to promote and raise funds for the cause of Teresa and the printing of her writings.

The ambassador of Philip III in Flanders began pressing to have Gracián come there, and finally he won his way. On 29 May 1607, Gracián left Spain for the last time. Soon after he arrived in Brussels, where he lived with the Carmelites of the observance, he became happily aware of the devotion to Teresa in that region and the opportunities to promote her writings. He began once more his apostolate of preaching, now against heresies. In the year of his arrival, he described in a letter his way of life in Flanders: "My health is very good in this land and since my desire is for nothing other than the service of God and here there are many opportunities for this, I am happy. Here we are always in the midst of battles—struggles against the heretics—and in this way and by writing against bad doctrine and arranging for the publication of what has been written, we pass our time. I sometimes preach to the discalced nuns....And I am happy when alone in my cell with its garden, where I spend my eremitical life—even eating there—occupying as much time as possible in prayer as I approach the end of my life which I hope in God will be this year." But he lived six more years of intense apostolic and contemplative life.

He promoted Teresa's writings, attended to the publication of those that remained unpublished, and arranged for translations into other languages. Continuing to work unsparingly for her beatification, he was again consoled to find so much more enthusiasm for her cause, this time in France and Flanders, than he had at the higher levels in Carmel in Spain.

Anne of Jesus, who was also in Flanders at this time, longed to bring the discalced Carmelites from the Spanish congregation to that region. In opposition to her on this point, Gracián worked to bring the discalced Carmelites from Italy. He had never favored the division of the Teresian Carmel into two congregations, but those in the Italian congregation agreed with Gracián and blamed the friars in Spain for the separation. Gracián preferred the Italian congregation because of their openness to the missions and other apostolic works. It was his opinion that if the discalced Carmelites did not go to foreign lands to shed their blood for the honor and glory of God and bring increase to the Catholic Church, they would not preserve their spirit at home or grow spiritually in numbers. Oddly enough, however, Gracián himself decided against joining either congregation, although he continued to work hard for the expansion of the discalced Carmelite nuns throughout central Europe. In 1608, he had been named bishop of Armenia. But that whole plan of the congregation for the propagation of the faith fell through. In 1614 Gracián's health began to weaken. Five months before his death, on 24 April 1614, he was able to share in the joy of Teresa's beatification. In September, he was struck down by a strange illness outside the city of Brussels, while on a journey of priestly ministry, and had to be lodged in a nearby house. He died the next day on 21 September at the age of 69.

Gracián always bore more of the dove in him than the serpent, but he was tenacious in his ideals. With an enormous capacity for work and an extraordinary physical resistance, he would give all his powers to a task if he judged it was good and noble. A few hours of sleep were enough and he was ready to go again. Everywhere, he made friends, but his friendship with Teresa is what history remembers him most for. His esteem for her is clear through his many letters from her that we now possess. For himself and for posterity, he took the pains to save them. Not for a moment did he ever doubt that she was worthy of being canonized or that she was the foundress from whom the discalced Carmelites, both friars and nuns, received their spirit.

On 15 December 1999, the Discalced Carmelite Order, after thorough study, officially revoked the sentence of expulsion from the order issued against Padre Jerónimo Gracián. It did this as an authoritative gesture to restore his good name and set right the injustice of which he was victim. The following year the order took the first steps to introduce his cause for canonization.

John of the Cross, St. (1542–1591). The first of the discalced Carmelite friars, John was born in Fontiveros (Avila), the third son of Gonzalo de Yepes and Catalina Alvarez. Because his life has become more widely known and researched, this sketch will mention only some main events. John was little more than two years old when his father died. In need of a better means of livelihood for her sons, John's mother, a weaver, moved to Arévalo and then Medina del Campo. In 1551 good fortune came John's way when he was enrolled in a catechism school in Medina for poor boys. This led to his employment as both an orderly and beggar for a hospital in the city. The new responsibility enabled him to enter a school operated by the Jesuits and study the humanities under their guidance (1559–63). But unexpectedly he entered the Carmelites at the age of twenty-one, taking the name Juan de Santo Matías. After his novitiate he was sent for studies to Salamanca. Ordained a priest in 1567, he returned to Medina to sing his first Mass. There he met Teresa who recruited him for a contemplative way of life for Carmelite friars similar to that of her nuns, with the exception of preaching and other priestly ministry. She brought him with her on their new foundation in Valladolid and there taught him and allowed him to see and experience the new style of Carmelite life established by her. At this time she made him a new habit, which she especially designed for the discalced Carmelite friars. The first house for friars was opened in Duruelo on 28 November 1568. John served as master of novices for the discalced friars in Duruelo, Mancera de Abajo, and Pastrana. In 1571 he was appointed rector of the new college in Alcalá for the discalced friars who would be pursuing studies. But soon after, in 1572, he was named by the nuncio Ormaneto confessor at the Incarnation in Avila to help Teresa in her work of reform there. He remained in this office until 1577 when, in early December, as a result of the chapter of Piacenza, he was unjustly seized as a renegade and imprisoned in the Carmelite monastery of the observance in Toledo. There he suffered until he managed a dramatic escape at night on 15 August 1578. While in prison he composed most of the majestic stanzas of his poem *The Spiritual Canticle*. After his escape he was sent to Andalusia as vicar of El Calvario. There he began his work of spiritual direction of the discalced Carmelites both friars and nuns, which led to his classic commentaries: *The Ascent of Mount Carmel, The Dark Night,* and *The Spiritual Canticle.*

In 1579 he was named rector of a new house of studies in Baeza for discalced Carmelites living in the south of Spain. In 1582, he was elected to be prior of the house in Granada. He had previously gone to Avila, in 1581, to urge Teresa to come down to Granada to make a foundation for her nuns there, but since she had other commitments at the time, she directed him to assist Anne of Jesus in making this new foundation, which the two of them did in January 1582. It was later in that same year that Teresa died. While in Granada (1582–88), John did most of his writing. In 1585 he was elected vicar provincial of Andalusia, but continued to live in Granada. This office kept him busy with much travel and a number of new foundations. During those years, crowded with many responsibilities demanding his attention, in the space of two weeks he composed his loftiest work, *The Living Flame of Love*. In 1588 he was called back to Castile to serve as prior of the house in Segovia and serve on the council of the vicar general for the discalced friars and nuns, Nicolás Doria. Because of disagreements among Doria, Gracián, and some of the discalced Carmelite nuns, he was considered a dissenter, set aside from the central government, and destined for the missions in Mexico. While plans were being made for this mission to Mexico, he withdrew to a solitary house in La Peñuela in Andalusia in June of 1591. At this time, Diego Evangelista began gathering any information he could that might be useful in calumniating him and having him expelled from the order. On 12 September John grew seriously ill with fever and an infection in his leg. Transferred to Ubeda where he could receive medical attention, he grew progressively worse until after much suffering he died on 14 December 1591. In 1593 his body was transferred to Segovia. He was beatified on 6 October 1674, and canonized on 27 December 1726. He was declared a Doctor of the Church on 24 August 1926.

Since none of Teresa's letters to John of the Cross have reached us, we are missing an important source of knowledge. But generally we can say that, for Teresa, John of the Cross was an expert exponent of spirituality, a spiritual, learned, and experienced man. She asserted that she had gone about here and there looking for light and then found it all in "little Seneca." In her letter to Anne of Jesus, she calls him a "divine and heavenly man" and affirms that in all Castile she had not found another spiritual director like him. For her, "he was a candid and pure soul, a man without malice or cunning," and "one of the purest souls in the Church." However, although she conceded absolute primacy to John in the area of spiritual direction, her preferred three in the area of government seem to have been Gracián, Doria, and Juan de Jesús Roca. It is hard to give any clear reason for this. In their spiritual teaching, John and Teresa were mutually influential. After her death, insofar as we know, John was the first promoter of the publication of her writings. In his *Spiritual Canticle* he praised her writings, and in his *Living Flame of Love* he praised her mystical graces and charism. Nonetheless both of them were spiritual geniuses in their own right and original in the presentation of their teaching.

Juan de Jesús (Roca). (1544–1614). Born in Sanahuja (Lerida), he studied first in Barcelona and then at the University of Alcalá, where he came to know Gracián. Entering the novitiate in Pastrana, he made his profession in 1573. He was prior at Mancera from 1575 to 1579. At the chapter in Almodóvar in 1576, he was appointed to watch over the monastic observance within the communities. But Teresa was not so pleased with his stress on austerity and penance. She did not want the friars to go barefoot and wanted them to have good meals (cf. Ltr. 161). She also objected to the many "tiresome decrees" he set down in his visitations. She said that just reading them wore her out. In 1579, with Diego de la Trinidad, he was named to go to Rome to plead the cause of the discalced Carmelites. In the midst of many difficulties, in great secrecy and in disguise, he carried out his mission successfully and with exceptional skill, obtaining the brief *Pia Consideratione* by which the discalced Carmelites were permitted to form a separate province. Teresa definitely thought it would be best if Gracián were elected as the first discalced provincial, but she was also well informed about the opposition to his election. Her second choice was Doria, and her third choice was Juan de Jesús (Roca). But this last choice was a most reluctant one; her opinion was that "he has no talent for government." She thought that if he had the assistance of Gracián or Doria, he might do all right because he was open to consultation. But then she adds that she was sure no one would vote for him. After Teresa's death, Roca was again sent to Rome on various occasions. And despite Teresa's remarks on his lack of talent for government, he went on to hold many positions as superior and to become the first provincial of Catalonia in 1588. He developed into an ardent advocate of missionary work on the part of the discalced Carmelites, an endeavor less in favor within the Spanish congregation than the Italian congregation of discalced Carmelites. He in fact audaciously proposed that his province join the Italian congregation. For this proposal he was deposed from his office of provincial in 1603 by the general of the Spanish congregation and exiled from his province. He never again held office but was allowed eventually to return to Catalonia. He died in Barcelona.

Leonor de San Gabriel. Born in Ciudad Real, she made her profession in Malagón. Small in stature and charming in her conversation, she accompanied Teresa to Seville and cared for her as her nurse in so orderly and conscientious a fashion that she seemed to Teresa like an angel. With affection Teresa began to refer to her as *mi Gabriela* (my Gabriel). After Teresa's death, Leonor left Seville to be Subprioress in Córdoba. She later served for a term as prioress in Sanlúcar and for several terms in Seville, where she died.

María Bautista (Ocampo) (1543–1603) The celebrated prioress of Valladolid and great friend of Teresa's was born in Torrijos (Toledo) to Teresa's cousin Diego de Cepeda. Her mother, Beatriz de la Cruz y Ocampo, died when she was five years old. She was then taken into the care of her aunt and uncle in La Puebla Montalbán (Toledo). Teresa met her there in 1549 when she made her pilgrimage to the Shrine of Guadalupe. Later she brought María to the Incarnation where her sister Leonor was already being educated. When in 1560 Teresa began to plan her reform project, María offered a thousand ducats from her inheritance. She entered St. Joseph's in 1563 and made her profession in 1564. Teresa took her with her for the foundation in Medina del Campo in 1567, and two years later, at the request of María de Mendoza, María transferred to Valladolid. She became prioress of Valladolid in 1571, at the time Teresa was made prioress of the Incarnation. Gifted with an uncommon combination of qualities, she was virtuous, intelligent, cautious, discreet, well organized, and a good administrator. She enjoyed a close friendship with Teresa, sharing with her as well a friendship with the renowned theologian Domingo Báñez. She felt perfectly at ease in giving her cousin advice, which sometimes Teresa found to be amusing. But Teresa sometimes had to reprove her lest she misuse her talents, turning them into a means of satisfying her own interests. What turned out to be unfortunate was the way Teresa was treated by her on her return in ill health from Burgos at the end of her life. María disdainfully sided with Beatriz de Castilla, who was determined to break Lorenzo's will and gain the inheritance destined for St. Joseph's in Avila. Teresa, of course, firmly resisted both María and Beatriz. Anne of St. Bartholomew, who was Teresa's nurse and companion in those last days, reported that María, who was prioress at Valladolid when Teresa and her nurse passed through, was loved very much by Teresa, but, on this occasion, reciprocated with no respect and ordered Teresa out of the house.

In the last years of her life, María was afflicted with a paralysis and rheumatism and much suffering. It is said that her aunt Teresa appeared to her, comforted her and told her that this was fitting because, since she loved her so much, she wanted her to be close to her in heaven.

María de San José (Salazar) (1548–1603). She was undoubtedly one of Teresa's most intimate friends. Gracián said of her that she was one of the holiest, purest, and most prudent women he had known in the order, and the one who suffered the most opposition in standing firm against a change in the laws left by Teresa. Born in Molina de Aragón (Guadalajara) or, according to others, in Toledo, it seems she was related to the Duke of Medinaceli, at least that she received an education characteristic of those who lived in the households of the Castilian nobility. When a little girl, she entered into the service of Doña Luisa de la Cerda and lived in her palace. There she met Teresa, who in 1562 was sent by her superiors as a companion to Doña Luisa to comfort her after her husband's death. Fourteen years old at the time, María developed a great admiration for Teresa and sometimes was a witness of her ecstasies. Six years later when Teresa returned to Toledo to arrange for a foundation in Malagón with Doña Luisa, María decided to join Teresa and her companions. It was not until two years later, however, that she received the habit. The investiture took place in Malagón in 1570 when she was twenty-two years old. In 1575 Teresa took her on the foundation in Beas with the intention of making her prioress of a further foundation that was planned for Caravaca. When Gracián intervened to order a foundation in Seville, Teresa chose instead to make her prioress there. Because of her intelligence, education, and other talents, she was referred to by Teresa as the "provincialess" (*provinciala*). And when nearing the time of her death, Teresa thought that María would be perfectly capable of taking her place. María saved a great number of Teresa's letters. In them she is forever being urged to take care of her health and try the various remedies prescribed by Teresa for her different illnesses. In some of her letters, Teresa joked with her over one display or another of her erudition. She also would accuse her of being crafty and lacking in openness. Teresa became most upset with her when she complained to the nuns in Seville that the house bought for them there and considered ideal by Teresa was unhealthy. Strange to say, in this matter, María de San José was probably more right than wrong. Teresa acknowledged that María de San José was cut out for dealing with Andalusians.

Despite any limitations she may have had, the prioress of Seville was a great figure among the nuns of the Teresian Reform. To none of the other nuns did Teresa express so much praise and cordial and intimate friendship. In 1578, Diego de Cárdenas, the provincial of the Carmelites of the observance in Andalusia, deposed her from the office of prioress because of false accusations that were made against her by Beatriz de la Madre de Dios. In the following year, Angel de Salazar was named vicar for the discalced friars and nuns. In reviewing the process against María, he concluded that removal from office was without foundation and restored her rights. On 9 June 1580, she was reelected prioress.

Her fidelity to Padre Gracián after Teresa's death brought her many troubles. They both felt the lack of Teresa's endorsement when they were in need of it. In December 1584, Gracián sent María as prioress on a new foundation in Lisbon, Portugal. Later, the chapter, which elected Nicolás Doria in the place of Gracián, was held in Lisbon. The dissension between Gracián and Doria that was to follow had its repercussions on María de San José. Though she tried to be a peacemaker, she was ordered by Doria in 1588 to have no more communication with Gracián, whom she had come to know so well in Seville. She played a role with Anne of Jesus in obtaining the brief from Sixtus V entitled "Salvatoris" (1591). The brief stated that no one has the authority to change or modify the constitutions received from Teresa. It riled Doria that there were efforts to preserve Teresa's constitutions from any changes that might be made by him, but not until 1593 were measures taken against her. She was confined to the monastery prison and deprived of communion. This punishment lasted for nine months, but then Doria died unexpectedly. The new general, Elías de San Martín, put an end to María's trials. She was elected prioress again in 1597. She was among those nuns desired by Jean de Brétigny for a foundation of Teresa's nuns in France, but the next general, Francisco de la Madre de Dios, opposed their going to France. Since authorization was then obtained by the French to take nuns from Portugal for a foundation in France, María de San José was transferred by the general out of Portugal to Talavera and then on to Cuerva, where she was received coldly by the prioress. María died shortly afterward. She left a number of writings that are highly regarded for their thought and charming style.

Mariano. See Ambrosio Mariano.

Maridíaz (Diaz, María) (1495–1572). Born in the tiny town of Vita (Avila), she devoted herself to a life of piety, spending a great deal of time before Jesus in the Blessed Sacrament and in care of the poor. For her spiritual directors, she chose, at various times, Gaspar Daza, St. Peter of Alcántara, Julián de Avila, and a number of Jesuits. Having acquired a reputation for sanctity, she was highly regarded in Avila. With a desire for greater poverty and fewer distractions, she sold her house and chickens. So that she then wouldn't have to beg, Padre Prádanos brought her to serve in the house of Doña Guiomar, where she suffered persecution on the part of the other servants. With advice from her spiritual directors, she left the house and began living in a gallery in the convent of San Millán where she had a view of the tabernacle. Teresa became her friend in 1557 while living in Doña Guiomar de Ulloa's house. When the people of Avila turned against Teresa over her foundation of St. Joseph's, they began to compare her unfavorably with Maridíaz, whom they extolled as living an austere and recollected life, in contrast to Teresa who was "restlessly chasing after novelties." She, rather than Teresa, was the one thought to be the true saint in Avila. People flocked to her with their problems, hoping to receive some words of comfort. She died at the age of seventy-seven.

Medina, Bartolomé de (1527–80). Born in Medina de Rioseco, he made his profession as a Dominican in 1546 in Salamanca. Opening his own class in theology at San Esteban, he explained things so well that the official class at the university was deserted. Filled with enthusiasm and diligently studious, he became one of the most prestigious professors of theology at the university. But he was not enthusiastic about Teresa when she came to Salamanca to make her foundation there. He complained that she "was one of those poor women who run around from place to place when it would be better for them to stay home and say their prayers." Having heard of his opposition to her, Teresa arranged to speak with him, hoping that if there were anything about which she was in error he would be the one who would certainly point it out to her. His interview with Teresa so changed him that he became afterward one of her greatest admirers. In 1574, while she was in Alba, he walked twenty-one kilometers every week in order to hear her confession. In one letter, we find her sending him a trout that she had received from the duchess, hoping that he might write her a line or two in return. He died in Salamanca of the tertian fevers, a form of malaria.

Mendoza, Alvaro de (d. 1586). The bishop who was closest to Teresa and from whom she received the most favors, he came from a highly influential family in Spain. He was appointed bishop of Avila in 1560. A robust man, he nonetheless, at the same time, manifested much piety and charity, sponsoring many humanitarian and social works. In 1562, influenced by Peter of Alcántara and won over by Teresa herself, he gave her decisive support in her endeavors. Accepting her new foundation in Avila under his authority when the provincial refused to grant it, he even provided the bread for the community. Yet at first he did oppose the foundation, fearing that Avila was too poor to support another community of nuns. He protected and defended Teresa against detractors and helped her with unbounded generosity.

In 1577 he was appointed bishop of Palencia and, at his urgings, Teresa founded a monastery in Palencia in 1580, and then through his mediation, she founded one in Burgos in 1582. When the persecution of Teresa was at its peak , he had the delicacy to write to King, Philip II, defending Teresa and her work. So great was his love and esteem for her that he arranged to be buried on the epistle side in the sanctuary of the new chapel in St. Joseph's in Avila to which he had contributed.

Mendoza, María de. The sister of Don Alvaro de Mendoza, bishop of Avila, she married Don Francisco de los Cobos, the great commander of León and secretary of state, administrator of the treasury, and close advisor to Charles V. In instructions the latter gave to his son Philip II, he warned him against the dangerous side of Cobos and of the dangerous influence his wife might have on him. Don Francisco died in 1547.

One gets the impression on reading Teresa's letters that the widow did not then turn suddenly to a life of piety. In fact, her life, like that of so many, can be divided into two sections. The first part was one of worldliness and self-seeking. The second part was one of conversion, surrender to God, and service under the influence of grace. Teresa in her letters at times had to encourage her to practice resignation to God's will in her trials and illnesses so that she might grow in holiness through them.

Doña María first became acquainted with Teresa through her brother Don Alvaro when Teresa was making her foundation in Avila. When Doña María's brother, Don Bernardino, died in 1568, she sponsored a foundation of a community of Teresa's nuns on a property outside of Valladolid. But because the site was unhealthy on account of its proximity to the river Pisuerga, she housed the nuns in her palace until she could buy another house for them, in 1569, into which they moved. Years later when Teresa was sent back to the Incarnation as prioress to help remedy the bad financial situation of that large community, Doña María helped Teresa free the nuns from their indigence by putting food on their table. It seems she may have died in 1578, since Teresa's last letter to her is in March of that year and in her letters to the prioress in Valladolid from 1579 through 1581, she neither sends regards to nor mentions Doña María.

Nicolás (Nicolao) de Jesús María (Doria) (1539–1594) Born in Genoa, Doria came to Spain in 1570 to make a fortune. Settling in Seville, he became a financier. After three years, following a mishap in which he almost perished in a shipwreck, he underwent a conversion. Renouncing his fortune, he gave it to the poor and took up studies for the priesthood. He was ordained afterward in Seville. In Seville he met Ambrosio Mariano, also an Italian, who recommended him to the archbishop as someone who could manage the episcopal finances and free the archdiocese from its heavy debts. Doria was able to do this so successfully that Philip II also sought his advice in financial affairs and brought him to Madrid to make use of his services at a time when the financial situation of the nation was verging on a state of crisis. After a year the king wanted to give him a bishopric as a testimony of gratitude for his services, but Doria decided to embrace the religious life. He was thinking at first of joining the Jesuits. Instead, in 1576, he left Madrid and returned to Seville where he then met Teresa. She afterward used to refer to him as Nicolao. Asking to be received among the discalced Carmelites, he entered their monastery of *Los Remedios* in Seville in 1577.

No sooner did he make his profession when he began to receive important positions within the order. It was to him that Teresa turned when all the other leaders of the discalced friars were under arrest or in exile. He succeeded in disguising his real reasons for being in Madrid and, while living in a monastery of the Carmelites of the observance, managed the affairs of Teresa's friars without raising the least suspicion. Efforts were made to send him to Rome to enter into negotiations there in favor of Teresa's reform, but the nuncio, who needed him, did not want him to leave Spain. From 1579–80 he was prior of Pastrana. In 1581, when the discalced friars and nuns became a separate province, he was elected the first councillor. Teresa thought at the time that he would be a good companion and advisor to Gracián and that the two would complement each other. He would be able to restrain Gracián, who some thought was too impulsive and active. But Gracián was also very gracious and gentle; in fact, too gentle for those who wanted more austerity among the friars. Time proved the two to be incompatible. To free himself of Doria, in 1582, Gracián arranged for him to go to Rome as his ambassador to represent there the causes of the discalced friars, especially when they were falsely accused by others. In 1583, Doria was sent to Genoa to make a foundation of discalced Carmelite friars there. And in one of the last projects of his life, he brought the discalced Carmelite nuns to Genoa. In the chapter celebrated in Lisbon in May 1585, at Gracián's suggestion, Doria was elected provincial—almost unanimously. Since he was in Italy at the time, he returned to Spain. In October the chapter was continued in Pastrana under his leadership. He divided the province into four regions with four vicar provincials, among whom was John of the Cross (Andalusia) and Gracián (Portugal). In March 1587, after the chapter, in response to a plea for more help from the friars who were in Mexico, Doria arranged to send Gracián there as his vicar. The ruling prince of Portugal, however, needed the services of Gracián and prevented his departure for Mexico.

In 1588 in a chapter in Madrid, Doria was elected vicar general of the discalced friars. At this point he revised the whole governmental system of the discalced friars and nuns. Gracián sided with the nuns in opposing their restructuring by Doria. They felt he was making changes that contradicted the constitutions left to them by St. Teresa. In 1591, Doria started a process against Gracián, which culminated in his being expelled from the order on 17 February 1592. The expulsion of Gracián and the investigations of St. John of the Cross cast their shadows over whatever good qualities Doria had and whatever benefits he had brought to the order.

In June 1593, he assisted at the general chapter in which the discalced friars separated completely from the observant Carmelites and became a separate congregation. This move was confirmed on 20 December 1593 by Clement VIII. Doria was then named general of the discalced Carmelites. He convoked a general chapter for the discalced friars to be held in Madrid in May 1594. Withdrawing for fifteen days of retreat to the friars Desert (eremitical house) of Bolarque, a concept supported by him, Doria then traveled on to Pastrana. On his journey from Pastrana to Alcalá, he fell from his donkey, on which he was traveling in a spirit of poverty, suffered injuries and subsequently died in Alcalá on at the age of fifty-five.

Ormaneto, Nicolás (Niccoló) (d. 1577). "The holy nuncio" was a friend of St. Charles Borromeo and his coadjutor in the reform of Milan. He had been in England with Cardinal Pole and also had assisted at the Council of Trent. Later he was named bishop of Padua. Arriving in Spain as nuncio for the Holy See in 1572, he soon got diligently involved in the reform of religious orders. Becoming an admirer of St. Teresa, he helped her, and her friars and nuns, to every extent that he could. Just when he was most needed by Teresa, when the conflict between the discalced and observant Carmelites was reaching its peak, he died. He left all that he owned to the poor, requiring Philip II, as a result, to pay the cost of his funeral.

Ortiz, Diego (d. 1611). The son-in-law of Alonso Alvarez Ramírez, the executor for Martín Ramírez. The latter was a Toledan merchant who left his money for a foundation of Teresa's nuns in Toledo. Diego was co-executor and more unyielding in his opinion than Alonso. With the power given him by Alonso, he proceeded to make many demands that Teresa didn't feel she could agree to. However, she also points out that he was very good and a theologian (F. 15.4).

Ovalle, Beatriz de (1560–1639). Born in Alba de Tormes in 1560, Beatriz was the fifth daughter of Teresa's sister Juana and brother-in-law Juan de Ovalle. Teresa gave her this name in memory of her own mother. This niece loved music and found her joy in it, never thinking of the religious life. Teresa felt much affection for her and one day, when the girl was ten, she clasped her hands in hers and said, "You must live and be a nun." But the words did not please Beatriz. When she was twenty, a prestigious gentleman, named Don Gonzalo, a family friend, came to the Ovalle home. His wife, who was insanely jealous, found him with Beatriz. The girl was maligned by her and accused of having an illicit affair with her husband. At first, neither Beatriz nor her parents paid any attention to the accusation. But the incident, of course, fueled much gossip, and Beatriz became the victim of a calumny. Although Teresa did not doubt her niece's innocence, she was disturbed over the matter and thought it would be wise if her niece were removed from these surroundings. But the parents thought that doing this would only make the accusations seem true. In the end Beatriz moved to Avila in 1582. Teresa's death affected her deeply and after many interior struggles she entered the Carmel of Alba de Tormes in 1585 at the age of twenty-five. She was received without a dowry because she was the foundress's niece. In 1591 she went as subprioress to the new foundation in Ocaña, becoming prioress there in 1600. In 1607, she was elected prioress of Toledo where the community needed a person with practical talent and efficiency. Their house was in a deplorable condition. She found a new house for the nuns into which they moved in 1608. In 1610, she returned to Ocaña as prioress and in 1615 was elected prioress of Santa Ana in Madrid. She served as prioress there at various times until her death.

Ovalle, Gonzalo de (1556–85) One of the two surviving children of Teresa's sister Juana, he was living in the house Teresa bought while it was being prepared to serve as the monastery of St. Joseph's in Avila. One day when he was about four years old his father found him hanging unconscious from the lintel of a door frame. He brought him to Teresa who took him in her arms tenderly, embraced, and prayed over him for about an hour and a half until little by little the small child began to give signs of life. Teresa then handed him over to his parents. They never were sure whether he had been actually dead or not. Around 1575, his father managed to have him placed in the service of the Duke of Alba. He remained in this post until his death at the age of twenty-eight. He was said to have lived a most exemplary life.

Ovalle, Juan de (d. 1595). Teresa's brother-in-law was born in Alba de Tormes and served under Charles V in Germany before marrying Juana. Though he had a difficult temperament, unstable, suspicious, and jealous, he and his wife made an effort to live a pious Christian life, and were generous in giving alms and caring for poor orphans. But in their efforts to sustain a status equal to that of the *hijosdalgo*, they never fared well and were often in financial difficulty. Teresa gives the impression that he was touchy and self-important but well meaning.

Padilla, Casilda de (b. 1562). Born in Valladolid into one of the most aristocratic families in Spain. She entered the discalced nuns in Valladolid at the age of thirteen, over the opposition of her family, after a dramatic escape from her mother and governess. The strange story is described by Teresa in chapter 11 of her *Foundations*. Casilda made her profession at age fifteen. Although spoken of so highly by Teresa, she did not persevere. Losing her initial fervor, she allowed herself to be influenced by her mother, María de Acuña, who was from the family of the Count of Buendía, and obtained a brief from Rome in 1581 permitting her to transfer to the monastery of the Franciscan nuns of San Luis in Santa Gadea del Cid (Burgos). All of this came as a shock to Teresa. Casilda became the abbess. In 1616 she obtained another brief from Rome allowing to leave her monastery to seek a remedy for her health from the waters of Fitero. After convalescing there she withdrew to live with the Conceptionist nuns in Madrid.

Padilla, Juan Calvo de (b. 1520). A Castilian priest who supported Teresa in her work of reform and held in high regard by Philip II. He had been a missionary in Africa and America before his initiative in Spain as a reformer. In his zeal, he often went beyond the bounds of discretion, stirred up much hostility, and more than once got himself in trouble with the Inquisition.

Pantoja, Hernando (d. 1582). Born in Avila, in 1517 he entered the Carthusian monastery, Santa María de las Cuevas, on the outskirts of Seville. From 1567 to 1580 he served as prior there. Teresa came to know him when she made her foundation in Seville in 1575. He was among the first to come to the aid of Teresa and her companions with their new foundation when they were still being treated coldly by everyone else. He provided for many of their needs and introduced them to other people who could be of assistance. Teresa grew very fond of him. In the problems that arose at the Carmel in Seville in 1579, she wrote to him begging for his help and prayers for the community there. She was amazed by all his kindnesses and referred to him as "my prior" or "my holy prior." In her *Foundations* she asks the nuns not to fail to keep him in their prayers and be thankful to him. In 1580 he had a fall and became incapacitated. From then on he had to be carried to the choir. He died a little more than a month after Teresa.

Philip II (1527–98). King of Spain, son of the emperor Charles V and Isabel of Portugal, he ascended the throne of his father in 1556. He never felt any contradiction between his profound Catholic belief and his high-handed actions with respect to the church. His continuous hostility to aspects of papal policy was inherited from his father. "Secular princes," he emphasized to his ambassador in Rome, "are not bound to carry out the mandates of the pope in temporal matters." An unswerving supporter of the spiritual authority of the papacy, he could not brook its refusal to support him blindly. Within Spain, Philip felt himself completely free to act as he liked in church matters. When he gave support to reforms within the church in Spain, he did not hesitate to sanction the use of troops against monasteries and convents. Possessing total control over appointment of bishops, he nonetheless always consulted carefully before naming to sees. He also came to accept the inevitability of toleration in specific circumstances. If England were invaded, he decided in 1576, there must be no religious persecution. He was also able to move towards accepting a form of toleration in the Netherlands. Likewise he accepted—albeit reluctantly—the need to coexist with Muslims (in Spain) and Jews (in Italy and north Africa) as subjects. His confessors, like those of other Catholic rulers, occupied a special place in government. They were always allotted a place on committees where moral questions were on the agenda. Philip was by temperament tranquil, subdued, and ever in control of himself. He spoke little, and when he did he always expressed himself carefully and courteously. It was precisely his silence that unnerved others They were given the right to speak first which made them feel immediately under scrutiny. A story goes around that even Teresa was unnerved in his presence: "I began to speak to him when his penetrating gaze, of those that penetrate to the soul, settled on me, so I lowered my eyes and rapidly stated what I wanted." But the story is unauthentic. The king's reserve, however, was natural, not affected. Teresa had to turn to him on various occasions for help with the trust of someone seeking help from a father. At times seeking protection for her reform, at other times for individuals, such as John of the Cross or Gracián, who were being either persecuted or calumniated, she happily found that Philip II did not disappoint her hopes. He even went so far as to pay all the expenses of the chapter of separation. Teresa asserted that had it not been for the king all of her work would have collapsed. After her death, he seemed to favor Doria in the latter's conflict with Gracián. On the whole, Philip II refused to engage in any propaganda battle to enhance his reputation, and thus he left the field wide open to the English and the Dutch. Their journalism produced an image of him and Spain that has since been characterized as "the Black Legend."

Quiroga, Gaspar de (1507–94). Born in Madrigal (Avila), he studied in Salamanca and as a young man entered the Colegio de Santa Cruz de Valladolid, where he stayed for seven years. Cardinal Tavera appointed him vicar general and also canon of Toledo. After the cardinal's death he was named capitular vicar. Philip II appointed him visitator of the kingdom of Naples and then both judge for the royal council and inquisitor general. When Archbishop Carranza died in 1577, Quiroga was appointed Archbishop of Toledo and Primate of Spain. But he was obliged to spend most of his time at the court, where he served also as president of the Council of Italy. Although he wanted to spend longer periods in Toledo tending to his church, Quiroga was forced to live mainly in Madrid, within easy reach of the king who valued his services. He was made a cardinal by Gregory XIII in 1577.

Teresa met him in 1580 on her way back from the foundation in Villanueva de la Jara. She and Gracián went to see him to request permission for a foundation of her nuns in Madrid which was within his jurisdiction. At this time he told her that he had read her *Life* when it was denounced to the Inquisition and found that her teaching was safe, true, and beneficial. He asked her to pray for him always. Nonetheless, he was not as cooperative with her as she would have liked. Stubborn and intractable despite all of Teresa's requests and letters, under one pretext and then another, he refused to authorize the foundation Teresa so longed for. He later also opposed his niece Elena de Quiroga's entrance into the monastery of the discalced Carmelite nuns in Medina del Campo in 1581. El Greco immortalized him in a portrait where he appears pale with a long white beard looking like a prophet of old.

Rojas y Sandoval, Cristóbal (1502–80). Born in Fuenterrabí (Guipúzcoa), the son of the Marquis of Denia, he did his studies at Alcalá and on their completion entered the service of Charles V as chaplain, accompanying him on his expedition to Flanders. In 1545 he was appointed bishop of Oviedo, and attended the Council of Trent. In 1562, he was appointed successor to his uncle who had just died while bishop of Córdoba, and then in 1571, he was made archbishop of Seville. Although he was a charitable and zealous man of exemplary life, he was displeased at hearing that Teresa had arrived with her nuns in Seville in 1575 with the intention of founding a new monastery without an endowment, and he was determined to prevent it. One day after about a month had passed, he decided to visit the nuns. So impressed and charmed was he by

Teresa's spirit that he changed his mind totally and allowed the foundation to be made without an endowment. He provided the nuns with wheat and money and from that time on favored them. When the nuns moved to another house in June 1576, the archbishop offered to preside in the procession. On their arrival at the entrance of the new monastery, Teresa knelt down and asked the archbishop for his blessing. After giving it, in the presence of all the people, he knelt down humbly and asked Teresa for hers. When in 1580 Philip II traveled to Portugal to take possession of that kingdom, he chose the talented Cristóbal Rojas to accompany him. In that year the brief for the separation of the discalced friars into a separate province arrived, and the king put the archbishop in charge of the procedures. On his journey to Castile to carry out his mission, Cristóbal Rojas fell sick. Forced to interrupt his travel in Cigales, he died there in September.

Rubeo, Juan Bautista (Giovanni Battista Rossi) (1507–78). An untiring apostle, he was born in Ravenna and entered the Carmelites at the age of ten. He received his doctorate in Padua. In 1546 he was named procurator general of the order and began lecturing at the Sapienza in Rome. The Carmelite general chapter in 1564, under the presidency of St. Charles Borromeo, unanimously elected him general of the order. He lost no time in obtaining faculties from the Holy See to visit, reform, and correct the houses of the order. His cherished desires were to bring the order back to its origins, to stress solitude, affective prayer, devotion to Mary, and the apostolate. This appealed to him much more than merely promoting fulfillment of the laws newly set forth by the Council of Trent. In 1564 he began his visit to Spain, and on 10 June 1566 he had an audience with Philip II. Proceeding to Andalusia, where the Carmelites were torn by rival factions and resistance to reform, he convoked a provincial chapter for 22 September at which over 200 Carmelites took part. His efforts to correct abuses angered the guilty parties and caused them to make appeals to the king, complaining of Rossi and calling on the king himself to set up a visitation. As a result, Philip II lost confidence in Rossi and initiated his own plans for the reform of religious orders in Spain. Unaware of the king's attitude, Rossi began his visitation of Castile and on 27 April 1567 authorized Teresa to found other houses for her nuns, provided they be under the jurisdiction of the order, and the number in each community be restricted to no more than twenty-five nuns. A month later he limited the region where the new houses could be founded to Castile, but later he extended this to all parts. Because of the troubles among the friars in Andalusia, he did not want to grant permission for new foundations of discalced friars. But at Teresa's request on 10 August 1567, he wrote from Barcelona giving her permission to found two houses of "contemplative Carmelite friars" in Castile. In 1569 in a letter to the prioress of Medina, Rossi wrote: "She [Teresa of Jesus] does more good for the order than all the Carmelite friars in Spain together." And Teresa esteemed him just as highly. But later because of the many jurisdictional complexities that arose from the king's desire to reform the Carmelites in Spain, passions were aroused and Rossi was so misinformed that he approved measures harmful to what Teresa was trying to bring about. She never lost her high esteem for Rossi and explained and appealed to him through her letters. Rossi died unexpectedly on 4 September 1578 as a consequence of an accident in which he fell from his mule and broke his leg. Teresa was deeply saddened when she received the news and always lamented the pain she thought she had caused the general because of the misunderstandings that had arisen and her inability to explain things to him personally or get her letters through to him.

Salazar, Angel de (1519–ca. 1600). One of the most praiseworthy of the Carmelites in Spain among the observants, Angel de Salazar was born in Valdesanas (Burgos) and received the Carmelite habit in La Moraleja in 1535. He studied at Salamanca and later in Rome where he received the degree of Doctor in Theology. For most of his life he held positions of responsibility as either prior or provincial. In the beginning, when Teresa explained to him her project for a new community, he favored it. But later, when the uproar arose against it in Avila, he wavered and withdrew his support. He zigzagged his way through all the problems that emerged during the years of Teresa's efforts as foundress of the discalced Carmelite friars and nuns. At times he supported and helped her, but at other times he created difficulties for her. When in 1569 Pius V named Dominicans as apostolic visitators of the Carmelites, Rossi, the Carmelite general, named Angel de Salazar, in whom he had full confidence, his representative and visitator for Spain. It was Angel de Salazar who prompted the apostolic visitator Pedro Fernández to appoint Teresa prioress of the Incarnation in Avila in 1571. On his return from the chapter of Piacenza in 1575, he committed the indiscretion of talking in Madrid about the measures that the chapter had taken against Teresa before she herself was officially informed. Nonetheless, when after many disturbances the nuncio Sega appointed Angel de Salazar vicar general of the discalced friars and nuns, the latter were all pleased, and Teresa spoke warmly of his character and ability. The date of his death is unknown; the last record of him is from 1595.

Salazar, Gaspar de (1529–93). Born in Toledo, and while studying at Alcalá, he decided to enter the Jesuits, which he did in 1552. The chronicler described him as being very devoted to the interior life with God, from whom he received many favors in prayer, and also as very intelligent and competent in business matters. In 1562 he was transferred to Avila to be rector there of the Jesuit college of San Gil. Because of difficulties that arose between the college and the bishop, Don Alvaro de Mendoza, Salazar was removed from that office after only nine months. But in that short time, he came to Teresa's aid by putting her spiritual director, Baltasar Alvarez, at ease about her, assuring him that he had nothing to fear. And when Teresa spoke to him of her experiences, he consoled her greatly and seemed to her to have a special gift of discerning spirits (L. 33.8–9). In 1565, he was appointed rector of the Jesuit college in Madrid. He eventually held this position as well in a number of other places, but in Cuenca, in 1575, he was accused of being too severe and removed from office. It doesn't seem, though, that Salazar was always as admirable as Teresa's description of him in her *Life*. After his removal from office, he got mixed up in an unsuccessful attempt to get the constitutions of the Jesuits changed, which may help to explain his desire to leave the Society. There is overwhelming evidence that he made determined efforts to enter Teresa's reform. But in a letter written by him to his general in 1579 he declared that while the discalced Carmelites may have endeavored to get him into their order, he himself had never any intention of leaving the Society of Jesus to go to a people who though good were very disorganized. He went on to declare that he had never desired office in the Society and had always protested against being appointed rector anywhere. Actually Teresa was disturbed by his thought of transferring to her friars and did her best to dissuade him. Salazar died in Alcalá in 1593.

Salcedo, Francisco de (d. 1580) Born in Avila, he married a cousin of Teresa's aunt. He studied theology for twenty years at the Dominican school in Avila. The first one in whom Teresa confided when her mystical life began in full, he was the one who was also most skeptical about her experiences and caused her the greatest suffering. He was convinced of the devil's involvement. Peter of Alcántara had to go to great lengths to assure him that Teresa's experiences were indeed from God. In the end, since he was always well intentioned, he did change his opinion and was ever faithful in trying to help Teresa with her undertakings. She wrote of him in her *Life*: "This gentleman is so prayerful and charitable that his goodness and perfection shine throughout the whole town" (23.6). When he started referring to himself as being old and infirm, Teresa in one reply joked with him: "Don't keep telling me that you are old, which leaves me in total dismay. As though there were some security in being young!" In 1570, after his wife died, he was ordained a priest. In 1576 he got tangled up in a troublesome lawsuit in which he lost a great part of his possessions. Teresa wrote to her brother in Avila urging him to show much kindness to Don Francisco, and regretted that he didn't bear the trial with greater courage. She believed it was sent to him by the Lord. When he died, the rumor went around that he had left the nuns a fortune and so their benefactors stopped trying to help them. The poor community ended up in dire straits, for the legacy they received was much too small to meet their needs.

Sega, Felipe (Filippo) (ca. 1537–96). Born in Bologna, he became bishop of Ripa and nuncio to Flanders before being appointed nuncio to Spain in 1577 as successor to Ormaneto. He entered Spain with a bias against Teresa and her reform, the source of which was Cardinal Buoncompagni, a relative of his and nephew of the pope. But the entire conflict that had developed in Spain among the Carmelites was so complex that he had little inkling of what he was getting into. He supported Tostado who was seeking to put into effect the decisions of the chapter of Piacenza. It was he who called Teresa "a restless, gadabout woman." He considered the discalced friars who took part in the chapter of Almadóvar in 1578 delinquents and rebels, never listened to their defense, and imprisoned their leaders in different monasteries of the observant Carmelites. Through the intervention of the king, an investigating committee was set up, and the friars as a result were placed under the care of Angel de Salazar, a former provincial of the observant Carmelites in Castile. Salazar dealt with the matter gently and promoted greater peace between the two groups of friars. Sega then mellowed somewhat and acquiesced when the discalced formed a separate province. After leaving Spain, he served in Portugal, Germany, and France. He was made a cardinal in 1591 and died in Rome.

Teresa (Teresita) de Jesús (de Cepeda) (1566–1610). The daughter of Teresa's brother Lorenzo, Teresita was born in Quito (modern Ecuador). Her mother died while she was still an infant. She first met her aunt Teresa in Seville in 1575. The nuns immediately grew fond of her and took her into the monastery to live with them, even though she was only nine years old. She traveled with Teresa and her father on the way back to Castile. After remaining a while in Toledo with Teresa and the community of nuns there, she went on to Avila with her father and lived at St. Joseph's, while Teresa remained in Toledo for business purposes. After living for some years at St. Joseph's, she received the habit, having pleased all the nuns by her delightful disposition. She was charming both in body and soul, and her exotic accent from America added to the charm. But she manifested as well, at times, a somewhat critical and independent spirit. On the final journey with Teresa from Burgos to Alba de Tormes, they stopped off at Valladolid. There Doña Beatriz de Castilla was causing a stir and threatening a law suit over the part of Lorenzo's legacy that was destined for St. Joseph's in Avila should Francisco have no heir. Teresita sided with the prioress María Bautista against Teresa's insistence that Lorenzo's wishes be respected. Teresita afterward always regretted that she had done this. Wanting to return to Avila quickly for Teresita's profession, Teresa was ordered instead to go to Alba. There she suffered her final illness and death. Only a few weeks after Teresa's death, despite all the attempts by relatives to persuade Teresita to return to the world so that the money left by her father could belong to them instead of the nuns at St. Joseph's, Teresita went ahead and made her profession. In 1602 she was elected sub-prioress at St. Joseph's in Avila. She died there eight years later.

Toledo, García de. A typical aristocrat in soul and blood, García de Toledo was a nephew of the Count of Oropesa. He went to America with the viceroy of Mexico and made his profession as a Dominican there in 1535. Returning to Spain, he became subprior in 1555 at Santo Tomás, the Dominican house in Avila, and served as one of Teresa's trusted confessors. Suddenly and unexpectedly, he entered the pages of Teresa's *Book of her Life* when she met him in a church in Toledo in 1562. To him we owe the expanded version of her *Life*, with its extra little treatise on prayer (chs. 11–22) and its final chapters on the foundation of St. Joseph's (chs. 32–40). Once Teresa received a message from God for him. The message was brief but all from God. And the witness said, "he began to weep, for it penetrated to the depths of his being. And he is a tough man who could rule the world." In 1569 he accompanied his cousin Francisco to Peru where the cousin had been appointed viceroy. He became provincial there besides having held other offices. He returned to Spain in 1581 and retired to the Dominican house at Talavera de la Reina, where he died.

Tostado, Jerónimo (1523–82). Born in Lisbon, he made his vows in 1545 and is said to have acquired his doctorate at Paris. He was afterward invited to lecture in the province of Catalonia. When the general, Rossi, made his visitation in Barcelona in 1567, Tostado was prior there. The general gave him, in addition to his office of prior, the office of reformer general of Catalonia. Tostado accompanied the general on his visitations in Italy, 1572–75, and was his socius at the general chapter of Piacenza. On 10 December 1575, Rossi appointed him visitator, reformer, and commissary general of the Spanish provinces. Tostado then had the power to suppress all the discalced foundations that were marked for suppression by the council of Piacenza. But the king managed to prevent him from exercising his powers. In 1576 he was elected provincial of Catalonia again. After the discalced friars and nuns were allowed to become a separate province in 1580, Rossi's successor reappointed him visitator and reformer of Spain, but he died, before Teresa, in Naples on 24 February.

Ulloa, Guiomar de (b. 1529). One of Teresa's best friends, Doña Guiomar was born in the town of Toro (Zamora) in 1529. Noted for her beauty and ostentatious manner, she married at the age of eighteen Francisco Dávila, a large property owner at Salobralejo. When Don Francisco died in 1554, he left her a widow at twenty-five with a small fortune and three children.

Experiencing a conversion, she renounced any further marriage and began to devote herself to works of charity. Her daughter Elvira entered the monastery of the Incarnation, where Doña Guiomar came to know St. Teresa. Teresa stayed in her home from 1555–58 as companion to her daughter, who was staying there with the provincial's permission. Doña Guiomar provided a great part of the income for Teresa's new foundation in Avila and solicited the brief from Rome for its establishment. It was she who arranged for Teresa to meet and speak with St. Peter of Alcántara. Teresa asserted that God gave her many favors in prayer and that she herself received enlightenment from her in matters about which learned men were ignorant. In 1578 Doña Guiomar entered St. Joseph's in Avila, but had to leave because of bad health. She took St. John of the Cross for her confessor while he was in Avila. In 1585 she wrote her memoirs of St. Teresa for Teresa's biographer, Padre Ribera, but after that nothing more is known of her.

Velázquez, Alonso (d. 1587). One of the strong lights of the Church in Spain, Alonso Velázquez was born in Tudela del Duero of poor parents. Having done his studies in Alcalá, he became a professor of philosophy there. When Teresa was in Toledo, he was canon at the cathedral of Toledo, and despite a busy life, took time out to come and hear her confession once a week, happy to give her whatever guidance she needed. In a letter to Gracián (Ltr. 117), Teresa tells of the extraordinary way in which it happened that Velázquez came to be her confessor. He was a solid help to her in the many trials she was undergoing at the time. One of the reasons he was so helpful was that he always assured her with passages from Scripture, which he knew so well. In 1578 he was made bishop of Burgo de Osma, and was instrumental in Teresa's foundation in Soria. The final account we have of the state of Teresa's soul was written by her for Velázquez in 1581 when he was bishop of Osma (ST. 65). After Teresa's death, in 1583, he became archbishop of Santiago de Compostela. Failing health and the loss of sight in one eye led him to resign his see in 1587 and retire to Talavera de la Reina where he died that same year.

Sources for the Biographical Sketches

Efrén de la Madre de Dios y Steggink, Otger. *Tiempo y Vida de Santa Teresa*, Segunda Edición Revisada y Aumentado. Madrid: BAC, 1977.

Peers, E. Allison. *Handbook to the Life and Times of St. Teresa and St. John of the Cross*. London, England: Burns Oates, 1954.

Salvador de la Virgen del Carmen. *Teresa de Jesús*. 2 vols. Vitoria: Diputación Foral de Alava, Consejo de Cultura, 1964–68.

Silverio de Santa Teresa. *Historia del Carmen Descalzo en España, Portugal y América*. 15 vols. Burgos: Monte Carmelo, 1935–49.

—*Obras de Santa Teresa de Jesús*. 9 vols. Burgos: Monte Carmelo, 1915–24.

—*Vida de Santa Teresa de Jesús*. 5 vols. Burgos: El Monte Carmelo, 1935–37.

Index

Index

A letter in bold type indicates that the letter itself is addressed to the person after whose name it appears.

The Institute of Carmelite Studies promotes research and publication in the field of Carmelite spirituality. Its members are Discalced Carmelites, part of a Roman Catholic community–friars, nuns and laity–who are heirs to the teaching and way of life of Teresa of Jesus and John of the Cross, men and women dedicated to contemplation and to ministry in the Church and the world. Information concerning their way of life is available through local diocesan Vocation Offices or from the Vocation Directors' Offices:

5345 S. University Avenue, Chicago, IL 60615

166 Foster Street, Brighton, MA 02135

P.O. Box 3420, San Jose, CA 95156-3420

5151 Marylake Drive, Little Rock, AR 72206